Tolley's Company Secretary's Handbook

Ninth Edition

by

Jerry P L Lai FCIS
KPMG

Tolley

A member of the Reed Elsevier plc group

Published by
Tolley
2 Addiscombe Road
Croydon Surrey CR9 5AF England
(0181) 686 9141

Typeset in Great Britain by
Phoenix Photosetting, Chatham, Kent

Printed in Great Britain by
Redwood Books, Trowbridge, Wiltshire

ISBN 0 75450 237–6

Preface

The role and responsibilities of the company secretary continue to evolve as the legislation and other regulations affecting companies change to meet the demands of today's ever competitive business environment. The Cadbury Committee, and more recently the Hampel Committee, recognise the important role of the secretary. The secretary is responsible for ensuring that corporate governance procedures are appropriate for the company, as well as interpreting and applying the Code of Best Practice drafted by the Committee. Inevitably, this places more demands upon the knowledge and expertise required of the secretary, who must therefore be suitably qualified and well informed to fulfil this role.

The purpose of this book is to provide the company secretary with a comprehensive handbook on the wide range of duties and responsibilities which typically fall to the secretary. It is intended that this book should be an initial source of advice on company secretarial matters and other business issues. Where further explanation is required, I would recommend that recourse is made to the relevant statutes or to the company's professional advisers. As before, we seek to improve on future editions of the book and I would very much welcome readers' comments and criticisms.

For this edition, I have once again maintained overall editorial control whilst still updating some of the chapters. Steve Martin FCIS and Claire Cranidge ACIS have continued to provide significant contribution in the update of this edition.

This ninth edition seeks to encompass *inter alia* the changes made to legislation during 1999. Corporate Governance continues to be a developing area and this edition therefore reflects the publication of the Hampel Report and the subsequent Combined Code for listed companies. It hopefully highlights the continuing role that the Secretary plays in this arena and the importance of keeping up to date with changes. It also includes changes in tax legislation and highlights the various consultative documents issued by Companies House. Again, based on the feedback that I have received, I have kept the chapters very much in the same order as the previous edition.

Finally, I would once again like to thank Stephen Barc of Butterworths–Tolley for his assistance on the Employment chapter, Tony Bannard and Emma Wise of this firm for their valued contributions and all the other members of the Company Secretarial team of KPMG at St Albans for their support whilst updating this edition.

October 1999   *Jerry PL Lai FCIS*
                                                              KPMG

Contents

Contents

Abbreviations and References

ABBREVIATIONS

ACT	=	Advance Corporation Tax
(FS)AVC	=	(Free Standing) Additional Voluntary Contribution
CA 1948	=	Companies Act 1948
CA 1967	=	Companies Act 1967
CA 1980	=	Companies Act 1980
CA 1981	=	Companies Act 1981
CA 1985	=	Companies Act 1985
CA 1989	=	Companies Act 1989
CIC	=	Close Investment Holding Company
DSS	=	Department of Social Services
EEIG	=	European Economic Interest Grouping
ERA 1996	=	Employment Rights Act 1996
EWC	=	Expected week of confinement
FSA 1986	=	Financial Services Act 1986
GMP	=	Guaranteed Minimum Pension
IA 1986	=	Insolvency Act 1986
ICTA 1988	=	Income and Corporation Taxes Act 1988
LGHA 1989	=	Local Government and Housing Act 1989
LPI	=	Limited price indexation
LTA 1954	=	Landlord and Tenant Act 1954
Ltd	=	Limited
NI	=	National Insurance
OPAS	=	Occupational Pensions Advisory Service
OPB	=	Occupational Pensions Board
PLC	=	Public Limited Company
PSO	=	Pension Schemes Office
RPI	=	Retail Price Index
S(s)	=	Section(s)
Sch	=	Schedule
SAS	=	Statement of Auditing Standard
SERPS	=	State Earnings Related Pension Scheme
SI	=	Statutory Instrument
SMA	=	State Maternity Allowance
SMP	=	Statutory Maternity Pay
SSCBA 1992	=	Social Security Contributions and Benefits Act 1992
SSP	=	Statutory Sick Pay
Table A	=	Table A to the Companies (Tables A to F) Regulations 1985
TURERA 1993	=	Trade Union Reform and Employment Rights Act 1993
VAT	=	Value Added Tax

REFERENCES

AC	=	Law Reports, Appeal Cases
AER	=	All England Law Reports
BCC	=	British Company Law Cases (CCH Editions Ltd)
BCLC	=	Butterworths Company Law Cases
Ch/ChD	=	Law Reports, Chancery Division
EGLR	=	Estates Gazette Law Reports
HL	=	House of Lords
ICR	=	Industrial Cases Reports
IRLR	=	Industrial Relations Law Reports
KB	=	Law Reports, King's Bench Division
LR	=	Law Reports (followed by court abbreviation)
QB/QBD	=	Law Reports, Queen's Bench Division
WLR	=	Weekly Law Reports

Chapter 1

The Company Secretary

Definition and authority

General

1.1 In 1877 the Master of the Rolls described the company secretary as:

> 'a mere servant; his position is that he is to do what he is told, and no person can assume that he has any authority to represent anything at all'.

This view of the ostensible authority of the company secretary in law remained for some considerable time. However, since the beginning of the century, the company secretary's profile has risen considerably.

The first recognition of this increasing importance by the courts came in the case of *Panorama Developments (Guildford) Ltd v Fidelis Furnishing Fabrics Ltd [1971] 2 QB 711* where, in the Court of Appeal, Salmon LJ described the company secretary as:

> 'the chief administrative officer of the company'.

Lord Denning MR said:

> 'He regularly makes representations on behalf of the company and enters into contracts on its behalf which come within the day-to-day running of the company's business . . . He is certainly entitled to sign contracts connected with the administrative side of a company's affairs . . . All such matters now come within the ostensible authority of a company's secretary.'

Thus, the company secretary can be said to have an ostensible authority on behalf of a company to enter into contracts which are of an administrative nature. This authority could be said to extend to such matters as the employment of administrative staff (e.g. accounting staff) ordering of office/factory equipment and stationery and the arrangement of the company's insurance. The secretary's ostensible authority does not, however, extend to contracts of a managerial nature. To enter into such contracts the secretary must be given express authority by the directors.

The position of the modern company secretary's authority would therefore appear to be as follows.

(*a*)   If the secretary has express authority from the board, he may enter into contracts of both an administrative and managerial nature on behalf of the company, and the company will be bound by his acts.

(*b*)   When the secretary has no express authority, his ostensible authority will allow him to enter into contracts of an administrative nature on behalf of the company, and the company will be bound by such acts.

Should the secretary act beyond his ostensible authority, and without an express authority, the position appears to be that the company will be bound by his acts but he may be held personally liable by the company for any resultant loss.

Since the publication of the 'Cadbury Report', incorporating recommendations on corporate governance, even greater emphasis has been placed on the role of the company secretary. An example of this is that the code stipulates that all directors should have access to the company secretary, and that any question regarding his removal should be a matter for all the board.

It goes further to suggest that the company secretary has a key role to play in ensuring that board procedures are both followed regularly and reviewed and that the company secretary will be a source of advice to the chairman and to the board on the implementation of the Code of Best Practice. (See Chapter 6 and Appendix 6B.)

Statutory recognition

1.2   The recognition of the authority of the secretary also extends to legislation, with the company secretary being recognised by several Acts of Parliament.

Companies Act 1985

1.3   Section 283(1) of the Companies Act 1985 states that every company must have a secretary. Whilst not imposing any specific duties upon him, the Act does state that the secretary is authorised to sign various documents on behalf of a company (for example, CA 1985, s 234A(1) states that the directors' report may be signed on behalf of the board by the secretary).

As an officer of the company the secretary can be held jointly liable for defaults which the company commits under the Act (for example, CA 1985, s 363(4) makes the secretary of the company liable for failure to deliver an annual return). Accordingly, a common assumption is that the secretary is the person responsible for maintaining a company's statutory books and records which are required to be maintained under the Act. Interestingly, the Act does not specify this as being a duty of the secretary but of the company. However, the directors will usually delegate this duty to the secretary and, as an officer of the company, the secretary would be liable for any default in carrying out those duties.

*Insolvency Act 1986 and Company Directors Disqualification
Act 1986*

1.4 Both of these Acts provide that where a body corporate is guilty of a
certain offence and it is proved that the offence was committed with the
consent or connivance of, or was attributable to any neglect on the part of any
director, manager, company secretary or other similar officer, that person will
be guilty of an offence and may be proceeded against and punished
accordingly.

Other legislation

1.5 The company secretary is also recognised as a responsible officer of
the company in other miscellaneous Acts of Parliament, examples being:

(*a*) Trade Descriptions Act 1968;

(*b*) Unsolicited Goods and Services Act 1971;

(*c*) Data Protection Act 1998; and

(*d*) Taxes Management Act 1970.

Other roles

1.6 As well as the recognition that the company secretary now has in
law, in modern practice it is increasingly common for the company secretary
to have considerable managerial responsibilities within a company and also
be given certain express powers in areas such as investments and
commercial contract arrangements. The additional roles will usually be
defined in the secretary's contract, or terms and conditions of employment.
Thus, today, the secretary can, in many ways, be described as forming the
backbone of the organisation.

Appointment and qualifications

General

1.7 Section 283(1) of the Companies Act 1985 provides that every
company must have a secretary. Certain restrictions are also imposed by this
section.

(*a*) A sole director of a company may not also be the secretary (section
283(2)).

(*b*) No company may have as secretary, a corporation, the sole director of
which is a sole director of the company (section 283(4)(a)).

(*c*) Similarly, a company is prohibited from having as sole director, a
corporation, the sole director of which is secretary to the company
(section 283(4)(b)).

The Companies Act 1989, s 27(1) also restricts appointment in that a person
who is an auditor of the company, cannot also be the secretary.

Regulation 99 of Table A provides model regulations surrounding the appointment of the company secretary:

> 'Subject to the provisions of the Act, the secretary shall be appointed by the directors for such term, at such remuneration and upon such conditions as they may think fit; and any secretary so appointed may be removed by them.'

Thus, under Table A, the directors of a company have the power to appoint and remove the secretary. In doing so, they must have regard to the Companies Act 1985. For a private company this causes no particular problem so long as the provisions of section 283(2) and (4)(a) of the CA 1985 (see above) are not contravened.

In the case of a *public company*, CA 1985, s 286 imposes a further duty upon the directors to ensure that the secretary is a person who appears to them to have the requisite experience and knowledge to fulfil the role and who either:

(i)   on 22 December 1980 held the office of secretary, assistant or deputy secretary of the company; or

(ii)   for at least three out of the five years preceding his appointment as secretary, held the office of secretary of a company other than a private company; or

(iii)   is a person, who by virtue of previous offices held, appears to the directors to be capable of discharging the functions required of the secretary; or

(iv)   is a barrister, advocate or solicitor called or admitted in any part of the United Kingdom; or

(v)   is a member of any of the following bodies:

> (A)   Institute of Chartered Secretaries and Administrators (ICSA), or
>
> (B)   Institute of Chartered Accountants in England and Wales (ICAEW), or
>
> (C)   Institute of Chartered Accountants in Scotland (ICAS), or
>
> (D)   Institute of Chartered Accountants in Ireland (ICAI), or
>
> (E)   Chartered Institute of Cost and Management Accountants (CIMA), or
>
> (F)   Chartered Association of Certified Accountants (ACCA), or
>
> (G)   Chartered Institute of Public Finance and Accountancy (CIPFA).

These qualifications would also appear to apply in the circumstances where a private company re-registers as a public company (see 2.49 THE COMPANY CONSTITUTION).

A company may, if it wishes, make further regulations in its articles of association for the appointment and removal of the secretary.

Procedure on appointment

1.8   The first secretary of a company is appointed by the completion of the appropriate section on the form 10 submitted to Companies House in the application for registration (see 2.42 THE COMPANY CONSTITUTION). His appointment is deemed to commence from the date the company is incorporated.

Subsequent appointments are made by the appropriate resolution of the board, i.e.:

'It was Resolved that .... be and is hereby appointed Secretary of the company in the place of .... who resigned as Secretary on .... 199 .'

Following appointment, the details of the new secretary must be entered in the register of directors and secretaries (CA 1985, s 290) and a return in the prescribed form (form 288a) must be made to Companies House within 14 days of the date of the change (CA 1985, s 288(2)).

The notification must contain the following details in respect of the secretary:

(*a*)   in the case of an individual, his present Christian name and surname, any former Christian name or surname and his usual residential address; or

(*b*)   in the case of a corporation or a Scottish firm, its corporate or firm name and address of its registered or principal office.

(CA 1985, s 290).

Similarly, any change in the details of the secretary required in (*a*) or (*b*) above must also be notified to Companies House on a form 288c within 14 days of their occurrence and the details entered in the register of directors and secretaries.

In February 1997 the DTI published a consultative document proposing changes to the law on disclosure of directors' and company secretaries' home addresses.

The paper proposed to allow companies to request that home addresses be kept off the public record if they send the Registrar an alternative service address and proposed to abolish the requirement for companies to record home addresses in the statutory registers.

The DTI has now announced, however, that the requirement forcompanies to file the home addresses of their directors and company secretaries should continue.

Where the company is listed, it may be thought appropriate to notify the London Stock Exchange of the appointment as it could be regarded as an important change in the holding of an executive office, however this is not obligatory.

Removal and resignation

1.9   Unless otherwise stated in a company's articles of association the secretary may be removed by a resolution of the board, i.e.:

'It was resolved that .... be and is hereby removed as Secretary of the company with immediate effect.'

The Companies Act 1985 makes no special procedure which must be followed, as in the removal of a director (see 6.9 THE DIRECTORS).

A secretary may also resign office at any time.

The resignation or removal of a secretary must be notified to Companies House on a form 288b within 14 days of the date of resignation or removal.

Although removal from office is a remarkably simple procedure the secretary may have recourse against the company under any service contract or contract of employment for breach of contract.

It should be noted, however, that the 'Cadbury Report' recommends that in the case of the removal of a secretary this should be an item for the whole of the board to decide.

Assistant and deputy secretary

1.10   Specific recognition is given by section 283(3) of the Companies Act 1985 of the office of assistant or deputy secretary:

'Anything required or authorised to be done by or to the secretary may, if the office is vacant or there is for any other reason no secretary capable of acting, be done by or to any assistant or deputy secretary.'

Unless otherwise stated in the articles of association an assistant or deputy secretary may be appointed and removed in the same manner as the secretary, although it appears that under the Act their appointments need not be notified to Companies House. The articles of association may delegate the power to appoint assistants or deputy secretaries to the secretary.

Joint secretary

1.11   Where a company has joint secretaries then section 290 of the Companies Act 1985 requires the details of each to be entered in the register of directors and secretaries and accordingly notified to Companies House (form 288a). It follows then that their authority is joint, and hence all acts should be done together e.g. signing and giving of notices. However, if it is the company's intention for the joint secretaries to act jointly and severally, express authority to that effect should be given in the articles or recorded in the board minute appointing them.

Scope of duties and responsibilities

General

1.12   The duties and responsibilities of a company secretary vary widely from company to company and will commonly be defined in the secretary's contract of employment or by the board of directors of the company. The secretary has become increasingly recognised by statute as being the officer of the company responsible for certain activities (see 1.1 above). However, in general, the extent and nature of a company secretary's duties are not defined in law and, accordingly, the secretary must look to his contract of employment and the company's articles of association to ascertain his precise responsibilities in any company. The secretary as an 'officer' of the company (CA 1985, s 744) can be said to be jointly and severally liable with the other officers of a company for ensuring the performance of certain activities.

The Companies Act 1985 imposes a number of duties on the secretary or upon him as an alternative to another person including:

(*a*)   the completion and signing of the annual return of the company (CA 1985, s 363(2)(c));

(*b*)   the signing of the directors' report in the company's annual accounts (CA 1985, s 234A(1));

(*c*)   the completion and signing of various Companies House forms;

(*d*)   the making of applications on behalf of the company to Companies House; and

(*e*)   the making of various statutory declarations on behalf of the company (e.g. CA 1985, s 12(3)(b)).

These are the basic duties, the actual scope of the secretary's duties will differ from company to company but will normally include:

 (i)   the maintenance of the statutory registers of the company;

 (ii)   attendance at board meetings, the formulation of agendas, taking minutes of the meeting, preparation of articles and notices to shareholders, and ensuring that correct procedures are followed both at board and general meetings;

(iii)   the custody of the company seal; and

(iv)   the authentication and retention of documents.

Maintenance of the statutory registers

1.13   The Companies Act 1985 requires that every company maintain the following registers:

(*a*)   register of members (CA 1985, s 352);

(*b*)   register of charges (CA 1985, s 407);

(*c*)   minute books of the proceedings of meetings of the members of the company (CA 1985, s 382);

(*d*)   accounting records (CA 1985, s 221);

(*e*)   register of directors and secretaries (CA 1985, s 288);

(*f*)   register of directors' interests and debentures of the company (CA 1985, s 325);

(*g*)   if the company is a public company, a register of interests in voting shares (CA 1985, s 211).

The secretary should ensure that all the registers are correctly maintained and that they are kept at the location specified by the Act. The secretary must also ensure that the requirements of the Act relating to the inspection of the registers are complied with at all times and, where notifiable changes are made, that Companies House is informed within the time limits specified in the Act (see Chapter 3 for details).

Meetings and minutes

1.14   The secretary of a company is usually expected to make the arrangements for meetings of the directors and members of the company. He is also expected to attend the meetings and take minutes. At general meetings it is usual for the secretary to read the notice to the meeting. Where possible a secretary should attempt to prepare agendas prior to meetings, setting out the items of business that are to be considered in a logical, clear and concise order.

The secretary should keep a file of documents that require the attention of the directors so that no items of concern are overlooked at board meetings. Agendas for board meetings should be prepared and circulated in advance, together with any papers or reports relating to the proposed items of discussion. The chairman's and secretary's copies of the agenda should have spaces, so as to allow notes to be made.

At the end of the meeting the secretary should use the chairman's copy of the agenda and his own to prepare the minutes.

The minutes should be completely impartial and in most circumstances should not include details of the discussions leading to decisions.

Extreme care should be taken in preparing minutes so as to make them as clear and concise as possible. The chairman of the meeting should then sign the minutes presented at the next board meeting, and the secretary should place them in the minute book.

Minutes do not need to be read out at the next meeting or approved by anybody other than the chairman but should, as a matter of good practice, be circulated to the other persons present at the meeting to allow them to comment on their content.

No amendments should be made to the minutes except to correct obvious errors and these should be initialled by the chairman before he signs them. Once the minutes have been signed they cannot be altered and any subsequent changes must be approved by a resolution at a meeting.

The statutory requirements relating to minutes are contained in 3.49–3.53 THE STATUTORY RECORDS.

The company seal

1.15   Section 36A of the Companies Act 1985 no longer makes it compulsory for a company to have a common seal. It may, however, have one if it so wishes. If a company has a seal it must have the name of the company engraved in legible characters on it (CA 1985, s 350).

The seal will normally be kept by the secretary who should keep a record of all the documents to which the seal is affixed. This may be conveniently done in a register of sealings.

Where a company does not have a seal, documents which are expressed as being executed 'on behalf of the company' and signed by a director and the secretary (or by two directors) and which are accordingly treated as being under seal, should be entered in the register of sealings (see Chapter 11).

The directors of a company should authorise the execution of such documents and those under seal.

If a company transacts business abroad, it may (if permitted by its articles of association) have one or more seals for use overseas and may authorise a person overseas to affix it to any document. Such a seal will be a facsimile of the common seal with the addition of the name of the place where it is to be used.

The secretary should, at all times, ensure the adequacy of the security of the seal to prevent it being fraudulently affixed to documents.

Authentication and retention of documents

1.16   The secretary is authorised by section 41 of the Companies Act 1985 to authenticate any document requiring authentication by the company. Such authentication need not be under the seal of the company. As such authentications are requested frequently by banks etc. many secretaries have stamps made which state that a document is 'certified to be a true original copy . . . . Secretary'.

One of the main administrative duties of a secretary may be to ensure that documents that need to be retained for a requisite period are so retained and then destroyed at the appropriate time (see Appendix 11A COMMERCIAL CONSIDERATIONS).

Stationery

1.17   Sections 349 and 351 of the Companies Act 1985 require every company to mention certain details in its business stationery. Failure to do so renders every officer of the company in default liable to a fine. Thus the main responsibility for ensuring that a company's stationery meets the requirements of the Act will usually fall to the secretary (see 2.17 THE COMPANY CONSTITUTION).

Administrative responsibilities

1.18   In addition to the statutory duties detailed above, the modern day company secretary will also find himself engaged in the following administrative responsibilities.

Compliance

(*a*)   Making certain that the company complies with the memorandum and articles of association and drafting amendments to ensure that they are kept up to date.

(*b*)   Where the company's securities are listed on The Stock Exchange ensuring compliance with the 'Listing Rules', releasing information to the market and ensuring security in respect of unreleased price-sensitive information.

Shares/Shareholders

 (i)   Dealing with transfers, transmissions and forfeiture of shares, issuing share certificates, attending to shareholders' queries and requests, and where some of these functions are delegated to Registrars, the secretary will be responsible for liaison with them to settle matters of particular sensitivity.

 (ii)   Communicating with the shareholders through the issue of circulars, payment of dividends, distribution of documentation regarding rights/capitalisation issues and general shareholder relations.

(iii)   Monitoring movements on the register of members to identify any possible 'stake-building' in the company's shares, making enquiries of shareholders as to beneficial ownership of holdings under section 212 of the Companies Act 1985, maintaining a register of material interests under section 211 (CA 1985), and making timely announcements to The Stock Exchange.

(iv)   Implementing changes in the company's share and loan structure, and administering directors' and employees' share option schemes.

(v) Where the company is involved in an acquisition or disposal, the secretary will have a number of responsibilities, especially in ensuring the effectiveness of all documentation and due diligence disclosures.

Directors

(A) Preparing the directors' report and co-ordinating the printing and distribution of the company's interim statements and annual report and accounts in consultation with the company's advisers.

(B) Keeping directors up to date on new developments in corporate governance and advising directors of their duties, responsibilities and personal obligations.

(C) Acting as a channel of communication for non-executive directors and providing them with relevant information.

Miscellaneous

(I) Administering the registered office, including dealing with official correspondence received.

(II) Maintaining a record of the group structure.

(III) Involvement in payroll, credit control, corporate finance, commercial law, contract vetting/drafting/negotiating, litigation, property management, employment law, personnel administration, pensions, insurance and risk management, office administration and company car schemes.

(IV) Assessing a company's ability to deal with the Year 2000 problem and advising on the action to be taken. Issues of particular concern will include disclosure to be made in the accounts as to whether the company is 'Year 2000 compliant', questions to be asked at the AGM and by the company's auditors, ensuring that the board addresses the issue and are aware of their duties in the serious event of failure to deal with the problem.

Liabilities

1.19   The secretary, as an officer of the company, may be liable with the directors to default fines for non-compliance with the Companies Act 1985 in several of the aforementioned situations (see 1.18 above). The penalties vary accordingly and are governed by section 730 and Schedule 24 of the Companies Act 1985. He will, without doubt, fall within the meaning of the expression 'any officer of the company who knowingly or wilfully authorised or permits the default, refusal or contravention mentioned in the enactment' (CA 1985, s 730(5)).

The fiduciary duties owed by a director are not dissimilar to those which may be applied to the position held by the company secretary. Therefore, the company secretary must, as an officer of the company, act in good faith in the interests of the company and not act for any collateral person. He must avoid any conflicts of interest and must not make profits from dealings for and on behalf of the company.

It should be noted that a company can take out and maintain insurance for its officers against any liability arising from negligence, default and breach of duty, subject to the appropriate provision being contained within the company's articles.

As a cautionary note the secretary when making contracts on behalf of the company should always ensure that he does so as the company's agent otherwise he could be held personally liable.

Chapter 2

The Company Constitution

The limited company

General

2.1　　Incorporation is the process by which a company may be formed and become a separate legal entity in its own right; distinct from its owners. This principle of the company being a separate legal person was established in 1897 in the case of *Salomon v Salomon and Co Ltd [1897] AC 22*. The Companies Acts have since established the procedure by which a company can be created and this is specified in Part I of the Companies Act 1985, section 1(1) of which states:

> 'Any two or more persons associated for a lawful purpose may, by subscribing their names to a memorandum of association and otherwise complying with the requirements of this Act in respect of registration, form an incorporated company, with or without limited liability.'

Section 1(3A) of the Companies Act 1985 (inserted by the Schedule to the Companies (Single Member Private Limited Companies) Regulations 1992 (SI 1992 No 1699) now allows one person to form a private company limited by shares or by guarantee by subscribing his name to the memorandum, so long as he complies with the registration requirements of the Act. These provisions were introduced on 15 July 1992. The single person may be a natural or a legal person.

The responsibility for recording minutes and decisions made in general meetings, together with the drawing up of any contract in writing outside of normal conditions between himself and the company, will then lie with the sole member or his representative. Single member private limited companies are considered more fully later (see 7.7 MEMBERSHIP).

To effect the incorporation of a limited liability company, the Companies Act 1985, like its predecessors, requires the preparation and presentation of certain documents to Companies House. When the Registrar is satisfied that the documents fulfil the requirements of the Act, a certificate of incorporation will be issued. This can be regarded as a company's 'birth certificate' and is conclusive evidence that the requirements of the Companies Act in respect of registration have been complied with and that the company is authorised to be registered (CA 1985, s 13(7)). The basic aim of the incorporation process is to ensure that sufficient information appears on the public file, maintained by Companies House, to enable the public to make an assessment of the company and of the risks attendant in dealing with it (see Chapter 5).

Reasons for incorporation

2.2   In Great Britain, businesses may take many different legal forms. For most people considering which form of business to use, the choice usually faced is whether to go into business as either:

(*a*)   a sole trader; or

(*b*)   a partnership; or

(*c*)   a limited liability company.

Other types of business organisation do exist, for example, Industrial and Provident Societies and Building Societies. However, in comparison to (*a*) to (*c*) above, their use is limited for most purposes.

Many factors exist in deciding what identity a business should take, for example, taxation considerations. In this decision process the advantages and disadvantages of the incorporation must be examined carefully, and professional advice should be sought where appropriate. The main advantages and disadvantages of incorporation are as follows.

Advantages

(i)   The limited liability of the members, where the company is limited.

(ii)   The ability to raise capital from outside the existing membership.

(iii)   The ability to borrow money in the company's name.

(iv)   A company is taxed in its own right as distinct from its members.

(v)   The continuance of the existence of the business notwithstanding the death or bankruptcy of all or any of its existing members.

Disadvantages

(A)   Requirements of the Companies Acts to disclose information about the company.

(B)   A greater formality is involved in setting up, running and winding up a company.

(C)   Various tax considerations may prove a disincentive.

(D)   The requirement to undergo a formal audit of the accounts each year (subject to exemptions for certain categories of small company and dormant companies (see 4.14 and 4.25 ACCOUNTS AND AUDITORS).

Classification of companies

2.3   Under the Act there exist three basic types of company which may be incorporated, being:

(*a*)   a company limited by shares;

(*b*)   an unlimited company; and

(*c*)   a company limited by guarantee and having no share capital.

Of the three types, the most commonly used for trading entities in Great Britain is the company limited by shares. However, there are two distinct classifications of company within this type, being the private limited company and the public limited company. Both unlimited companies and companies limited by guarantee are (by virtue of the definition given by the Companies Act 1985 to public companies) private companies.

The Act does, however, provide for the registration of certain other classifications of company. These companies fall into the following categories:

(i)   oversea companies having a place of business in Great Britain;

(ii)   an Isle of Man or Channel Islands company having a place of business in England and Wales and/or Scotland.

The registration of these types of company are discussed more fully in 2.55 below.

Additionally CA 1985, s 680 allows for the registration of companies either:

(A)   consisting of two or more members, which were in existence on 2 November 1862, including any company registered under the Joint Stock Companies Acts; and

(B)   any company formed after 2 November 1862, in pursuance of any Act of Parliament, or of letters patent, or being otherwise duly constituted according to law, and consisting of two or more members.

The procedural requirements for the registration of these types of company are laid out in CA 1985, s 681.

The Act also makes provision for the re-registration of companies as follows:

(I)   of a private company limited by shares as a public company limited by shares (CA 1985, ss 43–47);

(II)   of a public company limited by shares as a private company limited by shares (CA 1985, ss 53–55);

(III)   of a limited company as an unlimited company (CA 1985, ss 49, 50); and

(IV)   of an unlimited company as a limited company (CA 1985, ss 51, 52).

The re-registration of companies is dealt with in 2.50 *et seq* below.

The public limited company

2.4   According to section 1(3) of the Companies Act 1985 a public company is a company limited by shares or limited by guarantee and having a share capital whose memorandum of association states it to be a public company, for which the provisions of the Act have been complied with in its registration.

The provisions of the Act as regards the registration of public companies are basically the same as for private companies. However, certain significant differences exist in relation to

(*a*)   capital; and

(*b*)   commencement of trading.

These points are discussed more fully in 2.49 below.

The private limited company

2.5   Section 1(3) of the Companies Act 1985 states that by definition a private company is a company 'that is not a public company'.

The differences in the classification of companies limited by shares were first introduced by the Companies Act 1980, the provisions of which are now incorporated in the Companies Act 1985, to give effect to the European Community 2nd Company Law Directive of 1976 which was aimed at public companies.

The reasons why the classifications were introduced are now mainly historic. However, the basic difference between the two is that under CA 1985, s 81 it is an offence for a private company to offer or to allot any of its shares or debentures to the public, whether for cash or otherwise. Section 81 has been repealed for most purposes by sections 143(3) and 170(1) of the Financial Services Act 1986 but the basic principles introduced by section 81 of the Act remain the same.

Additionally, the provisions of the Companies Act 1989 relating to the de-regulation of companies, and in particular the elective regime, only apply to private companies.

Liability

2.6   The concept of limited liability is one which relates to the liability of the membership of a company to contribute to the assets of the company should it be wound up. The amount of the members' liability is determined by the liability clause contained in the company's memorandum of association and differs in its nature according to whether the company is one which is limited by shares, limited by guarantee or unlimited.

(a)   Limited by shares

A company limited by shares is formed on the basis that the liability of the members is limited to the amount (if any) unpaid on the shares held by them. A member's liability does not extend beyond any amounts unpaid on shares should the company be wound up.

(b)   Limited by guarantee

The liability of the members is limited to an amount which the members each undertake to contribute to the assets of the company should it be wound up. In effect, each member makes a guarantee to pay a specified amount to the company.

(c)   Unlimited

No limit to the liability of the members exists, thus the membership of such a company may, in the event of the company being wound up, find themselves liable to pay or contribute towards the debts of the company and the winding-up costs.

The privilege of obtaining limited liability, however, is only available where a company is limited by shares or by guarantee.

It should be borne in mind that, given the current practice of the banks to seek personal guarantees from directors and/or shareholders, the attractions of limited liability may be somewhat short-lived.

Nature of companies

2.7   The Register of Companies maintained by Companies House currently contains around one million companies which have been registered under the Companies Acts. Of this figure, around 99% are private companies (of which private companies limited by shares form the overwhelming majority). Public companies represent only 1% of companies registered. However, this is an increase from previous years. In 1985 public companies represented only 0.5% of companies registered.

The reason for this overwhelming use of the private company limited by shares comes out of the balance of the ability of the company to raise initial capital compared with the company limited by guarantee and the less onerous requirements of the Act compared with the public company. This difference has further been reinforced by various provisions of the Companies Act 1989 (see Chapter 7).

(a)   Capital

By definition, the members of a company limited by guarantee do not contribute any funds to the capital of the company on the assumption of their membership. They instead make a guarantee to do so should the company be wound up. Thus, the introduction of new members to the company will not, in itself, assist the company to raise capital.

For a company limited by shares, subject to certain requirements imposed by the Act (see 8.8 CAPITAL), members are usually asked to pay a cash consideration to the company in return for the allotment of shares.

Thus, the incorporation and use of a company limited by guarantee will only be appropriate where the company will be obtaining its funds by other means than the issue of shares. As such, the guarantee company is commonly used where funds are raised by fees or subscriptions and thus is suited to the incorporation of a club, society, association, institute or other 'not for profit' organisation. Guarantee companies are commonly used where charitable status will be required.

(b)   Companies Act requirements

The requirements of the Act vary in certain respects in relation to private and public limited companies in that the Act imposes additional requirements upon public companies in the disclosure of information and capital requirements.

Incorporation requirements

General

2.8   The registration of a limited company is effected by the delivery to the Registrar of Companies of the documents specified by the Companies Act 1985, the company's compliance with the various procedures contained therein and the payment to the Registrar of Companies of the appropriate fee (£20 as at the time of this publication).

Prior to proceeding to registration, however, several matters must first be considered.

The company name

2.9   In general, a company may register itself under any name it chooses. The Companies Act 1985, the Business Names Act 1985 and the common law do, however, place certain restrictions on the use of company and business names.

Companies Act 1985

2.10   Section 26 of the Companies Act 1985 defines several circumstances in which a company shall not be registered under CA 1985 by a name:

(*a*)   which includes, otherwise than at the end of the name, any of the following words or expressions — 'Limited', 'Unlimited' or 'Public Limited Company' (CA 1985, s 27 allows the abbreviations 'Ltd' and 'PLC' to be used as alternatives to the full forms); or

(*b*)   which is the same as a name already appearing on the index of company names maintained by the Registrar of Companies; or

(*c*)   the use of which, in the opinion of the Secretary of State, would constitute a criminal offence or is considered offensive.

Also, without the prior approval of the Secretary of State, a company may not be registered by a name:

(*d*)   which in the opinion of the Secretary of State would be likely to give the impression that the company is connected in any way with HM Government or with any local authority; or

(*e*)   which includes any word or expression which is specified for the time being by the Secretary of State (see Appendix 2B).

Prior to registration of a company, it is important that a check be undertaken on the index of names maintained by the Registrar of Companies under section 714 of the CA 1985, to ensure that the name required is not already being used. However, the Registrar also maintains a 'proposed name' index for companies which have lodged the relevant documents for registration but which have not yet been processed. While a name may not appear on the statutory index, it still may not be available for use.

It should be noted that the Registrar does not consult the Trade Marks Index when considering an application for a company name, and the registration of a name does not mean that trade marks do not already exist. It is therefore advisable to make a search at the Trade Marks Registry if in doubt. (See 11.18 COMMERCIAL CONSIDERATIONS.)

Business Names Act 1985

2.11   As well as the restrictions placed on the use of company names under the Companies Act 1985, the Business Names Act 1985 furtherintroduces a system for regulating the use of names under which companies, partnerships and individuals may carry on business in Great Britain. As regards a company registered under the Companies Act these regulations apply to it in circumstances where the company carries on business in a name other than its corporate name.

The main provisions of this Act as it applies to companies are:

(*a*)   except with the prior written approval of the Secretary of State a company may not carry on business under a name which would be likely to give the impression that the business is connected with Her Majesty's Government or with any local authority or the name includes any word or expression specified in regulations made by Statutory Instrument.

Failure to acquire consent by the Secretary of State for a name needing approval is a criminal offence;

(*b*)   where a company is using a name other than its corporate name it must state in legible characters on all its business letters, written orders for the supply of goods and services, invoices, receipts and demands for payment of debts arising in the course of business, the corporate name of the company and an address within Great Britain at which the service of documents relating to the business will be effective (usually the registered office address). This is in addition to a company's stationery requirements as specified in the Companies Act (CA 1985, ss 349 and 351); and

(*c*)   at any premises where the business is carried on to which the customers of the business or suppliers of any goods or services to the business have access, to display in a prominent position so that it may easily be read, a notice containing those names and addresses specified above. The company must also, on request, supply such names and addresses to any person who, in the course of business, may ask for them.

It should also be noted that under section 33 of the CA 1985 it is an offence for any person who is not a public company to carry on any trade, profession or business with a name which contains the words 'Public Limited Company' (or its abbreviation).

Further, section 34 of the 1985 Act prevents any person trading or carrying on a business to use the word 'Limited' (or its abbreviation) unless duly incorporated with limited liability.

Too like names

2.12   Section 28(2) of the Companies Act 1985 gives the Secretary of State a power, in certain circumstances, to direct a company to change its name. This power is exercisable where a company has been registered with a name that is either 'the same as' or 'too like' a name already appearing on the Register of Companies at the time the name was first registered.

Names which are considered 'the same as' or 'too like' will usually be brought to the Registrar's attention by the company for whom the name is 'the same as' or 'too like' lodging an objection and requesting that the company name be changed. In submitting an objection, the objecting party should give support to his objection by detailing his reasons for the application and giving evidence of any confusion between the companies that has arisen (or his reasons for expecting confusion to arise in the future).

It should be noted that it is the company which was last registered who will be directed to change its name. Thus, in submitting an objection it is important to consider whether the objection may lead to a counter-objection resulting in the originally objecting company being directed to change its name.

It is important to note that the power of the Secretary of State to direct a company to change its name in these circumstances is only exercisable for a period of twelve months from the date of registration of the name which is 'the same as' or 'too like' an existing name. Thus, objections lodged after this twelve-month period will be disregarded. However, in circumstances where the Secretary of State considers that misleading information was provided to him for the purpose of securing the registration of a company with a particular name or that undertakings or assurances given in this connection were not fulfilled, then the power of the Secretary of State to direct that the name of a company be changed is extended to five years from the date of registration in that name.

Failure to comply with a direction from the Secretary of State to change a company name may render the directors of the company so directed liable to a fine.

The criteria which the Registrar of Companies will apply in determining whether a company is 'the same as' or 'too like' an existing name is that the existence of the two names is likely to lead to confusion between the companies. Thus, factors such as the types of business carried on and the geographical locations and area of operation of the businesses will be considered.

Examples of circumstances, subject to the above criteria, in which names will be considered 'the same as' or 'too like' others are where:

(a)   *The names are the same*

    e.g.   PL Lai Limited and
            PL Lai Company, Limited.

(b)   *The names are phonetically identical*

e.g.   KPMG <u>Peat</u> Marwick Limited and
       KPMG <u>Pete</u> Marwick Limited.

(c)   *The names contain only a slight variation in spelling which does not make a significant difference*

e.g.   Aquiss Limited and
       Aquis Limited.

(d)   *The names contain a word (or words) which are regarded as a distinctive element and that element is not sufficiently qualified*

    e.g.   Aquis Limited and
            Aquis <u>Holdings</u> Limited.

    In this circumstance the addition of the word 'Holdings' to the name would not sufficiently qualify the name, the word 'Aquis' being considered the distinctive element.

Should a more distinctive qualification be added, then the names may then be considered sufficiently distinctive

e.g.   Aquis <u>Engineers</u> Limited and

Aquis <u>Secretaries</u> Limited.

Oversea company names

2.13   In the case of an oversea company registering as a branch, or as a place of business, pursuant to Part XXIII of the Companies Act 1985 (see 2.55 below), such registration will not be permitted in the oversea company's name if it differs from an existing registered company name only by the substitution of the overseas equivalent of 'Limited', 'Unlimited' or 'Public Limited Company' (or their permitted abbreviations).

e.g.   Aquis <u>S.A.</u> and

Aquis <u>PLC</u>.

Additionally, the provisions of CA 1985, s 26 (see 2.10 above) apply to the registration of oversea company names (CA 1985, s 694).

Misleading name

2.14   Pursuant to the power given to him by CA 1985, s 32 the Secretary of State (acting through the Registrar of Companies) may *at any time* direct a company to change its name if, in his opinion, the continued use of the name gives a misleading indication of the nature of the activities a company undertakes and that this is likely to cause harm to the public.

Where such a direction is made it must normally be complied with within six weeks. The company receiving the direction does, however, in such circumstances, have a right of appeal to the court, within three weeks of receiving the direction, to have it set aside. This contrasts with any direction to change a company name given under section 28 of the Act where no right of appeal to the court exists.

Exemption from using the word 'Limited' in a company name

2.15   Section 30 of the Companies Act 1985 specifies certain circumstances in which a company may be exempted from the use of the word 'Limited' in its name.

To qualify for such an exemption the company making the application must be a private company *limited by guarantee* and must satisfy the following conditions:

(*a*)   the objects of the company are the promotion of either commerce, art, science, education, religion, charity or of any profession;

(*b*)   the memorandum and articles of association state that:

(i) any profits or other income will be applied in promoting the company's objects;

(ii) the payment of dividends to the members is prohibited; and

(iii) on a winding-up, all the assets of the company will be transferred to another body having similar objects or of which the objects are the promotion of a charity.

Furthermore, a company which was a private company limited by shares on 25 February 1982, may also be exempt, but only if it did not include the word 'Limited' in its name due to a licence it had under section 19 of the Companies Act 1948 and it complies with the above conditions: (*a*) and (*b*).

In support of the application a company must submit to the Registrar of Companies a statutory declaration made by either a director or secretary of the company (or a solicitor engaged in the company's formation) on form 30(5)(a) (revised March 1995) which confirms that the above requirements have been met.

Should a company which has obtained an exemption from using the word 'Limited' in its name fail to continue to fulfil the conditions required to so exempt it, then the Registrar of Companies may direct the company to change its name to include the word 'Limited' at its end.

Passing off

2.16   Although through the various means and protections afforded to them by the Companies Act 1985, a company can protect its name by objecting to the registration of a company with a similar name, such protections are not open to a company when faced with the position that an *unincorporated* business is using a similar name (for example, possibly the same name with the exception of the words 'Limited' or 'Public Limited Company').

In such circumstances, no right of objection exists through the Registrar of Companies. However, the common law principle of 'passing off' may apply. In such circumstances, action may be taken by the objecting company through the courts which seeks to restrain the use of a particular name by another party, on the basis that a person may not represent himself as carrying on the trade or business of another. Such actions will usually succeed where it can be shown that the use of a particular name has or will mislead the public (*Ewing v Buttercup Margarine Co Ltd [1917] 2 Ch 1*).

Insolvency Act 1986

2.17   Under section 216 of Insolvency Act 1986 a person who at any time in the preceeding 12 months has been a director of a company which has gone into insolvent liquidation, is disallowed:

(i) from being a director of any other company which is known by a prohibited name; or

(ii)   from taking part in the promotion, formation and management of any such company; or

(iii)   from being involved in the carrying on of a business, which is not a company, under a prohibited name.

A prohibited name is the name by which the company was known in the 12 months prior to the liquidation or one which is so similar to suggest association with that company.

The restriction lasts for 5 years from the day the company went into liquidation and if a director contravenes any of the above regulations he is liable to imprisonment or a fine, or both.

Publication of company name

2.18   Under the provisions of the Companies Act 1985 a company must fulfil certain obligations imposed by the Act to publish its name, and other prescribed details, on its business stationery. Failure to do so renders every officer of the company in default, liable to a fine.

CA 1985, s 349 requires that a company's name must appear in legible characters upon:

(*a*)   all business letters;

(*b*)   all notices and other official publications;

(*c*)   all bills of exchange, promissory notes, endorsements, cheques and orders for money or goods purporting to be signed by or on behalf of the company; and

(*d*)   all bills of parcels, invoices, receipts and letters of credit.

CA 1985, s 351 further requires the following details to appear in legible characters on companies' business letters and order forms:

(i)   place of registration (i.e. England and Wales or Scotland);

(ii)   registered number;

(iii)   registered office address;

(iv)   where the company is exempt from the use of the word 'Limited' as part of its name, a statement must appear that the company is limited (e.g. 'a company limited by guarantee');

(v)   if the company is an 'investment company' (within the definition of CA 1985, s 266), a statement must appear that it is such a company.

There is no obligation on companies to state on their business stationery the names of any of the directors. However, should a company opt to do so (otherwise than as the signatory or in the text) then the names of *all* the directors must appear, including those of any shadow directors (CA 1985, s 305).

Similarly, a company having a share capital is under no obligation to state its share capital on its stationery. However, should it choose to do so, then any reference made must be to the *paid-up* share capital (CA 1985, s 351(2)).

Companies using E-mail as a means of communication, should note that business letters and order forms sent by electronic messaging should still comply with the statutory requirements laid down by the Companies Act 1985. The Criminal Evidence Act 1985, which came into force on 31 January 1997, makes it clear that computer generated documents are admissible in proceedings and can be treated in the same way as paper documents.

Similarly it is considered best practice to include on faxes the information you would show on business letters and with an order form placed on a web site the same details as required by s 351.

Section 111 of the Companies Act 1989 substituted sections 30, 30A, 30B and 30C for the original section 30 in the Charities Act 1960. The 1960 Act has since been consolidated into the Charities Act 1993 (see 11.9 COMMERCIAL CONSIDERATIONS). Section 68 of the 1993 Act requires that a charity incorporated under the Companies Act 1985 (or to which the provisions of the Companies Act apply), where its name does not include the word 'charity' or the word 'charitable', must state the fact that it is a charity on all business stationery as required under section 349 of the Companies Act 1985 and in all conveyances purporting to be executed by the company. Section 349(2) to (4) of the Companies Act 1985 applies in relation to a contravention of this section.

CA 1985, s 348 further requires a company to paint or affix its name outside every office or place from which it carries on business. The name painted or affixed must be placed in a conspicuous position and be legible. Failure to comply with this section renders the company and every officer of that company who is in default liable to a fine.

It should be noted that these provisions are in addition to any provisions with which a company must comply pursuant to the Business Names Act 1985 (see 2.11 above).

Change of company name

2.19   In accordance with section 28 of the Companies Act 1985 a company may, by a special resolution of its members, change its name (see precedent A, Appendix 2D). When changing a company name, a similar process to that described above to ensure the name's availability and acceptability must be undertaken. When passed, a copy of the special resolution changing the company name must be filed at Companies House (CA 1985, s 380(4)(a)) within 15 days of its passing, together with a cheque for £10 (as at the time of this publication) in payment of the appropriate fee.

Once the name has been approved, the Registrar of Companies will issue to the company a Certificate of Incorporation on Change of Name and alter the name of the company on the Register of Companies. The new company name becomes effective as from the date of issue of the Certificate of Incorporation on Change of Name (CA 1985, s 28(6)).

During company reorganisations it is often preferable for companies to simultaneously swap their names. This can be achieved by writing an explanatory letter to the Registrar enclosing the respective special resolutions.

A company which is listed must inform the Listing Authority of the name change and date from which it takes effect without delay and send them a copy of the change of name certificates. (Yellow Book, para 9.40).

The memorandum of association

2.20   Section 1 of the Companies Act 1985 states that any two or more persons who are associated for a lawful purpose may subscribe to the memorandum of association to form a limited or unlimited company so long as the other requirements for registration are complied with. They then become the first members of the company (see further 7.1 MEMBERSHIP). Where a private limited company is to be formed with only one member, this provision is modified by the new section 1(3A) of CA 1985 inserted by the Companies (Single Member Private Limited Companies) Regulations 1992 (SI 1992 No 1699) which allows the single member to subscribe alone to the memorandum.

This document constitutes a company's charter with the outside world, being more particularly the persons with whom a company will transact, either directly or indirectly, in the course of its business.

CA 1985, s 2 provides that the memorandum of association of a company must state:

(*a*)   the name of the company;

(*b*)   in the case of public companies only, a statement that the company is a Public Limited Company (CA 1985, s 25);

(*c*)   whether the domicile of the company is to be in England and Wales, or in Scotland;

(*d*)   the objects of the company;

(*e*)   that the liability of the members is limited;

(*f*)   in the case of a company limited by shares, the amount of authorised share capital with which the company is to be incorporated and how the shares are to be divided, or for a company limited by guarantee, the amount each member undertakes to contribute to the assets of the company in the event of it being wound up;

(*g*)   the names of the subscribers and, in the case of a company limited by shares, the number of shares to be taken by each (a minimum of one share must be taken by each subscriber).

Sub-paragraphs (*e*) to (*g*) above do not apply in the case of an unlimited company.

These statements are set out in the form of separate clauses in the memorandum and are examined in more detail below. The basic formats of the memorandum of association are, however, set out in The Companies (Tables A to F) Regulations 1985 (SI 1985 No 805), being:

(i) Table B in the case of a private company limited by shares;

(ii) Table C in the case of a company limited by guarantee;

(iii) Table E in the case of an unlimited company; and

(iv) Table F in the case of a public company limited by shares.

These tables set out the minimum of detail, and the format, that must appear in a company's memorandum of association pursuant to CA 1985, s 3.

The name clause

2.21 This is the first clause of the memorandum of association and is a statement that:

'The company's name is XYZ Limited/Public Limited Company'.

Unless otherwise approved by an application pursuant to sections 30 and 31 of the Companies Act 1985 a private company must conclude its name with the word 'Limited' or its abbreviation 'Ltd'. Exemptions from the use of the word 'Limited' exist in certain circumstances for a company limited by guarantee (see 2.15 above). Similarly the name of a public company must end in either 'Public Limited Company' or its abbreviation 'PLC'.

An unlimited company is forbidden to use the words 'Limited' or 'Public Limited Company' (or their abbreviations) in its name.

The public company clause

2.22 This clause is only required when the company being incorporated is to be a public company and is a statement of this fact i.e.:

'The company is to be a public company'.

The registered office clause

2.23 This clause establishes the domicile of a company (i.e. in which country it will be registered) and is a statement that the registered office of the company will be situated in either:

(*a*) England and Wales; or

(*b*) Scotland.

A statement that the registered office of the company is to be situated in the United Kingdom is not acceptable in this clause as it does not sufficiently identify with which companies registry (i.e. England and Wales *or* Scotland) the company is to be registered.

There is no requirement for the full postal address of the registered office to be included in this clause.

The objects clause

2.24   This is generally not one clause but a series of clauses which set out a company's objectives, being the business(es) it proposes to carry on and any incidental or ancillary powers which it may require to allow it to conduct its business(es).

The clauses can be split into three categories:

(a)   *The main objects clause(s)*

These clauses set out what the main business(es) and activities of the company will be.

(b)   *The subsidiary objects clause(s)*

These clauses set out the many ancillary activities which a company is authorised to undertake to enable it to achieve its stated main objects. For example, the power to borrow and lend money, purchase and sell property, acquire and promote other businesses and to give guarantees.

(c)   *The 'catch all' clause*

This clause will allow a company to do anything which could be regarded as incidental to the main objects and is usually included as a protection against the company overstepping the boundaries of the main and subsidiary objects clauses.

The main purpose behind the objects clause relates to the doctrine of *ultra vires* which states that any act of a company which is outside the scope of its objects is *ultra vires* ('beyond the powers') and void. This doctrine developed as a safeguard for the members of a company as a means of controlling, via a statement of the purpose of the company in its objects clause, the businesses in which a company (through its directors) could become involved (*Ashbury Railway Carriage and Iron Co v Riche (1875) LR 7 HL 653*). In effect, this doctrine allowed contracts to be declared void and set aside where a company had acted *ultra vires*. For third parties transacting in good faith with a company this posed the problem that by using this doctrine companies could escape their contractual responsibilities.

However, in response to this problem, the application of this doctrine has been changed in recent years by case law (*Bell Houses Ltd v City Wall Properties*

Ltd [1966] 2 QB 656) and most notably by section 9(1) of the European Communities Act 1972 (now CA 1985, s 35) which introduced safeguards for third parties who transacted with a company in good faith not realising the act to have been *ultra vires* of the company and accordingly void. Following the introduction of this legislation third parties were given the right to enforce the performance of a contract on a company notwithstanding that the company may have been acting *ultra vires*.

The Companies Act 1989, however, introduced further changes to the current position.

The Companies Act 1989

2.25   Following the introduction of sections 108 to 110 of the Companies Act 1989 in February 1991 the doctrine of *ultra vires* has undergone a further significant change.

CA 1989, s 108 introduced a substitution of CA 1985, s 35 which has effectively substantially abolished the previously established principle of *ultra vires* by stating that:

'(1)   The validity of an act done by a company shall not be called into question on the ground of lack of capacity by reason of anything in the company's memorandum',

and in section 35A(1) that:

'In favour of a person dealing with a company in good faith, the power of the board of directors to bind the company, or authorise others to do so, shall be deemed to be free of any limitation under the company's constitution'.

Thus, the 1989 Act effectively freed the board of directors from any limitation contained in the company's memorandum of association to bind it in any transactions with third parties while at the same time giving to third parties the protection that any acts done by the directors of a company cannot be declared void and set aside on the basis that they are *ultra vires*. This principle applies even where the third party is aware that the act is beyond the scope of the company's constitution.

However, these reforms are aimed at protecting third parties dealing with a company and not at giving directors unlimited scope for binding the company. Sections 35(2) and (3) and 35A(4) and (5) of the CA 1985 (as introduced by CA 1989, s 108) make the directors personally liable to account to a company's shareholders in circumstances where they have exceeded the powers given to them in the memorandum of association to bind the company. Thus, although the capacity of a company to transact with third parties cannot now be questioned, a company can hold its directors personally liable for any *ultra vires* acts they commit (CA 1985, s 35(3)) or can restrain them from doing any act which may be beyond the company's powers (CA 1985, s 35(2)).

The greater protection now afforded to third parties by sections 35 and 35A of the CA 1985 do not, however, apply to *ultra vires* transactions entered into between directors (and any persons connected with them) and the company. Under CA 1985, s 322A (as introduced by CA 1989, s 109) any such transactions will still be voidable at the instance of the company (see 11.6 COMMERCIAL CONSIDERATIONS).

The general commercial company

2.26   As a consequence of these changes, CA 1985, s 3A (as introduced by CA 1989, s 110) allows a company to state its objects in a much shortened form. The objects clause can now merely be a statement that:

'the object of the company is to carry on business as a general commercial company'.

Where the memorandum of association contains such a statement a company is deemed to be able to carry on any trade or business whatsoever and have the power to do all such things as are incidental or conducive to the company or of any trade or business.

Section 4 of the CA 1985 has also been amended by CA 1989, s 110 in that the objects clause may now be amended for any reason and not just for the reasons previously specified by that section. The subject of alteration of the objects clause is covered further below at 2.27.

It has yet to be seen how the changes will develop into company law. However, many companies may wish to continue to use the 'long form' method of objects clauses to provide them with some form of protection in restricting the capacity of directors to bind the company. It would be hard to hold a director personally liable where the objects of the company are for a general commercial company. Where 'long form' objects exist, however, the directors may find themselves becoming personally liable to the company where they exceed the powers given to them.

Alteration of the objects clause

2.27   Following the introduction of a revised section 4 of CA 1985, a company may, by a special resolution of its members, alter the objects clause of its memorandum of association for any reason (see precedent B, Appendix 2D). Prior to the coming into force of this section, the Act specified the only circumstances in which the objects clause could be altered.

Following the passing of a special resolution altering the objects clause, a copy must be filed at Companies House within 15 days of the date of passing (CA 1985, s 380(4)(a)) together with a print of the memorandum of association as altered (CA 1985, s 6(1)(a)).

Any alteration made in a company's objects clause may however, under CA 1985, s 5, be cancelled on the authority of the court following an application for cancellation by the holders of not less than 15% in nominal value of the company's issued share capital. Any such application may not be made by any person who voted in favour of the change and must be made within 21 days after the date of passing of the special resolution.

Upon an application for cancellation being made, the court may make an order confirming or rejecting the alteration, either in whole or in part, subject to such conditions it may decide (CA 1985, s 5(4)).

The limitation of liability clause

2.28   This is a statement that the liability of the members is limited and, in the case of both private and public companies limited by shares, is a statement that:

'The liability of the members is limited'.

This clause on its own does not state to what extent the liability of the members is limited. Section 74(2) of the Insolvency Act 1986, however, defines the extent of a member's liability and in the case of a company limited by shares states that it is the amount (if any) unpaid on the shares in respect of which he is liable as a past or present member. The liability as a past member does not apply to any debts or liabilities incurred after he ceased to be a member and, in any case, only applies where he ceased to be a member within a period of one year from the commencement of the winding up of the company.

In the case of companies limited by guarantee the statement of liability is rather different as it amounts to a declaration that in the event of a winding-up the members each undertake to contribute to the assets of the company (section 74(3) of the Insolvency Act 1986). However this contribution, and accordingly the liability of each member, will be restricted to the amount specified in the capital clause (see 2.29 below). This amount, when determined and included in the clause cannot be altered without the member's consent in writing (CA 1985, s 16(2)).

The capital clause

2.29   This clause sets out the amount of authorised (or nominal) capital with which a company limited by shares is incorporated and the division of this capital into shares of a specified amount e.g.:

'The share capital of the company is £1,000 divided into 1,000 ordinary shares of £1 each'.

The authorised share capital does not have to be stated in sterling and can be divided into different fixed amounts of non-sterling currencies. However, the minimum capital requirement of a public company is £50,000 and hence this minimum amount must be stated in sterling, although further share capital can be in other currencies.

The class(es) into which the shares are divided need not be determined in the capital clause (e.g. ordinary and preference). Such definitions may be more conveniently introduced in the articles of association together with the rights attaching to the shares.

The relevance of the authorised capital figure is that no shares may be issued in excess of the amount stated, although periodic increases of the authorised share capital are allowed by CA 1985, s 121 (see 8.38 CAPITAL). When incorporating a company, the amount of funds the company wishes to raise by way of share capital should be the guiding principle in determining the level at which the authorised capital should be fixed.

Private companies

2.30   No restriction exists with regard to either the maximum or minimum amounts of authorised capital.

In the case of a company limited by guarantee, this clause is a statement of the amount each member undertakes to contribute to the assets of the company should it be wound up whilst he is a member or within one year after he ceases to be a member, for payment of the debts or liabilities of the company contracted while he was a member.

Public companies

2.31   Section 11 of the Companies Act 1985 requires that a company being registered as a public limited company must state in its memorandum that its share capital is of an amount not less than the authorised minimum.

Section 118 of the CA 1985 further defines the authorised minimum as being £50,000 (or such other figure as the Secretary of State may from time to time determine).

Further requirements exist as to the paid-up capital of a public company before it may commence trading activities. These are discussed in 2.49 below.

The association clause

2.32   This clause forms the statement of intent of the subscribers to the memorandum of association (being the first members of a company) to be formed into a company.

In the case of a company limited by shares, section 2(5)(b) and (c) of the Companies Act 1985 requires that each subscriber take a minimum of one share (a minimum of two subscribers are required for public companies) and that each subscriber write his name opposite the number of shares he has agreed to take.

Section 2(6) of the CA 1985 further requires that each subscriber sign the memorandum in the presence of at least one witness, who must attest the signatures.

Form of memorandum

2.33   For an example of a model 'long form' memorandum of association for a private company limited by shares see Appendix 2C.

The articles of association

2.34   This document sets out a company's regulations for its internal management, and will commonly cover such matters as the rights of shareholders, procedure upon an issue or transfer of shares, rights attaching to shares, the appointment, removal and powers of the directors, and the conduct of board and general meetings.

Table A

2.35   This is contained in the Companies (Tables A to F) Regulations 1985 (SI 1985 No 805) and is a model set of articles for a company limited by shares. It applies to both public and private companies limited by shares and, with certain modifications as introduced by Tables C and E, to private companies limited by guarantee and unlimited companies respectively. For companies registered prior to the enactment of the 1985 Act, the Table A contained in the Companies Act under which the company was registered applies, unless the current form of Table A has been adopted by the company into its articles.

Pursuant to CA 1985, s 8 a company may adopt all or any of the regulations contained in Table A as its articles of association. Table A will therefore only apply to the extent that it is not modified or excluded by a company's articles of association.

Thus a company may either:

(*a*)   register its own articles, in which case the provisions of Table A will only apply where matters detailed in Table A are not omitted from, or specifically included in, the articles; or

(*b*)   adopt Table A in its entirety, or in a modified form.

If no articles are registered, then Table A will apply in its entirety and will automatically become the regulations of the company.

Thus, companies have a fairly free hand to draft such provisions as they may require into their articles of association. However, in constructing articles the following overriding principles should be borne in mind:

(i)   no effect can be given to any regulations in the articles which conflict with any statutory requirements; and

(ii)   should any regulations in the articles conflict with any provisions in its memorandum of association, then the provisions of the memorandum prevail.

Should a company on incorporation decide that it wishes to register its own articles, CA 1985, s 7(3) states that they must be printed, divided into paragraphs, numbered consecutively, signed by each subscriber to the memorandum of association in the presence of a witness and dated.

The Companies Act 1989 prospectively inserted a new section 8A into the Companies Act 1985. This section provides that regulations may be prescribed for a Table G containing model articles of association for partnership companies. A partnership company is defined as a company limited by shares whose shares are intended to be held to a substantial extent by or on behalf of its employees. The DTI is still considering, in the light of a consultation on the introduction of Table G conducted in 1995, whether to propose amending legislation.

Private companies

2.36   Many private companies limited by shares find it convenient to adopt articles of association in a shortened format. The reason for this is to simplify, as far as possible, the administration surrounding the company. This applies both where the company is a subsidiary within a group of companies or is in a 'stand alone' situation.

Many companies, however, deem it necessary to have strict procedures laid down for the administration of their affairs in such matters as:

(*a*)   share capital and class rights;

(*b*)   allotment and transfer of shares;

(*c*)   meetings of members and directors;

(*d*)   appointment and removal of directors;

(*e*)   powers of directors; and

(*f*)   general administration.

Due consideration must be given to such matters in giving instructions for the drafting of articles of association.

Public companies

2.37   No additional requirements are imposed on public companies to have included in their articles of association any specific provisions. However, should a public company be intending to apply for a listing on The London Stock Exchange or Alternative Investment Market, then the articles must comply with the regulations contained in The Stock Exchange's 'Listing Rules' (Yellow Book) or AIM rules. For example, no restrictions may exist on the transferability of fully paid shares.

Companies limited by guarantee

2.38   The rules on articles of association apply equally to a company limited by guarantee as they do to a company limited by shares. However, as a basic difference exists in the nature of the companies' memberships in so far as a company limited by guarantee has no shares, it is necessary for Table A to be modified in this respect. AccordinglyTable C in the Companies (Tables A to F) Regulations 1985 was drawn up to accommodate these necessary modifications.

Alteration of articles

2.39   Under section 9 of the Companies Act 1985 a company may at any time, but subject to its memorandum of association, by special resolution alter all or any of the conditions contained in its articles of association (see Precedents C and D, Appendix 2D). No reason for the alteration need be given and any alterations made are deemed as valid as if they had been originally contained in the articles and are also subject to further alteration by a special resolution (see 7.57 MEMBERSHIP). A company may not deprive itself or fetter its ability to alter its articles by any arrangement contained in its articles, in favour of its members or a third party. Thus, any attempt to make part of the articles unalterable is void (*Allen v Gold Reefs of West Africa [1900] 7 Ch 656*). Any article requiring a greater majority than is necessary to pass a special resolution is also void. When altered, a copy of the amended articles of association, together with a print of the special resolution which effected the alteration, must be delivered to Companies House (CA 1985, s 18 and s 380).

Companies quoted on The London Stock Exchange must obtain prior clearance from the Quotations Department for any proposed alterations to the articles, and once approved by the members revised copies of the articles must be delivered to The Stock Exchange.

Completion and filing of the incorporation documents

2.40   In making an application to register a company under the Companies Act 1985, section 10 requires the submission to the Registrar of Companies of a statement of the first directors, secretary and registered office of the company together with its memorandum and articles of association (unless Table A is to be adopted in its entirety). Section 12 of the CA 1985 further requires the completion and submission to the Registrar of Companies of a statutory declaration with these documents.

Section 11 of the CA 1985 also states that a *public* company must meet the minimum authorised capital requirement before it may be registered (currently £50,000).

Particulars of the first directors, secretary and registered office

2.41   In accordance with section 10(2) of and Schedule 1 to the Companies Act 1985 the following details are required to be given to the Registrar of Companies on form 10 (revised March 1995).

The details which must be given are as follows.

Directors

2.42

(*a*)   full name;

(*b*)   residential address;

(*c*)   business occupation;

(*d*)   nationality;

(*e*)   other UK directorships currently held or which have been held within the previous five years; and

(*f*)   date of birth.

In 1997, the DTI consulted on allowing companies to supply a service address for directors which would be placed on the public register instead of their home address. However, it was decided that the requirement for filing home addresses should remain. In addition, the paper proposed abolishing the requirement to provide the director's business occupation, nationality and particulars of other directorships. It has subsequently been decided that the requirement to file other directorships should be revoked.

For a public company section 282(1) of the CA 1985 imposes the requirement that the minimum number of directors needed is two. No such requirement exists for private companies where, subject to any provisions in the company's articles of association, the minimum number of directors needed is one (CA 1985, s 282(3)).

Changes to the directors of a company (appointment, removal and resignation) subsequent to registration are dealt with in 6.3 and 6.9 THE DIRECTORS.

Company secretary

2.43   The particulars required to be disclosed about the secretary of a company are his full name and residential address. A consultative document was published in 1997 which proposed to abolish the requirement to provide a residential address for the public record and instead provide an alternative service address (see 2.42 above), however it was decided that the requirement should remain unchanged.

The position and qualifications of the company secretary are dealt with more fully in Chapter 1.

Registered office

2.44   The full postal address of the first registered office of the company must be detailed.

If the company is to be domiciled and accordingly registered in England and Wales, the address of the registered office must be in either England or Wales. Similarly if the company is to be domiciled in Scotland the address of the registered office must be in Scotland. Accordingly, the address given must be consistent with the domicile stated in the company's memorandum of association.

The address of the registered office (but not the country of domicile) may subsequently be changed by resolution of the directors of the company.

Where a change in the location of a company's registered office occurs, section 287 of the Act requires notice of the change to be given to the Registrar of Companies on the prescribed form (form 287). The change does not become effective until the form of notification is filed at Companies House. However, until the end of a period of 14 days, beginning with the date on which notification of the change is filed at Companies House, a person may validly serve upon the company any document at its previous registered office address (section 287(4)).

Memorandum and articles of association

2.45   Section 2 of the Companies Act 1985 requires the memorandum and articles of association to be in the form and executed as specified by the Act (see 2.20 above).

An important point to note about the memorandum and articles of association is that when they are registered at Companies House they bind the members of a company to the same extent as they would have been bound had they been signed and sealed by each member. Thus, anyone entering into membership of the company, subsequent to the company's registration, is as bound to observe the provisions contained in the company's memorandum and articles as the subscribers who signed the original documents.

Declaration of compliance

2.46   Before the Registrar of Companies may issue the certificate of incorporation of a company, section 12 of the Companies Act 1985 states that he must first be satisfied that all the requirements of the Act have been complied with. For this purpose CA 1985, s 12 requires that a statutory declaration in the prescribed form (form 12, revised March 1995) be submitted. Such declaration must be completed by either a solicitor engaged in the formation of the company, or by a person named as a director or secretary of the company on the form 10.

The declaration must be made before a Notary Public, Commissioner for Oaths or Justice of the Peace who will also execute the form as confirmation of the declaration having been made.

Upon completion, the declaration is accepted by the Registrar of Companies as evidence that the requirements of the Act as regards the registration procedures have been complied with.

Capital duty

2.47   Prior to the Finance Act 1988, a company limited by shares was required to pay capital duty upon its applying for registration. This duty was charged at the rate of 1% on the value paid by the company on the issue of its share capital. Capital duty was abolished for all companiesapplying for registration and for all issues of shares made by a limited company on or after 16 March 1988 and has not been replaced by any other duty.

Certificate of incorporation

2.48   Upon the submission of the forms 10, 12 and the memorandum and articles of association, together with payment of the appropriate fee to the Registrar of Companies (£20 as at the time of publication) he will issue to the company its certificate of incorporation. This certificate contains details of the company's name and allocates to it a registered number, which is unique to that company. Should the name of the company subsequently be changed, this registered number will remain the same.

The certificate of incorporation is conclusive evidence that the requirements of the Act have been complied with and that a company is duly registered (in the case of a public company the certificate is also conclusive proof that the company is a public company — (CA 1985, s 13(7))). It is effectively the 'birth certificate' of a company and from the date of its issue a company becomes a body corporate in its own right with all the attendant rights attached. Thus a company will have obtained its own legal identity which is distinct from that of its members.

A *private company* may commence trading activities from the date of issue of this certificate. However, a *public company* may not commence trading activities or exercise any of its borrowing powers until the provisions of CA 1985, s 117, relating to a public company's minimum share capital requirements, have been fulfilled.

Minimum share capital requirements for a public company

2.49   Pursuant to section 117 of the Companies Act 1985 a *public company* may not commence business or exercise any of its borrowing powers unless the Registrar of Companies has issued to it a certificate under this section (commonly known as the 'trading certificate').

To apply for a trading certificate a public company must submit to the Registrar of Companies a statutory declaration in the prescribed form, being form 117 (revised March 1995) which states:

(*a*)   that the nominal value of the company's allotted share capital is not less than the authorised minimum (currently being £50,000 sterling);

(*b*)   the amount of the share capital which is paid up;

(*c*)   the amount (or an estimate) of the preliminary expenses payable by the company and to whom they have been paid or are payable; and (*d*)   the amount of or benefit paid, given or intended to be paid or given to any promoter of the company and the consideration for the payment of the benefit.

The Registrar of Companies further requires that, before the issue of the trading certificate, at least one-quarter of the nominal value of each issued share pursuant to (*a*) above is paid up (i.e. at least £12,500 in aggregate). Furthermore, the Registrar will refuse to issue the trading certificate unless all of the minimum paid up capital requirements have been strictly complied with. Section 101 of the CA 1985 further provides that a public company shall not allot a share except as paid up to one-quarter of its nominal value.

The statutory declaration must be made by a director or secretary of the company in the presence of a Notary Public, Commissioner of Oaths or Justice of the Peace.

Upon the issue of the trading certificate a public company may commence its business activities.

Re-registration

Re-registration of a private limited company as a public limited company

2.50   Under section 43 of the Companies Act 1985 a private company having a share capital and which has not previously been re-registered as unlimited may, by special resolution of its members, re-register as a public company. The resolution must be delivered to the Registrar within 15 days of its being passed, and the company must make an application in the prescribed form to the Registrar of Companies.

The special resolution must alter the memorandum and articles so as to bring them into line with that suitable for use by a public company (see Precedent E, Appendix 2D). It should thus be altered so that:

(*a*)   the memorandum states that the company is to be a public company (i.e. insertion of a 'public company' clause, see 2.22 above);

(*b*)   the allotted share capital is increased if, prior to the application for re-registration being made, it is below the statutory minimum (currently £50,000). The allotted share capital must be paid up to at least one-quarter of the nominal value of each share (see 2.49 above) as well as the whole of any premium on it (or an undertaking to pay the premium); and

(*c*)   appropriate alterations are made in the company's articles in the circumstances (e.g. minimum number of directors as two).

Once the memorandum and articles have been amended as appropriate an application can then be made in the prescribed form (form 43(3), revised March 1995), signed by a director or secretary of the company and delivered to the Registrar of Companies together with:

(i)   a printed copy of the memorandum and articles as altered;

(ii)   a copy of the company's balance sheet prepared to a date being not more than seven months before the company's application forre-registration, together with a copy of an unqualified report by the company's auditors in relation to that balance sheet;

(iii)   a copy of a written statement made by the company's auditors, certifying that the balance sheet ((ii) above) shows that the company's net assets were not less than the aggregate of its called-up share capital and its undistributable reserves;

(iv)   a copy of the valuation report relating to the value of the consideration if shares have recently been allotted in accordance with CA 1985, s 44;

(v)   a statutory declaration on a form 43(3)(e) — revised March 1995, sworn by a director or secretary stating that:

　　(A)   the special resolution has been passed;

　　(B)   that the statutory conditions for re-registration have been satisfied in relation to share capital;

　　(C)   that there has not been any change in the company's financial position between the balance sheet date and the date of application that has resulted in the net assets becoming less than the aggregate of its called-up share capital and 'undistributable reserves'; and

(vi)   a remittance filing fee of £20 (as at the time of this publication).

'Undistributable reserves' are those reserves which cannot lawfully be distributed by way of dividend to the company's members.

Once satisfied that the requirements of section 43 of the CA 1985 have been complied with, the Registrar of Companies will issue a new certificate of incorporation stating that the company is a public limited company. Such a change in status being effective as from the date of issue of the certificate. The certificate is conclusive evidence that the company is a public company and any alterations in the memorandum and articles of association take effect accordingly. The company can commence business immediately without having to obtain a trading certificate.

Re-registration of a public limited company as a private limited company

2.51   Under section 53 of the Companies Act 1985, a public company may re-register as a private company by passing a special resolution to alter its memorandum so that it no longer states that the company is a public company (see Precedent F, Appendix 2D). The resolution must also make any other alteration to the memorandum and articles which are requisite in the circumstances to bring it into line with a private company.

A copy of the special resolution should be sent to the Registrar of Companies together with an application on the prescribed form (form 53 —

revised March 1995), signed by a director or secretary of the company and accompanied by a registration fee of £20 (as at the time of this publication). A printed copy of the altered memorandum and articles of association must also be attached.

Where the above special resolution has been passed, an application can be made to the court for its cancellation within 28 days by:

(*a*)   the holders of no less than 5% in nominal value of the company's issued share capital or any class thereof; or

(*b*)   5% of its members if it is not limited by shares; or

(*c*)   not less than 50 of the company's members.

If such an application has been made the company must notify the Registrar of Companies on the prescribed form (form 54).

The courts, on hearing the application, have the power to either cancel or confirm the resolution or make such order as it considers appropriate. Additionally, the company must deliver to the Registrar an office copy of the court order cancelling or confirming the resolution (if appropriate).

Once the period of 28 days after the passing of the resolution has expired and there is no application or the courts have confirmed the resolution, and the Registrar is satisfied that the company can be re-registered, he will issue a certificate of incorporation stating that the company is a private company. Such change in status takes effect from the date of the issue of the certificate (CA 1985, s 55).

The certificate is conclusive evidence that the company is a private company and the alterations in the memorandum and articles as set out in the resolution become effective.

Re-registration of an unlimited company as a private company

2.52   Under section 51 of the Companies Act 1985 an unlimited company may, by passing a special resolution, re-register as a private limited company (see Precedent G, Appendix 2D). It is not possible for a company which has previously re-registered itself as unlimited under CA 1985, s 49 (see 2.53 below) to re-register as a private limited company again.

The special resolution must state whether the company is to be limited by shares or by guarantee. Alterations must be made to the memorandum and articles of association to comply with the requirements of the Companies Act 1985 in respect of a company limited by shares or a company limited by guarantee.

A copy of the special resolution should be lodged with the Registrar of Companies within 15 days of its passing, together with the application on the prescribed form (form 51, revised March 1995) and a printed copy of the altered memorandum and articles of association.

The fee for re-registration is £20 (as at the time of this publication).

The Registrar will issue a certificate of incorporation appropriate to the circumstances, which is conclusive evidence that the company is limited.

Re-registration of a private limited company as an unlimited company

2.53   Under section 49 of the Companies Act 1985, a private limited company may make an application to the Registrar for the company to be re-registered as unlimited, so long as it has not been registered as limited by virtue of section 51 (see 2.52 above).

The difference with this type of re-registration is that all the members must approve the registration by signing the prescribed form of assent (form 49(8)(a), revised March 1995). The memorandum and articles of association must also be altered to bring them in line with those of an unlimited company with or without a share capital (see Precedent H, Appendix 2D).

Having procured the above, an application on form 49(1) signed by a director or the secretary can be lodged with the Registrar together with the form 49(8)(a) as described above. A statutory declaration by the directors on form 49(8)(b) must also be submitted and a printed copy of the memorandum and articles of association as altered.

The fee for re-registration is £20 (as at the time of this publication).

Upon receipt of the various documents the Registrar will issue a certificate of incorporation appropriate to the changed status of the company, being conclusive evidence that the requirements of the Act have been complied with.

Same day registration

2.54   Companies House now offers a same day service where incorporations, change of name and re-registration of companies can be effected on the same day.

The appropriate completed statutory documents can be taken to Companies House offices at London, Cardiff or Edinburgh before 3 pm (see Appendix 5B for addresses). The documents are inspected at the counter and providing the necessary requirements are met, a certificate is issued on the same day. The fee for this service is £100 (as at the time of this publication) or £200 in the case of a re-registration accompanied by a change of name. It should be noted that registration of a place of business or branch can only be effected on the same day if the documents are taken to Cardiff or Edinburgh.

Registration of an oversea company

General

2.55   On 1 January 1993, The Oversea Companies and Credit and Financial Institutions (Branch Disclosure) Regulations 1992 (SI 1992 No 3179) came into force. These regulations complement the previous procedures for oversea companies to register as a place of business. Companies may now be required to either register under the old rules as a place of business or be subject to branch registration under the 1992 regulations.

Registration of an oversea company conducting business in the United Kingdom is only required if it falls into either the place of business or branch regime. To establish whether registration is needed there must be some physical or visible appearance in connection with a particular premises, a degree of permanence or some identification as being a location of the company's business.

Once the need for registration has been determined, then the oversea company must establish whether it should register as a branch or as a place of business. Essentially, a place of business is one where the oversea company carries out incidental or ancillary functions to the company's business as a whole e.g. an administrative office, warehouse facilities or a share transfer or registration office for the company.

Operations falling outside the place of business definition and organised to conduct business in Great Britain on behalf of the company (which is Limited) must be registered as a branch. A branch will be organised so it is able to conduct business on behalf of the company to enable a person to deal directly with the branch here instead of the company in its home state.

Additionally, depending on the structure of the oversea company, certain establishments may only be able to register as a place of business.

The requirements for registration of either a place of business or a branch are examined in more detail below.

The accounting requirements for oversea companies are examined separately in Chapter 4 (see 4.26 ACCOUNTS AND AUDITORS).

Place of business registration

2.56   Certain companies are not permitted to register under the branch regime. These include the following:

(*a*)   unlimited companies incorporated outside Great Britain;

(*b*)   companies incorporated in Northern Ireland or Gibraltar; and

(*c*)   limited companies incorporated outside the United Kingdom, whose operations only fall into the place of business regime, and who do not have a branch in Northern Ireland.

Particulars required for registration

2.57   Within one month of establishment of a place of business in Great Britain the oversea company is required to deliver the following documents to the Registrar of Companies.

A return in the prescribed form (form 691), containing the following:

(*a*)   a list of the names, residential addresses, dates of birth, and business occupations (or, if none then, other directorships) of each director (including shadow directors) and the name and residential address of the secretary;

(*b*)   a list of the names and addresses of each person resident in the United Kingdom who is authorised to accept the service of process and any notice on behalf of the company;

(*c*)   a statutory declaration made by a director or secretary of the company (or a representative described in (*b*) above) stating the date on which that place of business was established; and

(*d*)   a certified copy of the charter, statutes or memorandum and articles of association of the company or such other instrument constituting or defining the company's constitution. If the instrument provided is not written in English, a certified translation must also be delivered.

The fee for registration of a place of business is £20 (as at the time of this publication).

The office of the Registrar of Companies to which the documents must be delivered will depend upon whether the company has established its place of business in England and Wales (documents sent to Companies House in Cardiff) or Scotland (documents sent to Companies House in Edinburgh). Where a company has a place of business in both parts of Great Britain the documents are required to be delivered to both Registrars. It is also possible to register a place of business on the same day if the documents are taken to Cardiff or Edinburgh.

Name of the company

2.58   An oversea company required to register itself as a place of business must effect the registration in the name of the corporate body which is registered overseas.

Section 26 of CA 1985 relating to the prohibition of registration of certain company names applies equally to the registration of a company name by an oversea company as it does to a UK company (see 2.9 *et seq* above).

Should the company's name be unacceptable for use in Great Britain, notice may be served on the company to adopt a business name for use in Great Britain. The notice will be issued by the Secretary of State within twelve months of the date of registration or within twelve months of notifying the Registrar of any change of name. The notice will state the reasons given why the name is unacceptable, and will prevent the company from carrying on business in Great Britain using that name, after normally two months of the notice being served. A company may then send in form 694(4)(a) stating the name, other than its corporate name, under which it proposes to carry on business in Great Britain, and will be subject to the Business Names Act 1985 as any person of a UK incorporated company operating under a business name (see 2.11 above).

Alteration of registered particulars

2.59   Should any changes occur in any of the particulars registered at Companies House for an oversea company, a return in the prescribed form must be made to the Registrar of Companies pursuant to section 692 of the CA 1985.

The changes and the prescribed forms specified for notification are as follows:

(*a*)   form 692(1)(a) — any change to the charter or statutes registered, to be accompanied by an amended and certified copy of the instrument (together with a certified translation where appropriate);

(*b*)   form 692(1)(b) — any change to the directors or secretary (or any of their registered particulars);

(*c*)   form 692(1)(c) — any change to the name and address of the person in Great Britain authorised to accept service of documents on behalf of the company;

(*d*)   form 692(2) — any change to the corporate name of the company; and

(*e*)   form 225 — any change to the accounting reference date of a company.

Disclosure requirements

2.60   All companies covered by the place of business regime must comply with the following:

(*a*)   at every place of business the company's registered name and its country of incorporation must be displayed;

(*b*)   the company's name and country of incorporation must be stated on all bill-heads, letter paper and all notices and other official publications of the company;

(*c*)   if the liability of the company's members is limited, this must be stated at (*a*) above and on (*b*) above; and

(*d*)   in every prospectus inviting subscriptions for its shares or debentures in Great Britain, the country in which the company is incorporated should be stated.

Closing a place of business

2.61   A company must notify the Registrar of Companies when it ceases to have a place of business in Great Britain. The obligations of the company to deliver documents will only cease from the date that this fact is notified to the Registrar.

Branch registration

2.62   Every limited company which opens a branch in Great Britain and which is incorporated outside the United Kingdom and Gibraltar, is required to register under the branch regime.

Particulars required for registration

2.63   A form BR1, consisting of two sections (Part A: Company Details and Part B: Branch Details) must be submitted to the Registrar of Companies within one month of opening the branch. Registration can be effected the same day so long as the documents are taken to Cardiff or Edinburgh.

Part A: Company Details, requires the following information to be completed:

(*a*)   the corporate name and country of incorporation of the company, its legal form, identity of the register and its registration number;

(*b*)   a list of the names, residential addresses, dates of birth, business occupations, nationality, other directorships (if any) for each director, together with the extent of the authority that the director has to represent the company and whether the powers are exercised alone or jointly (see 2.57 above). Shadow directors are also included in these requirements;

(*c*)   the name and residential address of the secretary of the company; and

(*d*)   whether the company is a credit or financial institution under section 699A of the CA 1985.

In addition, oversea companies not incorporated in the EU, must also disclose the following on Part A of the form:

(i)   the governing law of the company;

(ii)   the accounting requirements in its home state, in accordance with its parent law; and

(iii)   the address of the principal place of business in its country of incorporation, the company's objects, issued share capital and currency.

If details of the company's accounting period are not given then a form 225 should be submitted giving details of the accounting reference date.

Part B: Branch Details, requires the following information to be completed:

(A)   the names and addresses of all persons resident in the UK that are authorised to accept service of documents, and of all persons authorised to represent the company in the UK together with the scope of their authority; and

(B)   the address of the branch, the business that is carried out there and the date that it opened.

Additionally, a certified copy of the constitution of the company, a copy of the latest accounts which have been publicly disclosed, together with certified translations (if applicable) must be submitted with the form.

The fee for registration of a branch is £20 (as at the time of this publication).

The branch registration regime requires an oversea company to file information about each branch that it has in Great Britain, providing each location has its own separate management structure and distinct reporting lines back to the parent company. To avoid duplication of documents the form does allow particulars to be filed with reference to those filed in respect of another branch. If however, the locations are linked within a uniform management structure then all the operations will amount to one branch and only one registration will be required. In these circumstances the registration is made to the appropriate Registrar, depending on where the principal place of business is located.

Name of the company

2.64   The rules applying to the name of an oversea company requiring to register itself as a place of business also apply to a branch (see 2.58 above for details).

Alteration of registered particulars

2.65   Should any changes occur in any of the particulars registered at Companies House then a return in the prescribed form must be made to the Registrar of Companies within 21 days.

The changes and the prescribed forms specified for notification are:

(*a*)   form BR2 — any alteration to the constitutional particulars;

(*b*)   form BR3 — any alteration of company particulars;

(*c*)   form BR4 — any change of directors or secretary or of their particulars;

(*d*)   form BR5 — any change of address or branch particulars;

(*e*)   form BR6 — any change of person authorised to accept service or to represent the branch or any change in their particulars; and

(*f*)   form BR7 — any change in the branch where the constitutional documents have been registered.

Disclosure requirements

2.66   The branch must comply with the following:

(*a*)   at every place of business the company's registered name and its country of incorporation must be displayed;

(*b*)   the company's name and country of incorporation must be stated on all billheads, letter paper and all notices and other official publications;

(*c*)   if the liability of the company's members is limited, this must be stated at (*a*) above and on (*b*) above; and

(*d*)   the place of registration and registration number of the branch must be stated on letter paper and order forms.

Also, every company incorporated outside the EU must state the following on its letter paper and order forms:

  (i)   the legal form of the company;

 (ii)   the location of its head office; and

(iii)   the fact that it is being wound up if applicable.

Additionally, if the company is not incorporated in the EU and which is required by the law of the country in which it is incorporated to be registered it shall also state on its letter paper and order forms:

(A)   the company's registration number; and

(B)   the identity of the registry in which it is registered in its home state.

Closing a branch

2.67   A company must notify the Registrar of Companies if it closes a branch in Great Britain. The obligations on the company for delivery of documents will cease only from the date that this fact is notified to the Registrar. Similarly where a company ceases to have a branch but continues to have a place of business, it must register under the place of business regime.

General requirements for oversea companies

Registration of charges by an oversea company

2.68   Currently the Companies Act 1985 requires an oversea company which has established a place of business in Great Britain to send details of certain charges to the Registrar. The charges are those of the company and will apply whether or not it has been registered under the place of business or branch regime.

Part IV of Schedule 15 to the Companies Act 1989 provisionally introduced a number of new measures for the registration of charges for oversea companies, whether registered as a branch or a place of business. These provisions (if brought into force) will oblige an oversea company, when it registers in accordance with section 691 and Schedule 21A of the Companies Act 1985, to also deliver particulars of charges over property.

Service of documents on an oversea company

2.69   Any process or notice served on an oversea company subject to branch registration or place of business registration is sufficiently served if:

(a)   addressed to any person whose name has been delivered to the Registrar to accept service of process on the company's behalf in respect of the business of the branch or place of business and of any notices required to be served on it; and

(b)   left at or sent by post to the address for that person which has been so delivered.

If, at any time, the appropriate person's name and address has not been delivered to the Registrar; or this information has been delivered but the person has died or ceased to reside at the address given; or the named person has refused to accept service on the company's behalf; or for any reason service cannot be given, then the document may be served by either leaving it or sending it by post to any place of business established by the company in Great Britain.

Northern Ireland registration

2.70   Northern Ireland has its own regimes with respect to place of business and branch registration. An oversea company having a branch in Northern Ireland and a place of business in Great Britain must register the branch in Northern Ireland but need not register as a place of business in Great Britain.

If a Northern Ireland company has a place of business in Great Britain, then it is required to register as a place of business (however large its operations) as the branch registration regime only applies to limited companies incorporated outside the UK.

Isle of Man and Channel Islands companies

2.71   The treatment accorded to companies registered in the Isle of Man or the Channel Islands differs in certain respects from that accorded to oversea companies in that the provisions of the Companies Act 1985 requiring documents to be forwarded or delivered to the Registrar of Companies apply to such companies as if they were incorporated under the Act (CA 1985, s 699(1)). The provisions of the Act apply to Isle of Man or Channel Island companies where they have established a place of business in either England and Wales or Scotland (or both) as if they were registered there. Registration of Isle of Man and Channel Islands companies is effected in the same manner as an oversea company.

However, a few exceptions in the documents that need to be delivered to the Registrar of Companies do exist under CA 1985, s 699(3). Documents relating to the following issues need not be delivered by an Isle of Man or Channel Islands company that has established a place of business. These are as follows:

(*a*)   resolution altering a company's objects (CA 1985, s 6(1));

(*b*)   alteration of the memorandum and articles of association by statute or statutory instrument (CA 1985, s 18);

(*c*)   directors' duty to file accounts (CA 1985, s 242(1)). It should be noted, however, that the provisions of the Act in respect of the filing of accounts by an oversea company (CA 1985, s 702) do apply;

(*d*)   notice to the Registrar of Companies of a change in its directors or secretary (CA 1985, s 288(2)). However, CA 1985, s 692(1)(b), relating to oversea companies applies in this respect; and

(*e*)   copies of certain resolutions and agreements to be sent to the Registrar so far as applicable to a resolution altering a company's memorandum or articles of association. CA 1985, s 692(1)(a) as it relates to oversea companies, however, applies.

These exceptions do not apply if the oversea company falls within the branch definition (see 2.55 above).

The European Economic Interest Grouping

General

2.72   Created on 25 July 1985 by the Council of Ministers of the European Community, the European Economic Interest Grouping ('EEIG') facilitates cross-frontier co-operation between firms engaged in similar activities within the European Union (EU). The instrument became available on 1 July 1989, and is part of the construction of the single European market programme.

The idea behind the instrument is to enable firms within the EU, particularly small and medium-sized firms, to group together in order to develop their own common activities and to increase profits by combining resources and services. The instrument provides a pre-established legal framework and flexible operational procedures. The purpose of a grouping is consequently not to make profits for itself, but to allow member companies to organise and co-ordinate projects, and to monitor their execution. Moreover, companies wishing to participate in cross-border co-operation will be able to overcome the difficulties presented by the legal systems of individual EU States.

Regulations

2.73   All legal bodies governed by public or private law can become members of EEIGs and a grouping may be created in any sector, be it agriculture, trade, industry or services. The official address of the EEIG must be within a European Union Member State although it need not correspond to the place where the principal activity is carried out. Members of an EEIG should be active within the Union prior to the creation of the grouping. Companies and other legal entities should be incorporated according to the legislation of a Member State. In addition, at least two members of a grouping should be based in different Member States. EEIGs are governed by European Union law, although only minimal obligations with regard to the organisation and management of the grouping are imposed.

Organisation

2.74   The grouping must have at least two 'organs'.

(*a*)   *College of members.* This is the ruling body and is analogous to a company acting in general meeting with each member having the right to vote. The conditions for the taking of decisions are largely left to the grouping contract, and the college may take any decision in order to achieve the objectives of the grouping.

(*b*)   *Management.* The managers are responsible for the day-to-day running of the grouping and may represent the EEIG in dealing with third parties. The contract of the grouping will determine the conditions for the appointment and removal of management.

Finance

2.75   An EEIG may be formed without capital, and is not even required to have any assets. Members have great flexibility regarding the method of financing the activities of the grouping, thus enabling funds to be used more effectively. As a result of this, members' liability is joint and several for the grouping's debts to third parties.

Taxation

2.76   The relevant EU regulations state that EEIGs are to be 'fiscally transparent'; properties are to be taxable and losses allowable only in the hands of their members. This is given effect in the UK by provisions included in the Finance Act 1990.

Where an EEIG is trading, the trade is regarded as being carried on by the members in partnership, and its profits are taxed accordingly. Thus, for capital gains purposes the existing partnership rules apply i.e. gains realised by the partnership are apportioned to the partners, but no gain or loss is treated as arising where a partner joins or leaves the partnership, or where there is a change in profit-sharing ratios, unless payment is made (except in certain cases where assets are revalued in the partnership accounts).

Normal rules (such as the requirement for expenditure to be incurred wholly and exclusively for the purpose of the member's trade) apply when considering the availability of relief for contributions by a member to the

EEIG's running expenses, or entitlement to capital allowances on the member's share of the grouping's assets.

Legal capacity

2.77   The instrument gives full legal capacity to the grouping from the date of its registration. To register, the grouping must request enrolment at the appropriate Registry of the Member State where it has its official address. For example, if the grouping is in the United Kingdom it will be registered with the Registrar of Companies at Companies House, Cardiff. Certain information about the grouping will then be published in a journal carrying legal notices, for example, the *London Gazette*.

An EEIG may have rights and obligations, place contracts and carry out legal acts in accordance with the objects determined by the members, in all EU Member States. It may also operate outside the Union in the exploration, research and penetration of new markets.

Post incorporation considerations

2.78   Shortly after a company has been duly registered and its certificate of incorporation issued, the directors of the company (as detailed on form 10) should hold their first board meeting. The purpose of this meeting is to record the position of the company at incorporation and to make the decisions necessary to enable the company to commence its business.

Accordingly, items which will commonly appear on the agenda for the first board meeting for consideration are:

(*a*)   the election of a chairman;

(*b*)   the certificate of incorporation and memorandum and articles of association produced to the meeting and if a public limited company the obtaining of a trading certificate discussed;

(*c*)   any further appointments of directors considered;

(*d*)   the common seal of the company adopted;

(*e*)   the registered office address confirmed or changed;

(*f*)   the company's accounting reference date fixed and the appropriate notification prepared and filed with the Registrar of Companies (see 4.2–4.5 ACCOUNTS AND AUDITORS);

(*g*)   auditors appointed;

(*h*)   bankers appointed to the company and an account opened;

(*j*)   statutory registers obtained and written up (see Chapter 3);

(*k*)   any arrangements for obtaining further capital discussed. If necessary, the relevant instructions should be given for the preparation of a prospectus and for application to be made to the Stock Exchange for a

The Company Constitution   **2.78**

listing and if appropriate brokers, underwriters and share registrars appointed (public companies only, see 8.20–8.27 CAPITAL);

(*l*)   if the company was formed to acquire a business then the terms of the purchase agreement should be agreed;

(*m*)   any pre-incorporation contracts made by the promoters of the company should be adopted and the need for directors' service contracts considered;

(*n*)   VAT registration application considered and also the company's arrangements for the payment of corporation tax, PAYE and National Insurance and the company's insurance arrangements discussed;

(*o*)   the necessity of applying for the registration of any trade or service marks discussed and, if required, trade mark agents instructed; and

(*p*)   business stationery complying with the Companies Act 1985 (CA 1985, s 349) and the Business Names Act 1985 ordered (see 2.18 above).

It should be noted that upon incorporation the directors and secretary of the company named in form 10 submitted to the Registrar of Companies are deemed appointed. Likewise, the subscribers to the memorandum of association are deemed the first members of the company. Any subsequent changes must then be made in accordance with the company's memorandum and articles of association and the Companies Act 1985.

Appendix 2A

Checklist for incorporation

General

The total number of effective incorporations for 1998/99 was 222,000 (1997/98 — 205,300) (England and Wales and Scotland). The average monthly rejection rate for documents submitted in respect of new incorporations for 1998/99 was 7.4% (1997/98 — 6.9%); this represents over 16,000 new companies applications in each year.

The following guide is designed purely as a reference point in ensuring the completeness of the documents required to be filed with the Registrar of Companies in applying for the registration of a private or public limited company. Reference to the detailed notes in the main text of this chapter is recommended.

Type of company

Is the company to be a private or public company limited by shares, or a private company limited by guarantee? Determine the purpose and capital requirements of the company.

Company name

(*a*)   Is the proposed name available? Check index at Companies House for availability. (See 2.9 above.)

(*b*)   Does the proposed name require prior approval? (See 2.10 above.)

(*c*)   Would the use of the name constitute a criminal offence or is it forbidden? (See 2.10 above.)

Statement of first directors, secretary and registered office (Form 10)

(i)   Have all the details required for the directors and secretary been entered and the form signed by each? (See 2.41 above.)

(ii)   Is the registered office address within the country of domicile stated in the memorandum of association? (See 2.44 above.)

(iii)   Has the form been signed by the subscribers to the memorandum of association *or* by an agent acting on their behalf?

Memorandum of association

(A)   Has the name of the company been correctly stated?

(B)   Have the names and addresses of the subscriber or subscribers been clearly stated, their signatures obtained and the number of shares they have each agreed to take been entered against their names?

(C) Has the name and address of the witness to the subscribers' signatures been entered and his signature obtained?

(D) Has the date of signature by the subscribers been stated?

(E) Does the capital clause meet the minimum authorised share capital requirements? (public companies only, see 2.49 above).

Articles of association

(I) Are they in the correct format for the type of company (i.e. Table A or C, see 2.34 *et seq* above)?

(II) As (B), (C) and (D) in 'Memorandum of association' above.

Statutory declaration

(1) Has this been made by either a director or secretary of the company (as named in form 10) or by a solicitor on their behalf?

(2) Has the declaration been signed in the presence of a Notary Public, Commissioner for Oaths or Justice of the Peace and been dated?

Fees

A cheque for £20 (this is the amount as at the date of publication) made payable to 'Companies House' must be submitted with the incorporation documents.

Appendix 2B

Restricted company names

Words requiring the consent of the Secretary of State before their use is allowed in a company name

(i) *Words implying national or international pre-eminence*

British	International	Scottish
England	Ireland	United Kingdom
English	Irish	Wales
European	National	Welsh
Great Britain	Scotland	

(ii) *Words implying business pre-eminence or representative or authoritative status*

Association	Federation
Authority	Institute
Board	Institution
Council	Society

(iii) *Words implying specific objects or functions*

Assurance	Holding
Assurer	Insurance
Benevolent	Insurer
Chamber of Commerce	Industrial & Provident Society
Chamber of Commerce,	Patent
Training and Enterprise	Patentee
Chamber of Industry	Post Office
Chamber of Trade	Re-assurer
Charity	Reassurance
Charter	Reinsurance
Chartered	Re-insurer
Chemist	Register
Chemistry	Registered
Co-operative	Sheffield
Foundation	Stock Exchange
Friendly Society	Trade Union
Fund	Trust
Group	

Words requiring the consent of the Secretary of State where consent will only be granted with the written or non-objection of the relevant department or body. Any correspondence should be submitted with the registration documents.

Word or expression	*Relevant body for companies to be registered within England or Wales*	*Relevant body for companies to be registered within Scotland*
Royal, Royale, Royalty, King, Queen, Prince, Princess, Windsor, Duke, His/Her Majesty	Home Office A Division Room 730 50 Queen Anne's Gate London SW1H 9AT (if based in England)	Scottish Office Home Department Civil Law and Legal Aid Division Saughton House Broomhouse Drive Edinburgh EH11 3XD
	Welsh Office Crown Buildings Cathays Park Cardiff CF1 3NQ (if based in Wales)	
Police	Home Office Police Department Strategy Group Room 510 50 Queen Anne's Gate London SW1H 9AT	Scottish Home and Health Department Police Division Regent Road St Andrews House Edinburgh EH1 3DG
Special School	Department for Education and Employment Schools 2 Branch Sanctuary Buildings Great Smith Street Westminster London SW1P 3BT	As for England and Wales
Contact Lens	The Registrar General Optical Council 41 Harley Street London W1N 2DJ	As for England and Wales
Dental, Dentistry	The Registrar General Dental Council 37 Wimpole Street London W1M 8DQ	As for England and Wales

Word or expression	Relevant body for companies to be registered within England or Wales	Relevant body for companies to be registered within Scotland
District Nurse, Health Visitor, Midwife, Midwifery, Nurse, Nursing	The Registrar & Chief Executive United Kingdom Central Council for Nursing, Midwifery and Health Visiting 23 Portland Place London W1N 4JT	As for England and Wales
Health Centre	Office of the Solicitor Department of Health & Social Security 48 Carey Street London WC2A 2LS	As for England and Wales
Health Service	NHS Management Executive Department of Health Eileen House 80–94 Newington Causeway London SE1 6EF	As for England and Wales
Pregnancy, Termination, Abortion	Department of Health Area 423 Wellington House 133–155 Waterloo Road London SE1 8UG	As for England and Wales
Charity, Charitable	Charity Commission Registration Division St Albans House 57–60 Haymarket London SW1Y 4QX	Inland Revenue Claims Branch Trinity Park House South Trinity Road Edinburgh EH5 3SD
or For companies *not* intending to register as a charity	Charity Commission 2nd Floor 20 Kings Parade Queens Dock Liverpool L3 4DQ	
Apothecary	The Worshipful Society of Apothecaries of London Apothecaries Hall Blackfriars Lane London EC4V 6EJ	The Royal Pharmaceutical Society of Great Britain Law Department 1 Lambeth High Street London SE1 7JN

Word or expression	Relevant body for companies to be registered within England or Wales	Relevant body for companies to be registered within Scotland
Polytechnic	Department for Education and Science FHE 1B Sanctuary Buildings Great Smith Street Westminster London SW1P 3BT	As for England and Wales
University	Privy Council Office 68 Whitehall London SW1A 2AT	As for England and Wales

Words, the use of which is governed by other legislation and may constitute a criminal offence. Consultation with the relevant bodies shown is advised. The Department of Trade & Industry reserves the right to seek the advice in each case direct from the relevant body if necessary.

Word or expression	Relevant body	Relevant legislation
Architect	Architects Registration Council of the United Kingdom 73 Hallam Street London W1N 6EE	Section 1 Architects Registration Act 1938
Credit Union	The Registrar of Friendly Societies Victoria House 30–34 Kingsway London WC2B 6ES Assistant Registrar of Friendly Societies 58 Frederick Street Edinburgh EH2 1NB (for Scottish registered companies)	Credit Union Act 1979
Olympiad, Olympiads, Olympian, Olympians, Olympic, Olympics *or translation thereof*	British Olympic Association 1 Wandsworth Plain London SW18 1EH	Olympic Symbol etc. (Protection) Act 1995* *Also protects Olympic Symbol of five interlocking rings and motto 'Citius Altius Fortius'*

Appendix 2B

Word or expression	Relevant body	Relevant legislation
Veterinary Surgeon, Veterinary, Vet	The Registrar Royal College of Veterinary Surgeons 62–64 Horseferry Road London SW1P 2AF	Sections 19, 20 Veterinary Surgeons Act 1966
Dentist, Dental Surgeon, Dental Practitioner	The Registrar General Dental Council 37 Wimpole Street London W1M 8DQ	Dentist Act 1984
Drug, Druggist, Pharmaceutical, Pharmaceutist, Pharmacist, Pharmacy	The Director of Legal Services The Royal Pharmaceutical Society of Great Britain 1 Lambeth High Street London SE1 7JN The Pharmaceutical Society 36 York Place Edinburgh EH1 3HU (for Scottish registered companies)	Section 78 Medicines Act 1968
Optician, Ophthalmic Optician, Dispensing Optician, Enrolled Optician, Registered Optician, Optometrist	The Registrar General Optical Council 41 Harley Street London W1N 2DJ	Opticians Act 1989
Bank, Banker, Banking, Deposit	Bank of England Supervision & Surveillance Threadneedle Street London EC2R 8AH	Banking Act 1987
Red Cross, Geneva Cross, Red Crescent, Red Lion and Sun	Seek advice of Companies House	Geneva Conventions Act 1957
Anzac	Seek advice of Companies House	Section 1 Anzac Act 1916
Insurance Broker, Assurance Broker, Re-Insurance Broker, Re-Assurance Broker	Seek advice of The Insurance Brokers Registration Council 15 St Helen's Place London EC3A 6DS	Sections 2 & 3 Insurance Brokers (Registration) Act 1977

Word or expression	Relevant body	Relevant legislation
Chiropodist, Dietician, Medical Laboratory Technician, Occupational Therapist, Orthoptist, Physiotherapist, Radiographer, Remedial Gymnast	Room 12.26 HAP4 Division Department of Health Hannibal House Elephant and Castle London SE1 6TE	Professions Supplementary to Medicine Act 1960 if preceded by Registered, State or Registered
Institute of Laryngology, Institute of Otology, Institute of Urology, Institute of Orthopaedics	Seek advice of University College London Gower Street London WC1E 6BT	University College London Act 1988
Patent Office, Patent Agent	IPCD Hazlitt House 45 Southampton Buildings London WC2A 1AR	Copyright, Designs and Patents Act 1988
Building Society	Seek advice of Building Societies Commission Victoria House 30–34 Kingsway London WC2B 6ES	Building Society Act 1986

(Choosing a Company Name — Notes for Guidance CHN2.)

Crown Copyright. Reproduced with the permission of the Controller of Her Majesty's Stationery Office.

Format of Memorandum of Association

The Companies Act 1985

Private Company Limited by shares

Memorandum of Association of [name of company] **Limited**

1   The name of the Company is [name of company] LIMITED.

2   The registered office of the Company will be situated in [England and Wales]/[Scotland].

3   The objects for which the Company is established are:

(a) To carry on the business of an investment and holding company in all its branches, and to acquire by purchase, lease, concession, grant, licence or otherwise such businesses, options, rights, privileges, lands, buildings, leases, underleases, stocks, shares, debentures, debenture stock, bonds, obligations, securities, reversionary interests, annuities, policies of assurance and other property and rights and interests in property as the Company shall deem fit and generally to hold, manage, develop, lease, sell or dispose of the same; and to vary any of the investments of the Company, to act as trustees of any deeds constituting or securing any debentures, debenture stock or other securities or obligations; to establish, carry on, develop and extend investments and holdings and to sell, dispose of or otherwise turn the same to account, and to co-ordinate the policy and administration of any companies of which this Company is a member or which are in any manner controlled by, or connected with the Company.

(b) To carry on any other trade or business whatsoever which can in the opinion of the Board of Directors be advantageously carried on in connection with or ancillary to any of the businesses of the Company.

(c) To purchase or by any other means acquire and take options over any property whatever, and any rights or privileges of any kind over or in respect of any property.

(d) To apply for, register, purchase, or by other means acquire and protect, prolong and renew, whether in the United Kingdom or elsewhere any patents, patent rights, brevets d'invention, licences, secret processes, trade marks, designs, protections and concessions and to disclaim, alter, modify, use and turn to account and to manufacture under or grant licences or privileges in respect of the same, and to expend money in experimenting upon, testing and improving any patents, inventions or rights which the Company may acquire or propose to acquire.

(e) To acquire and undertake the whole or any part of the business, goodwill, and assets of any person, firm, or company carrying on or proposing to carry on any of the businesses which the Company is authorised to carry on and as part of the consideration for such acquisition to undertake all or any of the liabilities of such person, firm or company, or to acquire any interest in, amalgamate with, or enter into partnership or into any arrangement for sharing profits, or for co-operation, or for subsidising or otherwise assisting any such person, firm or company, and to give or accept, by way of consideration for any of the acts or things aforesaid or property acquired, any shares, debentures, debenture stock or securities that may be agreed upon, and to hold and retain, or sell, mortgage and deal with any shares, debentures, debenture stock or securities so received.

(f) To improve, manage, construct, repair, develop, exchange, let on lease or otherwise, mortgage, charge, sell, dispose of, turn to account, grant licences, options, rights and privileges in respect of, or otherwise deal with all or any part of the property and rights of the Company.

(g) To invest and deal with the moneys of the Company not immediately required in such manner as may from time to time be determined and to hold or otherwise deal with any investment made.

(h) To lend and advance money or give credit on such terms as may seem expedient and with or without security to customers and others and to invest and deal with money and assets of the Company not immediately required in any manner and to receive money and securities on deposit or loan, at interest and otherwise upon such terms as the Company may approve.

(i) To borrow and raise money in such manner as the Company shall think fit and to secure the repayment of any money borrowed, raised or owing by mortgage, charge, standard, security, lien or other security upon the whole or any part of the Company's property or assets (whether present or future), including its uncalled capital, or by the creation and issue on such terms and conditions as may be thought expedient of debentures or debenture stock, perpetual or otherwise, or other securities of any description.

(j) To enter into or accept any guarantees or indemnities and to guarantee support or secure, either with or without the Company receiving any consideration or advantage, and whether by personal covenant or by mortgaging or charging all or any part of the undertaking, property and assets (present and future), including its uncalled capital, of the Company, or by both suchmethods, the performance of the obligations of and the repayment or payment of the principal amounts of and premiums, interest and dividends on any securities or other liabilities of any person, firm or company including (but without prejudice to the generality of the foregoing) any company which is for the time being the Company's holding company within the meaning of section 736 of the Companies Act 1985 or another subsidiary as defined by the said section of the Company's holding company or otherwise associated with the Company in business.

(k) To draw, make, accept, endorse, discount, negotiate, execute and issue promissory notes, bills of lading, warrants, debentures, and other negotiable or transferable instruments.

(l) To apply for, promote, and obtain any Act of Parliament, Provisional Order, or Licence of the Department of Trade or other authority for enabling the Company to carry any of its objects into effect, or for effecting any modification which may seem calculated directly or indirectly to promote the Company's interest, and to oppose any proceedings or application which may seem calculated directly or indirectly to prejudice the Company's interests.

(m) To enter into any arrangements with any Government or authority (supreme, municipal, local, or otherwise) that may seem conducive to the attainment of the Company's objects or any of them and to obtain from any such government or authority any charters, decrees, rights, privileges or concessions which the Company may think desirable and to carry out, exercise, and comply with any such charters, decrees, rights, privileges or concessions which the Company may think desirable.

(n) To subscribe for, take, purchase, or otherwise acquire and hold shares or other interests in or securities of any other company having objects altogether or in part similar to those of the Company or carrying on any business capable of being carried on so as directly or indirectly to benefit the Company or enhance the value of its property and to co-ordinate, finance and manage the businesses and operations of any company in which the Company holds any such interest.

(o) To act as agents or brokers and as trustees for any person, firm or company, or to undertake and perform sub-contracts.

(p) To remunerate any person, firm or company rendering services to the Company either by cash payment or by the allotment to him or them of shares or other securities of the Company credited as paid up in full or in part or otherwise as may be thought expedient.

(q) To pay all or any expenses incurred in connection with the promotion, formation and incorporation of the Company, or to contract with any person, firm or company to pay the same, and to pay commissions to brokers and others for underwriting, placing, selling, or guaranteeing the subscription of any shares or other securities of the Company.

(r) To support and subscribe to any charitable or public object and to support and subscribe to any institution, society, or club which may be for the benefit of the Company or its Directors or employees, or may be connected with any town or place where the Company carries on business; to give or award pensions, annuities, gratuities, and superannuation or other allowances or benefits or charitable aid and generally to provide advantages, facilities and services for any persons who are or have been Directors of, or who are serving or have served the Company or the holding company of the Company or a fellow subsidiary of the Company or of the predecessors in the business of the Company or of any such subsidiary, holding or fellow subsidiary company and to the wives, widows, children and other relatives and dependants of such persons; to make payments toward insurance; and to set up, establish, support and maintain superannuation and other funds or schemes (whether contributory, or non-contributory) for the benefit of any such persons and of their wives; widows; children and other relatives and dependants; and set up, establish support and maintain profit sharing or share purchase schemes for the benefit of any of the employees of the Company or of any such subsidiary, holding or fellow subsidiary and to lend money to any such employees or to trustees on their behalf to enable any such purchase schemes to be established or maintained.

(s) To promote any other company for the purpose of acquiring the whole or any part of the business or property and undertaking any of the liabilities of the Company, or undertaking any business or operations which may appear likely to assist or benefit the Company or to enhance the value of any property or business of the Company, and to place or guarantee the placing of, underwrite, subscribe for, or otherwise acquire all or any part of the shares or securities of any such company as aforesaid.

(t) To sell or otherwise dispose of the whole or any part of the business or property of the Company, either together or in portions, for such consideration as the Company may think fit, and in particular for shares, debentures, or securities of any company purchasing the same.

(u) To distribute among the Members of the Company in kind any property of the Company of whatever nature.

(v) To procure the Company to be registered or recognised in any part of the world.

(w) To do all or any of the things or matters aforesaid in any part of the world and either as principals, agents, contractors or otherwise, and by or through agents, brokers, sub-contractors or otherwise and either alone or in conjunction with others.

(x) To do all such things as may be deemed incidental or conducive to the attainment of the Company's objects or any of them.

The objects set forth in each sub-clause of this clause shall not be restrictively construed but the widest interpretation shall be given thereto, and they shall not, except where the context expressly so requires, be in any way limited or restricted by reference to or inference from any other object or objects set forth in such sub-clause or from the terms of any other sub-clause or the object or objects therein specified or ancillary to the objects or powers mentioned in any other sub-clause, but the Company shall have as full a power to exercise all or any of the said sub-clauses as if each sub-clause contained the objects of a separate company. The word 'company' in this Clause, except where used in reference to the Company, shall be deemed to include any partnership or body of persons, whether incorporated or unincorporated and whether domiciled in the United Kingdom or elsewhere.

4   The liability of the Members is limited.

5   The Share Capital of the Company is [£ total amount (e.g. £100)] divided into [number of shares (e.g. 100)] [class (e.g. ordinary)] shares of [£ nominal value (e.g. £1)] each.

We, the subscribers to this Memorandum of Association, wish to be formed into a Company pursuant to this Memorandum; and we agree to take the number of shares shown opposite our respective names.

Names and addresses of Subscribers	Number of shares taken by each person

Dated this   day of   199 .

Witness to the above Signatures:

Appendix 2D

PRECEDENT – Form of Resolution for Submission to Companies House

Number of Company [   ]

THE COMPANIES ACT 1985
COMPANY LIMITED BY SHARES
ORDINARY/SPECIAL/EXTRAORDINARY/ELECTIVE
RESOLUTION[1]
OF

[   ] LIMITED/PUBLIC LIMITED COMPANY[1]

Passed [DATE]   199 .

At an [ANNUAL] [EXTRAORDINARY][1] GENERAL MEETING of the above named Company, duly convened and held at [ADDRESS] on [DATE] at [TIME] the following resolution was duly passed as an ORDINARY/ SPECIAL/EXTRAORDINARY/ELECTIVE[1] (*) RESOLUTION. viz:

RESOLUTION

      [TEXT OF RESOLUTION]*

. . . .
Chairman

---

[1] *Delete as appropriate.*
* *See overleaf for the special resolutions relevant to this chapter.*

Precedents of Special Resolutions

A. Special Resolution for Change of Company Name

'That with the sanction of the Department of Trade the name of the company be and is hereby changed to [   ].'

B. Special Resolution to Change the Objects Clause in Memorandum of Association

'That the main objects of the Memorandum of Association of the company be and is hereby altered by the deletion of the existing clause [   ] and the insertion of the following new clause [   ]:

New Clause [   ]

(Detail)'

C. Special Resolution for the Alteration of part of the Articles of Association

'That regulations [to   ] in the existing Articles of Association be and are hereby deleted and that the following regulations be and are hereby inserted in their stead:

New Regulations [*to*   ]

(Detail)'

D. Special Resolution for the Adoption of new Articles of Association

'That the existing Articles of Association be and are hereby deleted in their entirety and that the new Articles of Association as initialled by the Chairman and presented to the meeting be and are hereby adopted in place thereof.'

E. Special Resolution for the Re-registration of a Private Company as a Public Company

'That pursuant to the provisions of Section 43 of the Companies Act 1985 the Company be and is hereby re-registered as a public company and that the Memorandum of Association of the Company be altered as follows:

(a)   by deleting the existing clause 1 and substituting therefor the following clauses to be numbered 1 and 2:

    1.   The name of the company is [   ] PUBLIC LIMITED COMPANY.

    2.   The Company is to be a public company.

(b)   by renumbering the existing clauses 2, 3, 4 and 5 as clauses, 3, 4, 5 and 6 respectively.'

F. Special Resolution for the Re-registration of a Public Company as a Private Company

'That the Company make an application to the Registrar of Companies pursuant to the provisions of Section 53 of the Companies Act 1985 to be re-registered as a private company and that the Memorandum of Association be thereupon altered as follows:

(a) by deleting the existing clauses 1 and 2 and substituting therefor the following clause to be numbered 1:

　1.　The name of the Company is [　　　　　　] LIMITED.

(b) by renumbering the existing clauses 3, 4, 5 and 6 as clauses 2, 3, 4 and 5 respectively.'

G. Special resolution of the Re-registration of an unlimited company as a Private Limited Company

'That pursuant to the provisions of Section 51 of the Companies Act 1985 the company be and is hereby re-registered as a private company limited by shares with an authorised share capital of £100 and that the Memorandum of Association of the Company be altered as follows:

(a) by deleting the existing clause 1 and substituting the following clause to be numbered 1:

　1.　The name of the Company is [　　　　　　] LIMITED.

(b) by adding thereto the following additional clauses to be numbered 4 and 5 respectively:

　4.　The liability of the members is limited.

　5.　The share capital of the company is [£　　　　] divided into [　　　　　　] shares of [£　　　　　] each.'

H. Special resolution for the Re-registration of a Private Limited Company as an unlimited company

'That pursuant to the provisions of Section 49 of the Companies Act 1985 the company be and is hereby re-registered as an unlimited company and that the Memorandum of Association of the Company be altered as follows:

(a) by deleting the existing clause 1 and substituting therefor the following clause to be numbered 1:

　1.　The name of the Company is [　　　　　　].

(b) by deleting the existing clause 4 and renumbering the existing clause 5 as clause 4.' (The original Clause 4 being the limited liability clause which is no longer needed.)

Chapter 3

The Statutory Records

Form and inspection of registers

3.1   The concept underlying the regulations set down in the Companies Act 1985 is that information should be readily available to shareholders and other interested persons, and thus the Companies Act 1985 requires every company to keep certain information in the form of registers. The registers must be in a form which allows them to be examined easily and it is important that care is taken to maintain the registers properly as this will be the best safeguard against accusations of impropriety.

Section 722(1) of the CA 1985 provides that any register required to be kept under the Act may be kept either by recording entries in bound books or recording the matters in question in any other manner. CA 1985, s 722(2) further provides that if entries are recorded otherwise than in bound books, then appropriate precautions must be taken to guard against falsification and facilitating their discovery.

Section 723 of the CA 1985 requires that if any register kept pursuant to the Act is otherwise than in legible form (i.e. stored on a computer) then it must be capable of being produced in a legible form e.g. a print-out. The Companies (Registers and Other Records) Regulations 1985 (SI 1985 No 724) introduced provisions about the location of registers kept otherwise than in legible form and notification that the registers are in a non-legible form must be given to the Registrar of Companies together with notification of the place for inspection.

Inspection rights were introduced by section 723A of the CA 1985 (as inserted by CA 1989, s 143(1)) and by the Companies (Inspection and Copying of Registers, Indices and Documents) Regulations 1991 (SI 1991 No 1998), from 1 November 1991.

The Regulations set out certain obligations of companies in relation to the inspection and copying of their records by members and non-members. They set out the circumstances in which companies are obliged to provide copies of entries on the various registers and prescribe the fees that they may charge for the provision of copies of entries on registers and for copies of other documents. Section 723A(6) of the Companies Act 1985 (as inserted by CA 1989, s 143(1)) provides that companies can provide more extensive facilities than they are obliged to provide under these Regulations or charge fees that are less than those prescribed under these Regulations.

The Companies (Inspection and Copying of Registers, Indices and Documents) Regulations 1991 (SI 1991 No 1998) apply an obligation to make a register, index or document available for inspection when required by the following sections of the Companies Act 1985:

(a) s 169(5) — contract for purchase by company of its own shares;

(b) s 175(6) — statutory declaration and auditors' report relating to payment out of capital;

(c) s 191(1) — register of debenture holders;

(d) s 219(1) — register of interests in shares and reports;

(e) s 288(3) — register of directors and secretaries;

(f) s 318(7) — directors' service contracts;

(g) s 356(1) — register and index of members;

(h) s 383(1) — minute books; and

(j) s 325 and paragraph 25 of Part IV of Schedule 13 — register of directors' interests.

The company must make the register, index or document available for inspection for not less than two hours between 9 am and 5 pm on each business day (i.e. any day except a Saturday, Sunday, Christmas Day, Good Friday or any other day which is a bank holiday in the part of Great Britain where the company is registered) (Companies (Inspection and Copying of Registers, Indices and Documents) Regulations 1991, Regs 2, 3(2)(a)).

The company must also permit a person inspecting the register, index or document to copy any information made available for inspection by means of taking notes or by transcribing the information, but the company is not obliged to provide any additional facilities for this purpose, other than those provided for the purposes of facilitating inspection (Companies (Inspection and Copying of Registers, Indices and Documents) Regulations 1991, Reg 3(2)(b), (3)).

Register of members

General

3.2   Section 352 of the Companies Act 1985 requires every company to keep a register of its members. For a company limited by shares, the section further provides that the following particulars be kept in respect of each member:

(a) name and address. The section does not detail the exact particulars required but the intent of the Act is that members should be sufficiently identified to avoid doubt;

(*b*)   date upon which each person was first registered as a member;

(*c*)   number of shares held by each member and the class of share held (if distinguished);

(*d*)   the amount paid, or agreed to be considered as paid, on each share held;

(*e*)   the date upon which each person ceased to be a member; and

(*f*)   amount and class of stock held by each member. This applies where a company has converted some of its shares into stock.

Section 361 of the Act states that entry of these particulars in the register is *prima facie* evidence of them but is not conclusive, and thus anyone dealing with the company will be taken to know that:

(i)   shares may be transferred in accordance with the articles;

(ii)   a member may, in certain circumstances, repudiate his shares and have his name removed from the register;

(iii)   there may be persons registered without their consent who may have their names removed;

(iv)   a person who has been incorrectly entered in contravention of section 84 may be removed under section 85; and

(v)   where the entry is conditional, membership is not complete.

Single member companies

3.3   If the number of members of a private company limited by shares or by guarantee falls to one, there shall upon the occurrence of that event be entered in the company's register of members with the name and address of the sole member:

(*a*)   a statement that the company has only one member; and

(*b*)   the date on which the company became a company having only one member.

If the membership increases from one to two or more members, there shall upon the occurrence of that event be entered in the company's register of members, with the name and address of the same member, a statement that the company has ceased to have only one member together with the date on which that event occurred.

Index of members

3.4   Section 354 of the Act requires that every company having more than 50 members (usually only public companies) must keep an index of the names of its members, unless the register is in such a form as to constitute an index on its own (e.g. alphabetical order).

The index must be updated in accordance with any changes in the register of members within 14 days of the updating of the register and must, at all times, be kept at the same place as the register.

Designated accounts

3.5   Members sometimes request that accounts in the register of members of companies be split into separately designated accounts in the same name with each account bearing a different reference. A company is not bound to grant such requests unless the articles expressly provide for this. No formal instrument is required to move shares from one account to another as there is no change of ownership.

Care must be taken when splitting an account into designated accounts as no entry must appear to give expressed, implied or constructive notice of a trust as this is contrary to the provisions of CA 1985, s 360.

Location and inspection

3.6   Section 353(1) of the Companies Act 1985 requires that the register of members be kept at the company's registered office. However, if the work of making up the register is done at another office of the company, it may be kept there. Furthermore, if the company arranges with some other person (e.g. share registrars) to maintain the register for the company, then it may be kept at that person's office. Inspection rights were changed by CA 1989, s 143 by the insertion of section 723A into the Companies Act 1985.

CA 1985, s 353(2) provides that if the register is kept otherwise than at the registered office, then the Registrar of Companies must be notified of the location at which it is kept, except where the register has always been held at the registered office or if the register was in existence on 1 July 1948. In such cases no notice need be sent until there is a change (CA 1985, s 353(3)).

This is, however, subject to the proviso that the register of members must be kept within the country of the company's domicile (i.e. England and Wales, or Scotland as appropriate) (CA 1985, s 353(1)).

If the company defaults in respect of this obligation, the company and every officer are liable to a default fine (CA 1985, s 353(4)).

Section 356(1) of the CA 1985 requires that the register must be open for inspection:

(*a*)   by any member of the company without charge; and

(*b*)   by any other person on payment of £2.50 for each hour or part thereof during which the right of inspection is exercised, or such lesser charge as the company may prescribe, for not less than two hours during the period between 9 am and 5 pm on each business day (CA 1985, s 356(1), as amended by CA 1989, s 143; Companies (Inspection and Copying of Registers, Indices and Documents) Regulations 1991 (SI 1991 No 1998), Regs 2, 3).

Neither the index of members' names nor the register of members is required to be laid out to show whether a member has given an address in a particular geographical location, has a holding of a certain size, is of a particular nationality, is a natural person or not, or is of a particular gender (Reg 4(2)).

The right to inspect the register is further extended by CA 1985, s 356(3) which allows members or any other person to request copies of it from the company, and the index or any part, on payment of:

  (i)   £2.50 for the first 100 entries or part thereof copied;

 (ii)   £20.00 for the next 1,000 entries or part thereof copied;

(iii)   £15.00 for every subsequent 1,000 entries or part thereof copied;

(or such lesser sum as the company may decide).

The company is not obliged, when providing copies of the whole or any part of the register of members, to extract entries by reference to any of the matters in Regulation 4(2) listed above, and set out in Regulation 4(3).

When copies are requested they do not have to be provided by the company immediately, but within ten days following the day upon which the request was received by the company (CA 1985, s 356(3)).

Where a register is kept in a non-legible form as permitted by CA 1985, s 723, the right of inspection is construed as a right to inspect a reproduction of the register in a legible form.

Penalties are imposed in case of default of the above provisions and, in addition, a judge may order an immediate inspection of the register or may direct that the copies requested be sent to the persons requiring them.

Closing the register

3.7   Section 358 of the Companies Act 1985 allows a company, for any time or times during a year, to close its register of members for any period not exceeding (in total) 30 days in each year.

If the company decides to close the register, it must give notice of its intention by advertisement in a newspaper which circulates in the district of the company's registered office.

Advantage is sometimes taken of this section when the company's registration office is hard pressed e.g. in the period just before the payment of a dividend. The advantage gained is, however, somewhat restricted as action still has to be taken in relation to the registration of probates, notices of changes of address etc.

Many companies, therefore, now set a date on which shareholders must be registered to qualify for a dividend or the right to apply for new shares, rather than closing their books.

In addition, these arrangements only apply as between the company and the registered members. Where a company's shares which are quoted on the Stock Exchange are sold, the rights to dividend and other benefits are governed by the contract of the parties or where the contract is silent, by the rules of the Stock Exchange.

Rectification of the register

3.8   The underlying purpose of the public disclosure of the members of a company is to allow creditors to be aware of whom and what they are dealing with. It is, therefore, vital that the register of members is maintained correctly at all times.

An error cannot be corrected by the company without applying to the court. Section 359 of the Companies Act 1985 grants the court power to order the correction of a company's register of members if:

(*a*)   the name of any person is, without sufficient cause, entered in or omitted from the register; or

(*b*)   default is made or an unnecessary delay occurs in entering the fact that a person has ceased to be a member.

The court may order such a rectification before and after the winding-up of a company. Any person may apply to the court, as may the company itself, and in fact this facility is frequently invoked.

When making an order for rectification the court can appoint any person to rectify the register. There must, of course, be a register to be rectified and thus, if the register has been destroyed, a new register will have to be prepared.

Removal of names

3.9   An entry relating to a former member may be removed from the register of members after the end of 20 years from the date on which he ceased to be a member (CA 1985, s 352(6)).

Entries of share warrants

3.10   A company may issue share warrants to members in respect of any fully-paid shares if so authorised by its articles. The share warrant entitles the bearer to the shares specified within it.

When a warrant is to be issued, the name of the member should be struck out of the register of members (CA 1985, s 355).

The following information should then be entered in the register:

(*a*)   the issue of the warrant;

(*b*)   the shares included in the warrant; and

(*c*)   the date of issue of the warrant.

Subject to the company's articles a bearer can become a member of the company by surrendering his warrant and will be entered on the register.

Changes in registered particulars

3.11   In order to prevent the register of members gradually becoming inaccurate due to changes in the registered particulars of members, it is necessary that all such changes are notified to the company. The most common types of changes requiring registration are as follows:

(*a*)   a change in a member's address; and

(*b*)   a change in a member's name.

Any notice of change of address should be signed by the appropriate member so as to reduce the risk of fraud and, in practice, it is advisable for a company to send out a form for the member to complete and return.

A change of the name of a member will require more formal documentary proof before the register of members is amended, such as the production of a marriage certificate, together with a written request by the member for the amendment to be made. Where a corporate member has changed its name, the usual procedure will be the production of the change of name certificate.

All alterations in the register of members should only be made after the directors of the company have approved them, as the secretary (or such other nominated person) has no power to alter the register without the authority of the board of directors.

Registration of trusts

3.12   Section 360 is one of the more important sections of the Companies Act 1985. This prohibits the entry of any trust on the register of members of the company. The section has the following effects:

(*a*)   the company is relieved of the duty of enquiring whether a transfer of shares by a trustee is within his powers;

(*b*)   the beneficiary who is not registered as the holder of shares has no connection with, or rights in, a company in which shares are held on trust for him; and

(*c*)   the registered holder is liable to the company for calls on the shares.

The section should be read in conjunction with the articles of the company which usually go beyond the provisions of the section by stating that the company is not required to recognise any right in a share except an absolute right in the registered holder. This will, however, not prohibit a company from recognising such rights should it so wish.

CA 1985, s 360 does not prevent an executor from having his name entered in the register without qualification, if the articles so allow.

Overseas branch registers

3.13   A company which has a share capital and whose objects include doing business in any of the countries in Her Majesty's dominions as specified in Part I of Schedule 14 to the Companies Act 1985 may maintain a branch register of members who are resident in the territory in which it transacts business (CA 1985, s 362).

Prior to the 1985 Companies Act such registers were called 'Dominion Registers'. It is at the discretion of the company whether it maintains such registers; it is not obliged to do so.

Any company which establishes an overseas branch register is required, within 14 days of such establishment, to give notice to the Registrar of Companies of the situation of the office where it is kept. Any changes or the discontinuance of the register must also be notified in the same manner.

The overseas branch register is deemed to be part of the register of the company and can be rectified by any competent court. Overseas branch registers must be maintained in the same manner as the register, with the exception that notice of the closing of the overseas branch register should be inserted in a newspaper circulating in the district where the overseas branch register is kept.

No transaction in respect of shares registered in an existing overseas branch register may be registered in another register and the shares must be distinguished from those appearing in the principal register.

A copy of every entry in an overseas branch register must be sent to the company's registered office as soon as practicable and a duplicate of the Dominion Register kept at the office where the company's principal register is kept (CA 1985, Sch 14, Pt II).

Duplicate registers

3.14   A company may keep its complete register in two places; one at the registered office and another at an office abroad. The 'duplicate' register has no statutory basis and should not be confused with the copy of an overseas branch register.

In law only one register exists i.e. the original register at the registered office of the company.

Register of directors and secretaries

General

3.15   Every company has to keep a register, known as the register of directors and secretaries, in which the following details for every person who is a director or secretary of the company must be shown (CA 1985, s 289(1)).

(*a*)   If the director is an individual:

    (i)   his present Christian name (this includes a forename) (CA 1985, s 289(2)(a)) and surname (surname in the case of a peer or person usually known by a title means that title) (CA 1985, s 289(2)(b));

    (ii)   any former Christian name or surname (this does not include, in the case of a peer or person having a British title, the name by which he was known before taking or succeeding to the title). The requirement also does not apply where a person's name was changed before he reached 18 or was changed or disused not less than twenty years ago. A married woman does not have to show her maiden name;

    (iii)   his usual residential address (the DTI published a consultative document proposing changes to the law on disclosure of directors' and company secretaries' home addresses. However the proposals were not adopted);

    (iv)   his nationality;

    (v)   his business occupation;

    (vi)   any other directorships currently held or held during the previous five years (this will soon not be necessary as there will be legislation to do away with this requirement following the DTI consultative document published in February 1997 of which this was one of the proposed changes that came through). Section 289(3) of the Companies Act 1985 gives certain exemptions here in respect of directorships of dormant companies or other companies within the same group;

    (vii)   date of birth. (The Companies Act 1989, Schedule 19, para 2, requires *all* directors to disclose their dates of birth, as from the commencement date of the Schedule on 1 October 1990.)

Should the director be a corporation, then the details required are its corporate name and the address of its registered or principal office.

(*b*)   For each secretary:

    (i)   present Christian name and surname (and any former names); and

(ii)   residential address (see (iii) above).

Should a corporation be a secretary then the same details are required as those for a corporate director.

The register should also note the dates of appointment and resignation/removal of each director and secretary.

Location and inspection

3.16   The register must be kept at the company's registered office (CA 1985, s 288(1)).

The register must be open to the inspection of the members of the company without charge and by other persons on the payment of £2.50 for each hour or part thereof during which the right of inspection is exercised or such lesser sum as the company may determine.

The register must be open for inspection for not less than two hours between 9 am and 5 pm on each business day. (For the right to make copies of this register, see 3.1 above.)

Changes

3.17   The Registrar of Companies must be notified (and the register of directors and secretaries accordingly updated) if there is:

(*a*)   a change in the directors or the secretary/secretaries of the company; or

(*b*)   a change in any of the information contained in the register.

The notification must show the date of change (CA 1985, s 288(2)) and where a new director or secretary is being appointed it must include a consent to act in the appropriate capacity. If a corporation is being appointed, the consent should be signed on its behalf by an officer of that corporation.

CA 1985, s 288(2) also requires that such notifications are forwarded in the prescribed form (forms 288a (appointment), 288b (resignation) and 288c (change of particulars)) to Companies House within 14 days of the date of the change.

Register of directors' interests

General

3.18   Every company is obliged to maintain a register of directors' interests in the shares or debentures of the company or a related company (CA 1985, s 325) and for this purpose, under section 324 of the Companies Act 1985, a director must notify the company in writing of his interests in the shares or debentures of the company and its associated companies and must state that the notice is given in fulfilment of the obligation. Directors also have to notify companies of theinterests of their wives and children (CA 1985, s 328), and shadow directors are also included.

Directors of companies which have a listing on either the full securities market or Alternative Investment Market should, in dealing with shares of that company or any of its subsidiaries, further comply with the provisions of the 'Model Code for Securities Transactions by Directors of Listed Companies' as set out in the appendix of Chapter 16 of The Stock Exchange's Listing Rules publication (the Yellow Book) or the AIM rules as appropriate.

The purpose of the register of directors' interests is to allow members and the general public to be aware of the extent that the directors of the company are interested in the shares and debentures and have rights to subscribe for further shares and debentures of the company.

The interpretation of the word 'interested' is crucial in determining the obligation of the directors. CA 1985, Sch 13, paras 1(1) and (2) state that any interest of any kind is included notwithstanding the existence of any restraints or restrictions to which the exercise of the right is or may be subject. For example, a person is to be considered 'interested' in shares or debentures if:

(*a*)   he is the beneficiary of a trust, the property of which includes any interest in shares or debentures (CA 1985, Sch 13, para 2); or

(*b*)   a body corporate owns the shares or debentures and the body corporate is accustomed to acting in accordance with his directions or if one third of the voting rights of the body corporate are owned by him (CA 1985, Sch 13, para 4); or

(*c*)   he has entered into a contract to purchase them (CA 1985, Sch 13, para 3(1)); or

(*d*)   he has the right to call for their delivery to him or his order, exercisable presently or in the future (CA 1985, Sch 13, para 6(2)); or

(*e*)   he is entitled to exercise any rights in those shares or debentures (except rights of proxy or to act as company representative to vote at meetings (CA 1985, Sch 13, para 3(1)); or

(*f*)   he has a joint interest in such shares or debentures.

A director need not notify a company of interests which come to his attention after he has ceased to be a director. Also the following interests do not have to be notified:

(i)   an interest in reversion or remainder in shares or debentures where a director has a life interest in the income of trust property comprising the shares or debentures (CA 1985, Sch 13, para 9); or

(ii)   an interest as a bare trustee or a custodian trustee (CA 1985, Sch 13, para 10); or

(iii) an interest subsisting by virtue of an authorised unit trust scheme within the meaning of the Financial Services Act 1986 (CA 1985, Sch 13, para 11); or

(iv) certain other interests under statutory schemes.

In addition, the Companies (Disclosure of Directors' Interests) (Exceptions) Regulations 1985 (SI 1985 No 802) added a number of other exceptions to those set out above.

Time for notification and penalties for non-notification

3.19   Notification must be given within five days of the relevant date.

The relevant date is as follows:

(*a*)   in the case of existing interests, the day following the director's appointment;

(*b*)   in the case of subsequent interests, the day following that on which the event giving rise to the obligation occurred;

(*c*)   if the director was unaware of the interest or event at the relevant date, the day following that on which he became aware of it.

(CA 1985, Sch 13, paras 14 and 15.)

Saturdays, Sundays and Bank Holidays are excluded in calculating the period for notification (CA 1985, Sch 13, para 16).

A director who fails to give the appropriate notification within the above period or who makes a false statement to a company is guilty of an offence punishable on summary conviction or on conviction on indictment by imprisonment or a fine or both (CA 1985, ss 324(7) and 328(6)).

Contents and location of the register

3.20   The register must contain the following information:

(*a*)   the name of the director;

(*b*)   the information given by the director; and

(*c*)   the date the information is entered in the register.

The entries must be made in chronological order against each name (CA 1985, Sch 13, para 21).

The entry must be made within three days from the day following that on which the interest is received by the company (again excluding Saturdays, Sundays and Bank Holidays) (CA 1985, Sch 13, para 22).

The company also has the obligation to register the following matters without notification:

(i)   the grant to a director of a right to subscribe for shares or debentures of the company (CA 1985, s 325(3)); or

(ii)   the exercise of such a right (CA 1985, s 325(4)).

Where a listed company has received notification of a director's interest, it must notify the appropriate investment exchange of the information, which may then publish the information.

The register must be kept at the company's registered office or, if the register of members of the company is not kept there, at the place where the register of members is kept. The Registrar of Companies must be notified of the register's location in the latter case (CA 1985, Sch 13, para 27).

An index of the names in the register must be maintained with the register, unless the register itself is in the form of an index, and any alterations must be made to the index within 14 days of the amendment of the register itself (CA 1985, Sch 13, para 28).

Inspection of register

3.21   The register must be made available for inspection to the same extent and in the same manner as the register of members (CA 1985, Sch 13, para 25) (although the register of directors' interests is never closed). The rules regarding copies of the register, the powers of the court to compel inspection and the supply of copies are also exactly the same as in the register of members (CA 1985, s 326(6) and Sch 13, para 26).

The register must be produced at the beginning of every annual general meeting of the company and during the meeting be open for inspection by any person attending (CA 1985, Sch 13, para 29).

Penalties for non-compliance

3.22   There are various penalties for non-compliance with the obligations imposed in relation to the register, which may be incurred by the company and every officer in default (CA 1985, s 326).

The Department of Trade & Industry may appoint inspectors to investigate failure to comply with section 324 of the Companies Act 1985.

Register of charges

General

3.23   This is an area which has undergone alteration and sections will be changed and renumbered by the Companies Act 1989, although the new provisions have not as yet come into force (see 9.15).

Section 411 of the Companies Act 1985, inserted by CA 1989, s 101, will impose an obligation upon all companies to keep a register of all fixed and floating charges, whereas at present only limited companies have to maintain such registers (CA 1985, s 407). The current provisions are outlined at 3.27 below.

Section 406 of the CA 1985 further requires companies to keep copies of every instrument creating a charge which requires registration with the Registrar of Companies pursuant to the Act. CA 1989, s 101 will extend this requirement when this provision comes into force so that a company will also have to keep copies of *all* instruments which create a charge, whether or not they have to be registered with the Registrar of Companies.

Location

3.24 Sections 406(1) and 407(1) of the Companies Act 1985 respectively require that a company keep copies of all charges which must be registered pursuant to the Act and the register of charges at its registered office.

Contents of register

3.25 Section 407(2) of the Companies Act 1985 requires that the following details be entered in the register of charges for each charge affecting the property or undertaking of a company:

(*a*)   short description of the property charged;

(*b*)   amount of the charge; and

(*c*)   name(s) of the person(s) entitled to the charge (except in the case of bearer securities).

Charges for the purposes of CA 1985, s 407(2) are charges specifically affecting the property of the company and floating charges on the company's undertaking or property. However, this does not only mean charges required to be registered at Companies House but extends to all charges which fit the definition.

Inspection

3.26 Section 408 of the Companies Act 1985 requires that a company have available for inspection at its registered office the register of charges and copies of any charge documents, for not less than two hours during normal business hours in each day.

Creditors and members of the company have the right to inspect the register and any copy charge documents required to be kept by the company without payment. However, any other person wishing to inspect them may be charged no more than 5p per inspection (or such lesser sum as the company may determine). The right to obtain copies of the charges register and any charge documents of which the company has to maintain copies will be extended to all persons by CA 1989, s 101. Previously this right was restricted to members and creditors.

Register of interests in shares

General

3.27   Section 211 of the Companies Act 1985 requires a *public company* only to maintain a register for the purpose of recording notifications of interests in shares.

Prior to the 1981 Act there was a register of substantial individual interests which related to interests at 10% or more in the capital of the company. The 1981 Act increased the notifiable information and in 1985 the previous provisions were repealed by CA 1985, Part VI.

The underlying purpose of the register is to prevent takeovers by stealth.

Sections 198–202 of the CA 1985 (sections 199(2) and 202 amended by CA 1989, s 134), impose a general obligation upon persons to notify a *public company* of the following within two days of the occurrence of any of the following events:

(*a*)   if they acquire a 3% interest (or more) in the shares of the company;

(*b*)   if they cease to hold a 3% interest (or more) in the shares of the company;

(*c*)   if they hold a 3% interest in the shares of the company and the percentage level of the holding changes; or

(*d*)   if they exercise a share option.

An 'interest' is taken as including any interest held by a person's spouse, infant child or step-child and also includes any corporate interests (in certain circumstances). CA 1985, s 203 explains the details.

The Disclosure of Interests in Shares (Amendment) Regulations 1993 (SI 1993 No 1819), whose main purpose is to implement the requirements of the Major Shareholding Directive, came into force on 18 September 1993. These regulations amend Part VI of the Companies Act 1985 and introduce an additional disclosure threshold of 10% for non-material interests. The 3% disclosure threshold remains for interests which under the new provisions are characterised as material. Non-material interests include interests held by investment managers, unit trust managers and those categories of persons who currently enjoy full exemption which cannot continue under the Directive as voting rights are controlled.

Contents of register of interests

3.28   When a company receives a notification from a person in satisfaction of the above obligation the company must within three days record the following information:

(*a*)   the name of the person;

(*b*)   the information; and

(*c*)   the date of inscription.

(CA 1985, s 211(1).)

If the company is informed that the person making the notification is no longer a member of a concert party agreement the company must record the information against his name wherever it appears.

The register must also include the information that it receives as a result of a CA 1985, s 212 inquiry in the register; such information being recorded in a separate part of the register against the name of the registered holder. The information required by CA 1985, s 213 is:

(i)   the fact that the company gave notice under CA 1985, s 212 to that person requiring particular information;

(ii)   the date the notice was given; and

(iii)   any information received by the company as a result of the giving of the notice in so far as the information relates to the present interests held by any persons in shares that are comprised in the company's share capital.

Index

3.29   Entries must be made in chronological order in respect of each name and the register must be kept in index form or else have a separate index (CA 1985, s 211(5) and (6)).

Location and inspection

3.30   The register is required to be kept at the same location as a company's register of directors' interests (CA 1985, s 211(8)).

The register of interests in shares is required to be made available to members of the company without charge for not less than two hours between 9 am and 5 pm on any business day and to non-members on the payment of £2.50 per hour (CA 1985, s 219).

The fee for copies made by non-members is £2.50 for the first 100 copies, £20 for the next 1,000 and £15 for every subsequent 1,000 copies.

However, an exemption exists in paragraphs 3 and 10 of Schedule 5 to the Companies Act 1985 which allows a company not to make the register available for inspection in certain circumstances. The relevant exemption is the exemption of a company from the requirement to disclose in its accounts particulars of shareholdings in subsidiaries or other bodies corporate incorporated or carrying on business outside the United Kingdom, in circumstances where disclosure would be harmful to the business of the company.

Removal of entries from the register

3.31   Under section 218 of the Companies Act 1985, entries in the register of interests must not be deleted except in accordance with section 217 of the CA 1985 which permits deletions in the following circumstances:

(*a*)   a company may remove an entry where more than six years have elapsed since the date of inscription and either:

   (i)   the entry recorded the fact that the person in question ceased to have an interest subject to the notification requirement, or

   (ii)   it has been superseded by a later entry under CA 1985, s 211;

(*b*)   where a notification under CA 1985, Part VI gives the name and address of another person and states that the person is interested in its shares, the company must within 15 days notify the other person of the entry made (CA 1985, s 217(2)). The other person may then apply to the company to have his name removed from the register on the grounds that the entry was incorrect (CA 1985, s 217(3)); and

(*c*)   where a person who is identified in the register as party to a concert party agreement under CA 1985, s 204 ceases to be such a party, he may apply to have the information recorded that he is no longer party to the agreement (CA 1985, s 217(4)).

If the company fails to make the alterations requested under section 217(3) and (4) of the CA 1985, an application may be made to the court who may order the appropriate amendment to be made (CA 1985, s 217(5)).

Where an entry is removed from the register the company must also amend the index within 14 days (CA 1985, s 217(6)).

Any entry wrongly removed must be restored to the register as soon as is reasonably practicable. Unauthorised deletions and failure to restore are punishable by default fines (CA 1985, s 218(3)).

Penalties for non-compliance

3.32   If default is made in complying with the requirements to maintain a register of interests in shares, the company and every officer who is in default is liable on summary conviction to a fine not exceeding one-fifth of the statutory minimum or, on conviction contravention, a daily default fine not exceeding one-fiftieth of the statutory maximum.

Investigations by a company of interests in its own shares

3.33   Under section 212 of the Companies Act 1985 a public company may issue a notice in writing to any person whom it knows, or has reasonable cause to believe, to be interested in the shares of the company (or has been so interested in the three years prior to the notice). It does not, however, have to show real ground for its belief as long as it is not frivolously or vexatiously sought.

Such notice may require the recipient to:

(*a*)   indicate whether he is or was so interested;

(*b*)   give particulars of his own past or present interest in shares in the company held by him at any time during the previous three years;

(*c*)   give particulars of any other interests subsisting in the shares; and

(*d*)   in relation to past interests, to provide particulars and the identity of any person who held the interest immediately upon the addressee ceasing to hold it.

Members holding not less than one-tenth of the voting rights of the company may require the company to exercise its powers under section 212 (CA 1985, s 214(1)).

The members making the requisition must not only specify the manner in which they wish the powers to be exercised but also give reasonable grounds for requiring the company to exercise the powers (CA 1985, s 214(2)(c)). On the conclusion of the investigation the company must then prepare a report of the information received. Such report must then be made available at the registered office of the company within a reasonable time after the end of the investigation (CA 1985, s 215(1)).

There are further provisions relating to the time scale for investigations and reports contained in sections 214 and 215 of the CA 1985 and there is a default fine for non-compliance (CA 1985, ss 214(5) and 215(8)).

Penalties for failure to provide information under section 212

3.34   There are two types of penalty for failure to provide the information required under section 212 of the Companies Act 1985.

First, failure to supply the information permits the company to apply to the court for an order directing that the shares in question shall be subject to the restrictions imposed by CA 1985, Part XV. Such restrictions are as follows:

(*a*)   the shares may not be transferred;

(*b*)   no voting rights shall be exercisable in respect of the shares;

(*c*)   no bonus shares may be issued in respect of the shares; and

(*d*)   no payments whatsoever in respect of the shares shall be made except in liquidation.

Second, there are criminal penalties in respect of failure to comply with a CA 1985, s 212 request and the making of statements known to be false in a material matter or recklessly made.

There is a statutory defence if the defendant can prove that the requirement to give the information was vexatious or frivolous (CA 1985, s 216(4)). There is also a provision for exemption from the obligation to give information, with the exemption being made by the Secretary of State (CA 1985, s 216(5)).

Register of debenture holders

General

3.35   The Companies Acts do not impose a requirement to keep a register of debenture holders. However, when a debenture is created, the terms of the document constituting the debenture invariably include an obligation to maintain such a register.

Once such an obligation has arisen section 190 of the Companies Act 1985 applies. CA 1985, s 190 contains provisions relating to where the register may be kept, rights of inspection and the duty to notify the Registrar of the register's location.

Contents of register of debenture holders

3.36   The Companies Act 1985 does not specify the information that must be included in a register of debenture holders, as such requirements are normally included in the debenture document.

Location and inspection

3.37   The register of debenture holders must be kept at either of the following two locations:

(*a*)   at the company's registered office; or

(*b*)   at the place where the work in making it up is done.

If the register is not kept at the registered office, notice of its location must be given to the Registrar, as should notice of any change in its location.

Under section 190(1) and (2) of the Companies Act 1985, a company registered in England and Wales may not keep such a register in Scotland nor may a company registered in Scotland keep a register of debenture holders in England or Wales.

The register of debenture holders must be open to the inspection of a registered debenture holder or shareholder without payment of a fee and to any other person on payment of £2.50 for each hour or part thereof during which the right of inspection may be exercised.

The register must be available for inspection subject to such reasonable restrictions as the company in general meeting may impose, provided that a minimum of two hours in each day shall be allowed for inspection. The register can, however, be closed (and thus not available for inspection) in accordance with the articles of the company or the document(s) securing the debenture(s) during such period or periods not exceeding 30 days in total in any year.

The company is not obliged to present its register of debenture holders for inspection in a manner which groups together entries by reference to whether a debenture holder has given an address in a particular geographical location, is of a particular nationality or gender, has a holding of a certain size, or is a natural person or not (Companies (Inspection and Copying of Registers, Indices and Documents) Regulations 1991, Reg 4(2)).

The company must provide any registered debenture holder or any shareholder with a copy of the register or part of it on payment of exactly the same fee as in the Register of Members (see 3.6 above). The company is not obliged, when providing such copies, to extract entries by reference to any of the matters listed above in relation to Regulation 4(2) and (3).

In addition, every debenture holder is entitled to have forwarded to him a copy of any trust deed securing any issue of debentures on payment of 10 pence per hundred words or part thereof copied (see 3.6 above for inspection and copying requirements).

Accounting records

General

3.38   Every company is required to maintain accounting records which must be sufficient to show and explain the company's transactions and must be such as to:

(*a*)   disclose with reasonable accuracy at any time, the financial position of the company at that time; and (*b*)   enable the directors to ensure that any balance sheet and profit and loss account prepared under CA 1985, Part VII comply with the requirements of that Act.

(CA 1985, s 221(1), as inserted by CA 1989, s 2.)

The accounting records must contain entries from day to day of all sums of money received and expended by the company and the matters in respect of which the receipt and expenditure takes place, and a record of all the assets and liabilities of the company.

If a company deals in goods the records must also contain:

  (i)   statements of stock held by the company at the end of each financial year of the company;

 (ii)   all statements of stocktakings from which any such statement of stock has been or is to be prepared; and

(iii)   except in the case of goods sold by way of ordinary retail trade, statements of all goods sold and purchased, showing the goods and the buyers and sellers in sufficient detail to enable all these to be identified.

(CA 1985, s 221(3), as inserted by CA 1989, s 2.)

Form of accounting records

3.39   The Companies Act 1985 does not prescribe any precise form that accounting records should take, it does however provide that accounting records may be kept either by making entries in bound books or by recording the matters in any other manner (CA 1985, s 722(1)). Where the accounting records do not take the form of entries in a bound book adequate precautions must be taken to guard against falsification and to facilitate their discovery (CA 1985, s 722(2)).

Section 723(1) of the CA 1985 permits data to be recorded otherwise than in a legible form provided it is capable of being reproduced in legible form, thereby allowing such information to be stored electronically.

In practice, the method chosen will depend on many factors such as the size of the company and the degree of sophistication required for management purposes.

Duty in relation to subsidiary undertakings

3.40   The Companies Act 1989 inserted in CA 1985 the requirement that a parent company which has a subsidiary undertaking to which the consolidation requirements of the Companies Act 1985 do not apply, must take reasonable steps to secure that the undertaking keeps such accounting records as to enable the directors of the parent company to ensure that any balance sheet and profit and loss account prepared in accordance with CA 1985 complies with the requirements of CA 1985, ss 229 and 243.

Retention of accounting records

3.41 Accounting records must be retained for three years by a private company and for six years by a public company; the period running from the date on which the records were made. There is an exception to this i.e. where a direction as to the disposal of records is made under the winding-up rules under section 411 of the Insolvency Act 1986. In addition, a company must ensure that it complies with any other statutory requirements relating to the retention of accounting records, for example, the Taxes Management Act 1970, the Value Added Tax Act 1983 and PAYE Regulations etc. (see 11.16 and Appendix 11A COMMERCIAL CONSIDERATIONS).

Location and inspection of accounting records

3.42 A company's accounting records must be kept at the company's registered office or such place as the directors consider fit. They must at all times be open to inspection by the company's officers (CA 1985, s 222(1), inserted by CA 1989, s 2) which include all directors and managers, as well as the secretary of the company. It has been held that an auditor who is appointed under the Act is an officer of the company but he also has a specific right of access at all times enshrined in section 389A(1) of the Companies Act 1985, inserted by CA 1989, s 120 (*R v Shacter* [*1960*] 2 *QB* 252).

A member of a company does not have such a right of inspection and Article 109 of Table A (as set out in SI 1985 No 805) states that 'No member shall (as such) have any right of inspecting any accounting records or other book or document of the company except as conferred by statute or authorised by the directors or by ordinary resolution of the company'. It is, however, open to a company's articles of association to give members a right to inspect the company's accounting records although this right ceases on the voluntary winding-up of a company. (See also 4.24 ACCOUNTS AND AUDITORS and 7.6 MEMBERSHIP for members' rights in respect of the accounts.)

If the accounting records of a company are kept outside Great Britain accounts and returns with respect to the business dealt with in those accounting records must be sent to, and kept at, a place in Great Britain, and must at all times be open to inspection by the company's officers (CA 1985, s 222(2)).

These accounts and returns must:

(*a*) disclose with reasonable accuracy the financial position of the business at intervals of not more than six months; and (*b*)   enable the directors to ensure that the company's balance sheet and profit and loss account comply with the requirements of CA 1985.

(CA 1985, s 222(3)).

Failure to keep proper accounting records

3.43   Every officer of a company who is in default in respect of accounting records is guilty of an offence unless he acted honestly and his default is excusable. The officer will also be guilty of an offence if he has intentionally caused default by the company in relation to the provisions for maintenance of accounting records, or if he has failed to take all reasonable steps to secure compliance with them (CA 1985, s 221(5)).

Anyone summarily convicted of an offence under this section is liable to imprisonment for up to six months, or a fine or both; and on conviction on indictment liable to imprisonment for up to two years, or a fine or both (CA 1985, s 221(6)).

Apart from the liability arising from the failure to carry the statutory obligation outlined above, penalties may also arise for offences antecedent to or in the course of the winding-up of the company.

Directors' service contracts

General

3.44   Every company must make available for inspection of its members the terms of service contracts with its directors including shadow directors (CA 1985, s 318). This requirement does not, however, include contracts which have less than twelve months to run or which can be terminated by the company within the following twelve months without payment of compensation.

The following must be available:

(*a*)   if the service contract is in writing, a copy of the contract; and

(*b*)   if the service contract is not in writing, a written memorandum of its terms.

(CA 1985, s 318(1)(a) (b)).

Any amendments to the contract must also be shown (CA 1985, s 318(10)). It is important that this obligation is fulfilled with fairness so as to give the members an accurate understanding of the obligations of the company to the director and thus, if all the terms of the contract are not contained in the contract, then a memorandum detailing the additional terms should be provided.

The obligation extends to service contracts with subsidiaries of the company (CA 1985, s 318(1)(c)). If, however, the contract requires the director to work mainly or completely outside the United Kingdom the company need only make available a memorandum stating the name of the director, the provisions of the contract concerning its duration and, if appropriate, the name of and place of incorporation of the subsidiary (CA 1985, s 318(5)).

Location and inspection of service contracts

3.45   Copies of all service contracts and memoranda must be kept together (CA 1985, s 318(2)) by companies at one of the following places:

(*a*)   the registered office;

(*b*)   any other place where the register of members is kept; or

(*c*)   the company's principal place of business provided that this is situated in the part of the United Kingdom in which the company is registered.

(CA 1985, s 318(3)).

If the documents are not kept at the registered office, then the Registrar of Companies must be notified of the address at which they are held (CA 1985, s 318(4)).

All members of the company are entitled to inspect the documents for not less than two hours between 9 am and 5 pm on any business day without payment of a fee (CA 1985, s 318(7)). The court can compel an immediate inspection in the case of refusal to allow such inspection (CA 1985, s 318(9)).

Penalties

3.46   Failure to comply with the obligations relating to inspection of the above documents has penal consequences for the company and every officer in default (CA 1985, s 318(8)).

Contracts for the purchase of the company's own shares

3.47   Should a company have entered into any contracts for the purchase of its own shares, they must be held at the registered office of a company for a period of ten years after the contract is completed (CA 1985, s 169). In a public company any person may inspect them, but if the company is private, the right of inspection is confined to members. The right of inspection applies for not less than two hours between 9 am and 5 pm on any business day.

Redemption or purchase of shares

3.48   Where a company has passed a resolution to redeem or purchase its shares out of capital under section 175 of the Companies Act 1985, a copy of the statutory declaration and auditors' report must be retained at the company's registered office from the date of publication of notice in the *Gazette* until five weeks after the date of the resolution for payment out of capital. These documents must be available for inspection by any member or creditor of the company without charge for not less than two hours between 9 am and 5 pm on any business day (CA 1985, s 175(6)).

Minutes

General

3.49   Section 382 of the Companies Act 1985 requires every company to keep minutes of the proceedings of its general meetings and of the meetings of its directors and managers. If it fails to do so, the company and every officer in default may be liable to a fine.

Form and security of minutes

3.50   The minutes (like other company registers and records covered by section 722 of the Companies Act 1985) can be kept either in a bound book or in some other manner, for example, in a loose-leaf folder into which typed sheets can be inserted as a record of each successive meeting.

If the minutes are not kept in the form of a bound book, CA 1985, s 722(2) states that adequate precautions must be taken for safeguarding against falsification and facilitating its discovery.

Minutes as evidence

3.51   Section 382(2) of the Companies Act 1985 states that the minutes of a meeting, which have been signed by the chairman of the meeting (or signed at the next meeting by the chairman), are evidence of its proceedings.

As CA 1985, s 382(2) uses the simple word 'evidence', the implication is that in the case of a dispute as to the content of a minute further proof may be needed. Other evidence may, therefore, be produced to rebut or correct the minutes, even though they may have been signed by the chairman. For example, a member who was present at a meeting might testify that a resolution was not put to the vote, although it is recorded in the minutes as having been done.

To prevent subsequent argument over a matter which cannot be proved or disproved afterwards, the articles of association of the company may introduce a regulation to provide that the minutes are 'conclusive evidence' of the business transacted at a meeting in certain circumstances.

The matter most likely to give rise to argument is whether the chairman's declaration of a result of a vote on a show of hands was correct (i.e. that a resolution was carried or not carried, or that a required majority was or was not obtained).

Regulation 47 of Table A provides that unless a poll is demanded at the time, a declaration by the chairman of the result of a vote on a show of hands, once recorded in the minutes of the meeting, shall be conclusive evidence of the result without further proof.

Section 378(4) of the CA 1985 introduces a further safeguard for a company by stating that a declaration by the chairman that an extraordinary or special resolution has been carried is, unless a poll is called, conclusive evidence of the fact.

A member may, however, still challenge the minutes of a meeting, even if they have been declared to be conclusive evidence, if he can show that they are a false record or have been fraudulently prepared or that the chairman's declaration is incorrect by its own terms (i.e. in conflict with the result which it purports to verify).

Written resolutions

3.52   In place of a board meeting, the directors of a company may substitute 'resolutions in writing'. The power to do so must, however, be contained in a company's articles of association. Regulation 93 of Table A provides a model for this authority:

'A resolution in writing signed by all the directors entitled to receive notice of a meeting of directors or of a committee of directors shall be as valid and effectual as if it had been passed at a meeting of directors or (as the case may be) a committee of directors duly convened and held and may consist of several documents in the like form each signed by one or more directors . . .'.

A similar procedure can be adopted for general meetings. However, for private companies, they are regulated in this respect by the provisions of sections 381A to 382A of the Companies Act 1985 (sections 381A to 381C and 382A inserted by CA 1989, s 113) and public companies by the power in their articles of association. However, there have been recent changes in this area (see Chapter 7 at 7.59).

Resolutions in writing of the directors and the members must be recorded in a company's minute books in the same way as minutes.

Location and inspection of minutes

3.53   Pursuant to section 383 of the Companies Act 1985 a company is required to keep the minutes of its general meetings at its registered office and to make them available for inspection by members, without charge, for at least two hours between 9 am and 5 pm on each business day.

The section grants members a right to inspect the minutes of general meetings of a company of which they are members and to be supplied with a copy of any minutes of a general meeting within seven days of making the request. In providing such copies a company may levy such charge of 10 pence per hundred words or part thereof copied.

It should be noted that the rights of members to inspect minutes are confined solely to minutes of general meetings. Members have no right to inspect the minutes of board meetings; this is a right that only extends to the directors.

Chapter 4

Accounts and Auditors

Annual accounts

General

4.1   Section 226(1) of the Companies Act 1985 requires the directors of a company to prepare a profit and loss account in respect of each financial year and a balance sheet as at the end of the financial year; these are referred to as the company's individual accounts.

A company's first financial year begins on its date of incorporation and ends on the last day of its first accounting reference period (the 'accounting reference date' see 4.2 below) or, if the directors so wish, on a day which is not more than seven days before or after the end of that period. Each successive financial year begins on the day after the date to which the preceding balance sheet was made up and ends.

Accounting reference date

4.2   A company's accounting reference periods are determined according to its accounting reference date. The current rules for the adoption by a company of its accounting reference date and hence the corresponding accounting reference period were introduced by the Companies Act 1985 (Miscellaneous Accounting Amendments) Regulations 1996 (SI 1996 No 189).

Section 224 of the Companies Act 1985 states that the accounting reference date of a company is the last day of the month in which the anniversary of its incorporation falls. A company's accounting reference period must not exceed 18 months and while section 224(4) states that a company's first such period must be more than six months, this is subject to the provisions of section 225 (see 4.3 below). Subsequent accounting reference periods are successive periods of twelve months beginning immediately after the end of the previous accounting reference period and ending with the company's accounting reference date.

Since 1 April 1992, Companies House has not accepted accounts which for the relevant accounting period are made up to a date other than the accounting reference date shown on the public file. A company may, however, treat its accounting reference period as ending at any time within seven days either side of its given accounting reference date by virtue of section 223(2) and (3) of the Act (see 4.1 above).

Alteration of the accounting reference date

4.3 Section 225 of the Companies Act 1985 governs any subsequent changes to lengthen or shorten the accounting period of a company. The current rules relating to changing the accounting reference date of a company were introduced by the Companies Act 1985 (Miscellaneous Accounting Amendments) Regulations 1996 (SI 1996 No 189). The rules for the alteration of an accounting reference date whether during or after the end of an accounting reference period are broadly similar and the form (form 225) prescribed to notify the change to Companies House is the same in each case.

The form 225 must state whether the current or previous accounting reference period is to be shortened, so as to come to an end on the first occasion on which the new accounting reference date falls or fell after the beginning of the period, or is to be extended, so as to come to an end on the second occasion on which that date falls or fell after the beginning of the period.

A notice stating that the current or previous accounting reference period is to be extended is ineffective if given less than five years after the end of an earlier accounting reference period of the company which was extended under section 225, unless:

(*a*)   the form 225 was given by a company which is a subsidiary undertaking or parent undertaking of another EEA undertaking and the new accounting reference date coincides with that of the other EEA undertaking or, where that undertaking is not a company, with the last day of its financial year;

(*b*)   an administration order is in force under Part II of the Insolvency Act 1986; or

(*c*)   the Secretary of State directs that it should not apply, which he may do with respect to a notice which has been given or which may be given.

An 'EEA undertaking' is defined as an undertaking established under the law of any part of the United Kingdom or the law of any other EEA State. An 'EEA State' is a State which is a Contracting Party to the Agreement on the European Economic Area signed at Oporto on 2 May 1992, as adjusted by the Protocol signed at Brussels on 17 March 1993 and by Council Decision Number 1/95 of 10 March 1995.

Alteration during an accounting reference period

4.4 A company may by notice in the prescribed form (form 225) given to the Registrar, specify a new accounting reference date having effect in relation to the company's current accounting reference period and subsequent periods.

Alteration after the end of an accounting reference period

4.5   A company may by notice in the prescribed form (form 225) given to the Registrar, specify a new accounting reference date having effect in relation to the company's previous accounting reference period and subsequent periods. A company's 'previous accounting reference period' means that immediately preceding its current accounting reference period.

A notice may not be given for a previous accounting reference period if the period allowed for laying and delivering accounts and reports in relation to that period has already expired.

Form and content of accounts

4.6   Pursuant to section 226(3) of the Companies Act 1985 a company's individual accounts must comply with the requirements of CA 1985, Sch 4 with respect to the form and content of the balance sheet and profit and loss account and also any additional information which has to be given in the notes to the accounts.

'A true and fair view'

4.7   Section 226(2) of the Companies Act 1985 requires that the balance sheet gives a true and fair view of the company's state of affairs as at the end of the financial year and the profit and loss account gives a true and fair view of the company's profit or loss for the financial year.

The requirement to give a 'true and fair view' is considered of paramount importance. Thus, CA 1985, s 226(4) and (5) goes on to say that:

(*a*)   where compliance with the provisions of CA 1985, Sch 4 as to matters to be included in the company's accounts are not sufficient to give a true and fair view, the necessary additional information must be given in the accounts, or a note to the accounts; and

(*b*)   where, in special circumstances, compliance with the above provisions is inconsistent with the requirement to give a true and fair view, the directors shall depart from the provisions to the extent necessary to give a true and fair view. Particulars of any such departure and the reasons for it must be stated in a note to the accounts.

Accounts must be prepared with regard to the accounting standards issued by the Accounting Standards Board (ASB). When the ASB replaced the Accounting Standards Committee on 1 August 1990, it adopted the Statements of Standard Accounting Practice (SSAPs) existing on that date. The ASB now develops and issues Financial Reporting Standards which will eventually supersede all existing SSAPs.

The ASB issued its first standard, FRS 1—Cashflow statements, on 26 September 1991, to replace SSAP10 (Statement of source and application of funds). Further standards have since been issued, for instance:

  (i) FRS 2, Accounting for subsidiary undertakings;

 (ii) FRS 3, Reporting for financial performance;

(iii) FRS 4, Capital instruments;

 (iv) FRS 5, Reporting the substance of transactions;

  (v) FRS 6, Acquisitions and mergers;

 (vi) FRS 7, Fair values in acquisition accounting;

(vii) FRS 8, Related party disclosures;

(viii) FRS 9, Associates and joint ventures;

 (ix) FRS 10, Goodwill and intangible assets;

  (x) FRS 11, Impairment of fixed assets and goodwill;

 (xi) FRS 12, Provisions, contingent liabilities and contingent;

(xii) FRS 13, Derivatives and other financial instruments: disclosures;

(xiii) FRS 14, Earnings per share; and

(xiv) FRS 15, Tangible fixed assets.

Group accounts

4.8   In addition to the requirement to prepare individual accounts, the directors of a company must, if at the end of the financial year the company is a UK registered parent company, prepare group accounts pursuant to section 227(1) of the Companies Act 1985. Group accounts must be consolidated accounts comprising:

(*a*)   a consolidated balance sheet dealing with the state of affairs of the parent company and its subsidiary undertakings; and

(*b*)   a consolidated profit and loss account dealing with the profit or loss of the parent company and its subsidiary undertakings.

(CA 1985, s 227(2)(a)(b).)

An exemption does, however, exist where a group qualifies as a small or medium-sized group pursuant to CA 1985, s 248 (see 4.21 below).

The Companies Act 1989 considerably redefined the CA 1985 definitions relating to parent company/subsidiary company relationships and the requirement to prepare group accounts. There are now five definitions of the circumstances in which group accounts must be prepared, whereas prior to the coming into force of the present regulations there were only two.

Under the current definitions (CA 1985, s 258), an undertaking is a parent undertaking in relation to another undertaking, a subsidiary undertaking, in all of the following cases.

  (i)   If it holds a majority of the voting rights in the undertaking.

(ii)   If it is a member of the undertaking and has the right to appoint or remove a majority of its board of directors.

(iii) If it has the right to exercise a dominant influence over the undertaking:

    (A)   by virtue of provisions contained in the undertaking's memorandum or articles; or

    (B)   by virtue of a control contract.

(iv)   If it is a member of the undertaking and controls alone, pursuant to an agreement with other shareholders or members, a majority of the voting rights in the undertaking.

(v)   If it has a participating interest (being around 20% of the issued share capital) in the undertaking, and:

    (I)   it actually exercises a dominant influence over it; or

    (II)   it and the subsidiary undertaking are managed on a unified basis.

These definitions apply only for the purposes of determining whether group accounts should be prepared. For general purposes the definitions of subsidiary, holding company and wholly-owned subsidiary given in sections 736 and 736A of the CA 1985 apply.

The group accounts prepared must represent a true and fair view of the group's affairs.

Exemption for subsidiaries of EU undertakings

4.9   A parent company is exempt from the requirement to prepare group accounts if it is itself a subsidiary undertaking and its immediate parent undertaking is established under the law of an EU Member State, where:

(*a*)   the company is a wholly-owned subsidiary of that parent undertaking;

(*b*)   the parent undertaking holds more than 50% of the shares in the company and notice requesting the preparation of group accounts has not been served on the company by shareholders holding in aggregate:

    (i)   more than half of the remaining shares in the company; or

    (ii)   5% of the total shares in the company.

    Such notice must be served no later than six months after the end of the financial year before that to which it relates.

The exemption does not apply to a company any of whose securities are listed on a stock exchange in any EU Member State and is also conditional upon compliance with all of the following conditions:

(A)   that the company is included in consolidated accounts for a larger group drawn up to the same date, or to an earlier date in the same financial year, by a parent undertaking established under the law of an EU Member State;

(B)   that those accounts are drawn up and audited, and that parent undertaking's annual report is drawn up, according to that law, in accordance with the provisions of the Seventh Directive;

(C)   that the company discloses in its individual accounts that it is exempt from the obligation to prepare and deliver group accounts, and the name of the parent undertaking is disclosed as well as:

   (i)   its country of incorporation, if outside Great Britain, or

   (ii)   the address of its principal place of business, if unincorporated; and

(D)   that the company delivers to the Registrar of Companies, within the period allowed for delivering its individual accounts, copies of those group accounts and of the parent undertaking's annual report, together with the auditors' report on them. A certified translation of these documents is required if they are in a language other than English.

Small and medium-sized companies

4.10   Sections 246 to 249 of the Companies Act 1985 enable a company which falls within the definition of a small or medium-sized company under CA 1985, s 247 to deliver abbreviated accounts to Companies House. However, the requirement to prepare and issue full accounts to the members of the company still applies. Alternatively, a small company is permitted to prepare and issue modified accounts (see 4.11 below) to both its members and Companies House, by virtue of The Companies Act 1985 (Accounts of Small and Medium-Sized Enterprises and Publication of Accounts in ECUs) Regulations 1992 (SI 1992 No 2452). In addition, certain categories of small company may obtain exemption from audit (see 4.14 below).

The Companies Act 1985 (Accounts of Small and Medium-Sized Companies and Minor Accounting Amendments) Regulations 1997 (SI 1997 No 220) came into force on 1 March 1997. These provisions apply to annual accounts and reports approved by the board of directors on or after 1 March 1997. A company may for financial years ending on or before 24 March 1997 prepare and deliver to the Registrar of Companies such annual accounts and reports as it would have been required to prepare and deliver had the amendments made by these regulations not been brought into force.

The regulations inserted several new sections into the Act dealing with the accounting provisions for small and medium-sized companies. In particular, these sections set out in full the provisions governing the accounts and reports to be prepared and delivered by such companies. Section 246 and Schedules 8 and 8A to the Act address in full the provisions applicable to small companies, while section 246A deals with those applicable to medium-sized companies.

The new sections also amend the statements required in the balance sheet of such companies (and in the directors' report in the case of small companies). Reference is now made to the accounts being prepared in accordance with the special provisions applicable to small and medium-sized companies under the amended sections.

Section 247B restates the provisions concerning the special auditors' report required when a small or medium-sized company delivers abbreviated accounts to the Registrar of Companies. However, the auditors are no longer required to make a report to the directors and the special auditors' report delivered to the Registrar need no longer in all cases be accompanied by or set out in full the auditors report required under section 235. The section 235 report will be required if it is qualified or contains a statement under section 237(2) or section 237(3) (see 4.51 and 4.52 below).

To qualify as a small or medium-sized company the company may not be:

(*a*)   a public company; or

(*b*)   a banking or insurance company; or

(*c*)   an authorised person under the Financial Services Act 1986; or

(*d*)   a company which is a member of an ineligible group.

(CA 1985, s 247A(1).)

An ineligible group is defined by CA 1985, s 247A(2) as a group which contains either:

 (i)   a public company, or

 (ii)   a body corporate which can offer its shares or debentures to the public, or

(iii)   an institution authorised under the Banking Act 1987, or an insurance company to which Part II of the Insurance Companies Act 1982 applies, or an authorised person under the Financial Services Act 1986.

Small company

4.11   In order to qualify as small in relation to a particular year, a company must have been:

(*a*)   small since incorporation; or

(*b*)   small in that year, and in the year before; or

(*c*)   small in the two years before that year; or

(*d*)   small in that year, and small in any two years out of the three years before that year.

'Small' means that at least two of the following three conditions are fulfilled:

 (i)   turnover does not exceed £2.8 million;

 (ii)   balance sheet total does not exceed £1.4 million;

(iii)   average number of employees during the relevant period does not exceed 50.

(CA 1985, s 247(3).)

The limits applicable to small companies in respect of turnover and the balance sheet total were increased to comply in full with EU Directive 90/604/EEC, when SI 1992 No 2452 came into force on 16 November 1992.

Abbreviated accounts

4.12   A small company is permitted under section 246, CA 1985 to lodge abbreviated accounts with Companies House and such abbreviated accounts must contain:

(*a*)   an abbreviated balance sheet with notes, together with a statement above the directors' signatures on the balance sheet that they have relied on the exemptions for individual accounts on the grounds that the company is entitled to the benefit of those exemptions as a small (or medium-sized) company; and

(*b*)   a special auditors' report stating that the requirements for exemption are satisfied, which should be reproduced on the full accounts prepared for the members.

A copy of the profit and loss account and the directors' report is not required for disclosure purposes.

Modified accounts

4.13   Small companies are permitted to issue modified accounts to their members and to lodge such accounts at Companies House. Such modified accounts comprise:

(*a*)   a modified version of the balance sheet with notes, together with a statement that advantage has been taken, in the preparation of the accounts, of special exemptions applicable to small companies;

(*b*)   a directors' report, which contains a statement that advantage has been taken, in the preparation of the report, of special exemptions applicable to small companies; and

(*c*)   a statement of the grounds on which, in the directors' opinion, the company is entitled to those exemptions, which may be shown either in the balance sheet or in the directors' report.

The provisions allow certain items in the balance sheet and the notes on the balance sheet to be combined, and the auditors are required to report on the company's entitlement to these exemptions. However, the exemptions are not as extensive as those for abbreviated accounts and the full version of the profit and loss account is still required.

Certain categories of small company

4.14   The latest in a line of audit exemption regulations are the Companies Act 1985 (Audit Exemption) (Amendment) Regulations 1997 (SI 1997 No 936). Previously, the Companies Act 1985 (Audit Exemption) Regulations 1994 (SI 1994 No 1935), which came into force on 11 August 1994, inserted sections 249A to 249D and substituted section 388A into the Companies Act 1985; and the Companies Act 1985 (Audit Exemption) (Amendment) Regulations 1994 (SI 1994 No 2879), which came into force on 12 November 1994, and the Companies Act 1985 (Audit Exemption) (Amendment) Regulations 1995 (SI 1995 No 589), which came into force on 30 March 1995, made further minor amendments.

The Companies Act 1985 (Audit Exemption) (Amendment) Regulations 1997 (SI 1997 No 936) came into force on 15 April 1997 and apply to financial periods ending on or after 15 June 1997. The main impact of the regulations was to extend the availability of the total audit exemption to companies with an aggregate turnover of not more than £350,000, while retaining the partial audit exemption for charitable companies with a gross income of not more than £250,000.

For financial periods ending before 15 June 1997, a company's turnover in the year the exemption is claimed must either be:

(*a*)   not more than £90,000 to be entitled to the total audit exemption; or

(*b*)   more than £90,000 but not more than £350,000 to entitle the company to a limited review by a reporting accountant.

For a company which is a charity, references to turnover are substituted by references to gross income and for such a company to meet the report conditions its gross income must not be more than £250,000.

It was recently reported in the *Financial Times* (10 May 1999) that the government is giving consideration to increasing the threshold for audit exemption from the current turnover limit of £350,000 to £4 million.

The following sections 4.15 to 4.19 reflect the current provisions.

Criteria for small company

4.15   Certain categories of small company are entitled to a total exemption from an audit of its accounts under section 249A(1) of the Companies Act 1985. For a company to take advantage of this exemption, it must satisfy the following conditions:

(*a*)   it must qualify as a small company in relation to that year for the purposes of section 246 (see 4.11 above); and

(*b*)   its turnover in that year must be not more than £350,000; and

(*c*)   its balance sheet total for that year must be not more than £1.4 million; and (*d*)   the company must not have been at any time within that year:

　　(i)   a public company;

　　(ii)   a banking or insurance company;

　　(iii)   a parent company or subsidiary undertaking;

　　(iv)   an authorised person or an appointed representative under the Financial Services Act 1986; or

　　(v)   otherwise subject to a statute-based regulatory regime (section 249B).

The exemption from audit has been made available to companies within a group by the Companies Act 1985 (Audit Exemption) (Amendment) Regulations 1997 (SI 1997 No 936). A company which is a parent company or subsidiary undertaking for any period within a financial year may take advantage of the audit exemption if it was a member of a group satisfying the following conditions:

(*a*)   the group qualifies as a small group, in relation to that financial year, for the purposes of section 249 and is not, and was not at any time within that year, an ineligible group within the meaning of section 248(2); and

(*b*)   the group's aggregate turnover in that year (calculated in accordance with section 249) is not more than £350,000 net (or £420,000 gross); and

(*c*)   the group's aggregate balance sheet total for that year (calculated in accordance with section 249) is not more than £1.4 million net (or £1.68 million gross).

Additionally, a company which is a subsidiary undertaking and was dormant within the meaning of section 250 throughout the financial period in question (see 4.25 below) is entitled to the audit exemption under section 249(1). This follows amendment of section 249B by the Companies Act 1985 (Miscellaneous Accounting Amendments) Regulations 1996 (SI 1996 No 189) which extended the audit exemption to dormant subsidiaries within a group. The effect of this amendment, and this position has been clarified by SI 1997 No 936, is that the directors of dormant companies may seek exemption from audit under either section 249A or section 250.

The list in section 249B of companies not permitted to take advantage of the audit exemption in section 249A is more extensive than the list in section 250. The advantage of not seeking members' approval under section 250 must therefore be weighed against the more restrictive application of section 249A. A dormant company which is not entitled to the exemption from audit under section 249A may nonetheless take advantage of the exemption available under section 250. Therefore public and private companies which are members of an ineligible group will need to pass a special resolution under section 250 to obtain an exemption from audit.

A charitable company will be entitled to the total audit exemption provided its gross income is not more than £90,000. For charitable companies with a gross income of more than £90,000 but not more than £250,000, the audit exemption will be conditional upon the company's accounts receiving a limited review by a reporting accountant (see 4.17 below). The maximum figures for turnover or gross income are proportionately adjusted where the company's financial period is less than a year.

Directors' statement in accounts

4.16 The directors of a company entitled to the exemptions in section 249A of the Act must state in the company's balance sheet that for the year in question the company was entitled to the audit exemption and that no notice has been deposited by the members in relation to the accounts for that financial year (see 4.19 below). They must also acknowledge their responsibilities for ensuring that the company keeps accounting records which comply with section 221 of the Companies Act 1985 and for preparing accounts which give a true and fair view of the state of affairs of the company at the end of the financial year and of its profit and loss for the financial year. A statement to this effect must appear in the balance sheet immediately above the signature of the director signing the accounts on behalf of the board of directors.

Report of reporting accountant

4.17 Section 249A(2) of the Companies Act 1985 requires that, for a company which is a charity with a gross income of more than £90,000 but not more than £250,000, a report is prepared by a reporting accountant (see 4.18 below). The reporting accountant must state whether in his opinion:

(*a*) the accounts of the company for the financial year in question are in agreement with the accounting records kept by the company; and

(*b*) having regard only to, and on the basis of information contained in those accounting records:

   (i) those accounts have been properly drawn up in a manner consistent with the provisions of the Act so far as applicable to the company; and

   (ii) the company satisfied the requirements for the exemptions conferred by section 249A and did not fall within any category within section 249B at any time during the financial year.

The report must state the name of the reporting accountant and be signed by him. Where the reporting accountant is a body corporate or partnership, any reference to signature of the report or any copy of the report by the reporting accountant is a reference to signature in the name of the body corporate or partnership by a person authorised to sign on its behalf.

Reporting accountant

4.18   A reporting accountant must either be a member of an accounting body who is entitled to engage in public practice and is not ineligible for appointment as a reporting accountant, or any person (whether or not a member of that body) who is subject to, and eligible under, the rules of that body in seeking appointment or acting as auditor in accordance with the requirements of the Companies Act 1985. The relevant accounting bodies are:

(*a*)   the Institute of Chartered Accountants in England and Wales (ICAEW);

(*b*)   the Institute of Chartered Accountants in Scotland (ICAS);

(*c*)   the Institute of Chartered Accountants in Ireland (ICAI);

(*d*)   the Association of Chartered Certified Accountants (ACCA);

(*e*)   the Association of Authorised Public Accountants (AAPA);

(*f*)   the Association of Accounting Technicians (AAT);

(*g*)   the Association of International Accountants (AIA); and

(*h*)   the Chartered Institute of Management Accountants (CIMA).

Notice by members requiring audit

4.19   Any member or members holding not less than 10 per cent in the aggregate in nominal value of the company's issued share capital or any class of it or if the company does not have a share capital of not less than 10 per cent in number of the members of the company, may by notice in writing deposited at the company's registered office require the company to obtain an audit of its accounts for that year. The notice must be given during the financial year but no later than one month before the end of that year and where such a notice has been deposited, the company is not entitled to the audit exemptions (section 249B(2)).

Medium-sized company

4.20   In order to qualify as medium-sized in relation to a particular year, a company must have been:

(*a*)   medium-sized since incorporation; or

(*b*)   medium-sized in that year, and in the year before; or

(*c*)   medium-sized in the two years before that year; or

(*d*)   medium-sized in that year, and medium-sized in any two years out of the three years before that year.

Medium-sized qualification requires at least two of the following three conditions to be satisfied:

(i)   turnover does not exceed £11.2 million;

(ii)   balance sheet total does not exceed £5.6 million;

(iii)   number of employees during the relevant period does not exceed 250.

(CA 1985, s 247(3).)

The limits applicable to medium-sized companies in respect of turnover and the balance sheet total were increased by SI 1992 No 2452 (see 4.11 above).

The abbreviated accounts of a medium-sized company require:

(A)   a balance sheet (as for a small company) (see 4.12 above);

(B)   a profit and loss account, which may be abbreviated and need not disclose turnover;

(C)   a special auditors' report; and

(D)   a directors' report.

(CA 1985, s 246A.)

Small and medium-sized groups

4.21   A parent company need not prepare, or deliver, group accounts if the group headed by it qualified as a small or medium-sized group, and also does not include:

(*a*)   any public company;

(*b*)   any body corporate which can offer its shares or debentures to the public; or

(*c*)   any institution authorised under the Banking Act 1987, an insurance company to which Part II of the Insurance Companies Act 1982 applies, or any authorised person under the Financial Services Act 1986.

(CA 1985, s 248(2).)

In order to qualify as small or medium-sized in relation to a particular year, the group must have been:

(i)   small or medium-sized since incorporation; or

(ii)   small or medium-sized in that year, and in the year before; or

(iii)   small or medium-sized in the two years before that year; or

(iv)   small or medium-sized in that year, and small or medium-sized in any two years out of the three years before that year.

(CA 1985, s 249.)

Small group

4.22   In order to qualify as a small group, a group must meet at least two of the following three conditions:

(*a*)   aggregate turnover does not exceed £2.8 million net (or £3.36 million gross);

(*b*)   aggregate balance sheet total does not exceed £1.4 million net (or £1.68 million gross);

(*c*)   aggregate average number of employees does not exceed 50.

Medium-sized group

4.23   In order to qualify as a medium-sized group, a group must meet at least two of the following three conditions:

(*a*)   aggregate turnover does not exceed £11.2 million net (or £13.44 million gross);

(*b*)   aggregate balance sheet total does not exceed £5.6 million net (or £6.72 million gross);

(*c*)   aggregate average number of employees does not exceed 250.

The above limits in respect of turnover and the balance sheet total of both small and medium-sized groups reflect increases introduced during 1992 by statutory instrument (SI 1992 No 2452), and are found at CA 1985, s 249(3).

The Department of Trade and Industry has recently published a consultation document, 'Raising the Threshold Levels for SMEs' and is seeking views on raising the threshold for companies which qualify as small or medium.

Disclosure requirements

4.24   If a parent company is exempt from the requirement to prepare group accounts, it is entitled to issue full individual accounts to its members and to lodge abbreviated individual accounts with Companies House (see 4.12 and 4.20 above). Where the auditors are of the opinion that the directors were not entitled to the exemption conferred by CA 1985, s 248, the auditors must state that fact in their report. (CA 1985, s 237(4A), as inserted by SI 1996 No 189).

However, where a small company is not entitled to the above exemption but is required to prepare group accounts, it may nonetheless take advantage of provisions (SI 1992 No 2452) relating to modified accounts. If a small company has prepared modified individual accounts (see 4.13 above) and is preparing group accounts for the same year, it is permitted to prepare and issue modified group accounts to its members. Similar provisions apply to the preparation of modified group accounts and to the preparation of a consolidated balance sheet.

Dormant companies

4.25   A *private* company other than a banking or insurance company, or an authorised person under the Financial Services Act 1986 may, in the circumstances defined by section 250 of the Companies Act 1985, pass a special resolution exempting itself from the obligation to appoint auditors (see precedent A, Appendix 4A).

Section 250 did not previously permit public companies which were dormant within the meaning of this section to exempt themselves from the requirement to appoint auditors. This restriction was repealed by the Companies Act 1985 (Miscellaneous Accounting Amendments) Regulations 1996 which brought this amendment into force with effect from 2 February 1996.

A company which is exempt from this obligation is entitled to prepare accounts which are not subject to audit and do not contain an audit report. It is further entitled to lay such accounts before the members of the company in general meeting and to deliver such accounts to the Registrar of Companies.

The circumstances defined by CA 1985, s 250 (as amended by The Companies Act 1985 (Amendment of Sections 250 and 251) Regulations 1992 (SI 1992 No 3003)) in which a company can take advantage of this exemption are that:

(*a*)   the company has been dormant since its incorporation; or

(*b*)   the company has been dormant since the end of the previous financial year, qualifies as a 'small' company and is not required to produce group accounts.

A special resolution may be passed at a general meeting of the company at any time after copies of the annual accounts and reports for that year have been sent out in accordance with section 238(1).

A company which is not entitled to prepare abbreviated accounts for a small company, by virtue of the restrictions on a company which is a member of an ineligible group (see 4.10 above), may nonetheless take advantage of the exemption from the obligation to appoint auditors afforded to the company by its dormant status.

'Dormant' is defined by CA 1985, s 250(3) as meaning that no accounting transactions which would be required by section 221 to be entered in the accounting records of the company have occurred during the relevant period (i.e. either since incorporation ((*a*) above) or the end of the previous financial year ((*b*) above)).

A copy of the resolution must be sent to Companies House within 15 days of the date it was passed (CA 1985, s 380(4)(a)).

If the company ceases to be dormant, or becomes a public company or a banking or insurance company, or becomes an authorised person under the Financial Services Act 1986, the directors must appoint an auditor to serve until the next general meeting at which accounts are laid. Failing this, the company in general meeting may appoint an auditor.

Oversea companies

4.26   The Oversea Companies and Credit and Financial Institutions (Branch Disclosure) Regulations 1992 (SI 1992 No 3179), which came into force on 1 January 1993, introduced regulations governing the registration and compliance requirements of oversea companies conducting business in Great Britain (see 2.54 THE COMPANY CONSTITUTION). The regulations distinguish a place of business from a branch, and different rules apply to the accounts required to be disclosed in Great Britain. These are outlined below.

Place of business

4.27   An establishment deemed to constitute a place of business is required to comply with section 700 of the Companies Act 1985. However, the Secretary of State has exercised his power under this section to grant many exemptions to oversea companies by The Oversea Companies (Accounts) (Modifications and Exemptions) Order 1990 (SI 1990 No 440). For each financial year, an oversea company must prepare accounts and a directors' report, together with an auditors' report, in accordance with the rules set out in CA 1985, Sch 9, prior to its amendment by the Companies Act 1989.

The directors' report and the auditors' report are not required for filing purposes, nor is disclosure required in the notes to the accounts of particulars of directors' remuneration or of loans to, and similar transactions with, directors. Other exemptions relate to the disclosure of turnover and taxation, as well as particulars of investments in subsidiaries and other corporate bodies, and the identity of the company's ultimate holding company. As a consequence, the documents generally required for the purposes of disclosure would comprise:

(*a*)   a balance sheet;

(*b*)   a profit and loss account; and

(*c*)   notes to the accounts.

The accounts to be prepared are those for the company as a whole. The accounts for the place of business are not sufficient for filing purposes, although they are usually required for tax purposes. Group accounts are required where at the end of the financial year an oversea company has subsidiary undertakings, but this requirement is subject to the same exemptions as are available to British companies.

A place of business is required to deliver the accounts and reports prepared to Companies House. If these are in a language other than English, a certified translation into English must be annexed to the original language version (The Companies (Forms) Regulations 1985 (SI 1985 No 854), Reg 6).

The period allowed for delivery to Companies House is 13 months from the end of the accounting reference period to which the accounts relate. However, if the oversea company's first accounting reference period is for more than 12 months, the period allowed in respect of that first period is 13 months from the anniversary of the company establishing a place of business in Great Britain. A fee of £15 as at the time of this publication is payable to Companies House upon filing.

Branch

4.28   Where an oversea company establishes a branch in Great Britain, its annual filing obligations will be governed by Schedule 21D of the CA 1985, as inserted by the Oversea Companies and Credit and Financial Institutions (Branch Disclosure) Regulations 1992 (SI 1992 No 3179). The documents comprising the accounts will depend upon whether or not disclosure of the accounts is required under the parent law of the oversea company in its country of incorporation. If disclosure is not required, the accounts to be filed at Companies House will be those required under the place of business regime (see above) and such accounts will require delivery within the same time limits.

However, if disclosure of the accounts is required in the country of incorporation, the accounts must be the full accounts of the oversea company, including the directors' report and an auditors' report, unless modified accounts are permitted in the company's country of incorporation, in which case, such modified accounts will be sufficient for disclosure in Great Britain. The due date for filing at Companies House will be by reference to the date of first disclosure in the country of incorporation. Within three months of that date, the accounts must be delivered to Companies House with the appropriate filing fee (£15 as at the time of this publication).

Credit or financial institutions

4.29   If an oversea company is a credit or financial institution, then different rules will apply and these principally relate to the disclosure requirements (CA 1985, Sch 21C, as inserted by SI 1992 No 3179). Where audited accounts are not required under the parent law of the oversea company, the accounts required to be delivered in Great Britain will be the same as those under the place of business regime, and will therefore be subject to delivery at Companies House within 13 months of the end of the relevant accounting reference period.

On the other hand, should audited accounts be required under the oversea company's parent law, the accounts to be delivered to Companies House must be the full, or where permitted, modified accounts of the oversea company. If such audited accounts are subjectto disclosure and registration in the home state, then the due date for filing at Companies House is within three months of the date of first disclosure in the country of incorporation. Where the parent law merely requires disclosure of the accounts, then these must be available for inspection at the branch in Great Britain.

Approval of accounts

4.30   Under section 233(1) of the Companies Act 1985 a company's annual accounts must be approved by the board of directors and signed on behalf of the board by a director of the company. For this purpose, the company's annual accounts comprise its individual balance sheet and profit and loss account, together with any group accounts. The signature must be on the company's individual balance sheet (CA 1985, s 233(2)) and although the consolidated balance sheet is often signed there is not a requirement to do so.

Every copy of a company's balance sheet which is laid before a company's general meeting or is otherwise published, circulated or issued must state the name of the person who signed the balance sheet on behalf of the board.

The accounts must also bear a statement as to the date they were signed. This is commonly stated above the director's signature on the balance sheet, or is sometimes given in a note to the accounts.

The directors' report

4.31   Pursuant to section 234(1) of the Companies Act 1985 all companies must prepare a directors' report in respect of each financial year. The contents of the report are set out in section 234 of, and Schedule 7 to, CA 1985 as amended by the Companies Act 1985 (Miscellaneous Accounting Amendments) Regulations 1996 (SI 1996 No 189) and the Companies Act 1985 (Directors' Report) (Statement of Payment Practice) Regulations 1997 (SI 1997 No 571). In summary the contents now required are:

(*a*)   a fair review of the development of the business of the company during the financial year and of its position at the end of it;

(*b*)   the principal activities of the company during the year;

(*c*)   the names of the persons who were directors at any time during the year and their interests (if any) in any shares and debentures (or options) of the company;

(*d*)   the amount (if any) which the directors propose should be paid as a dividend;

(*e*)   a statement of the market value of fixed assets where this is substantially different from the balance sheet amount;

(*f*)   details of any political or charitable contributions made, exceeding in aggregate £200 during the year; and

(*g*)   details of any acquisitions of its own shares which a company has made during the year.

For companies which employ an average of more than 250 employees in each week of the financial year, the directors' report must also give details as to the employment of disabled persons and of employee involvement in the company's management.

Further, public companies or large subsidiaries of public companies must disclose the company's payment policy and practice.

Pursuant to CA 1985, s 234A(1), the directors' report must be approved by the board of directors and signed on their behalf by either a director or the secretary of the company. Every copy of the report which is laid before the company in general meeting or which is published, circulated or issued, must bear the name of the person who signed it on behalf of the board (CA 1985, s 234A(2)). It is usual for the directors' report to be approved and signed on the same date as the balance sheet.

The auditors' report

4.32   Under section 384 of the Companies Act 1985, every company except certain categories of small company and dormant companies are required to appoint an auditor (see 4.40 below). The auditor pursuant to section 235(1) of the CA 1985, is required to make a report to the company's members on all annual accounts of the company, of which copies are to be laid before the company in general meeting, or sent to the members during their tenure of office (see 4.50 below).

The report is required to state whether in the auditors' opinion the annual accounts have been properly prepared in accordance with the Companies Act 1985 and whether a true and fair representation of the state of affairs of the company is given.

The auditors' report must state the name(s) of the auditors and be signed by them pursuant to CA 1985, s 236(1). Every copy of the report which is delivered to the members or is published, issued or circulated, must bear the name of the auditors who signed it (CA 1985, s 236(2)), and must be signed on a date on or after the date the balance sheet and directors' report are approved by the board of directors.

However, it should be noted that the Auditing Practices Board (APB) in the first of its Statements of Auditing Standards (SASs), 'Auditors' Report on Financial Statements', dispensed with the common practice of auditors to sign the audit report as made at an effective date. The SAS additionally adopted the recommendations of the Cadbury Report in relation to directors' and auditors' responsibilities (see 4.33 below) and gave auditors greater flexibility over the wording to be used in expressing an opinion on a set of accounts.

Corporate governance

4.33   The report of the Cadbury Committee (see 6.13 THE DIRECTORS) made several recommendations relating to statements to be made in a company's report and accounts by the directors and the auditors in their respective reports. However, the statements to be made by the directors and the auditors are now subject to the requirements of the Combined Code.

The Combined Code was published on 25 June 1998 and will apply to companies listed on the London Stock Exchange in relation to accounting periods ending on or after 31 December 1998. As a consequence, Rule 12.43A was introduced into the Listing Rules which requires companies to produce:

1.   A narrative statement which describes how the principles in section 1 of the Code have been applied by the company and provides an explanation so that shareholders can evaluate how the principles have been applied.

2.   A statement of compliance which indicates the extent to which the company has complied with section 1 of the Code during the accounting period. In particular, a company will be required to disclose its compliance with the Code provisions while identifying those provisions with which it has not complied. The statement should also indicate the period during which the company did not comply with the Code provisions.

3.   A report on the directors' remuneration which provides certain specified information about the remuneration packages paid to the directors. This requirement of the Listing Rules is disapplied in the case of investment companies (including investment trusts) with boards of non-executive directors.

The statement of compliance, and its review by the company's auditors, is a continuing listing obligation of The London Stock Exchange with regard to certain specified code provisions. In addition, the directors' report should contain a statement of their responsibilities for the accounts, the effectiveness of the company's system of internal control, and indicate whether the business is a going concern, together with any assumptions or qualifications to support this statement.

Likewise, the auditors are required to provide a statement of their reporting responsibilities and to give an opinion on the directors' statement, as well as reviewing the compliance statement as far as it is possible for them to objectively verify compliance with the Code.

The ICAEW has recently produced draft guidance to assist companies in implementing the internal controls requirements of the Combined Code. The Code has extended the internal control so that in addition to financial controls companies are required to report on their operational controls, compliance controls and risk management. The guidance prepared by the Turnbull Committee is currently in draft form but will shortly be available in final form at which point the Stock Exchange will produce further guidance. It is intended that the guidance will apply in respect of accounting periods ending on or after 23 December 2000.

Duty to lay accounts

4.34   In respect of each financial year, section 241 of the Companies Act 1985 requires the directors of a company to lay copies of the company's annual accounts and the directors' and auditors' reports for that year before the company in general meeting. It is common practice for a company's accounts to be laid before the annual general meeting, although this is not a specific requirement.

Duty to file accounts

4.35   Section 244 of the Companies Act 1985 requires the directors, in respect of each financial year, to deliver to the Registrar of Companies a copy of the company's annual accounts and directors' and auditors' reports. The individual balance sheet and directors' report must bear the live signatures of the persons who signed them on behalf of the board. The auditors' report must also bear the live signatures of the auditors who signed it.

The Companies Act 1985 (Welsh Language Accounts) Regulations 1992 (SI 1992 No 1083), which inserted section 255E into CA 1985 and made minor amendments to sections 242 and 243, was subsequently revoked following publication of The Welsh Language Act 1993 (Commencement) Order 1994 (SI 1994 No 115(C.5)) which brought into force various sections of The Welsh Language Act 1993. Section 255E was repealed. The replacement regulations, The Companies (Welsh Language Forms and Documents) Regulations 1994 (SI 1994 No 117) permit any company, other than a listed company, whose memorandum of association states that its registered office is to be situated in Wales to deliver to Companies House its accounts and reports in Welsh only. The Registrar of Companies is required under the Act to obtain a translation of these documents into English.

In addition, section 242B was inserted into CA 1985 by The Companies Act 1985 (Accounts of Small and Medium-Sized Enterprises and Publication of Accounts in ECUs) Regulations 1992 (SI 1992 No 2452). A company is now permitted to deliver and publish an additional copy of its accounts in which the amounts have been translated into ECUs, together with the accounts required to be lodged with Companies House under CA 1985, s 242.

Companies House will now accept accounts made up in Euro for accounting periods ending on or after 1 January 1999.

Time limits for laying and filing accounts

4.36   Section 244 of the Companies Act 1985 fixes the periods allowed from the end of a company's financial year on its accounting reference date, to lay and file its accounts and report. These are:

(*a*)   for a *private* company, ten months after the end of the relevant accounting reference period; and

(*b*)   for a *public* company, seven months after the end of the relevant accounting reference period.

Where a company's first accounting reference period exceeds twelve months, the period allowed for laying and delivering the accounts and reports is ten months for a private company and seven months for a public company from the first anniversary of the company's incorporation, or, in both types of company, three months from the end of the accounting reference period, whichever expires last.

The impact of this rule is that for private companies the maximum period between the date of the company's incorporation and the date it must file its accounts at Companies House is 22 months; this is commonly known as the '22 month rule'. For public companies, the maximum period between these two dates is generally 19 months, although where a public company's first accounting reference period is for more than 16 months, this extends to a maximum of 21 months.

These time limits are strictly interpreted by reference to calendar months. For instance, a private company with an accounting reference date of 30 September is required to file its annual accounts by 30 July of the following year, not 31 July. On the other hand, where the accounts of a private company are for a financial year ending on 30 April, the accounts must be lodged with Companies House by 28 February. These rules must be interpreted correctly in view of the civil penalties which apply in relation to accounts which are filed late.

Where a company has business interests outside the United Kingdom, a three-month extension to these limits may be claimed by the delivery to the Registrar of Companies of a notice in the prescribed form (form G244). Such notice must be delivered to Companies House within the same period allowed for the filing of the company's annual accounts.

Failure to file the accounts within the above periods can result in the Registrar of Companies using one of the sanctions available to him under the Act (see 5.2 DISCLOSURE AND REPORTING REQUIREMENTS). The penalties for failure to file on time are specified in the Table of Penalties (Appendix 5C DISCLOSURE AND REPORTING REQUIREMENTS).

Revision of defective accounts

4.37   The directors of a company may prepare revised accounts or a revised directors' report where it appears to them that these documents do not comply with the requirements of the Companies Act 1985 (CA 1985, s 245). If these have been laid before the members in general meeting or delivered to the Registrar of Companies, the revisions to be made are restricted to:

(*a*)   the correction of any part of the accounts or report which does not comply with the requirements of the Act; and

(*b*)   the making of any necessary consequential amendments.

The Companies (Revision of Defective Accounts and Report) Regulations 1990 (SI 1990 No 2570) specified the requirements which apply to the preparation, laying and delivery of revised accounts or a revised report. These regulations were subsequently amended by the Companies Act (Miscellaneous Accounting Amendments) Regulations 1996 (SI 1996 No 189). The requirements will depend in part on whether revision is by replacement of the original accounts and report or revision by a supplementary note indicating the corrections made to the original accounting documents.

Sections 233 and 234A of the Companies Act 1985, which relate to the approval and signing of the accounts and directors' report, shall apply to the revised accounts and report respectively, except that where revision is by supplementary note, the signature shall apply in respect of the supplementary note. Where the accounts and report have been laid before the members in general meeting or delivered to the Registrar of Companies, the following statements are required in the revised accounting documents:

(i)   in the case of revision by replacement:

(A)   that the revised accounts or report replace the original accounting documents for the financial year in question;

(B)   that, in respect of revised accounts, they are now the statutory accounts of the company for that financial year;

(C)   that the revised accounts or report have been prepared as at the date of the original accounting documents and not at the date of revision;

(D)   the defects in the original accounts or report which caused them not to comply with the requirements of CA 1985; and

(E)   any significant amendments made consequential upon the remedying of those defects;

(ii)   in the case of revision by supplementary note:

(A)   that the note revises certain aspects of the original accounts or report of the company and is to be treated as forming part of the document in question; and

(B) that the accounts or report have been revised as at the date of the original accounting documents and not as at the date of revision.

A company's current auditors are required to make a report, or (as the case may be) a further report under section 235 of the Companies Act 1985 to the members of the company under these regulations, on any revised accounts or reports prepared under section 245 of the Act. If the auditors' report on the original annual accounts was not made by the company's current auditors, the directors of the company may resolve that the auditors' report on the revised accounts and report is made by the company's previous auditors, provided that they agree to do so and continue to be qualified for appointment as auditor of the company.

Following approval of the revised accounting documents, the directors shall:

(1) where the original accounts and report were sent to all persons entitled to receive such documents under CA 1985, s 238:

    (*aa*) send to any person who was entitled to receive the original documents under section 238, a copy of the revised accounts or report in the case of revision by replacement, or a copy of the supplementary note where revision is by supplementary note, together with a copy of the auditors' report on those documents, not more than 28 days after the date of the revision; and

    (*bb*) send to any person who at the date of revision is entitled to receive copies of accounts and reports under section 238, the documents referred to in (1)(*aa*) above not more than 28 days after the revision;

(2) where the original accounts and report have been laid before the members in general meeting in compliance with section 241 of the Act, lay the documents referred to in (1)(*aa*) above before the next general meeting held after the date of revision at which any annual accounts for a financial year are laid, unless the revised documents have been laid before an earlier general meeting;

(3) where the original accounts and report have been delivered to the Registrar of Companies as required by section 242 of the Act, deliver to the Registrar within 28 days of the revision, copies of the documents referred to in (1)(*aa*) above.

The statutory instrument also contains similar regulations affecting the abbreviated accounts of small and medium-sized companies, summary financial statements and the unaudited accounts of dormant companies. Following amendment of these regulations by the Companies Act 1985 (Audit Exemption) Regulations 1994 (SI 1995 No 2879), the regulations include provisions to deal with certain categories of small company which are exempt from the audit requirement.

The Secretary of State may give notice to the directors of a company under section 245A where a question arises as to the compliance of the company's accounts and report with the requirements of CA 1985. Following notice under this section, the Secretary of State or a person authorised under section 245B may make application to the court for a declaration that the accounts do not comply with the Act and an order requiring the directors to prepare revised accounts.

The Financial Reporting Review Panel is an authorised person for the purpose of section 245B, by virtue of The Companies (Defective Accounts) (Authorised Person) Order 1991 (SI 1991 No 13). This statutory instrument also deems the Panel a person authorised to receive and investigate complaints about the annual accounts of companies (CA 1985, s 245C). Any accounts referred to the Panel may result in the auditors being reported to their professional body, who as recognised supervisory bodies may exercise their ultimate sanction to deregister auditors.

Partnerships and unlimited companies

4.38   The Partnerships and Unlimited Companies (Accounts) Regulations 1993 (SI 1993 No 1820) which came into force on 21 July 1993 affect limited and unlimited companies which fall within the following definitions of a 'qualifying partnership' and a 'qualifying company'.

(*a*)   A qualifying partnership is a partnership governed by the laws of any part of Great Britain in which each of its members is either:

   (i)   a limited company, or

   (ii)   an unlimited company, or a Scottish firm, each of whose members is a limited company.

(*b*)   A qualifying company is an unlimited company incorporated in Great Britain in which each of its members is:

   (i)   a limited company, or

   (ii)   another unlimited company, or a Scottish firm, each of whose members is a limited company.

The regulations will require members of a qualifying partnership to prepare, deliver and publish audited accounts for financial years commencing on or after 23 December 1994, and an unlimited company which is a qualifying company by virtue of these regulations will be required to deliver accounts and reports to the Registrar of Companies (CA 1985, s 254(3)(b), as amended by the regulations). The regulations are drafted so that any member of a qualifying partnership or a qualifying company which is a comparable undertaking incorporated in or formed under the law of any country or territory outside Great Britain is subject to the requirements of these regulations.

The members of a qualifying partnership at the end of any financial year of the partnership are required for that year to prepare in respect of the partnership the same annual accounts and reports as are required to be prepared by companies formed and registered under the Companies Act 1985 within ten months after the end of the financial year. Each limited company which is a member of a qualifying partnership at the end of any financial year of the partnership must append to the copy of its annual accounts, which is next delivered to the Registrar of Companies in compliance with CA 1985, s 242, a copy of the accounts of the partnership prepared for that year.

The members of a qualifying partnership are exempt from the requirements to prepare, deliver and publish the partnership's accounts if the partnership is dealt with on a consolidated basis in group accounts prepared by a member of the partnership which is established under the law of an EU Member State, or a parent undertaking of such a member which is so established. Where a qualifying partnership's head office is in Great Britain and each of its members is an undertaking comparable to a limited company which is incorporated in a country or territory outside the United Kingdom but not within the EU, or an undertaking comparable to an unlimited company or partnership, which is incorporated in or formed under the law of such a country or territory, and each of whose members is such an undertaking, the latest accounts of the partnership must be available for inspection by any person at the head office of the partnership.

Summary financial statements

4.39   Under section 251 of the Companies Act 1985 a listed company is authorised to issue summary financial statements in place of full accounts. The scope of this section was extended by Regulation 3 of The Companies Act 1985 (Amendment of Sections 250 and 251) Regulations 1992 (SI 1992 No 3003), which came into force on 4 December 1992, so that holders of a company's listed debentures are now entitled to receive summary financial statements.

A public company whose shares or debentures, or any class of whose shares or debentures are listed, may issue such statements to any entitled person, being those persons specified in CA 1985, s 238(1), namely:

(*a*)   every member of the company;

(*b*)   every holder of the company's debentures; and

(*c*)   every person who is entitled to receive notice of general meetings.

The procedure under which summary financial statements may be prepared and issued is set out in The Companies (Summary Financial Statements) Regulations 1995 (SI 1995 No 2092) which replaced The Companies (Summary Financial Statements) Regulations 1992 (SI 1992 No 3075). The earlier regulations continue to apply in respect of financial years commencing on a date prior to 23 December 1994.

The 1995 regulations, which restate the provisions of SI 1992 No 3075, provide that so long as no restriction exists in a company's memorandum and articles of association and, in the case of debenture holders, in the instrument governing the company's debentures, it may, subject to fulfilling certain requirements, issue to entitled persons summary financial statements. Schedules 1 to 3 of the regulations detail the form and content required of these statements.

The 1995 Regulations streamline the procedures whereby a company consults with its shareholders to determine whether a shareholder wishes to receive the full report and accounts or summary financial statements in place of them, while at the same time clarifying the content required of such statements.

The requirements which a company wishing to issue summary financial statements must fulfil are as follows.

(i) The company must have ascertained that the entitled person does not wish to continue to receive copies of the full accounts.

(ii) The time limits specified by CA 1985, s 244 must not have expired (see 4.36 above).

(iii) The summary statements must be approved by the board. The original must be signed by a director and all copies must state the name of the director who signed.

(iv) The summary statements must contain a prominent statement that the entitled persons have a right to the full report and accounts if they so wish, and that they should consult them for a full understanding of the affairs of the company which the summary does not provide.

(v) The statements must contain a clear and conspicuous statement of how members and debenture holders can obtain a copy of the company's last full accounts and reports, and of how they can elect to receive such accounts in place of summary financial statements for future years.

The regulations prescribe the manner in which the wishes of entitled persons can be ascertained as to whether or not they wish to receive summary financial statements or not i.e:

(A) any relevant notification in writing by the entitled person to the company that he wishes to receive summary financial statements only (or full accounts in place of them). Such notice must be received by the company before the first date on which copies of the full accounts are sent out in compliance with section 238(1) of the CA 1985;

(B) consultation by notice accompanied by a printed reply card or form, specifying a date by which the company must receive a response to the consultation. The date must be at least 21 days after the service of the notice and not less than 28 days before the first date on which copies of the full accounts for the next financial year are sent out in compliance with section 238(1); or

(C) a relevant consultation comprising a copy of the full accounts and reports, a specimen of the summary financial statements on those accounts and a printed card or form to notify the company that he wishes to receive full accounts for the next and future years. If no response is received to this consultation, he will receive summary financial statements.

The auditor

General

4.40 Section 384 of the Companies Act 1985 requires that every company must appoint an auditor. However, exemptions do exist for certain categories of small company and dormant companies. Section 25(1) of the CA 1989 introduced the qualification that a person to be eligible for appointment as a company auditor must be a member of a recognised supervisory body, as defined by CA 1989, s 30 (see 4.42 below). However, no person may be appointed as auditor of a company if he is an officer or employee of the company, or a partner or employee of an officer or employee of that company. A partnership of which such a person is a partner or a body corporate may also not be appointed as an auditor (see 4.44 below).

Appointment

4.41 Under section 385(3) of the Companies Act 1985, the first auditors of a company may be appointed by the directors at any time, to hold office until the *first* general meeting of the company at which accounts are presented (see precedent B, Appendix 4A). The directors may also appoint an auditor to fill a casual vacancy in the office of auditor which has been caused by the death or resignation of the previous auditor (CA 1985, s 388).

Section 385(2) of the CA 1985 requires a company in general meeting to appoint (or reappoint) auditors at each general meeting at which accounts are laid, to hold office until the next such general meeting (see precedent C, Appendix 4A). However, under CA 1985, s 386, a *private company* may now elect to dispense with the obligation to appoint or reappoint auditors each year (see 7.58 MEMBERSHIP).

Should the members fail to appoint or reappoint auditors, the company must, within seven days, give notice of the fact to the Secretary of State who may exercise his power under CA 1985, s 387 to appoint an auditor.

The provisions apply to the appointment as company auditor of a partnership constituted under the law of England and Wales or Northern Ireland, or under the law of any other country or territory in which a partnership is not a legal person (CA 1989, s 26(1)). In Scotland, a partnership is a legal person and, thus, any change in the partners does not affect the appointment of the partnership.

The appointment is (unless a contrary intention appears) an appointment of the partnership as such and not of the partners (CA 1989, s 26(2)). Where the partnership ceases, the appointment is to be treated as extending to:

(*a*)   any partnership which succeeds to the practice of that partnership and which is eligible for the appointment; and

(*b*)   any person who succeeds to that practice having previously carried it on in partnership and who is eligible for the appointment.

For this purpose, a partnership is to be regarded as succeeding to the practice of another partnership only if the members of the successor partnership are substantially the same as those of the former partnership; and a partnership or other person is to be regarded as succeeding to the practice of a partnership only if it or he succeeds to the whole or substantially the whole of the business of the former partnership (CA 1989, s 26(4)).

Thus, in order for a partnership automatically to succeed to another partnership which has ceased, it is necessary for the partners of the successor partnership to consist 'substantially' of the same persons as the former partnership and for the whole or substantially the whole of the business of the former partnership to be taken by the new partnership. A partnership in England and Wales generally ceases where there is any change in the composition of the partnership, or on its dissolution.

Where the partnership ceases and no person succeeds to the appointment, the appointment may with the consent of a client company be treated as extending to a partnership or other person (that is, an individual or body corporate) eligible for the appointment, who succeeds to the business of the former partnership or to such part of it as it is agreed by the company shall be treated as comprising the appointment (CA 1989, s 26(5)).

Eligibility for appointment

4.42   Under section 25(1) of the Companies Act 1989 a person is eligible for appointment as a company auditor only if he:

(*a*)   is a member of a recognised supervisory body (that is, recognised by the Secretary of State); and

(*b*)   is eligible for the appointment under the rules of that body.

A recognised supervisory body must have rules to the effect that a person is not eligible for appointment as a company auditor unless:

(i)   in the case of an individual, he holds an 'appropriate qualification';

(ii)   in the case of a firm:

    (A)   the individuals responsible for company audit work on behalf of the firm hold an 'appropriate qualification', and

    (B)   the firm is controlled by 'qualified persons'.

In respect of the above definitions an 'appropriate qualification' and, accordingly, a 'qualified person' are deemed under section 31 of the CA 1989 to be a person who:

(I) was, by virtue of membership of a body recognised for the purposes of CA 1985, s 389(1)(a) (which is now repealed), qualified for appointment as an auditor of a company under that section immediately before 1 January 1990, and immediately before the commencement of CA 1989, s 25; or

(II) holds a recognised professional qualification obtained in the United Kingdom; or

(III) holds an approved overseas qualification and satisfies any additional educational requirements applicable.

The bodies of accountants which are designated as recognised supervisory bodies are:

(1) the Institute of Chartered Accountants in England and Wales (ICAEW);

(2) the Institute of Chartered Accountants of Scotland (ICAS);

(3) the Association of Chartered Certified Accountants (ACCA);

(4) the Institute of Chartered Accountants in Ireland (ICAI);

(5) the Association of Authorised Public Accountants (AAPA).

A 'recognised supervisory body' is a body corporate or unincorporated association which is recognised by the Secretary of State, is established in the UK and which maintains and enforces rules as to:

(*aa*) the eligibility of persons to seek appointment as company auditors, and

(*bb*) the conduct of company audit work,

which are binding on persons seeking appointment or acting as company auditors, either because they are members of that body or because they are otherwise subject to its control (CA 1989, s 30(1)).

Register of auditors

4.43 Sections 35 and 36 of the Companies Act 1989 require recognised supervisory bodies to keep and maintain a register of individuals and firms eligible for appointment as company auditor, and of individuals holding an appropriate qualification, who are responsible for company audit work on behalf of such firms (see 4.18 above).

Such registers must be maintained at the principal UK office of the relevant body and must be available for inspection by any person for at least two hours between 9 am and 5 pm on any business day. The recognised supervisory body must ensure that the entries in the register are arranged, for inspection purposes, alphabetically and by reference to recognised supervisory bodies. An obligation is imposed by statutory instrument upon all such bodies to co-operate with each other to ensure that each recognised supervisory body enters the required information on the register maintained by that body.

Such bodies are also required to provide to the public the names and addresses of the directors and members of the firm, where the firm is a body corporate, and of the partners, in the case of a partnership. This information must be available for inspection alphabetically and by reference to the firm.

In maintaining the register of auditors, each recognised supervisory body must exercise reasonable care to ensure the accuracy of theregister and to ensure that all persons or firms named in the register are eligible for appointment as company auditor. Any amendments to entries in the register must be effected within ten business days of the body becoming aware of the relevant change.

Independence of auditors

4.44   A person is ineligible for appointment as company auditor of a company if he is:

(*a*)   an officer or employee of the company; or

(*b*)   a partner or employee of such a person, or a partnership of which such a person is a partner,

or if he is ineligible, by virtue of the above, for appointment as company auditor of any associated undertaking of the company (CA 1989, s 27(1)).

An 'officer' of a company includes a director, manager or company secretary (CA 1985, s 744). Because an auditor is for some purposes regarded as an officer of the company, the Companies Act 1989 provides that, for the purpose of the foregoing, an auditor of a company is not to be regarded as an officer or employee of the company (CA 1989, s 27(1)). It follows that an auditor cannot also be secretary of the same company.

A person is also ineligible for appointment as auditor of a company if there exists between

(i)   him or any associate of his, and

(ii)   the company or any associated undertaking,

a connection of any such description as may be specified by regulations, in the form of a statutory instrument, made by the Secretary of State. The regulations may make different provisions for different cases (CA 1989, s 27(2) and (4)). At the time of writing, no regulations have been made.

Pursuant to CA 1989, s 27(3) 'associated undertaking', in relation to a company, means:

(A)   a parent undertaking or subsidiary undertaking of the company (see 4.8 above); or

(B)   a subsidiary undertaking of any parent undertaking of the company.

'Associate' is defined as follows.

(I)   In relation to an individual 'associate' means:

   (1)   that individual's spouse or minor child or stepchild;

   (2)   any body corporate of which that individual is a director; and

   (3)   any employee or partner of that individual.

(II)   In relation to a body corporate 'associate' means:

   (1)   any body corporate of which that body is a director;

   (2)   any body corporate in the same group as that body; and

   (3)   any employee or partner of that body or of any body corporate in the same group.

(III)   In relation to a Scottish firm, or a partnership constituted under the law of any other country or territory in which a partnership is a legal person, 'associate' means:

   (1)   any body corporate of which the firm is a director;

   (2)   any employee of or partner in the firm; and

   (3)   any person who is an associate of a partner in the firm.

(IV)   In relation to a partnership constituted under the law of England and Wales or Northern Ireland, or the law of any other country or territory in which a partnership is not a legal person, 'associate' means any person who is an associate of any of the partners.

Acting when disqualified

4.45   A person may not act as company auditor if he is ineligible for appointment to that office (CA 1989, s 28(1)). If during his term of office a company auditor becomes ineligible for appointment to the office, he must thereupon vacate office and must forthwith give notice in writing to the company concerned that he has vacated it by reason of ineligibility (CA 1989, s 28(2)).

Contravention of these provisions carries a penalty (CA 1989, s 28(3) and (4)), but it is a defence for a person to show that he did not know and had no reason to believe that he was, or had become, ineligible for appointment (CA 1989, s 28(5)). The onus of proof is thus on the defendant.

Vacation of office through ineligibility requires a statement of any circumstances which the outgoing auditor considers should be brought to the attention of members or creditors of the company (see 4.47 below).

Power of Secretary of State to require second audit

4.46   Where a person appointed auditor of a company was, for any part of the period during which the audit was conducted, ineligible for appointment as auditor of the company, the Secretary of State may require the company to engage the services of someone who is eligible for that appointment. The company has 21 days in which to comply with the direction (CA 1989, s 29(1)).

Pursuant to section 29(1) of the Companies Act 1989 the person engaged must either:

(*a*)   audit the relevant accounts again; or

(*b*)   review the first audit and report (giving his reasons) whether a second audit is needed.

Removal and resignation

4.47   Section 391 of the Companies Act 1985 allows for the removal from office of an auditor before the expiry of his term of appointment by the passing of an ordinary resolution by the company in general meeting (see Precedent D, Appendix 4A). However, special notice (see 7.39 MEMBERSHIP) must be given to the company (see precedent E, Appendix 4A), and the company must notify its members whenever a resolution is to be proposed at a general meeting, for the appointment of an auditor who was not the previously appointed auditor of the company or for the removal of an auditor before the expiry of his term of office.

Special notice is required to be given of the proposal of such a resolution (CA 1985, s 391A) and notification must be given to Companies House in the prescribed form within 14 days of the passing of the resolution (CA 1985, s 391(2)).

In practice such an occurrence is rare. The most common procedure where a company wishes to change its auditors is that the directors will request the auditors to resign voluntarily. The directors will then exercise their power to appoint new auditors to fill the resulting casual vacancy.

Under CA 1985, s 392, whenever an auditor ceases to hold office, *for whatever reason*, he is required to deposit at the registered office of the company a statement that there are no circumstances connected with his ceasing to hold office which he considers should be brought to the notice of members or creditors of the company, or disclose any such circumstances. Where the auditor discloses any circumstances a copy of the statement must be filed with the Registrar of Companies within 28 days.

Where an auditor resigns his office, the company must within 14 days of receipt of the auditor's notice of resignation file a copy with Companies House (CA 1985, s 392(3)). Should the auditor's notice contain a statement of circumstances connected with his resignation, the company must also (unless the court holds it to be defamatory) send a copy to every person entitled to receive a copy of the accounts.

Section 392A of the CA 1985 allows an auditor, who has included in the notice of his resignation a statement of the circumstances connected with it, the following discretionary rights:

(*a*)   to circulate to members a statement, of reasonable length, of the reasons for his resignation (unless, upon application to the court, it is held to be defamatory);

(*b*)   to requisition a general meeting, at which he may explain the reasons for his resignation; and

(*c*)   to attend and speak at the general meeting at which his resignation or the appointment of his successor is to be considered.

Elective regime

4.48   A private company may dispense with the obligation to appoint or re-appoint auditors each year by passing an elective resolution under CA 1985, s 386 (see 7.58 MEMBERSHIP). Where such an election is in force, a member may, by depositing the appropriate notice with the company, require the directors to convene an extraordinary general meeting to consider whether the appointment of the auditors should be brought to an end (CA 1985, s 393). If, at such a meeting, it is decided to bring the appointment to an end, the appointment will be deemed terminated from the next general meeting at which the auditors would be due to be re-appointed or, if an election not to hold annual general meetings is in force, from the end of the time for appointing auditors.

However, where there is a change in the auditors during the period in which the election is in force, for instance, following the resignation of the current auditors or where the current auditors are not seeking re-appointment, the CA 1985 would appear to be silent with regard to the appointment of new auditors. In normal circumstances, the special notice provisions under sections 388(3) and 391A(1)(b) would apply, however, where a company is also not required to hold an annual general meeting in each year nor to lay accounts before the members in general meeting, this requirement would override the advantage of passing such elective resolutions.

In the above circumstances, the appointment of new auditors may be made by the directors, although, section 388(3)(b) requires that an auditor appointed by the directors to fill a casual vacancy is subject to re-appointment at a general meeting for which special notice has been given. It could be argued however that, while the election is in force andproviding the elective resolution did not specify the auditors by name, the new auditors are deemed to be re-appointed in each year, unless a resolution is passed under section 250 to dispense with the appointment of auditors or the elective resolution is revoked under section 393. Alternatively, the following procedure based on the stated legislation may be adopted.

(*a*)   Auditors are required to deposit notice at the company's registered office at any time in the case of resignation and at least 14 days prior to the date on which their re-appointment is deemed to take place where the auditors are not seeking re-appointment.

(*b*)   Upon receipt of such notice, the directors should notify the members and any member should then, by giving notice to the company at its registered office, direct that:

(i)   an annual general meeting be convened, by virtue of the provisions of CA 1985, s 366A; and

(ii)   a resolution for the appointment of new auditors be considered at the annual general meeting (special notice provisions under section 388 or section 391A).

Where a change in auditors in the above manner is anticipated and any doubt exists as to the approach to be adopted, it would be prudent to apply the special notice provisions in conjunction with the rights granted to the members of the company under the elective regime.

Meetings and resolutions

4.49   A company's auditors are entitled to receive all notices of, and other communications relating to, any general meeting which a member of the company is entitled to receive, to attend any general meeting of the company and to be heard at any general meeting which they attend on any part of the business of the meeting which concerns them as auditors (CA 1985, s 390(1)).

The auditors of a private company have certain rights in relation to a proposed written resolution under section 381A of the Companies Act 1985 as amended by the Deregulation (Resolutions of Private Companies) Order 1996 (SI 1996 No 1471). The requirement to involve the auditors in any written resolution was removed, although the auditors are now entitled to receive a copy of the resolution, or to otherwise be informed of its contents, at or before the time the resolution is supplied to a member for signature (see 7.59 MEMBERSHIP).

Auditors' report

4.50   The auditors are required to report to the company's members on all accounts of the company, copies of which are to be laid before thecompany in general meeting during their tenure of office (CA 1985, s 235(1)) (see 4.32 above).

Thus, even where auditors are appointed at every general meeting at which accounts are laid, it is possible that if a company is behind in preparing its accounts, or it decides to have a shortened accounting period, that the auditors may be required to report on more than one set of accounts during their term of office. Where a private company has elected not to appoint auditors annually, the auditors will be required to report on all accounts to be laid before the company in general meeting during their successive terms of office.

Where there is in force an election by a private company to dispense with the laying of accounts before the company in general meeting, the auditors are required to report to the company's members on all accounts sent to the members and others during the auditors' tenure of office (CA 1985, s 252(3)(a)).

The auditors' report is required to state:

(*a*)   whether, in the opinion of the auditors, the annual accounts have been properly prepared in accordance with the Companies Act 1985; and, in particular,

(*b*)   whether a 'true and fair view' is given (see 4.7 above):

   (i)   in the case of an individual balance sheet, of the state of affairs of the company as at the end of the financial year;

   (ii)   in the case of an individual profit and loss account (see below), of the profit or loss of the company for the financial year; and

   (iii)   in the case of group accounts, of the state of affairs as at the end of the financial year, and the profit or loss for the financial year, of the undertakings included in the consolidation as a whole, so far as concerns members of the company.

The Statement of Auditing Standards, 'Auditors' Report on Financial Statements', requires auditors to report on their audit responsibilities as well as those of the directors and to provide a full description of their audit opinion (see 4.32 above).

The annual accounts are defined as the company's individual accounts and, where applicable, its group accounts (CA 1985, s 262(1)). The auditor is not required to report on a company's individual profit and loss account where the company is required to prepare and does prepare, group accounts (CA 1985, s 230(3)).

Under section 236(1) of the Companies Act 1985 the auditors' report must state the names of the auditors and be signed by them.

Every copy of the auditors' report which is laid before the company in general meeting, or which is otherwise circulated, published or issued, must state the names of the auditors (CA 1985, s 236(2)). The 'names of the auditors' would appear to refer to the name under which a partnership or body corporate practises but, in the case where an individual is the auditor, the individual's name must be referred to (CA 1985, s 236(5)).

The copy of the auditors' report which is delivered to the Registrar of Companies must state the names of the auditors and be signed by them (CA 1985, s 236(3)). There are penalties on the company and its officers (which could include the auditor) for non-compliance with the foregoing.

Consistency of directors' report with accounts

4.51   Pursuant to section 237(1) of the Companies Act 1985 in preparing their report, the auditors must carry out such investigations as will enable them to form an opinion as to:

(*a*)   whether proper accounting records have been kept by the company and proper returns adequate for their audit have been received from branches not visited by them; and

(*b*)   whether the company's individual accounts are in agreement with the accounting records returns.

If the auditors form a negative opinion in relation to any of these matters, they must state that fact in their report (CA 1985, s 237(2)).

Information and explanations not received

4.52   If the auditors fail to obtain all the information and explanations which, to the best of their knowledge and belief, are necessary for the purposes of their audit, they must state that fact in their report (CA 1985, s 237(3)).

SAS 120 — Consideration of law and regulations, requires the auditors to obtain written confirmation from the directors on non-compliance with relevant law and regulations; this may be by way of board resolution passed at the same time as the accounts are approved by the directors. The auditors should ensure that the directors giving the representation have taken appropriate steps to inform themselves by making the necessary enquiries.

Remuneration of directors and transactions with directors and officers

4.53   If the requirements of the Companies Act 1985 relating to the disclosure of directors' remuneration and the disclosure of particulars of transactions with directors and officers are not complied with in the accounts, the auditors are required to include in their report, so far as they are reasonably able to do so, a statement giving the required particulars (CA 1985, s 237(4)).

Auditors' rights to information

4.54   The auditors of a company have right of access at all times to the company's books, accounts and vouchers, and are entitled to require from the company's officers such information and explanations as they think necessary for the performance of their duties as auditors (CA 1985, s 389A(1)).

It is an offence, punishable by imprisonment or a fine (or both), if an officer of a company knowingly or recklessly makes to the company's auditors a statement (whether orally or in writing) which conveys or purports to convey any information or explanations which the auditors require, or are entitled to require, as auditors of the company, and which is misleading, false or deceptive in a material particular (CA 1985, s 389A(2)).

Remuneration of auditors

4.55   The remuneration (including expenses) of auditors appointed by the company in general meeting must be fixed by the company in general meeting, or in such manner as the company in general meeting may determine (CA 1985, s 390A(1) and (4)). In practice, the usual approach is for the general meeting to give authority to the directors to fix the remuneration of the auditors.

Where the auditor is appointed by the directors (for example, as first auditor or to fill a casual vacancy) or by the Secretary of State, the remuneration (including expenses) of the auditors may be fixed by the directors or by the Secretary of State, as the case may be. The amount of the remuneration (including expenses) of the company's auditors in their capacity as such must be stated in a note to the company's annual accounts (CA 1985, s 390A(3) and (4)).

The amount for remuneration is to include the estimated money value of benefits in kind. The nature of any such benefit must also be disclosed.

Small companies are exempt from the requirement to disclose the remuneration of auditors in abbreviated accounts (the Companies Act 1985 (Accounts of Small and Medium-Sized Enterprises and Publication of Accounts in ECUs) Regulations 1992 (SI 1992 No 2452)).

Remuneration for non-audit work

4.56   Under section 390B of the Companies Act 1985 the Secretary of State for Trade and Industry has the power to require the disclosure of the amount of any remuneration received by a company's auditors or their associates in respect of services other than those as auditor of the company. Regulations requiring such disclosure were introduced by The Companies Act 1985 (Disclosure of Remuneration for Non-Audit Work) Regulations 1991 (SI 1991 No 2128). The Cadbury Committee reporting on remuneration received by auditors for non-audit work recommended that these regulations are reviewed and amended so that the relative significance of a company's audit and non-audit fees to an audit firm can be assessed.

For a financial year beginning on or after 1 October 1991, the regulations require disclosure of the total remuneration paid to the company's auditors or their associates during that year and the previous financial year in respect of non-audit services provided to the company and to any associated undertaking of the company of which the company's auditors or their associates are auditors.

Such disclosure is to be made in the notes to the annual accounts of a company and does not require the disclosure of any such remuneration for a financial year commencing prior to 1 October 1991. The regulations apply in relation to benefits in kind as to payments in cash, and in relation to any such benefit require disclosure of its nature and its estimated money value.

A company which qualifies as a small or medium-sized company is not required to disclose remuneration for non-audit work for the financial year in which it is entitled to the exemptions granted under section 246 of the Act.

The definition of an associate is widely drafted and resembles the provisions of section 346 of the Companies Act 1985 relating to persons who are regarded as connected to a director of a company. An associate of a company's auditors in the relevant financial year, at any time in the financial year, will depend upon the form in which the auditors exist, and is:

(*a*)   where the company's auditor is an individual:

     (i)   any partnership in which the auditor was a partner; and

(ii)   any body corporate in which the auditor or any associate of his was entitled to exercise or control the exercise of 20% or more of the voting rights at any general meeting and any body corporate which was in the same group as any such body corporate;

(*b*)   where the company's auditors are a partnership:

   (i)   any other partnership which had a partner in common with the auditors;

  (ii)   any body corporate which was a partner in the auditors;

 (iii)   any body corporate in which, whether alone or with any associate of the auditors, the auditors or any partner in the auditors was entitled to exercise or control the exercise of 20% or more of the voting rights at any general meeting;

 (iv)   any body corporate which was in the same group as any such body corporate as defined in (*b*)(ii) and (*b*)(iii) above; and

  (v)   any partner in the auditors;

(*c*)   where the company's auditors are a body corporate:

  (i)   any partnership in which the auditors were a partner;

  (ii)   any partnership in which a director of the auditors was a partner;

 (iii)   any body corporate which was in the same group as the auditors;

 (iv)   any body corporate which was an associated undertaking of the auditors or of a body corporate in the same group as the auditors;

  (v)   any body corporate in which any director of the auditors either alone or with any associate of the auditors was entitled to exercise or control the exercise of 20% or more of the voting rights at any general meeting and any body corporate which was in the same group as any such body corporate; and

 (vi)   any director of the auditors;

(*d*)   regardless of the form in which the company's auditors exist, any person who was entitled to receive 20% or more of the auditors' profits and any person of whose profits the auditors were entitled to receive 20% or more.

The auditors of a company are under an obligation to provide the directors of the company with any information necessary to identify the auditors' associates for the purposes of disclosure in the accounts of the company. However, the definition of 'associate' was slightly amended by The Companies Act 1985 (Disclosure of Remuneration for Non-Audit Work) (Amendment) Regulations 1995 (SI 1995 No 1520). It excludes any corporate body in which any partner or director in the company's auditors is able to exercise, or control the exercise of, 20% or more of the voting rights at any general meeting solely in his capacity as an insolvency practitioner, a receiver, a manager, or a judicial factor.

Appendix 4A

Precedents

A. Dormant Company — Non-Appointment of Auditors

'That in accordance with the provisions of Section 250(1)(a) of the Companies Act 1985, the company being a dormant company within the meaning of the said section, Section 388A(1) of the Companies Act 1985 shall apply and accordingly no auditors shall be appointed.'

B. Resolution for Appointment of First Auditors

'That [name of individual auditors or partnership] be and are hereby appointed auditors of the company to hold office until the conclusion of the first general meeting at which accounts are laid before the company.'

C. Resolution for Re-appointment of Auditors

'That [name of individual auditors or partnership] be and are hereby re-appointed auditors of the company to hold office until the conclusion of the next general meeting at which accounts are laid before the company and that the Directors be and are hereby authorised to fix their remuneration.'

D. Resolution for Removal of Auditors

'That [existing auditors' names] be and are hereby removed as auditors of the company with immediate effect and that [new auditors' names] be and are hereby appointed as auditors of the company in their stead to hold office until the conclusion of the next general meeting at which accounts are laid before the company and that the Directors be and are hereby authorised to fix their remuneration.'

E. Special Notice for the Removal of Auditors

'The Directors

Limited

Dear Sirs

I hereby give notice pursuant to Section 379 and Section 391A of the Companies Act 1985 of my intention to propose the following ordinary resolution at the next Annual General Meeting of the Company.

RESOLUTION

That Messrs [existing auditor's names] be and are hereby removed from office as auditors of the company [and that [new auditor's names] be appointed as auditors of the company in their place to hold office until the conclusion of the next General Meeting at which Accounts are laid before the company at a remuneration to be fixed by the Directors].

Dated this   day of

.... ,

Chapter 5

Disclosure and Reporting Requirements

Disclosure and Companies House

General

5.1 An essential element of the incorporation process and the subsequent operation of a limited liability company is that of the disclosure of information about it. The principle behind this is that, in dealing with a company which has been granted limited liability status, the public must be able to make an assessment of the company and of any risks attendant in dealing with it.

The legislation which sets down the majority of disclosure requirements for limited liability companies is the Companies Act 1985 (CA 1985) which is an Act that consolidated previous Companies Act legislation. The Companies Act 1985 has itself been amended in certain respects by the Companies Act 1989 and by statutory instrument.

The disclosure requirements of the Act are basically twofold. Firstly, a company is required to place certain information about itself (broadly relating to its management, capital structure and activities), on a public file maintained at Companies House and secondly, it is also required to make certain disclosures in statutory registers which it must maintain itself (see Chapter 3).

The Companies Registration Offices were first established in 1844 in order to administer companies established under the Joint Stock Companies Act 1844 which, for the first time, provided companies with a cheap and easy method of incorporation with limited liability status, which previously could only be obtained by either a Royal Charter or a Special Act of Parliament.

Companies House today is an Executive Agency of the Department of Trade and Industry for whom it performs two basic roles:

(a) the incorporation, re-registration and striking off of companies and the registration of documents required to be filed under companies, insolvency and related legislation; and

(b) the provision to the public of information about these companies, for which Companies House enforces compliance with statutory requirements.

However, the Deregulation and Contracting Out Act 1994 provides for the contracting out of certain functions of the Registrar of Companies (see 5.4 below).

Companies House also provides assistance and information to those involved in the administration of companies and has produced a series of publications in this connection (see Appendix 5A).

The main office of Companies House is located in Cardiff where the Registrar of Companies for England and Wales is based. A separate Registrar of Companies for Scotland is based in offices in Edinburgh. In addition to these offices, a series of satellite offices also exist in the main regional centres. The addresses of these offices and the services provided at each can be found in Appendix 5B.

The London office of Companies House has moved address and is now based at Companies House, London Information Centre, 21 Bloomsbury Street, London WC1B 3XD. Companies House in London will still be able to provide a same day incorporation and change of name registration service. One consequence of the move is that the London microfiche library has been sold and will move to Cardiff in August 1999. From then, all microfiche requests will need to be made to Cardiff.

However, more documents will be available through Companies House Direct as all documents registered since 1995 have been placed on to the on-line system. It is presently possible to obtain the mortgage index, charge details and the register of directors through this system.

Companies Act compliance and enforcement

5.2   The Companies Act 1985 requires each company registered under the Companies Acts to disclose certain specified information about itself. These requirements can be split into two broad categories being:

(*a*)   annual filing requirements (see 5.5 below); and

(*b*)   occasional filing requirements (see 5.12 and Appendix 5D below).

Companies House continues to devote considerable efforts to ensuring that companies fulfil their annual filing and this has resulted in an increase of companies being compliant. Based on the average year to date, Companies House achieved a compliance rate for accounts of 96.2% for the period to 31 January 1998. For the same period, 94.1% of companies had submitted their annual returns, while 91.1% of companies were fully compliant.

To ensure companies comply with their disclosure requirements, Companies House has considerable powers under the Act. The main sanctions available to Companies House are as follows.

(i)   *Default order*

Under the provisions of section 713 and section 242(3) of the CA 1985, the Registrar of Companies may, after service of notice on the company if the default continues for more than 14 days from the date of the notice, apply to the court for an order requiring the officers of a company to deliver a specified document within a given time.

(ii)   *Penalties*

(A)   *Criminal penalties*

The Registrar of Companies may proceed through the courts to prosecute any company officers who have failed to file at Companies House any documents which they are obliged to file under the Act. Successful prosecutions result in the officers concerned receiving a criminal record and render them liable to a fine as specified in the Punishment of Offences Table in CA 1985, Sch 24 (see Appendix 5C).

The statutory maximum prescribed under section 32 of the Magistrates' Courts Act 1980 was increased from £2,000 to £5,000 when the Criminal Justice Act 1991 (Commencement No 3) Order 1992 (SI 1992 No 333) brought into force section 17 of the Criminal Justice Act 1991. In addition, various offences in Schedule 24 of CA 1985 refer to the standard scale which under the Criminal Justice Act 1991, s 17 is as follows.

Level on the Scale	Amount of Fine
1	£ 200
2	£ 500
3	£1,000
4	£2,500
5	£5,000

A maximum fine of £5,000 per offence exists for failing to deliver, in the specified time, an annual return or the annual financial statements. After conviction, continued default in the delivery of the above overdue documents can result in additional fines of up to £500 per day from the date of default being imposed.

(B)   *Civil penalties*

The Registrar of Companies is empowered under CA 1985, s 242A, to impose upon a company a civil penalty without recourse to the court for its failure to file the annual financial statements within the required period. A different scale of penalties apply to private and public limited companies, and these are as follows.

Length of Period	Public Co	Private Co
Not more than 3 months	£ 500	£ 100
3 to 6 months	£1,000	£ 250
6 to 12 months	£2,000	£ 500
More than 12 months	£5,000	£1,000

Such penalties can be enforced from the first day of default and are calculated by reference to the length of default. These penalties will be strictly enforced and no mitigating circumstances, such as the size of the company or the nature of its business, will be taken into account. However, the Registrar will in limited circumstances exercise his discretion and may waive the filing penalty where accounts are received within three days of the deadline and the company has not previously incurred a penalty.

Upon receipt of the accounts by Companies House, a notice will be issued to the company at its registered office, followed by a final notice two weeks later. Any penalties still outstanding after 30 days from the date of notification of the amount due will be referred to the Lewis Group, the debt collection agency appointed by Companies House, who will pursue such debts in the courts if necessary.

The collection agents are seeking to improve the effectiveness of their collection procedures by introducing a range of measures. These include garnishee orders, oral examinations and for persistent late filing the prosecution of individual directors. Under a garnishee order, the court will be asked to grant an order requiring the company's bank to pay the penalty and any associated legal costs from the company's bank account. An oral examination will involve a director of the company attending court to undergo a strict examination of the assets, liabilities and means of the company.

(iii) *Disqualification*

Under the provisions of section 3 of the Company Directors' Disqualification Act 1986, a director who has been prosecuted and convicted three or more times in a five-year period for a failure to deliver documents to Companies House may be disqualified by the court from being a director or taking part in the management of a company for up to five years.

Similarly, the court may also make a disqualification order against any director who has received three or more default orders under the provisions of sections 242(3) and 713 of the CA 1985, in the last five years.

(iv) *Dissolution*

Where the Registrar of Companies believes that a company is no longer in business or in operation, he is empowered under section 652 of the CA 1985 to remove a company from the Register of Companies. This has the effect of deregistering the company and thus depriving it of its legal status. Reinstatement of a company in such circumstances can be both costly and time-consuming. However, without reinstatement any property or rights held by the company prior to its dissolution become *bona vacantia* and pass to the Crown. Application for reinstatement may be made by either the company, a director or member at any time up to 20 years from the date of dissolution. (See 9.16–9.33 BORROWING AND SECURITY.)

A company's failure to file annual returns, accounts, or to respond to any communication from Companies House, will commonly result in the company being struck off.

Thus, it can be seen that Companies House has considerable powers to enforce the disclosure requirements of the Companies Act 1985.

Other powers of Companies House

5.3   Companies House also has powers in other areas.

(*a*)   *Company names*

The Registrar of Companies has considerable powers to either reject an application made for the incorporation of a company under a particular name or to force a company to change its name in certain circumstances. The Registrar's powers in this connection are discussed in 2.12 and 2.14 THE COMPANY CONSTITUTION.

(*b*)   *Document examination*

Section 706 of the CA 1985 gives the Registrar of Companies the power to determine the format and legibility of documents filed with Companies House in satisfaction of any requirement of the Companies Act 1985.

Under section 706, the Registrar is empowered to refuse to accept for filing any documents which do not conform with the following guidelines.

(i)   Documents must be on paper which is white or otherwise of a background density not greater than 0.3.

(ii)   Documents must be on paper with a matt finish.

(iii)   Each page must be on A4 size paper.

(iv)   Each page must have a margin all round of not less than 10mm wide. If the document is bound, the bound edge must have a margin of not less than 20mm.

(v)   Letters and numbers must be clear, legible and of uniform density.

(vi)   Letters and numbers must not be less than 1.8mm high, with a line width of not less than 0.25mm.

(vii)   Letters and numbers must be black or otherwise providing reflected line density of not less than 1.0.

For glossy accounts, Companies House have indicated that they will accept a photocopy of the accounts provided this document contains 'live' (i.e. original) signatures.

Where documents filed do not satisfy the criteria set by the Registrar of Companies the documents may be rejected and a period of 14 days allowed from the date of rejection for a suitable replacement to be filed. If this is not done, the original document will be deemed not to have been delivered to the Registrar. Failure to do so can result in a default action being taken against the company and its officers 14 days from the service of the notice.

(c) *Fees*

The Act also grants the Registrar of Companies the power to levy statutory charges upon companies in certain circumstances. The fees specified in the Companies (Fees) Regulations 1991 (SI 1991 No 1206) have been amended by further regulations and more recently by the Companies (Fees) (Amendment) Regulations 1996 (SI 1996 No 1444). The circumstances and the fees payable are as follows.

UK companies	*Charge*	*Same day charge*
Registration of a company on its formation	£20.00	£100.00
Re-registration of a private company as a public company	£20.00	£100.00
Re-registration of a public company as a private company	£20.00	£100.00
Re-registration of a limited company as unlimited	£20.00	£100.00
Re-registration of an unlimited company as limited	£20.00	£100.00
Registration of a company's change of name	£10.00	£100.00
Registration of an annual return	£15.00	–
Oversea companies	*Charge*	
Registration of an oversea company as a place of business in Great Britain	£20.00	£100.00
Registration of an oversea company as a branch in Great Britain	£20.00	£100.00
Registration of a name under which an ovesea company proposes to carry on business in Great Britain	£20.00	£100.00
Re-registration of a name under which an oversea company proposes to carry on business in Great Britain	£20.00	£100.00
Registration of the annual accounts of an oversea company	£15.00	–

(*d*)   *Inspection of company records*

The public records of companies registered in the UK are held in microfiche form and may be inspected by any person at Companies House. For companies registered in England and Wales, a company search can be undertaken at Companies House in Cardiff or London, or ordered through one of the satellite offices detailed in Appendix 5B. For companies registered in Scotland, a search can be undertaken at Companies House in Edinburgh or ordered through the satellite office in Glasgow.

Information about companies may also be obtained by accessing a computerised retrieval system, Companies House Direct (formerly known as CHORUS), which can be viewed at Companies House, or provided by subscription to a user direct to the user's own computer system. The information presently available includes general details about a company, such as the company's name, registered number, date of incorporation, its accounting reference date, and the last received annual return and accounts.

In addition, Companies House Direct allows access to images of company accounts, the mortgage index and details of company directors. A register of directors and company secretaries includes lists of all directorships and secretaryships of individual officers as well as their home addresses, while a register of disqualified directors detailing all disqualification orders made under the Company Directors' Disqualification Act 1986 is also available.

A fee is payable in respect of each company for which a company search is undertaken (starting at £5.00 for a microfiche copy of a company record).

Contracting out

5.4   Schedule 16 of the Deregulation and Contracting Out Act 1994 inserted provisions into section 704 of the Companies Act 1985 which enable the Registrar of Companies to contract out certain functions to any person authorised by him. Where an order is made under section 69 of the Deregulation and Contracting Out Act 1994, a person is authorised by the Registrar of Companies to accept delivery of any class of documents which are required under the Companies Act to be delivered to the Registrar.

The Contracting Out (Functions in relation to the Registration of Companies) Order 1995 (SI 1995 No 1013) came into force on 5 April 1995. The Order permits the Registrar of Companies for England and Wales to authorise the exercise by another person, or that person's employees, of certain functions conferred on the Registrar including:

(*a*)   receiving any return, accounts or other document required to be filed with, delivered or sent, or notice of any matter required to be given, to the Registrar;

(*b*) the incorporation of companies and the change of name of companies by or under Chapters I and II of Part I of the Act; and

(*c*) the re-registration and change of status of companies by or under Part II and sections 138, 139 and 147 of the Act.

The Order excludes from contracting out certain functions of the Registrar of Companies for Scotland, while enabling the Secretary of State to contract out certain functions where his approval is required in the following circumstances:

(i) to prohibit the registration of a company with a name which would be likely to give the impression that it is connected with local or national government; and

(ii) to permit an extension of the period allowed for laying and delivering accounts and reports following an application by a company for such an extension.

While a number of Companies House services have been put out to competitive tender, these services have been successfully retained in-house.

Recent developments

5.5 Companies House, in line with its Executive Agency status, is continuing to look at ways of improving the speed and quality of the information it provides to the public. Companies House has been investigating the possibility of accepting for filing on a company's records documents submitted in electronic form. This method for filing documents was introduced into the Companies Act 1985 (section 707) by section 125(2) of the Companies Act 1989.

The Electronic Filing Project which ran during 1996 involved a number of presenters filing at Companies House various forms using an electronic method of filing. The forms presented comprised forms 287, 288(b), 288(c) and 88(2). The project concluded that documents can be successfully received electronically and automatically validated and placed on a company's record with a high degree of certainty. There are a number of legal issues that require addressing such as the use of alternative forms of authenticating such documents other than by signature or by statutory declaration. Additionally, Companies House will conduct detailed discussions with presenters on the administrative and technical issues before such a project is launched.

Companies House has set itself the objective of moving to electronic media and will seek to cease using paper and fiche media as the primary storage and distribution medium during 1999. To this end, Companies House has engaged a number of outside contractors to look at various products and services offered by Companies House and improving or extending their coverage. For instance, the CD-ROM Directory was launched in January 1997 and currently offers basic information on current and recently dissolved companies. It is issued on a quarterly basis and Companies House intends that it will replace the current directory issued on microfiche.

Companies House launched its Electronic Filing Service in October 1998. At present, the service allows forms 287, 288a, b and c and form 363a. The ability to file electronically will be supplemented by a validation process, will involve a method of prepayment in the case of annual returns and will be subject to companies having the minimum PC requirements for the system to operate.

There are three new variants to the forms used to effect a change in a company's registered office address (form 287(I) and the forms required to notify the appointment and resignation of company officers (forms 288ab(I)). These new forms allow intelligent character recognition for electronic input. In addition, companies which use the Companies House Direct service can now order for downloading, viewing or printing from their PC copies of company accounts.

Another project aims to increase the amount of information electronically stored as data. In particular, the mortgage register is available online through Companies House Direct. It is also intended that snapshots of issued capital and shareholder data will be made available on Companies House Direct and this will enable such data to be pre-printed on shuttle documents.

The annual return

General

5.6   Section 363 of the Companies Act 1985 requires every company to make up and deliver to Companies House in each calendar year an annual return made up to a date no later than its 'return date' which is determined by reference to either:

(*a*)   the company's date of incorporation; or

(*b*)   the anniversary of the return date of the last filed annual return.

A company's return date may be changed by shortening the period between annual returns to less than a twelve month period; extensions beyond a twelve month period are not permitted.

The annual return must be signed by either a director or the secretary of the company. While a 'shadow director' is deemed to be a director of a company for the purposes of sections 363 to 365 of the Act, a 'shadow director' may not sign the annual return (section 365(3)). The return must be filed at Companies House within 28 days of the return date accompanied by the prescribed fee (£15, as at date of publication). Failure to do so renders the company and its officers liable to default proceedings (see 5.2 above).

Type of return

5.7   Under the Companies (Forms Amendment No 2 and Company's Type and Principal Business Activities) Regulations 1990 (SI 1990 No 1766), provision was made for the introduction of the new-style annual return, form 363a, and two variants of this form, namely 363b and 363s (the 'shuttle document'). Following the publication of the Companies (Forms) (Amendment) Regulations 1995 (SI 1995 No 736), which came into force on 1 April 1995, the annual return is required to be made on the forms prescribed by the Companies (Forms) (No 2) Regulations 1991 (SI 1991 No 1259) for forms 363b and 363s and the form 363a prescribed by the later regulations.

The regulations revoked earlier versions of form 363a with effect from 1 April 1996, while revoking the versions of forms 363b and 363s as prescribed by SI 1990 No 1766 with effect from 1 April 1995. Forms 363b and 363s as prescribed by the Companies (Forms) (No 2) Regulations 1991 will continue to apply. The forms differ in that form 363a is a blank annual return, while forms 363s and 363b are pre-printed to the extent indicated in 5.8 and 5.9 below. The form and content of the annual return which applies in all cases are described in 5.11 below.

During 1997, Companies House sought views on the possible abolition of the requirements for companies to enter on the annual return:

(*a*)   details of transfers of shares since the made up date of the last annual return; and

(*b*)   a list of the persons who have ceased to be members of the company since the made up date of the last annual return.

The consultation concluded that this information should be retained on the annual return.

Form 363s (the 'shuttle document')

5.8   This form has been designed as a computer generated form, which is issued by Companies House to each company shortly before its 'return date'. It contains the following pre-printed details about the company:

(*a*)   company details including:

(i)   company name and registered number;

(ii)   registered office address;

(iii)   the company's return date;

(iv)   company type and principal activity; and

(*b*)   details of officers:

(i)   particulars of the company secretary;

(ii)   particulars of each director.

The details relating to the issued share capital of the company and changes in the shareholders or their holdings are not pre-printed. The information contained in the form is based on those details contained in the last annual return filed at Companies House and will generally take account of any changes filed at Companies House since the last annual return. The company secretary should however ensure that the pre-printed details correspond with the entries in the company's statutory registers and complete the remainder before signing and returning the form to Companies House.

Form 363b

5.9 This form contains fewer pre-printed details than shown on form 363s and in particular does not include details of the company'sofficers or the type of company and its principal activities. The form is sent by Companies House to the company for completion of the remaining particulars.

Form and content of return

5.10 Each annual return must state the date to which it is made up (being a date no later than the 'return date') and, in addition, must contain the following information.

(*a*)   The address of the company's registered office.

(*b*)   The type of company and its principal business activities (see note (A) below).

(*c*)   The name and address of the company secretary (see note (B) below).

(*d*)   The name and address of every director of the company (see note (B) below).

(*e*)   In the case of each individual director:

    (i)   his nationality, date of birth and business occupation, and

    (ii)   such particulars of other directorships and former names as are required to be contained in the company's register of directors.

(*f*)   In the case of any corporate director, such particulars of other directorships as would be required to be contained in the register of directors in the case of an individual.

(*g*)   If the register of members is not kept at the company's registered office, the address of the place where it is kept.

(*h*)   If any register of debenture holders (or a duplicate of any such register or a part of it) is not kept at the company's registered office, the address of the place where it is kept.

(*j*)   If the company has elected:

    (i)   to dispense under CA 1985, s 252 with the laying of accounts and reports before the company in general meeting; or

    (ii)   to dispense under CA 1985, s 366A with the holding of annual general meetings,

    a statement to that effect (see 7.58 MEMBERSHIP).

(CA 1985, s 364).

Notes

(A) The information as to the company's principal business activities may be given by reference to one or more categories of the Standard Industrial Classification code.This requirement was introduced by the Companies Act 1989 because the abbreviated accounts which a small company is entitled to file with the Registrar of Companies are not required to include a directors' report which would otherwise contain this information.

(B) A person's 'name' and 'address' mean, respectively:

(i) in the case of an individual, his Christian name (or other forename) and surname and his usual residential address;

(ii) in the case of a corporation or Scottish firm, its corporate or firm name and its registered or principal office;

(iii) in the case of a peer, or an individual usually known by a title, the title may be stated instead of his Christian name (or other forename) and surname or in addition to either or both of them;

(iv) where all the partners in a firm are joint secretaries, the name and principal office of the firm may be stated instead of the names and addresses of the partners.

In addition to the above, the annual return of a company having a share capital must contain the following particulars with respect to its share capital and members.

(I) The total number of issued shares of the company at the date to which the return is made up and the aggregate nominal value of those shares.

(II) With respect to each class of shares in the company:

(i) the nature of the class; and

(ii) the total number and aggregate nominal value of issued shares of that class at the date to which the return is made up.

(III) A list of the names and addresses of every person who:

(i) is a member of the company on the date to which the return is made up; or

(ii) has ceased to be a member of the company since the date to which the last return was made up (or, in the case of the first annual return, since the incorporation of the company).

If the names are not arranged in alphabetical order, the return must have annexed to it an index sufficient to enable the name of any person in the list to be found easily.

(IV) The number of shares of each class held by each member of the company at the date to which the return is made up, and the number of shares of each class transferred since the date to which the last annual return was made up (or, in the case of the first annual return, since the incorporation of the company), by each member or person who has ceased to be a member, and the dates of registration of the transfers (both acquisitions and disposals).

The annual return may, if *either* of the *two* immediately preceding annual returns has given the full particulars of the members required above, give only such particulars as relate to persons ceasing to be or becoming members since the date of the last annual return *and* to shares transferred since that date. Thus, in such cases, the annual return would not need to include the foregoing particulars in relation to continuing members whose shareholdings have remained unchanged. This exception is not available for more than two consecutive years (that is, the full particulars must be given at least once in every three years).

Notification of other changes

5.11   The Companies (Forms Amendment No 2 and Company's Type and Principal Business Activities) Regulations 1990 (SI 1990 No 1766) provided that a form 363s (the 'shuttle document') issued by the Registrar of Companies is a prescribed form for the purpose of notifying certain changes in the company's details provided the form is issued by the Registrar to the company. The provisions were extended by the Companies (Forms) Regulations 1991 (SI 1991 No 879) and further amended by the Companies (Forms) (No 2) Regulations 1991 (SI 1991 No 1259). As a consequence, the 'shuttle document' is a prescribed form for the purpose of notifying the following:

(*a*)   a change in the company's registered office address (usually on form 287);

(*b*)   the resignation of the secretary or the directors, or any changes in their particulars such as their home address (usually on the relevant variant of form 288); and

(*c*)   the location of the register of debenture holders or the register of members, where they are kept at an address other than the registered office (usually on forms 190 and 353 respectively).

Form 363b is a prescribed form only for the purpose of notifying any change in the company's registered office provided the form is issued by the Registrar to the company.

The appointment of a secretary or a director must be notified on form 288a since the form 363s is not a prescribed form for this purpose. In addition, the requirement to inform Companies House of the above changes within 14 days of the occurrence of the change still applies.

Information annexed to annual return

5.12   Section 231 of the Companies Act 1985 requires disclosure of information about related undertakings in a company's accounts in accordance with the provisions of Schedule 5 of the Act. By virtue of section 231(5), if the directors are of the opinion that due to the number of undertakings to be disclosed compliance would result in information being unduly excessive, the information need only be given in respect of:

(*a*)   the undertakings whose result or financial position, in the directors' opinion, principally affected the figures shown in the company's accounts; and

(*b*)   undertakings excluded from consolidation under section 229(3) or (4).

If advantage is taken of this exemption, the notes to the accounts should contain a statement that the information given relates to only these undertakings. In addition, the full information, comprising the information disclosed in the accounts as well as the information not so disclosed, must be annexed to the company's next annual return, being the return delivered to the Registrar after the accounts in question have been approved by the directors in accordance with section 233 of the Act.

Failure to disclose the full information with the annual return will render the company and every director who is in default liable to a fine and, for continued contravention, to a daily default fine.

General filing administration

Prescribed forms

5.13   The Companies Act 1985 specifies various circumstances in which a company must make a return to Companies House. These returns must be made on the forms specified by The Companies (Forms) Regulations 1985 (SI 1985 No 854), as amended. Various regulations (including SI 1987 No 752, SI 1988 No 1359 and SI 1990 No 572) have replaced existing forms or introduced new forms to accommodate changes in companies legislation and the Companies (Forms Amendment No 2 and Company's Type and Principal Business Activities) Regulations 1990 (SI 1990 No 1766) introduced the current annual returns. In addition the main regulations (SI 1985 No 854) were amended by The Companies (Forms) (Amendment) Regulations 1992 (SI 1992 No 3006), which introduced new forms for the registration of an oversea company as either a place of business or a branch (see 2.54–2.66 THE COMPANY CONSTITUTION).

More recently, the Companies (Forms) (Amendment) Regulations 1995 (SI 1995 No 736) which came into force on 1 April 1995 revised a number of forms to make them easier to use and revoked the earlier versions of these forms with effect from 1 April 1996. The exception to this is in the case of annual returns where two sets of regulations prescribed versions of forms 363b and 363s. Forms 363b and 363s prescribed by the earlier statutory instrument (SI 1990 No 1766) were revoked with effect from 1 April 1995. In addition, the form 288 has been redesigned so that the appointment, resignation and changes in the particulars of a director or secretary are notified on three separate forms, namely, 288a, 288b and 288c respectively.

The Companies (Welsh Language Forms and Documents) Regulations 1994 (SI 1994 No 117) introduced additional prescribed forms for the purposes of complying with sections 287(3), 288(2) and 363(2) of the Companies Act 1985. The forms, 287CYM, 288CYM and 363CYM, are in Welsh as well as in English, and may be completed in Welsh without an accompanying certified English translation where the company's memorandum states that its registered office is to be situated in Wales. In such cases, the Registrar is required to obtain a translation into English. The Companies (Welsh Language Forms and Documents) (Amendment) Regulations 1995 (SI 1995 No 734) recently amended the above forms and introduced further Welsh variants of companies forms.

Following amendments to the rules for changing a company's accounting reference date, the Companies (Forms) (Amendment) Regulations 1996 (SI 1996 No 594) prescribed a replacement form 225 with effect from 1 April 1996. This form is intended for use by both companies incorporated under the Companies Act as well as oversea companies which have established a branch or a place of business in Great Britain.

There are over 80 circumstances specified under the Companies Act 1985 when a return is required to be made in a prescribed form. (See Appendix 5D below for a comprehensive list of these.) The form numbers given under the Companies (Forms) Regulations 1985 refer to the relevant section under the Act which requires the return to be made. Accordingly, for fuller explanations of the circumstances under which the returns are required, reference should be made to the Act.

Registration of resolutions

5.14   In addition to the prescribed forms mentioned above and contained in Appendix 5D, section 380 of the Companies Act 1985 requires that a copy of every resolution to which CA 1985, s 380 applies, must within *15 days* of it being passed, be filed with Companies House. The resolutions and agreements which must be registered pursuant to CA 1985, s 380 are:

(*a*)   special resolutions;

(*b*)   extraordinary resolutions;

(*c*)   elective resolutions or resolutions revoking elective resolutions;

(*d*)   resolutions or agreements agreed to by all members of the company, which would otherwise have required to be passed as either special or extraordinary resolutions;

(*e*)   resolutions or agreements agreed to by all the members of a class of shareholders, which would otherwise have required a particular majority; and all resolutions or agreements which are not agreed to by all members, but which are nonetheless binding on all members of a particular class of share;

(*f*)   a resolution passed by the directors to change the name of a company to include the word 'limited', where directed to do so by the Secretary of State;

(*g*)   a resolution to give, vary or revoke the authority of directors to allot shares pursuant to CA 1985, s 80;

(*h*)   a resolution of the directors under CA 1985, s 147(2) to alter the memorandum of association of a public company, when it ceases to be a public company through the acquisition of its own shares;

(*j*)   a resolution to give, vary, revoke or renew a company's authority under CA 1985, s 166 to purchase its own shares; and

(*k*)   a resolution for the voluntary winding-up of the company passed pursuant to section 84(1)(a) of the Insolvency Act 1986.

In addition, the procedure for an increase in the share capital of a company requires the company to send a copy of the ordinary resolution authorising the increase to Companies House together with the notice of the increase (form 123) within 15 days of the resolution being passed. For further information on general meetings and resolutions please refer to Chapter 7.

Summary

5.15   Filing administration is a key element of a company secretary's role and is one which, if neglected, can result in considerable penalties being imposed upon both the company and its officers (see Appendix 5C).

To avoid any penalties, three key points must be borne in mind:

(*a*)   all forms and accounts must be filed within the specified time limit;

(*b*)   all forms and accounts must bear the appropriate original signatures and be dated; and

(*c*)   all forms and accounts must be in a form approved by Companies House and the information contained on them be clear and legible (see 5.3(*b*) above).

Disclosure and The Stock Exchange

General

5.16   A company listed on the London Stock Exchange, in addition to its obligations under the Companies Act 1985, is required to comply with the requirements of the Listing Rules, which replaced the Admission to Securities Listing (the 'Yellow Book') on 1 December 1993. The Rules, still known as the Yellow Book, have been reorganised into a more user-friendly format and incorporate many of the previously unwritten rules of the Stock Exchange.

One of the main conditions of listing is the requirement to observe the continuing obligations set out in the Rules, which the Exchange emphasise 'is essential to the maintenance of an orderly market in securities and to ensure that all users of the market have access to the same information at the same time'. The Stock Exchange may take action against any company which fails to comply with any continuing obligation it is required to observe (see 5.19 below).

Notification of any matter required to be disclosed to the Exchange is made to the Company Announcements Office ('CAO') and companies are advised to follow the procedural guidelines of the Regulatory News Service. Announcements may be delivered by hand in hard copy form or made by facsimile. However, the Exchange's preferred method is by electronic means, since these enable the CAO to process the information more quickly and efficiently for onward transmission to the market.

The electronic methods available are Direct Link, Telecom Gold and Telex. The use of Telecom Gold requires the company to telephone the Exchange to inform the CAO that an announcement has been made to its mailbox, while Direct Link makes the information immediately available to the CAO. The company should use the Announcement Validation Service ('AVS') numbers issued to it when making announcements to validate the source of such information.

Continuing obligations

5.17   The Listing Rules require a company to notify the CAO without delay of any information which will enable the company's shareholders and the public to make an assessment of its position, and of any major new developments which are not public knowledge and lead to substantial price movements in the company's listed securities and, for a company with listed debt securities, also have a significant effect on its ability to meet its commitments.

In general, these obligations are in addition to any specific requirements of the Listing Rules to notify The Stock Exchange. The Exchange may, however, permit a company to dispense with the requirements to make information public where the directors can satisfy the Exchange that its disclosure may be prejudicial to the company's legitimate business interests. The circumstances in which a company must notify the CAO are numerous and will include the following.

(*a*)   Any proposed change in the capital structure of the company, any change in the rights attaching to any class of listed securities and the basis of allotment of listed securities offered generally to the public for cash. Such changes must be notified without delay.

(*b*)   Any information about substantial share interests in the company's share capital which are disclosed to the company under section 198 of the Companies Act 1985, and any information obtained by the company under section 212 of the Act about the beneficial ownership of such shares (see 3.27–3.34 THE STATUTORY RECORDS). This information must be notified to the CAO without delay.

(*c*)   Any decisions of the directors relating to dividends, profits and other matters requiring announcement must, wherever possible, be notified before 5.30 pm on the day of the board meeting at which these matters are considered; otherwise the relevant announcement must be made before 7.30 am on the following business day.

The Rules require all circulars, notices, reports, announcements or other documents issued by the company to be forwarded to the CAO at the same time as they are issued. In addition, all resolutions passed by the company in general meeting, with the exception of resolutions which comprise the ordinary business of an annual general meeting, must be forwarded to the CAO without delay after the meeting in question. In each case, six copies of these documents are required.

The London Stock Exchange published in September 1998 an updated version of its continuing obligations guide. This guide is a useful summary of the key obligations which listed companies are required to comply with and is a helpful aid to company secretaries in ensuring that they meet the deadlines required by the Listing Rules.

Financial information

5.18   A listed company is required to issue an annual report and accounts as well as a report covering the first six months of each financial year. The annual accounts must be published no later than six months after the end of the financial year, while the half-yearly report must be published within four months of the end of the relevant financial period. In exceptional circumstances, the Exchange may allow an extension to these time limits.

The company must notify the CAO immediately following board approval of the preliminary statement of its annual results, the announcement of the half-yearly results and any decision relating to the payment of a dividend on the company's listed equity securities.

The ASB has recently published its recommendations for the information to be disclosed in the preliminary announcements made by companies listed on the London Stock Exchange. It sets the minimum requirements for the information to be given in such announcements which provides more detail than is currently required under the Listing Rules. In particular, the ASB recommends that the announcement should include:

1.   A narrative commentary highlighting the main factors which have influenced the company's performance during the financial period in question and the company's position at the end of the period.

2.   A summary profit and loss account which provides greater disclosure than currently recommended by the Listing Rules.

3.   A statement of total recognised gains and losses which reports any material gains and losses which have been recognised during the financial period (other than those already indicated in the profit and loss account).

4.   A summary balance sheet showing significant movements in key indicators and applying similar classifications to those used in the annual financial statements.

Where the interim report is audited, the announcement to the Company Announcements Office and any related press releases must include the auditors report in full. However, where the auditors have merely reviewed the interim report then a copy of the review report must be provided in full when the announcement is made to the CAO.

Monitoring and enforcement

5.19   The Stock Exchange monitors the information provided to it and will make contact with a company should the company fail to comply with the requirements of the Listing Rules. For instance, the Continuing Obligations team will write to the company where notifications of major shareholdings are incomplete or the company secretary may be contacted by telephone where there appears to be a deficiency in the timing or content of announcements.

The Exchange is empowered to censure any company for its failure to observe any applicable obligation of the Listing Rules, to publish the fact that the company has been censured and to suspend or cancel the company's listing. The Exchange may also take action against the directors of the company concerned.

Appendix 5A

Publications available from Companies House

Ref. No.   *Description*

Incorporation/Registration

CHN1	New Companies
CHN2	Choosing a Company Name
CHN3	Sensitive Words and Expressions
CHN4	Change of Company Name
CHN5	Public Limited Companies
CHN6	European Economic Interest Groupings
CHN7	Publication of Company Name and Particulars to be Shown on Company Stationery
CHN8	Exemption from Using the Word 'Limited' in a Company Name
CHN9	The New Company – Looking Forward
CHN10	Single-member Companies

Unincorporated Businesses

CHN11	Business Names and Business Ownership
CHN12	The Registration of Newspapers
CHN13	Limited Partnerships

Officers' Responsibilities

CHN14	Flat Management and Similar Companies
CHN15	Directors and Companies House
CHN16	Company Secretaries' Duties and Responsibilities
CHN17	Auditors
CHN18	Document Quality

Document Registration

CHN19	Disclosure Requirements
CHN20	Accounting Reference Dates
CHN21	Dormant Company Accounts
CHN22	Late Filing Penalties
CHN23	Company Charges and Mortgages
CHN23(S)	Company Charges (Scotland)
CHN24	Resolutions
CHN25	Oversea Companies

Ref. No.   *Description*

Company Closure

CHN27   Striking Off, Dissolution and Restoration
CHN27(S)   Striking off, Dissolution and Restoration (Scotland)
CHN28   Liquidation and Insolvency
CHN28(S)   Liquidation and Insolvency (Scotland)

Other Issues

CHN29   Microfiche Records
CHN30   Share Capital
CHN31   Use of Welsh
CHN32   Products and Services Information and Price List

The above publications can be obtained by telephoning (01222) 380801 or viewed on their own dedicated web site (http://www.companies-house.gov.uk). The Registrar of Companies also publishes a regular newsletter 'The Register' aimed at advising readers of current developments in company law and the activities of Companies House. Those interested can be requested to be put on the mailing list by writing to: The Register, Room 3.92, Companies House, Crown Way, Cardiff CF4 3UZ.

Appendix 5B

Companies House office locations

England & Wales

Crown Way Maindy Cardiff CF14 3UZ (Tel: 01222 380801)	Head Office for England & Wales providing all services.
21 Bloomsbury Street London WC1 3XD (Tel: 01222 380801)	Company Search and Document filing facilities.
75 Mosley Street Manchester M2 2HR (Tel: 0161 236 7500)	Company Search and Document filing facilities.
Birmingham Central Library Chamberlain Square Birmingham B3 3HQ (Tel: 0121 233 9047)	Company Search and Document filing facilities.
25 Queen Street Leeds LS1 2TW (Tel: 0113 233 8338)	Company Search and Document filing facilities.

Scotland

37 Castle Terrace Edinburgh EH1 2EB (Tel: 0131 535 5800)	Head Office for Scotland providing all services.
7 West George Street Glasgow G2 1BQ (Tel: 0141 221 5513)	Company Search and Document filing facilities.

Stock Exchange

London Stock Exchange Ltd
Old Broad Street
London
EC2N 1HP
(Tel: 0171 797 1000)

Punishment of offences under the Companies Act 1985

The statutory maximum is £5,000, as currently set by the Criminal Justice Act 1991.

Section of Act creating offence	General nature of offence	Mode of prosecution	Punishment	Daily default fine (where applicable)
6(3)	Company failing to deliver to Registrar notice or other document, following alteration of its objects.	Summary.	One-fifth of the statutory maximum.	One-fiftieth of the statutory maximum.
18(3)	Company failing to register change in memorandum or articles.	Summary.	One-fifth of the statutory maximum.	One-fiftieth of the statutory maximum.
19(2)	Company failing to send to one of its members a copy of the memorandum or articles, when so required by the member.	Summary.	One-fifth of the statutory maximum.	
20(2)	Where company's memorandum altered, company issuing copy of the memorandum without the alteration.	Summary.	One-fifth of the statutory maximum for each occasion on which copies are so issued after the date of the alteration.	

28(5)	Company failing to change name on direction of Secretary of State.	Summary.	One-fifth of the statutory maximum.	One-fiftieth of the statutory maximum.
31(5)	Company altering its memorandum or articles, so ceasing to be exempt from having 'limited' as part of its name.	Summary.	The statutory maximum.	One-tenth of the statutory maximum.
31(6)	Company failing to change name, on Secretary of State's direction, so as to have 'limited' (or Welsh equivalent) at the end.	Summary	One-fifth of the statutory maximum.	One-fiftieth of the statutory maximum.
32(4)	Company failing to comply with Secretary of State's direction to change its name, on grounds that the name is misleading.	Summary.	One-fifth of the statutory maximum.	One-fiftieth of the statutory maximum.
33	Trading under misleading name (use of 'public limited company' or Welsh equivalent when not so entitled); purporting to be a private company.	Summary.	One-fifth of the statutory maximum.	One-fiftieth of the statutory maximum.

Section of Act creating offence	General nature of offence	Mode of prosecution	Punishment	Daily default fine (where applicable)
34	Trading or carrying on business with improper use of 'limited' or 'cyfyngedig'.	Summary.	One-fifth of the statutory maximum.	One-fiftieth of the statutory maximum.
54(10)	Public company failing to give notice, or copy of court order, to Registrar, concerning application to re-register as private company.	Summary.	One-fifth of the statutory maximum.	One-fiftieth of the statutory maximum.
80(9)	Directors exercising company's power of allotment without the authority required by section 80(1).	1. On indictment. 2. Summary.	A fine. The statutory maximum.	
81(2) *(repealed for certain purposes)*	Private limited company offering shares to the public, or allotting shares with a view to their being so offered.	1. On indictment. 2. Summary	A fine. The statutory maximum.	
82(5) *(repealed for certain purposes)*	Allotting shares or debentures before third day after issue of prospectus.	1. On indictment. 2. Summary.	A fine. The statutory maximum.	

86(6) *(repealed for certain purposes)*	Company failing to keep money in separate bank account, where received in pursuance of prospectus stating that stock exchange listing is to be applied for.	1. On indictment. 2. Summary.	A fine. The statutory maximum.	
87(4) *(repealed for certain purposes)*	Offeror of shares for sale failing to keep proceeds in separate bank account.	1. On indictment. 2. Summary.	A fine. The statutory maximum.	
88(5)	Officer of company failing to deliver return of allotments, etc., to Registrar.	1. On indictment. 2. Summary.	A fine. The statutory maximum.	One-tenth of the statutory maximum.
95(6)	Knowingly or recklessly authorising or permitting misleading, false or deceptive material in statements by directors under section 95(5).	1. On indictment. 2. Summary.	2 years or a fine; or both. 6 months or the statutory maximum; or both.	
97(4) *(repealed for certain purposes)*	Company failing to deliver to Registrar the prescribed form disclosing amount or rate of share commission.	Summary.	One-fifth of the statutory maximum.	

Section of Act creating offence	General nature of offence	Mode of prosecution	Punishment	Daily default fine (where applicable)
110(2)	Making misleading, false or deceptive statement in connection with valuation under section 103 or 104.	1. On indictment. 2. Summary.	2 years or a fine; or both. 6 months or the statutory maximum; or both.	
111(3)	Officer of company failing to deliver copy of asset valuation report to Registrar.	1. On indictment. 2. Summary.	A fine. The statutory maximum.	One-tenth of the statutory maximum.
111(4)	Company failing to deliver to Registrar copy of resolution under section 104(4), with respect to transfer of an asset as consideration for allotment.	Summary.	One-fifth of the statutory maximum.	One-fiftieth of the statutory maximum.
114	Contravention of any of the provisions of sections 99 to 104, 106.	1. On indictment. 2. Summary.	A fine. The statutory maximum.	
117(7)	Company doing business or exercising borrowing powers contrary to section 117.	1. On indictment. 2. Summary.	A fine. The statutory maximum.	
122(2)	Company failing to give notice to Registrar of reorganisation of share capital.	Summary.	One-fifth of the statutory maximum.	One-fiftieth of the statutory maximum.

123(4)	Company failing to give notice to Registrar of increase of share capital.	Summary.	One-fifth of the statutory maximum.	One-fiftieth of the statutory maximum.
127(5)	Company failing to forward to Registrar copy of court order, when application made to cancel resolution varying shareholders' rights.	Summary	One-fifth of the statutory maximum.	One-fiftieth of the statutory maximum.
128(5)	Company failing to send to Registrar statement or notice required by section 128 (particulars of shares carrying special rights).	Summary.	One-fifth of the statutory maximum.	One-fiftieth of the statutory maximum.
129(4)	Company failing to deliver to Registrar statement or notice required by section 129 (registration of newly created class rights).	Summary.	One-fifth of the statutory maximum.	One-fiftieth of the statutory maximum.
141	Officer of company concealing name of creditor entitled to object to reduction of capital, or wilfully misrepresenting nature or amount of debt or claim, etc.	1. On indictment. 2. Summary.	A fine. The statutory maximum.	

Section of Act creating offence	General nature of offence	Mode of prosecution	Punishment	Daily default fine (where applicable)
142(2)	Director authorising or permitting non-compliance with section 142 (requirement to convene company meeting to consider serious loss of capital).	1. On indictment. 2. Summary.	A fine. The statutory maximum.	
143(2)	Company acquiring its own shares in breach of section 143.	1. On indictment.	In the case of the company, a fine. In the case of an officer of the company who is in default, 2 years or a fine; or both.	
		2. Summary.	In the case of the company, the statutory maximum. In the case of an officer of the company who is in default, 6 months or the statutory maximum; or both.	
149(2)	Company failing to cancel its own shares, acquired by itself, as required by section 146(2); or failing to apply for re-registration in the case there mentioned.	Summary.	One-fifth of the statutory maximum.	One-fiftieth of the statutory maximum.

		1. On indictment.	Where the company is convicted, a fine. Where an officer of the company is convicted, 2 years or a fine; or both.	One-fiftieth of the statutory maximum.
151(3)	Company giving financial assistance towards acquisition of its own shares.	2. Summary.	Where the company is convicted, the statutory maximum. Where an officer of the company is convicted, 6 months or the statutory maximum; or both.	
156(6)	Company failing to register statutory declaration under section 155.	Summary.	The statutory maximum.	
156(7)	Director making statutory declaration under section 155, without having reasonable grounds for opinion expressed in it.	1. On indictment. 2. Summary.	2 years or a fine; or both. 6 months or the statutory maximum; or both.	
169(6)	Default by company's officer in delivering to Registrar the return required by section 169 (disclosure by company of purchase of own shares).	1. On indictment. 2. Summary.	A fine. The statutory maximum.	One-tenth of the statutory maximum.

Section of Act creating offence	General nature of offence	Mode of prosecution	Punishment	Daily default fine (where applicable)
169(7)	Company failing to keep copy of contract, etc., at registered office; refusal of inspection to person demanding it.	Summary.	One-fifth of the statutory maximum.	One-fiftieth of the statutory maximum.
173(6)	Director making statutory declaration under section 173 without having reasonable grounds for the opinion expressed in declaration.	1. On indictment. 2. Summary.	2 years or a fine; or both. 6 months or the statutory maximum; or both.	
175(7)	Refusal of inspection of statutory declaration and auditors' report under section 173, etc.	Summary.	One-fifth of the statutory maximum.	One-fiftieth of the statutory maximum.
176(4)	Company failing to give notice to Registrar of application to court under section 176, or to register court order.	Summary.	One-fifth of the statutory maximum.	One-fiftieth of the statutory maximum.
183(6)	Company failing to send notice of refusal to register a transfer of shares or debentures.	Summary.	One-fifth of the statutory maximum.	One-fiftieth of the statutory maximum.

Section	Description	Mode of prosecution	Penalty	Daily default fine
185(5)	Company default in compliance with section 185(1) (certificates to be made ready following allotment or transfer of shares, etc.).	Summary.	One-fifth of the statutory maximum.	One-fiftieth of the statutory maximum.
189(1)	Offences of fraud and forgery in connection with share warrants in Scotland.	1. On indictment. 2. Summary.	7 years or a fine; or both. 6 months or the statutory maximum; or both.	
189(2)	Unauthorised making of, or using or possessing apparatus for making, share warrants in Scotland.	1. On indictment. 2. Summary.	7 years or a fine; or both. 6 months or the statutory maximum; or both.	
191(4)	Refusal of inspection or copy of register of debenture holders, etc.	Summary	One-fifth of the statutory maximum.	One-fiftieth of the statutory maximum.
210(3)	Failure to discharge obligation of disclosure under Part VI; other forms of non-compliance with that Part.	1. On indictment. 2. Summary	2 years or a fine, or both. 6 months or the statutory maximum; or both.	
211(10)	Company failing to keep register of interests disclosed under Part VI; other contraventions of section 211.	Summary.	One-fifth of the statutory maximum.	One-fiftieth of the statutory maximum.

Section of Act creating offence	General nature of offence	Mode of prosecution	Punishment	Daily default fine (where applicable)
214(5)	Company failing to exercise powers under section 212, when so required by the members.	1. On indictment. 2. Summary.	A fine. The statutory maximum.	
215(8)	Company default in compliance with section 215 (company report of investigation of shareholdings on members' requisition).	1. On indictment. 2. Summary.	A fine. The statutory maximum.	
216(3)	Failure to comply with company notice under section 212; making false statement in response, etc.	1. On indictment. 2. Summary.	2 years or a fine; or both. 6 months or the statutory maximum; or both.	
217(7)	Company failing to notify a person that he has been named as a shareholder; on removal of name from register, failing to alter associated index.	Summary.	One-fifth of the statutory maximum.	One-fiftieth of the statutory maximum.

218(3)	Improper removal of entry from register of interests disclosed; company failing to restore entry improperly removed.	Summary.	One-fifth of the statutory maximum.	For continued contravention of section 218(2), one-fiftieth of the statutory maximum.
219(3)	Refusal of inspection of register or report under Part VI; failure to send copy when required.	Summary.	One-fifth of the statutory maximum.	One-fiftieth of the statutory maximum.
221(5) or 222(4)	Company failing to keep accounting records (liability of officers).	1. On indictment. 2. Summary.	2 years or a fine; or both. 6 months or the statutory maximum; or both.	
222(6)	Officer of company failing to secure compliance with, or intentionally causing default under, section 222(5) (preservation of accounting records for requisite number of years).	1. On indictment. 2. Summary.	2 years or a fine; or both. 6 months or the statutory maximum; or both.	
231(6)	Company failing to annex to its annual return certain particulars required by Schedule 5 and not included in annual accounts.	Summary	One-fifth of the statutory maximum.	One-fiftieth of the statutory maximum.

Section of Act creating offence	General nature of offence	Mode of prosecution	Punishment	Daily default fine (where applicable)
232(4)	Default by director or officer of a company in giving notice of matters relating to himself for purposes of Schedule 6, Part I.	Summary.	One-fifth of the statutory maximum.	
233(5)	Approving defective accounts.	1. On indictment. 2. Summary.	A fine.	
233(6)	Laying or delivery of unsigned balance sheet; circulating copies of balance sheet without signatures.	Summary.	One-fifth of the statutory maximum.	
234(5)	Non-compliance with Part VII, as to directors' report and its content; directors individually liable.	1. On indictment. 2. Summary.	A fine. The statutory maximum.	
234A(4)	Laying, circulating or delivering directors' report without required signature.	Summary.	One-fifth of the statutory maximum.	
236(4)	Laying, circulating or delivering auditors' report without required signature.	Summary.	One-fifth of the statutory maximum.	

238(5)	Failing to send company's annual accounts, directors' report and auditors' report to those entitled to receive them.	1. On indictment. 2. Summary.	A fine. The statutory maximum.	One-fiftieth of the statutory maximum.
239(3)	Company failing to supply copy of accounts and reports to shareholder on his demand.	Summary.	One-fifth of the statutory maximum.	
240(6)	Failure to comply with requirements in connection with publication of accounts.	Summary.	One-fifth of the statutory maximum.	
241(2) or 242(2)	Director in default as regards duty to lay and deliver company's annual accounts, directors' report and auditors' report.	Summary.	The statutory maximum.	One-tenth of the statutory maximum.
251(6)	Failure to comply with requirements in relation to summary financial statements.	Summary	One-fifth of the statutory maximum.	
288(4)	Default in complying with section 288 (keeping register of directors and secretaries, refusal of inspection).	Summary.	The statutory maximum.	One-tenth of the statutory maximum.
291(5)	Acting as director of a company without having the requisite share qualification.	Summary	One-fifth of the statutory maximum.	One-fiftieth of the statutory maximum.

Section of Act creating offence	General nature of offence	Mode of prosecution	Punishment	Daily default fine (where applicable)
294(3)	Director failing to give notice of his attaining retirement age; acting as director under appointment invalid due to his attaining it.	Summary.	One-fifth of the statutory maximum.	One-fiftieth of the statutory maximum.
305(3)	Company default in complying with section 305 (directors' names to appear on company correspondence, etc.).	Summary.	One-fifth of the statutory maximum.	
306(4)	Failure to state that liability of proposed director or manager is unlimited; failure to give notice of that fact to person accepting office.	1. On indictment. 2. Summary.	A fine. The statutory maximum.	
314(3)	Director failing to comply with section 314 (duty to disclose compensation payable on takeover, etc.); a person's failure to include required particulars in a notice he has to give of such matters.	Summary.	One-fifth of the statutory maximum.	

317(7)	Director failing to disclose interest in contract.	1. On indictment. 2. Summary.	A fine. The statutory maximum.	
318(8)	Company default in complying with section 318(1) or (5) (directors' service contracts to be open to inspection); 14 days' default in complying with section 318(4) (notice to Registrar as to where copies of contracts and memoranda are kept); refusal of inspection required under section 318(7).	Summary.	One-fifth of the statutory maximum.	One-fiftieth of the statutory maximum.
322B(4)	Terms of any unwritten contract between sole member of a private company limited by shares or by guarantee and the company not set out in a written memorandum in minutes of a directors' meeting.	Summary.	Level 5 on the standard scale (currently £5,000).	
323(2)	Director dealing in options to buy or sell company's listed shares or debentures.	1. On indictment. 2. Summary.	2 years or a fine; or both. 6 months or the statutory maximum; or both.	
324(7)	Director failing to notify interest in company's shares; making false statement in purported notification.	1. On indictment. 2. Summary.	2 years or a fine; or both. 6 months or the statutory maximum; or both.	

Section of Act creating offence	General nature of offence	Mode of prosecution	Punishment	Daily default fine (where applicable)
326(2), (3), (4), (5)	Various defaults in connection with company register of directors' interests.	Summary.	One-fifth of the statutory maximum.	Except in the case of section 326(5), one-fiftieth of the statutory maximum.
328(6)	Director failing to notify company that members of his family have, or have exercised, options to buy shares or debentures; making false statement in purported notification.	1. On indictment. 2. Summary.	2 years or a fine; or both. 6 months or the statutory maximum; or both.	
329(3)	Company failing to notify investment exchange of acquisition of its securities by a director.	Summary.	One-fifth of the statutory maximum.	One-fiftieth of the statutory maximum.
342(1)	Director of relevant company authorising or permitting company to enter into transaction or arrangement, knowing or suspecting it to contravene section 330.	1. On indictment. 2. Summary.	2 years or a fine; or both. 6 months or the statutory maximum; or both.	

			In the case of failure to keep the name painted or affixed, one-fiftieth of the statutory maximum.
342(2)	Relevant company entering into transaction or arrangement for a director in contravention of section 330.	1. On indictment. 2. Summary.	2 years or a fine; or both. 6 months or the statutory maximum; or both.
342(3)	Procuring a relevant company to enter into transaction or arrangement known to be contrary to section 330.	1. On indictment. 2. Summary.	2 years or a fine; or both. 6 months or the statutory maximum; or both.
343(8)	Company failing to maintain register of transactions, etc., made with and for directors and not disclosed in company accounts; failing to make register available at registered office or at company meeting.	1. On indictment. 2. Summary.	A fine. The statutory maximum.
348(2)	Company failing to paint or affix name; failing to keep it painted or affixed.	Summary.	One-fifth of the statutory maximum.
349(2)	Company failing to have name on business correspondence, invoices, etc.	Summary.	One-fifth of the statutory maximum.

Section of Act creating offence	General nature of offence	Mode of prosecution	Punishment	Daily default fine (where applicable)
349(3)	Officer of company issuing business letter or document not bearing company's name.	Summary	One-fifth of the statutory maximum.	
349(4)	Officer of company signing cheque, bill of exchange, etc. on which company's name not mentioned.	Summary.	One-fifth of the statutory maximum.	
350(1)	Company failing to have its name engraved on company seal.	Summary.	One-fifth of the statutory maximum.	
350(2)	Officer of company, etc. using company seal without name engraved on it.	Summary.	One-fifth of the statutory maximum.	
351(5)(a)	Company failing to comply with section 351(1) or (2) (matters to be stated on business correspondence etc.).	Summary.	One-fifth of the statutory maximum.	
351(5)(b)	Officer or agent of company issuing, or authorising issue of, business document not complying with those subsections.	Summary.	One-fifth of the statutory maximum.	

351(5)(c)	Contravention of section 351(3) or (4) (information in English to be stated on Welsh company's business correspondence, etc.).	Summary.	One-fifth of the statutory maximum.	For contravention of section 351(3), one-fiftieth of the statutory maximum.
352(5)	Company default in complying with section 352 (requirement to keep register of members and their particulars).	Summary.	One-fifth of the statutory maximum.	One-fiftieth of the statutory maximum.
352A(3)	Company default in complying with section 352A (statement that company has only one member).	Summary.	Level 2 on the standard scale (currently £500).	One tenth of level 2 on the standard scale.
353(4)	Company failing to send notice to Registrar as to place where register of members is kept.	Summary.	One-fifth of the statutory maximum.	One-fiftieth of the statutory maximum.
354(4)	Company failing to keep index of members.	Summary.	One-fifth of the statutory maximum.	One-fiftieth of the statutory maximum.
356(5)	Refusal of inspection of members' register; failure to send copy on requisition.	Summary.	One-fifth of the statutory maximum.	
363(3)	Company with share capital failing to make annual return.	Summary.	The statutory maximum.	One-tenth of the statutory maximum.

Section of Act creating offence	General nature of offence	Mode of prosecution	Punishment	Daily default fine (where applicable)
364(4)	Company without share capital failing to complete and register annual return in due time.	Summary.	The statutory maximum.	One-tenth of the statutory maximum
366(4)	Company default in holding annual general meeting.	1. On indictment. 2. Summary.	A fine. The statutory maximum.	
367(3)	Company default in complying with Secretary of State's direction to hold company meeting.	1. On indictment. 2. Summary.	A fine. The statutory maximum.	
367(5)	Company failing to register resolution that meeting held under section 367 is to be its annual general meeting.	Summary.	One-fifth of the statutory maximum.	One-fiftieth of the statutory maximum.
372(4)	Failure to give notice to member entitled to vote at company meeting, that he may do so by proxy.	Summary.	One-fifth of the statutory maximum.	
372(6)	Officer of company authorising or permitting issue of irregular invitations to appoint proxies.	Summary.	One-fifth of the statutory maximum.	

376(7)	Officer of company in default as to circulation of members' resolutions for company meeting.	1. On indictment. 2. Summary.	A fine. The statutory maximum.	
380(5)	Company failing to comply with section 380 (copies of certain resolutions etc. to be sent to Registrar of Companies).	Summary.	One-fifth of the statutory maximum.	One-fiftieth of the statutory maximum.
380(6)	Company failing to include copy of resolution to which section 380 applies in articles; failing to forward copy to member on request.	Summary.	One-fifth of the statutory maximum for each occasion on which copies are issued or, as the case may be, requested.	
381B(2)	Director or secretary of company failing to notify auditors of proposed written resolution.	Summary.	Level 3 on the standard scale (currently £1,000).	
382(5)	Company failing to keep minutes of proceedings at company and board meetings, etc.	Summary.	One-fifth of the statutory maximum.	One-fiftieth of the statutory maximum.
382B(2)	Failure of sole member to provide the company with a written record of a decision.	Summary.	Level 2 on the standard scale (currently £500).	
383(4)	Refusal of inspection of minutes of general meetings; failure to send copy of minutes on member's request.	Summary.	One-fifth of the statutory maximum.	

Section of Act creating offence	General nature of offence	Mode of prosecution	Punishment	Daily default fine (where applicable)
387(2)	Company failing to give Secretary of State notice of non-appointment of auditors.	Summary.	One-fifth of the statutory maximum.	One-fiftieth of the statutory maximum.
389(10)	Person acting as company auditor knowing himself to be disqualified; failing to give notice vacating office when he becomes disqualified.	1. On indictment. 2. Summary.	A fine. The statutory maximum.	One tenth of the statutory maximum.
389A(2)	Officer of company making false, misleading or deceptive statement to auditors.	1. On indictment. 2. Summary.	2 years or a fine; or both. 6 months or the statutory maximum; or both.	
389A(3)	Subsidiary undertaking or its auditor failing to give information to auditors of parent company.	Summary	One-fifth of the statutory maximum.	
389A(4)	Parent company failing to obtain from subsidiary undertaking information for purposes of audit.	Summary.	One-fifth of the statutory maximum.	

391(2)	Failing to give notice to Registrar of removal of auditor.	Summary.	One-fifth of the statutory maximum.	One-fiftieth of the statutory maximum.
392(3)	Company failing to forward notice of auditor's resignation to Registrar.	1. On indictment. 2. Summary.	A fine. The statutory maximum.	One-tenth of the statutory maximum.
392A(5)	Directors failing to convene meeting requisitioned by auditor.	1. On indictment. 2. Summary.	A fine. The statutory maximum.	
394A(1)	Person ceasing to hold office as auditor failing to deposit statement as to circumstances.	1. On indictment 2. Summary.	A fine The statutory maximum.	
394A(4)	Company failing to comply with requirements as to statement of person ceasing to hold office as auditor.	1. On indictment. 2. Summary.	A fine. The statutory maximum.	One-tenth of the statutory maximum.
399(3)	Company failing to send to Registrar particulars of charge created by it, or of issue of debentures which requires registration.	1. On indictment. 2. Summary.	A fine. The statutory maximum.	One-tenth of the statutory maximum.

Section of Act creating offence	General nature of offence	Mode of prosecution	Punishment	Daily default fine (where applicable)
400(4)	Company failing to send to Registrar particulars of charge on property acquired.	1. On indictment. 2. Summary.	A fine. The statutory maximum.	One-tenth of the statutory maximum.
402(3)	Authorising or permitting delivery of debenture or certificate of debenture stock, without endorsement on it of certificate of registration of charge.	Summary.	One-fifth of the statutory maximum.	
405(4)	Failure to give notice to Registrar of appointment of receiver or manager, or of his ceasing to act.	Summary.	One-fifth of the statutory maximum	One-fiftieth of the statutory maximum.
407(3)	Authorisation or permitting omission from company register of charges.	1. On indictment. 2. Summary.	A fine. The statutory maximum.	
408(3)	Officer of company refusing inspection of charging instrument, or of register of charges.	Summary.	One-fifth of the statutory maximum.	One-fiftieth of the statutory maximum.

415(3)	Scottish company failing to send to Registrar particulars of charge created by it, or of issue of debentures which requires registration.	1. On indictment. 2. Summary.	A fine. The statutory maximum.	One-tenth of the statutory maximum.
416(3)	Scottish company failing to send to Registrar particulars of charge on property acquired by it.	1. On indictment. 2. Summary.	A fine. The statutory maximum.	One-tenth of the statutory maximum.
422(3)	Scottish company authorising or permitting omission from its register of charges.	1. On indictment. 2. Summary.	A fine. The statutory maximum	One-fiftieth of the statutory maximum.
423(3)	Officer of Scottish company refusing inspection of charging instrument, or of register of charges.	Summary	One-fifth of the statutory maximum.	
425(4)	Company failing to annex to memorandum court order sanctioning compromise or arrangement with creditors.	Summary.	One-fifth of the statutory maximum.	
426(6)	Company failing to comply with requirements of section 426 (information to members and creditors about compromise or arrangement).	1. On indictment. 2. Summary.	A fine. The statutory maximum.	

Section of Act creating offence	General nature of offence	Mode of prosecution	Punishment	Daily default fine (where applicable)
426(7)	Director or trustee for debenture holders failing to give notice to company of matters necessary for purposes of section 426.	Summary.	One-fifth of the statutory maximum.	
427(5)	Failure to deliver to Registrar office copy of court order under section 427 (company reconstruction or amalgamation).	Summary.	One-fifth of the statutory maximum.	One-fiftieth of the statutory maximum.
429(6)	Offeror failing to send copy of notice or making statutory declaration knowing it to be false etc.	1. On indictment. 2. Summary.	2 years or a fine; or both. 6 months or the statutory maximum; or both.	One-fiftieth of the statutory maximum.
430A(6)	Offeror failing to give notice of rights to minority shareholder.	1. On indictment. 2. Summary.	A fine. The statutory maximum.	One-fiftieth of the statutory maximum.

444(3)	Failing to give Secretary of State, when required to do so, information about interests in shares, etc.; giving false information.	1. On indictment. 2. Summary.	2 years or a fine; or both. 6 months or the statutory maximum; or both.
447(6)	Failure to comply with requirement to produce documents imposed by Secretary of State under section 447.	1. On indictment. 2. Summary.	A fine. The statutory maximum.
448(7)	Obstructing the exercise of any rights conferred by a warrant or failing to comply with a requirement imposed under subsection (3)(d).	1. On indictment. 2. Summary.	A fine. The statutory maximum.
449(2)	Wrongful disclosure of information or document obtained under section 447 or 448.	1. On indictment. 2. Summary.	2 years or a fine; or both. 6 months or the statutory maximum; or both.
450	Destroying or mutilating company documents; falsifying such documents or making false entries; parting with such documents or altering them or making omissions.	1. On indictment. 2. Summary.	7 years or a fine; or both. 6 months or the statutory maximum; or both.

Section of Act creating offence	General nature of offence	Mode of prosecution	Punishment	Daily default fine (where applicable)
451	Making false statement or explanation in purported compliance with section 447.	1. On indictment. 2. Summary.	2 years or a fine; or both. 6 months or the statutory maximum; or both.	
455(1)	Exercising a right to dispose of, or vote in respect of, shares which are subject to restrictions under Part XV; failing to give notice in respect of shares so subject; entering into agreement void under section 454(2), (3).	1. On indictment. 2. Summary.	A fine. The statutory maximum.	
455(2)	Issuing shares in contravention of restrictions of Part XV.	1. On indictment. 2. Summary.	A fine. The statutory maximum.	
458	Being a party to carrying on of company's business with intent to defraud creditors, or for any fraudulent purpose.	1. On indictment. 2. Summary.	7 years or a fine; or both. 6 months or the statutory maximum; or both.	
461(5)	Failure to register office copy of court order under Part XVII altering, or giving leave to alter, company's memorandum.	Summary.	One-fifth of the statutory maximum.	One-fiftieth of the statutory maximum.

		One-fifth of the statutory maximum.	One-fiftieth of the statutory maximum.
651(3)	Person obtaining court order to declare company's dissolution void, then failing to register the order.	Summary.		One-fiftieth of the statutory maximum.
652E(1)	Person breaching or failing to perform a duty imposed by section 652B or 652C.	1. On indictment. 2. Summary.	A fine. The statutory maximum.	
652E(2)	Person failing to perform a duty imposed by section 652B(6) or 652C(2) with the intent to conceal the making of application under section 652A.	1. On indictment. 2. Summary.	7 years or a fine; or both. 6 months or the statutory maximum; or both.	
652F(1)	Person furnishing false or misleading information in connection with application under section 652A.	1. On indictment. 2. Summary.	A fine. The statutory maximum.	
652F(2)	Person making false application under section 652A.	1. On indictment. 2. Summary.	A fine. The statutory maximum.	
697(1)	Oversea company failing to comply with any of sections 691 to 693 or 696.	Summary.	For an offence which is not a continuing offence, one-fifth of the statutory maximum.	

Section of Act creating offence	General nature of offence	Mode of prosecution	Punishment	Daily default fine (where applicable)
697(1)–*contd*			For an offence which is a continuing offence, one-fifth of the statutory maximum.	One-fiftieth of the statutory maximum.
697(2)	Oversea company contravening section 694(6) (carrying on business under its corporate name after Secretary of State's directions).	1. On indictment. 2. Summary.	A fine. The statutory maximum.	One-tenth of the statutory maximum.
697(3)	Oversea company failing to comply with section 695A or Schedule 21A.	Summary.	For an offence which is not a continuing offence, one-fifth of level 5 of the standard scale (equivalent to £5,000). For an offence which is a continuing offence, one-fifth of level 5 of the standard scale.	£100
703(1)	Oversea company failing to comply with requirements as to accounts and reports.	1. On indictment. 2. Summary.	A fine. The statutory maximum.	One-tenth of the statutory maximum.
703D(5)	Oversea company failing to deliver particulars of change to registrar.	1. On indictment. 2. Summary.	A fine. The statutory maximum.	

703R(1)	Company failing to register winding-up or commencement of insolvency proceedings etc.	1. On indictment. 2. Summary.	A fine. The statutory maximum.	£100
703R(2)	Liquidator failing to register appointment, termination of winding-up or striking-off of company.	1. On indictment. 2. Summary.	A fine. The statutory maximum.	£100
720(4)	Insurance company etc. failing to send twice-yearly statement in form of Schedule 23.	Summary.	One-fifth of the statutory maximum.	One-fiftieth of the statutory maximum.
722(3)	Company failing to comply with section 722(2), as regards the manner of keeping registers, minute books and accounting records.	Summary.	One-fifth of the statutory maximum.	One-fiftieth of the statutory maximum.
Sch 14, Pt II, para 1(3)	Company failing to give notice of location of overseas branch register, etc.	Summary.	One-fifth of the statutory maximum.	One-fiftieth of the statutory maximum.
Sch 14, Pt II, para 4(2)	Company failing to transmit to its registered office in Great Britain copies of entries in overseas branch register, or to keep a duplicate of overseas branch register.	Summary.	One-fifth of the statutory maximum.	One-fiftieth of the statutory maximum.

Section of Act creating offence	General nature of offence	Mode of prosecution	Punishment	Daily default fine (where applicable)
Sch 21C, Pt I, para 7	Credit or financial institution failing to deliver accounting documents.	1. On indictment. 2. Summary.	A fine. The statutory maximum.	£100
Sch 21C, Pt II, para 15	Credit or financial institution failing to deliver accounts and reports.	1. On indictment. 2. Summary.	A fine. The statutory maximum.	£100
Sch 21D, Pt I, para 5	Company failing to deliver accounting documents.	1. On indictment. 2. Summary.	A fine. The statutory maximum.	£100
Sch 21D, Pt I, para 13	Company failing to deliver accounts and reports.	1. On indictment. 2. Summary.	A fine. The statutory maximum.	£100

Specified forms for use for returns to Companies House

In circumstances where a return is required to be made, the form numbers and the time limits allowed for filing (where applicable) are as follows. Where the form number no longer relates to the relevant section of the Act, the number in brackets under the form number gives the appropriate new section number. The most commonly used forms have been highlighted with an asterisk (*). The forms solely applicable to Scotland have been omitted, while some forms which have Welsh variants have been indicated with a #.

Form No.	Details of circumstances when used	Time limit for filing
6	Notice of application to the Court for cancellation or alteration to the objects of a company.	15 days
10*	Statement of first directors and secretary and intended situation of registered office.	On application
12*	Statutory Declaration of compliance with requirements on application for registration of a company.	On application
30(5)(a)#	Declaration on application for the registration of a company exempt from the requirement to use the word 'limited' or its Welsh equivalent.	On application
30(5)(b)#	Declaration on application for registration under CA 1985, s 680 of a company exempt from the requirement to use the word 'limited' or its Welsh equivalent.	On application
30(5)(c)#	Declaration on change of name omitting 'limited' or its Welsh equivalent.	On application
43(3)	Application by a private company for re-registration as a public company.	On application

Form No.	Details of circumstances when used	Time limit for filing
43(3)(e)	Declaration of compliance with requirements by a private company on application for re-registration as a public company.	On application
49(1)	Application by a limited company to be re-registered as unlimited.	On application
49(8)(a)	Members' assent to company being re-registered as unlimited.	On application
49(8)(b)	Form of statutory declaration by directors as to members' assent to re-registration of a company as unlimited	On application
51	Application by an unlimited company to be re-registered as limited.	On application
53	Application by a public company for re-registration as a private company.	On application
54	Notice of application made to the Court for the cancellation of a special resolution regarding re-registration.	28 days
88(2)*	Return of allotment(s) of shares.	One month
88(3)*	Particulars of a contract relating to shares allotted as fully or partly paid up otherwise than in cash.	One month
97	Statement of the amount or rate per cent of any commission payable in connection with the subscription of shares.	Before commission is paid
117*	Application by a public company for certificate to commence business and statutory declaration in support.	On application
122*	Notice of consolidation, division, sub-division, redemption or cancellation of shares, or conversion, or re-conversion of stocks into shares.	One month
123*	Notice of increase in nominal capital.	15 days

Form No.	Details of circumstances when used	Time limit for filing
128(1)	Statement of rights attached to allotted shares.	One month
128(3)	Statement of particulars of variation of rights attached to shares.	One month
128(4)	Notice of assignment of name or new name to any class of shares.	One month
129(1)	Statement by a company without share capital of rights attached to newly created class of members.	One month
129(2)	Statement by a company without share capital of particulars of a variation of members' class rights.	One month
129(3)	Notice by a company without share capital of assignment of a name or other designation to a class of members.	One month
139	Application by a public company for re-registration as a private company following a Court Order reducing capital.	On application
147	Application by a public company for re-registration as a private company following cancellation of shares and reduction of nominal value of issued capital.	On application
155(6)a	Declaration in relation to assistance for the acquisition of shares.	15 days
155(6)b	Declaration by the directors of a holding company in relation to assistance for the acquisition of shares.	15 days
157	Notice of application made to the Court for the cancellation of a special resolution regarding financial assistance for the acquisition of shares.	On application

Form No.	Details of circumstances when used	Time limit for filing
169	Return by a company purchasing its own shares.	28 days
173	Declaration in relation to the redemption or purchase of shares out of capital.	Prior to redemption or purchase
176	Notice of application to the Court for the cancellation of a resolution for the redemption or purchase of shares out of capital.	5 weeks
190	Notice of place where a register of holders of debentures or a duplicate is kept or of any change in that place.	On change occurring
190a	Notice of place for inspection of a register of holders of debenture which is kept in a non-legible form, or of any change in that place.	On change occurring
225#	Change of accounting reference date.	On application but prior to due date for filing accounts.
244	Notice of claim to extension of period allowed for laying and delivering accounts — oversea business or interests.	On application but prior to due date for filing accounts.
266(1)	Notice of intention to carry on business as an investment company.	On application
266(3)	Notice that company no longer wishes to be an investment company.	On application
287*# 287(I)	Notice of change in situation of registered office.	On application
288a* 288ab(I)	Appointment of director or secretary.	14 days
288b*#	Resignation of director or secretary.	14 days
288c*# 288c(I)	Change of particulars for director or secretary.	14 days

Form No.	Details of circumstances when used	Time limit for filing
318	Notice of place where copies of directors' service contracts and any memoranda are kept or any change in that place.	14 days
325	Notice of place where register of directors' interests in shares etc. is kept or of any change in that place.	On change
325a	Notice of place for inspection of a register of directors' interests in shares etc. which is kept in a non-legible form, or of any change in that place.	On change
353	Notice of place where register of members is kept or of any change in that place.	14 days
353a	Notice of place for inspection of a register of members which is kept in a non-legible form, or of any change in that place.	14 days
362	Notice of place where an overseas branch register is kept, of any change in that place, or of discontinuance of any such register.	14 days
362a	Notice of place for inspection of an overseas branch register which is kept in a non-legible form, or of any change in that place.	14 days
363a*# 363b*# 363s* 363s(I)	Annual Return.	Refer to 5.5 above
391	Notice of passing of resolution removing an auditor.	14 days
395*	Particulars of a mortgage or charge.	21 days
397	Particulars for the registration of a charge to secure a series of debentures.	21 days
397a	Particulars of an issue of secured debentures in a series.	21 days

Form No.	Details of circumstances when used	Time limit for filing
398	Certificate of registration in Scotland or Northern Ireland of a charge comprising property situate there.	21 days
400	Particulars of a mortgage or charge subject to which property has been acquired.	21 days
403a*	Declaration of satisfaction in full or in part of mortgage or charge.	On application
403b	Declaration that part of the property or undertaking charged (*a*) has been released from the charge; (*b*) no longer forms part of the company's property or undertaking.	On application
405(1)	Notice of appointment of receiver or manager.	7 days
405(2)	Notice of ceasing to act as receiver or manager.	On application
600(a)	Notice of appointment of liquidator — voluntary winding-up (members' or creditors') (Insolvency Act 1986, s 109).	14 days
652a	Application for striking off	On application
652c	Withdrawal of application for striking off	On application
680a	Application by joint stock company for registration under Part XXII of the Companies Act 1985, and Declaration and related statements.	On application
680b	Application by a company which is not a joint stock company for registration under Part XXII of the Companies Act 1985, and Declaration and related statements.	On application
684	Registration under Part XXII of the Companies Act 1985; List of members — existing joint stock company.	Prior to forms 680a and b
685	Declaration on application by a joint stock company for registration as a public company.	On application

Form No.	Details of circumstances when used	Time limit for filing
686	Registration under Part XXII of the Companies Act 1985; Statutory Declaration verifying list of members.	Prior to forms 680a and b, 684 and 685
691*	Return and declaration delivered for registration of a place of business of an oversea company.	One month of commencing business
692(1)(a)	Return of alteration in the charter, statutes, etc. of an oversea company.	21 days
692(1)(b)*	Return of alteration in the directors or secretary of an oversea company or in their particulars.	21 days
692(1)(c)*	Return of alteration in the names or addresses of persons resident in Great Britain authorised to accept service on behalf of an oversea company.	21 days
692(2)	Return of change in the corporate name of an oversea company.	21 days
694(4)(a)	Statement of name, other than corporate name, under which an oversea company proposes to carry on business in Great Britain.	On application
694(4)(b)	Statement of name, other than corporate name, under which an oversea company proposes to carry on business in Great Britain in substitution for name previously registered.	On application
703P(1)	Return by an oversea company that the company is being wound up.	14 days
703P(3)	Notice of appointment of a liquidator of an oversea company.	14 days
703P(5)	Notice by the liquidator of an oversea company concerning the termination of liquidation of the company.	14 days

Form No.	Details of circumstances when used	Time limit for filing
703Q(1)	Return by an oversea company which becomes subject to insolvency proceedings, etc.	14 days
703Q(2)	Return by an oversea company on cessation of insolvency proceedings, etc.	14 days
BR1*	Return delivered for registration of a branch of an oversea company.	One month of commencing business
BR2	Return by an oversea company subject to branch registration of an alteration to constitutional documents.	21 days after date on which notice could have been received in Great Britain
BR3	Return by an oversea company subject to branch registration, for alteration of company particulars.	21 days after date on which notice could have been received in Great Britain
BR4	Return by an oversea company subject to branch registration of change of directors or secretary or of their particulars.	21 days after date on which notice could have been received in Great Britain
BR5	Return by an oversea company subject to branch registration of change of address or other branch particulars.	21 days
BR6	Return of change of person authorised to accept service or to represent the branch of an oversea company or of any change in their particulars.	21 days
BR7	Return by an oversea company of the branch at which the constitutional documents of the company have been registered in substitution for a previous branch.	21 days

Chapter 6

The Directors

General

Definition of a director

6.1 Section 741 of the Companies Act 1985 defines a 'director' as any person occupying the position of director, by whatever name called. This would be determined by reference to facts, such as the nature of the duties performed by the person and the authority he exercises within the company. The scope of this definition is extended, by virtue of section 741(2), to include any person (known as a 'shadow director') in accordance with whose directions or instructions the directors of a company are accustomed to act.

Anyone deemed to be a director will be subject to the privileges and liabilities which attach to a director. For instance, section 744 states that a director is an officer of the company and that, as such, he is liable to the relevant penalties if he or the company is in default of the Companies Act 1985 (see Appendix 5C DISCLOSURE AND REPORTING REQUIREMENTS) or other legislation.

Shadow directors

6.2 A shadow director is also required to comply with the provisions of the Act applicable to directors, including the following:

(*a*) his details must be entered in the register of directors (section 288);

(*b*) he must disclose any interests in contracts of the company by written notice to the directors (section 317);

(*c*) any service contract must be available for inspection by the members (section 318);

(*d*) he is prohibited from dealing in share options (section 323); and

(*e*) he must disclose his holdings in shares and debentures of the company or its subsidiaries, and such details must be entered in the register of directors' interests (sections 324 and 325).

The term 'shadow director' may include outside persons or corporate bodies who, often for legitimate commercial reasons, influence the directors' actions or otherwise control the company. A controlling shareholder or a creditor may be regarded as a shadow director where the provisions of section 741 apply. However, there is little case law on this point.

In *Re Tasbian Limited (No 3)* *[1992] BCC 358*, the courts were concerned with the appointment of a 'company doctor' to Tasbian Limited by Castle Finance Limited, which had provided finance to the company. The person so appointed negotiated on behalf of the company with trade creditors, the DTI and the Inland Revenue; monitored its trading position on a regular basis; countersigned all company cheques; and proposed and implemented a new group structure.

The judge ruled that the activities of the company doctor could fall within the definition of a shadow director, and this ruling has been confirmed by the Court of Appeal.

For a person to be regarded as a shadow director, the directors must, as a body, be acting on his directions or instructions and must be accustomed to doing so. A person is not deemed to be a shadow director in circumstances where the directors act on advice given by him in a professional capacity, since there is no express or implied requirement for the directors to act. In addition, where the directors act in accordance with directions or instructions on an isolated occasion, a person will not be deemed a director.

Under section 741(3), a holding company will not be treated as a shadow director of its subsidiary companies by reason only of the directors of such subsidiaries being accustomed to act in accordance with its directions or instructions, for the purposes of the following:

(i)   directors' duty to have regard to interests of employees (section 309);

(ii) directors' long-term contracts of employment (section 319);

(iii) substantial property transactions involving directors (sections 320 to 322); and

(iv) general restrictions on powers of companies to make loans and other transactions involving directors (sections 330 to 346).

This section would appear to imply that other factors would need to be taken into account to determine whether or not the holding company should be regarded as a shadow director under the above sections.

Appointment

6.3   The Companies Act 1985 requires that every company other than a private company has at least two directors; in the case of private companies the minimum number of directors required is one. The Act further restricts a sole director from also occupying the position of secretary of the company.

The first directors of the company, as named in the incorporation documents filed with the Registrar of Companies, are deemed to have been appointed upon the incorporation of the company. Their appointments are effective from the date of issue of the company's certificate of incorporation. Subsequent appointments are made by the directors (see Precedent A, Appendix 6A), and/or the company in general meeting, in accordance with the provisions contained in the company's articles of association.

Where a director is required under the company's articles to hold a specified number of shares in the company, CA 1985, s 291 provides a period of two months within which the share qualification may be acquired. The articles may, however, specify a shorter period. Failure to comply with the relevant share qualification will result in the director automatically ceasing to hold office at the expiry of the relevant period.

Under CA 1985, s 292, the appointments of directors at a general meeting of a public company must be voted upon individually, unless all the members present at the meeting have first agreed to appoint the directors in a single resolution. Additionally, CA 1985, s 293 provides that no person can be appointed as a director of a public company if he has attained the age of 70 years, unless the appointment has been approved by the company at a general meeting, for which special notice was given of the intention to propose a resolution to appoint such a person as a director. These provisions do not apply to a private company unless it is a subsidiary of a public company.

Section 294 of the Act imposes upon a person, appointed or proposed to be appointed a director of a company, a duty to notify to the company the attainment of any retiring age applicable to him under section 293 or under the company's articles of association. Section 294(2) further implies that a director of a company not subject to the provisions of section 293, the articles having modified or disapplied the requirements of that section, is nonetheless required to give notice to the company under this section.

Within 14 days of the appointment of a director, the relevant notification (form 288a) must be filed with the Registrar of Companies, providing details of the director's name, address, date of birth and occupation, together with a list of directorships currently held and any past directorships held within five years prior to that appointment (see 3.15 THE STATUTORY RECORDS).

For companies listed on the London Stock Exchange, the appointment of a new director must be notified without delay to the Company Announcements Office. The announcement must disclose the date of appointment and whether the person appointed will be executive or non-executive as well as details of any functions or responsibilities held. A new director must also provide to the Securities and Futures Authority ('SFA') details of his past and present business activities within 14 days of his appointment. A new director's declaration must be submitted to the SFA every three years and following any changes in the details previously submitted, other than changes in his personal details, such as his residential address.

Rotation of directors

6.4   Many companies adopt articles of association which require a third of the directors of the company to retire by rotation at each annual general meeting and to be subject to re-appointment by the company in general meeting (see Precedent B, Appendix 6A). The appointment (and re-appointment) of a director is defined as ordinary business of the company, for which an ordinary resolution is required. Clauses 73 to 80 of Table A 1985 indicate the circumstances in which a director must retire at a company's annual general meeting. These are:

(a)   where a director is subject to retirement by rotation; and

(b)   where a director has been appointed by the board of directors since the last general meeting of the company.

At the first annual general meeting of a company to which the above clauses apply, all the directors of the company are required to retire from office and are subject to re-election by the members at the meeting. For subsequent annual general meetings, Table A requires that one third of directors, or the number nearest to one third are subject to retirement by rotation. However, there may be circumstances in which some of the directors are not caught by these provisions.

For instance, clause 84 of Table A provides that a managing director or a director holding executive office is not subject to retirement by rotation. In addition, directors who were appointed by the board of directors between annual general meetings are not included in calculating the number of directors required to retire by rotation, although they are subject to retirement under clause 78 of Table A. For example, for a company which has five directors, one of whom is the managing director, and two of whom were appointed since the last annual general meeting, the number of directors required to retire by rotation is one (being the number nearest to one third).

The directors subject to retirement by rotation are those who have been longest in office. For directors appointed on the same day, the director to retire would be decided by lot or by agreement among the directors. A director required to be re-elected at the annual general meeting will generally hold office until the end of the meeting in question should he or she not be re-elected. However, a retiring director, if willing to act, will be deemed re-appointed if the company does not fill the vacancy created by his or her retirement, unless it is resolved not to re-appoint the director or not to fill the vacancy.

It is essential that where directors are required to retire the company's articles are strictly adhered to, since failure to re-elect a director could have important consequences. In *Re New Cedos Engineering Co Ltd* [*1994*] *1 BCLC 797*, the directors of the company refused to register a transfer of shares. It was successfully argued that no valid board meeting had been held within the two month period in which registration of a share transfer may be refused, since the directors had ceased to hold office by failing to be re-elected at a general meeting.

While section 285 of the Companies Act 1985 and clause 92 of Table A provide that any acts of the directors are valid notwithstanding any defect in the appointment of any director which is subsequently discovered, the above case clearly demonstrates the need to follow any rotation clauses correctly. It would be prudent in such circumstances for any directors whose appointment is defective to be re-appointed by the board of directors or the members in general meeting, while also requesting the members to ratify any acts of those directors during the period in which they technically did not hold office (see Precedent C, Appendix 6A).

The rotation clauses enable the company to remove a director at the expiry of his period of office if it wishes to do so. In some cases, it may be inappropriate or inconvenient to retain such clauses in the company's articles, although it may be useful to have alternative powers of removal in the articles in addition to the statutory provisions (see 6.9 below). If rotation clauses are not needed, it is advisable to amend the company's articles to remove these provisions. Where they are required, however, they should be followed strictly bearing in mind the possible consequences of failing to re-elect directors.

Executive, non-executive and alternate directors

6.5   Regulation 84 of Table A permits the board of directors to appoint one or more of their number as managing director or to hold any other executive office, for instance, as finance director. Such directors are generally termed 'executive directors'. Regulation 72 further provides that the directors may delegate to executive directors such of their powers as they decide upon such terms and remuneration as they think fit. The terms of and remuneration for executive office are usually governed by a director's service agreement (see EMPLOYMENT AND HEALTH AND SAFETY at 14.18).

Such service contracts must be available for inspection at the company's registered office. Where any term of a director's service contract for a period exceeding five years states that the director's employment cannot be terminated by the company by notice or can only be terminated in specified circumstances, the agreement must first be approved by ordinary resolution of the company in general meeting (CA 1985, s 319). In addition, for any further contract entered into by the company with the director while the earlier contract has more than six months to run, the unexpired portion of the orginal contract is added to the period for which the subsequent contract will run. Any term which contravenes section 319 will be void to the extent that it contravenes the section, and any contract or further contract to which the relevant provisions apply are deemed to contain a term entitling the company to terminate it at any time by giving reasonable notice.

The Cadbury Committee in their Code of Best Practice (see Appendix 6B) proposed that where a director's term of office will exceed three years, shareholders' approval should be sought on the service contract. This was subsequently superseded in part by the requirements of the Greenbury Code (see Appendix 6D), and as a consequence The Listing Rules defines a director's service contract as 'a service contract with a director of the issuer with a notice period of one year or more with provisions for predetermined compensation or termination of an amount which equals or exceeds one year's salary and benefits in kind.' This position has not changed with the publication of the Combined Code.

The holding of executive office is dependent upon the holding of office as director and, as such, any director ceasing to hold office as a director, for whatever reason, will also cease to hold executive office at the same time. Executive directors are still subject to the provisions of the company's articles of association, although, where the articles require directors to retire by rotation, such rotation clauses will generally not apply to directors holding executive office. (Scc 6.4 above.)

Non-executive directors

6.6   Non-executive directors do not hold executive office but are selected by the board of directors for appointment so that the company may benefit from a wealth of commercial experience and expertise gained outside the company. Such directors have the same responsibilities and liabilities as executive directors in terms of their statutory and fiduciary duties, even though they are not usually as involved in the company's affairs as are executive directors. However, they have the same rights of access to information afforded to executive directors of the company.

The Cadbury Committee's Code of Best Practice advised companies to select non-executive directors through a formal selection procedure. Although the decision should be made by the board as a whole, selection may be by recommendation of a nomination committee. The Code recommends that the majority of such directors are sufficiently independent of the management of the company so that they can exercise an independent judgement in any decision before the board. To enable a non-executive director to exercise this level of independence, PRONED (Promotion of Non-Executive Directors) recommends that, in particular, a non-executive director:

(*a*)   should not have been employed by the company in an executive capacity within the five years prior to his appointment as a non-executive director;

(*b*)   should not have commercial relationships with the company, of a regular or continuing nature, where he or his employing firm act as professional advisers to the company, or of a significant nature, where he is employed by a company which is a customer of or a supplier to the company on whose board he sits; and

(c)   should not have a personal relationship with any other member of the board.

PRONED provides further guidance on the rights, terms and conditions of appointment of non-executive directors, and emphasises their role on various board committees, notably the audit committee, the remuneration committee and the nomination committee. While a number of organisations have endorsed the value of adequate non-executive director representation at board level, the importance of this role has again been recognised by the Greenbury Committee in their Report on Directors' Remuneration.

The Greenbury Committee recommended that, to avoid potential conflicts of interest, a company's board of directors should set up remuneration committees exclusively comprised of non-executive directors to determine on behalf of the board, and on behalf of the shareholders, the company's policy on executive and specific remuneration packages for each of the executive directors. Such non-executive directors should have no personal financial interest, other than as shareholders, in the matters to be decided, no potential conflicts of interest arising from cross-directorships and no day-to-day involvement in running the business. The Hampel Committee supported the recommendations of the earlier committees and the position with regard to non-executive directors remains unchanged.

Alternate directors

6.7   A company's articles may provide for the appointment of an alternate director, who is a person appointed by a director to act in accordance with his instructions on the board of directors in the absence of that director (Table A, regulation 65). The appointment may be made by notice to the company at its registered office and is usually subject to the approval of the board. The appointing director may also revoke the alternate's appointment at any time by notice to the company. Where the appointing director ceases to hold office, for whatever reason, any alternate director so appointed will automatically cease to hold office.

An alternate director is generally entitled to receive notice of all board meetings, and of all committee meetings of which his appointor is a member. He may be deemed for all purposes a director and therefore his appointment would be required to be entered in the register of directors and notified to the Registrar of Companies. He would also be responsible for his own acts and defaults and, for this reason, is not deemed an agent of the director appointing him.

Remuneration of directors

6.8   The directors may delegate the subject of remuneration to a remuneration committee made up wholly or mainly of non-executive directors, whose purpose is to recommend to the board appropriate remuneration for executive directors (see the Cadbury Committee's Code of Best Practice, Appendix 6B). For listed companies, the Greenbury Committee report goes further than this by recommending that a remuneration committee should be established and consist exclusively of non-executive directors. The committee should make a report each year to the shareholders on behalf of the board, the chairman of the remuneration committee should attend the company's annual general meeting to answer shareholders' questions about directors' remuneration. The report should form part of, or be annexed to, the company's annual report and accounts (Greenbury Committee Report, Part A 'Remuneration committee' and Part B 'Disclosure and approval provisions') and should give details of any service contracts with notice periods in excess of one year, giving reasons for the notice period. Although meetings of the committee may be open to executive directors, no such director may be involved in any decision on his own remuneration.

The remuneration to be paid to the directors of a company will usually fall into the following categories:

(*a*)   remuneration subject to the directors' determination:

   (i)   remuneration paid in respect of any executive office or services provided;

   (ii) benefits to directors who have held executive office or employment;

   (iii) expenses incurred within the discharge of directors' duties;

(*b*)   remuneration subject to approval in general meeting:

   (i)   any emoluments outside the scope of the above.

An alternate director is not entitled to receive any remuneration from the company for his services, unless there is provision in the company's articles of association.

Regulation 84 of Table A permits the directors to determine the terms and remuneration of any director holding the office of managing director or any other executive office and in respect of the provision by him of any services outside the scope of the ordinary duties of a director. Regulation 83 further provides that the directors may determine the expenses they are to be paid in connection with the discharge of their duties and regulation 87 authorises the directors to provide benefits, whether by payment of a gratuity, pension, insurance or otherwise on the retirement of any director who has held executive office or employment with the company.

The directors are generally entitled to such remuneration as the company in general meeting may by ordinary resolution determine (Table A, regulation 82). The level of remuneration may be determined in advance of the year in question, although, in practice, it is confirmed at the general meeting at which the accounts disclosing such remuneration are laid. Approval of the accounts will not in itself authorise the payment of remuneration which has not been otherwise authorised, unless the shareholders are aware that in approving the accounts they are also being asked to approve the directors' remuneration.

Disclosure of the total emoluments paid to the directors in any year is required in the notes to the accounts of a company. For the purpose of approving the directors' remuneration at any general meeting at which the accounts are considered, it will be necessary to establish whether such emoluments are subject to the directors' determination or approval in general meeting. It should also be noted that CA 1985, s 311 does not permit the payment of remuneration to a director (whether as a director or otherwise) without the deduction of tax.

As a consequence of the Greenbury Report on Directors' Remuneration, the Listing Rules of the Stock Exchange were amended to incorporate its recommendations. The Combined Code has amended the information required to be disclosed in relation to the remuneration of directors. For accounting periods ending on or after 31 December 1998, the Listing Rules require a company's annual report to include a report to the shareholders which must contain:

(i) a statement of the company's policy on executive directors' remuneration;

(ii) the amount of each element in the remuneration package for the period under review of each director by name, including, but not restricted to, basic salary and fees, the estimated money value of benefits in kind, annual bonuses, deferred bonuses, compensation for loss of office and payments for breach of contract or other termination payments, together with the total for each director for the period under review and for the corresponding prior period, and any significant payments made to former directors during the period under review; such details to be presented in tabular form, unless inappropriate, together with explanatory notes as necessary;

(iii) information on share options, including SAYE options, for each director by name in accordance with the recommendations of the Accounting Standards Board's Urgent Issues Task Force Abstract 10; such information to be presented in tabular form together with explanatory notes as necessary;

(iv) details of any long-term incentive schemes, other than share options details of which have been disclosed under (iii) above, including the interests of each director by name in the long-term incentive schemes at the start of the period under review; entitlements or awards granted and commitments made to each director under such schemes during the period, showing which crystallise either in the same year or subsequent years; the money value and number of shares, cash payments or other benefits received by each director under such schemes during the period; and the interests of each director in the long-term incentive schemes at the end of the period;

(v) explanation and justification of any element of remuneration, other than basic salary, which is pensionable;

(vi) details of any directors' service contract with a notice period in excess of one year or with provisions for pre-determined compensation on termination which exceeds one year's salary and benefits in kind, giving the reasons for such notice period;

(vii) the unexpired term of any directors' service contract of a director proposed for election or re-election at the forthcoming annual general meeting and, if any director proposed for election or re-election does not have a directors' service contract, a statement to that effect; and

(viii) a statement of the company's policy on the granting of options or awards under its employees' share schemes and other long-term incentive schemes, explaining and justifying any departure from that policy in the period under review and any change in the policy from the preceding year.

(ix) for defined benefit schemes (as in part I of schedule 6 to the Companies Act 1985):

    (a) details of the amount of the increase during the period under review (excluding inflation) and of the accumulated total amount at the end of the period in respect of the accrued benefit to which each director would be entitled on leaving service or is entitled having left service during the period under review;

    (b) and either:

        (i) the transfer value (less director's contributions) of the relevant increase in accrued benefit (to be calculated in accordance with Actuarial Guidance Note GN11 but making no deduction for any underfunding) as at the end of the period; or

        (ii) so much of the following information as is necessary to make a reasonable assessment of the transfer value in respect of each director:

            (a) current age;

            (b) normal retirement age;

            (c) the amount of any contributions paid or payable by the director under the terms of the scheme during the period under review;

            (d) details of spouse's and dependants' benefits;

(e) early retirement rights and options, expectations of pension increases after retirement (whether guaranteed or discretionary); and

(f) discretionary benefits for which allowance is made in transfer values on leaving and any other relevant information which will significantly affect the value of the benefits.

Voluntary contributions and benefits should be disclosed; and

(x) for money purchase schemes (as in part I of schedule 6 to the Companies Act 1985) details of the contribution or allowance payable or made by the company in respect of each director during the period under review.

Removal

6.9 The circumstances in which a director may vacate his office are generally stated in the company's articles of association and usually comprise the following statements which follow those specified by regulation 81 of Table A:

(*a*) he ceases to be a director by virtue of any provision of the Act or he becomes prohibited by law from being a director;

(*b*) he becomes bankrupt or makes any arrangement or composition with his creditors generally;

(*c*) he is, or may be, suffering from mental disorder and either:

(i) he is admitted to hospital under the Mental Health Act 1983; or

(ii) an order is made by a court having jurisdiction in matters concerning mental disorder for his detention or for the appointment of a person to manage his property or affairs;

(*d*) he resigns his office by notice to the company (see Precedent D, Appendix 6A); or

(*e*) he is absent from board meetings for six consecutive months without the permission of the board and the directors resolve that his office be vacated.

The company's articles may further provide that a director may be removed from office by extraordinary resolution of the company, or that his office may terminate upon service of notice at the company's registered office by the company's holding company or majority shareholder. In the absence of any provisions in the articles of association, a director may nonetheless be removed from office by provisions contained in the Companies Act 1985.

Under CA 1985, s 303, the members may by ordinary resolution remove a director from office before his term of office has expired (see Precedent E, Appendix 6A), provided that special notice (see Precedent F, Appendix 6A) has been given to the company at its registered office of their intention to propose such a resolution at a general meeting convened for that purpose. It should be noted that the provisions of section 381A relating to written resolutions of members of private companies do not extend to resolutions passed under section 303.

The director in question is entitled under this section to receive a copy of the special notice and to prepare and have circulated to the members a written representation (unless upon application to the court, such representation is held to be defamatory). Furthermore, the director is entitled to attend and speak at the meeting at which his removal will be proposed.

The power of removal under section 303 co-exists with any such power contained elsewhere and cannot be set aside by anything in the articles or in any agreement between the company and the director. In addition, it is not the purpose of this section to deprive a director of any right to compensation or damages in respect of his appointment as a director or any appointment terminating with that as a director.

The resignation or removal of a director must be notified to Companies House on form 288b within 14 days of the event and, in the case of a listed company, to the Company Announcements Office of the London Stock Exchange without delay.

Powers of directors

General

6.10   The directors are responsible for the operation and management of a company both on a day-to-day basis and in the long term. Directors have extensive powers to manage the company and these are derived from the company's memorandum and articles of association. For instance, regulation 70 of Table A empowers the directors to exercise all the powers of the company subject to the provisions of the articles.

Articles of association commonly contain specific provisions and restrictions relating to the exercise of their powers, for example, borrowing powers, although the limitation of legitimate actions is usually kept to a minimum so as to facilitate the efficient running of the company. There are also statutory provisions restricting the powers of directors to ensure that the company is managed for the benefit of shareholders and employees, including the Insolvency Act 1986, the Company Directors' Disqualification Act 1986 and the Financial Services Act 1986.

The wide powers given to directors to act on behalf of the company mean that they are responsible for the arrangements relating to the fulfilment of the company's statutory duties. They can therefore be liable to penalties should the company fail to comply, and are sometimes personally liable for the consequences of their actions (e.g. for wrongful trading under the Insolvency Act 1986).

The directors act as agents of the company and cannot do anything which is not authorised by the company's memorandum of association. Any act by them which is *ultra vires* the company will be void and ineffective, except where the transaction can be enforced by an outsider (see 11.2 COMMERCIAL CONSIDERATIONS).

The directors' powers cannot be overruled by the members as they do not act as agent for some or even all the members. As such, their powers to appoint one of their number as managing director, to declare interim dividends and to sue in the company's name, have been treated as exclusive to them, and resolutions passed by members conflicting with these decisions are therefore ineffective. The members are, however, at liberty to alter the company's memorandum and articles of association by special resolution.

Directors should appreciate the obligations and responsibilities required of their office and understand the professional duty of care which a director as an officer of a company must bring to his position. The directors will commonly turn to the company secretary to enable him to carry out his duties in a professional manner.

The role of the company secretary

6.11   The company secretary is also an officer of the company as defined by CA 1985, s 744 and, as such, he is liable to the various penalties incurred if he fails to comply with the requirements of the Companies Act 1985. It is his duty to draw the directors' attention to any action which is required to be taken, and he may be liable for damages resulting from his negligence, as well as any attempt, through the articles of association or any contract, to exempt any director, or other officer of the company, from liability in respect of negligence, default, breach of duty or of trust.

CA 1985, s 727, does, however, provide that the courts may grant relief in any proceedings against an officer of the company, if it appears that the officer, although liable in respect of negligence, default, breach of duty or of trust, acted honestly and reasonably and under the circumstances of the case ought to be excused.

It is generally the duty of the company secretary to ensure that the board of directors acts in accordance with company legislation and the company's memorandum and articles of association (see Chapter 1). He should act on the instructions of the directors in filing all formal returns as required by the Companies Acts and maintaining the prescribed registers and records as well as the minute book, the despatch of notices of general meetings and the company's report and financial statements.

The relationship of the secretary to the board of directors and to individual directors will vary according to the size of the company and to whether the directors are executive or non-executive (see 6.5 above). The directors will commonly rely on the secretary for information and advice on all company matters, especially where they do not have first-hand experience, and the Cadbury Report (see 6.13 below) emphasised that all directors should have access to the secretary on such matters. It also recognised the importance of the secretary's role in corporate governance matters (see Appendix 6B).

The secretary should therefore be able to advise, guide and warn the directors of the danger of disqualification and possible personal liability. The secretary must be a competent and reliable person, and must be able to assist the directors in carrying out their duties. He must be able to carry out his duties in a satisfactory manner, without being biased towards any one director, as he is ultimately responsible for the performance of most of the duties imposed by the Companies Acts, which are generally delegated to him by the directors (see 1.1 THE COMPANY SECRETARY).

Corporate Governance

6.12   Corporate governance is a developing area which has seen the formation of two further committees since the Committee on the Financial Aspects of Corporate Governance under the chairmanship of Sir Adrian Cadbury first considered this issue. The Study Group on Directors' Remuneration chaired by Sir Richard Greenbury and the Committee on Corporate Governance under Sir Ronald Hampel's chairmanship have sought to develop the principles of corporate governance further.

The Cadbury Report

The Report of the Committee on the Financial Aspects of Corporate Governance (the 'Cadbury Report') was published on 1 December 1992. It defined corporate governance as the system by which companies are directed and controlled, and identifies the three elements of governance as:

(*a*)   the board of directors;

(*b*)   the shareholders; and

(*c*)   the auditors.

The Cadbury Report, with its accompanying Code of Best Practice (see Appendix 6B) sought to clarify and redress the balance between the respective roles and responsibilities of the directors, the shareholders and the auditors. The report charged the directors with the responsibility for corporate governance, the shareholders with the responsibility to ensure that directors and auditors appointed by them fall within an appropriate governance structure with the auditors providing an external and objective check on the directors' statements.

The Code itself covers the role and structure of the board of directors, the appointment and independence of non-executive directors, the determination of the executive directors' remuneration (subsequently superseded by the Greenbury recommendations) and the financial reporting and controls to be exercised by the board. The Code was primarily aimed at UK-registered companies listed on the London Stock Exchange, although the Code and the report's recommendations was regarded as relevant to many companies, whether public or private.

Since, the Auditing Practices Board adopted the recommendations of the Cadbury Report in relation to directors' and auditors' responsibilities, a statement by the auditors on these matters has been required in their report on the accounts for financial periods ending on or after 30 September 1993.

The Greenbury Report

The Greenbury Report on Directors' Remuneration was published on 17 June 1995. It sought to allay public concerns about the remuneration of directors by seeking to 'identify good practice in determining Directors' remuneration and prepare a Code of such practice for use by UK PLCs'. The Code (see Appendix 6D) was primarily aimed at listed companies. Although its principles were also recommended for non-listed companies.

The Greenbury Code covers a number of areas comprising the composition and role of the remuneration committee, disclosure and approval provisions, remuneration policy and service contracts and compensation. The Code is intended to work alongside Cadbury although it has extended and replaced the section in the Cadbury Code dealing with the remuneration of executive directors.

The Hampel Report

The aim of the Hampel Committee was to review the implementation of the findings of the Cadbury and Greenbury Committees and the Report goes on to endorse the overwhelming majority of the two earlier reports and their findings. According to the Hampel Report the 'objective of the new principles and code, like those of the Cadbury and Greenbury codes, is not to prescribe corporate behaviour in detail but to secure sufficient disclosure so that investors and others can assess companies' performance and governance practice and respond in an informed way'.

The Report itself sets out seventeen principles (which follow) on which the final combined set of principles and code is based. The Code addresses the three elements of governance identified by Cadbury and covers the composition and role of the board of directors together with directors' remuneration; the role of, and relationship with, the company's shareholders; and the board's accountability and its relationship with the company's auditors, as well as the function of the auditors.

1 The board (Principle A.I)
Every listed company should be headed by an effective board which should lead and control the company. (Endorses Cadbury).

2 **Chairman and CEO (Principle A.II)**
There are two key tasks at the top of every public company – the running of the board and the executive responsibility for the running of the company's business. A decision to combine these roles in one individual should be publicly explained.

3 **Board balance (Principle A.III)**
The board should include a balance of executive directors and non-executive directors (including independent non-executives) such that no individual or small group of individuals can dominate the board's decision taking. (Endorses Cadbury).

4 **Supply of information (Principle A.IV)**
The board should be supplied in a timely fashion with information in a form and of a quality appropriate to enable it to discharge its duties. (Endorses Cadbury).

5 **Appointments to the board (Principle A.V)**
There should be a formal and transparent procedure for the appointment of new directors to the board. The Committee recommends as good practice the adoption of a formal procedure for appointments to the board, with a nomination committee making recommendations to the full board. Individuals should also receive appropriate training following appointment and then as necessary to ensure that they are aware of their duties and responsibilities as director of a listed company.

6 **Re-election (Principle A.VI)**
All directors should be required to submit themselves for re-election at regular intervals and at least every three years. Companies adopting Table A currently allow managing directors and executive directors to hold office without being required to retire by rotation.

7 **The level and make-up of remuneration (Principle B.I)**
Levels of remuneration should be sufficient to attract and retain the directors needed to run the company successfully. The component parts of the remuneration should be structured so as to link rewards to corporate and individual performance.

8 **Procedure (Principle B.II)**
Companies should establish a formal and transparent procedure for developing policy on executive remuneration and for fixing the remuneration packages of individual directors.

9 **Disclosure (Principle B.III)**
The company's annual report should contain a statement of remuneration policy and details of the remuneration of each director.

10 **Shareholder voting (Principle C.I)**
Institutional shareholders have a responsibility to make considered use of their votes.

11 **Dialogue between companies and investors (Principle C.II)**
Companies and institutional shareholders should each be ready, where practicable, to enter into dialogue based on the mutual understanding of objectives.

12 Evaluation of governance disclosures (Principle C.III)
When evaluating companies' governance arrangements, particularly those relating to board structure and composition, institutional investors and their advisers should give due weight to all relevant factors down to their attention. Investors should show some flexibility in interpreting the company's compliance with a code of best practice and ought to listen to the directors' explanations. Investors should then judge their explanations on their merits.

13 The AGM (Principle C.IV)
Companies should use the AGM to communicate with private investors and encourage their participation.

14 Financial reporting (Principle D.I)
The board should present a balanced and understandable assessment of the company's position and prospects. (Endorses Cadbury).

15 Internal control (Principle D.II)
The board should maintain a sound system of internal control to safeguard shareholders' investment and the company's assets. The Report states that this covers financial, operational and compliance controls and risk management.

16 Relationship with auditors (Principle D.III)
The board should establish formal and transparent arrangements for maintaining an appropriate relationship with the company's auditors. (Endorses Cadbury).

17 External auditors (Principle D.IV)
The external auditors should independently report to shareholders in accordance with statutory and professional requirements and independently assure the board on the discharge of their responsibilities in accordance with professional guidelines.

The Committee envisaged that the requirement for companies to confirm compliance with the Cadbury Code in the annual report and accounts will be superseded by a new requirement to make a statement to show how the principles of corporate governance are being applied and how the company is complying with the code. Any significant diversions from the code would need to be justified.

Combined Code

Following the publication of this final report the Committee produced a set of principles and code of good corporate practice which embraces the work of the Cadbury, Greenbury and Hampel Committee. The Committee submitted to the London Stock Exchange a Combined Code which sought to bring together Hampel and the earlier codes. The Stock Exchange followed this up with a consultation document inviting views on the cohesiveness of the draft Combined Code and when the code should apply to listed companies.

The final version of the Combined Code (see Appendix 6E) was published during June 1998 and a related amendment was made to the Listing Rules.

Listed companies will be required to comply with the new listing rule for accounting periods ending on or after 31 December 1998. However, as with the earlier Codes, it will be of relevance to non-listed companies.

The Combined Code differs from the code in the committee's final report in a number of respects. In particular, the Code makes clear that in relation to the role of chairman and chief executive officer there should be a clear division of responsibilities at the head of the company which will ensure a balance of power and authority such that no one individual has unfettered powers of decision. Companies should also avoid paying more remuneration to directors than is necessary to attract and retain directors of the required calibre and no director should be involved in deciding his or her own remuneration.

Other codes of best practice

In addition to the above Codes, a number of institutional investors have produced their own corporate governance guidelines against which they have indicated they will measure the effectiveness of boards of companies in which they invest. These guidelines are in some cases more exacting than the above Codes on particular issues of concern to institutional investors. Boards may find that they will need to address the concerns of their shareholders even though they are complying with or adhering to the codes and principles of Cadbury, Greenbury and Hampel.

Board meetings

6.13   The Companies Act 1985 does not impose a requirement on the directors for the holding of board meetings. Indeed, regulation 88 of Table A merely provides that 'subject to the provisions of the articles, the directors may regulate their proceedings as they think fit'. For many companies, it is usual for meetings to be conducted on an informal basis, particularly where the directors and shareholders are the same people, or there are few directors or the directors can otherwise make decisions without notice or formality.

Unless the articles of association provide otherwise, directors can only exercise their powers collectively by passing resolutions at board meetings or by written resolution signed by all the directors (see 6.20 below). The company's articles will generally empower the directors to regulate their proceedings in respect of meetings. They should ensure that they comply with rules relating to:

(*a*)   the chairman's appointment (see 6.16 below);

(*b*)   notice (see 6.17 below);

(*c*)   quorum (see 6.18 below);

(*d*)   voting rights (see 6.19 below); and

(*e*)   recording of decisions (see 6.20 below).

The board of directors may comprise both executive and non-executive directors (see 6.5 above) and its composition should be such that power and authority is not reserved for too few members of the board. For this reason, the Cadbury Report advised that where possible the offices of chairman and the chief executive are not occupied by the same person and that the views of the non-executive directors, who should be sufficiently independent, carry significant weight in the board's decisions.

Matters specifically reserved for the approval of the board include the approval of the interim and final financial statements as well as the approval and recommendation respectively of the interim and final dividend. In addition, the board is responsible for the general management of the company, the appointment and removal of board and committee members as well as the company secretary. The Cadbury Committee also recommended that major capital projects, major contracts in the ordinary course of business and major investments are subject to board approval (see Appendix 6C).

Committees

6.14   The board of directors are generally authorised by the company's articles of association to delegate their powers to a committee comprising one or more directors (Table A, regulation 72). Such a committee will be formed for a particular purpose, for instance, the consideration of an item of business which cannot be properly discussed at a full board meeting without further examination.

Prior to setting up any committee, the directors should determine its relationship with the board, such as its terms of reference and its reporting requirements, as well as the regulations governing the proceedings of the committee, such as the number of directors which will constitute the quorum. Where the committee comprises two or more directors, Table A provides that, subject to any conditions imposed by the directors, the provisions of the articles governing the proceedings of directors will apply to the committee.

The board of directors may delegate responsibilities for the determination of executive directors' pay to a remuneration committee – for listed companies the Greenbury Committee's Code of Best Practice made this a requirement, and the selection and recommendation of suitable candidates for appointment as directors to a nomination committee. The Cadbury Report principally dealt with the establishment of an audit committee to recommend to the board suitable auditors for appointment, to review the financial statements prior to submission to the board and to discuss any matters of concern with the auditors. All listed companies are advised to establish an audit committee composed of (at least three) non-executive directors, the majority of whom should be independent of the management of the company.

Secretary's duties

6.15   The secretary's duties will vary according to the business to be conducted at the meeting but he must be ready to advise the chairman and the board, if requested to do so, on procedural points and to give his views on any matters referred to him. He should be in a position to alert the chairman to any proposed action which is unlawful or in conflict with the company's memorandum and articles of association, or any trust deed or any shareholders' pre-emption rights in the transfer or allotment of shares.

He must be aware of matters such as the inclusion of any other business which is not already on the agenda, where a director is aiming to get a quick decision without having had time to carefully consider the matter. It follows that the secretary should have available all necessary documents to enable him to perform his duties as required.

He must ensure that all confidential papers are removed and kept safely once the meeting is over.

Chairman

6.16   The articles of association will generally provide for the appointment and removal of a chairman at meetings of the directors (Table A, regulation 91). The directors may appoint one of their number as chairman of the board and, in this role, he may preside at every meeting of the directors at which he is present. In his absence, Table A provides for the appointment of an alternative chairman for the purpose of conducting the board meeting.

The chairman must ensure that the meeting has been properly convened, in that notice of the meeting has been validly served on all directors in accordance with the company's articles. He should also establish that the meeting is properly constituted by ensuring that his appointment is valid and that the specified quorum is present at the meeting. He will be responsible for the regulation of the meeting and should therefore ensure that the meeting is conducted as required by the articles.

The chairman has a duty to ensure that the board meeting is a proper forum for debate. He should allow each director the opportunity to express his own views on any matter before the board, should he wish to, and to hear the views of other directors on that matter. He must not show partiality to any director, nor allow a director to monopolise the meeting so that debate is stifled.

The chairman may adjourn the meeting at any time should he feel that there is any cause to do so, subject to any conditions imposed by the company's articles.

Notice and agenda

6.17   Unlike general meetings of the members, there is no statutory provision for the period of notice to be given to directors. Board meetings can therefore be at short notice or on specified dates as determined, so long as the directors are given reasonable notice or are notified in accordance with any provisions made in the articles of association. Indeed, written notice need not be given to the directors, unless required by the company's articles. However, all directors must be aware that in coming together the intention is to transact business of the company.

The articles usually provide that any one director may summon a meeting directly or request the secretary to do so. If there is default in giving notice, the meeting will be irregular. The secretary should ensure that all directors are given reasonable notice, so that they have sufficient time to enable them to attend, even if they have indicated that they will not wish to attend, otherwise the meeting may be invalid. Some articles may provide that where a director is absent from the UK, notice need not be given to that director (Table A, regulation 88). The notice of the meeting must contain:

(*a*) the place of the meeting; and

(*b*) the day, date and time of the meeting; and may also include:

(*c*) the business to be transacted; and

(*d*) the details of any special business to be transacted.

The agenda for the meeting may be circulated with the notice of the meeting, or it may alternatively form part of the notice (see (*c*) and (*d*) above). Any papers required to enable the directors to formulate their views on items to be discussed should be circulated with the agenda. The agenda will enable the chairman to conduct the business of the meeting in a logical manner and ensure that nothing is overlooked. It also helps the secretary in that he can refer to it as a guide in the drafting of the minutes after the meeting.

The secretary should prepare a separate form of agenda for the chairman, which will be more detailed than those of the directors and contain the points to be taken into account in reaching a decision. There should be wide margins for use by the chairman should he wish to make any notes and the secretary should refer to such notes, when preparing the minutes of the meeting.

Quorum

6.18 The quorum (i.e. the number of directors required to be present to constitute a valid meeting) is generally fixed by the articles, and may provide the directors with the power to determine the quorum for board meetings (Table A, regulation 89). Table A provides that, unless the directors determine otherwise, two directors will comprise the quorum and permits, in the absence of their appointors, alternate directors to be counted in the quorum.

The quorum must be a 'disinterested' quorum entitled to vote on the matters to be discussed; thus the quorum must be comprised of directors who are entitled to vote on the particular matter before the meeting. If a director is interested in a contract and is not permitted by the articles to vote on it, he may not be counted for the purpose of the quorum with respect to that particular business (see 6.28 below). The meeting is irregular if the required quorum is not present and no business can be transacted.

A company's articles will generally specify the minimum number of directors required for the company, as in regulation 64 of Table A, or will enable the members to determine the minimum by ordinary resolution. For many companies, the minimum number of directors will be equivalent to the number of directors comprising the quorum. In the case of a private company, the articles may provide that the minimum is one, and the quorum will be adjusted to one to enable the transaction of business by a sole director.

Where the number of directors falls below the number fixed as the quorum, the directors will be unable to transact valid business either in a meeting of the board, or by written resolution of the directors. Regulation 90 of Table A provides that in this circumstance the continuing directors or the sole remaining director may act only for the purpose of appointing a director to fulfil the quorum requirement or to convene a general meeting.

Regulation 90 does not specify the business to be conducted at the general meeting but its purpose would presumably be to enable the directors to transact valid business. This may be achieved either by the members appointing a director to meet the quorum specified in the articles or to alter the provision in the articles so that the quorum is reduced to less than or equal to the number of directors then in office.

Where the number of directors falls below one, in the case of a sole director, it would then be necessary for the members to requisition a general meeting, by notice to the company at its registered office, to authorise the secretary to convene a meeting at which a resolution could be passed to appoint new directors.

Voting

6.19   Commonly, a company's articles of association will allow each director one vote on each resolution proposed at a board meeting with the chairman being entitled to a second or casting vote in the case of deadlock (Table A, regulation 88). Voting is usually by a show of hands, though the chairman may alternatively determine the mood of the meeting and declare the resolution carried or defeated on that basis.

The chairman may exercise his own vote in favour of a resolution and his casting vote either for or against the resolution. In exercising his casting vote, the chairman should consider whether or not the passing of a resolution by such a vote is in the best interest of the company, particularly where the directors propose to commit the company to a controversial or expensive course of action.

Similarly, each director owes a fiduciary duty to the company and should therefore exercise his vote in the interest of the company (see 6.24 below).

For instance, the articles will usually provide that a director cannot vote on a resolution concerning a matter in which he has a material interest which conflicts or may conflict with the interest of the company (Table A, regulation 94). The provision may be relaxed in specific cases by the articles. Regulation 94 specifies the circumstances where it should not apply.

Having reached decisions on the items of business before the board, it is essential that the directors ensure all such decisions are implemented. This may involve delegation to the secretary, such as in giving notice of a general meeting, or to a committee of directors where such business requires further consideration before a decision can be made (see 6.14 above). It is common for the minutes of board meetings to indicate the person responsible for implementing a particular decision.

Minutes

6.20   Section 382 of the Act requires that a record of all meetings of the directors are kept. It is the secretary's duty, as delegated by the directors, to keep a clear and concise record of the minutes of each meeting. Relevant dates and figures should be recorded, as well as the main considerations that led to a decision, and names should only be given if requested by the speaker, except where a formal resolution is proposed and seconded (see 1.14 THE COMPANY SECRETARY).

Regulation 93 of Table A empowers a company to send out one or more copies of a proposed written resolution to each director for his consideration, with his consent to the passing of the resolution being indicated by signature on the document (see 3.52 THE STATUTORY RECORDS). The resolution is deemed to have been passed, and thus valid and effective, on the date the document is signed by the last director. A recent case, *Hood Sailmakers Ltd v Axford [1996] 4 All ER 830*, examined the provisions of regulation 98 of Table A 1948 (the predecessor to regulation 93) and the impact upon it of regulation 106 (now regulation 88 of Table A 1985). Regulation 93 states that '[a] resolution in writing signed by all the directors entitled to receive notice of a meeting of the directors . . . shall be as valid and effectual as if it had been passed at a meeting of directors', while regulation 88 deems it unnecessary to give notice of such a meeting to a director who is absent from the United Kingdom. This would imply that if all directors save one were outside the UK written resolutions could be passed by the remaining director only. If this were the case, the effect would be to override the quorum requirement expressed in regulation 99 (now regulation 89). However, the *Hood Sailmakers* case has confirmed that all directions must sign this document for the resolutions to be valid.

A resolution in writing is equivalent to a resolution passed at a board meeting and should be entered in the minute book as would be a board minute. Resolutions in writing are normally used where it is inconvenient to summon a board meeting, such as where there is not enough time to give notice for some urgent business or it is not possible for the directors to meet in the same place. Similarly, where the business to be conducted is of a routine nature, this may be dealt with by written resolution. It is usual for decisions of a sole director to be made by written resolution, since a meeting of the directors would only comprise one director in any case.

The Act contains provisions requiring the minutes of all meetings of the company to be open to inspection by members of the company. However, no statutory right of inspection is given to the members to enable them to examine the minute book containing decisions of the directors. The directors' minute book is available for inspection by any director or alternate director of the company, and must be open for inspection by the company's auditors.

The minutes are defined in the Companies Act 1985 as 'evidence' of the decisions taken at a meeting. Their evidential value is considered more fully in 3.51 THE STATUTORY RECORDS.

Modern technology

6.21   The directors are empowered by regulation 88 of Table A to regulate their proceedings in whatever manner they think fit, subject to any provisions in the company's articles. As such, this would open to them the possibility of the use of modern technology to the conduct of board meetings. For instance, meetings may be held over the telephone or the use of video-conferencing facilities would enable the directors to hold a meeting 'round the table' over long distances.

Meetings conducted by telephone or video-conferencing facilities present a number of difficulties, the most obvious one being the definition of a meeting established in *Sharp v Dawes (1876) 2 QBD 26* (see 7.26 MEMBERSHIP), that a meeting involves the coming together of two or more persons. Such meetings would not only appear to fail this test but also the quorum requirement.

Meetings conducted by telephone, even on a conference call, present difficulties due to the inability of each director to see the other and although impersonation is a potential problem, a more practical problem would be misunderstanding any decisions agreed or being unable to hear clearly what is being said. Such meetings would practically only take place between two or three directors where it is possible to bring 'together' all directors of the company without prior notice of a meeting. Any meetings conducted by telephone which excluded any director may be invalidated by the notice provisions.

With video-conferencing facilities, it is possible to conduct a meeting between several locations in a manner similar to a meeting where the directors are physically present in the same room, thereby overcoming some of the practical problems inherent with meetings over the telephone. Such facilities would be useful where the number of directors is large and they are dispersed between, say, two or three locations. Meetings conducted in this manner would require more formality, since it would be necessary to give sufficient notice to all directors.

For meetings held between several locations, it would be difficult to determine where the meeting actually took place, or where the meeting is held across different time zones, the date or time of the meeting. To avoid ambiguity, it would be useful to establish rules relating to such meetings. For instance, the directors could determine that all meetings of a UK-incorporated company are deemed to be held in the UK and that the time of the meeting is to be expressed in Greenwich Meantime (GMT).

Where directors are separated by long distances, it is possible to pass decisions by written resolution of the directors. This would require sending copies of the resolution to each director by post and awaiting the return of each signed document before the resolution was passed. With the use of facsimile machines, it is possible to obtain a director's consent to a particular course of action within hours rather than days, by the transmission of a proposed resolution to each director and the receipt of a signed facsimile from each director. Any such signed resolutions should be supported by a copy of the resolution with the director's original signature.

Generally, it would be advisable, in the absence of any express provisions in the company's articles of association, for all meetings conducted by the above means to be confirmed in writing by the directors party to the decisions made, such as by written resolution of the directors. Alternatively, the directors should consider updating the articles to address such problems as the quorum requirement, so that they are able to take advantage of the flexibility offered by modern technology.

Duties of directors

General

6.22   There are certain duties which a person running a business is obliged to carry out regardless of the legal form of the business. Essentially, these duties are to comply with specific business legislation such as employment, health and safety at work, consumer, income tax and VAT legislation. The duties of a company director are, however, considerably more onerous than those of a sole trader or partner.

A director has certain legal duties but also has certain fiduciary duties and a duty of skill and care which cannot be so clearly defined. No contract can exempt a director from liability for negligence, default or breach of trust.

Fiduciary duty

6.23   In carrying out their duties, directors are in a fiduciary position, i.e. in a position of trust. Because of their fiduciary position, directors also owe certain duties to the company and must act *'bona fide'* in the interest of the company. The duty is owed primarily to the company and not to individual shareholders, or to creditors of the company (however, see 6.35 below). It is a subjective duty and the directors must act *'bona fide* in what they consider — not what the courts may consider — is in the interests of the company, and not for any collateral purpose' *per* Lord Greene MR in *Re Smith & Fawcett Ltd* [*1942*] *Ch 304.*

A director must not abuse his position as an agent of the company or trustee of the company's property. He must, therefore, not put himself in a position where there is a conflict of interest between his beneficiaries and his personal interests. Should any personal interests or conflicts arise, he is under an obligation to disclose the existence of the interest or conflict.

It appears that a fiduciary will not commit a breach of this rule merely by getting into a position of potential abuse, but that if he is in such a position, he is obliged to prefer the interest of the beneficiary. It therefore appears that a director will not be in breach of these rules if he were a director of a competing company. He may, however, find himself with conflicting duties to two separate beneficiaries.

The courts will only interfere if no reasonable director could possibly have concluded that a particular course of action was in the interest of the company.

In *Re W & M Roith Ltd* [*1967*] *1 WLR 432,* a director entered into a service contract with his company in order to provide a pension for his wife in the event of his death. He did not give any consideration to the fact that the contract was not for the benefit of the company and accordingly the contract was held not to be binding on the company.

The interest of the company is not necessarily the same as its shareholders. Directors may, therefore, have to balance fairly the different interests of the company as a going concern, different classes of shareholders and those of present and future shareholders.

Fair dealing

6.24   Directors, by their fiduciary position, must comply with the fair dealing rule and not abuse their position or attempt to profit personally from it without complying with the requirements relating to full disclosure to, and the approval of, the rest of the board or shareholders. Thus, directors must not aim to enrich themselves without the knowledge and consent of the shareholders, otherwise personal liability will arise from the fact that a profit has been made.

In *Regal (Hastings) Limited v Gulliver* [*1967*] *1 AER 378,* four of the directors and the company's solicitor had made a profit on the sale of a subsidiary company's shares to which they had subscribed in their own right. They were made to account for the profit. In summing up, Lord Russell said:

'The rule of equity which insists on those who by the use of a fiduciary position make a profit, being liable to account for that profit, in no way depends on fraud or absence of *bona fides*; or upon such questions or considerations as whether the profit would or should otherwise have gone to the plaintiff, or whether he took a risk or acted as he did for the benefit of the plaintiff, or whether the plaintiff has in fact been damaged or benefited by his action.'

In this case it was pointed out that, if the directors had obtained the consent of Regal's shareholders in general meeting, they could have retained their profit. This case also highlighted the fact that the directors' profits need not be at the expense of the company before they have to account for it.

Thus, essentially, a director is expected to act honestly and in a reasonable belief that he is acting for the benefit of the company. He must not act outside the company's objects or make a personal profit from a transaction, even if it also benefits the company.

Duty of skill and care

6.25   Whilst a director may not be liable for making an error of judgement, he is expected to perform his duties to the best of his ability on the basis of his knowledge and experience. In general, an executive director would normally be expected to have the skills necessary to carry out his job but even non-executive directors must exercise reasonable skill and care in the exercise of their duties.

The case of *Re City Equitable Fire Insurance Co Ltd [1925] Ch 407* defined the skill and care expected of a director as being the degree of skill and care that can reasonably be expected from the professional qualifications held by the director. This applies equally whether the director is a non-executive as well as an executive (*Dorchester Finance Co Ltd v Stebbing [1989] BCLC 498*). Furthermore, a greater degree of skill and care is expected from an executive director who is an experienced businessman than from an inexperienced non-executive director.

Thus, in general, although there are no clear guidelines to define the degree of skill and care expected of a director, the courts in determining possible liability will look at the qualifications and experience of the director and his status within the company (e.g. finance director or non-executive) to establish the degree of skill and care which he could reasonably have been expected to display.

Disclosure of directors' interests

General

6.26   Directors are responsible to the members of the company for their actions. They must, in carrying out their duties, bear in mind the interest of the members and employees of the company, and must at all times act in good faith for the benefit of the company.

The Companies Act 1985 imposes certain duties on directors so that they cannot exploit their privileged position within a company and to avoid conflicts of interest. To achieve this aim directors are obliged to make full disclosure of certain interests, so that others connected with the company are kept fully aware of the true interests of the director.

Directors therefore have a statutory duty in relation to:

(*a*)   disclosure of interests in shares and debentures (see 6.27 below);

(*b*)   disclosure of interests in contracts (see 6.28 below);

(*c*)   loans to directors (see 6.29 below);

(*d*)   obtaining approval of substantial property transactions (see 6.30 below); and

(*e*)   disclosure of option dealings (see 6.31 below).

A listed company must notify without delay the Company Announcements Office of The London Stock Exchange following disclosure to the company by a director under section 324 of the Companies Act 1985 (as extended by section 328 of the Act) of any information relating to any interests in the company's listed securities or of any options, rights or obligations relating to such securities of that director or of any person connected to him. Should the company receive this information otherwise than by disclosure by the director, the company is still required to make such information public.

A company listed on the London Stock Exchange is required by the Listing Rules to adopt a code of dealing in relation to the company's listed securities. The Model Code in the Appendix to Chapter 16 of the Listing Rules sets a minimum standard, although a company may adopt a code with more exacting rules. The code must be adopted by board resolution and will apply to dealings by the company's directors and by any employee of the company or any director or employee of a group company who by reason of his office or employment is likely to be in possession of unpublished price-sensitive information. The Model Code is now a continuing obligation and companies will no longer be required to adopt the Code each time it is amended.

Part V of the Criminal Justice Act 1993 introduced provisions relating to insider dealing and, by virtue of Schedule 6 to this Act, the Company Securities (Insider Dealing) Act 1985 is repealed in its entirety. Section 52 of the 1993 Act provides that an individual who has information as an insider is guilty of insider dealing if he deals in securities that are price-affected securities in relation to this information in circumstances where the acquisition or disposal of shares occurs on a regulated market, or he relies on a professional intermediary or is himself acting as a professional intermediary. It is also an offence if a person in possession of such information encourages another person to deal in these securities in the above circumstances or improperly discloses the information to another person.

Section 53 contains defences to the above offences and Schedule 1 to the Act also provides special defences to a person whose business is as a market maker, or who can show that the information was market information or that he acted in conformity with the price stabilisation rules under section 48 of the Financial Services Act 1986. An individual guilty of insider dealing shall be liable on summary conviction to a fine not exceeding the statutory maximum (currently £5,000) or imprisonment for a term of not more than six months or both; or on conviction on indictment to a fine or imprisonment for a term of not more than seven years or both.

Disclosure of interests in shares and debentures

6.27   Any person who becomes a director has a duty under section 324 of the Companies Act 1985 to notify the company of any interests he has in shares or debentures of the company, or of its holding or subsidiary company. Similarly, a director who alters his shareholdings in the company must also notify the company of the alteration. This obligation extends to include holdings held by 'connected persons' i.e. in trust or by a director's spouse, children and stepchildren.

The following information must be supplied by the director, and kept in the register of directors' interests:

(*a*)   particulars of interests subsisting on the date of appointment of the director;

(*b*)   details of subsequent acquisitions or disposals and the price paid;

(*c*)   details of assignment of rights granted by the company to subscribe for shares or debentures, giving the consideration received; and

(*d*)   details of the grant by any other company in the group of a right to subscribe for its shares or debentures.

The proper maintenance of the register of directors' interests depends on the director concerned making the notification. Failure to notify within the time limit (three days) renders the director liable to imprisonment or a fine or both.

It should be noted that it is not the secretary's duty to search for the information, only to record it once it has been provided by the directors concerned. (Also see 3.18 THE STATUTORY RECORDS.)

Disclosure of interests in contracts

6.28   Where a director has an interest (direct or indirect) in any contracts with the company, he is obliged in accordance with section 317 of the Companies Act 1985 to disclose at a meeting of the directors any interest in a contract or proposed contract with the company. For the purpose of CA 1985, s 317 'contract' includes any transaction or arrangement entered into on or after 22 December 1980.

The requirement to disclose includes indirect interests such as the interests of connected persons as defined in section 346, except where such a person is also a director of the company. A 'connected person' under CA 1985, s 346 is defined as follows:

'(2) A person is connected with a director of a company if, but only if, he (not being himself a director of it) is —

(*a*)   the director's spouse, child or step-child; or

(*b*)   except where the context otherwise requires, a body corporate with which the director is associated; or

(*c*)   a person acting in his capacity as trustee of any trust the beneficiaries of which include —

    (i)   the director, his spouse or any children or step-children of his, or

    (ii)   a body corporate with which he is associated, or of a trust whose terms confer a power on the trustees that may be exercised for the benefit of the director, his spouse, or any children or step-children of his, or any such body corporate; or

(*d*)   a person acting in his capacity as partner of that director or of any person who, by virtue of paragraph (a), (b) or (c) of this subsection, is connected with that director; or

(*e*)   a Scottish firm in which —

    (i)   that director is a partner;

    (ii)   a partner is a person who, by virtue of paragraph (a), (b) or (c) above, is connected with that director; or

    (iii)   a partner is a Scottish firm in which that director is a partner or in which there is a partner who, by virtue of paragraph (a), (b) or (c) above, is connected with that director.'

Notice must be given at the first meeting at which any contract placed by or with the company is discussed or the first meeting after the director (or the connected person) obtains an interest in the matter.

A company's articles of association can provide that the interested director shall not vote or be counted in the quorum at a meeting at which a contract in which he is interested is discussed, unless his interest is as a shareholder or he represents an associate company.

If the director does not disclose his interest, he is not covered by the protection in the articles of association which permit him to be interested in a contract and he may not be allowed to keep any private profit which he may make. If the breach of duty to disclose is subsequently discovered, the contract will be *prima facie* voidable and can be cancelled by the company, and the director will be liable to criminal proceedings and to a fine on conviction.

Directors' interests in a contract must be disclosed in the notes to audited accounts in accordance with CA 1985, s 232.

Loans to directors

6.29 The general rule is that a company is prohibited from making a loan to a director of a company or of its holding company (CA 1985, s 330(2)). The Act draws a distinction between loans made by private companies and loans made to directors of relevant companies. The position for loans by relevant companies is more restrictive, where a relevant company is defined as a public company or a company which falls into one of the following categories:

(*a*) the company is a subsidiary of a public company; or

(*b*) it is a subsidiary of a company which has as another subsidiary a public company; or

(*c*) it has a subsidiary which is a public company.

A relevant company is prohibited from making a quasi-loan to a director of the company or of its holding company, or making a loan or quasi-loan to any person connected with such a director. In addition, a relevant company is not permitted to enter into a credit transaction as creditor for such a director or a person connected with that director.

In certain circumstances (CA 1985, ss 332–338), the general prohibition on loans by a company to its directors is relaxed to allow for certain loans to be made, being:

(i) a quasi-loan by a *relevant* company to a director of the company or its holding company not exceeding a total of £5,000 provided the terms of the loan require reimbursement within two months of the loan being made (CA 1985, s 332);

(ii) a loan by a company to a director of the company or of its holding company not exceeding a total of £5,000 (CA 1985, s 334);

(iii) a transaction not exceeding a total of £10,000 entered into for a director by a *relevant* company in the ordinary course of business and on terms no more favourable than for any unconnected person (CA 1985, s 335);

(iv) a loan by a company for expenditure incurred, or to be incurred, by a director in the performance of his duties as an officer of the company, subject to such expenditure being approved by the company in general meeting and, in the case of a *relevant* company, not exceeding a total of £20,000. If approval is not given at the general meeting at which the transaction is disclosed or before the next annual general meeting, then the loan must be repaid within six months of the date of that meeting (CA 1985, s 337);

(v) a loan or quasi-loan to a director of a company or of its holding company (for a *relevant* company not exceeding a total of £100,000), where the ordinary business of the company includes the making of loans or quasi-loans, made in the ordinary course of business and on terms no more favourable than for any unconnected person of the same financial standing (CA 1985, s 338).

A quasi-loan in these circumstances is a transaction under which the company agrees to pay, or pays otherwise than in pursuance of an agreement, a sum for a director or agrees to reimburse, or reimburses otherwise than in pursuance of an agreement, expenditure incurred by another party for the director:

(A) on terms that the director (or a person on his behalf) will reimburse the company; or

(B) in circumstances giving rise to a liability on the director to reimburse the company.

(CA 1985, s 331(3).)

The rules on loans to directors also apply to:

(I) connected persons such as a spouse or minor children (see 6.29 above);

(II) any company in which he is interested in at least one-fifth of the equity share capital; and

(III) any company in which he can control the exercise of more than one-fifth of the votes.

Any transactions not covered by the exceptions in sections 332 to 338 of the Act are in breach of the Companies Act 1985 and are voidable. The directors concerned are also liable to make good any loss for which repayment is not obtained from a third party and to account for his own profit, unless he can prove that reasonable steps were taken to ensure that the Companies Act 1985 was being complied with.

Substantial property transactions

6.30   Should a director wish to purchase any non-cash asset from a company or to dispose of such an asset to the company, then the approval of the members by an ordinary resolution at general meeting is required (CA 1985, s 320(1)).

'Non-cash asset' means any property or interest in property other than cash e.g. lease, shares, patents, copyrights, the benefits of book debts etc. (CA 1985, s 739).

The following should be noted, when considering such a transaction:

(*a*) shareholders' approval is only required if:

(i) the value of the assets is more than £2,000 and exceeds the lesser of £100,000 or 10% of the company's net assets;

(ii) the transaction is not between companies within a wholly-owned group.

(*b*) a transaction which does not receive the approval of the members will generally be voidable; and

(*c*) in relation to the transaction, if the board of directors exceeds any limitation of its powers under the company's articles, it will be voidable at the instance of the company in accordance with CA 1985, s 322A (see 6.33 below).

Where (*c*) applies, the directors will be liable to account to the company for any gain made directly or indirectly from the transaction and shall indemnify the company for any loss or damage which arises. The transaction can be ratified by the members in general meeting.

Option dealings

6.31 Section 323 of the Companies Act 1985 makes it an offence for a director of a company to buy (but not to sell):

(*a*) a right to call for delivery at a specified price and within a specified time of a specified number of 'relevant shares', or a specified amount of 'relevant debentures'; or

(*b*) a right to make delivery at a specified price and within a specified time of a specified number of 'relevant shares' or a specified amount of relevant debentures; or

(*c*) a right (as he may elect) to call for delivery at a specified price and within a specified time of a specified number of 'relevant shares' or a specified amount of 'relevant debentures'.

'Relevant shares' are shares in the director's company or any other body corporate which is the company's subsidiary or holding company, of which there has been granted a listing on a stock exchange.

'Relevant debentures' are debentures in the director's company or any other body corporate which is the company's subsidiary or holding company of which there has been granted a listing on a stock exchange.

'Price' includes any consideration other than money.

Section 323 of the CA 1985 applies to a director's spouse, infant children and other connected persons (CA 1985, s 327) but it is a defence if the director can show that he had no reason to believe that the connected person was a director of the company in question.

The penalty for non-compliance of CA 1985, s 323 is a fine or imprisonment or both.

Intervention by the courts

6.32 Generally, the courts are reluctant to intervene in the acts or decisions of the directors, except in the following circumstances where the directors:

(*a*)   have not acted honestly and in good faith (*bona fide*);

(*b*)   have exceeded their powers derived from the company's memorandum and articles of association (see 6.33 below);

(*c*)   have caused the company to act illegally; or

(*d*)   have in their actions breached the rules as established in the case of *Associated Provincial Picture Houses Ltd v Wednesbury Corporation* [*1948*] *1 KB 223*, known as the *'Wednesbury Principles'*, being that the directors have:

  (i)   taken into account matters which they ought not to take into account and acted in their own or a third party's interest;

  (ii)   acted for an improper purpose;

  (iii)   refused to take into account or neglected to take into account matters which they ought to take into account;

  (iv)   done something which no reasonable board of directors could have considered to be in the company's interest, or which they actually thought would be injurious to its interests.

In order to safeguard their position directors should ensure that their reasons and the facts which they took into account, as well as the arguments against or for any proposed course of action, are fully recorded in time minutes of the board meeting.

Limitations on company's right to set aside a transaction

6.33   Section 35A of the Companies Act 1985 limits a company's right to have a transaction entered into by a third party acting in good faith with the company set aside by providing that:

(*a*)   the validity of an act of a company shall not be called into question on the grounds of lack of capacity by reason of anything in the company's memorandum (CA 1985, s 35(1)); and

(*b*)   in favour of a person dealing in good faith with a company, the power of the board of directors to bind the company, or authorise others to do so, shall be deemed to be free of any limitation under the company's constitution (CA 1985, s 35A(1)).

A shareholder may still bring proceedings to restrain acts which are beyond the company's capacity or beyond the directors' powers and the directors are therefore still under a duty to observe any limitations on their powers in the company's memorandum of association, as well as actions which, but for CA 1985, s 35(1), would be beyond the company's capacity. Such actions may only be ratified by special resolution of the company. Relief from liability relating to actions beyond the company's capacity may be agreed by a separate special resolution.

CA 1985, s 35A(1) does not, however, affect any liability incurred by the directors, where they have exceeded their power, although these actions can be ratified by ordinary resolution of the company.

(i) For the purpose of CA 1985, s 35A a person is not to be regarded as acting in bad faith merely because he knows that an act is beyond the powers of the directors. He is presumed to be acting in good faith unless the contrary is proven.

(ii) Limitations on the directors' powers under the company's memorandum and articles of association include limitations derived from:

(A) a resolution of the company in general meeting or meeting of any class of shareholders; or

(B) any agreement between the members of the company or any class of shareholders.

Exception to sections 35, 35A and 35B of the Companies Act 1985

6.34   Section 322A of the Companies Act 1985 seeks to restrict the circumstances in which a director may contract with the company of which he is a director, a person connected with him or a company with whom the director is associated (see 6.28 above) where the company has acted *ultra vires* and under which the company may not have the transaction set aside.

Section 322A applies in circumstances where a company enters into a transaction with a director of the company or of its holding company or a person connected with him (see 6.28 above), and the board of directors, in connection with the transaction, exceeds any limitation on its powers under the company's constitution.

This section states that such transactions are voidable at the instance of the company, notwithstanding the provisions of CA 1985, s 35A (see 6.32 above).

In relation to companies which are charities the operation of sections 35 and 35A of the CA 1985 will be restricted by section 65 of the Charities Act 1993 (see 11.9 COMMERCIAL CONSIDERATIONS). It provides that sections 35 and 35A of the CA 1985 shall not apply to charitable companies except in favour of a person who:

(*a*) gives full consideration in money or money's worth in relation to the act in question; and

(*b*) does not know that the act is not permitted by the company's memorandum or is beyond the powers of the directors or that the company is a charity.

A private company limited by shares or by guarantee, having only one member, is permitted to enter into contracts with that member. However, where the sole member is a director of the company and the company enters into any contract with that member which is not:

(i)   reduced to writing; nor

(ii)   made in the ordinary course of the company's business,

the company is required, by virtue of section 322B of the CA 1985, to set out the terms of the contract in a written memorandum or record such terms in the minutes of the first board meeting following the making of the contract. For this purpose, a sole member who is a shadow director will be treated as a director under this section.

Liability of directors

General

6.35   In carrying out his duties, certain standards are expected of a director. To avoid liability for acts done by him he must be able to show that he acted honestly and reasonably and that he ought fairly to be excused. He may be personally liable if he is negligent and makes a misrepresentation in that capacity.

Since the introduction of the Insolvency Act 1986 and the coming into force of the Company Directors' Disqualification Act 1986, there has been an increased possibility for directors to be disqualified and made personally liable for the company's debts. A liquidator or receiver has a statutory duty to report on the conduct of directors as well as shadow directors or failed companies. A report must be made to the Department of Trade and Industry if it is found that there have been activities which could lead to a director being declared unfit by the courts. (See 9.33 BORROWING AND SECURITY.)

Under the Company Directors' Disqualification Act 1986, the director of a company may be disqualified from acting as a director of any company for a period of between two and 15 years, depending upon the nature of the offence committed under this Act. The circumstances in which an application may be made for the director's disqualification are as follows:

(*a*)   he has been guilty of three or more defaults in complying with companies legislation in relation to the filing of documents with the Registrar of Companies during a period of five years prior to an application for his disqualification;

(*b*)   he is, or was, a director of a company which has at any time become insolvent and that his conduct as a director of that company makes him unfit to be concerned in the management of a company;

(*c*)   he has carried on business with the intention of defrauding the creditors of the company or any other person, or for a fraudulent purpose as defined under section 213 of the Insolvency Act 1986 (see 6.36 below); or

(*d*)   he was the director of a company which has gone into insolvent liquidation, and knew, or ought to have known that the company could not avoid insolvent liquidation; known as wrongful trading under section 214 of the Insolvency Act 1986 (see 6.36 below).

A director who acts whilst disqualified or whilst an undischarged bankrupt is liable to imprisonment or a fine, or both, and is personally liable for debts incurred by the company whilst he was involved in the management of the company. Any person (including the company secretary) who knowingly acts on the instructions of a disqualified director is also personally liable. In both cases the liability is joint and several with the company and any other person who is liable.

In deciding whether to disqualify a director (or shadow director) the courts will take into account several factors such as:

(i) breach of faith or duty owed by the director to the company;

(ii) the use of the company's assets for the director's own benefit;

(iii) the company's failure to keep proper records or file statutory returns;

(iv) failure to produce annual accounts;

(v) causing a company's insolvency;

(vi) failure to supply customers with their goods even though they have been paid for; and

(vii) in an insolvency, failure to comply with duties relating to statement of affairs, attendance at meetings, surrender of company property.

Under the Companies Act 1985, the director of the company may be liable to default fines or other penalties (see above) for his failure to:

(A) file documents in due time with the Registrar of Companies, such as the annual return, audited accounts, various notifications and resolutions;

(B) convene and hold an annual general meeting;

(C) register a charge, which is registrable under the Companies Act 1985; or

(D) afford pre-emption rights to the existing members of a company, pursuant to CA 1985, s 89(1).

In addition, a director may incur personal liability under the Insolvency Act 1986 for:

(I) wrongful trading (see 6.36 below);

(II) fraudulent trading (see 6.37 below); or

(III) acting while disqualified (also under the Company Directors' Disqualification Act 1986).

In the event that a company is struck off the register maintained at Companies House and is dissolved, either as a result of the Registrar of

Companies taking action against the company (CA 1985, s 652) or at the request of the directors (CA 1985, s 652A), the directors remain personally liable for any liabilities of the company for a period of 20 years from its dissolution. (See 9.26 BORROWING AND SECURITY.) Thisperiod of personal liability is reduced to two years if the company is removed from the register as a result of its liquidation under the procedures contained in the Insolvency Act 1986.

Most of the personal liability provisions of the Insolvency Act 1986 only apply where a company is in liquidation and involve the directors contributing to the company's assets for distribution by the liquidators.

Wrongful trading

6.36　　Section 214 of the Insolvency Act 1986 implies that directors owe a duty to creditors where a company has gone into insolvent liquidation and the director knew, or ought to have known, that there was no reasonable prospect that the company should avoid this situation.

On application by the liquidator, the court may make a director personally liable to contribute to the company's assets (and disqualification for up to 15 years) where that director knew, or ought to have concluded prior to the liquidation, that there was no reasonable prospect that the company would avoid going into insolvent liquidation. A director will not be made personally liable where he can show that he has taken every step prior to liquidation to minimise the potential loss to the company's creditors.

In *Re Produce Marketing Consortium Ltd (No 2)* *[1987]* *BCLC 520* the court, in deciding whether a director of an insolvent company knew that there was no reasonable prospect of the company avoiding liquidation, ruled that the director be judged by the standards of a person fulfilling that function with reasonable diligence, as well as the functions entrusted to that particular director. The two directors claimed they only became aware of the insolvent condition of the company when they received the draft accounts in January 1987. The court held that they must have had the knowledge at the time when the accounts should have been laid before the company in general meeting in July 1986, also that they were closely involved in the business and had delayed the preparation of the accounts.

It is a financial question as to whether a company is insolvent and any director with responsibility for accounting is therefore expected to display a great degree of diligence in this area and is thus more likely to be found liable for wrongful trading. However, the Insolvency Act 1986 makes no reference to trading in the knowledge that the company cannot meet its liabilities. Directors may be able to continue trading whilst a company is technically insolvent if there is a *reasonable* prospect that they can trade out of the difficulties, or that an arrangement with creditors will solve the problems. This is to prevent the abuse of limited liability, and it is a test for negligence rather than for fraud; as such, the tests are objective.

In order to reduce the risk of being found liable for wrongful trading, a director should:

(*a*)   ensure that his job description is accurately defined;

(*b*)   ensure that the company has a system for producing accounts and information timeously and within the limits set by the Companies Act 1985; and

(*c*)   insist on his concern being recorded in board minutes where he can see that the company is insolvent but the other directors disagree.

The standard of skill and care to be shown by a director to avoid liability is the highest that he possesses and that a person carrying out his functions can reasonably be expected to possess.

Fraudulent trading

6.37   Pursuant to section 213 of the Insolvency Act 1986, a liquidator may apply to the court for an order making a director personally liable to contribute to a company's assets (and disqualify him for up to 15 years) where he is of the opinion that the director was knowingly party to the carrying on of the company's business with *intent* to defraud creditors. In the case of *Re William C Leitch Bros [1932] 2 Ch 71* the 'intent' to defraud was held to be the continuance of business and the incurring of further debts when there is to the *knowledge* of the directors no reasonable prospect of creditors *ever* receiving payment of their debts.

In this way fraudulent trading can be contrasted to wrongful trading in that in wrongful trading no 'fraudulent intent' need be proved, only negligence.

The Companies Act 1985, s 458 also makes a director liable to imprisonment or a fine, or both, if the director was knowingly a party to carrying on business with fraudulent intent. This applies whether or not the company is in liquidation.

Liability as a signatory

6.38   Section 349(4) of the Companies Act 1985 requires that any bill of exchange, promissory note, endorsement, cheque or order for money or goods purporting to be signed by, or on behalf of the company, must state the company's name in legible characters.

Any officer of the company who fails to comply with CA 1985, s 349(4) is liable to a fine and, in default of payment by the company, may become personally liable to the holder of any such cheque or bill of exchange. (See 11.13 COMMERCIAL CONSIDERATIONS.)

Liability for contempt

6.39   If a company is judicially restrained from carrying out certain acts, or gives an undertaking to that effect and the director whose duty it is to take reasonable steps to ensure that the order is obeyed, deliberately fails to do so and the order is breached, then that director may be personally liable and is in contempt of his duties.

In *Attorney General for Tuvalu and another v Philatelic Distribution Corp and others* [*1990*] *BCLC 245* the Court of Appeal stated that although the director was not knowingly party to the breach, 'where a company was ordered not to do certain acts or gave an undertaking to like effect and a director was aware of the order or undertaking he was under a duty to take reasonable steps to ensure that the order was obeyed and if he wilfully failed to take those steps and the order or undertaking was breached he can be punished for contempt'. Accordingly the director in this case was committed to prison for contempt of court notwithstanding that he was not a party to the breach.

Indemnity for liability

6.40   Most companies' articles of association will generally include an indemnity clause indemnifying officers of the company where proceedings are brought against them so that they will not have to bear the costs of any legal action brought against them, and an insurance policy to that effect can be taken out by the company. Regulation 118 of Table A provides a model regulation on directors' and other officers' liability.

Policies may cover legal liability for 'wrongful acts' such as breach of trust, breach of duty, act, negligence, error, omission, mis-statement and misleading statement. It must be noted, however, that section 310 of the Act makes void any provision exempting an officer of the company from liability or indemnity, except where the officer is successful in defending the proceedings brought against him.

Section 310(3) of the Companies Act 1985 specifically authorises a company to purchase and maintain for its officers insurance policies against such liability (see 13.54–13.59 INSURANCE ADMINISTRATION). Where, in any financial year, a company has purchased or maintained any such insurance, that fact must be stated in the directors' report.

Precedents

A. Appointment of a Director

'It was Resolved that pursuant to regulation [   ] of the Articles of Association of the company [   ] be and is hereby elected a Director of the company with immediate effect.'

B. Re-Election of Retiring Directors

(i)   'It was Resolved that [   ] a Director who had been appointed since the last Annual General Meeting and in accordance with the company's Articles of Association, now retiring, be and is hereby re-elected a Director of the company.'

(ii) 'It was Resolved that [   ] a Director retiring by rotation in accordance with the company's Articles of Association, be and is hereby re-elected a Director of the company.'

(iii) 'It was Resolved that the Directors who had been appointed since the incorporation of the company and in accordance with the company's Articles of Association now retiring, be and they are hereby re-elected Directors of the company.'

C. Ratification of Directors Acts

'(i) That Messrs [   ] being the Directors who ceased to hold office by failing to be re-elected in accordance with the company's Articles of Association be and they are hereby appointed and re-elected as Directors of the company; and

(ii) All legal acts of the aforementioned persons acting as Directors of the company on behalf of the company in accordance with the authority given by the Memorandum and Articles of Association and exercised prior to the date of this resolution be and they are hereby ratified and confirmed notwithstanding any defects in any appointments that might otherwise cause their validity to be in doubt.'

D. Director's Resignation Letter

'The Directors
> Limited

199

Dear Sirs

I hereby tender my resignation as a Director of the company with effect from the close of business at today's date and confirm that I have no outstanding claims whatsoever against the company.

Yours faithfully

.....................................,'

E. Removal of a Director

'That [   ] be and he is hereby removed from his office as a Director of the company with immediate effect.'

F. Special Notice for the Removal of a Director

'The Directors
> Limited

199

Dear Sirs

I/We hereby give notice pursuant to Section 303 and Section 379 of the Companies Act 1985 of my/our intention to propose the following ordinary resolution at the next Annual General Meeting of the company.

> 'That [   ] be and he is hereby removed from his office as a Director of the company with immediate effect'.

Yours faithfully

.....................................,'

Report of the Committee on the Financial Aspects of Corporate Governance (The 'Cadbury Report')

The Code of Best Practice

1 The Board of Directors

1.1 The board should meet regularly, retain full and effective control over the company and monitor the executive management.

1.2 There should be a clearly accepted division of responsibilities at the head of the company, which will ensure a balance of power and authority, such that no one individual has unfettered powers of decision. Where the chairman is also the chief executive, it is essential that there should be a strong and independent element on the board, with a recognised senior member.

1.3 The board should include non-executive directors of sufficient calibre and number for their views to carry significant weight in the board's decisions.

1.4 The board should have a formal schedule of matters specifically reserved to it for decision to ensure that the direction and control of the company is firmly in its hands.

1.5 There should be an agreed procedure for directors in the furtherance of their duties to take independent professional advice if necessary, at the company's expense.

1.6 All directors should have access to the advice and services of the company secretary, who is responsible to the board for ensuring that board procedures are followed and that applicable rules and regulations are complied with. Any question of the removal of the company secretary should be a matter for the board as a whole.

2 Non-Executive Directors

2.1 Non-executive directors should bring an independent judgement to bear on issues of strategy, performance, resources, including key appointments, and standards of conduct.

2.2 The majority should be independent of management and free from any business or other relationship which could materially interfere with the exercise of their independent judgement, apart from their fees and shareholding. Their fees should reflect the time which they commit to the company.

2.3 Non-executive directors should be appointed for specified terms and re-appointment should not be automatic.

2.4 Non-executive directors should be selected through a formal process and both this process and their appointment should be a matter for the board as a whole.

[3 Executive Directors

3.1 Directors' service contracts should not exceed three years without shareholders' approval.

3.2 There should be full and clear disclosure of directors' total emoluments and those of the chairman and highest-paid UK director, including pension contributions and stock options. Separate figures should be given for salary and performance-related elements and the basis on which performance is measured should be explained.

3.3 Executive directors' pay should be subject to the recommendations of a remuneration committee made up wholly or mainly of non-executive directors.]

4 Reporting and Controls

4.1 It is the board's duty to present a balanced and understandable assessment of the company's position.

4.2 The board should ensure that an objective and professional relationship is maintained with the auditors.

4.3 The board should establish an audit committee of at least three non-executive directors with written terms of reference which deal clearly with its authority and duties.

4.4 The directors should explain their responsibility for preparing the accounts next to a statement by the auditors about their reporting responsibilities.

4.5 The directors should report on the effectiveness of the company's system of internal control.

4.6 The directors should report that the business is a going concern, with supporting assumptions or qualifications as necessary.

Section in square brackets [   ] superceded by the Greenbury Code of Best Practice.

Appendix 6C

Schedule of matters to be reserved for the approval of the Board of Directors

Companies Act requirements

1   Approval of interim and final financial statements.*
2   Approval of the interim dividend and recommendations of the final dividend.*
3   Approval of any significant change in accounting policies or practices.*
4   Appointment or removal of company secretary.*
5   Remuneration of auditors (where, as is usual, shareholders have delegated this power to the Board) and recommendations for appointment or removal of auditors.*

Stock Exchange

6   Approval of all circulars to shareholders and listing particulars (approval of routine documents such as periodic circulars re. scrip dividend procedures or exercise of conversion rights might perhaps be delegated to a committee).*
7   Approval of press releases concerning matters decided by the Board.*

Management

8   Approval of the group's commercial strategy and the annual operating budget.
9   Changes to the group's capital structure or its status as plc.
10 Appointments to boards of subsidiaries.
11 Terms and conditions of directors [and senior executives].*
12 Changes to the group's management and control structure.

Board membership and board committees

13 Board appointments and removals.*
14 Terms of reference of chairman, vice-chairman, chief executive and other executive directors.*
15 Terms of reference and membership of board committees.*

Cadbury recommendations

16 Major capital projects.
17 Material contracts of the company [or any subsidiary] in the ordinary course of business, e.g. bank borrowing (above £ . . . . .) and acquisition or disposal of fixed assets (above £. . . . .).

18   Contracts of the company [or any subsidiary] not in the ordinary course of business, e.g. loans and repayments (above £. . . . .); foreign transactions (above £. . . . .); major acquisitions or disposals (above £. . . . .).

19   Major investments [including the acquisition or disposal of interests of more than, e.g. 5% in the voting shares of any company or the making of any take-over bid].

20   Risk management strategy.

21   Treasury policies (including foreign exchange exposures).

Miscellaneous

22   Major changes in the rules of the company pension scheme, or changes of trustee or (where this is subject to the approval of the company) changes in the fund management arrangements.

23   Major changes in employee share schemes and the allocation of executive share options.

24   Formulation of policy regarding charitable donations.

25   Political donations.

26   Prosecution, defence or settlement of litigation (involving more than £. . . . . or being otherwise material to the interests of the company).

27   Internal control arrangements.

28   Health and safety policy.

29   Environmental policy.

30   Directors' and officers' liability insurance.

Note: items marked with an asterisk (*) are not considered suitable, in any event, for delegation to a committee of the Board because of Companies Act requirements or because, under the recommendations of the Cadbury Report, they are the responsibility of, e.g. an audit, nomination or remuneration committee, with the final decision on the matter required to be taken by the whole Board.

(Reproduced with the permission of the Institute of Chartered Secretaries and Administrators).

Appendix 6D

Report of the Study Group on Directors' Remuneration (The 'Greenbury Report')

The Code of Best Practice

A   The remuneration committee

A1   To avoid potential conflicts of interests, Boards of Directors should set up remuneration committees of Non-executive Directors to determine on their behalf, and on behalf of the shareholders, within agreed terms of reference, the company's policy on executive remuneration and specific remuneration packages for each of the Executive Directors, including pension rights and any compensation payments.

A2   Remuneration committee Chairmen should account directly to the shareholders through the means specified in this Code for the decisions their committees reach.

A3   Where necessary, companies' Articles of Association should be amended to enable remuneration committees to discharge these functions on behalf of the Board.

A4   Remuneration committees should consist entirely of Non-Executive Directors with no personal financial interest other than as shareholders in the matters to be decided, no potential conflicts of interest arising from cross-directorships and no day-to-day involvement in running the business.

A5   The members of the remuneration committee should be listed each year in the committee's report to shareholders (B1 below). When they stand for re-election, the proxy cards should indicate their membership of the committee.

A6   The Board itself should determine the remuneration of the Non-Executive Directors, including members of the remuneration committee, within the limits set in the Articles of Association.

A7   Remuneration committees should consult the company Chairman and/or Chief Executive about their proposals and have access to professional advice inside and outside the company.

A8   The remuneration committee Chairman should attend the company's Annual General Meeting (AGM) to answer shareholders' questions about Directors' remuneration and should ensure that the company maintains contact as required with its principal shareholders about remuneration in the same way as for other matters.

A9   The committee's annual report to shareholders (B1 below) should not be a standard item of agenda for AGMs. But the committee should consider each year whether the circumstances are such that the AGM should be invited to approve the policy set out in their report and should minute their conclusions.

B **Disclosure and approval provisions**

B1 The remuneration committee should make a report each year to the shareholders on behalf of the Board. The report should form part of, or be annexed to, the company's Annual Report and Accounts. It should be the main vehicle through which the company accounts to shareholders for Directors' remuneration.

B2 The report should set out the Company's policy on executive remuneration, including levels, comparator groups of companies, individual components, performance criteria and measurement, pension provision, contracts of service and compensation commitments on early termination.

B3 The report should state that, in framing its remuneration policy, the committee has given full consideration to the best practice provisions set out in sections C and D below.

B4 The report should also include full details of all elements in the remuneration package of each individual Director by name, such as basic salary, benefits in kind, annual bonuses and long-term incentive schemes including share options.

B5 Information on share options, including SAYE options, should be given for each Director in accordance with the recommendations of the Accounting Standards Board's Urgent Issues Task Force Abstract 10 and its successors.

B6 If grants under executive share option or other long-term incentive schemes are awarded in one large block rather than phased, the report should explain and justify.

B7 Also included in the report should be pension entitlements earned by each individual Director during the year, calculated on a basis to be recommended by the Faculty of Actuaries and the Institute of Actuaries.

B8 If annual bonuses or benefits in kind are pensionable the report should explain and justify.

B9 The amounts received by, and commitments made to, each Director under B4, B5 and B7 should be subject to audit.

B10 Any service contracts which provide for, or imply, notice periods in excess of one year (or any provisions for predetermined compensation on termination which exceeded one year's salary and benefits) should be disclosed and the reasons for the longer notice periods explained.

B11 Shareholders and other relevant business interests and activities of the Directors should continue to be disclosed as required in the Companies Acts and London Stock Exchange Listing Rules.

B12 Shareholders should be invited specifically to approve all new long-term incentive schemes (including share option schemes) whether payable in cash or shares in which Directors or senior executives will participate which potentially commit shareholders' funds over more than one year or dilute the equity.

C Remuneration policy

C1 Remuneration committees must provide the packages needed to attract, retain and motivate Directors of the quality required but should avoid paying more than is necessary for this purpose.

C2 Remuneration committees should judge where to position their company relative to other companies. They should be aware what other comparable companies are paying and should take account of relative performance.

C3 Remuneration committees should be sensitive to the wider scene, including pay and employment conditions elsewhere in the company, especially when determining annual salary increases.

C4 The performance-related elements of remuneration should be designed to align the interests of Directors and shareholders and to give Directors keen incentives to perform at the highest levels.

C5 Remuneration committees should consider whether their Directors should be eligible for bonuses. If so, performance conditions should be relevant, stretching and designed to enhance the business. Upper limits should always be considered. There may be a case for part-payment in shares to be held for a significant period.

C6 Remuneration committees should consider whether their Directors should be eligible for benefits under long-term incentive schemes. Traditional share option schemes should be weighed against other kinds of long-term incentive scheme. In normal circumstances, shares granted should not vest, and options should not be exercisable, in under three years. Directors should be encouraged to hold their shares for a further period after vesting or exercise subject to the need to finance any costs of acquisition and associated tax liability.

C7 Any new long-term incentive schemes which are proposed should preferably replace existing schemes or at least form part of a well-considered overall plan, incorporating existing schemes, which should be approved as a whole by shareholders. The total rewards potentially available should not be excessive.

C8 Grants under all incentive schemes, including new grants under existing share option schemes, should be subject to challenging performance criteria reflecting the company's objectives. Consideration should be given to criteria which reflect the company's performance relative to a group of comparitor companies in some key variable such as total shareholder return.

C9 Grants under executive share option and other long-term incentive schemes should normally be phased rather than awarded in one large block.

C10 Executive share options should never be issued at a discount.

C11 Remuneration committees should consider the pension consequences and associated costs to the company of basic salary increases, especially for Directors close to retirement.

C12 In general, neither annual bonuses nor benefits in kind should be pensionable.

D   Service contracts and compensation

D1 Remuneration committees should consider what compensation commitments their Directors' contracts of service, if any, would entail in the event of early termination, particularly for unsatisfactory performance.

D2 There is a strong case for setting notice or contract periods at, or reducing them to, one year or less. Remuneration committees should, however, be sensitive and flexible, especially over timing. In some cases notice or contract periods of up to two years may be acceptable. Longer periods should be avoided wherever possible.

D3 If it is necessary to offer longer notice or contract periods, such as three years, to new Directors recruited from outside, such periods should reduce after the initial period.

D4 Within the legal constraints, remuneration committees should tailor their approach in individual early termination cases to the wide variety of circumstances. The broad aim should be to avoid rewarding poor performance while dealing fairly with cases where departure is not due to poor performance.

D5 Remuneration committees should take a robust line on payment of compensation where performance has been unsatisfactory and on reducing compensation to reflect departing Directors' obligation to mitigate damages by earning money elsewhere.

D6 Where appropriate, and in particular where notice or contract periods exceed one year, companies should consider paying all or part of compensation in instalments rather than one lump sum and reducing or stopping payment when the former Director takes on new employment.

Committee on Corporate Governance: The Combined Code

Part 1   Principles of Good Governance

Section 1   Companies

A   Directors

The Board

1   Every listed company should be headed by an effective board which should lead and control the company.

Chairman and CEO

2   There are two key tasks at the top of every public company – the running of the board and the executive responsibility for the running of the company's business. There should be a clear division of responsibilities at the head of the company which will ensure a balance of power and authority, such that no one individual has unfettered powers of decision.

Board Balance

3   The board should include a balance of executive and non-executive directors (including independent non-executives) such that no individual or small group of individuals can dominate the board's decision taking.

Supply of Information

4   The board should be supplied in a timely manner with information in a form and of a quality appropriate to enable it to discharge its duties.

Appointments to the Board

5   There should be a formal and transparent procedure for the appointment of new directors to the board.

Re-election

6   All directors should be required to submit themselves for re-election at regular intervals and at least every three years.

B   Directors' Remuneration

The Level and Make-up of Remuneration

1   Levels of remuneration should be sufficient to attract and retain the directors needed to run the company successfully, but

companies should avoid paying more than is necessary for this purpose. A proportion of executive directors' remuneration should be structured so as to link rewards to corporate and individual performance.

Procedure

2   Companies should establish a formal and transparent procedure for developing policy on executive remuneration and for fixing the remuneration packages of individual directors. No director should be involved in deciding his or her own remuneration.

Disclosure

3   The company's annual report should contain a statement of remuneration policy and details of the remuneration of each director.

C   **<u>Relations with Shareholders</u>**

Dialogue with Institutional Shareholders

1   Companies should be ready, where practicable, to enter into a dialogue with institutional shareholders based on the mutual understanding of objectives.

Constructive Use of the AGM

2   Boards should use the AGM to communicate with private investors and encourge their participation.

D   **<u>Accountability and Audit</u>**

Financial Reporting

1   The board should present a balanced and understandable assessment of the company's position and prospects.

Internal Control

2   The board should maintain a sound system of internal control to safeguard shareholders' investment and the company's assets.

Audit Committee and Auditors

3   The board should establish formal and transparent arrangements for considering how they should apply the financial reporting and internal control principles and for maintaining an appropriate relationship with the company's auditors.

Section 2 Institutional Shareholders

E   **Institutional Investors**

Shareholder Voting

1   Institutional shareholders have a responsibility to make considered use of their votes.

Dialogue with Companies

2   Institutional shareholders should be ready, where practicable, to enter into a dialogue with companies based on the mutual understanding of objectives.

Evaluation of Governance Disclosures

3   When evaluating companies' governance arrangements, particularly those relating to board structure and composition, institutional investors should give due weight to all relevant factors drawn to their attention.

Part 2 Code of Best Practice

Section 1 Companies

A   **Directors**

A.1   **The Board**

Principle Every listed company should be headed by an effective board which should lead and control the company.

Code Provisions

A.1.1   The board should meet regularly.

A.1.2   The board should have a formal schedule of matters specifically reserved to it for decision.

A.1.3.   There should be a procedure agreed by the board for directors in the furtherance of their duties to take independent professional advice if necessary, at the company's expense.

A.1.4   All directors should have access to the advice and services of the company secretary, who is responsible to the board for ensuring that board procedures are followed and that applicable rules and regulations are complied with. Any question of the removal of the company secretary should be a matter for the board as a whole.

A.1.5   All directors should bring an independent judgement to bear on issues of strategy, performance, resources (including key appointments) and standards of conduct.

A.1.6   Every director should receive appropriate training on the first occasion that he or she is appointed to the board of a listed company, and subsequently as necessary.

A.2 Chairman and CEO

Principle **There are two key tasks at the top of every public company – the running of the board and the executive responsibility for the running of the company's business. There should be a clear division of responsibilities at the head of the company which will ensure a balance of power and authority, such that no one individual has unfettered powers of decision.**

Code Provision

A.2.1 A decision to combine the posts of chairman and chief executive officer in one person should be publicly justified. Whether the posts are held by different people or by the same person, there should be a strong and independent non-executive element on the board, with a recognised senior member other than the chairman to whom concerns can be conveyed. The chairman, chief executive and senior independent director should be identifed in the annual report.

A.3 Board Balance

Principle **The board should include a balance of executive and non-executive directors (including independent non-executives) such that no individual or small grop of individuals can dominate the board's decision taking.**

Code Provisions

A.3.1 The board should include non-executive directors of sufficient calibre and number for their views to carry significant weight in the board's decisions. Non-executive directors should comprise not less than one third of the board.

A.3.2 The majority of non-executive directors should be independent of management and free from any business or other relationship which could materially interfere with the exercise of their independent judgement. Non-executive directors considered by the board to be independent in this sense should be identified in the annual report.

A.4 Supply of Information

Principle **The board should be supplied in a timely manner with information in a form and of a quality appropriate to enable it to discharge its duties.**

Code Provision

A.4.1 Management has an obligation to provide the board with appropriate and timely information, but information volunteered by management is unlikely to be enough in all circumstances and directors should make further enquiries where necessary. The chairman should ensure that all directors and properly briefed on issues arising at board meetings.

A.5   **Appointments to the Board**

Principle   **There should be a formal and transparent procedure for the appointment of new directors to the board.**

Code Provision

A.5.1   Unless the board is small, a nomination committee should be established to make recommendations to the board on all new board appointments. A majority of the members of this committee should be non-executive directors and the chairman should be either the chairman of the board or a non-executive director. The chairman and members of the nomination committee should be identified in the annual report.

A.6   **Re-election**

Principle   **All directors should be required to submit themselves for re-election at regular intervals and at least every three years.**

Code Provisions

A.6.1   Non-executive directors should be appointed for specified terms subject to re-election and to Companies Act provisions relating to the removal of a director, and reappointment should not be automatic.

A.6.2   All directors should be subject to election by shareholders at the first opportunity after their appointment, and to re-election thereafter at intervals of no more than three years. The names of directors submitted for election or re-election should be accompanied by sufficient biographical details to enable shareholders to take an informed decision on their election.

B   **Directors' Remuneration**

B.1   **The Level and Make-up of Remuneration**

Principle   **Levels of remuneration should be sufficient to attract and retain the directors needed to run the company successfully, but companies should avoid paying more than is necessary for this purpose. A proportion of executive directors' remuneration should be structured so as to link rewards to corporate and individual performance.**

Code Provisions

Remuneration policy

B.1.1   The remuneration committee should provide the package needed to attract, retain and motivate executive directors of the quality required but should avoid paying more than is necessary for this purpose.

B.1.2   Remuneration committees should judge where to position their company relative to other companies. They should be aware what comparable companies are paying and should take account of relative performance. But they should use such comparisons with caution, in view of the risk that they can result in an upward ratchet of remuneration levels with no corresponding improvement in performance.

B.1.3   Remuneration committees should be sensitive to the wider scene, including pay and employment conditions elsewhere in the group, especially when determining annual salary increases.

B.1.4   The performance-related elements of remuneration should form a significant proportion of the total remuneration package of executive directors and should be designed to align their interests with those of shareholders and to give these directors keen incentives to perform at the highest levels.

B.1.5   Executive share options should not be offered at a discount save as permitted by paragraphs 13.30 and 13.31 of the Listing Rules.

B.1.6   In designing schemes of performance-related remuneration, remuneration committees should follow the provisions in Schedule A to this Code.

Service Contracts and Compensation

B.1.7   There is a strong case for setting notice or contract periods at, or reducing them to, one year or less. Boards should set this as an objective, but they should recognise that it may not be possible to achieve it immediately.

B.1.8   If it is necessary to offer longer notice or contract periods to new directors recruited from outside, such periods should reduce after the initial period.

B.1.9   Remuneration committees should consider what compensation commitments (including pension contributions) their directors' contracts of service, if any, would entail in the event of early termination. They should, in particular, consider the advantages of providing explicitly in the initial contract of such compensation commitments except in the case of removal for misconduct.

B.1.10   Where the initial contract does not explicitly provide for compensation commitments, remuneration committees should, within legal constraints, tailor their approach in individual early termination cases to the wide variety of circumstances. The broad aim should be to avoid rewarding poor performance while dealing fairly with cases where departure is not due to poor performance and to take a robust line on reducing compensation to reflect departing directors' obligations to mitigate loss.

B.2   **Procedure**

Principle   **Companies should establish a formal and transparent procedure for developing policy on executive remuneration and for fixing the remuneration packages of individual directors. No director should be involved in deciding his or her own remuneration.**

Code Provisions

B.2.1   To avoid potential conflicts of interest, boards of directors should set up remuneration committees of independent non-executive directors to make recommendations to the board, within agreed terms of reference, on the company's framework of executive remuneration and its cost; and to determine on their behalf specific remuneration packages for each of the executive directors, including pension rights and any compensation payments.

B.2.2   Remuneration committees should consist exclusively of non-executive directors who are independent of management and free from any business or other relationship which could materially interfere with the exercise of their independent judgement.

B.2.3   The members of the remuneration committee should be listed each year in the board's remuneration report to shareholders (B.3.1 below).

B.2.4   The board itself or, where required by the Articles of Association, the shareholders should determine the remuneration of the non-executive directors, including members of the remuneration committee, within the limits set in the Articles of Association. Where permitted by the Articles, the board may however delegate this reponsibility to a small sub-committee, which might include the chief executive officer.

B.2.5   Remuneration committees should consult the chairman and/or chief executive officer about their proposals relating to the remuneration of other executive directors and have access to professional advice inside and outside the company.

B.2.6   The chairman of the board should ensure that the company maintains contact as required with its principal shareholders about remuneration in the same way as for other matters.

B.3   **Disclosure**

Principle   **The company's annual report should contain a statement of remuneration policy and details of the remuneration of each director.**

Code Provisions

B.3.1   The board should report to the shareholders each year on remuneration. The report should form part of, or be annexed to, the company's annual report and accounts. It should be the main vehicle through which the company reports to shareholders on directors' remuneration.

B.3.2 The report should set out the company's policy on executive directors' remuneration. It should draw attention to factors specific to the company.

B.3.3 In preparing the remuneration report, the board should follow the provisions in Schedule B to this Code.

B.3.4 Shareholders should be invited specifically to approve all new long-term incentive schemes (as defined in the Listing Rules) save in the circumstances permitted by paragraph 13.13A of the Listing Rules.

B.3.5 The board's annual remuneration report to shareholders need not be a standard item of agenda for AGMs. But the board should consider each year whether the circumstances are such that the AGM should be invited to approve the policy set out in the report and should minute their conclusions.

C **Relations with Shareholders**

C.1 **Dialogue with Institutional Shareholders**

Principle **Companies should be ready, where practicable, to enter into a dialogue with institutional shareholders based on the mutual understanding of objectives.**

C.2 **Constructive Use of the AGM**

Principle **Boards should use the AGM to communicate with private investors and encourage their participation.**

Code Provisions

C.2.1 Companies should count all proxy votes and, except where a poll is called, should indicate the level of proxies lodged on each resolution, and the balance for and against the resolution, after it has been dealt with on a show of hands.

C.2.2 Companies should propose a separate resolution at the AGM on each substantially separate issue and should in particular propose a resolution at the AGM relating to the report and accounts.

C.2.3 The chairman of the board should arrange for the chairman of the audit, remuneration and nomination committees to be available to answer questions at the AGM.

C.2.4 Companies should arrange for the Notice of the AGM and related papers to be sent to shareholders at least 20 working days before the meeting.

D   **Accountability and Audit**

D.1   **Financial Reporting**

Principle   **The board should present a balanced and understandable assessment of the company's position and prospects.**

Code Provisions

D.1.1   The directors should explain their responsibility for preparing the accounts and there should be a statement by the auditors about their reporting responsibilities.

D.1.2   The board's responsibility to present a balanced and understandable assessment extends to interim and other price-sensitive public reports and reports to regulators as well as to information required to be presented by statutory requirements.

D.1.3   The directors should report that the business is a going concern, with supporting assumptions or qualifications as necessary.

D.2   **Internal Control**

Principle   **The board should maintain a sound system of internal control to safeguard shareholders' investment and the company's assets.**

Code Provisions

D.2.1   The directors should, at least annually, conduct a review of the effectiveness of the group's system of internal controls and should report to shareholders that they have done so. The review should cover all controls, including financial, operational and compliance controls and risk management.

D.2.2   Companies which do not have an internal audit function should from time to time review the need for one.

D.3.   **Audit Committee and Auditors**

Principle   **The board should establish formal and transparent arrangements for considering how they should apply the financial reporting and internal control principles and for maintaining an appropriate relationship with the company's auditors.**

Code Provisions

D.3.1   The board should establish an audit committee of at least three directors, all non-executive, with written terms of reference which deal clearly with its authority and duties. The members of the committee, a majority of whom should be independent non-executive directors, should be named in the report and accounts.

D.3.2   The duties of the audit committee should include keeping under review the scope of results of the audit and its cost

261

effectiveness and the independence and objectivity of the auditors. Where the auditors also supply a substantial volume of non-audit services to the company, the committee should keep the nature and extent of such services under review, seeking to balance the maintenance of objectivity and value for money.

Section 2   Institutional Shareholders

E   **Institutional Investors**

E.1   **Shareholder Voting**

Principle **Institutional shareholders have a responsibility to make considered use of their votes.**

Code Provisions

E.1.1   Institutional shareholders should endeavour to eliminate unnecessary variations in the criteria which each applies to the corporate governance arrangements and performance of the companies in which they invest.

E.1.2   Institutional shareholders should, on request, make available to their clients information on the proportion of resolutions on which votes were cast and non-discretionary proxies lodged.

E.1.3   Institutional shareholders should take steps to ensure that their voting intentions are being translated into practice.

E.2   **Dialogue with Companies**

Principle **Institutional shareholders should be ready, where practicable, to enter into a dialogue with companies based on the mutual understanding of objectives.**

E.3   **Evaluation of Governance Disclosures**

Principle **When evaluating companies' governance arrangements, particularly those relating to board structure and composition, institutional investors should give due weight to all relevant factors drawn to their attention.**

Schedule A: Provisions on the Design of Performance-related Remuneration

1   Remuneration committees should consider whether the directors should be eligible for annual bonuses. If so, performance conditions should be relevant, stretching and designed to enhance the business. Upper limits should always be considered. There may be a case for part payment in shares to be held for a significant period.

2   Remuneration committees should consider whether the directors should be eligible for benefits under long-term incentive schemes. Traditional share option schemes should be weighed against other kinds of long-term incentive scheme. In normal circumstances, shares granted or other forms of deferred remuneration should not vest, and options should not be exercisable, in under three years. Directors should be encouraged to hold their shares for a further period after vesting or exercise, subject to the need to finance any costs of acquisition and associated tax liability.

3   Any new long-term incentive schemes which are proposed should be approved by shareholders and should preferably replace existing schemes or at least form part of a well considered overall plan, incorporating existing schemes. The total rewards potentially available should not be excessive.

4   Payouts or grants under all incentive schemes, including new grants under existing share option schemes, should be subject to challenging performance criteria reflecting the company's objectives. Consideration should be given to criteria which reflect the company's performance relative to a group of comparator companies in some key variables such as total shareholder return.

5   Grants under executive share option and other long-term incentive schemes should normally be phased rather than awarded in one large block.

6   Remuneration committees should consider the pension consequences and associated costs to the company of basic salary increases and other changes in remuneration, especially for directors close to retirement.

7   In general, neither annual bonuses nor benefits in kind should be pensionable.

Schedule B: Provisions on what should be included in the Remuneration Report

1   The report should include full details of all elements in the remuneration package of each individual director by name, such as basic salary, benefits in kind, annual bonuses and long-term incentive schemes including share options.

2   Information on share options, including SAYE options, should be given for each director in accordance with the recommendations of the Accounting Standards Board's Urgent Issues Task Force Abstract 10 and its successors.

3   If grants under executive share option or other long-term incentive schemes are awarded in one large block rather than phased, the report should explain and justify.

4   Also included in the report should be pension entitlements earned by each individual director during the year, disclosed on one of the alternative bases recommended by the Faculty of Actuaries and the Institute of Actuaries and included in the Stock Exchange Listing Rules. Companies may wish to make clear that the transfer value represents a liability of the company, not a sum paid or due to the individual.

5   If annual bonuses or benefits in kind are pensionable the report should explain and justify.

6   The amounts received by, and commitments made to, each director under 1, 2 and 4 above should be subject to audit.

7   Any service contracts which provide for, or imply, notice periods in excess of one year (or any provisions for pre-determined compensation on termination which exceed one year's salary and benefits) should be disclosed and the reasons for the longer notice periods explained.

Committee on Corporate Governance The Combined Code – Reproduced with the permission of Gee Publishing Ltd.

Chapter 7

Membership

Members and the company

Definition of a member

7.1   Section 22 of the Companies Act 1985 defines a member as being either a subscriber to the memorandum of association or some other person who has *agreed* to become a member of the company and has been *registered* as such in the register of members. With the exception of the members of a company limited by guarantee, the members of a company are thus its shareholders.

A shareholding in a company can be acquired in several ways, either by:

(*a*)   subscription to the memorandum of association;

(*b*)   acquisition by way of allotment or transfer; or

(*c*)   transmission.

However, until the person acquiring the shares by either of the methods above (except by subscription to the memorandum of association) is entered in the register of members of the company then, although he could be described as a shareholder, he could not be described as a member (CA 1985, s 22(2)). A person subscribing to the memorandum of association, however, automatically becomes a member without registration being required (CA 1985, s 22(1)).

An important point arising out of this definition is that the Companies Act 1985 commonly refers to 'members' not 'shareholders' in specifying their rights. Thus, even though a person may have acquired 99% of a company's issued shares he cannot exercise any of his rights as a member until registered in the register of members as holding the shares. However, the rights of members are commonly tied in with the shares that they hold, both by the Act and by a company's articles of association.

For companies limited by guarantee the situation is slightly different as the members do not hold shares. Instead of shareholdings, each person who wishes to become a member of a company limited by guarantee gives a guarantee that, in the event of the company being wound up, he will contribute the amount specified in the memorandum of association to the company's assets (usually £1). However, as with a company limited by shares, until the person giving the guarantee is registered in the register of members, he does not acquire the status of a member. Again, the subscribers to the memorandum of association automatically become members without registration being required.

Institutional Shareholders

7.2 Shareholders are the owners of a company and therefore institutional shareholders are obliged to act responsibly and in the best interests of their investors. Guidelines have been produced by the Institutional Shareholders' Committee on the responsibilities of institutional shareholders in the United Kingdom. This code of best practice makes various recommendations such as having effective channels of communication with the board to enable a better understanding of each others aims and requirements, supporting the board by positive voting unless they have good reason to do otherwise and to consider all offers of a takeover bid objectively.

Institutional investors have a fiduciary responsibility to those on whose behalf they are investing and in June 1998 following a final report of the Hampel Committee, a Combined Code was produced and is now incorporated in the Listing Rules as Amendment 12 (see Appendix 6E). Included in this Combined Code are principles and code provisions applicable to institutional shareholders:

Principle
Institutional shareholders have a responsibility to make considered use of their votes.

Code Provisions
Institutional shareholders should endeavour to eliminate unnecessary variations in the criteria which each applies to the corporate governance arrangements and performance of the companies in which they invest.

Institutional shareholders should, on request, make available to their clients information on the proportion of resolutions on which votes were cast and non-discretionary proxies lodged.

Institutional shareholders should take steps to ensure that their voting intentions are being translated into practice.

Principle
Institutional shareholders should be ready, where practicable, to enter into a dialogue with companies based on the mutual understanding of objectives.

Principle
When evaluating companies' governance arrangements, particularly those relating to board structure and composition, institutional investors should give due weight to all relevant factors drawn to their intention.

Acquisition of shares

7.3   As mentioned above there are several different methods by which a person may acquire shares in a company and accordingly become a member of it.

(a)   *Subscription*

By subscribing to the memorandum of association of a company prior to its applying for registration, a subscriber automatically becomes a member on the date the company is incorporated (see 2.1 THE COMPANY CONSTITUTION and 7.1 above). In subscribing, the subscriber will state opposite his name how many shares he agrees to take and he will then sign the memorandum of association.

(b)   *Acquisition by allotment*

A person may become a member of a company by agreeing to purchase shares which the company has offered to issue. In effect, a contract is created between the company and the prospective member under which, in consideration for the payment by the member to the company of an agreed sum, the company will issue shares to the member. Usually the agreement to acquire shares in this manner (as required by CA 1985, s 22(2)) will be indicated by the completion of an application form for shares in response to an offer for sale made by the company. On the allotment of the shares, the company will register the applicant in the register of members, and it is from that date that the person becomes a member, not from the date of allotment.

(c)   *Acquisition by transfer*

Subject to any restrictions which may exist in a company's articles of association, an existing member may transfer, either for a consideration or otherwise, his shareholding in a company to another person. The transfer is effected by the completion of a stock transfer form (Stock Transfer Act 1963) by the transferor in favour of the transferee, the submission of the form (to the Inland Revenue) for stamp duty purposes and then the transferee's presentation of the form to the company together with the relevant share certificate for board approval and registration in the register of members (see 7.16 below).

(d)   *Transmission*

Although similar in many ways to a transfer of shares, a person may become entitled to the shares of another upon the death, bankruptcy or insanity of a member. In such circumstances, the person becoming entitled to the shares will submit to the company a notice of his entitlement (e.g. probate) together with a request that he now be registered in the register of members as the holder of the shares. Accordingly upon registration he becomes a member (see 7.23 below).

It is important to note that a person who has not agreed to become a member cannot be registered in the register of members as one. In such circumstances, the person who has been erroneously registered may force the company to take his name off the Register. Such rectification of the register however will, in most circumstances, require the consent of the court (CA 1985, s 359).

Cessation of membership

7.4   It would follow from the above and from section 22 of the Companies Act 1985 that a person will cease to be a member of the company upon his ceasing to be registered in the register of members. This can be brought about in several ways:

(*a*)   voluntary transfer of shares (as 7.3(*c*) above);

(*b*)   transmission on death or bankruptcy (as 7.3(*d*) above);

(*c*)   compulsory transfer of shares (e.g. enforcement of a lien); and

(*d*)   forfeiture (e.g. non-payment of calls due).

Restrictions upon membership

7.5   Generally speaking, any person or legal entity may be a member of a company, subject to them having sufficient legal capacity. Thus, with the exception of minors and persons who are either bankrupt or insane (where agreement to become a member would be voidable), any person or corporation can be a member. However, the Companies Act 1985 has introduced several restrictions relating to the capacity of companies in certain instances to hold shares.

(*a*)   *Holding its own shares*

CA 1985, s 143 expressly prohibits a company from holding its own shares. However, subsection (3) of this section goes on to qualify this statement somewhat by specifically excluding certain transactions as not being acquisitions within the meaning of section 143, so long as the shares acquired are fully paid.

CA 1985, s 162 further goes on to provide perhaps the most common exception to the general rule by providing a procedure whereby a company with appropriate provisions in its articles may purchase its own shares (see 8.48–8.56 CAPITAL).

CA 1985, s 143(2) states that any acquisition by a company of its own shares (unless being an exempt category) is void.

(*b*)   *Holding company*

CA 1985, s 23 states that a company cannot be a member of its own holding company. A slight exception to this general rule exists in circumstances where the subsidiary is holding the shares of its holding company purely as a personal representative or trustee of a third party and that neither the subsidiary nor the holding company has a beneficial interest in the shares held.

CA 1985, s 23(1) states that any transfer or allotment of shares (outside the limited exception) by a holding company to a subsidiary is void.

Shares

7.6   Under section 2(5) of the Companies Act 1985, every company is required to include a statement in its memorandum of association of the amount of share capital with which it proposes to be registered and that the share capital be capable of division into shares of a fixed amount. This constitutes a company's authorised (or nominal) share capital, for example:

'The share capital of the company is £1,000,000 divided into 1,000,000 ordinary shares of £1 each.'

The Act has many provisions relating to share capital (see below) but, apart from applying several general restrictions and obligations upon a company, does not specify the general rights which attach to shares. It is, in general, left to a company to determine what rights shall attach to its shares. Thus regulation 2 of Table A states:

'Subject to the provisions of the Act and without prejudice to any rights attached to any existing shares, any share may be issued with such rights or restrictions as the company may by ordinary resolution determine.'

Thus, so long as a company has an authorised share capital, then it is free to determine the rights attaching to its shares. This includes the currency in which the value of the shares will be stated, for example:

'The share capital of the company is $1,000 divided into 2 ordinary shares of $500 each.'

It is permissible for a company to denominate its capital in different fixed amounts of non-sterling currencies provided, in the case of a public company, the required statutory minimum (i.e. £50,000) is in sterling (see 2.30 THE COMPANY CONSTITUTION).

The DTI has announced that new legislation will be introduced to provide a simpler mechanism for the redenomination of companies' share capital.

Under existing legislation in order to convert share capital from one currency to another, private companies would need to cancel old shares and issue new ones, requiring shareholder and court approval. Furthermore public companies are currently obliged to have a minimum share capital of £50,000 and only additional share capital to this can be denominated in another currency.

The new legislation will allow companies to pass an ordinary resolution in general meeting to the effect that references to share capital denominated in one currency, will be to the equivalent amount in Euros or another currency. In the case of redenomination into Euro during any transitional period to UK membership of the single currency, a board resolution can be passed.

In addition, public companies will be permitted to denominate their minimum share capital in any currency not just sterling.

There would be no need for companies to issue new share certificates following redenomination.

Section 121 of the CA 1985 sets out the procedure by which the authorised share capital of a company may be increased or altered (see 8.37 CAPITAL).

The rights and liabilities attaching to shares by the Act and by the articles of association are discussed in 7.7 below.

Chapter VIII, sections 182 to 189 of the CA 1985 specify further requirements with which a company must comply in respect of its share capital.

(a)   Distinguishing numbers

CA 1985, s 182(2) requires that every issued share shall bear a distinguishing number. However, the section also provides that where all the issued shares are fully paid up and rank *pari passu* (equally between themselves) then the requirement for the shares to bear distinguishing numbers may be dispensed with.

(b)   Share transfers

CA 1985, s 182(1) states that shares are the personal estate of a member and, subject to the Stock Transfer Act 1963, they may be transferred by a member in the manner specified by a company's articles of association, for example, according to any pre-emption rights which may exist.

The Stock Transfer Act 1963 specifies the form that a share transfer must take and under CA 1985, s 183 it is unlawful for a company to register any transfer not in the specified form. Certain exceptions to this rule however exist under the Stock Transfer Act 1982 and where a person has become entitled to a share by operation of law (e.g. deceased member's executor) (CA 1985, ss 183(2) and (3)).

A company may specify the circumstances in its articles of association when it will and will not register transfers of shares. This power is subject however to CA 1985, s 187 which specifies the circumstances in which by operation of law a person must be recognised as having become entitled to shares (e.g. by grant of probate of a will) (see 7.23 below).

(c)   Share certificates

Within two months of the date of allotment or date of lodging of a transfer of any shares, a company is obliged to issue to the holder of the shares a certificate representing the shares which have been allotted or transferred (CA 1985, s 185(1)) (see 7.24 below).

In respect of a transfer of shares the 'date of lodging' is deemed to be the date upon which a *duly stamped* transfer is lodged.

Membership and share rights

Rights of members

7.7   The rights of the members of a company are usually linked with and expressed in terms of the rights attaching to the shares which they hold— although not exclusively so. For example, a member holding preference shares will have the same right to inspect the register of members of the company as a member holding ordinary shares, but the company's articles of association may give the two classes of shares different voting rights.

In companies limited by guarantee the rights of members attach solely to the member personally as no shares exist unless the company was formed before 22 December 1980. However, it is fairly common for such companies to create classes of membership which have lesser rights than full membership on such matters as voting; such membership is sometimes referred to as associate membership.

In essence, the rights and the liabilities attaching to shares and membership are defined by a combination of the Companies Act 1985 and a company's articles of association.

The Companies Act 1985 provides the members of a company with many rights specific to membership and also certain liabilities. The Act also provides for specific rights attaching to shares; these mainly relate to the variation of the rights of shareholders.

The principal rights of a member of a company are as follows.

(a)   Inspection of statutory books and records

The Act provides that a member may inspect various statutory registers of a company and request copies of the same (see Chapter 3) and to inspect directors' service contracts or written memoranda of the terms and conditions of a director's contract of service for both the company and any subsidiary of the company (CA 1985, s 318). A member may also request that a company provide him with a copy of its memorandum and articles of association (CA 1985, s 19).

(b)   To receive a copy of the annual accounts

CA 1985, s 238 provides that a member is entitled to receive a copy of the annual accounts of the company (see Chapter 4) at least 21 days before the general meeting at which they are to be laid (usually the annual general meeting).

A member may also request that the company provide him with a copy of the latest accounts of the company (CA 1985, s 239).

Additionally, if the accounts from a listed public company have been received in the form of a summary financial statement, then a member may notify the company in the relevant manner prescribed by The Companies (Summary Financial Statements) Regulations 1995 (SI 1995 No 2092), of either or both of the following matters:

(i)   that he wishes to receive full accounts and reports for the financial year covered by the summary financial statements; and/or

(ii) that he wishes to receive full accounts and reports for future financial years.

(c)   To receive notice of general meetings

Subject to any provisions to the contrary contained in the company's articles of association, a member is entitled, pursuant to CA 1985, s 370, to receive notice of all general meetings.

CA 1985, s 372 further provides that a member may appoint a proxy to attend a general meeting on his behalf. This right may be restricted in the articles of association to the extent that a member of a private company (unless authorised by the articles) may not appoint more than one proxy and also (unless authorised by the articles) a proxy may not vote except on a poll. A proxy may, however, join in the demand for a poll (see 7.32 below).

(d)   Elective regime

Where a private company has elected to dispense with the requirements of the Act relating to the holding of annual general meetings, the laying of the annual accounts before a general meeting and the annual appointment of auditors, a member may, by giving notice to the company, require that these elections be disapplied in respect of any year (see 7.60 below).

(e)   Unfair prejudice

Under CA 1985, s 459 a member has the right to petition the court to obtain relief where the member considers that any act (proposed or actual) will or has resulted in unfair prejudice to his interests or to the interests of the members generally.

(f)   Petition court

A member has the right under section 122 of the Insolvency Act 1986 to petition the court for the winding-up of a company if it is unable to pay its debts, if the members have fallen below two in the case of a public company or on just and equitable grounds.

Following the Law Commission's report on shareholder remedies, the DTI has issued a consultation document which includes most of the Law Commission's original recommendations. The proposals are intended to make it easier for minority shareholders to seek redress if they are not content with the way a company is being run. One recommendation is the introduction of an exit article to Table A providing a procedure allowing shareholders to make arrangements to deal with the situation where a disaffected shareholder wants to leave the company.

Liabilities of members

7.8   In addition to rights, a member also has certain liabilities imposed upon him by the Act as follows.

(a)   *Contributions on winding-up*

To contribute to the assets of the company in respect of any amounts outstanding on the shares which they hold in a winding-up (Insolvency Act 1986, s 74). Members of companies limited by guarantee would, in such circumstances, be liable to pay the amount of the guarantee which they have given. In certain circumstances persons who have been members within the twelve months preceding the winding-up can also be required to contribute to the assets of the company, but not beyond the amount which is unpaid on the shares which they held.

(b)   *To pay calls on shares*

To pay up when called upon to do so by the company, any amount outstanding on the shares which a member holds and which are unpaid (CA 1985, s 1(2)(a) and Table A, regulation 12).

(c)   *Carrying on business with less than two members*

CA 1985, s 24 imposes a personal liability upon a member of a public company where a company has carried on business for more than six months without having two members, such circumstances being in contravention of CA 1985, s 1(1). Under section 122 of the Insolvency Act 1986, there being only one member of a public company is grounds under which a petition may be made to the court to wind up a company.

Where a public company has only one member CA 1985, s 24 states that any person who, during the period the company had less than two members, is a member and knows that the company is carrying on business with less than two members, becomes jointly and severally liable with the company for the payment of the company's debts incurred during that period.

Provisions for single member private companies were implemented by the Companies (Single Member Private Limited Companies) Regulations 1992 (SI 1992 No 1699) which came into force on 15 July

1992. Accordingly, section 24 of the Companies Act 1985 and section 122 of the Insolvency Act 1986 no longer apply to private companies. A person who is liable for the debts of a private company under those provisions ceases to be liable for any such debts incurred from the date when these regulations came into force.

Other duties, however, will fall upon a single member to safeguard the company. For instance, the sole member of a private company will be liable to a fine if he fails to make a written record of decisions made in a general meeting. He may instead proceed by a written resolution where appropriate (CA 1985, s 382B, as inserted by the above regulations).

If the membership of a private company falls to one, a statement that this has occurred must be entered on the register of members together with the date when this change occurred. If subsequently the membership increases to two or more, another statement must be inserted into the register stating that the company ceased to have one member and the date when it occurred. There is also a fine for default of this provision (CA 1985, s 382B(2), as inserted by the above regulations).

Share rights

7.9   As well as the rights which attach to membership of a company, a member also has certain rights which attach to the shares which he holds. These rights are set out by a combination of the Companies Act 1985 and the articles of association.

Companies Act 1985

The rights set out in the Companies Act 1985 include the following.

Pre-emption rights

7.10   Under section 89 of the CA 1985 a company proposing to issue shares is obliged to offer the existing members a proportion of the shares equal to the member's current shareholding (see 8.5 CAPITAL). In certain circumstances a member's right may be disapplied pursuant to sections 91 and 95 of the CA 1985 (see 8.6–8.7 CAPITAL).

Variation of class rights

7.11   Special rights attached to a class of shares usually relate to dividends, voting, return of capital or distribution of surplus assets on a winding-up and will commonly be found in a company's articles of association. However they may be set out in the memorandum, or created by a special resolution. Where the rights are laid down asaforementioned, the provisions will determine how the shares can be varied. If it is unclear where the definition of rights is laid down, a scheme of arrangement, under section 425 of the CA 1985, may be necessary to clarify them.

(a)   *Special rights in the memorandum*

Where the memorandum provides for a variation procedure, the clause must be complied with. If the variation is connected with the giving, variation, revocation, or renewal of an authority for the purposes of section 80 of the CA 1985, or with a reduction of the company's share capital, then the variation can be effected by following the statutory procedure in 7.11(*b*) below.

If the memorandum does not include provisions relating to a variation of rights but these are instead included in the articles on incorporation, then that procedure as laid down must be followed. However if neither the memorandum nor the articles contain provisions then the special rights will have to be varied by *all* the members. It is possible for the memorandum to prohibit a variation altogether, in which case the only option would be by means of a scheme of arrangement or reconstruction under section 425 of the CA 1985.

(b)   *Special rights in the articles*

If the articles provide for a variation of rights procedure it usually takes the form of what is called a 'modification of rights article' whereby class rights can be changed by passing an extraordinary resolution at a separate class meeting or by obtaining written consent of three-quarters of the holders of the issued shares of that class. The expressed procedure as set out in the articles must be complied with and any meeting required to be held must be done so in accordance with the provisions relating to the holding of general meetings in the articles. However, there must be a quorum of two who between them hold at least one-third in nominal value of the issued shares of that class.

In the situation where the articles do not provide for a variation procedure, section 125(2) of the CA 1985 details the statutory procedure to be followed. This is very similar to what is commonly found in the articles and requires:

(i)   three-quarters of the holders of the issued shares of the class in question to consent in writing to the variation; or

(ii)   the passing of an extraordinary resolution at a separate class meeting sanctioning the variation.

It should be noted that a written resolution of the members under section 381A of the CA 1985 could be used but that would mean obtaining the signature of *all* shareholders, not just of that particular class.

(c)   *Objection to variation*

If the articles or memorandum state that a variation is subject to consent of a certain number of the holders of that class then section 127 of the CA 1985 may be applied. This gives minority members the right to challenge a decision to vary rights by making an application to the court within 21 days of the resolution being passed, to have the variation cancelled.

At least 15% of the dissentient holders of the issued shares concerned, who did not consent or vote for the resolution, must be party to the application. The court then has to decide whether the variation would unfairly prejudice the shareholders of the class represented. The variation will not have effect until it has been confirmed by the court.

Articles of association

7.12   The articles of association is the document which sets out a company's internal rules (see 2.33–2.38, 2.44 THE COMPANY CONSTITUTION) and accordingly the rights attaching to shares will usually be stated in them.

Voting

7.13   Regulations 54 to 63 of Table A set out the model voting rights attaching to shares. Regulation 54 states that 'subject to any rights or restrictions attaching to any shares' on a show of hands every member present at a general meeting has one vote (regardless of the number of shares held) and on a poll has one vote for each share of which he is the holder.

Where different classes of share exist the rights of members to vote on a show of hands is sometimes restricted (e.g. deferred shares) and different weightings can be attached to the number of votes shares of different classes carry on a poll (e.g. 'A' ordinary shares—one vote for every share held; 'B' ordinary shares—one vote for every ten shares held).

Regulation 57 further specifies that, unless all moneys due and payable in respect of shares held by a member have been paid, then that member's voting rights are suspended until such time as the amounts due have been paid. A company may specify in its articles other circumstances when voting rights may be suspended (e.g. public companies commonly reserve this right for circumstances when a member to whom a request under section 212 of the Act requiring the member to disclose the beneficial ownership of shares had not so disclosed beneficial ownership).

Dividends

7.14   Part VIII of the Companies Act 1985 sets out the statutory provisions relating to the payment of dividends by a company. Additionally, regulations 102 to 108 of Table A provide model regulations.

(a)   Statutory provisions

Section 263(1) of the CA 1985 provides that a company may not make a distribution except out of profits available for the purpose. A distribution is described in CA 1985, s 263(2) as being a distribution of a company's assets, whether in cash or otherwise. However, the following are specifically referred to in that section as not being distributions:

(i)   an issue of shares as fully or partly paid bonus shares (see 8.13 CAPITAL);

(ii) redemption or purchase of a company's own shares out of capital (CA 1985, s 171);

(iii) reduction of share capital (CA 1985, s 135); and

(iv) distribution of assets on a winding-up.

The profits available for distribution are defined as being a company's accumulated realised profits less its accumulated realised losses, so far as not previously distributed, capitalised or written off (CA 1985, s 263(3)). Sections 270 to 276 of the CA 1985 further specify that, for the purposes of determining the profit available for distribution, reference must be made to the company's last annual, or interim, or initial accounts prepared in accordance with Part VII of the CA 1985. A public company is required to deliver these accounts to Companies House where they are used for the purposes of determining a dividend.

Problems have arisen where PLC's have not filed interim accounts, which were required for justification of the payment of a dividend, prior to the distribution being made. Any dividend paid out in contravention of the provisions laid down in the Companies Act is illegal and therefore recoverable from the shareholders.

Further restrictions are imposed on distributions by a public company. CA 1985, s 264 states that a public company may only make a distribution at any time:

(i)   if at the time of the distribution the amount of its net assets is not less than the aggregate of its called up share capital and undistributable reserves; and

(ii) the distribution does not reduce the amount of the net assets to less than the aggregate of its called up share capital and undistributable reserves.

The undistributable reserves are defined by section 264(3) as being:

(A)   share premium account; or

(B)   capital redemption reserve; or

(C)   the amount by which the accumulated, unrealised profits exceed the accumulated unrealised losses (so far as not previously utilised, written off or reorganised as appropriate); or

(D)   any other reserve stated as not being capable of distribution either in the company's memorandum and articles or any statute.

A company which has an exemption from the use of the word 'limited' in its name under section 30 of the Act (see 2.15 THE COMPANY CONSTITUTION) is specifically required by the Act to have a clause in its memorandum and articles of association prohibiting it from paying dividends (section 30(3)(b)).

(b)   Articles of association

A company's articles of association will usually make provision for the declaration of a dividend and its payment. Regulations 102 to 108 of Table A set out model regulations in this respect. These regulations may be modified as required by a company (see 2.34 THE COMPANY CONSTITUTION).

(i)   Declaration

Regulation 102 of Table A provides that a company may by ordinary resolution declare dividends, but may not declare a dividend which exceeds the amount recommended by the directors. This is a matter commonly dealt with at the annual general meeting (see Precedent N, Appendix 7B).

(ii)   Interim dividends

Interim dividends are dividends which are paid between general meetings at which final dividends are declared. The power to pay interim dividends is one which is commonly delegated to the directors (regulation 103 of Table A) (see Precedent M, Appendix 7B).

(iii)   Right to receive dividends

The articles of association will usually set out the rights of different classes of shareholder to receive dividends. Regulation 104 of Table A provides that, subject to any rights attached to shares, dividends are declared and paid according to the amounts paid up on the shares for which the dividend is paid.

(iv)   Payment

Payment of dividends is usually made by way of dividend warrant which details the gross amount of the dividend due to the shareholder, the tax credit (see 10.9 COMPANY TAXATION) and the net amount payable, together with a warrant (or cheque) for the net amount.

(v)   Unclaimed dividends

Regulation 108 of Table A provides that any dividend not claimed within twelve years of its declaration can be forfeited and cease to remain owing by the company if the directors so resolve. This is a longer period than the minimum required by statute. Under the Limitation Act 1980 the time limit for recovery is six years in England. In Scotland the time limit is five years under the Prescription and Limitation (Scotland) Act 1973.

(vi) *Scrip Dividends*

These are also known as stock dividends and are shares which are issued fully paid to shareholders instead of a cash dividend. They are different to bonus issues as the shareholder is usually given the choice of electing to take shares or cash.

(vii) *Waiver of dividends*

Shareholders can waive their rights to receive a particular or future dividends in respect of all or part of their holdings. To be effective, the waiver should be in the form of a deed and should be executed and delivered to the company prior to the dividend being declared and paid (see Precedent N, Appendix 7B). The reason for this is to avoid any liability to tax due on declared dividends.

Alternatively the articles of association could be amended to include a provision giving shareholders the right to send notice to the company waiving their rights to a particular dividend, and consequently allowing the company to only declare and pay dividends to the shareholders who haven't given such a notice.

(viii) *Winding-up*

The rights of shareholders to participate in a distribution of the assets of a company on a winding-up will usually be determined by reference to any class rights existing in the articles of association. Regulation 117 of Table A provides that the liquidator may, with the sanction of an extraordinary resolution of the company, distribute the assets available for that purpose amongst the members. The usual presumption is that members holding shares with the same rights and paid up to the same extent rank equally on such a distribution with the amount paid relating to the proportion of shares held.

Class rights

7.15   The share capital of a company may be divided into such class of shares as the company may determine. This is commonly done by the share rights being determined in the articles of association, although the articles may provide otherwise (e.g. regulation 2 of Table A provides that shares may be issued with such rights or restrictions as the company may by ordinary resolution determine). In varying class rights account must be taken of section 125 of the CA 1985 (see 7.11 above).

The common classes of shares which a company's share capital may contain are as follows.

(*a*)   *Ordinary shares*

A company's ordinary share capital is commonly regarded as its 'risk' capital as the ordinary shares of a company will usually carry the main financial risk. They will normally confer on the holders full voting rights but will be subordinate to other classes of share in respect of dividends (e.g. preference shares). The ordinary shareholders usually stand to gain (or lose) the most on a winding-up, depending on the surplus assets available, as an ordinary share will usually participate past its capital value.

It is increasingly common for companies to divide their ordinary shares into different categories (e.g. 'A' ordinary shares and 'B' ordinary shares) and to attach different rights to each, for example, weighted voting rights between categories. Some companies have also issued non-voting ordinary shares, which bear all the characteristics of an ordinary share, but do not confer on the holder any right to vote at a general meeting. Companies are allowed to issue non-voting shares i.e. shares that do not carry any voting rights but this is rare in practice. Furthermore, the Stock Exchange Listing Rules provide that non-voting shares must be clearly designated as such.

(*b*)   *Preference shares*

The common characteristic of preference shares is that they carry the right to a fixed dividend and will usually rank in priority to other classes of share for repayment on a winding-up.

(i)   *Dividend*

The dividend due on preference shares is, unless stated to be non-cumulative, deemed cumulative; thus, should a company fail to pay the dividend due, the dividend will accrue to the shareholder and become payable (together with the next dividend due) at the next payment date. A preference dividend must be satisfied before a dividend can be paid to the ordinary shareholders. Non-cumulative dividends are deemed lost if a company is unable to pay them in any particular year. The right to a dividend once declared is usually expressed as a percentage e.g. 8% preference shares.

(ii)   *Voting*

Preference shares will not usually confer on the holders a right to vote at general meetings unless their dividend is in arrears, at which point they may be accorded such rights, or there is a proposed variation attaching to the shares.

(iii) *Winding-up*

Preference shares usually only confer on the holders the right to the repayment of the capital sum of the share together with any dividends in arrears. However, it is possible for the shares to be deemed 'participating' in which case they will (after repayment of capital and outstanding dividends) rank equally with the ordinary shares on a distribution of surplus assets.

(iv) *Conversion*

Preference shares may carry the right for the holders to convert them into ordinary shares at a particular time or upon the occurrence of a given event.

(c) *Redeemable shares*

Where authorised by its articles of association, a company may issue redeemable shares (CA 1985, s 159). A model power for the issue of redeemable shares is given by regulation 3 of Table A. The terms and manner of the redemption must be determined in the articles of association, but in any event must be determined before the shares are issued (CA 1985, s 159A, inserted by CA 1989, s 133) (this section, however, is not yet in force). No redeemable shares may be issued where a company has no non-redeemable shares in issue.

The rights attaching to redeemable shares on such matters as voting, rights to dividend and to participate in a winding-up should be determined in the articles. It is common for redeemable shares to be issued as a hybrid version of preference shares (i.e. redeemable preference shares) (see 8.58 and 8.59 CAPITAL).

(d) *Founder shares*

These are shares usually issued to the founders or promoters of a company which confer on the holders enhanced rights over other classes of share. It is common for founder shares to give to the holders proportionately increased voting rights over the ordinary shares and an entitlement to participate in surplus profits over a specified level.

(e) *Deferred shares*

Deferred shares are commonly shares which carry very few rights (i.e. their rights are deferred to the ordinary shares). A deferred share will usually carry no right to vote or participate in a distribution and only the right to repayment of their capital value on a winding-up.

(f) *Other types of shares*

In addition to the above, many hybrid forms of share which combine the characteristics of these different classes exist. Examples are as follows.

   (i)   Preferred ordinary shares.

   (ii)   Cumulative redeemable preference shares.

   (iii)   Cumulative redeemable participating preference shares.

   (iv)   Cumulative convertible non-participating preference shares.

   (v)   Non-cumulative convertible preference shares.

Such types of shares will commonly be used by venture capitalists when making an equity investment in a company.

Transfer and transmission of shares

Share transfers

7.16   Under section 182 of the Companies Act 1985 shares are deemed to be personal estate (moveable property in Scotland). They are transferable in the manner provided by the articles of association of a company. Section 183 of the CA 1985 states that a proper instrument must be completed and presented to the company unless the shares have been transmitted by operation of law.

The proper instrument of transfer required for fully paid shares of companies governed by the Companies Act 1985 is that set out in the Stock Transfer Act 1963. Under the 1963 Act the transferor's signature does not have to be witnessed nor be under seal and, where the shares concerned are fully paid, the transferee need not sign the form. Under CA 1985, s 183 it is unlawful for a company to register a transfer of shares not in this form (unless an exempt transfer under the Stock Transfer Act 1982).

Transfer procedure

7.17   A transfer of shares takes place when a shareholder who wishes to sell his shares completes a stock transfer form and gives it with his share certificate to the purchaser in exchange for the agreed price. The purchaser then completes the bottom half of the form with his name and address, dates it and then presents it for payment of the appropriate stamp duty at the Inland Revenue Stamp Office. Once the stock transfer form has been stamped it can then be presented, together with the appropriate share certificate, for registration with the company (see Precedent A2, Appendix 7B).

A new Stock Transfer form was introduced on 15 July 1996 for use where securities are transferred to a person who will hold them in uncertificated form. The address of the person to whom the securities are being transferred may be omitted.

If however the transferor only wishes to sell part of his shareholding then he must send the signed transfer to the company with his share certificate for endorsing with 'certificate lodged'. The stock transfer form is then returned, to be passed on to the transferee for the consideration, and can be presented to the company for registration.

Also, where the shares to be transferred are held jointly, then the stock transfer form must be signed by all the holders for the transfer to be valid.

If the shares being transferred are partly paid then the articles usually provide for both the transferor and transferee to sign the transfer form.

When a company receives a transfer for registration the following points should be borne in mind.

(*a*)   The details of the transferor and shares transferred should agree with the certificate(s) presented and the entry in the register of members.

(*b*)   The transfer form should be checked to ensure that it has been correctly completed and is stamped, denoting payment of the appropriate amount of stamp duty (see 7.19 below).

(*c*)   The company's records should be checked to ensure that there are no liens or other restrictions on the shares being transferred.

(*d*)   If the company has restrictions on transfers in its articles of association the transfer should be checked to ensure that it does not contravene any such provisions (see 7.18 below).

Once the company secretary is satisfied that the transfer is in order, it should be presented to the directors for their approval to its registration (see Precedent A, Appendix 7B). Once this approval has been obtained, the register of members of the company should then be updated and amended, as appropriate, with the details of the new member being entered. The share certificate of the former member should be cancelled and filed with the stock transfer form. If the certificate of the former member has been lost or destroyed then the member should be asked to complete an indemnity (see Precedent B, Appendix 7B). Only once the old share certificate (or an indemnity) has been lodged should a new certificate be prepared and issued. This must be done within two months of the transfer being lodged. The certificate will require signature by a director and the secretary of the company (or two directors) and be expressed as being executed by the company. The certificate can then be sent to the new member.

Pre-emption rights

7.18   Many private companies and some public companies (except those that are listed where shares must be freely transferable) insert into their articles of association pre-emption rights which apply in circumstances where an existing shareholder wishes to sell all or part of his shareholding. In such situations the pre-emption rights will commonly require that the shareholder who wishes to sell must first offer his shares to the other shareholders in proportion to their existing holdings and in accordance with rules laid down in the articles with regard to notices, time limits etc.

Where pre-emption rights exist they must be observed, a company will be able to refuse to register a transfer of shares where the rights have been disregarded. This right of refusal is in addition to any other rights of refusal a company has contained in its articles of association (regulations 24 and 25 of Table A). It should be noted that the directors' refusal to register a transfer must be in good faith, and for the benefit of the company. Where registration of a transfer in contravention of any existing pre-emption rights occurs, it is open to aggrieved members to contest its validity.

Stamp duty on transfer

7.19   The person responsible for maintaining a company's register of members (usually the company secretary) is bound to ensure that all transfers accepted for registration are either stamped with the appropriate duty or certified as being exempt from stamp duty. He can request the adjudication of a transfer where he doubts that it has been properly stamped.

The current rates of stamp duty are set out in Appendix 7A to this chapter. Gifts *inter vivos* are exempt from stamp duty and are not subject to adjudication and the levy of a fixed stamp duty of 50p. Such transfers may be submitted immediately for registration and need not be presented to the stamp office. The appropriate certificate on the reverse of the form must, however, be completed.

There are certain other transactions which are also exempt and are no longer subject to a fixed duty of 50p; these are also listed in the Appendix.

Crest

7.20   CREST is the electronic settlement system which allows shareholders to hold and transfer their securities in dematerialised form. CREST was introduced on the London Stock Exchange on 15 July 1996 and the previous settlement system, TALISMAN, closed on 11 April 1997.

The legal procedures for the CREST system are contained in the Uncertificated Securities Regulations 1995 (SI 1995 No 3272) which provide for the system to be run by an approved operator. The operator is CRESTCo Ltd, a private company owned by various firms connected with all sectors of the equities market. CRESTCo has issued a manual which sets out the procedures in detail and the rules which apply.

Joining CREST

7.21   In order for a company to be eligible to join CREST (to become a 'participating issuer') its articles of association will need to permit securities to be transferred through CREST and thus the articles will no doubt need amending. Normally, this would be done by the members passing a Special Resolution, but the regulations allow for the board to pass the relevant resolution and for notice of the directors' resolution to be given to all members either before or within 60 days of it being passed. The passing of the resolution effectively overrides any provisions in the company's articles inconsistent with CREST. CRESTCo has issued draft forms of notification.

The shareholders can resolve to revoke or reverse the directors' resolution by passing an ordinary resolution. A copy of the directors' resolution or of a resolution of the members preventing or reversing the directors' resolution must be filed with the Registrar within 15 days of it being passed.

In addition to joining CREST, the issuer must also submit a separate application form to CRESTCo for each class of securities concerned.

Readers should note that a directors' resolution is not effective for loan stock or other securities whose rights are not set out in the articles. Instead, appropriate alterations will need to be made to the instrument creating the terms of the said securities. Similarly, a directors' resolution cannot be used if changes are required to the procedures for conversion and/or redemption of shares. Instead the articles would have to be altered by members' resolution.

In due course, the company should seek to remove any unnecessary or obsolete articles after entering into CREST.

Deposits of certificated shares into CREST are exempt from 50p stamp duty charge, normally imposed for no sale transfer. In addition they will not be liable to stamp duty reserve tax (SDRT) unless 0.5% or 1.5% SDRT applies e.g. because they are transfers for consideration in money or money's worth (see Appendix 7A).

Statutory Registers

7.22   An entry on the register of members maintained by the participating issuer (e.g. the Registrar which has entered into thenecessary agreement with CRESTCo Ltd) is *prima facie* evidence of title to the units of security which he is recorded as holding in uncertificated form.

The Registrar will update the register of members upon receiving an operator instruction. If relating to a transfer of title to uncertificated units of a security, this is the point at which legal title passes to the transferee.

Transmission of shares and the registration of documents

7.23   Transmission of shares occurs when shares are 'transferred' by operation of law rather than by an act of a shareholder. For example, transmission encompasses the change in ownership in shares upon a shareholder's:

(*a*)   death;

(*b*)   bankruptcy; or

(*c*)   becoming of unsound mind and the subject of an order of the Court of Protection.

Where transmission occurs the entitled party must produce to the company whose shares he is interested in documentation to validate his claim. Where such documentation is received the following general points should be considered.

(i)   It should be ensured that the details of the shareholder concerned are the same in both the documentation submitted, the relevant share certificate(s) and the register of members.

(ii)   The share certificate(s) of the member concerned should be requested if not received at the same time as the documentation.

(iii)   The documents received should be recorded in a register of documents (date of receipt, type of document and date of return). Once the details of the documentation have been recorded in both the register of documents and register of members, a registration stamp or similar endorsement should be put onto the document.

(iv)   The share certificate should be endorsed in favour of the appropriate person and the company's registration stamp (as in (iii) above) impressed upon it. The endorsement on the share certificate should equate to the amended entry in the register of members (e.g. Messrs Y and Z, deceased).

(v)   The documentation and endorsed share certificate should be returned to the person entitled and an entry of the date they were returned made in the register of documents.

The common circumstances in which transmission will occur and the documentation required together with other circumstances when documentation may be presented to a company are discussed below.

(A)   *Probate*

Grants of probate (or in Scotland, Confirmation) enable a person or persons named in the will of a deceased person to act as executor in respect of the estate of the deceased. A grant of probate includes a copy of the will and is issued over the impressed seal of the Family Division of the High Court. To help executors, 'office copies' of the grant will often be issued bearing an impression of the seal of the Court. Office copies do not include a copy of the will, but as the terms of the will are generally of no consequence to a company, office copies are sufficient for registration purposes as they indicate who is empowered to deal with the deceased's estate and should be accepted by the company as satisfactory evidence of the grant (CA 1985, s 187).

On production of a probate for registering similar checks should be made as detailed in points (i) to (v) above. In addition the following is recommended:

(I) The date of death and registration of the probate should be entered in the appropriate folio of the register of members together with the name and address of the executor(s) to be described as 'executor of . . . . deceased'. After the name of the member the word 'deceased' should be included. Legally they remain the registered shareholder.

(II) The share certificate should be endorsed with the same details i.e. date of death and registration of probate, name and address of executor(s).

(III) Once the company has applied its registration stamp to the probate it should be returned to the person who lodged it together with the endorsed share certificate and if appropriate a new dividend mandate.

(IV) Letters of request may be sent to the executor(s) if personal registration is required (See (E) below).

(B) *Letters of administration*

Letters of administration (or in Scotland, Confirmation) are granted to a person to administer the estate of a person who has died without leaving a valid will (intestate) or without naming executors. Office copies of letters of administration are usually available in the same manner as for grants of probate.

(C) *Confirmation*

This is the equivalent Scottish document to English probate and letters of administration.

(D) *Bona vacantia*

Where a person domiciled in England and Wales has died without leaving a will and with no successor, then the High Court will appoint either the Treasury Solicitor, or the officers of the Duchy of Lancaster or the Duke of Cornwall to administer the estate of the deceased. The High Court will issue a document of *bona vacantia* to this effect. The equivalent Scottish document is *ultimus haeres*.

(E) *Letters of request*

A letter of request is a document sent by an executor or administrator to a company authorising and requesting the company to enter their names as the holders of the shares standing in the name of the deceased in the register of members. The letter must be signed by all the executors/administrators of the deceased and should only be registered if a grant of representation (e.g. probate) has already been registered by the company.

The procedure for registration is similar to that which applies in the case of non-market transfers. Any subsequent change in the registered holder can then only be effected by a transfer in the normal way.

(F)   *Death of holding in joint account*

When a joint shareholder dies, the company does not have to concern itself with his executors or administrators. The remaining shareholder has full power to deal with the shares as the legal interest in shares passes to them by right of survivorship. A company will normally receive a certificate of death and upon receipt the name and address of the appropriate member should be deleted in the register of members.

(G)   *Change of name of shareholder*

A shareholder can change his name in a number of ways, for example, by marriage, the grant of an honour, succession to a title or by deed poll. When a company receives evidence of a name change the register of members and the member's share certificate should be amended as appropriate.

(H)   *Change of address of shareholder*

Notifications of change of address should be signed personally by the shareholder. If there are circumstances that give rise to concern regarding the authenticity of the notification, then the shareholder should be sent the company's own form for completion.

(I)   *Court of Protection orders*

The Court of Protection makes orders appointing receivers to deal with the income of persons described as 'the patient' when a person is proved to be incapable (through mental disorder) of managing his property and affairs. The equivalent Scottish document is known as an appointment of a judicial factor or *curator bonis.*

(J)   *Lien*

A notice of lien is merely written advice that share certificates have been deposited with a person as security for a loan or other advance. Such a notice should not be acknowledged by a company as this would be contrary to the provisions of section 360 of the Companies Act 1985.

It may be desirable, however, to keep an unofficial note of the notice in case the company wishes to exercise a lien over the shares or is asked to issue a duplicate certificate.

(K) *Bankruptcy order*

The effect of a bankruptcy order is to vest the property in the shares in a trustee for the benefit of the shareholder's creditors. Either the original order or an authenticated office copy of it or a copy of the *London* (or *Edinburgh*) *Gazette* should be presented to a company. The equivalent Scottish document is an act and warrant appointing a trustee in bankruptcy.

(L) *Stop notice*

A stop notice is an official notice given by the court preventing the transfer of (and sometimes the payment of dividends on) a shareholding because of the interest of a third party in the shares. There is no similar Scottish document.

(M) *Injunction*

An injunction or restraining order may be made by the court preventing the transfer of a shareholding. The order or an authenticated copy are sufficient for registration purposes. The equivalent Scottish document is an Interdict.

While the order is in force no transfer of the shareholding can be registered.

(N) *Rectification of register*

A court may order that the register of members of a company be rectified by the removal or addition of a person. The original order or an authenticated copy may be registered.

(O) *Restrictions on shares*

Under sections 210 and 445 of the CA 1985, the Department of Trade and Industry, or the court, may order that the rights of transfer, renunciation, exchange and voting be removed from particular shares.

In the event of the withdrawal of the order, this should be acknowledged to the sender and the entries made in respect of it deleted from the register.

(P) *Powers of attorney*

A power of attorney is the appointment by an individual or body corporate of a person or persons to act on his or its behalf on the terms and for the period specified in the power.

Share certificates

7.24   A share certificate must contain at least the following information:

(*a*)   a certificate serial number;

(*b*)   the name of the company;

(*c*)   the name of the registered holder;

(*d*)   the number and description of the shares (this should be shown twice as a security measure);

(*e*)   a statement of the extent to which the shares are paid up; and

(*f*)   the date of the issue.

Companies that are listed on the Stock Exchange must also comply with the requirements of the Stock Exchange's Listing Rules ('the Yellow Book').

The full name of the shareholder should be shown on the certificate together with any titles he may have (decorations or professional qualifications do not have to be shown). Where the shareholder is a body corporate, its full unabbreviated name should be shown. For joint holders it is only necessary to show the name of the first-named holder, although it is common practice to include the names of all the joint holders. Many certificates show the shareholder's registered address. This is the full address that appears in the register of members. Increasingly, share certificates do not show the address of shareholders as it has been recognised that addresses tend to become out of date very quickly.

(1)   *Execution of certificates*

Under section 186 of the CA 1985, a share certificate issued under the common seal of a company is *prima facie* evidence of amember's title to the shares which the certificate represents. Accordingly, it is very important that precautions are taken for the accurate completion and security of share certificates. Companies are under no obligation to seal certificates but doing so gives the certificate greater evidential standing. Where a company has dispensed with the requirement to have a common seal (CA 1985, s 36A(3)), then a share certificate will be validly executed when signed by either two directors or one director and the company secretary and expressed as being executed on behalf of the company (CA 1985, s 36A(4)).

If a certificate is signed without the director's authority, it will be void and not binding on the company (*South London Greyhound Racecourses Ltd v Wake [1931] 1 Ch 496*). However, where a certificate is issued under the authority of the directors, even if fraudulently obtained, then the company is estopped from denying the holder's title. This can occur in circumstances where a transferee has lodged a forged transfer with the company or where the company secretary has fraudulently obtained the director's authority. Thus, it is now common practice for larger companies to have a forged transfer insurance policy to cover potential liabilities arising from the issue of share certificates.

(2) *Securities seal*

Although companies are no longer obliged to have company seals many public companies have adopted and continue to use 'securities seals'. Such seals are useful where the register of members is maintained by external Registrars, as the seal can then be kept in the custody of the Registrar who may seal the certificates without the need to send the certificates to the company for execution. The London Stock Exchange used to require listed companies to seal share certificates but this has since been abolished. Where seals are used, it is quite common for signatures to be omitted. Authority for this must be granted by the articles of association of the company.

(3) *Issue*

Under section 185 of the CA 1985, a company is required to have share certificates ready within two months after the date of allotment of shares or the date on which a valid transfer form is presented for registration. For listed companies the requirements are slightly more onerous as certificates must be available within one month after the expiry of any right of renunciation of renounceable documents, or within 14 days of the presentation of a valid transfer form.

Companies may issue more than one certificate in respect of each holding if authorised by their articles. Private companies are permitted to charge fees for these services. Listed companies are prohibited from charging a fee for replacing certificates.

(4) *Duplicate certificates*

Regulation 7 of Table A provides that where a share is defaced, worn out, lost or destroyed then it may be renewed. When this occurs the shareholder should be asked to complete an indemnity in return for which a duplicate certificate (marked as such) can be prepared and issued to the member (see Precedent B, Appendix 7B).

General meetings

General

7.25   A general meeting is a meeting of the members of the company called either in circumstances specified by the Act or the memorandum and articles of association, at which the members will consider, and if thought fit, pass resolutions.

The Companies Act 1985 makes provision for three types of general meeting and the circumstances in which they must be held:

(*a*)   annual general meeting (see 7.41 below);

(*b*)   extraordinary general meeting (see 7.47 below); and

(*c*)   separate general meeting of the holders of a class of share (see 7.52 below).

A company may, in its memorandum and articles of association, introduce further situations where a general meeting must be called to consider specific items of business.

Convening of general meetings

7.26   A general power to convene general meetings vests in the directors of a company who must call a general mee9ting when required to do so by the Act or the company's articles of association, or when the directors wish. Regulation 37 of Table A provides a model power for the directors to call general meetings.

In certain circumstances, general meetings may be convened by the members, the court and on the requisition of the auditors (see 7.47 below).

Section 369 provides for the giving of notice of meetings to members (see 7.35 below).

Quorum

7.27   A general meeting cannot be validly held unless a quorum of members is in attendance. A long-established principle of the common law is that a meeting is only validly constituted by the attendance of two or more persons (*Sharp v Dawes (1876) 2 QBD 26*). A company may determine its quorum requirements in the articles of association. Regulation 40 of Table A provides for a minimum of two members present either in person or by proxy to be a quorum.

Should a company's articles of association make no provision as to quorum, then under section 370(4) of the Companies Act 1985, the quorum is deemed to be two members personally present. An interesting point is that this definition makes no provision for proxies being counted in a quorum.

In the case of a private company, one person may be a quorum regardless of any provision in the articles if the company has only one member (CA 1985, s 370A; the Companies (Single Member Private Limited Companies) Regulations 1992 (SI 1992 No 1699)).

The Act specifies two other circumstances in which one member may be a quorum, as follows:

(*a*)   a general meeting called on the direction of the Secretary of State under CA 1985, s 367; and (*b*)   a general meeting called on the order of the court under CA 1985, s 371 (see 7.51 below).

Proxies

7.28   Section 372(1) of the Companies Act 1985 provides that a member entitled to attend and vote at a general meeting is entitled to appoint another person to attend and vote on his behalf. The proxy need not also be a member.

For a private company the right of a proxy extends to his also being able to speak at the meeting. This right does not, however, extend to the proxy of a member of a public company.

However, section 372(2) of the CA 1985 imposes certain restrictions on proxies, being:

(*a*)   a member in a company not having a share capital has no right to appoint a proxy;

(*b*)   a member of a private company is not entitled to appoint more than one proxy to attend on the same occasion; and

(*c*)   a proxy is not entitled to vote except on a poll. A proxy may however demand, or join in the demand for, a poll (CA 1985, s 373(2)).

A company may extend these rights in its articles of association.

The notice calling a general meeting of a company limited by shares must contain a statement that a member is entitled to appoint a proxy (CA 1985, s 372(3)). To be valid, a form of proxy must be lodged with the company by a specific time prior to the holding of the meeting (usually 48 hours — Table A, article 62), thus allowing for the company to check the validity ofappointments. Any provision in a company's articles which seeks to extend the period to longer than 48 hours is void (CA 1985, s 372(5)). However, the period may be shortened (e.g. to 24 hours).

(For a sample form of appointment of a proxy see Precedent C, Appendix 7B.)

In recent years questions have arisen as to the validity of faxed proxy appointments. More specifically when the original signed copy is not physically deposited at the designated office within the specified time laid down in the Articles. For the purposes of Part 8 of the Insolvency Rules 1986 it has been held that a faxed proxy form is acceptable if the signature placed thereon carries some distinctive or personal marking which has been placed there by, or with the authority of the creditor. Although this ruling does not apply to meetings held under the Companies Act 1985, the company's articles could be altered to allow for faxed proxies.

The Companies Act does not prevent the use of electronic proxies and E-Vote, a subsidiary of Thomson Financial Services, will be launching an electronic voting system whereby proxy votes will be able to be lodged electronically via the internet with registrars.

For companies employing registrars it will be the registrars who are initially responsible for checking proxy cards against the Register of Members and counting the postal proxy votes prior to the general meeting. If the proxy voting is close or the resolutions being proposed are controversial a poll may be demanded, in which case, scrutineers should be appointed by the company to check the proxy voting for any irregularities, and to carry out the poll count at the meeting itself (see 7.32 below).

When the shares of a company are traded on the (Alternative Investment Market) AIM or if the company is listed, it is obliged to send to all persons entitled to vote together with the notice, proxy forms providing for two-way voting on all resolutions to be proposed at the meeting (Chapter 13, para 28 of the London Stock Exchange's Listing Rules and the AIM Rules) (Table A, Art 61). The form must also state that if it is returned with no indication as to how the proxy shall vote, the proxy will exercise his discretion as he thinks fit. The articles commonly provide for the instrument of proxy to be signed by the appointer, and sealed in the case of a corporation.

Section 372(6) of the CA 1985 states that where proxies are sought at the company's expense and specify that a particular person is to act as a proxy, the invitation must be extended to all the members entitled to appoint a proxy for the meeting.

Where proxies have been revoked, regulation 63 of Table A provides that a vote given or a poll demanded by a proxy or an authorised representative of a corporation shall be valid where the authority of the person voted has been previously determined, unless a notice was duly deposited before the commencement of the meeting or any adjourned meeting at which the vote is given or the poll demanded.

If there are no provisions contained within the articles of association after the meeting has begun but before an adjourned meeting or a poll, notification of a revocation will only be effective if received before the meeting has started, since the adjournment and poll are regarded as continuations of the meeting.

If a member is present in person at the meeting he may vote despite having appointed a proxy. Where a member votes at the meeting, the proxy's authority will be impliedly revoked and if the proxy also votes this will invalidate his vote (*Cousins v International Brick Co Ltd [1931] 2 Ch 90*).

Authorised representative

7.29   A corporation which is a member of a company may, under section 375 of the Companies Act 1985, appoint a person to be its representative at any meeting of a company which it is entitled to attend. Such representatives may be appointed by resolution of the directors of the appointing corporation (see Precedent D, Appendix 7B).

It is advantageous from the appointing company's point of view to appoint a representative instead of a proxy. This stems from the fact that a corporate representative holds the same rights at a meeting as those of a registered shareholder. He may speak at the meeting and may vote on a show of hands and be counted in the quorum.

Additionally, the usual 48-hour notification rule for proxies to be appointed does not apply to a corporate representative, although it is common practice for the representative to submit prior to the meeting some proof of authority from his appointor.

Voting

7.30   There are two forms of voting at a general meeting, being a show of hands and a poll. A company may determine the voting rights of members (usually related to the class of share held) in its articles of association. Table A provides model voting powers in regulations 54–63.

Show of hands

7.31   Regulation 54 of Table A provides that, on a show of hands, every member present in person (or by an authorised representative) has one vote. Unless conferred by the articles, proxies have no right to vote on a show of hands. The chairman will usually count the hands raised and declare the result.

On a poll

7.32   Regulation 54 provides that each member has one vote for every share which he holds on a poll. This procedure recognises the weighted rights of the larger shareholder who, on a show of hands, may be defeated by a larger number of smaller shareholders. On a poll, votes may be cast either personally, or by proxy (Table A, regulation 59 and CA 1985, s 372).

The articles of association may make provision for the procedure on a poll but section 373 of the Companies Act 1985 states that any provision in the articles is void so far as it seeks to:

(*a*)   restrict the circumstances in which a poll may be demanded to other than on the question of the appointment of the chairman of the meeting or the adjournment of the meeting;

(*b*)   make ineffective a demand for a poll:

   (i)   by not less than five members entitled to vote;

   (ii)   by a member or members representing at least 10% of the total voting rights of members having the right to vote;

(iii)   by members holding shares paid up to the extent of more than one-tenth of the total sum paid up on all the shares conferring a right to vote at the meeting.

Under section 373(2) of the CA 1985 a proxy may demand or join in the demand for a poll.

The voting process will generally be managed by the company's registrars and/or scrutineers appointed for this purpose. Firstly the validity of the demand should be checked by referring to the authority laid down in the articles and the identity of the person demanding the poll. The poll may be taken immediately, at the conclusion of the meeting, or at another time fixed by the chairman.

If the poll is to be held straight away, voting cards will be issued for completion and collected for checking, including those which the chairman has for the shareholders who appointed him as proxy.

Any spoilt or incomplete cards will not be included together with any cards completed by members not shown on the register of members at the register's closing date.

Having counted the votes, the registrar, or appointed scrutineer, will produce a certificate recording the exercise of the votes. The Chairman will then declare the result of the poll.

Casting vote

7.33   Regulation 50 of Table A allows, in the case of an equality of vote, the chairman to have a second or casting vote. In the event that the articles of association do not provide for a casting or second vote to the chairman then he will not be entitled to one.

Majority requirements

7.34   The Companies Act 1985 and a company's articles of association require resolutions to be passed by specified majorities. For the types of resolution, the majorities required and the circumstances in which they may be used see 7.56 *et. seq.* below.

Notice of meetings

7.35   Every general meeting which a company holds requires notice to be given to each person entitled to attend. The notice must be given within specified time limits and must contain certain particulars. The regulations surrounding the notice of meetings are found both in Chapter IV of Part XI of the Companies Act 1985 and a company's articles of association.

The articles of association of a company may not reduce the length of notice required to be given to less than the minimum required by section 369 of the

CA 1985. However, they may increase the length of notice required. The minimum periods of notice pursuant to CA 1985, s 369 are as follows:

(*a*)   In the case of an annual general meeting, or a general meeting at which a special resolution is to be proposed, *21 days'* notice.

(*b*)   In the case of a general meeting, other than an annual general meeting or a general meeting at which a special resolution is to be proposed, *14 days'* notice.

It should be noted that one of the provisions contained within the Combined Code (see Appendix 6E) states that companies should arrange for the notice of the AGM and related papers to be sent to shareholders at least 20 working days before the meeting, thus giving shareholders more time to consider the contents of what they have been sent.

If the articles of association of a company are silent on the dates upon which the service and receipt of the notice will be deemed to have occurred, then such dates may not be included in the period of notice. However, the articles of association will usually indicate whether the period of notice is to include or exclude the day of posting of the notice, the day of service and the day of the meeting itself.

Pursuant to CA 1985, s 369, a notice issued to convene a general meeting must be in writing.

Agreement to short notice

7.36   A meeting called by shorter notice than that specified by sections 369 and 378 of the Companies Act 1985 or the articles of association will only be valid if the following conditions are met.

(*a*)   In the case of an annual general meeting, the short notice has been agreed to by all the members of the company entitled to attend and vote (CA 1985, s 369(3)(a)) (see Precedent E.2, Appendix 7B).

(*b*)   In the case of any other general meeting, the short notice has been agreed to by a majority of the members holding not less than 95% of the nominal value of the shares having a right to attend and vote at the meeting (CA 1985, s 369(4) and 378(3)) (see Precedent E.1, Appendix 7B).

Under the elective regime the majority of members required to authorise short notice for an extraordinary general meeting of a *private* company may, with the consent of all of the members of the company, be reduced to not less than 90% of the nominal value of the shares having a right to attend and vote at the meeting (CA 1985, s 369(4) and s 378(3)). (See 7.60 below.)

Entitlement to receive notice

7.37   Unless the articles of association determine otherwise, a notice of a general meeting must be given to every member of the company and to all persons entitled to a share in consequence upon the death or bankruptcy of a member and to the directors and auditors (CA 1985, s 370(2); Table A, regulation 38).

Table A, regulation 112 additionally states that:

(*a*)   where joint holders of a share are concerned, the notice should be given to the first named in the register of members; and

(*b*)   if a member has a registered address outside of the United Kingdom he shall not be entitled to receive such notice unless he has given to the company an address within the United Kingdom where notices may be given to him.

Regulation 116 of the 1985 Table A provides that a notice may be given by the company to a bankrupt or deceased person's trustee or personal representative to an address provided by them. However, in the absence of such an address, the notice may be given as if the bankruptcy or death had not occurred.

Furthermore, section 370(1) and (2) of Companies Act 1985, state that even though a member may not be entitled to attend a meeting unless the articles otherwise provide, he will still be entitled to receive notice. If a notice of a general meeting forms part of the statutory accounts, a footnote should be inserted to the effect that it is sent only for information to the holders of shares who are not entitled to attend and vote at the meeting.

If a person is entered into the register of members after notices have been despatched he is not entitled to receive the notice of the meeting. However, his usual rights of attendance and voting and to be counted in the quorum will still be applicable.

The company may also see fit to give notice of meetings to their solicitors and other advisers.

Table A, regulation 39 gives some form of relief in that if by accident any person so entitled to receive notice, failed to receive it, that fact shall not invalidate the proceedings at the meeting.

Contents of notice

7.38   The name of the company together with details of the time, place and date of the meeting must be stated on the notice together with the general nature of the business to be transacted. If the meeting is to be an annual general meeting this must also be described as such (CA 1985, s 366(1)). Pursuant to section 372(3) of the Companies Act 1985 a statement that a member entitled to attend and vote at the meeting has the right to appoint a proxy to attend and vote in his stead must appear on thenotice. The notice should, by convention, be signed by or on behalf of the convening authority (CA 1985, s 41). This will usually be the secretary on behalf of the directors of the company. (See Precedent F, Appendix 7B.)

In order for a notice to be valid it must state clearly the business to be transacted at the meeting, giving enough information to enable it to be fully understood. Where the proposed resolution contained in the notice is not self-explanatory it is customary to also attach an explanatory statement to the notice. This is necessary to enable members to make an informed decision whether or not to attend the meeting.

It used to be necessary for listed companies to state in their notice convening an annual general meeting the place and time at which copies of directors' service contracts will be available for inspection, or a negative statement if there are no such contracts available. The requirement to include such a note has now been removed following Amendment 8 to the Listing Rules.

If it is the intention to move a special, extraordinary or elective resolution at a meeting, sections 378(2) and 379A(2) require the notice to be described as such. Furthermore, the text of any of the above described resolutions must be set out accurately and contain the entire substance of the resolution. There can be no substantial amendments of these resolutions after the notice of the general meeting at which the resolutions are to be proposed is served.

Circulars

7.39   If the company is listed, it is a requirement that for any business other than routine business at an annual general meeting, the notice must be accompanied by an explanatory circular or if the business is to be considered on the same day as the annual general meeting an explanation must be incorporated into the directors' report (Chapter 14, para 17 of the London Stock Exchange's Listing Rules).

It is common practice, that where business is to be conducted at a meeting which is non-routine or complex, a circular is also despatched in conjunction with the notice, to provide shareholders with clear explanations as to why the business is being transacted. If any director has an interest in the resolution this is also likely to be disclosed in the circular.

Section 376 of the Companies Act 1985 also imposes a duty on a company to circulate at the requisition of the specified number of members, resolutions proposed to be moved or a statement with respect to business at any general meeting. This will be at the expense of the requisitionists (see 7.44 and 7.48 below). However, the DTI has recently investigated several proposals which have considered whether the costs of circulating the shareholders' resolution should be borne by the company.

Special notice

7.40   The Companies Act 1985 requires that, in certain circumstances, special notice be given *to* the company of the intention to propose certain ordinary resolutions at a general meeting. The circumstances in which special notice must be given are:

(*a*)   the removal of a director (CA 1985, s 303(2));

(*b*)   appointing or approving the appointment of a director of a public company (or a subsidiary of a public company) who has attained the age of 70 (CA 1985, s 293);

(*c*)   removing an auditor before the expiration of his term of office (CA 1985, s 391A(1)(a));

(*d*)   the appointment of an auditor other than the retiring auditor (CA 1985, s 391A(1)(b));

(*e*)   filling a casual vacancy in the office of auditor (CA 1985, s 388(3)(a)); and

(*f*)   re-appointing as auditor a retiring auditor appointed by the directors to fill a casual vacancy (CA 1985, s 388(3)(b)).

Section 379(1) of the CA 1985 states that, where special notice is required to be given of any resolution, then the resolution is not valid unless notice of the intention to propose it has been given to the company at least 28 days before the meeting at which it is to be proposed. However, CA 1985, s 379(3) states that, where the meeting is called for a date 28 days or less after the special notice has been given, the notice is deemed properly given notwithstanding that CA 1985, s 379(1) has not been complied with.

On receipt of a special notice, the company must give its members notice of the resolution at the same time and in the same manner as it gives notice of the general meeting at which it is to be proposed. If this is not practicable, the company may give notice in a newspaper with an appropriate circulation, or by such other means as the company's articles of association specify at least 21 days before the meeting (CA 1985, s 379(2)). Notice of the relevant resolution must also be given to the persons to be affected by the said resolution i.e. the director to be removed, the auditor to be removed, the retiring/resigning auditor and their replacement.

Annual general meetings

7.41   Section 366 of the Companies Act 1985 requires a company to hold an annual general meeting ('AGM') once in every calendar year, and to describe it as the annual general meeting in the notice convening the meeting.

A company's first AGM may be held at any time within 18 months of its incorporation. Thereafter, an annual general meeting must be held in each calendar year. However, CA 1985, s 366(3) allows an interval of up to 15 months between the AGM of one year and that of the next, subject to an annual general meeting being held in each calendar year.

Business of the meeting

7.42   It is possible to call an extraordinary general meeting of a company whenever necessary, but it is usual to defer non-urgent business until the AGM. Accordingly, the AGM is the one occasion in a year when the directors must appear before shareholders and give them an account of their management of the company.

The Act does not specify what business is required to be transacted at an AGM, this is left to individual companies to include in their articles of association, although interestingly, Table A in the Companies (Tables A to F) Regulations 1985 provides no model regulations in this respect.

It is usual (though not obligatory) to include consideration of a company's annual accounts in the business of the AGM. The directors are required by section 241 of the Companies Act 1985 to lay the accounts before a general meeting in each year, and a link between this and the annual general meeting is obviously intended although not stated by the Act.

As well as the receipt of the annual accounts of a company, other business commonly transacted at the annual general meeting includes:

(*a*)   the declaration of a final dividend (Table A, regulation 102);

(*b*)   the re-election of any retiring directors (Table A, regulations 73 to 80);

(*c*)   the approval of directors' remuneration (Table A, regulation 82); and

(*d*)   the re-appointment of auditors and the fixing of their remuneration (CA 1985, s 385(2)).

Other business which a company can conveniently deal with at the AGM are items such as:

(i)   authorising the directors to allot shares up to a specified level during the year (CA 1985, s 80) (see 8.4 CAPITAL);

(ii)   disapplying pre-emption rights in respect of allotments of shares up to a specified level (CA 1985, s 89) (see 8.7 CAPITAL); and

(iii)   passing elective resolutions (CA 1985, s 379A) (see 7.60 below).

Public companies commonly include items dealing with the directors' authority to allot shares and the disapplication of pre-emption rights in the business of every AGM so as to effectively roll over these authorities in each year.

(For a sample notice of the annual general meeting of a private limited company see Precedent F, Appendix 7B.)

Conduct of the AGM

7.43   The AGM is usually the one time of the year when the shareholders have the opportunity to speak on the business to be transacted and, where companies allow, for general questions to be asked on matters such as the past and future performance of the company and directors' remuneration.

It is extremely important therefore that careful preparation and planning are carried out well in advance of the meeting itself in order that the meeting can run as smoothly as possible.

In September 1996 the ICSA published a *Guide to Best Practice for Annual General Meetings* which contains 24 best practice points as well as other recommendations including how to communicate with shareholders, the timing and notice of the AGM, dealing with shareholders' questions and establishing procedures for dealing with disturbances.

Circulation of members' resolutions

7.44   Under section 376 of the Companies Act 1985, a company has a duty on the requisition in writing of a specified number of members and at the members' expense:

(*a*)   to circulate to members of the company entitled to receive notice of the next annual general meeting, notice of any resolution which may properly be moved and is intended to be moved at that meeting; and

(*b*)   to circulate to members entitled to have notice of any general meeting sent to them, any statement of not more than 1,000 words with respect to the matter referred to in any proposed resolution, or the business to be dealt with at that meeting.

The number of members required to requisition the company in this matter is as follows:

(i)   not less than one twentieth of the total voting rights of all the members having a right to vote at the meeting at which the requisition relates; or

(ii)   not less than 100 members holding shares on which there has been paid up an average sum per member of not less than £100.

A copy of the requisition signed by the requisitionists must be deposited at the registered office of the company not less than six weeks before the meeting, where it requires notice of a resolution, and in other cases one week before the meeting. There should also be left with the requisition a sum reasonably sufficient to cover expenses.

A company may apply to the court for leave not to circulate such a resolution or statement if they (or some other person who is aggrieved) feel the resolution or statement is of a defamatory nature.

Default

7.45 If a company fails to hold an AGM in any year as required by the Act, the company and any officers of the company in default may, under section 366(4) of the Companies Act 1985, be liable to a fine.

If there is a default in holding an AGM, the Secretary of State, pursuant to section 367 of the CA 1985, may, on the application of a member of the company, call or direct the calling of the meeting.

If, under these directions, an AGM is held a year late (i.e. in the calendar year following the year in which the meeting should have been held), it does not rank as the AGM of that year as well, unless:

(*a*) the company passes a resolution to that effect at the meeting (CA 1985, s 367(4)); and

(*b*) a copy of the resolution passed is delivered to the Registrar of Companies within 15 days of its passing (CA 1985, s 367(5)).

Without such a resolution, the company must hold a second AGM, as the actual AGM of that year (i.e. in addition to the meeting carried over from the previous year).

Companies Act 1989

7.46 Under the elective regime which was introduced on 1 April 1990 by section 115(2) of the Companies Act 1989, (now section 366A of the CA 1985) a *private* company may elect to dispense with the requirement to hold an annual general meeting in each year (see 7.60 below).

Extraordinary general meetings

7.47 A general meeting which is not specified in the notice of the meeting as being an annual general meeting is deemed to be an extraordinary general meeting ('EGM') (Table A, regulation 36).

The directors have a discretion to call an EGM at any time, and as often as they may wish (Table A, regulation 37). In practice, however, they will only call an EGM if there is urgent business which cannot conveniently be left for consideration at the next AGM.

There are circumstances in which the directors are required to call an EGM for a particular purpose, but, unlike an AGM, there are no provisions in the Act requiring EGMs to be held at specific intervals. An EGM may transact whatever business is set out in the notice of the meeting.

In any of the following circumstances, the directors *are* required to convene an EGM.

7.48   *Membership*

(*a*)   On the requisition of members of the company who hold at least *one-tenth* of the shares in the company carrying voting rights (CA 1985, s 368) (see 7.48 below);

(*b*)   On the resignation of an auditor who resigns in certain circumstances (CA 1985, s 392A(2)) (see 7.49 below);

(*c*)   Within 28 days of the directors becoming aware that the net assets of a public company are half (or less) of its called-up share capital (CA 1985, s 142) (see 7.50 below); and

(*d*)   In compliance with an order of the court (CA 1985, s 371) (see 7.51 below).

Requisition of an EGM by the members

7.48   Under section 368 of the Companies Act 1985, members holding at least one-tenth of the paid-up share capital carrying voting rights at a general meeting may deposit at the registered office a requisition, signed by all of the requisitionists, requiring the directors to convene an EGM.

The requisition must specify the objects of the meeting and thus it is usual to set out in the requisition the text of the resolution(s) which the requisitionists propose to move at the EGM. The requisition must further be signed by all the members requisitioning the meeting and be deposited at the registered office of the company.

The directors must, upon receipt of a valid requisition, convene an EGM for the objects specified in the requisition, although the directors may add further resolutions if they wish. The notice to convene the EGM must be issued by the directors within 21 days of the deposit of the requisition. Paragraph 9 of Schedule 19 to the Companies Act 1989 introduced a provision which requires the directors to hold the meeting within 28 days of the dispatch of this notice (CA 1985, s 368(8)).

Should the directors fail to convene an EGM following receipt of a valid requisition, the requisitionists, or a majority of them representing more than half their total voting rights, may convene the meeting, to be held within three months of the date of a deposit of the requisition. In such an instance, the requisitionists may recover from the directors any reasonable expenses which they have incurred in convening the meeting. However, the business of the EGM must be confined to the purposes specified in the requisition.

The most common reason for a requisition under section 368 of the CA 1985 is to remove directors from office (by an ordinary resolution, of which special notice is required under CA 1985, s 303). There is, however, no limit on the business for which an EGM may be requisitioned.

EGM on resignation of the auditor

7.49 If a company's auditors resign, they are obliged by section 394 of the Companies Act 1985 to state in their notice of resignation whether or not there are any circumstances which they consider should be brought to the notice of members or creditors of the company. If there are such circumstances, a statement of what they are must be included.

If the auditor's notice of resignation states that there are circumstances which he thinks must be brought to the attention of the members or creditors, section 392A(2) of the CA 1985 allows him, with his notice, to deposit a requisition calling on the directors to convene an EGM to receive and consider the auditor's explanation of the circumstances surrounding his resignation.

The directors are then required to issue a notice within 21 days of the deposit of the requisition by the auditor, to convene an EGM to be held within 28 days from the issue of that notice (CA 1985, s 393(2)(a)).

EGM on the financial situation of a public company

7.50 Section 142 of the Companies Act 1985 imposes an obligation on the directors of a *public company* to convene an EGM as a result of their becoming aware that the net assets of the company have fallen to, or below, the value of half its called-up share capital for the purpose of considering whether any, and if so, what steps must be taken to deal with the situation.

In such a circumstance the directors must issue the notice to convene the meeting within 28 days of their becoming aware that the assets have fallen below the specified level and the meeting must be called for a date not more than 56 days from the date on which the directors became so aware.

EGM by order of the court

7.51 The court has an inherent power to order a general meeting of a company to be convened. However, it will not normally interfere in a dispute between directors and shareholders, as the shareholders have their own power to requisition a meeting as specified above.

The court has a general statutory power under section 371 of the Companies Act 1985, either on its own motion or upon the application of a director or member of the company who would have power to vote at the meeting, to order that a general meeting be held and to give instructions for the conduct of the meeting.

This power is normally used to order that meetings be held when there is only one member available or willing to attend a general meeting and there is no other way of obtaining a quorum. Such a general meeting could not otherwise be held (*Re El Sombrero Ltd* [*1958*] *Ch 900* and *Re Opera Photographic Ltd* [*1989*] *5 BCC 601*).

Separate general meetings

7.52   There are several circumstances under the Companies Act 1985 when a company must hold a separate general meeting of the holders of a class of share. The articles of association may further specify circumstances when class meetings must be held.

Variation of rights

7.53   Section 125 of the CA 1985 provides that in circumstances where a variation of the rights of a class of share is proposed, a class meeting must be held to pass an extraordinary resolution approving the variation (see 7.58 below).

Reconstructions

7.54   Section 425 of the CA 1985 provides that the court may, on the application of creditors or members or a class of creditors, convene class meetings (and creditors' meetings) in circumstances where a company is proposing a compromise between itself and its creditors (or a class of them) or its members (or a class of them) which requires a 75% majority of those attending and voting to make the compromise or arrangement binding.

The procedure for the convening, holding and passing of resolutions at class meetings are the same as for general meetings (unless the articles of association provide otherwise) except that the right to receive notice of and to vote at the meeting are usually restricted to the holders of the class of share in question.

Adjournment of meetings

7.55   An adjournment of a meeting is, by common law, only a continuation of the original meeting, so unless otherwise provided for in the articles of association, there is no need to give notice of the adjourned meeting. Any irregularity in the convention of the original meeting will also affect the adjourned meeting. Proxies for the original meeting may be used for the adjournment. Regulation 45 of Table A and common law gives the chairman the power to adjourn a general meeting from time to time and from place to place. If, however, the chairman improperly attempts to adjourn a meeting, another chairman may be elected by the members and the meeting continued. In the case that the meeting has been adjourned properly, members would not be able to remain and carry on the proceedings. Additionally, if a poll is demanded on the question of adjournment, it should be taken immediately (Table A, regulation 51).

Where a meeting is adjourned for 14 days or more, at least seven days' clear notice must be given specifying the time and place of the adjourned meeting and the general nature of the business to be transacted (Table A, regulation 45). Otherwise no new notice needs to be given, unless new business is proposed different to that proposed in the notice of the original meeting.

Furthermore, regulation 41 of Table A states that if there is not a quorum present after half an hour from the time appointed for the meeting, or if during a meeting the quorum ceases to be present, the meeting shall be adjourned to the same day and time the following week or a time and place as the directors may determine.

Resolutions

General

7.56   Various decisions of a company are required by the Companies Acts, and the articles of association of a company, to be made by the members passing resolutions in general meeting. The articles of a company will normally determine the procedure and majorities required for particular resolutions. However, there are basically three types of resolution which are recognised, being ordinary, special and extraordinary resolutions. On 1 April 1990 the Companies Act 1989 introduced a further type of resolution known as an elective resolution. This form of resolution is only available to a *private company* (see 7.58 below).

Ordinary resolution

7.57   An ordinary resolution is the normal means of securing the members' approval to business transacted at a general meeting. The ordinary resolution may be used for purely routine business (e.g. approval of the annual accounts), but may also suffice as approval of certain important or contentious business (e.g. the removal of a director).

No definition of an 'ordinary resolution' is contained in the Companies Act 1985, but any resolution which is not defined as an 'extraordinary resolution' or a 'special resolution' is deemed to be an ordinary resolution.

An ordinary resolution is carried by a simple majority of the votes cast at a general meeting, whether by a show of hands or on a poll.

As a general rule, it is not necessary to deliver a signed copy of an ordinary resolution to Companies House although there are a few exceptions, being:

(*a*)   an increase in authorised capital pursuant to CA 1985, s 121 (CA 1985, s 123);

(*b*)   the authorisation of directors to allot shares pursuant to CA 1985, s 80 (CA 1985, s 80(8)); and

(*c*)   the voluntary winding-up of a company pursuant to section 84(1)(a) of the Insolvency Act 1986 (Insolvency Act 1986, s 84(3)).

Unless the Act or a company's articles of association specify that an extraordinary or special resolution is required for a particular item of business, an ordinary resolution will usually suffice.

The articles of the company may provide that a special or extraordinary resolution shall be required in certain circumstances (e.g. in the instance of an increase of capital). But in some situations the Act expressly overrides the articles in providing that an ordinary resolution is sufficient. For example, section 303 of the CA 1985 states that a director may be removed by an ordinary resolution of the company notwithstanding anything to the contrary in the articles of association.

Extraordinary resolution

7.58   An extraordinary resolution differs from an ordinary resolution in that it must be specifically described as such in the notice of a general meeting. It must be carried at the general meeting by a majority of at least three-quarters of the votes cast (CA 1985, s 378(1)).

The two occasions under the law where an extraordinary resolution is required are:

(*a*)   when a company resolves that it be wound up voluntarily, it being unable to carry on its business because of its liabilities (Insolvency Act 1986, s 84(1)(c)); and

(*b*)   at a meeting of the holders of a particular class of shares, to sanction a variation of the rights attached to those shares under CA 1985, s 125(2)(b) (or any corresponding provisions of the articles).

No period of notice is prescribed, so an extraordinary resolution, if it is to be proposed at an extraordinary general meeting, requires 14 days' notice to be given. In this way, it differs from a special resolution as it does not in itself require more than 14 days' notice of the meeting at which it is to be proposed.

A signed copy of an extraordinary resolution must be delivered to the Registrar of Companies within 15 days of its passing (CA 1985, s 380(4)(b)).

Special resolution

7.59   A resolution is deemed a special resolution pursuant to section 378(2) of the Companies Act 1985 when it is described as such in the notice of the meeting. A special resolution to be passed must be carried by a three-quarters majority of votes cast at a general meeting. Twenty-one days' clear notice is also required of a general meeting at which a special resolution is to be proposed.

A printed and signed copy of a special resolution must be delivered to Companies House within 15 days of its passing (CA 1985, s 380(4)(a)). The

Companies Act 1985 specifically requires a special resolution to be passed to effect various actions of a company. Instances where a special resolution is required are:

(*a*)   an alteration to the objects clause contained in the memorandum of association (CA 1985, s 4);

(*b*)   an alteration to the articles of association (CA 1985, s 9);

(*c*)   a reduction of its capital subject to confirmation of the court (CA 1985, s 135);

(*d*)   various alterations of the company's status by re-registration (e.g. from a private to a public company) (see 2.49 THE COMPANY CONSTITUTION);

(*e*)   a change of name (CA 1985, s 28);

(*f*)   a purchase of its own shares (CA 1985, s 164);

(*g*)   in the case of a *private company*, the provision of financial assistance for the purchase of its own shares (CA 1985, s 155);

(*h*)   in disapplication of pre-emption rights (CA 1985, s 95); and

(*j*)   in exempting a dormant company from appointing auditors (CA 1985, s 250).

A company's articles of association may introduce further instances when a special resolution is required.

Elective resolution

7.60   Section 116 of the Companies Act 1989 introduced into the Companies Act 1985 (section 379A) a new type of resolution called an 'elective resolution'. An elective resolution is one which must be agreed to at the general meeting at which it is passed, in person or by proxy, by *all* of the members entitled to attend and vote at that meeting. Only a *private* company may pass an elective resolution.

An elective resolution may be passed where a private company wishes:

(*a*)   to fix the duration of the authority of the directors to allot shares, as greater than five years (CA 1985, s 80A) (see Precedent G, Appendix 7B);

(*b*)   to dispense with the requirement to lay accounts and reports before the company in general meeting (CA 1985, s 252) (although under CA 1985, s 253(2) a member has the right to require the laying of accounts at a general meeting) (see Precedent H, Appendix 7B);

(*c*)   to dispense with the requirement to hold an annual general meeting (CA 1985, s 366A) (under section 366A(3) a member may require a company to hold an annual general meeting in any year) (see Precedent J, Appendix 7B);

(*d*)   to dispense with the requirement to appoint auditors annually (CA 1985, s 386) (although under CA 1985, s 393(1) a member has the right to require that the appointment of auditors so appointed, be terminated and their re-appointment considered at a general meeting) (see Precedent K, Appendix 7B); and

(*e*)   to reduce the majority required to consent to the holding of a general meeting at short notice, from members holding 95% to not less than 90% in nominal value of shares having the right to attend and vote at a general meeting (CA 1985, s 369(4)) (see Precedent L, Appendix 7B).

The period of notice required for such a resolution to be passed in general meeting is at least 21 days' notice in writing (CA 1985, s 379A(2)(a)). However, new amending legislation came into force on 19 June 1996 contained in the Deregulation (Resolutions of Private Companies) Order 1996 (SI 1996 No 1471) which enables less than 21 days' notice to be given provided that all members entitled to attend and vote at the meeting so agree. The resolution must be described as an elective resolution and the terms of the resolution stated in the notice. Alternatively, the resolution may be passed using a written resolution (see 7.61 below).

The effective dates when the elections become operative are laid down in the relevant sections of the Act. However, it should be noted that an election to dispense with the laying of accounts has effect in relation to the accounts and reports in respect of the financial year in which the election is made and subsequent financial years. Hence if the company has a December year end it would need to pass the elective resolution before the end of the financial year concerned for them not to be laid in the following year.

A company may revoke elective resolutions by passing an ordinary resolution. An elective resolution is automatically revoked if a private company re-registers as a public company.

A signed copy of an elective resolution must be delivered to Companies House within 15 days of its passing. Similarly, any resolution revoking an elective resolution must also be filed (CA 1985, s 380(4)(bb)).

Written resolutions

7.61   Section 381A of the Companies Act 1985 provides that from 1 April 1990 anything which may be done by resolution of a *private* company in general meeting (or by resolution of a meeting of any class of members of the company) may, instead of a meeting being held, be done by a written resolution signed by or on behalf of *all* members of the company who, at the date of the resolution, would be entitled to attend and vote at a general meeting. Previous notice is not required of such a resolution and the signatures need not be on a single document, provided each is on a document which accurately states the terms of the resolution. The date of the passing of the resolution is taken as being the date upon which the last member signs.

As exceptions to this rule, a written resolution may *not* be used for the removal of a director or auditor from office, or to lay accounts.

In the following specified circumstances, if a written resolution is used, then the adaption of the relevant procedural requirements, as set out in the Companies Act 1985, must also be followed. The revised procedural requirements are set out in Part II of Schedule 15A to the CA 1985 and relate to the following.

(*a*)   Disapplication of pre-emption rights.

(*b*)   Financial assistance for the purchase of a company's own shares.

(*c*)   Authority for the off-market purchase of a company's own shares.

(*d*)   Approval for payments out of capital.

(*e*)   Approval of a director's service contract.

(*f*)   Funding director's expenditure in performing his duties.

Section 381B of the CA 1985 used to require that a copy of any proposed written resolution must be sent to the company's auditors with a sanction that if they considered that the resolution concerned them as auditors, then within seven days of receipt of the notice they could require the resolution to be considered in general meeting.

This process proved to be burdensome on private companies wishing to use the written resolution procedure and hence new regulations were brought into force on 19 June 1996 following approval of the Deregulation (Resolutions of Private Companies) Order 1996 (SI 1996 No 1471).

Section 381B was substituted for new regulations which impose a duty on the directors and secretary of the company to send the company's auditors a copy, or otherwise inform them, of the contents of the written resolution, at or before the time that resolution is supplied to a member for signature. Non-compliance with this section is a criminal offence, but will not affect the validity of the resolution. As a result of this new section, auditors will no longer be able to give notice to the company requiring a meeting to be held, or be able to attend and be heard at that meeting.

Section 381C was also amended to make clear that the statutory written resolution under section 381A and 381B may be used notwithstanding any provision in a private company's memorandum and articles of association, but does not prejudice any power conferred by any such provision. In other words, more relaxed procedures in a company's articles are unaffected, and this section only overrides provisions contained in articles which are more onerous or where written resolutions are not permitted.

Written resolutions must be recorded in the company's minute book and as they are used to give effect to what otherwise would be either ordinary, special, extraordinary or elective resolutions, the usual provisions of section 380 of the CA 1985 apply to the registration of the resolution passed at Companies House.

Amendment of resolutions

7.62   An ordinary resolution may be amended even if the text of the resolution has been set out in the notice of the meeting.

The text of an extraordinary, special or elective resolution must be set out in the notice of the meeting at which the resolution is to be considered. This has the result that there can be no substantial amendment of these resolutions after the notice of the general meeting at which the resolution is to be proposed is posted, since the amended resolution would no longer be the same one of which notice had been given.

Resolutions passed at adjourned meetings

7.63   Section 381 of the Companies Act 1985 provides that where a resolution is passed at an adjourned meeting of either the company, its directors or at a class meeting, then the resolution is deemed passed on the date on which it was passed (i.e. the date of the adjourned meeting being held and not at any earlier date).

Registration of resolutions

7.64   Section 380 of the Companies Act 1985 requires that a copy of every resolution to which the section applies must, within 15 days of it being passed, be filed with Companies House (see 5.12 DISCLOSURE AND REPORTING REQUIREMENTS).

Unanimous agreement of the members

7.65   The procedures for convening, constituting and conducting a company meeting are intended to safeguard a minority of members, who may disagree with the resolutions passed at a general meeting or who may not be able to attend the meeting. Their safeguards are that the resolution must be passed by a simple or three-quarters majority or by unanimous agreement; proper notice must be given for the meeting; a quorum of members must be present; and a vote on the resolutions proposed must be taken in the proper manner. If there are flaws in this procedure, the resolution may be invalid and accordingly will not be binding upon them.

Should, however, every member of a company who is entitled to attend and vote at a general meeting be in agreement with a resolution, it ispointless to invalidate the meeting because of some technical flaw in the procedure. This is illustrated by the case of *Re Express Engineering Works* [*1920*] *1 Ch 466*, where a unanimous decision of a board meeting (all the members of the company being directors) was accepted in place of a resolution in general meeting.

In addition, the courts have recognised that the informal but unanimous agreement of the members, or an irregular general meeting which has produced the unanimous agreement of the members, will be accepted as a binding decision instead of a resolution duly passed at a general meeting.

Signed resolutions procedure

7.66   For companies with a small membership to which the written resolution procedure specified by section 381A of the Companies Act 1985 does not apply (see 7.61 above), an alternative to holding general meetings may be introduced in the articles of association. The alternative where *authorised by the articles of association* (Table A, regulation 53) is to circulate a print or prints of a proposed resolution to each member of the company for their signature.

Thus the inclusion of regulation 53 of Table A (or a similar regulation) in a company's articles of association allows the company, where all the members agree to the passing of a particular resolution, to avoid the need to hold a general meeting.

The signed resolution should be preserved in the minute book, since it serves in place of a resolution passed at a general meeting. A copy of such a resolution must also be filed with Companies House if required by the Act.

For private limited companies section 381C(1) of the CA 1985, specifically states that, for a private company CA 1985, s 381A and s 381B apply, notwithstanding anything contained in the company's memorandum and articles of association, but do not prejudice any power conferred by any provision of the memorandum and articles of association.

Minutes of general meetings

7.67   Section 382 of the Companies Act 1985 obliges a company to enter minutes of all general meetings into a book made for that purpose. Section 382A imposes a further requirement for a company to record written resolutions in the same way as those for general meetings.

Minutes are only *'prima facie'* evidence of the proceedings of a meeting and a member may still challenge the validity of these minutes (see 3.51 THE STATUTORY RECORDS).

Stamp duties on share transfers

Rates of duty

Transfers on sale of shares (unless falling into the categories specified in (ii) and (iii) below) are liable to *ad valorem* stamp duty at the rate of 50p per £100 or part of £100 of the consideration.

Exempt transfers

The Stamp Duty (Exempt Instruments) Regulations 1987 (SI 1987 No 516) provide that certain documents (including a transfer operating as a voluntary disposition *inter vivos*) executed on or after 1 May 1987 are not liable to stamp duty. Exempt documents must bear an appropriate certificate and once certified, can be sent direct to the company secretary or Registrar for registration.

The categories of exempt transactions are as follows.

(*a*)   The vesting of property subject to a trust in the trustees of the trust on the appointment of a new trustee, or in the continuing trustees on the retirement of a trustee.

(*b*)   The conveyance or transfer of property the subject of a specific devise or legacy to the beneficiary named in the will (or his nominee).

(*c*)   The conveyance or transfer of property which forms part of an intestate's estate to the person entitled on intestacy (or his nominee).

(*d*)   The appropriation of property within section 84(4) of the Finance Act 1985 (death: appropriation in satisfaction of a general legacy of money) or section 84(5) or (7) of that Act (death: appropriation in satisfaction of any interest of surviving spouse and in Scotland also of any interest of issue).

(*e*)   The conveyance or transfer of property which forms part of the residuary estate of a testator to a beneficiary (or his nominee) entitled solely by virtue of his entitlement under the will.

(*f*)   The conveyance or transfer of property out of a settlement in or towards satisfaction of a beneficiary's interest, not being an interest acquired for money or money's worth, being a conveyance or transfer constituting a distribution of property in accordance with the provisions of the settlement.

(*g*)   The conveyance or transfer of property on and in consideration only of marriage to a party to the marriage (or his nominee) or to trustees to be held on the terms of a settlement made in consideration only of the marriage.

(*h*)   The conveyance or transfer of property within section 83(1) of the Finance Act 1985 (transfer in connection with divorce etc.).

(*i*)   The conveyance or transfer by the liquidator of property which formed part of the assets of the company in liquidation to a shareholder of that company (or his nominee) in or towards satisfaction of the shareholder's rights on a winding-up.

(*j*)   The grant in fee simple of an easement in or over land for no consideration in money or money's worth.

(*k*)   The grant of a servitude for no consideration in money or money's worth.

(*l*)   The conveyance or transfer of property operating as a voluntary disposition *inter vivos* for no consideration in money or money's worth nor any consideration referred to in section 57 of the Stamp Act 1891 (conveyance in consideration of a debt etc.).

(*m*)   The conveyance or transfer of property by an instrument within section 84(1) of the Finance Act 1985 (death: varying disposition).

If a transaction falls within one of the above categories a certificate in the following form should be contained within the transfer document:

'I/We, hereby certify that this instrument falls within category [initial of category] in the Schedule to the Stamp Duty (Exempt Instruments) Regulations 1987.
Signature   [transferor or transferor's Solicitor]
Description   [e.g. transferor, solicitor for the transferor]
Dated   '

The certificate may be signed by the transferor or grantor, or by a solicitor on his behalf. (An authorised agent may also sign the certificate provided he states the capacity in which he signs.)

Fixed duty transfers

Transfers falling within any of the following categories attract a fixed duty of 50p.

(*a*)   Transfer by way of security for a loan or re-transfer to the original transferor on repayment of a loan.

(*b*)   Transfer, not on sale and not arising under any contract of sale and where no beneficial interest in the property passes: (i) to a person who is a mere nominee of, and is nominated only by, the transferor; (ii) from a mere nominee, who has at all times held the property on behalf of the transferee; (iii) from one nominee to another nominee of the same beneficial owner where the first nominee has at all times held the property on behalf of that beneficial owner.

As with a transfer exempt from stamp duty, to establish that a transfer is only liable to a fixed duty of 50p a certificate should be completed which details the facts of the transaction. It should be noted that as from 1 October 1999 fixed duties will be increased to £5.00.

Purchase of own shares

Stamp duty is payable on a purchase by a company of its own shares. The statutory return (form 169) constitutes the document which is liable to stamp duty and is accordingly treated as the instrument transferring the shares on sale for stamp duty purposes (Finance Act 1986, s 66). The form should be sent to the Inland Revenue for stamping with a cheque for the appropriate amount of stamp duty prior to lodging with the Registrar. Companies House will not accept unstamped forms.

Stamp duty reserve tax

The Finance Act 1986 (section 86) introduced stamp duty reserve tax (SDRT) which is charged at the rate of 50p per £100 (or part thereof) on certain share transactions which do not attract stamp duty. SDRT is charged on certain agreements to transfer securities, where there is no transfer document and so no liability to stamp duty (e.g. shares held in electronic form under CREST). Renounceable letters of allotment and transactions closed within a stock exchange account are examples of items which attract reserve tax.

The Uncertificated Securities Regulations 1995 (SI 1995 No 3272) amend company law to allow for shares to be held in uncertificated form and to be transferred through an approved paperless transfer system.

The Stamp Duty Reserve Tax (Amendment) Regulations 1997 came into force on 20 October 1997 and made changes to the 1986 regulations to take account of paperless share dealing. Now the operator of CREST or a similar electronic system is liable to collect and pay SDRT incurred on chargeable transactions.

The two month period allowed for transfer documents to be produced and stamped before SDRT is charged does not apply unless there is still a stamped transfer document, in which case the stamp duty paid will cancel the SDRT charge.

To simplify calculations by the CREST operator, SDRT rates will be changed to a flat percentage e.g. 0.5%, but stamp duty rates will remain the same.

Transfers arising from an agreement between persons who are not resident in the UK which are settled through CREST will be liable to SDRT.

Interests and penalties (revised as from 1 October 1999)

Interest will be charged on duty that is not paid within 30 days of the execution of a document subject to stamp duty. The amount of interest will be rounded down where necessary to a multiple of £5.00, however no interest will be payable on calculated amounts of less than £25.00.

Penalties for late stamping will apply to all documents submitted late for stamping. There will be a maximum penalty of £300.00 (or the amount of duty owed if less) on documents submitted up to a year late, or £300.00 (or the amount of duty owed if more) where the documents are presented more than a year late.

Further information on the above can be found in the new leaflet published by the Inland Revenue Stamp office, entitled Stamp Duty Interests and Penalties, S010 99.

Precedents

A.1. Transfer of Shares

It was resolved that the undernoted duly stamped transfer of ordinary shares of £1 each in the company be and are hereby approved, and registered in the books of the company. It was further resolved that a share certificate for the transferee be sealed and signed on behalf of the company in accordance with the Articles of Association of the company and issued in due course, and that the share certificate held by the transferor be cancelled accordingly:

No. of Transfer	*Transferor*	*Transferee*	*No. of Shares*
1	Jerry Lai	Claire Cranidge	100
	Aquis Court	Aquis Court	
	31 Fishpool Street	31 Fishpool Street	
	St Albans	St Albans	
	Hertfordshire	Hertfordshire	
	AL3 4RF	AL3 4RF	

A.2. Stock Transfer Form

CON 40 (1963)

STOCK TRANSFER FORM

(Above this line for Registrars only)

Certificate lodged with the Registrar

Consideration Money £ ......100............

(For completion by the Registrar/Stock Exchange)

Name of Undertaking.	PL LAI LIMITED

Description of Security.

ORDINARY SHARES OF £1.00 EACH

Number or amount of Shares, Stock or other security and, in figures column only, number and denomination of units, if any.

Words

ONE HUNDRED

Figures

100

(100 units of £1)

Name(s) of registered holder(s) should be given in full: the address should be given where there is only one holder.

If the transfer is not made by the registered holder(s) insert also the name(s) and capacity (e.g. Executor(s)) of the person(s) making the transfer.

In the name(s) of

JERRY LAI
AQUIS COURT
31 FISHPOOL STREET
ST ALBANS
HERTFORDSHIRE
AL3 4RF

I/We hereby transfer the above security out of the name(s) aforesaid to the person(s) named below.

Signature(s) of transferor(s)

1. ....
2. ....
3. ....
4. ....

Stamp of Selling Broker(s) or, for transactions which are not stock exchange transactions, of Agent(s), if any, acting for the Transferor(s)

A body corporate should execute this transfer under its common seal or otherwise in accordance with applicable statutory requirements.

Date ....1 SEPTEMBER 1998

Full name(s), full postal address(es) (including County or, if applicable, Postal District number) of the person(s) to whom the security is transferred.

Please state title, if any, or whether Mr., Mrs., or Miss.

Please complete in typewriting or in BLOCK CAPITALS.

CLAIRE CRANIDGE
AQUIS COURT
31 FISHPOOL STREET
ST ALBANS
HERTFORDSHIRE
AL3 4RF

I/We request that such entries be made in the register as are necessary to give effect to this transfer.

Stamp of Buying Broker(s) (if any)

Stamp or name and address of person lodging this form (If other than the Buying Broker(s))

Reference to the Registrar in this Form means the registrar or registration agent of the undertaking NOT the Registrar of Companies at Companies House.

FORM OF CERTIFICATE REQUIRED WHERE TRANSFER IS EXEMPT FROM STAMP DUTY

Instruments executed on or after 1st May 1987 effecting any transactions within the following categories are exempt from stamp duty:—

A. The vesting of property subject to a trust in the trustees of the trust on the appointment of a new trustee, or in the continuing trustees on the retirement of a trustee.

B. The conveyance or transfer of property the subject of a specific devise or legacy to the beneficiary named in the will (or his nominee). Transfers in satisfaction of a general legacy of money should not be included in this category (see category D below).

C. The conveyance or transfer of property which forms part of an intestate's estate to the person entitled on intestacy (or his nominee). Transfers in satisfaction of the transferees entitlement to cash in the estate of an intestate, where the total value of the residuary estate exceeds that sum, should not be included in this category (see category D below).

D. The appropriation of property within section 84(4) of the Finance Act 1985 (death: appropriation in satisfaction of a general legacy of money) or section 84(5) or (7) of that Act (death: appropriation in satisfaction of any interest of surviving spouse and in Scotland also of any interest of issue).

E. The conveyance or transfer of property which forms part of the residuary estate of a testator to a beneficiary (or his nominee) entitled solely by virtue of his entitlement under the will.

F. The conveyance or transfer of property out of a settlement in or towards satisfaction of a beneficiary's interest, not being an interest acquired for money or money's worth, being a conveyance or transfer constituting a distribution of property in accordance with the provisions of the settlement.

G. The conveyance or transfer of property on and in consideration only of marriage to a party to the marriage (or his nominee) or to trustees to be held on the terms of a settlement made in consideration only of the marriage. A transfer to a spouse after the date of marriage is not within this category, unless made pursuant to an ante-nuptial contract.

H. The conveyance or transfer of property within section 83(1) of the Finance Act 1985 (transfers in connection with divorce etc.).

I. The conveyance or transfer by the liquidator of property which formed part of the assets of the company in liquidation to a shareholder of that company (or his nominee) in or towards satisfaction of the shareholder's rights on a winding-up.

L. The conveyance or transfer of property operating as a voluntary disposition *inter vivos* for no consideration in money or money's worth nor any consideration referred to in section 57 of the Stamp Act 1891 (conveyance in consideration of a debt etc.).

M. The conveyance or transfer of property by an instrument within section 84(1) of the Finance Act 1985 (death: varying disposition).

(1) Delete as appropriate.

(2) Insert "(A)", "(B)" or appropriate category.

(3) Delete second sentence if the certificate is given by the transferor or his solicitor.

(1) I/We hereby certify that the transaction in respect of which this transfer is made is one which falls within the category(2) .... above. (1)I/We confirm that (1)I/We have been duly authorised by the transferor to sign this certificate and that the facts of the transaction are within (1)my/our knowledge (3)

Signature(s) ....

Description ("Transferor", "Solicitor", etc.) ....

....

....

....

....

Date ....19................

NOTES

(1) If the above certificate has been completed, this transfer does not need to be submitted to the Controller of Stamps but should be sent directly to the Company or its Registrars.

(2) If the above certificate is not completed, this transfer must be submitted to the Controller of Stamps and duly stamped. (See below.)

FORM OF CERTIFICATE REQUIRED WHERE TRANSFER IS NOT EXEMPT BUT IS NOT LIABLE TO *AD VALOREM* STAMP DUTY

Instruments of transfer, other than those in respect of which the above certificate has been completed, are liable to a fixed duty of 50p when the transaction falls within one of the following categories:—

(a) Transfer by way of security for a loan or re-transfer to the original transferor on repayment of a loan.

(b) Transfer, not on sale and not arising under any contract of sale and where no beneficial interest in the property passes: (i) to a person who is a mere nominee of, and is nominated only by, the transferor; (ii) from a mere nominee who has at all times held the property on behalf of the transferee; (iii) from one nominee to another nominee of the same beneficial owner where the first nominee has at all times held the property on behalf of that beneficial owner. (NOTE—This category does not include a transfer made in any of the following circumstances: (i) by a holder of stock, etc., following the grant of an option to purchase the stock, to the person entitled to the option or his nominee; (ii) to a nominee in contemplation of a contract for the sale of the stock, etc., then about to be entered into; (iii) from the nominee of a vendor, who has instructed the nominee orally or by some unstamped writing to hold stock, etc., in trust for a purchaser, to such purchaser.)

(1) Delete as appropriate.

(2) Insert "(a)", "(b)".

(3) Here set out concisely the facts explaining the transaction. Adjudication may be required.

(1) I/We hereby certify that the transaction in respect of which this transfer is made is one which falls within the category(2) .... above. (1)I/We confirm that (1)I/we have been duly authorised by the transferor to sign this certificate and that the facts of the transaction are within (1)my/our knowledge.

(3) ....

....

....

....

Signature(s) ....

Description ("Transferor", "Solicitor", etc.) ....

....

....

....

Date ....

©1996 **OYEZ** The Solicitors' Law Stationery Society Ltd, Oyez House, 7 Spa Road, London SE16 3QQ

1996 Edition 10.96 F32696

5036018

Conveyancing 40

B. Indemnity for Lost Certificate

'I, [Name of member] do hereby request that the company (or its Registrars) issue to me a duplicate certificate No. [certificate number] for [no. of shares] shares in the capital of the Company, the certificate having been mislaid, destroyed or lost, and in consideration of the Company so doing, I hereby indemnify the said Company against all claims and demands, monies, losses, damages, costs and expense which may be brought against or be paid, incurred, or sustained by the said Company by reason or in consequence of the said certificate having been mislaid, destroyed or lost, or by reason or in consequence of the issuing to me of the said duplicate certificate, or otherwise howsoever in relation thereto. I further undertake and agree, if the said certificate shall hereafter be found, forthwith to deliver up the same or cause the same to be delivered up to the company, its Registrars or their successors and assigns without cost, fee or reward.

Dated this   day of   199

[Signature of member]'

C. Form of Proxy for use at Extraordinary/Annual General Meeting

'I, [Name of member]
of [Member's address]
hereby appoint [name of proxy]
of [proxy's address]
or failing him the duly appointed Chairman of the meeting, as my proxy to attend and vote for me on my behalf at the Extraordinary/Annual General Meeting of the company to be held at [place of meeting]
on [date of meeting]   at [time am/pm of meeting]
and at every adjournment thereof.

Dated this   day of   199

[Signature of member]'

D. Resolution of Board Appointing An Authorised Representative

'That [name of representative] be and is hereby appointed, pursuant to Section 375 of the Companies Act 1985, to act as the company's representative at any meeting of the members of [name of company].
This appointment shall remain in force until the company shall resolve otherwise or until [name of officer of the company] vacates the office of Director/Secretary/other officer of the company.'

E.1. Consent to Short Notice of an Extraordinary General Meeting

'We, the undersigned, being a majority in number of the members of the above-named company and entitled to attend and vote at the Extraordinary General Meeting of the said company convened by a Notice of Meeting [date of notice] and to be held on [date of meeting] and together holding 95 per cent and upward in nominal value of the shares giving that right, hereby agree to the holding of such meeting and to the proposing and passing of the Resolutions on the day and at the time and place set out in such Notice, notwithstanding that less than the statutory period of the notice thereof has been given to us.

Dated this   day of   199

[Name of member]   [Name of member]
(Member)   (Member)'

E.2. Consent to Short Notice of an Annual General Meeting

'We, the undersigned, being all the members for the time being of the company having the right to attend and vote at the Annual General Meeting of such company convened to be held at [place of meeting] on [date of meeting] at [time of meeting] (the attached notice being the notice convening the meeting), hereby agree:

(*a*)   in accordance with Section 369(3)(a) of the Companies Act 1985 to the holding of such meeting notwithstanding that less than the statutory period of notice thereof has been given, and

(*b*)   to accept service of documents in accordance with Section 238(4) of the Companies Act 1985 notwithstanding that the said documents were sent less than 21 days before the meeting.

Dated this   day of   199

[Name of member]   [Name of member]
(Member)   (Member)'

F. Notice of an Annual General Meeting

NOTICE IS HEREBY GIVEN THAT THE ANNUAL GENERAL MEETING OF [name of company]
WILL BE HELD AT [place of meeting]
ON [date of meeting] 199   AT [time of meeting] AM/PM'

BUSINESS

1   To receive and adopt the Directors' Report and the Audited Statement of Accounts for the year/period ended [   ].

2   To re-elect a Director.

3   To confirm the Directors' remuneration.

4   To declare a dividend.

5   To reappoint the retiring Auditors and authorise the Directors to fix their remuneration.

Dated this   day of   199

REGISTERED OFFICE   BY ORDER OF THE BOARD
[name of company]

SECRETARY [Signature of Secretary]

Note: A member entitled to attend and vote is entitled to appoint a proxy to attend and on a poll vote in his/her place. Such proxy need not be a member of the company.'

G. Extension of Directors' Authority to Allot Shares

'That in accordance with the provisions of Section 80A of the Companies Act 1985 the Directors be and they are hereby unconditionally authorised for the purposes of Section 80 of the said Act to allot shares up to the amount of the authorised Capital of the Company (£   ) at any time or times from the date of this resolution'.

H. Dispensation with the Laying of Accounts Before a General Meeting

'That in accordance with the provisions of Section 252 of the Companies Act 1985 the Company hereby dispenses with the laying of accounts and reports before the company in General Meeting in respect of the year ending [   ] 199 and subsequent financial years'.

J. Dispensation with the Requirement to Hold Annual General Meetings

'That in accordance with the provisions of Section 366A of the Companies Act 1985 the Company hereby dispenses with the holding of the Annual General Meeting for 199 and subsequent years'.

K. Dispensation with the Requirement to Appoint Auditors Annually

'That in accordance with the provisions of Section 386 of the Companies Act 1985 the Company hereby dispenses with the obligation to appoint auditors annually and that during the term that such dispensation is in force the Directors be and they are hereby authorised to fix the auditors remuneration'.

L. Reduction of Percentage of Members Required to Consent to Short Notice

'That in accordance with the provisions of Sections 369(4) and 378(3) of the Companies Act 1985 the majority required for the authority to hold general meetings/class meetings upon Short Notice be and it is hereby reduced from 95 per cent to 90 per cent'.

M. Board Resolution for an Interim Dividend

'It was Resolved that an interim dividend for the year ended [date of accounting period] of [amount] on the ordinary shares of the company be [paid] [declared payable] on [date] to all members whose name appears in the Register of Members on [date].'

N. Declaration of a Final Dividend at General Meeting

'It was Resolved that [the final dividend] [the dividend recommended by the directors on (date)] of [amount] for the year ended [date of accounting period] be [paid] [declared payable] on the ordinary shares of the company to all members whose names appear in the Register of Members on [date] and that such dividend be paid on [date of payment].'

Precedent N, Appendix 7B

The Directors

Deed of Waiver

I, [   ] of [   ] being the registered holder of
[   ] shares of £ [   ] each in the capital of
Limited whose Registered Office is situated at [   ] ('the Company'), do hereby absolutely and irrevocably waive my right and entitlement to the final dividend of [   ]p per share recommended by the Directors and if considered fit to be approved by the shareholders at the Annual General Meeting to be held on   199 .

Signed by me as a deed this   day of   199
(*signature*)

in the presence of:

Witness: _____

Name: _____

Address: _____

Chapter 8

Capital

Maintenance of capital

8.1   A general principle of company law is that capital, once raised, must be maintained. The issued share capital of a company is the fund to which creditors can look for payment of their debts. 'The whole of the subscribed capital of a company with limited liability, unless diminished by expenditure on the objects of the company shall remain available for the discharge of its liabilities' (*per* Kitto J in *Davis Investments Pty Limited v Commissioner of Stamp Duties (NSW 1957–58)*). Shares must not be issued at a discount (i.e. for less than their nominal amount) (CA 1985, s 100) although payment in full is not required on allotment.

Serious loss of capital

8.2   Under section 142 of the Companies Act 1985, should the net assets of a public company fall to a level of half or less of its called-up share capital, then the directors have a duty imposed upon them by section 142 to convene a general meeting to consider what steps should be taken to deal with the situation. A problem that exists here for the directors of a public company is in determining the time at which the net assets have fallen to below one-half of the share capital. For the purposes of CA 1985, s 142 it would seem reasonable to assume that it is from the date that the audited accounts show this position as being the trigger date for the directors becoming aware of the situation. Upon discovery of the fact, the directors must within 28 days convene a general meeting, to be held on a date no later than 56 days from the date of discovery.

Issue of capital

8.3   Capital is issued by the directors of the company and is represented by the shares which are taken up by the shareholders. The directors may not issue shares beyond the amount fixed as the authorised capital of the company and the directors must be duly authorised to make the issue. In certain circumstances, the existing shareholders may have a right to have allotted to them a proportionate part of a new issue of shares (the application of pre-emption rights if incorporated into the articles of association). In addition, there are restrictions on offering shares to the public at large (see 8.9 below).

Section 88 of the Companies Act 1985 requires a company making an allotment of shares, to lodge with the Registrar of Companies *within one month*, a return of the allotment made in the prescribed form (form G88(2)). This return states the number and nominal amount of the shares allotted, the names and addresses of the allottees, and the amount (if any) paid or due and payable on each share whether on account of the nominal value of the shares or by way of premium.

If shares are allotted *otherwise than in cash*, a contract in writing constituting the title of the allottee to the allotment, together with the contract in respect of which the allotment was made, a return (form G88(3)) must also be lodged with the Registrar of Companies. The form G88(3) states the number and nominal amount of the shares so allotted, the extent to which they are to be treated as paid up, and the consideration for which they have been allotted. This shall be completed and lodged with the Registrar of Companies also within one month.

A consultation was conducted in August 1996 by Companies House on proposed changes to section 88. The outcome of the consultation is still unknown. The proposed change to the requirements relating to returns on allotments is to either:

(*a*)   simplify the requirement, so that only the overall amount of any allotment will be notified to the Registrar of Companies within one month of the allotment. The details of the new allottees would then have to be included in the list of members on the next annual return; or

(*b*)   abolish completely the requirement in section 88(2) to deliver a return of allotments to the Registrar of Companies which shows details of the allotments within one month of the allotment.

Authority to allot shares

8.4   Before allotting any shares, the directors of the company must ensure that they have the authority to do so. Section 80(1) of the Companies Act 1985 prevents the directors of a company allotting any 'relevant securities' (see below) unless authorised by either the company in general meeting or the articles of association of the company.

The power of the directors to allot shares is restricted by the statutory rules contained in sections 80 and 80A of the CA 1985 (inserted by CA 1989, s 115). Under CA 1985, s 80(1) directors are not permitted to allot 'relevant securities' unless they have been authorised to do so, either by the company in general meeting, or the company's articles of association.

Such authority may be general or specific to a particular issue and may also be conditional or unconditional. The authorisation must state either the maximum number or amount of shares that may be allotted and the expiry date of the authorisation. The expiry date may not be more than five years either from the date of incorporation of the company or from the date on which the resolution is passed by a general meeting of the company (see Precedent A, Appendix 8A). An authority given in pursuance of CA 1985, s 80 may be revoked or varied at any time by the company in general meeting.

The authority may be renewed by the company in general meeting for further periods of no longer than five years, but such extensions of time must state the amount of securities that may be allotted within the period. It is common for many *public companies* to renew this authority each year at the annual general meeting (i.e. to effectively 'roll' the authority annually).

'Relevant securities' are defined as shares in the company other than those shown in the memorandum to have been taken by the subscribers to it or shares allotted in pursuance of an employee share scheme, and any right to subscribe for, or to convert any security into, shares in the company other than shares so allotted (CA 1985, s 80(2)).

The provisions of CA 1985, s 80(3) to (8) set out the requirements relating to the authority to allot, although these provisions may be relaxed in the case of a *private company* by passing an elective resolution under CA 1985, s 80A (see 7.58 MEMBERSHIP), and in summary are:

(*a*)   the authority may be for a particular exercise of the power or for its exercise generally, and may be unconditional or subject to conditions;

(*b*)   the authority must state the maximum amount of relevant securities that may be allotted under it and the date on which it will expire;

(*c*)   the authority shall not be given for a period exceeding five years, either from the date of incorporation where the authority is contained in the articles or five years from the date of the resolution giving the authority. In the case of a private company which has passed elective resolution under section 80A the authority may be given for an indefinite period or for a fixed period exceeding five years;

(*d*)   the authority may be revoked or varied by ordinary resolution of the company;

(*e*)   the authority may be renewed or further renewed by means of an ordinary resolution for a further period not exceeding five years but the resolution must state or restate the amount of relevant securities which may be allotted under it.

The directors may allot relevant securities notwithstanding that the authority has expired, provided that the allotment is pursuant to an offer or agreement made by the company before the authority expired.

A director who knowingly and wilfully contravenes CA 1985, s 80 is liable to a fine, but the validity of any allotment so made is not affected if the directors do not have sufficient authority to allot.

Pre-emption rights on issue

8.5   Section 89 of the Companies Act 1985 provides that a company which is proposing to allot 'equity securities' must first make an offer of those securities, on the same or more favourable terms in proportion to the nominal value held, to each person holding relevant shares, and shares shall not be allotted until the period allowed for acceptance of any such offer has expired, or all the offers made have either been accepted or refused.

The issue of any shares carrying the right to a fixed dividend and shares to be acquired under an employee share scheme do not fall within the definition of equity securities.

Exclusion

8.6   Under section 91 of the Companies Act 1985 the pre-emption rights may, as applying to a *private company*, be excluded by a provision contained in the memorandum or articles. Moreover, any requirement or authority in the memorandum or articles, if it is inconsistent with the statutory pre-emption provisions, will have effect as a provision excluding those provisions.

In practice, the articles of association of many private companies exclude the provisions of section 89(1) of the CA 1985 and may well provide non-statutory provisions.

Disapplication

8.7   If the directors of a company, public or private, are generally authorised for the purposes of section 80 to allot shares, they may be given power by the articles or by a special resolution of the company to allot equity securities without application of the pre-emption provisions. Where the directors are authorised for the purposes of CA 1985, s 80, whether generally or otherwise, the company may by special resolution resolve that the pre-emption provisions shall not apply to a specified allotment of equity securities (CA 1985, s 95) (see Precedent B, Appendix 8A). In this case the directors must circulate, with the notice of the meeting at which the special resolution is proposed, a written statement giving:

(*a*)   their reasons for making the recommendation;

(*b*)   the amount to be paid to the company in respect of the equity securities to be allotted; and

(*c*)   the directors' justification of that amount.

In the case of public companies, it is common practice to link a resolution for the disapplication of pre-emption rights to a resolution authorising the directors to allot shares under CA 1985, s 80 and to propose such resolutions at the annual general meeting. However, for listed companies, the Stock Exchange will not regard a special resolution under CA 1985, s 95 as valid for a period longer than that ending 15 months from the date of the passing of the resolution or the next annual general meeting, whichever is earlier.

Certain cases will require specific shareholder approval, such as transactions with directors and substantial shareholders. Guidelines on pre-emption have been produced by the Stock Exchange and representatives of the institutional shareholders which, in general, approve of an annual disapplication provided it is restricted to anamount of shares not exceeding

5% of the issued ordinary share capital shown in the latest published accounts. A company is expected to observe cumulative limits in any rolling three-year period and not make use of more than 7[frac1/2]% of issued ordinary share capital by way of non-pre-emptive issues for cash in any such period.

Payment

8.8   Shares allotted by a company and any premium on them may be paid up in money or money's worth including goodwill and know-how. A public company is prohibited from accepting an undertaking by a person to do work or perform services for the company in payment for its shares, or any premium on them, and if it does so, the holder of shares is liable to pay to the company an amount equal to their nominal value and any premium treated as paid up by the company and interest at the appropriate rate. A company's shares may not be allotted at a discount (CA 1985, s 100(1)). A public company may also not allot shares except as paid up at least as to one-quarter of its nominal value and the whole of any premium on it (CA 1985, s 101(1)).

The Registrar of Companies is aware of the payment up of share capital that had purportedly been satisfied by means of the allottee giving an undertaking to pay on demand the cash equivalent of one-quarter of the nominal value. The Registrar after having sought legal advice does not regard such undertaking as amounting to money or money's worth and has been advised that the use of this scheme is unlawful.

A public company is restricted from allotting shares as fully or partly paid-up otherwise than in cash if the consideration for the allotment is or includes an undertaking which is to be, or may be, performed more than five years after the date of allotment (CA 1985, s 102(1)). If the company allots shares in contravention of this provision the allottee remains liable to pay the company an amount equal to their nominal value plus any premium and interest at the appropriate rate (CA 1985, s 102(2)).

A non-cash consideration for shares in a public company must be valued in accordance with the provisions of section 108 of the Companies Act 1985 before allotment. The valuation must be made by an independent person and a report must be made to the company during the six months immediately preceding the allotment of shares. A copy of the report must be sent to the proposed allottee. A copy of the report must also be delivered to the Registrar of Companies at the same time as the return of allotments.

An 'independent person' is defined as a person qualified at the time of the report to be appointed, or continue to be, an auditor of the company. If it appears to the independent person to be reasonable for the valuation to be made by someone who has requisite knowledge and experience to value the consideration and who is not an officer orservant of the company or its holding or subsidiary company, he may accept such valuation as the basis for his report.

(CA 1985, ss 99 to 108.)

The transfer from a person who is a subscriber to the memorandum in the case of a public company formed as such, or a person who is a member of the company on the date of re-registration in the case of a company re-registered as a public company, to a public company of non-cash assets where the consideration is equal to at least one-tenth of the nominal value of the company's issued share capital is prohibited, unless the conditions of section 104 of the CA 1985 have been complied with, during an initial period of two years from the date of incorporation or re-registration as a public company.

The conditions of CA 1985, s 104 are as follows:

(*a*)   the consideration must be independently valued under CA 1985, s 109;

(*b*)   the report with respect to the consideration must have been made during the six months immediately preceding the date of the agreement for the transfer of a non-cash asset;

(*c*)   the terms of the agreement must be approved by an ordinary resolution of the company; and

(*d*)   copies of the resolution and report must be circulated to the members not later than the giving of notice of the meeting at which the resolution is proposed.

Allotment of shares

Private company

8.9   The ability of private companies to make allotments of shares is restricted by the provisions of section 81 of the Companies Act 1985 and section 170 of the Financial Services Act 1986 which state that a private company commits an offence if it offers any shares for sale to the public.

Public company

8.10   Public companies may allot or offer to allot shares to the public. However, before they may do so, they must comply with the prospectus requirements of Part IV of the Financial Services Act 1986 or the Public Offers of Securities Regulations 1995 (see 8.14–8.18 below).

Issue of shares to existing shareholders

8.11   There are basically two forms of share issue to existing shareholders whereby the shareholders may retain the same proportion of total equity as prior to the issue. These are rights and bonus issues.

Rights issue

8.12   This is a form of raising additional capital from existing shareholders.

When offering shares in a rights issue, a company sends an explanatory letter to each member with a provisional allotment letter detailing the number of shares to which the member is entitled to subscribe and the price at which the shares are being offered. Attached to the letter will be forms of acceptance and renunciation. Should a member not exercise his right to the shares he may renounce them in favour of someone else. Ultimately, the member (or renouncee) will complete the form of acceptance and application and lodge it with the company, together with his payment for the shares.

The offer must conform to four requirements:

(*a*)   it must be in writing;

(*b*)   it must be delivered personally or by post;

(*c*)   it must specify a period being not less than 21 days within which the offer may be accepted; and

(*d*)   the offer must be on a 'rights basis' in proportion to the member's existing holding as a fraction of the holdings of all members eligible to receive the offer.

After the period of the offer has expired, the company may utilise any shares not accepted by the members to whom they were offered, either to issue them to outsiders or in different proportions between members.

Members have no automatic right to be offered shares which other members have not accepted. However, provisions in the articles of association may be included to such effect.

Bonus issue

8.13   A bonus issue (sometimes called either a capitalisation or scrip issue) is also an allotment of shares to existing members in proportion to their present holdings. It differs from a rights issue in that no additional capital funds from outside the company are raised by the issue. Its purpose is to capitalise profits or reserves which would otherwise be available for distribution to the members. Thus no payment is required from the members for the bonus shares.

The shares being issued are paid up by the company applying either a credit balance from the profit and loss account or from reserves to the payment of the shares, which are then allotted to members. No statutory authority for this procedure exists, but it can only be done if the appropriate power to do so exists in the company's articles of association (Table A, regulation 110). The power in the articles ofassociation will also determine such matters as the requirement of the directors to obtain the authority of a general meeting before capitalising reserves and the proportions in which the bonus shares may be distributed. Bonus shares may not be issued at a discount (CA 1985, s 100) and a public company may not allot bonus shares as paid unless they are paid up to at least one-quarter of their nominal value (CA 1985, s 101).

The reserves which are capitalised may either be distributable profits, non-distributable reserves or a quasi-capital fund such as a share premium account or capital redemption reserve. The decision to capitalise, however, rests with the shareholders in general meeting.

Regulation of offers — the statutory framework

Introduction

8.14 Generally, only a public limited company may make a public offer of shares (referred to hereafter as 'securities') because there are restrictions imposed on private companies offering securities to the public.

Securities may be either 'listed' or 'unlisted'. Listed securities are securities which are admitted to the Official List of the Stock Exchange; other securities are referred to as unlisted securities. Different statutory provisions apply depending on whether the securities to be offered are to be listed or unlisted. The relevant statutory provisions are briefly considered in turn below; where applicable, reference is made to where the provisions are dealt with in greater detail elsewhere in the chapter.

Listed securities

8.15 The statutory provisions relating to listed securities are set out in Part IV (sections 142 to 157) of the Financial Services Act 1986. (These provisions replaced the provisions set out in Part III of the Companies Act 1985 and have since been amended by the Public Offers of Securities Regulations 1995.) The relevant securities to which Part IV applies are set out in Schedule 1 to the 1986 Act, and are as follows:

(*a*) shares and stock in the share capital of a company (para 1);

(*b*) debentures (para 2);

(*c*) warrants or other instruments entitling the holder to subscribe for investments falling within (*a*) and (*b*) above (para 3); and

(*d*) certificates which represent the above-mentioned securities (para 5) (but note that these securities are excluded from listing by the Stock Exchange listing rules referred to below).

No securities to which Part IV applies are to be admitted to listing except in accordance with the provisions of Part IV (section 142(1)).

Any application for listing is to be made to the Board of the Stock Exchange (which is the 'competent authority' (section 142(6)) in accordance with the provisions of Part IV and of rules made by the Stock Exchange for the purposes of those provisions ('listing rules'). The listing rules require that as a condition of admission to listing, a document known as 'listing particulars' must be submitted to the Stock Exchange; broadly, listing particulars are the equivalent to a prospectus where unlisted securities are being issued. Listing rules and listing particulars, and the provisions of Part IV relating to them, are dealt with in greater detail in 8.20 *et seq.* below.

Unlisted securities   1537

8.16   The issue of unlisted securities is regulated by the Public Offers of Securities Regulations 1995 (SI 195 No 1357) which came into force on 19 June 1995 and implements the Public Offers Directive (Council Directive 89/298/EEC). The regulations replace Part III of the Companies Act 1985, while also repealing Part V of Financial Services Act 1986 (which was never brought into force).

Part II of the new regulations apply to securities which have not been admitted to the Official List and are not the subject of an application for listing. The relevant unlisted securities subject to these regulations are set out in Schedule 1 of the Financial Services Act 1986 (see 8.15 above).

Registration and publication of prospectus

8.17   A prospectus is required in relation to securities offered to the public in the United Kingdom, although the regulations set out the circumstances where an offer is deemed not to be an offer to the public and therefore exempt from the requirement to register and publish a prospectus. The offeror who may or may not be the issuer is required to deliver for registration a copy of the prospectus to the Registrar of Companies prior to its publication.

Registration must occur before an offer of the securities is made. The prospectus must then be made available to the public free of charge from the time the securities are first offered to the public. The regulations also provide circumstances, for instance, where there is a significant inaccuracy in the original prospectus, where a supplementary prospectus is required to be delivered to the Registrar for registration.

Form and content of prospectus

8.18   Prospectuses must be drawn up in accordance with Part II of the Regulations which require more extensive disclosure than under Part III of the Companies Act 1985 but are less onerous than for listing particulars. The regulations impose on the persons responsible for the prospectus a general duty to disclose all relevant information similar tothat imposed on those responsible for listing particulars under section 146 of the Financial Services Act 1986.

Schedule 1 of the regulations sets out the information to be included in the prospectus, while also providing circumstances in which there are exemptions to giving certain information. In general, the prospectus should contain general information about the name and registered office address of the issuing company together with details of the offeror if different from the issuer and the date of publication of the prospectus.

The prospectus should disclose the persons responsible for the prospectus and their advisers, the securities to which the prospectus relates and the offer as well as provide general information about the issuer and its capital. In addition, disclosure is required of details of the issuer's principal activities, its assets and liabilities, financial position and profits and losses together with details of its administration, management and supervision.

The capital markets

8.19   An issue of securities can take a number of different forms:

(*a*)   public offer, by direct invitation by the company or an offer for sale by an issuing house;

(*b*)   placing or selective marketing, usually to institutional investors;

(*c*)   fixed price tender;

(*d*)   rights issue to the existing holders.

The primary market is the Stock Exchange Listed Market; minimum requirements as to the expected market value of securities apply and therefore a listing is only open to larger companies. Smaller companies may seek a quotation for their unlisted securities on the Alternative Investment Market (AIM) which replaces the Unlisted Securities Market (USM) and is designed to provide a regulated market with less onerous requirements for admission than for the Official List (see 8.28 below).

Official listing of securities

General

8.20   As mentioned in 8.15 above, Part IV of the Financial Services Act 1986 contains the statutory requirements relating to the listing of securities on the Official List of the Stock Exchange. An application for listing must be made in accordance with section 143 of the FSA 1986 to the competent authority in such manner as the listing rules may require. The Board of the Stock Exchange has been designated the competent authority for the purposes of Part IV, and one of its functions is the making of listing rules. The listing rules are contained in The Stock Exchange's 'Listing Rules' (the Yellow Book).

The Stock Exchange is primarily a market-place for trading the securities of companies. The requirements set out in the Yellow Book seek to secure the confidence of investors in the conduct of the market. They ensure that all applicants for listing are of a certain minimum size, have an adequate trading record and provide sufficient information about their history, prospects and financial condition to form a reliable basis for market evaluation. The second function, achieved by requiring all listed companies to accept the continuing obligations set out in Chapter 9 of the Yellow Book, is to ensure that all marketings of securities are conducted on a fair and open basis.

Reasons for seeking a public listing

8.21

(*a*)   The character of the company may have changed. What started as a small business may have expanded to the extent that it is more suited to operate in the public domain.

(*b*)   The status is improved, which helps commercial and financial transactions.

(*c*)   The company has access to the market for additional capital which the existing shareholders may be unable or unwilling to provide.

(*d*)   The company may wish to make acquisitions and to be able to offer quoted shares as consideration.

(*e*)   A market in the company's shares may improve the effectiveness of executive or employee share schemes.

(*f*)   The shareholders may wish to realise a part of their investment; a flotation generally achieves a better price than a private sale.

(*g*)   The proprietors can retain effective control by holding a substantial stake whilst still realising their objectives.

(*h*)   A flotation may assist the proprietors in dealing with problems of succession.

Disadvantages of a public listing

8.22

(*a*)   There is a considerable burden on the senior management in preparing for the flotation which may adversely affect the smooth running of the business.

(*b*)   The process of going to the market is expensive.

(*c*)   Public shareholders are more likely to expect a dividend so that the cash available for retention may be reduced.

(*d*)   Institutions and analysts need to be convinced of the company's worth and the proprietors and company will be subject to close scrutiny.

(*e*)   The Stock Exchange rules on the disclosure of information have to be complied with.

(*f*)   Dealings in the company's shares by directors are restricted by the Stock Exchange Model Code on directors' dealing.

Basic conditions to be fulfilled by an applicant

8.23

(*a*)   The expected market value of securities for which listing is sought must be at least £700,000 in the case of shares and £200,000 in the case of debt securities. However, securities of a lower value may be admitted to listing provided the Board of the Stock Exchange is satisfied that adequate marketability can be expected.

(*b*)   The securities must be freely transferable.

(*c*)   A company must have published or filed accounts covering a period of three years preceding application for listing. The Board of the Stock Exchange may accept a shorter period if it is desirable in the interests of the company or of investors and the Board is satisfied that investors will have the necessary information to enable them to arrive at an informed judgement on the company.

(*d*)   At least 25% of any class of shares must be in the hands of the public not later than the time of admission.

Listing particulars

8.24   Listing particulars must not be published until they have received the formal approval of the Listing Department of the Stock Exchange in their final form. All new applicants were in the past required to publish listing particulars in accordance with Chapter 5 of the Yellow Book.

The Public Offers of Securities Regulations 1995 which implement the Public Offers Directive came into force on 19 June 1995, and made changes to the provisions of Part IV of the Financial Services Act 1986 in the context of public offers of securities which are the subject of an application for an official listing.

The principal change is the requirement that an issuer applying for listing of securities to be offered to the public in the UK for the first time is obliged to publish a prospectus rather than listing particulars before admission. The above regulations also introduced a regime for the pre-vetting of prospectuses by the Stock Exchange where no application for listing on the Exchange is involved. The purpose of this is to establish mutual recognition in other EU/EEA member states of UK prospectuses.

The contents requirements of listing particulars are set out in detail in Chapter 6 of the Yellow Book. A summary of the requirements is as follows.

Part A

Details of the persons responsible for the listing particulars, the auditors and other advisers.

The directors must make a declaration that they accept responsibility for the information contained in the document and that to the best of their knowledge and belief the information is in accordance with the facts and does not omit anything likely to affect the import of such information.

Part B

The securities for which application is being made.

Part C

General information about the issuer and its capital.

Part D

The group's activities.

Part E

Financial information concerning the issuer or group.

Part F

The management.

Part G

The recent development and prospects of the group.

Parts H–N

Additional information concerning debt securities.

Reference should be made to the Yellow Book for the detailed requirements of the contents.

In addition to the information specified by the listing rules as a condition of the admission of any securities to the Official List, section 146 of the FSA 1986 requires that any listing particulars shall contain all such information as investors and their professional advisers would reasonably require and reasonably expect to find for the purpose of making an informed assessment of the assets, liabilities, financial position, profits and losses and prospects of the issuer of the securities and the rights attaching to those securities.

Application procedure and publication

8.25   Chapter 7 of the Yellow Book sets out the detailed procedure for application. Certain documents, including copies of the listing particulars, must be submitted for approval at least 14 days prior to the intended publication of listing particulars. An application for admission to listing signed by a duly authorised officer and an application by the sponsoring member firm signed by a partner or director of the member firm must be lodged with the Listing Department at least two business days prior to the hearing of the application by the Board of the Stock Exchange. In the case of securities of a class not already listed, the application must be supported by two firms of market-makers who are prepared to register as dealers in the security.

Once approved, the listing particulars must be published. The publication requirements vary according to the method by which the securities are to be brought to the market.

Persons responsible for particulars

8.26   The persons responsible for listing particulars are:

(*a*)   the issuer of the securities to which the particulars relate;

(*b*)   each person who is a director of the company at the time when the particulars are submitted to the competent authority;

(*c*)   each person who has authorised himself to be named, and is named in the particulars as a director, or as having agreed to become a director of the company, either immediately or at a future date;

(*d*)   each person who accepts, and is stated in the particulars as accepting, responsibility for, or for any part of, the particulars;

(*e*)   each person, not falling within any of the foregoing categories who has authorised the contents of, or any part of, the particulars.

Persons responsible for listing particulars may be held liable to pay compensation to any person who has acquired any securities and suffered loss in respect of them as a result of any untrue or misleading statement in the particulars or omission from them.

Registration of particulars

8.27   On or before the date on which listing particulars are published as required by the listing rules, a copy of the particulars must be delivered for registration to the Registrar of Companies, and a statement that a copy of the particulars has been delivered to the Registrar of Companies must be included in the particulars.

The Alternative Investment Market (AIM)

General

8.28   The Unlisted Securities Market (USM) closed entirely at the end of 1996. The USM was replaced on 19 June 1995 by the Alternative

Investment Market (AIM) which is the market provided by the London Stock Exchange for transactions in AIM securities, being securities admitted to trading subject to the AIM Rules. AIM is a market designed primarily for emerging or smaller companies and the rules of this market are less demanding than those of the Official List or the former Unlisted Securities Market (USM).

Admission to trading on AIM

8.29   A company seeking admission of its securities to trading on AIM must satisfy on admission and continue to satisfy the Stock Exchange that it meets the following conditions:

(*a*)   it must be duly incorporated or otherwise validly established according to the relevant laws of its place of incorporation or establishment. An issuer which is a company incorporated in the UK must be a public company, while issuers incorporated or established outside the UK must be permitted to offer securities to the public;

(*b*)   the securities for which admission to AIM is sought must be freely transferable although any shares held by a shareholder which are subject to the restrictions imposed by section 212 of the Companies Act 1985 may be discounted;

(*c*)   there must be no securities in issue of the class that are admitted to trading on AIM;

(*d*)   the issuer of AIM securities must have a nominated adviser and a nominated broker, although these roles may be performed by the same firm (see 8.30 below).

Companies seeking a listing on the Official List are required to demonstrate an acceptable trading record and meet other criteria, while the AIM Rules impose no minimum requirements on companies seeking admission to trading on AIM. However, a company which has as its main activity an independent business which has not been earning revenue for at least two years, must ensure that all persons who at the time of admission to trading on AIM are directors and employees agree not to dispose of their interest in AIM securities for a period of one year after admission to AIM subject to certain exemptions. Also, companies must now disclose any significant discrepancy between a company's actual performance and any public profit forecast.

At least ten days prior to admission, a new applicant must make a public announcement (via the Exchange's regulatory news service) giving details of its name and business; directors; major shareholders; promoters; and nominated adviser and broker.

Nominated adviser and nominated broker

8.30   A nominated adviser must be independent of the issuer and must be a member firm of the Exchange or a person authorised under the Financial Services Act 1986. A nominated adviser must be entered on a list maintained by the Exchange and owes to the Stock Exchange the responsibilities set out in Chapter 16 of the AIM Rules. A nominated broker is a member firm of the Stock Exchange which assumes the responsibilities set out in Chapter 17 of the Rules.

If a company ceases to have either a nominated adviser or a nominated broker, trading in its securities will be suspended by the Exchange. Failure to replace either a nominated adviser or a nominated broker within one month of ceasing will result in the discontinuation of those securities to trading.

Application for entry to AIM

8.31   An application for admission to AIM must be made in writing in a form prescribed by the Exchange and must be accompanied by an admission document if required. It must be received by the Exchange not less than 72 hours prior to the date the company wishes the securities to be admitted to trading.

When a company applies for admission it must publish a document in English containing information required by the Public Offers of Securities Regulations 1995 (SI 1995 No 1537) together with the additional information required by Chapter 16 of the AIM Rules. However, an admission document need not be published by an issuer applying for admission to trading on AIM of securities of a class already admitted, unless the issuer is required to publish a prospectus by virtue of the above regulations.

Continuing obligations

8.32   The main obligations after entry to AIM are outlined in Chapter 16 of the AIM Rules. In particular, the directors must:

(*a*)   issue accounts within six months of the year end;

(*b*)   publish a half-yearly report within four months of the period end;

(*c*)   advise the Exchange without delay of the resignation, dismissal or change of any nominated adviser or nominated broker;

(*d*)   obtain shareholders' consent before issuing options or convertible loan stock; and

(*e*)   register all share transfers within 14 days of receipt.

The Rules also oblige the directors to disclose details of dividends, results, changes in capital structure, the cancellation of existing securities, material acquisitions or realisations of assets, directors' dealings in shares, changes in directors and any purchase by the company of its own shares.

Venture capital

General

8.33 The term 'venture capital' is generally associated with investments made in unquoted companies with which a high level of risk is attached, but for which a high return is expected. No two investments made by venture capitalists will be the same, but such investments will generally have the following features:

(*a*) equity participation or an option to convert debt into equity;

(*b*) a medium to long-term (five or ten years) investment horizon; and possibly

(*c*) active involvement in the management by the investor.

Companies qualifying for venture capital

8.34 Any kind of business can successfully approach the venture capital market, provided it has an attractive investment proposal. Finance is available at most stages of development, such as:

(*a*) start-up, requiring initial capital;

(*b*) development and expansion, where additional capital is required to assist in the company's growth;

(*c*) re-financing to release existing investors;

(*d*) rescue of an unprofitable business with the prospect of a turn-around;

(*e*) buy-out by the management or buy-in by another interested party.

Sources of venture capital

8.35 Venture capital originated in the United States of America, and in the United Kingdom was only available from a few sources until the mid-1970s. However, the United Kingdom can now boast a wide range of providers of venture capital, including divisions or subsidiaries of clearing banks, merchant banks, major public companies, pension funds, insurance companies and investment trusts and Business Expansion Scheme funds.

Each fund has its own investment criteria, varying as to:

(*a*) the size of investment, although as a broad guideline investments over £100,000 represent the lower threshold;

(*b*) the preferred industry sector;

(*c*) the state of development of the business;

(*d*) the degree of involvement in the management of the business;

(*e*) the overall return required, which itself will determine the percentage equity required.

In general, the higher the level of risk, the higher the return that will be expected. As an indication, a 20% compound rate of return would be expected of a low risk investment, rising to 60% or more for higher risks in, for example, a company starting up a new product/market. While some running yield on the investment may be sought, the overall return required will be estimated having regard to the expected length of the investment and profitable realisation by some form of 'exit route'.

Exit routes

8.36   The venture capitalist will at some stage want to realise his investment in an acceptable manner. Typically, a fund will look for one of the following exit routes, depending on the suitability of the company:

(*a*)   Stock Exchange flotation (see 8.20 above);

(*b*)   Alternative Investment Market (see 8.28 above);

(*c*)   purchase of own shares (see 8.48 below);

(*d*)   acquisition by another company.

Alterations to capital

General

8.37   Section 121 of the Companies Act 1985 allows a company limited by shares to alter its share capital in any of the following ways:

(*a*)   increasing its authorised share capital by the creation of new shares;

(*b*)   consolidating and dividing its share capital into shares of a larger amount than its existing shares;

(*c*)   sub-dividing its shares, or any of them, into shares of a smaller amount;

(*d*)   converting all or any of its paid-up shares into stock and reconverting that stock into paid-up shares of any denomination;

(*e*)   cancelling shares not taken or agreed to be taken by any person and diminishing the amount of the share capital accordingly.

Any such alterations must be authorised by the company's articles of association and be approved by a resolution of the company in general meeting. The type of resolution required to approve the alteration (i.e. ordinary, special or extraordinary) will depend on the provisions of the articles of association, but will usually be an ordinary resolution.

Alterations must be notified to the Registrar of Companies within one month of their occurrence, an exception being notification of an increase in authorised capital (CA 1985, s 121(2)(a)) which must be made within 15 days (see 8.38 below).

Increase of authorised share capital

8.38   The need to increase the authorised share capital will usually arise when a company wishes to make an issue of shares but has insufficient share capital not yet allotted.

The company, if authorised by its articles of association, can effect an increase in its authorised share capital by passing the relevant ordinary resolution in general meeting.

Example

> 'That the capital of the company be and it is hereby increased from £1,000 to £10,000 by the creation of an additional 9,000 ordinary shares of £1 each.'

A print of the resolution authorising the increase, together with notification of the increase in the prescribed form (form G123), must be filed with the Registrar within 15 days of the passing of the resolution (CA 1985, s 123).

As an increase in the authorised share capital is effectively an amendment of the capital clause in a company's memorandum of association, a duly amended copy of the company's memorandum and articles of association must also be prepared and filed with the Registrar of Companies.

Consolidation and division

8.39   This is not a very common occurrence but would be used in circumstances where a company wished to combine shares with a low nominal value into fewer shares with a higher nominal value. Following consolidation, the register of members will require amendment and share certificates may also need to be recalled for amendment if any of the shares consolidated are in issue.

Example

> 'That the 100,000 ordinary shares of 10 pence each be and are hereby consolidated and divided into 10,000 shares of £1 each.'

Sub-division

8.40   Shares may be sub-divided by a company because shares of a smaller denomination are becoming more popular. The procedure is similar to that on conversion into stock and consolidation. The register of members will need to be amended and share certificates may also require amendment if any of the shares that are sub-divided are in issue.

Example

'That the 100 ordinary shares of £10 each be and are hereby sub-divided into 1,000 ordinary shares of £1 each.'

Conversion and reconversion

8.41   Stock can only be created from fully paid shares. The procedure followed is much the same as with a consolidation of shares except that it is not necessary to call in share certificates, nor will fractions occur.

Historically, the advantage gained by converting shares into stock lay in the fact that prior to the Companies Act 1948, stock did not require to be numbered, whereas shares did. However, the 1948 Act introduced a provision allowing companies to dispose of the requirement to number shares and thus the main advantage of stock was diminished.

Stock may also be reconverted into paid-up shares of any denomination, and the procedure is similar to that on conversion into stock.

Cancellation

8.42   The procedure on a cancellation of, as it were, unwanted *unissued* share capital follows the preceding matters, but naturally does not involve any calling in of share certificates or any amendment to the register of members.

Example

'That the 10,000 ordinary shares of £1 each in the authorised capital of the company which have not been taken or agreed to be taken by any person be and are hereby cancelled and that the authorised share capital of the company be diminished by £10,000 accordingly.'

A cancellation of capital should not be confused with a reduction of *issued* share capital under section 135 of the Companies Act 1985, which requires confirmation by the court (see 8.45 below).

Notification of changes

8.43   The above matters, if the articles of association permit, can be effected by ordinary resolution. With the exception of an increase in authorised capital, there is no requirement for a print of such resolutions to be filed with the Registrar of Companies (unless a special or extraordinary resolution is required by the articles of association when filing would be required pursuant to section 380(4)(a) and (b) of the Companies Act 1985). However, notification must be given to the Registrar in the prescribed form (form G122) (CA 1985, s 122).

Reduction of capital

General

8.44   A company's capital may be altered under section 135 of the Companies Act 1985 by a reduction of its issued share capital. This type of alteration must be authorised by the company's memorandum and articles of association and be approved by a special resolution of the company (see Precedent C, Appendix 8A). Any such reductions are, however, subject to confirmation by the court.

A company's issued share capital may be reduced in any of the following ways:

(*a*)   by extinguishing or reducing the liability on any of its shares in respect of share capital not paid-up;

(*b*)   by the cancellation of any paid-up share capital which is lost or unrepresented by available assets;

(*c*)   by paying up any paid-up share capital which is in excess of the company's needs.

If it finds it necessary, the company may alter its memorandum by reducing the amount of its share capital and accordingly of its shares.

Application for court order confirming the reduction

8.45   In accordance with section 136 of the Companies Act 1985, where a company has passed a special resolution reducing its capital by one of the methods described above, an application must be made to the court for an order confirming the reduction.

If the courts so direct or if the proposed reduction involves either:

(*a*)   diminution of liability in respect of unpaid share capital; or

(*b*)   the payment to a shareholder of any paid-up capital;

then the following applies:

(i)   at a date fixed by the court, every creditor who is entitled to any claim which would be admissible in proof against the company in a winding-up is entitled to object to the reduction of capital;

(ii)   the courts will settle a list of creditors entitled to object and may publish notices fixing days within which those creditors not entered on the list are to request that their names be entered and where they are to be excluded from the right to object to a reduction of capital.

The court has the power to dispense with the consent of a creditor on the company securing payment of his debt if:

(A)   the company admits the full amount of the debt or is willing to provide for it;

(B)   the company does not admit to the debt but the court fixes an amount after enquiry and adjudication as if the company were being wound up by the court.

Court order confirming reduction

8.46   Under section 137 of the Companies Act 1985, the court may issue an order confirming the reduction if it is satisfied with respect to every creditor who under section 136 is entitled to object to the reduction of capital, that either:

(*a*)   his consent to the reduction has been obtained; or

(*b*)   his debt or claim has been satisfied or determined.

The court may order the company to add the words 'and reduced' to its name for a period of time if it thinks appropriate, and may also request that the company publish the reasons for the reduction of capital.

Under section 138 of the Companies Act 1985 the Registrar will register the court order confirming the reduction in capital upon the production of a copy of the order and minutes approved by the court showing:

(i)   the amount of the share capital;

(ii)   the number of shares into which the share capital is divided and the amount of each share;

(iii)   the amount (if any) paid on the shares.

The reduction becomes effective upon registration and in confirmation the Registrar issues to the company a certificate as conclusive evidence of the alteration.

Should a public company make application for its share capital to be reduced below the authorised minimum (i.e. £50,000), then the Registrar of Companies will not register such a reduction unless an application for the company to be re-registered as a private company is also submitted at the same time (see 2.50 THE COMPANY CONSTITUTION).

Variation of class rights

8.47   A company may, pursuant to section 125 of the Companies Act 1985 vary the rights attaching to any class or classes of existing shares. This topic is covered in 7.10 MEMBERSHIP.

Purchase of own shares

General

8.48   A general rule against a limited company purchasing its own shares is contained in section 143 of the Companies Act 1985, and is fundamental to the principle that capital must be maintained (see 7.4 MEMBERSHIP and 8.1 above).

There are, however, a number of exceptions to this rule:

(*a*)   acquisition of fully paid-up shares otherwise than for valuable consideration (CA 1985, s 143(3));

(*b*)   redemption or purchase in accordance with Chapter VII, Part V of the CA 1985;

(*c*)   acquisition of shares in a reduction of capital duly made (see 8.44 above);

(*d*)   purchase of shares in pursuance of a court order under section 5 of the CA 1985 (alteration of objects), section 54 of the CA 1985 (litigated objection to resolution for company to be re-registered as private) or section 461 of the CA 1985 (relief to members unfairly prejudiced);

(*e*)   forfeiture of shares, or acceptance of shares surrendered in lieu, in pursuance of the articles, for failure to pay any sum payable in respect of the shares.

The provisions enabling companies to purchase their own shares were brought in by the Companies Act 1981, following the Green Paper issued by the Government in June 1980 on 'The Purchase by a Company of its Own Shares' (Cmnd 7944), which recommended a change in the law to 'make investment and participation in such [private] companies more attractive by providing shareholders with a further means of disposing of their shares and by permitting the remaining members to maintain control and ownership of the business'.

There are a number of circumstances in which the purchase of own shares provisions might prove useful, in particular, for small and medium-sized private companies, where the unmarketability of unquoted shares is a burden. These include:

 (i)   the buying out of a dissident shareholder, who may be harming the company's business;

 (ii)   the buying out of the shares of a deceased shareholder where the personal representatives or beneficiaries under the will do not wish to keep them;

(iii)   the buying out of the shares of a proprietor of a company who is retiring to make way for new management;

(iv)   proprietors who might be unwilling to admit outsiders to a permanent share of the profits can obtain short-term equity finance with the possibility of the option of selling shares back to the company;

(v)   outsiders who might be reluctant to become locked into an unquoted company will be more ready to invest if an additional market for their shares exists.

Although the considerations relating to the marketability of shares will not be applicable in the case of a public company, it may be advantageous to such a company to issue redeemable equity rather than permanent equity or loan capital to meet a need for medium-term finance.

Company law requirements

8.49   Part VII of the Companies Act 1985 specifies the procedures which must be followed. These provisions are designed to safeguard the interests of creditors and other shareholders.

Power to purchase shares

8.50   Section 162 of the Companies Act 1985 gives power to a public or private company limited by shares or by guarantee and having a share capital, if authorised by its articles of association, to purchase its own shares (including any redeemable shares). Redeemable shares can therefore be purchased prior to their redemption date. Specific authority must be given by the company's articles of association. Regulation 35 of Table A in The Companies (Tables A to F) Regulations 1985 (SI 1985 No 805) contains the following authority:

'Subject to the provisions of the Act, the company may purchase its own shares (including any redeemable shares) and, if it is a private company, make a payment in respect of the redemption or purchase of its own shares otherwise than out of distributable profits of the company or the proceeds of a fresh issue of shares.'

Following the purchase, there must be at least one member of the company holding non-redeemable shares.

Procedure

8.51   The procedure is different, depending on whether the transaction is an off-market purchase or a market purchase.

The terms of a proposed contract for an off-market purchase (which, pursuant to section 163 of the Companies Act 1985, means all purchases of shares made other than on a recognised investment exchange) must be authorised by a special resolution of the company (see Precedent D, Appendix 8A) passed either at a general meeting of the company or, in the case of a private company, by written resolution in accordance with section 381A of the CA 1985, before the contract is entered into. In the case of a public company, the authority conferred by the resolution must specify a date on which the authority is to expire and that date must not be more than 18 months after the date on which the resolution is passed.

The authority may be varied, revoked or renewed by special resolution (CA 1985, s 164(2)).

The shares to be purchased are disenfranchised for the vote on the special resolution. A vendor shareholder who holds shares other than those to be purchased can only vote on a poll in respect of those shares (CA 1985, s 164(5)).

If the resolution is to be passed at a general meeting, a copy of the proposed contract or a written memorandum of the terms must be made available for inspection by members of the company at the company's registered office for not less than 15 days ending with the date of the meeting and at the meeting itself (CA 1985, s 164(6)) (see 3.47 THE STATUTORY RECORDS for inspection rights details). There is no provision for the shareholders to waive this requirement so, even if consent to short notice of the meeting is given, the 15-day period must still be adhered to. However, provided the procedural requirements of section 381A of the CA 1985 (inserted by CA 1989, s 113) are followed, a private company may pass the resolution by written resolution (see 7.59 MEMBERSHIP). An adaptation of the procedural requirements contained in Schedule 15A to the CA 1985 (inserted by CA 1989, s 114) dispenses with the 15-day inspection period, provided the documents are supplied to each member signing the resolution at or before the time at which the resolution is supplied to him for signature. The vendor shareholder is not regarded as a member who would be entitled to attend and vote on the resolution and he need not, therefore, sign the written resolution. If the procedural requirements are not observed the resolution is ineffective.

If the company was incorporated before 1 July 1985 and has not updated its articles of association, it must reserve the power to authorise a purchase of its own shares. If the articles of association also contain pre-emption rights, the consent of all the members to waive those rights should be obtained. The following conditions must also be met:

(*a*)   the shares to be purchased must be fully paid (CA 1985, s 159(3));

(*b*)   the terms of purchase must provide for payment on completion (CA 1985, s 159(3));

(*c*)   the purchase price must be met out of distributable profits or from the proceeds of a fresh issue of shares made for the purpose (CA 1985, s 160). A private company may also make a purchase out of capital if the stricter procedural requirements of sections 171 to 177 of the CA 1985 are followed;

(*d*)   once purchased, the shares must be cancelled and the issued share capital of the company is reduced accordingly (CA 1985, s 160(4)). An issue of new shares for the purpose of making the purchase may be made up to the nominal amount of the shares to be purchased without first increasing the authorised capital.

At the time of writing, the DTI has published a consultative document concerning possible changes on companies purchasing their own shares. It basically allows companies to retain the purchased shares 'in treasury' with the possibility of subsequent resale (subject to a limit of ten per cent of the issued shares).

It is thought that the ability to hold repurchased shares in treasury for resale would provide additional flexibility, in that companies could carry a higher level of debt since they could subsequently resell the treasury shares fairly quickly if interest rates rose, necessitating a reduction in the company's gearing level.

Contingent purchase contract

8.52   This is a contract entered into by a company relating to any of its shares which does not amount to a contract to purchase those shares, but under which the company may become entitled or obliged to purchase those shares. Purchase in pursuance of a contingent purchase contract may only be made if the contract is approved in advance by a special resolution before the contract is entered into (CA 1985, s 165).

Market purchases

8.53   This requires only the authority of an ordinary resolution. The authority must:

(*a*)   specify the maximum number of shares authorised to be acquired;

(*b*)   determine both the maximum and minimum prices which may be paid for the shares; and

(*c*)   specify a date on which it is to expire.

(CA 1985, s 166(3).)

The authority may be general or limited to the purchase of shares of a particular class or description and may be unconditional or subject to conditions (CA 1985, s 166(2)).

The maximum and minimum price may be determined by:

(i)   specifying a particular sum; or

(ii)   providing a basis or formula for calculating the amount of the price without reference to any person's discretion or opinion.

(CA 1985, s 166(6)(a), (b).)

Disclosure

8.54   The special resolution authorising an off-market purchase or a contingent purchase contract must be filed with the Registrar of Companies within 15 days of its passing (CA 1985, s 380(4)(h)). The ordinary resolution for a market purchase must also be filed within 15 days.

Pursuant to section 169 of the Companies Act 1985, within 28 days of the shares purchased being delivered to the company, the company must deliver to the Registrar of Companies a return on the prescribed form (form 169) stating with respect to shares of each class purchased:

(*a*)   the number and nominal value of the shares;

(*b*)   the date on which they were delivered to the company.

In the case of a public company the return must also state:

 (i)   the aggregate amount paid by the company for the shares; and

(ii)   the maximum and minimum prices paid in respect of shares of each class purchased.

Where a company enters into a contract for the off-market purchase of its own shares or a contingent purchase contract or a contract authorising the company to make a market purchase of its own shares, the company shall keep a copy of the contract or, if it is not in writing, a memorandum of its terms, at its registered office from the conclusion of the contract until the end of a period of ten years after the completion of all purchases under it. These copies must be open for inspection without charge to any member of the company and, if it is a public company, by any other person (CA 1985, s 169(4)) (see 3.47 THE STATUTORY RECORDS for inspection rights details).

Failure by company to purchase its own shares

8.55   Should a company having made an agreement to purchase its own shares fail to do so, then the company is in breach of contract. Under section 178(2) of the Companies Act 1985 a company may not be held liable in damages for its failure to purchase the shares. However, this subsection does not prevent an aggrieved shareholder from enforcing performance of the contract, excepting that the court may not grant an order for specific performance if the company can show that it is unable to meet the costs of the purchase out of its distributable profits (CA 1985, s 178(3)).

Where a company is wound up and shares are outstanding for purchase, then the shareholder may enforce the terms of the purchase against the company unless:

(*a*)   the purchase was to take place at a date later than that of the winding-up; or

(*b*)   the company was unable up to the date of commencement of the winding-up to lawfully make a distribution equal in value to the price at which the shares were to have been purchased.

(CA 1985, s 178(4) and (5).)

In such circumstances the debt due to the shareholder becomes a deferred debt in the liquidation.

Taxation

8.56   The introduction of the purchase of own-share provisions was accompanied by some major changes in tax law which allow the purchase price for shares in unquoted trading companies to be treated as a capital payment and therefore subject to capital gains tax, rather than as a distribution which would give rise to a charge to advance corporation tax on the company and a liability to income tax to the vendor shareholder on any amount in excess of the nominal value plus premium on subscription.

Redemption of shares

General

8.57   The provisions relating to the purchase of own shares are closely tied to the provisions under sections 159 and 160 of the Companies Act 1985 permitting redemption of shares.

Any limited company, provided it is authorised to do so by its articles of association, may issue shares which are to be redeemed or are liable to be redeemed at the option of the company or the shareholder. Regulation 3 of Table A in the Companies Act (Tables A–F) Regulations 1985 gives such authority. No redeemable shares may be issued unless there are issued shares of the company which are not redeemable (CA 1985, s 159(2)).

Redeemable shares may not be redeemed unless they are fully paid and the terms of redemption must provide for payment on redemption (CA 1985, s 159(3)).

Terms and manner of redemption

8.58   Section 159A of the Companies Act 1985 (inserted by CA 1989, s 133(2)) (not yet in force) sets out conditions as regards the terms and manner of redemption which must be satisfied before redeemable shares may be issued. These are:

(*a*)   the date on or by which, or dates between which, the shares are to be or may be redeemed must be specified in the articles, or, if the articles so provide, may be fixed by the directors, in which case the date or dates must be fixed before the shares are issued;

(*b*)   any other circumstances in which the shares are to be or may be redeemed must be specified in the articles;

(*c*)   the amount payable on redemption must be specified in or determined in accordance with the articles. The articles must not provide for this amount to be determined by reference to any person's discretion or opinion;

(*d*)   any other terms and conditions of redemption must be specified in the articles.

Financing of redemption

8.59 The general rule is that redeemable shares may only be redeemed out of distributable profits, or out of the proceeds of a fresh issue of shares made for the purposes of the redemption (CA 1985, s 160(1)(a)). However, a private company may redeem or purchase its own shares out of capital under section 171 of the Companies Act 1985. Pursuant to section 160(1)(b) of the CA 1985, any premium payable on redemption must be paid out of distributable profits of the company, except that if the redeemable shares were issued at a premium, any premium payable on redemption may be paid out of the proceeds of a fresh issue of shares made for the purposes of the redemption (CA 1985, s 160(2)), provided this does not exceed the lesser of:

(*a*) the aggregate of premiums received on the issue of the shares redeemed; and

(*b*) the current amount of the company's share premium account (including any sum transferred to that account in respect of premiums on the new shares).

(CA 1985, s 160(2)(a), (b).)

Failure to redeem

8.60 Should a company fail to redeem any shares falling due for redemption, then the situation is the same as for a company failing to fulfil an agreement to purchase its own shares (see 8.55 above).

Capital redemption reserve

8.61 When shares are redeemed or purchased wholly out of profits, the amount by which the issued share capital is reduced on cancellation of the shares shall be transferred to 'the capital redemption reserve' (CA 1985, s 170(1)). The capital redemption reserve is treated as share capital except that it may be applied in paying up fully paid bonus shares to be allotted to members of the company.

Where shares are redeemed or purchased wholly or partly out of the proceeds of a fresh issue of shares, the amount to be transferred to the capital redemption reserve is the difference between the nominal value of the shares redeemed or purchased and the proceeds of the fresh issue (CA 1985, s 170(2)).

If a private company redeems or purchases its own shares out of capital, different rules apply.

(*a*) If the total of the permissible capital payment plus the proceeds of a fresh issue is less than the nominal value of the shares to be redeemed or purchased the difference must be transferred to the capital redemption reserve (CA 1985, s 171(4)).

(*b*)   If the total of the permissible capital payment plus the proceeds of a fresh issue is greater than the nominal value of the shares redeemed or purchased, the amount of any capital redemption, share premium account, or fully paid share capital and any amount representing unrealised profits of the company for the time being standing to the credit of any revaluation reserve maintained by the company, may be reduced by the amount by which the permissible capital payment exceeds the nominal value of the shares (CA 1985, s 171(5)).

Redemption or purchase of own shares out of capital

General

8.62   A private company may, if expressly authorised to do so by its articles of association, make a payment in respect of the redemption or purchase of its own shares otherwise than out of its distributable profits or the proceeds of a fresh issue of shares (i.e. out of capital) (CA 1985, s 171(1)).

The payment which may be made out of capital is such an amount taken together with:

(*a*)   any available profits of the company; and

(*b*)   the proceeds of any fresh issue of shares made for the purpose of the redemption or purchase,

as is the price of redemption or purchase. This payment is known as the permissible capital payment.

(CA 1985, s 171(3)(a), (b).)

There are special rules contained in section 172 of the Companies Act 1985 for determining the availability of profits. The question must be determined by reference to profits, losses, assets and liabilities, provisions of Schedule 4, paragraphs 88 and 89, namely depreciations, diminution in asset values, retentions to meet liabilities, share capital and reserves as disclosed in relevant accounts i.e. such accounts as are necessary to enable a reasonable judgement to be made as to the amounts of those items. The directors are required to make a statutory declaration specifying the amount of the permissible capital payment within three months of the date of the accounts (CA 1985, s 172(6)).

Procedure

8.63

(*a*)   The directors must make a statutory declaration in the prescribed form (form 173) specifying the amount of the permissible capital payment, stating that, having made full inquiries into the affairs and prospects of the company, they have formed the opinion:

(i)   that there will be no grounds on which the company could be found unable to pay its debts immediately following the payment out of capital;

(ii)   as regards its prospects for the year following the payment that, having regard to their intentions with respect to the management of the company's business during that year, the company will be able to carry on business as a going concern and be able to pay its debts as they fall due, throughout the year.

(CA 1985, s 173(3)(a), (b).)

The directors' statutory declaration must have annexed to it a report addressed to the directors by the company's auditors, stating that they have inquired into the company's state of affairs, that the amount specified in the declaration is the permissible capital payment and that it has been, in their view, properly determined and they are not aware of anything to indicate that the directors' opinion is unreasonable in the circumstances (CA 1985, s 173(5)).

Should a director make such a declaration without having reasonable grounds for the opinion expressed in the declaration, then he is liable to imprisonment or a fine, or both (CA 1985, s 173(6)).

(b)   The payment out of capital must be approved by a special resolution passed on or within a week of the date on which the directors make the statutory declaration (CA 1985, s 174(1)). The member holding shares to which the resolution relates is disenfranchised from voting on the special resolution (CA 1985, s 174(2) and (3)). The statutory declaration and auditors' report must be available for inspection at the meeting at which the resolution is passed, or, if the written resolution procedure under section 381A of the Companies Act 1985 (see 7.59 MEMBERSHIP) is used they must be supplied to the member at or before the time when the resolution is presented to him for signature (CA 1985, s 174(4)).

(c)   Within one week of the date of passing of the special resolution above, the company must publish a notice in the *London Gazette*:

(i)   stating that the company has approved a payment out of capital for the purpose of acquiring its own shares;

(ii)   specifying the amount of the permissible capital payment for the shares and the date of the resolution;

(iii)   stating that the statutory declaration of the directors and the auditors' report are available for inspection at the company's registered office;

(iv)   stating that any creditor of the company may, at any time within the five weeks immediately following the date of the resolution for payment out of capital, apply to the court for an order prohibiting the payment.

In addition, the company must also publish a similar notice in an appropriate national newspaper or give notice in writing to each of its creditors (CA 1985, s 175(1), (2) and (3)).

(*d*)   A copy of the statutory declaration of the directors and the auditors' report must be delivered to the Registrar of Companies not later than the 'first notice date' which is the day on which the company first publishes the *London Gazette* notice or the national advertisement, or notice to creditors, whichever is the earlier (CA 1985, s 175(4) and (5)). The statutory declaration and auditors' report must be kept at the registered office throughout the period beginning with the first notice date and ending five weeks after the date of the resolution and shall be open to inspection of any member or creditor (CA 1985, s 175(6)) (see 3.47 THE STATUTORY RECORDS for inspection rights details).

(*e*)   The payment out of capital for the purchase or redemption of the shares must be made no earlier than five nor more than seven weeks after the date of the resolution (CA 1985, s 174(1)).

Objections by members or creditors

8.64   Following the passing of a resolution approving a payment out of capital for the redemption or purchase of its shares, any member who did not consent to nor vote in favour of the resolution and any creditor may, pursuant to section 176 of the Companies Act 1985, within five weeks apply to the court for cancellation of the resolution.

The court has various powers under section 177 of the CA 1985 where an objection is lodged. It may approve arrangements for the purchase of dissentient members, or for the protection of dissentient creditors, it may make an order on such terms and conditions as it thinks fit, confirming or cancelling the resolution, and in confirming the resolution, it may alter or extend any date or period of time specified in the resolution.

Financial assistance by a company for the purchase of its own shares

General

8.65   Chapter VI of Part V of the Companies Act 1985 (sections 151 to 158) contains provisions relating to a company giving financial assistance for an acquisition in itself or in its holding company. The rules cover the giving of such assistance by limited companies as well as by unlimited companies.

Where a person is acquiring or is proposing to acquire shares in a company, it is unlawful for the company or any of its subsidiaries to give him any financial assistance directly or indirectly for the purpose of that acquisition, before or at the same time as the acquisition takes place (CA 1985, s 151(1)). Where a person has acquired shares in a company and any liability has been incurred by that person or any other person for the purpose of that acquisition, it is unlawful for the company or any of its subsidiaries to give financial assistance directly or indirectly for the purpose of reducing or discharging the liability so incurred (CA 1985, s 151(2)). The reference to 'person' is not limited to individuals but includes companies and other bodies corporate.

For the purpose of the foregoing:

'(*a*)   a reference to a person incurring a liability includes his changing his financial position by making an agreement or arrangement (whether enforceable or unenforceable, and whether made on his own account or with any other person) or by any other means, and

(*b*)   a reference to a company giving financial assistance for the purpose of reducing or discharging a liability incurred by a person for the purpose of the acquisition of shares includes its giving such assistance for the purpose of wholly or partly restoring his financial position to what it was before the acquisition took place.'

(CA 1985, s 152(3).)

Thus, the recipient of the financial assistance need not necessarily be the acquirer of the shares in order for the provisions of the 1985 Act to apply.

If a company contravenes these provisions, it is liable to a fine and every officer of the company who is in default is liable to a fine or imprisonment or both (CA 1985, s 151(3)).

Financial assistance

8.66   Financial assistance is defined by section 152(1) of the Companies Act 1985 as including:

' (i)   financial assistance given by way of gift;

 (ii)   financial assistance given by way of guarantee, security or indemnity, other than an indemnity in respect of the indemnifier's own neglect or default, or by way of release or waiver;

(iii)   financial assistance given by way of loan or any other agreement under which any of the obligations of the persons giving the assistance are to be fulfilled at a time when in accordance with the agreement any obligation of another party to the agreement remains unfulfilled, or by way of the novation of, or the assignment of rights arising under, a loan or such other agreement; or

(iv)   any other financial assistance given by a company the net assets of which are thereby reduced to a material extent or which has no net assets.'

Under section 152(2) of the CA 1985, 'net assets' are defined as the aggregate of the company's assets less the aggregate of its liabilities, including provisions for liabilities and charges. This refers to the actual value of the company's net assets, as distinct from their book value.

Permitted transactions

8.67   Under section 153 of the Companies Act 1985 there are, however, some important exceptions and exemptions particularly for private companies. The following types of transaction are specifically excepted from the prohibition (CA 1985, s 153(3)):

(*a*)   a distribution of a company's assets by way of dividend lawfully made, or a distribution made in the course of the company's winding-up;

(*b*)   the allotment of bonus shares;

(*c*)   a reduction of capital confirmed by order of the court under section 137 of the CA 1985;

(*d*)   a redemption or purchase of the company's own shares made in accordance with CA 1985;

(*e*)   anything done in pursuance of an order of the court under section 425 of the CA 1985 (power of company to compromise with creditors and members);

(*f*)   anything done under an arrangement made in pursuance of section 110 of the Insolvency Act 1986 (liquidator accepting shares as consideration for sale of company property) or under an arrangement made between a company and its creditors which is binding on the creditors by virtue of Part I of the Insolvency Act 1986.

Also under section 153(1) of the CA 1985 a company is permitted to give financial assistance for the purpose of an acquisition of shares in itself or its holding company if:

(i)   the company's principal purpose in giving that assistance is not to give it for the purpose of any such acquisition, or the giving of the assistance for that purpose is only an incidental part of some larger purpose of the company, *and*

(ii)   the financial assistance is given in good faith in the interests of the company giving the assistance.

Where a person has already acquired shares in a company, the company or a subsidiary of the company, pursuant to section 153(2) of the CA 1985, is not prohibited from giving financial assistance if:

(A)   its principal purpose in giving that assistance is not to reduce or discharge any liability incurred by any person for the purpose of the acquisition, or the reduction or discharge of any such liability is only an incidental part of some larger purpose of the company giving the assistance, and

(B)   the assistance is given in good faith in the interests of the company giving the assistance.

These exceptions are intended to remove from the scope of the prohibition a transaction which has the incidental consequence, but not the main purpose, of providing financial assistance for an acquisition of the company's shares. An example might be where, for normal commercial reasons, a group of companies needs to increase its general level of borrowings after the acquisition of a new company and the new company assists in obtaining or securing the new borrowings.

Where the lending of money is part of the ordinary business of a company, the company is not prohibited from lending money in the ordinary course of its business (CA 1985, s 153(4)(a)). Restrictions exist on what may be done by a public company (see 8.70 below).

Employee share schemes

8.68   Under section 153(4)(b) of the Companies Act 1985 a company is not prohibited from providing financial assistance for the purposes of any employees' share scheme provided it does so in good faith in the interests of the company. Again, restrictions exist on what may be done by a public company (see 8.70 below).

A further exception in relation to the provision of financial assistance to employees was introduced into the 1985 Act (section 153(4)(bb)) by section 196 of the Financial Services Act 1986 (and modified by the 1989 Act). Under this exception, a company and any of its subsidiaries are permitted to provide financial assistance for the purposes of or in connection with anything done by the company (or a company in the same group) for the purpose of enabling or facilitating transactions in shares in the first-mentioned company between, and involving the acquisition of beneficial ownership of, those shares by:

(*a*)   the *bona fide* employees or former employees of that company or of another company in the same group; or

(*b*)   the wives, husbands, widows, widowers, children or stepchildren under the age of 18 of any such employees or former employees.

For the purposes of this exception, a company is in the same group as another company if it is a holding company, or subsidiary of that company, or a subsidiary of a holding company of that company (CA 1985, s 153(5), substituted by CA 1989, Sch 18, para 33).

Loans to employees (other than directors)

8.69   A company is not prohibited from making loans to persons (other than directors) employed in good faith by the company to enable them to acquire fully paid shares in the company or its holding company to be held by them by way of beneficial ownership (CA 1985, s 153(4)(c)).

Special restriction for public companies

8.70   The exceptions described above are subject to a special restriction for public companies. A public company may take advantage of these exceptions only if the company has net assets which are not thereby reduced or, to the extent that its net assets are reduced, if the financial assistance is provided out of its distributable profits (CA 1985, s 154(1) and (2)).

For the purpose of this restriction, the following definitions apply.

(*a*)   'Distributable profits' are those profits out of which the company could lawfully make a distribution equal in value to the financial assistance and includes, in a case where the financial assistance is or includes a non-cash asset, any profit which, if the company were to make a distribution of the asset, would under section 276 and Schedule 4 be available for that purpose (CA 1985, s 152(1)(b)).

(*b*)   'Distribution' has the meaning given by section 263(2) of the CA 1985 (CA 1985, s 152(1)(c)).

(*c*)   'Net assets' means the amount by which the aggregate of the company's assets exceeds the aggregate of its liabilities (taking account of both assets and liabilities to be as stated in the company's accounting records immediately before the financial assistance is given) (CA 1985, s 154(2)).

(*d*)   'Liabilities' includes any amount retained as reasonably necessary for the purpose of providing for any liability or loss which is either likely to be incurred or certain to be incurred but uncertain as to amount or as to the date on which it will arise (CA 1985, s 154(2)).

Private companies

8.71   In addition to the exceptions set out above, there are special provisions which allow a private company to give financial assistance for an acquisition of shares in the company (or its private holding company), subject to appropriate safeguards for members and creditors.

The conditions under which a private company may give financial assistance for an acquisition of shares in the company or, if it is a subsidiary of another private company, in that other company, are set out in sections 155 to 158 of the Companies Act 1985 (section 155(1)). A company may give financial assistance only if the company has net assets which are not thereby reduced or, to the extent that they are reduced, if the assistance is provided out of distributable profits (sections 154(2) and 155(2)).

A subsidiary may not give financial assistance for an acquisition of shares in a company which is its holding company if, between the two companies, there is an intermediate holding company which is a public company (CA 1985, s 155(3)).

Special or written resolution

8.72   Unless the company proposing to give the financial assistance is a wholly-owned subsidiary, the giving of assistance must be approved by special resolution of the company in general meeting (CA 1985, s 155(4)). A copy of the special resolution must be forwarded to the Registrar of Companies within 15 days after it is passed (CA 1985, s 380(1)). As an alternative to a special resolution passed in general meeting, the approval may be given by way of a written resolution agreed to by all members of the company who are entitled to attend and vote at general meetings of the company (see 7.59 MEMBERSHIP).

Where the financial assistance is to be given by a company in respect of an acquisition of shares in its holding company, that holding company and any intermediate holding company between those two companies must (except for any company which is a wholly-owned subsidiary) also approve the assistance by passing a special resolution (or written resolution) (CA 1985, s 155(5)).

The special resolution (or written resolution) must be passed on the date the directors make their statutory declaration, or within the week following, but the resolution will not be effective:

(*a*)   unless the statutory declaration of the directors and the report of the auditors are available for inspection by members of the company at the meeting at which the resolution is passed (or, in the case of a written resolution, unless those documents are supplied to each relevant member at or before the time at which the resolution is supplied to him for signature); or

(*b*)   if, on application, the resolution is cancelled by the court.

(CA 1985, s 157(1), (4) and Sch 15A, para 4.)

A prescribed minimum of the company's shareholders (broadly, those holding 10% of any class of its shares) may apply to the court for the cancellation of the resolution as above. Applicants may not include any person who consented to or voted in favour of the resolution (CA 1985, s 157(2) and (3)). Thus, in cases of a written resolution, application may be made only by persons holding shares which do not carry a right to vote at general meetings of the company.

Statutory declaration

8.73   The directors of the company proposing to give the financial assistance and, where the assistance is to be in respect of an acquisition of shares in its holding company, the directors of that holding company and of any intermediate holding company between those two companies, are required, before the financial assistance is given, to make a statutory declaration in the prescribed form (form 155(6)(a) or, for the holding company, form 155(6)(b)) (CA 1985, s 155(6)). The declaration by the directors must contain the prescribed particulars of the assistance to be given and of the business of the company of which they are directors and they must identify the person to whom the assistance is to be given. The declaration must state that the directors have formed the opinion, as regards the company's initial situation immediately following the date on which the assistance is proposed to be given, that there will be no ground on which the company could then be found to be unable to pay its debts, and either:

'(a) if it is intended to commence the winding-up of the company within 12 months of that date, that the company will be able to pay its debts in full within 12 months of the commencement of the winding-up, or

(b) in any other case, that the company will be able to pay its debts as they fall due during the year immediately following that date.'

(CA 1985, s 156(2).)

In forming their opinion, the directors must take into account the same liabilities (including the company's contingent and prospective liabilities) as would be relevant, under section 122 of the Insolvency Act 1986 (winding-up by the court), to the question of whether the company is unable to pay its debts (CA 1985, s 156(3)).

A director who makes a statutory declaration without having reasonable grounds for the opinion expressed is liable to imprisonment or a fine, or both (CA 1985, s 156(7)).

The statutory declaration must have annexed to it a report by the company's auditors (addressed to the directors) stating that they have enquired into the company's state of affairs and are not aware of anything to indicate that the opinion expressed by the directors in their declaration (that is, as to the ability of the company to pay its debts), is unreasonable in all the circumstances (CA 1985, s 156(4)).

The statutory declaration of the directors and the report of the auditors must be delivered to the Registrar of Companies, together with a copy of any related special resolution passed by the company (as described earlier), within 15 days of the passing of the resolution or, where no such resolution is required to be passed, within 15 days of the making of the declaration (CA 1985, ss 156(5) and 380(1)). Failure to comply with this requirement carries penalties (CA 1985, s 156(6)).

Pursuant to section 158 of the Companies Act 1985 the financial assistance may *not* be given:

(a) before the expiry of four weeks from the date on which the last relevant authorising special resolution was passed unless, in respect of each special resolution, every member of the company who is entitled to vote at its general meetings voted in favour of the resolution;

(*b*)   where an application for the cancellation of any such resolution is made, before the final determination of the application, unless the court otherwise orders; and

(*c*)   later than eight weeks after the date on which the earliest of the relevant statutory declarations by the directors of the company or its holding company was made, unless the court, following an application by a dissentient shareholder, otherwise orders.

Precedents

A. Directors' Authority to Allot Shares

'That the Directors be and they are hereby unconditionally authorised for the purposes of Section 80, Companies Act 1985 to allot shares up to the amount of the authorised share capital of the company (£   ) at any time or times during the period of five years from the date of this resolution.'

B. Disapplication of Pre-emption Rights

'That the rights of pre-emption contained in Section 89(1), Companies Act 1985 and Article [   ] of the Articles of Association of the Company shall not apply to the allotment of [   ] ordinary shares of £1 each to be made by the Directors on [   ] 1998.'

C. Reduction of Capital

'That the capital of the company be reduced from [£   ] divided into [   ] ordinary shares of £1 each (which are all issued and paid up in full) to [£   ] divided into [   ] ordinary shares of 10 pence each and that such reduction be effected by returning to the holders of the said shares paid-up capital to the extent of 90p per share and by reducing the nominal amount of the said shares from £1 to 10 pence accordingly.'

D. Off-market Purchases of Own Shares

'That the off-market purchase(s) of shares in the capital of the company on the terms of the proposed contract(s) to be made between the company and [ ] as laid before the meeting and initialled by the chairman for the purpose of identification be and are hereby approved.'

Chapter 9

Borrowing and Security

Borrowing

General

9.1   A company may require loan capital to achieve its objectives in addition to the share capital put into the company by its shareholders. Such loan capital may be secured or unsecured and where security is required by the lender this is usually achieved by way of a charge over the company's assets. A chargeholder will generally enforce his security on the occurrence of specified events and this may lead to the company's liquidation and subsequent dissolution. However, liquidation is not the only method whereby a company is dissolved since the company may be struck off and dissolved under Part XX of the Companies Act 1985. These matters are considered later in this Chapter.

Power to borrow

9.2   A company may proceed to borrow and give security for borrowing in its own name, provided it has sufficient authority to do so in its memorandum and articles of association. In general terms, a trading company has such authority as an implied power, as the borrowing of money can be regarded as incidental to its trading activities. This general assumption was extended into statute, by virtue of sections 108 to 110, and 112 of the Companies Act 1989; the implications of which are that as a company can no longer act *ultra vires*, then it must have an implied power to borrow (see 11.1 COMMERCIAL CONSIDERATIONS).

However, the directors of a company may still be held personally liable by the members of the company, for committing the company to an act which is not expressly authorised in the memorandum and articles of association. In terms of borrowing outside a company's powers, a director could incur substantial liability. It would therefore seem prudent practice to ensure that, for the protection of a director's position, an express power to borrow is given, and that any limit on the amount which may be borrowed is not exceeded.

It is common practice for the directors to be given an express power to borrow up to a specified limit, beyond which the authority of a generalmeeting is required. A company's memorandum of association will generally contain a statement to the effect that 'the directors may borrow on behalf of the company and in the company's name such amounts as may be necessary for the business of the company'. Such an express power clearly gives the directors sufficient authority to exercise their borrowing powers on the company's behalf.

For a private limited company, no power to borrow need exist beyond that given in its memorandum and articles of association. A company originally registered as a public limited company must, however, be in possession of a trading certificate under section 117 of the Companies Act 1985 before it may exercise its borrowing powers (see 2.48 THE COMPANY CONSTITUTION). Where a public company borrows without holding a trading certificate, the validity of the transaction cannot be questioned. However, the company and the officers responsible for the default become liable to prosecution (CA 1985, s 117(7) and (8)).

Forms of borrowing

9.3   Where the appropriate authority exists, a company may borrow in such manner as it thinks fit. Thus, borrowing can take the form of a mortgage on specific property, a floating charge on all a company's property or by way of a bond, debenture or debenture stock and either with or without security. If unsecured, it is usually called an 'unsecured note' or 'loan note'.

(*a*)   *Bank loan or overdraft.* These methods would not normally meet the company's long-term loan requirements, as banks are usually averse to the making of long-term loans for the purpose of capital developments. Moreover, the bank would almost certainly require some form of security, such as personal guarantees from the directors.

(*b*)   *Issue of debentures.* This method would probably meet requirements more adequately where a large loan is required for an extended period — where, for example, it is required for extensive capital development.

Debentures

9.4   A debenture is defined by section 744 of the Companies Act 1985 as including debenture stock, bonds and any other securities of a company, whether constituting a charge on the assets of the company, or not. In common usage, a debenture is usually regarded as a document which is described as a debenture and is used to evidence or acknowledge a debt. A debenture can either be secured or unsecured and either registered or unregistered. Some common terms used in relation to debentures are given below.

(*a*)   *Debenture*

A debenture in its purest form is issued for a fixed amount and is not divisible or transferable into smaller amounts than its face value. It is usually issued in respect of a loan or series of loans and may be either secured or unsecured.

(*b*)   *Debenture stock*

Debenture stock is a divisible form of a debenture (as described in (*a*) above). However, unlike a debenture, debenture stock will usually be created by a trust deed which sets out the conditions of issue, repayment and the payment of interest and its transferability (see 9.6 below). The form of transfer of debenture stock is specified in the Stock Transfer Act 1963 and transfers are generally exempt from stamp duty.

(*c*)   *Registered debentures*

Most debentures and debenture stock are issued as registered in the name of the holder, rather than in bearer form. This has the advantage for both the issuing company and the holder that as registered debentures are recorded in a company's statutory books, the title of the holder is recorded and thus is more secure should the document evidencing the existence of the debt be lost or damaged.

(*d*)   *Convertible debentures/debenture stock*

These are a hybrid form of debentures/debenture stock that give an option to the holder to convert his debenture into shares in the company at a stated time or times and in a specified formula.

(*e*)   *Secured debentures*

Debentures can be secured by either fixed or floating charges, or by a combination of both.

(i)   *Fixed charge*

This will secure a particular item of property of the company (e.g. a building) and will restrict the company's ability to deal with it without the consent of the debenture-holder.

(ii)   *Floating charge*

This is a form of security that exists over the whole of the property and assets of a company as opposed to a particular item.

Fixed and floating charges are considered more fully in 9.7 to 9.10 below.

(*f*)   *Unsecured debentures*

Unsecured debentures give no right of security to the holder. Because of this, unsecured debentures usually carry a higher rateof interest than secured debentures/debenture stock, due to the increased risk of loss of the capital sum. Unsecured debentures are commonly referred to as unsecured loan stock.

(*g*) *Redeemable debentures*

Although it is possible for a company to issue perpetual (i.e. irredeemable) debentures, it is rare in practice. Commonly, debentures/debenture stock when issued will be expressed to be redeemable on a specified date or dates or upon the occurrence of a specified event or events. Alternatively, debentures can carry a right to conversion (see (*d*) above) or to partial redemption and partial conversion.

The funding for redemption will commonly be made out of a sinking fund which is established in the terms of issue. A sinking fund is an account to which specified sums must be set aside by the company in order to finance the redemption.

Shares or debentures?

9.5   When deciding between shares and debentures as a method of raising capital, the following factors ought to be considered.

(*a*) *Redemption.* If the company would prefer to have the opportunity to clear off the debt within a given period, debentures would obviously meet this requirement, as redeemability is an important feature of that type of security.

Against this, it might be argued that the advantage of redeemability can be gained by the issue of redeemable shares, but the rather stringent conditions laid down in the Companies Act 1985 for their issue and redemption frequently rule them out.

(*b*) *Interest.* Another way of making debentures more attractive than shares is to offer interest at a fixed rate which is payable (usually half-yearly) irrespective of the company's trading results.

Preference shares might be considered as an alternative, but the fixed dividend on such shares is dependent upon the company's trading results and may be passed over or carried forward.

(*c*) *Security.* If the company is in a position to offer adequate security to prospective debenture-holders, that would be yet another way of making debentures more attractive than shares.

On the other hand, the directors might regard the creation of a charge upon the company's assets as a disadvantage, in that it is likely to be restrictive as regards the assets so charged. If, however, the security is in the form of a floating charge, this disadvantage can be put aside.

(*d*) *Economy.* Because the advantages of security and regular fixed rate interest can be included with debenture stock provisions,debentures can usually be issued at a lower rate of interest — that is, as compared with the rate of dividend that it would be necessary to offer to prospective preference shareholders.

(*e*) *Membership.* As debenture-holders are merely 'loan creditors' of the company, the raising of funds by way of debentures does not extend the membership and, therefore, by the same token there is no further spread of voting power.

Against this, it must be accepted that the preference shares of many companies carry no voting power. Furthermore, in recent years an increasing number of companies have appeared to favour the issue of non-voting ordinary shares.

(*f*)   *Convertibility.* A debenture is available which might prove attractive to the investor who is undecided between debentures and shares. This is the convertible debenture (see 9.4(*d*) above).

(*g*)   *Taxation.* Debenture interest is chargeable against profits, whereas dividend on shares is regarded as a distribution of profits — a very important consideration as regards taxation.

Issue of debentures

9.6   Generally speaking, there are no provisions in the Companies Act 1985 relating to the issue of debentures. However, where an issue of debenture stock to the public is proposed, the regulations of the Financial Services Act 1986 relating to the issue of prospectuses apply. The regulations contained in the Stock Exchange's 'Listing Rules' apply where the company making the issue is listed.

The trust deed creating the debenture stock will commonly detail the terms of issue. However, where a company is proposing to issue debentures which carry an option or right to convert the debenture stock into shares, then the provisions of section 80 of CA 1985 regarding the directors' authority to allot shares apply (see 8.4 CAPITAL).

The purpose of the trust deed is to vest the charged property of the company in the names of trustees on behalf of the holders of the debenture stock and to set out the conditions regarding repayment, the payment of interest and the transferability of the debenture stock. A trust deed is not always required in the issue of debenture stock. However, the creation of one does offer a number of advantages:

(*a*)   the trust deed will usually contain a legal mortgage, which will generally rank in priority to other forms of security;

(*b*)   the appointment of trustees ensures that there is someone with a specific duty to act should the security be in jeopardy; and

(*c*)   the trustees can also act for the debenture-holders as a body to protect their interests.

Security

General

9.7   Where a company borrows money, whether by way of the issue of debentures or by some other means (e.g. bank overdraft), it is common practice for the company to have to give some form of security for the borrowing. Again, it could be argued that there is an implied power for companies to grant security in a similar fashion to the power to borrow (see 9.2 above). However, because of the potential personal liability of directors where they act outside the power contained in a company's memorandum of association, it is advisable that this power is expressly stated.

Security may be given on any of the property of the company, be it real or personal, present or future, and can be secured either by way of a charge on specific property (fixed charge) or by way of a floating charge.

Fixed charges

9.8 A fixed (or specific) charge is a charge which is granted over a particular property or asset of a company (e.g. a building) and is equivalent to a mortgage which a bank or building society would grant to an individual.

Once a charge has been created, a company cannot deal with the charged asset without the prior consent of the charge holder.

It is common practice, where a fixed charge has been created to secure the issue of a series of debentures, for the trust deed (see 9.6 above) to contain a clause appointing trustees for the debenture-holders in whom the fixed charge will vest. This has the advantage that should a debenture- holder transfer his debenture, then a transfer of the security is not also required, as would be the case if the trustees did not have this right.

A fixed charge holder ranks as the highest class of creditor in a winding-up. A fixed charge has priority over winding-up expenses and other creditors' claims, including preferential debts — which broadly comprise of taxation and employee charges, and floating charges. However, where several fixed charges exist on the same property or asset, then the priority of ranking will depend upon the order of ranking established at the creation of the charges, provided such charges are registered at Companies House within the prescribed period (see 9.11 below).

Floating charges

9.9 A floating charge is a charge which does not relate to any specific property or assets of the company but relates to the entire undertaking of the company. Thus, as a floating charge does not relate to specific assets, the company is not restricted in its freedom to deal with its assets in conducting its business. The terms of the deed creating a floating charge will usually specify the circumstances in which the charge will crystallise (i.e. attach to the property of the company subject to the charge). When crystallisation occurs, the floating charge effectively becomes a fixed charge and will give the holder the right to take possession of his security and to appoint a receiver to realise the security.

Subject to any fixed charges which may exist, a floating charge ranks in priority, in a winding-up, to ordinary and other secured creditors. Floating charges, whether crystallised or not, rank after winding-up expenses and preferential debts.

Enforcing security

9.10 An administrative receiver is appointed by or on behalf of debenture-holders as a receiver or manager of the whole or most of a company's property where such debentures are secured by a floating charge or by such a charge and one or more other securities (Insolvency Act 1986, s 29). An administrative receiver is normally appointed by the court on the application of a mortgagee or debenture-holder:

(*a*) when repayment of the principal sum and/or payment of interest is in arrears;

(*b*) when the security has crystallised into a specific charge by a winding-up order or resolution; or

(*c*) where the security is at risk.

Another method of appointing a receiver is for the debenture-holder to execute a deed of appointment granting the receiver authority to act.

Under a fixed charge a receiver has no authority to manage the company but as long as the debenture confers this right, a receiver under a floating charge may be appointed as both receiver and manager. If a receiver is appointed in this way, under a floating charge, he can then manage the business provided that the charge is over the goodwill or business of the company. In practice, most bank debentures contain a fixed charge over certain identified assets and a floating charge over the general undertaking of the company.

Registration of charges

General

9.11 Every company registered under the Companies Act 1985 is required by section 407 of the CA 1985 to maintain a register of charges and to enter in it particulars of charges specifically affecting the property of the company, and of all floating charges on the company's undertaking or any of its property (see 3.23–3.26 THE STATUTORY RECORDS). Additionally, sections 395 to 399 of the 1985 Act require that if a company creates a fixed or floating charge over its assets, the charge must be registered with the Registrar of Companies *within 21 days* of its creation.

Pursuant to CA 1985, s 396, charges which require registration are:

(*a*) a charge securing any issue of debentures;

(*b*) a charge on the uncalled capital of a company;

(c)   a charge created or evidenced by an instrument which, if executed by an individual, would require registration as a bill of sale;

(d)   a charge on land or any interest in it (excluding rent);

(e)   a charge on book debts of the company;

(f)   a floating charge on the company's undertaking or property;

(g)   a charge on calls made but not paid;

(h)   a charge on a ship or aircraft, or any share in a ship; and

(j)   a charge on goodwill, or any patent, trade mark, service mark, registered design, copyright or design right or any licence under or in respect of any such right.

CA 1985, s 396(4) also deems that a charge includes a mortgage for the purposes of the Act.

Registration

9.12   A charge is registered by the delivery to the Registrar of Companies of the original charge document, together with a form 395 which contains the following details:

(a)   the date upon which the charge was created;

(b)   the amount of the debt it secures;

(c)   short particulars of the property to which the charge relates; and

(d)   the person(s) entitled to it.

(CA 1985, s 397.)

Section 401 of the Companies Act 1985 further requires that the Registrar of Companies keep a register of charges in which these details for each charge registered with him must be entered. The issue by the Registrar of Companies of a certificate of registration of a charge is conclusive evidence that the charge has been duly registered, and that the particulars are complete.

If the Registrar of Companies detects any error or omission in the documents presented to him for the registration of a charge, he will return the documents to the presenter for correction and subsequent resubmission. Unless the documents in corrected form are received at the registry within *21 days* of the creation of the charge, the Registrar will decline to register the charge.

Failure to register a charge

9.13   If a charge required to be registered pursuant to sections 395 and 396 of the Companies Act 1985 is not presented for registration *within 21 days* of creation, it becomes *void* against the liquidator or administrator and any creditor of the company. Furthermore, the loan secured by the void charge becomes *immediately repayable* by the company pursuant to CA 1985, s 395(2).

The position of the holder of an unregistered charge therefore depends on the course of events. He can demand immediate repayment or enforce his security against the company, unless the company should go into liquidation, in which case any other creditor who has obtained a right over the same asset will have priority. The position of the holder of an unregistered charge is therefore precarious.

Failure to register a charge pursuant to sections 395 to 398 of the CA 1985 renders the company and each of its officers liable to a fine under CA 1985, s 399(3).

It is possible to apply to the court for an order to extend the time limit for registration (i.e. to permit registration after the 21-day period has expired). An explanation of the reasons for the failure to register in time must be given. The court will usually permit late registration, unless there was a fraud, or the company has meanwhile gone into liquidation. In permitting late registration, the court will not deprive another creditor of his priority claim, if it is obtained after the 21-day period for the registration of an earlier charge has expired (CA 1985, s 404).

Although the direct consequences of the failure to register a charge affect the holder of the charge, the company also suffers in that the loan secured by the charge becomes *immediately repayable*, even though it was lent for a fixed period, and the company and its officers may be fined.

Satisfaction of a charge

9.14   A registered charge must be cleared from the register maintained by the Registrar of Companies on repayment of the full amount owing under the charge, or on the release of the property which is subject to the charge.

The requirement of section 403 of the Companies Act 1985 for the registration of the satisfaction of a charge is that either a director or the secretary of the company must make a statutory declaration in the prescribed form (being a form 403a or form 403b as appropriate). The declaration is then presented to the Registrar, who will enter amemorandum of satisfaction on the company's register of charges which he maintains.

Form 403a is used when a debt has been paid off, and form 403b when part of the property or undertaking subject to the charge has been released from it, or the property subject to the charge has been disposed of by the company.

Two practical points should be noted:

(*a*)   there is no time limit for delivering a statutory declaration. If it is overlooked at the time, it can be done even years later. Meanwhile, however, the file at Companies House will give misleading information; and

(*b*) it is not necessary to obtain the formal consent of the former holder of the charge to clear it from the file at Companies House. If the procedure for clearance is effected improperly, the charge holder may apply to the court for the reinstatement of the charge on the file and also claim damages from the company's officers if their action has caused him loss.

The satisfaction of a charge should also be recorded in the register of charges which is required to be maintained by the company.

Proposed changes

9.15   Part IV of the Companies Act 1989 provisionally introduced into the Companies Act 1985 new regulations affecting the registration of charges. At the time of writing, the legislation is still not in force and whether these provisions of the Companies Act 1989 will ever be brought into force is debatable. The options considered include:

(*a*) retaining the present legislation in Part XII of the Companies Act 1985 (see 9.11–9.14 above);

(*b*) retaining the main core procedural provisions of the present legislation, including the conclusive certificate (see 9.12 above), while incorporating certain improvements of the Companies Act 1989 together with a system of provisional registration; or

(*c*) introducing a more radical option involving the replacement of the present system (registration only after the creation of the charge) with a notice filing system where registration is effected either before or after the creation of the charge.

Any change would aim to provide more adequate disclosure of the creation of such charges as well as clarification of the law. In the meantime, a summary of the changes proposed by the Companies Act 1989, so far as they are currently known, is given below.

(i) *Charges requiring registration*

The list of charges requiring registration, although different in format, contains few changes. Notably, the categories have been redrawn so that book debts and intellectual property are specifically included. Securities on ships and aircraft have been removed.

(ii) *Registration*

Charges will still require to be registered by the delivery of a return to the Registrar of Companies, although the original charge document will no longer be required to be filed. The particulars of the charge will only require the signature of either the company *or* the chargee.

As the Registrar will therefore not be checking for any errors or omissions in the charge document, the issue of a certificate of registration of a charge will no longer be 'conclusive evidence' that the particulars of the charge are complete. Accordingly, the issue of a certificate by the Registrar will only be conclusive proof that the particulars of the charge were delivered no later than the date stated in the certificate (CA 1985, s 397, as inserted by CA 1989, s 94).

(iii)   *Failure to register a charge*

The 21-day time limit for the registration of charges after their creation remains. Failure to register a charge within the 21-day period will result in it becoming void against:

(A)   an administrator or liquidator of the company; and

(B)   any person who for value acquires an interest in, or right over, the property subject to the charge.

As before, where a charge becomes void, any monies secured under it become immediately repayable.

However, it will now be possible to register a charge outside the 21-day period without having to apply to the court for an order extending the registration period. When a charge is registered outside the 21-day period it ceases to be void. However, the charge may still be invalid against the persons stated in (A) and (B) above should insolvency proceedings have begun prior to registration, or if a person acquires an interest in, or right over, the property subject to the charge prior to registration (CA 1985, s 399, as inserted by CA 1989, s 95).

(iv)   *Errors and omissions*

If the particulars of a charge which are registered contain any errors or omissions which render the registered particulars of the charge either inaccurate or incomplete, then the charge is void to the extent of the error or omission against an administrator, liquidator or person acquiring an interest in, or right over, property subject to the charge, unless the court otherwise decides (CA 1985, s 402, as inserted by CA 1989, s 97).

Such errors or omissions can, however, be corrected by the delivery to the Registrar of Companies of further particulars of the charge. The notice of such particulars will require to be signed by both the company *and* the chargee.

(v)   *Satisfaction of a charge*

Section 403 of the CA 1985, as inserted by section 98 of the CA 1989, has altered the rules surrounding the notification of the satisfaction of a charge.

A memorandum will require delivery to the Registrar of Companies and will require signature on behalf of both the company *and* the chargee.

However, indications are that the memorandum will not require verification by way of a statutory declaration (this point is subject to confirmation).

Upon the delivery of a memorandum to the Registrar of Companies, he will pass a copy of it bearing a note of the date it was delivered to him, to the company, chargee and any other person having an interest in the charge.

(vi) *Oversea companies*

Schedule 15 to the CA 1989 inserted Chapter III into Part XXIII of the 1985 Act, which introduces new provisions for the registration of charges created by oversea companies over property situated in Great Britain. The charges which are subject to registration are the same as those which must be registered under Part XII of the Act by companies incorporated in Great Britain.

These provisions were modified by the Oversea Companies and Credit and Financial Institutions (Branch Disclosure) Regulations 1992 (SI 1992 No 3179), which provide that the legislation relating to the registration of charges will apply to oversea companies whether they are, or will be, registered as a place of business or a branch.

However, the period in which particulars of the charge must be delivered, in the prescribed form, to the Registrar of Companies is determined as follows:

(A) for a charge over property of an oversea company at the date it delivers documents for registration as a place of business or a branch, at the same time as such documents are delivered;

(B) for a charge created by a registered oversea company, within 21 days of the date the charge is created;

(C) for a charge created over property acquired by a registered oversea company, within 21 days of the date of the charge's creation or the date of acquisition; and

(D) for a charge over property of a registered oversea company, which does not fall within any of the above categories (for instance, property normally situated in the country of incorporation), and is held in Great Britain for a continuous period of four months, before the end of that period.

Subject to other minor modifications, the provisions of sections 399 to 419, as inserted by CA 1989, will apply substantially to the registration of charges by oversea companies.

Dissolution

General

9.16   There are a number of circumstances in which a company may be struck off the register of companies and dissolved. In each case, the method by which dissolution is achieved involves following through procedures set out in the Companies Act 1985 or the Insolvency Act 1986 (IA 1986). The company may resolve to dissolve the company or the dissolution may be imposed on the company by its creditors or by the court. The circumstances giving rise to a company's dissolution generally fall into the following categories:

(*a*)   the Registrar of Companies has cause to believe the company is no longer carrying on business and proceeds to strike the company off the register (see 9.17 below);

(*b*)   the company is no longer trading, has no assets nor liabilities, and the directors resolve to apply to the Registrar for the company to be struck off (see 9.18 below); or

(*c*)   the company is being wound-up under the provisions of the Insolvency Act 1986 (see 9.32 below).

A company may be dissolved and struck off under the Companies Act 1985 where it has no assets or liabilities, although a company with assets will generally be wound up under the provisions of the Insolvency Act 1986. It is important to note that the assets of a company which is inadvertently struck off either at the request of the company's directors or by the Registrar of Companies will become the property of the Crown (see 9.30 below). A company's dissolution may be effected by the Registrar in circumstances prescribed by the Companies Act 1985, although the Registrar has in the past permitted the dissolution of companies under an informal procedure at the request of the company's directors (see 9.18 below).

Striking off by Registrar

9.17   Where the Registrar of Companies has reasonable cause to believe that a company is not carrying on business or is in operation, he may send to the company a letter inquiring whether or not this is the case. This is generally indicated by the failure of the company to submit to Companies House an annual return or annual accounts within the required time limits. Failure by the company to respond to this letter within one month of sending this letter will result in the Registrar sending a second letter to the company within 14 days of the end of that month.

Should the Registrar receive from the company confirmation that the company is no longer in business or in operation, or should he receive no response within one month of sending the second letter, he may then publish in the *London Gazette* and send to the company by post notice that at the expiration of three months from the date of the notice the company will be struck off the Register of Companies and dissolved.

Where a company is being wound up and the Registrar has reasonable cause to believe that no liquidator is acting, or that the affairs of the company are fully wound up and the returns required to be made by the liquidator have not been made for a period of six consecutive months, the Registrar shall publish in the *Gazette* and send to the company or the liquidator (if any) notice of his intention to strike off and dissolve the company at the expiration of three months.

Following the expiration of the time mentioned in the notice, the Registrar may strike the company's name off the register and publish notice to that effect in the *London Gazette*. On publication of this notice, the company is dissolved.

Striking off at directors' request

9.18   The Registrar previously accepted requests from directors of a company for the company to be struck off the register where the company was no longer trading and had no assets nor liabilities. In this circumstance, the Registrar required a director to sign a form DISS 1 confirming that this is the case, following which the Registrar proceeded to strike off the company in a similar manner to that where the Registrar initiated this course of action (see 9.17 above).

However, the process of striking off a company at the directors' request was changed following publication of the Deregulation and Contracting Out Act 1994 which received Royal Assent on 3 November 1994. It introduced a number of deregulatory measures including a formal striking off procedure which came into force on 1 July 1995 (see 9.19 to 9.25 below).

Striking off procedure

9.19   Section 13 and Schedule 5 of the Deregulation and Contracting Out Act 1994 amended the Companies Act 1985 by inserting sections 652A to 652F into the Companies Act 1985. While some of the provisions mirror the earlier legislation, the striking off procedure imposes certain responsibilities upon the directors of such companies. The key elements of the procedure are examined below.

Application in prescribed form

9.20   On application by a private company, the Registrar of Companies may strike the company's name off the register of companies (CA 1985, s 652A). An application by a company shall be made on the company's behalf by its directors or by a majority of them in the prescribed form (form 652a), and submitted to the Registrar together with a filing fee of £10. During the three months prior to the application, the company must not have:

(*a*)   changed its name;

(*b*)   traded or otherwise carried on business;

(*c*)   made a disposal for value of property or rights which, immediately before ceasing to trade or otherwise carry on business, it held for the purpose of disposal for gain in the normal course of trading or otherwise carrying on business; or

(*d*)   engaged in any other activity, except one which is:

(i)   necessary or expedient for the purpose of making an application under section 652A or deciding whether to do so;

(ii)   necessary or expedient for the purpose of concluding the affairs of the company;

(iii)   necessary or expedient for the purpose of complying with any statutory requirement; or

(iv)   specified by the Secretary of State by order for the purposes of section 652B(1).

A company shall not be treated as trading or otherwise carrying on business by virtue only of the fact that it makes a payment in respect of a liability incurred in the course of trading or otherwise carrying on business.

Other circumstances when application not permitted

9.21   An application may not be made at a time when in relation to the company any of the following is the case:

(*a*)   an application has been made to the court under section 425 of the Companies Act 1985 for the sanctioning of a compromise or arrangement and the matter has not been finally concluded;

(*b*)   a voluntary arrangement in relation to the company has been proposed under Part I of the Insolvency Act 1986 and the matter has not been finally concluded;

(*c*)   an administration order in relation to the company is in force under Part II of the Insolvency Act 1986 or a petition for such an order has been presented and has not been finally dealt with or withdrawn;

(*d*)   the company is being wound up under Part IV of the Insolvency Act 1986, whether voluntarily or by the court, or a petition under that Part for the winding up of the company by the court has been presented and not finally dealt with or withdrawn;

(*e*)   there is a receiver or manager of the company's property; or

(*f*)   the company's estate is being administered by a judicial factor.

For (*a*) above, the matter is finally concluded if the application has been withdrawn, it has been finally dealt with without a compromise or arrangement sanctioned by the court, or a compromise or arrangement has been so sanctioned and has together with anything required to be done under any provision made in relation to the matter by order of the court, been fully carried out.

For (*b*) above, the matter is finally concluded if no meetings are to be summoned under section 3 of the Insolvency Act 1986, meetings summoned under that section fail to approve the arrangement with no, or the same, modifications, an arrangement approved by meetings summoned under that section, or in consequence of a direction under section 6(4)(b) of that Act has been fully implemented, or the court makes an order under s 6(5) of that Act revoking approval given at previous meetings and, if the court gives any directions under s 6(6) the company has done whatever it is required to do under those directions.

Notice of application

9.22   A person who makes an application under section 652A is required to give notice of the application by providing, within seven days from the day on which the application is made, a copy of the application to every person who, at any time on that day, is:

(*a*)   a member of the company;

(*b*)   an employee of the company;

(*c*)   a creditor of the company;

(*d*)   a director of the company, other than any director who is party to the application;

(*e*)   a manager or trustee of any pension fund established for the benefit of the employees of the company; or

(*f*)   a person of a description specified by regulations made by the Secretary of State.

A document shall be treated as given to a person if it is delivered to him or left at his proper address or sent by post to him at that address.

Withdrawal of application

9.23   A person who is a director of the company at the end of the day on which a person other than himself becomes a person within the categories listed in 9.22 (*a*)–(*f*) above, must provide to that person a copy of the application within seven days from that day. These duties shall cease to apply if the application is withdrawn before the end of the period for giving the copy application.

Should any of the events occur under which application for striking off shall not be made (see 9.20–9.21 above) a person who at the end of the day on which such an event occurs shall ensure that the company's application is withdrawn forthwith. An application under section 652A is withdrawn if notice of withdrawal in the prescribed form (Form 652c) is given to the Registrar of Companies.

Offences

9.24   A person who breaches or fails to perform a duty imposed on him by section 652B or 652C is guilty of an offence and liable to a fine. It is a defence for the accused to prove that he did not know, and could not reasonably have known, of the existence of the facts which led to the breach, or in failing to perform a duty imposed on him that he took all reasonable steps to perform that duty. A person failing to give notice of an application to any party who, at the time of the application or subsequently, fell within the categories 9.22 (*a*)–(*f*) above with the intent to conceal the application will be liable to imprisonment or a fine, or both. Should a person make an application in circumstances where he is not permitted to do so, or fails to withdraw an application when such circumstances subsequently arise, would be guilty of an offence. Other offences include making a false application to the Registrar of Companies or giving false or misleading information in connection with such an application.

Notice by Registrar

9.25   The Registrar shall not strike off a company until after the expiration of three months from the publication by him in the *London Gazette* of a notice stating that he may exercise his power under section 652A in relation to the company and inviting any person to show cause why he should not do so. Where the Registrar strikes a company off the register he shall publish notice of that fact in the *Gazette* and the company to which the notice relates is dissolved.

Liability of officers and members

9.26   The liability (if any) of every director, managing officer and member of the company continues and may be enforced as if thecompany had not been dissolved for a period of 20 years from the dissolution of the company (see 9.29 below). If there is no officer of the company whose name and address are known to the Registrar of Companies, the letter or notice may be sent to each person who subscribed to the memorandum of association at the address shown in the subscription clause of the memorandum.

Objection to dissolution

9.27   Where a company has been struck off the register of companies, an application may be made:

(*a*)   for the dissolution to be declared void; or

(*b*)   for the company to be restored to the register.

An application may be made by the liquidator of a company or by any other person appearing to the court to be interested for the court to make an order on such terms as the court thinks fit that the dissolution of the company be declared void. Once an order has been made, the liquidator or the interested person may take proceedings against the company as if it had not been dissolved. The person making the application to the court is under a duty to deliver to the Registrar of Companies an office copy of the order for registration within seven days after the making of the order or such further time as the court may allow. Failure to do so will render the person liable to a fine and, for continued default, to a daily default fine.

Application to declare dissolution void

9.28   An application to declare a company's dissolution void may not be made after the end of a period of two years from the date of the dissolution of the company, unless it is for the purpose of bringing proceedings against the company:

(*a*)   for damages in respect of personal injuries including any disease and any impairment of a person's physical or mental condition; or

(*b*)   for damages under the Fatal Accidents Act 1976 or The Damages (Scotland) Act 1976.

Such applications may be made at any time, although no order shall be made on any such application if it appears to the court that the proceedings would fail by virtue of any enactment as to the time within which the proceedings must be brought.

Re-instatement of dissolved company

9.29   Any member or creditor of a company which has been struck off the register may apply to the court before the expiration of 20 years from publication in the *Gazette* of a notice under section 652 or under section 652A(4) for the company to be re-instated where they feel aggrieved by the company having been struck off. The court if satisfied that the company was at the time of the striking off carrying on business or in operation or otherwise that it is just that the company be restored to the register, may order that the company's name be so restored. Restoration may also be effected where in making an application under section 652A a duty required to be performed was not so performed or there was a breach of duty.

Following the delivery of an office copy of the order to the Registrar of Companies for registration, the company is deemed to have continued in existence as if its name had not been struck off. The court may by the order make such directions and provisions as seem just for placing the company and all other persons in the same position as nearly as may be as if the company's name had not been struck off.

Property of dissolved company

9.30   When a company is dissolved, all property and rights whatsoever vested in or held on trust for the company immediately before its dissolution (including leasehold property, but not including property held by the company on trust for any other person) are deemed to be *bona vacantia* and:

(*a*)   belong to the Crown, or to the Duchy of Lancaster or to the Duke of Cornwall for the time being (as the case may be); and

(*b*)   vest and may be dealt with in the same manner as other *bona vacantia* accruing to the Crown, to the Duchy of Lancaster or the Duke of Cornwall.

The person in whom any property or right is vested by section 654 may dispose of, or of an interest in, that property or right notwithstanding that an order may be made under section 651 for the dissolution to be declared void or under section 653 for the company to be restored to the Register of Companies. Where such an order is made it does not affect the disposition (but without prejudice to the order so far as it relates to any other property or right previously vested in or held on trust for the company), and the Crown or, as the case may be, the Duke of Cornwall shall pay to the company an amount equal to:

(i)   the amount of any consideration received for the property or right or interest therein; or

(ii)   the value of any such consideration at the time of the disposition, or, if no consideration was received, an amount equal to the value of the property, right or interest disposed of, as at the date of the disposition.

Disclaimer of property by Crown

9.31   Where property becomes *bona vacantia* and vests in the Crown under section 654 of the Act, the Crown may disclaim its title to the property by notice signed by the Crown's representative, being the Treasury Solicitor or in relation to property in Scotland the Queen's and Lord Treasurer's Remembrancer. The right to execute a notice of disclaimer may be waived by or on behalf of the Crown either expressly or by taking possession or other act evincing that intention.

Since 5 February 1997, the Treasury Solicitor has not sought to collect *bona vacantia* if the known net assets of a dissolved company are less than £500. The Treasury Solicitor will not object to a bank or building society making payment to the former shareholders of a dissolved company of a sole asset (whether in one or more accounts) of less than £500 without reference to the Treasury Solicitor should a request be received by the bank or building society for such a payment.

A notice of disclaimer is only effective if it is executed within 12 months of the date on which the vesting of the property under section 654 came to the notice of the Crown representative, or where an application in writing is made to the Crown representative by a person interested in the property requiring him to decide whether or not he will disclaim, within three months after the receipt of the application. This period of three months may be extended by the court which would have had jurisdiction to wind up the company if it had not been dissolved.

A notice of disclaimer shall be delivered to the Registrar of Companies and retained and registered by him. Copies of the notice are required to be published in the *London Gazette* and to all persons who have notified the Crown's representative of their claim to be interested in the property. Where notice of disclaimer is executed under section 656 relating to any property, that property is deemed not to have vested in the Crown.

Dissolution following winding-up

9.32 The liquidation or winding-up of a company is effected under Part IV of the Insolvency Act 1986, following which the company is struck off the register of companies and dissolved. Under the provisions of this Part, there are three methods of winding-up companies, which are as follows:

(*a*) members' voluntary winding-up;

(*b*) creditors' voluntary winding-up; and

(*c*) winding-up by the court.

Voluntary winding-up may occur where the company's articles specify a fixed period for the company, that period has expired and the members have resolved to wind up the company; the company resolves by special resolution that it be wound up; or the company resolves by extraordinary resolution that it cannot by reason of its liabilities continue in business (IA 1986, s 84).

The circumstances in which a company may be wound up by the court are specified in IA 1986, s 122 and include the following:

(i) the company has by special resolution resolved that it be wound up by the court; (ii)the company has been a public company since its original incorporation and has not been issued with a certificate under CA 1985, s 117 (see 2.48 THE COMPANY CONSTITUTION) and more than one year has expired since it was incorporated;

(iii) the company does not commence business within a year of incorporation, or suspends business for a whole year;

(iv) except in the case of a private company limited by shares or by guarantee the number of members is reduced below two;

(v) the company is unable to pay its debts; or

(vi) the court is of the opinion that it is just and equitable that the company should be wound up.

The effect of a resolution being passed to wind up a company, or of the presentation to the court of a petition to wind up the company, is that the winding-up is deemed to commence from that moment (IA 1986, ss 86 and

129). Accordingly, the business of the company must cease, except as far as it may be required for the beneficial winding-up of the company (IA 1986, s 87).

Liability of directors in winding-up

9.33   In conducting a winding-up, a liquidator is obliged to investigate the records of the company. He should consider whether any transactions were effected at an under-value or at preferential rates and whether any charges are void due to failure to register the charge or, in the case of floating charges, were created within one year of the beginning of the liquidation in favour of any person (within two years for a connected person). The liquidator should also consider whether there is any evidence of:

(*a*)   wrongful trading (see 6.37 THE DIRECTORS);

(*b*)   fraudulent trading (see 6.38 THE DIRECTORS); or

(*c*)   misfeasance (improper performance of a lawful act).

The liquidator has a duty to report any fraud or criminal act that he discovers in the course of a winding-up to the Department of Public Prosecutions (IA 1986, ss 218 and 219). Where the company is being wound up by the court the conduct must be reported to the Official Receiver. If the liquidator or the Official Receiver considers that the conduct of a director has been such as to make him unfit to be concerned in the management of a limited company, he must inform the Secretary of State.

Chapter 10

Company Taxation, Taxation of Company Cars, PAYE and National Insurance

Corporation tax

General

10.1 Corporation tax is a tax which is levied on the worldwide profits of a UK resident company wherever the profits arise. The treatment of companies which are not resident in the UK is obviously different, but they too are chargeable to corporation tax on any profits which arise in the UK from a trade or business carried on by the non-resident company through a UK branch or agency.

For the purposes of corporation tax, 'profits' include both income and chargeable gains arising from the disposal of assets and 'company' means any body corporate or unincorporated association (although certain exceptions do exist, see *Conservative and Unionist Central Office v Burrell [1982] 1 WLR 522*). A partnership, although an unincorporated body, is subject not to corporation tax but to income tax. Before the 1996/97 fiscal year, all partners were jointly and severally liable for tax on the profits of the partnership. With the advent of self assessment for individuals, a partner is now only liable for tax on his share of the partnership's profits, although he remains jointly and severally liable for taxes which are partnership expenses for example, PAYE and VAT. Local authorities and the charitable activities of registered charities are exempt from corporation tax. 'Profits' do not, however, include dividends or other distributions received from UK companies ('franked investment income') upon which tax will already have been paid (see 'advance corporation tax' at 10.10 below).

A company which is incorporated in the UK is generally regarded as UK resident for corporation tax purposes. Where a company is incorporated outside the UK it will generally be regarded as UK resident if its central management and control is exercised in the UK.

An exception applies where a company which would be regarded as UK resident under these rules would also be treated as resident elsewhere under any double tax arrangements. In such circumstances, the company is treated, for UK tax purposes, as resident not in the UK, but elsewhere.

Assessment

10.2   Corporation tax is assessed on the profits of a company arising in its accounting period and is then charged at the rate appropriate for the financial years in which the accounting period falls. A company's accounting period is deemed to commence on the date a company begins to trade, or otherwise becomes liable to corporation tax, or immediately after the previous accounting period finishes. An accounting period is deemed to finish on the earliest of the following dates:

(*a*)   twelve months from the date of commencement of the accounting period; or

(*b*)   the company's accounting reference date; or

(*c*)   the company beginning/ceasing to trade, or otherwise ceasing to be within the charge to corporation tax; or

(*d*)   the company beginning or ceasing to be resident in the UK.

Where a company makes up its accounts for a period that exceeds twelve months then the accounting period will be split into successive periods of twelve months and a final period of any shorter excess.

For corporation tax purposes, a financial year commences on 1 April in each year and runs to 31 March in the following year (e.g. 1 April 1999 to 31 March 2000 is the 1999 financial year).

Calculation of corporation tax

10.3   In calculating the profits of a company which are liable to corporation tax, the following items, referred to here as taxable income, must be included:

(*a*)   trading income less capital allowances (Schedule D, Case I Profits), from which are deducted any trading losses brought forward from previous years;

(*b*)   income from property less allowable expenses (Schedule A);

(*c*)   unfranked investment income (i.e. investment income other than distributions to which a tax credit is attached, which constitute franked investment income, and certain intra-group distributions which are not brought into the corporation tax computation), consisting mainly of interest and similar payments received either gross or under deduction of basic rate tax. Where received under deduction of tax, the interest etc. has to be grossed up in the corporation tax computation. Tax is deducted from, for example, loan stock and debenture interest, government and local authority securities and building society interest (Schedule D, Case III); and

(*d*)   income from overseas securities and possessions (Schedule D, Cases IV and V) and other miscellaneous items (Schedule D, Case VI).

As well as its taxable income, a company is also assessable on its chargeable gains (i.e. capital gains) less any allowable capital losses. These are subject to corporation tax rather than capital gains tax. The taxable income and gains together constitute the profits chargeable to corporation tax.

From these chargeable profits may be deducted any allowable charges on income, being generally all amounts paid by the company where income tax has already been deducted (excluding interest) (e.g. patent royalties and annuities), trading losses of the current accounting period, certain trading losses from later accounting periods and current year trading losses surrendered by other companies within the same tax group and non trade deficits on loan relationships, Schedule A losses or excess management charges of an investment company. For accounting periods ended on or before 31 March 1996, annual interest (e.g. debenture and loan stock interest and mortgage interest) was also treated as a charge on income.

A company may set against its corporation tax liability:

(i) any income tax already suffered on unfranked investment income received (see (*c*) above), so far as not already set against the company's liability to account for income tax on such payments made by it; and

(ii) advance corporation tax in respect of distributions made in the period to 5 April 1999 after offsetting credits on franked investment income and subject to a maximum equal to the prevailing lower rate of income tax applied to the chargeable profits plus any surplus advance corporation tax brought forward at 1 April 1999, after taking account of the Shadow ACT regime (see 10.15 below).

Administration

10.4 Significant changes in corporation tax assessment and collection occurred on the introduction of Pay and File after September 1993 and on the introduction of corporation tax self assessment for accounting periods ending on or after 1 July 1999.

Pay and File

10.5 For accounting periods ending on or after 1 October 1993 companies must pay tax, without assessment, no later than nine months and one day after the end of the accounting period. In addition, they have to file a tax return (on form CT200 or an approved substitute) normally within twelve months of the end of the accounting period; or within three months of the issue by the Inland Revenue of the notice to make a return (form CT203) if later.

In practice, therefore, companies will have to have their tax liability substantially calculated within nine months of the end of the accounting period in order to meet correctly their tax liability. In addition, it is proposed that for accounting periods ending on or after 1 July 1999, companies will be required to include a self-assessment of their liability to corporation tax with their tax return.

A company is liable to interest on all tax remaining unpaid nine months and one day after the end of the accounting period, whether or not an assessment has been raised. There are also fixed penalties where the return is not submitted on time, ranging from £100 for up to three months' delay, to a maximum of £200 for a first default. These figures increase to £500 and £1,000 respectively if the company is late in filing returns in three or more successive periods. In addition, if the return is still outstanding at the later of the due date for filing and eighteen months after the end of the return period, a penalty of 10% of the tax unpaid at that date is due. This penalty increases to 20% if the return continues to be outstanding for a further six months (normally twenty-four months after the end of the return period).

Assessments for accounting periods ending on or after 1 October 1993 will, in general, be issued in agreed figures, although they will still be needed to finalise the position unless no liability arises. An appeal can be made against an assessment, stating the grounds for the appeal, within 30 days after the date of the issue of the assessment.

The new self assessment regime will apply to UK companies for accounting periods ending after 1 July 1999.

Companies will still have the same broad requirements to file tax returns and make claims and elections under self assessment as under Pay and File.

However, under the new self assessment regime a company will be required to calculate, notify and pay its own tax liabilities without the need for the Inland Revenue to issue assessments. A company will also be required to keep documentation to support the returns made.

This represents a final shift in responsibility to the taxpayer. The presumption will be that the submitted return reflects the company's correct corporation tax liability and that the tax paid is correct.

To police the system, the Inland Revenue has been given a fixed period in which it may enquire into any return and can make enquiries without needing to give a reason. The Inland Revenue views its right to have access to underlying documentation and other documentation as an important requirement if self assessment is to work.

At the end of that period, or at the end of any enquiry, the taxpayer has some degree of finality. The position is made less certain by the Inland Revenue's discovery powers under which they may issue discovery determinations or assessments for up to 21 years after the end of an accounting period where negligent or fraudulent conduct is found.

Corporation tax self assessment

10.6   It is proposed that companies liable to the full rate of corporation tax (see 10.7 below) will be required to pay their tax in quarterly instalments for accounting periods ending on or after 1 July 1999. Payments would commence six months and fourteen days from the start of the accounting period. Transitional provisions would phase in the new regime over several years to reduce the cash flow impact for companies affected.

Rate

10.7   There are two rates of corporation tax which apply to companies, termed the full rate and the small companies rate (see 10.16 below). The rates are as follows:

Financial Year(s)	Full Rate	Small Companies Rate
1982	52%	38%
1983	50%	30%
1984	45%	30%
1985	40%	30%
1986	35%	29%
1987	35%	27%
1988 to 1989	35%	25%
1990	34%	25%
1991 to 1995	33%	25%
1996	33%	24%
1997	31%	21%
1998	31%	21%
1999	30%	20%

The full rate applies where company 'profits' exceed an upper limit, set at £1,500,000 for the financial year 1998. The small companies rate applies where profits do not exceed a lower limit, set at £300,000 for the financial year 1998. These figures are reduced where there areassociated companies. A different marginal rate of tax applies where profits fall between the two thresholds (see 10.15 below). Profits for these purposes are profits chargeable to corporation tax, plus franked investment income from non-group companies and foreign income dividends (see 10.13 below).

The government has also announced that a new 'starting' rate of corporation tax has been introduced with effect from the 2000/01 fiscal year (see below).

Advance corporation tax

General

10.8   Until 5 April 1999, advance corporation tax ('ACT') was generally payable whenever a company resident in the UK made a 'qualifying distribution', except when a company pays an intra-group dividend and a group election was in force (Income and Corporation Taxes Act 1988, s 247) in which case the dividend can be paid without accounting for ACT. In addition, a special exemption applied in respect of ACT which would otherwise be payable on certain dividends paid by entities known as International Headquarters Companies. The definition of a qualifying distribution is very broad, but the main categories were:

(*a*)   dividends;

(*b*)   any distribution in respect of shares in the company the cost of which is borne by the company;

(*c*)   the issue of redeemable shares or any securities unless there is new consideration for the issue;

(*d*)   the repayment of share capital followed by a bonus issue; and

(*e*)   the transfer of assets or liabilities between a company and its members where the market value received exceeds any new consideration given.

Certain items were not treated as distributions, examples being:

(i)   distributions made in respect of share capital on liquidation or dissolution;

(ii)   qualifying donations to charity; and

(iii)   certain purchases by a private limited company of its own shares for the benefit of the trade of the company.

From 8 October 1996, where the purchase or redemption by a company of its own shares is classified as a distribution, that distribution is treated as a Foreign Income Dividend ('FID'). This treatment also applies to certain other distributions which are connected with arrangements relating to a transaction in securities. The consequences for the company of FID treatment are detailed at 10.12 below.

For distributions after 5 April 1999 ACT has been abolished. In addition, FIDs have also been abolished from the same date.

Rate

10.9   The rate of ACT is expressed as that fraction of the amount of the qualifying distribution which is set for the financial year during which the distribution is made:

Financial Year(s)	*Rate*
1979 to 1985	3/7ths
1986	29/71sts
1987	27/73rds
1988 to 1992	25/75ths
1993	22½/77½ths
1994 to 1998	20/80ths

Any ACT payable in respect of a distribution made before 6 April in a financial year in which the rate is changed is, however, calculated at the rate fixed for the preceding financial year.

Up to and including financial year 1992 the rate of ACT was linked to the basic rate of income tax. From financial year 1994 this linking is to the lower rate, currently 20%. In financial year 1993 the ACT rate had no direct relationship with either the lower or the basic rate but was set at 22.5% of the gross dividend.

Payment

10.10   ACT applied to all qualifying distributions made by a company. The aggregate of the distribution made plus the ACT payable in respect of it is known as a franked payment. Exceptions to this rule applied to certain dividends paid out of foreign source profits.

The company had to account the ACT to the Inland Revenue on a quarterly basis. The returns were made on form CT61(Z) and had to be made up to the following dates: 31 March, 30 June, 30 September and 31 December (and, where a company's accounting period ended on a different date, to that date).

The return had to be submitted with the payment within 14 days of the return date.

Franked investment income (FII)

10.11   Where a company received a qualifying distribution from another company (to which a tax credit was attached), the related tax credit is set off against any ACT due to be accounted for by the recipient in respect of its own franked payments in the same accounting period. A qualifying distribution plus the tax credit attached to it was franked investment income (FII). Under the new regime, FII attributable to a dividend made after 5 April 1999 cannot be used to 'frank' dividend payments in this way.

ACT and corporation tax

10.12   If, during an accounting period, franked payments made by a company exceeded its franked investment income, then the net ACT accounted for to the Inland Revenue could be set off against the company's mainstream corporation tax liability for the period.

However, the maximum ACT set-off equalled to the amount of ACT which would have been payable if the franked payments made were equal to the corporation tax profits for the accounting period.

Any surplus ACT which arose (i.e. ACT that exceeded the maximum set-off) could, subject to certain conditions, either be carried back or carried forward and set off against corporation tax of other accounting periods. Alternatively, it was generally possible for surplus ACT to be surrendered to a subsidiary company.

Foreign Income Dividends

10.13 A company paying a dividend out of foreign source profits could elect for that dividend to be treated as a FID. Broadly, the consequences for the company of FID treatment were:

(*a*) ACT was payable as for any normal dividend;

(*b*) FIDs payable could be franked only by FIDs received, not by other qualifying dividends received; and

(*c*) surplus ACT resulting from the payment of a FID out of foreign source profits was repayable by the Inland Revenue.

The abolition of ACT

10.14 The liability to account for ACT on dividends has been abolished from 6 April 1999 as was the FID regime. Equally, any dividends received from this date cannot be used to frank any dividends paid prior to 6 April 1999.

Many companies will have surplus ACT brought forward at 6 April 1999. The right to reduce the company's corporation tax liability by reference to this surplus will be restricted by the introduction of the shadow ACT regime.

Broadly, companies will still be allowed to deduct real surplus ACT from future corporation tax liabilities but only to the extent that they could have done so had the ACT regime continued in effect from 6 April 1999.

When a company makes a distribution after 6 April 1999, it is treated as having paid shadow ACT at a rate of 25% of the net distribution. If the company receives FII in an accounting period it is only treated as having paid shadow ACT on distributions in that accounting period to the extent that franked payments exceed franked investment income (distributions received plus the reduced 10% tax credit).

The shadow ACT is set against the company's corporation tax liability for that accounting period. Although this does not actually reduce the company's corporation tax liability, the shadow ACT will restrict the amount of 'real' surplus ACT brought forward which can be offset against the tax liability.

Income tax

10.15 Where a company makes annual payments, for example, payments of interest to another company, it is required to deduct income tax and account for this on its CT61(Z) return. For payments made after 5 April 1996, companies should generally deduct tax at the lower rate of income tax on payments of interest and at the basic rate on other annual payments. Previously the basic rate applied to all payments. Where a company receives payments net of income tax, for example, building society interest, it can set the tax deducted against any income tax payable in that accounting period. Any tax deducted which is unutilised at the end of the accounting period can be set against the company's corporation tax liability. (Such receipts of payments net of income tax should be grossed up and included in the calculation of the corporation tax liability.)

Small companies rate

General

10.16 The rate of corporation tax payable by a company depends on the level of its taxable profits. A separate UK resident company, which is not a close investment-holding company ('CIC') (see 10.22 below), pays tax at the small companies rate if its profits in the financial year 1999 are no more than £300,000, (financial year 1998 — £300,000). This threshold is generally reduced where a company is associated with another company (see 10.18 below). A company which is a CIC at the end of its accounting period is charged to corporation tax at the full rate, irrespective of its profit levels.

Rates of tax

10.17 Companies with 'profits' (defined below) of no more than £300,000 in the financial year 1999 (financial year 1998 — £300,000) will pay corporation tax at the small companies rate of 20%. The full rate of corporation tax (see 10.7 above) applies to companies with profits greater than £1,500,000 in the financial year 1999 (financial year 1998 — £1,500,000).

When a company's profits for the 1999 financial year are between £300,000 and £1,500,000, tax is charged on the excess over £300,000 so that the benefit of the 20% rate is gradually reduced, until at £1,500,000 it is eliminated. An effective marginal rate of tax of 32.5% (financial year 1998 — 33.5%) exists for profits in this band. The thresholds of £300,000 and £1,500,000 relate to a full year and are reduced proportionately for shorter periods and for associated companies.

For the purposes of the small companies rate and the marginal rate, a company's profits are its trading income, any capital gains and other income chargeable to corporation tax and the grossed up amount of any UK dividends receivable, other than from fellow group members.

Associated companies

10.18 Where the company has associated companies, the thresholds of £300,000 and £1,500,000 are divided by the number of associated companies. In determining how many associated companies there are for the purposes of the small companies rate:

(*a*) companies dormant throughout the relevant accounting period are ignored;

(*b*)   non-UK resident companies are included;

(*c*)   investment and holding companies are included;

(*d*)   companies are included if they were associated for any part of the accounting period.

Generally a company is regarded as an associated company of another if one of the two has control of the other or both are under the control of the same person or persons. Control for these purposes is as defined in 10.21 below.

Starting Rate

10.19   The government has announced that a new starting rate of 10% will apply to companies (other than controlled foreign companies) with taxable profits of up to £10,000 for the year commencing 1 April 2000.

A marginal rate of 22.5% will apply to profits between £10,000 and £50,000.

A company's profits and its £10,000 and £50,000 thresholds will be computed for these purposes in the same way as that used for the small companies rate of tax.

Close companies

General

10.20   The close company legislation was originally introduced to ensure that individuals could not avoid the higher rates of income tax by retaining income to be taxed in companies under their control. Until 1989, shareholders could be taxed on certain undistributed income by means of an 'apportionment' of that income. The apportionment provisions were repealed in the Finance Act 1989, but new provisions were introduced for certain investment holding companies. However, the provisions relating to loans made to, or benefits obtained by, participators have been retained.

Most close companies are private companies, but companies on the Alternative Investment Market and the former Unlisted Securities Market may also be close. In some circumstances, a fully listed company may be a close company.

Definition of a close company

10.21   Broadly, a close company is a company which is resident in the UK and which is either under the 'control' of five or fewer 'participators' or under the 'control' of participators who are its 'directors', whatever their number. A company is also close where those participators are entitled to the greater part of the assets on a winding-up of the company.

A 'participator' is generally defined as a person having a share or interest in the capital or income of a company, including an indirect interest (such as a loan creditor).

A person is taken to have 'control' of a company if he exercises, or is able to exercise or is entitled to acquire, direct or indirect control over the company's affairs. This includes possession of or the right to acquire the greater part of the share capital, voting power or rights to the assets on a winding-up.

A 'director' includes not only any person who occupies the position of director (by whatever name called), but also any person in accordance with whose directions or instructions the directors are accustomed to act (i.e. a shadow director within the meaning of section 741 of the Companies Act 1985) and anyone involved in the management of the company who owns or controls at least 20% of its ordinary share capital.

A company cannot be close if it is:

(*a*)   a non-resident company for UK tax purposes; or

(*b*)   a company controlled by one or more non-close companies (other than by reason of non-residence) and only close by taking a non-close company as one of the five or fewer controlling participators; or

(*c*)   a quoted company in which 35% or more of the voting rights attaching to the ordinary share capital are held by the public. The definition of public contains a number of restrictions to exclude holdings owned by persons who have an interest in or connection with the company.

Close investment-holding companies

10.22   A close investment-holding company ('CIC') is a close company which exists wholly or mainly for the purposes of investment other than in land and buildings which are to be let to third parties. A company which deals in land or carries on any other type of trade is not treated as a CIC. Nor is a company which holds shares in, or makes loans to, its subsidiaries which are themselves not CICs, as long as the holding company exists wholly or mainly for the purpose of holding shares in or making loans to such subsidiaries, or co-ordinating the administration of such subsidiaries.

Where a company is a CIC at the end of its accounting period, then the company is charged to corporation tax at the full rate in respect of accounting periods beginning after 31 March 1989.

Loans to participators

10.23   If a close company makes a loan or advances money to a participator, or to an associate of a participator, other than a participator or associate which is a company non-resident in the UK, it has to pay to the Inland Revenue an amount of tax calculated as if the loan were a distribution on which ACT had to be paid. For accounting periods ending before 31 March 1996, the tax also applied to loans or advances to non-resident companies. This tax cannot be set against any other tax liability and represents a cash penalty for, broadly, as long as the loan is outstanding. If the loan is repaid, an equivalent proportion of the tax is repaid. Since 5 April 1999 if the loan is waived the tax is repaid in full it cannot be recovered and a further tax charge could result to the participator. The rules specify the dates of payment and repayment of this tax for loans and advances made in accounting periods ending on or after 31 March 1996. The tax is payable nine months and one day after the end of the accounting period in which the loan was made unless the loan has been repaid in full before this nine-month date. Repayments of the tax are due nine months after the accounting period in which the loan was repaid or waived. For accounting periods ending after 30 September 1993 and before 31 March 1996 this tax was due and payable fourteen days after the end of the accounting period in which the loan or advance is made. For earlier accounting periods, the tax was due within fourteen days after the issue of a notice of assessment.

These provisions are designed to prevent shareholders withdrawing money from a close company by way of loan in an attempt to avoid the tax payable on distributions. The provisions do not apply if, broadly, a loan does not exceed £15,000 and it is made to a director or employee of the close company who works for it full time and who does not own more than 5% of the ordinary share capital in the company. Company law restrictions on loans to directors should, however, always be considered (see 6.30 THE DIRECTORS).

Benefits to participators

10.24 Expenses incurred by a close company in the provision of benefits, such as living expenses or accommodation, for any participator or his associate, will be disallowed for corporation tax purposes and will be treated as distributions, unless they are charged to income tax under Schedule E. For this purpose, the value of the deemed distribution is equivalent to the value of the relevant benefit for income tax purposes, and, like other distributions, made up to 5 April 1999 required the payment of ACT.

Tax losses

General

10.25 Companies often make tax losses (especially in their early years), and it is important that these losses are used effectively. Appropriate elections are required so that losses can be used efficiently.

Corporation tax losses

10.26 A trading loss is computed for corporation tax purposes in the same manner as a trading profit and may be utilised in the following ways.

(*a*) A company may set a trading loss incurred in an accounting period against any profits (including capital gains) of the same accounting period.

(*b*) A company incurring a trading loss for which it cannot claim full relief against profits of the same accounting period may set the unused losses against any profits of the preceding year during which it was carrying on the same trade, setting the losses against the most recent profit first.

Losses cannot be carried back against profits which have already been set against trade charges.

Prior to 2 July 1997, trading losses could be carried back over three years (see (*d*) below).

(*c*)   Prior to 2 July 1997, where a UK resident company received in an accounting period more franked investment income (FII) than it made franked payments, a claim could be made to set off trading losses and certain unrelieved expenses against this surplus. The effect of such a claim was that the tax credit attaching to as much of the surplus FII as was offset by the losses was payable to the company. Since relief is given at the 'tax credit' rate (25% for the financial years 1988 to 1992, reducing to 20% thereafter) rather than the corporation tax rate (31% or 21%), the alternative course of carrying forward the losses for relief against subsequent trading profits needed to be considered. The FII set off option was abolished by the Finance (No 2) Act 1997 — however, there are transitional provisions for accounting periods ending on or after 2 July 1997 but beginning before that date. The three year carry back is retained for terminal losses, i.e. those incurred in the final twelve months of the company's trade.

(*d*)   For accounting periods ended before 2 July 1997, unused losses could be set off against profits for the preceding three years (see (*b*) above). There are transitional provisions for accounting periods ending on or after 2 July 1997 but beginning before that date.

(*e*)   Group relief is available to groups of companies headed by a UK-resident parent company which owns, directly or indirectly, at least 75% of the ordinary share capital of each subsidiary company and which meets certain other requirements. Trading losses, trade and non-trade charges on income in excess of profits, and management expenses in excess of profits of an investment company may be surrendered to fellow members of the group and used to reduce their profits of the same accounting period.

(*f*)   A company incurring a trading loss in an accounting period shall, to the extent it is not otherwise utilised as above, set the loss against any income from the same trade in succeeding accounting periods. Relief must be taken at the earliest opportunity. It is not permissible, for example, to defer claiming relief for a particular period so as to obtain relief for charges on income which do not relate to the company's trade.

(*g*)   Where a loss is incurred during the last twelve months in which a company trades, to the extent which it cannot be used against the profits of the accounting period in which it arises, the loss may be carried back and set against the profits of the accounting period falling wholly or partly in the period if three years immediately before the loss arises. In determining the loss in the twelve months prior to cessation, charges paid wholly and exclusively for trade purposes can also be carried back.

(*h*)   Where a trading company pays charges on income which exceed the profits of the period against which they are deductible, the company may treat as a trading expense the smaller of the excess and the total trade charges, i.e. those incurred wholly and exclusively for the purposes of the trade. This amount is then eligible for loss relief as in (*f*) above. The excess of such charges over profits is not available for relief against the profits of preceding accounting periods as outlined in (*b*) above, otherwise than as part of a terminal loss on a cessation of trade (see (*g*) above).

Restrictions on setting trading losses against total profits

10.27   Relief for trading losses is restricted in the following circumstances:

(*a*)   a loss incurred in a trade assessable under Schedule D, Case V (i.e. a trade controlled outside the UK) can only be relieved against future profits of the same trade;

(*b*)   a loss incurred in a trade not being run on a commercial basis with a view to profit can only be relieved against profits of the same trade.

Excess management expenses of investment companies

10.28   An investment company is a company whose business comprises the making of investments and which derives most of its income from them. An investment company is not regarded as carrying on a trade in respect of this business activity which, therefore, cannot give rise to trading losses. In computing its taxable profits, an investment company is entitled to deduct its expenses of management (which arc not defined by the legislation). Where the management expenses exceed the company's total profits for the period they are carried forward to the next accounting period and treated as if they were expenses actually incurred in the later period. Alternatively, excess management expenses can be surrendered as group relief, as noted in 10.26(*e*) above.

Deficits on non-trading loan relationships

10.29   Under the regime which deals with the taxation of corporate debt, for accounting periods commencing on or after 1 July 1997, net debits (i.e. losses) arising from non-trading loan relationships can be relieved in the following ways:

(*a*)   by set off against the company's total profits for the accounting period;

(*b*)   by surrender as group relief;

(*c*)   by carry back against profit arising in the preceding year from non-trading loan relationships; and

(*d*)   by carry forward for relief against non-trading profits (i.e. non-trading income and capital gains) of the next accounting period.

The period in (*c*) above extended back to 1 April 1996 for deficits arising in accounting periods ending before 2 July 1997. There are transitional provisions for the treatment of deficits in periods straddling that date.

Relief for such losses must be claimed and can generally be taken in a combination of methods (*a*) to (*d*) above. Any deficits which are not relieved in the ways listed above are carried forward and treated as non-trading deficits arising in subsequent accounting periods.

Capital losses

10.30   Allowable capital losses are deducted from chargeable gains of the same or any subsequent (but not earlier) accounting period. No claim is necessary and the deduction is made automatically. Special rules apply to determine the availability of capital losses for companies which join a tax group.

Miscellaneous loss reliefs

10.31

(*a*)   Where Schedule A losses arise, i.e. where allowable expenditure exceeds the rent receivable under a lease of a UK property, the losses would be pooled and relieved against current and future profits. They would also be available as group relief. Before 1 April 1998, Schedule A losses were streamed according to the class of lease to which they related. The losses were only available to set against rent under the same lease in a subsequent period or against current year or subsequent rental income of leases of the same class of lease to that on which the loss arose.

(*b*)   Where in any accounting period a company incurs a loss in any transaction chargeable to corporation tax under Schedule D, Case VI, the company shall set the loss against any Case VI income in the same or any subsequent accounting period. Relief must be taken at the earliest opportunity.

(*c*)   By concession, deficiencies of income from letting of overseas property (taxed under Case V) may be carried forward for set-off against future income from the same property.

Time limits

10.32   Many of the above claims must be made within two years of the end of the accounting period in which the loss was incurred, although some may be made within six years of the end of the accounting period. Under Pay and File and CTSA, some claims, for example group relief, must be made on the corporation tax return (form CT200) itself.

Value added tax

General

10.33   Value added tax ('VAT') is an indirect tax on the supply, importation and acquisition of certain goods and services from EU Member States. It is charged on taxable supplies of goods or services made in the UK by a taxable person in the course of a business and, by one of two different procedures, on imported goods, whether the importer is in business or is a private individual. It is also chargeable on certain services imported by persons (not necessarily taxable) in the course of a business.

HM Customs and Excise ('Customs') administer the tax which operates within a framework of registration and self-assessment by periodic returns. A taxable person must account for VAT chargeable on his taxable supplies (output tax) but is entitled to credit for VAT suffered on goods or services which he purchases (input tax) to the extent, broadly, that such goods and services are utilised in making such taxable supplies (see 10.37 below). VAT suffered on supplies used directly in the making of exempt supplies is not generally recoverable. There is a strict compliance code with heavy penalties.

Meaning of 'supply'

10.34   There are two kinds of supply: goods and services. To be liable to UK VAT the supplies must be made in the UK. The place of supply is determined according to special rules. The passing of title to goods pursuant to an agreement, either immediately or at some future time, as in a hire-purchase agreement, is a supply of goods. 'Supply of services' is a wide concept, including the hiring of goods and transfers of rights over intangible property. Transactions are supplies if there is consideration, whether in money or not, but the legislation also treats certain other transactions as if they were supplies. Examples are a gift of business assets; the assets of a business remaining when it is deregistered for VAT; and fuel provided to staff for their private use. Certain transactions are specifically not treated as supplies, including the transfer of a business as a going concern where certain conditions are satisfied, the receipt of dividends, profit sharing, cash settlements and inter-branch transactions carried on wholly in the UK.

Liability of a supply

10.35   Supplies of goods or services fall into four categories.

(*a*)   *Standard-rated* — Tax is charged so that the value of the supply plus the tax is equal to the consideration. For imported goods the value is the invoice price (plus other import duties, commission, freight etc.) or the value according to the customs valuation rules. The rate is currently 17.5% of the value of the supply.

(*b*)   *Zero-rated* — These supplies are specified by legislation and currently include food, books, certain supplies of buildings for domestic or charitable use, transport, medicines and exported goods subject to proof of export. As of 1 April 1994, domestic, residential and charity non-business use of fuel and power ceased to be zero-rated and became liable to VAT at a reduced rate of 5% from 1 September 1997 (previously 8%). Zero-rated supplies are taxable but the rate of tax is nil and they count towards the taxable turnover of the business.

(c)   *Exempt* — These currently include most interests in land (although there is an option to tax the grant of interests in commercial land and buildings at the standard rate), insurance, postage (only where conveyed by the Post Office), some financial and insurance services, certain supplies of education and some supplies related to healthcare. Exempt supplies do not form part of taxable turnover.

(d)   *Outside the scope* — From 1 January 1993 certain supplies of services by UK taxable persons are treated as made outside the UK. This status generally applies if the recipient of the service is either a VAT registered person elsewhere in the EU or is based outside the EU. In these circumstances, such supplies fall outside the scope of UK VAT, although they may fall within the VAT regime of another country. VAT incurred by the supplier on purchases of goods and services used in making these supplies is recoverable if the supply would have been taxable if made in the UK or if it falls within the special rules for financial or insurance services made to a person who belongs outside the EU.

Where several supplies are charged at a single inclusive price, an apportionment may sometimes be necessary.

Taxable persons and registration

10.36   Taxable persons are those carrying on business (i.e. companies, partnerships or individuals) that are, or are required to be, VAT registered. Businesses must notify Customs where their taxable turnover exceeds the registration limits on either historic or forecast future turnover.

Under the historic test a business is liable to register for VAT if, at the end of any month, the value of its taxable supplies in the last twelve months, has exceeded £51,000 (prior to 1 April 1999 the threshold was £50,000). It must notify Customs within 30 days of the end of that month. Under the future turnover test a business is liable to register if at any time there are reasonable grounds for believing that the value of the business's taxable supplies will exceed £51,000 (formerly £50,000) in the next 30 days. The business must notify Customs within 30 days of that date. Businesses may choose to register for VAT if they are making taxable supplies below the deregistration threshold of £49,000 or intend to make taxable supplies in the future.

A business making only exempt supplies is not entitled to VAT registration. A business whose supplies are wholly or mainly zero-rated must notify Customs if it exceeds the limits but may be excused registration. However, in this situation, registration is generally beneficial since the business can obtain repayment of input tax. A business which makes supplies of goods or services outside the UK and, therefore, outside the scope of UK VAT should consider registration on avoluntary basis if those supplies would have been taxable if made in the UK or if they fall within the special rules for financial or insurance services made to a person who belongs outside the EU. This is because it, too, could probably obtain repayments of input tax from Customs.

Input tax and partial exemption

10.37   Input tax is VAT suffered by a taxable person on goods or services supplied to him, or imported by him, which are used or to be used for the purpose of his business. The rules relating to the recovery of input tax are complex and it is recoverable only to the extent that it is attributable to three categories: taxable supplies, supplies outside the UK which would be taxable or, in certain circumstances, exempt if made in the UK and certain transactions carried out in warehouses. Certain input tax (e.g. on purchased cars, except those purchased for resale, leasing or by firms for whom cars are a key part of their business, such as driving schools, or business entertaining) may not be deducted. From 1 August 1995, only 50% of input tax on leased cars can be deducted where there is private use. Before claiming credit in the VAT return the business should hold a valid tax invoice from the supplier as evidence of entitlement. There are rules regarding what must be shown on a tax invoice. These include the supplier's VAT registration number, the date of supply, the name and address of the supplier and customer, details of the goods or services sold and the total amount of tax charged.

A business which makes a mix of taxable and exempt supplies is 'partly exempt' and may suffer a restriction on the amount of input tax recovered. If a restriction is necessary, recovery in each VAT accounting period is provisional and such businesses are normally required to recalculate their entitlement by reference to a 'longer period' (usually a calendar year beginning on the 1st day of April, May or June, depending on the VAT accounting periods of the business).

Record keeping, returns and compliance

10.38   A VAT registered person is required to keep accounting records for up to six years which must be available for inspection by Customs who make periodic control visits. With Customs' approval, records may be maintained in microfilm or computerised form. When registering a business, Customs will prescribe VAT accounting periods (although these may be changed on request) which are usually quarterly. However, a business in a repayment position may apply for monthly accounting periods. Businesses must declare the amount of output tax due and the amount of input tax being claimed on their return. Businesses must also show on the return the value of goods supplied to and acquired from other EU Member States.

Output tax is due on all supplies, with the exception of zero-rated and exempt supplies, which have taken place (i.e. whose tax point has occurred) in the period of the return. This return must be submitted toCustoms with payment of the net tax shown as due before the last day of the month following the end of the VAT period. Traders who agree to pay Customs by credit transfer get an extra seven days to pay, although the return deadline is not extended. Where the input tax exceeds the output tax, Customs will make a refund with a 5% repayment supplement if there is undue delay on their part. Retailers and certain businesses dealing in second-hand goods are required to use special schemes for calculating the amount of output tax due.

From October 1992 very large traders (whose total VAT liability in the last year exceeded £2 million) have been required to make monthly payments of VAT on account. From 1 June 1996 traders have had the option of paying their actual monthly liability instead of the set payments.

Up to 31 December 1992, provided various requirements were satisfied, including particularly obtaining adequate evidence of export, a UK business was able to zero-rate its exports of goods. As of 1 January 1993, to zero-rate supplies of goods to other EU Member States UK businesses must obtain their customer's VAT registration number and quote it on the invoice. Otherwise, VAT must be charged at the standard rate. For supplies to non-EU Member States the rules applicable for pre-31 December 1992 exports continue to apply.

As of 1 January 1993, most UK businesses which sell goods to customers in other EU Member States are also required to furnish to Customs an EU Sales List ('ESL') on form VAT 101. Submission of an ESL is normally required for each calendar quarter and it must be received by Customs within six weeks of the period to which it relates. In addition, businesses which ship significant values of goods, currently £225,000 (from 1 January 1998) or more per annum for each of 'imports' and 'exports', between the UK and other EU Member States are required to complete very detailed monthly Supplementary Statistical Declarations, known as Intrastats. These Intrastats, prepared separately for movements of goods into and out of the UK, must be submitted to Customs by the 10th working day of the next calendar month. There are criminal penalties for default in submission of, or inaccurate, returns. It is important to note that goods moved to and from branches in other EU Member States must also be recorded on the ESL and Intrastat returns.

Recovery of overpaid VAT

10.39   Customs are required to repay VAT overpaid (unless this would unjustly enrich the claimant) if claims are made within three years of the overpayment. If the overpayment occurred as a result of a mistake then the claimant has three years to submit a claim from the date of discovering the mistake. The three year time limit was introduced from 18 July 1996 for claimants who normally pay VAT and 1 May 1997 for repayment traders.

Penalties and interest

10.40   Offences and defaults in connection with VAT attract heavy penalties. From 25 July 1985, penalties for criminal offences (fraudulent evasion and knowingly or recklessly making false statements or returns) were substantially increased. Other defaults are no longer criminal matters and are dealt with by a system of financial penalties and surcharges imposed directly by Customs and notified by assessment. Many of these are tax-geared and cumulative. The most important are set out below.

(*a*)   *Failure to register* — The penalty is £50 or, if greater, a percentage of the net accrued tax due from the date registration should have been effected. The percentage varies depending on how late the registration is; not more than 9 months late, 5%; more than 9 but not more than 18 months late, 10%; more than 18 months late, 15%. For penalties assessed before 1 January 1995, these penalties were 10%, 20% and 30% respectively. From 1 January 1996, this penalty is extended to such a failure by the transferee in relation to the transfer of all or part of a business as a going concern.

(*b*)   *Failure to render a return* or pay tax by the due date may attract a default surcharge. Following a default, Customs may issue a surcharge liability notice that fixes a surcharge period extending over the next year. A further default in that period triggers an automatic surcharge of 2% of the tax due. The surcharge period may then be extended and the next default within that period attracts a surcharge of 5%. For each subsequent default within the surcharge period, the surcharge rises by 5% up to a maximum of 15%. The current rate of default surcharge became effective on 1 October 1993; for tax liabilities arising before this date, higher rates applied. Therefore it usually requires a year of timely returns before the position is normalised.

Where a liability to surcharge arises, Customs do not issue a surcharge assessment at the 2% or 5% rates for an amount of less than £200. In these circumstances a default is recorded, a surcharge liability extension notice is issued and the rate of surcharge on the subsequent defaults in the surcharge notice period increases accordingly.

(*c*)   *Evasion involving dishonesty* — This covers cases falling short of fraud to a criminal level of proof (although Customs can choose to proceed with this civil offence even if criminal fraud could be proved) but involving an element of dishonesty. The penalty is 100% of the tax evaded with mitigation to such amount (including nil) as Customs and Excise in their discretion consider reasonable.

(*d*)   *Regulatory breach*—A penalty of £5 a day applies for a breach of a regulatory requirement. This is increased to £10 a day on the second breach and £15 a day for the third and subsequent such breaches within a two-year period, subject to a maximum penalty of 100 days and a minimum penalty of £50.

(*e*)   *Failure to preserve records* — Fixed penalty of £500.

(*f*)   *Underdeclaration/overclaiming of tax:*

   (i)   *Misdeclaration penalty.* For misdeclarations in VAT accounting periods beginning on or after 1 December 1993, a penalty will be incurred where a return is made understating liability to tax or overstating repayment of tax credits if the tax which would have been lost (had the error not been discovered) equals or exceeds the lesser of £1 million and 30% of the 'Gross Amount of Tax' ('GAT'). GAT is the total amount of input tax plus output tax which should have been stated in the return for that period.

   If, however, the error arises as a result of Customs issuing the taxpayer with an assessment which understates the liability and this is not brought to Customs attention within 30 days of the date of the assessment, the test is whether the tax which would have been lost equals or exceeds the lesser of £1 million and 30% of the 'True Amount of Tax' ('TAT'). TAT is the true output tax less input tax for the period in question.

In both the above instances the penalty imposed is 15% of the tax which would have been lost if the inaccuracy had not been discovered.

For periods beginning before 1 December 1993, the penalties were always based on the level of error compared to the TAT, although different tests and penalty rates applied.

A person is not liable to a penalty:

(A) if he is convicted of an offence or assessed to a penalty for *Tax evasion: conduct involving dishonesty*; or

(B) if he has a reasonable excuse for the error; or

(C) if, at the time when he had no reason to believe that Customs were enquiring into his affairs, he furnished them with full information with respect to the inaccuracy concerned.

Additionally, penalties are not normally imposed where:

(I) the error does not exceed £2,000 in a VAT period;

(II) the error is discovered in the period between the end of the VAT return quarter in question and the due date for the following return; or

(III) the error has been corrected by a compensating error in respect of the same transaction in the next VAT return period such that no overall loss of VAT arises.

(ii) *Repeated misdeclaration.* A misdeclaration which exceeds the lesser of 10% of the GAT and £500,000 is regarded as a 'material inaccuracy'. Where there is a material inaccuracy in respect of an accounting period beginning on or after 1 December 1993 and Customs issue a notice and there are two or more further material inaccuracies in the eight periods following the issue of the notice, a penalty will arise. In such circumstances the penalty is charged in respect of the second and subsequent material inaccuracies during the currency of the notice. The penalty is 15% of the tax which would have been lost for the VAT accounting period in question if the inaccuracy had not been discovered.

For periods beginning before 1 December 1993, the basis for calculating the penalty and the rate of penalty were different.

(iii) *Default interest.* Simple interest at variable rates is charged on VAT underdeclared or overclaimed, calculated from the date when it should first have been paid. It is chargeable even if penalties are also imposed. On 7 September 1994 Customs issued a News

Release stating that where an assessment did not represent commercial restitution (i.e. the tax underdeclared by one taxable person could be recoverable by another taxable person) they may not seek to impose interest. This treatment is, however, discretionary.

(g)   *Use of incorrect certificates* — A penalty equal to the tax undercharged is payable if a person to whom a supply is, or is to be, made gives a supplier an incorrect certificate showing that it qualifies for zero-rating or exemption.

(h)   *Inaccuracies in ESLs* — Broadly, if the information in a minimum of three returns is materially misleading and Customs have issued timely warning notices to the taxpayer after the first and second offences, a penalty of £100 can arise if a third inaccurate ESL is submitted within two years of the issue of the second notice. After a penalty, the business must submit accurate returns for two years to set the 'penalty clock' back to the starting position.

(j)   *Failure to submit ESLs* — Where an ESL is not received by Customs by the due date and, following the issue by Customs of a default notice, the business fails to submit the return within the next 14 days, a penalty becomes due. The first such default attracts a daily penalty of £5. Subsequent failures before the first anniversary of the notice attract daily penalties of £5, £10 and £15 respectively for the first, second and third subsequent defaults. For each occasion of default, penalties are subject to a minimum of £50 and a maximum of 100 days.

Defences to all these penalties are very limited except that those in (f)(i) and (f)(ii) can be avoided if the tax error is voluntarily disclosed,when the taxpayer has no reason to suspect that his tax affairs are being investigated by Customs. Penalties may not be deducted in computing any profit or gain for direct tax purposes and are in addition to the amount of any assessment which Customs may raise for any underdeclaration of tax or overclaim of input tax.

Importation

10.41   From 1 January 1993, as a result of the completion of the EU Single Market, VAT on purchases of goods by a VAT registered business from other EU states is no longer collected on importation. Instead, the acquiring business is required to account for 'acquisition' VAT on such purchases through the VAT return (as if the business had sold the goods to itself). Such VAT can be reclaimed as input tax if it satisfies the normal conditions for recovery.

Also from 1 January 1993, EU suppliers selling goods to UK non-registered customers must charge VAT at the supplier's appropriate domestic VAT rate.

For goods imported from outside the Single Market, VAT is collected at the port of importation if the goods would be standard rated if supplied in the UK, and any person, whether VAT registered or not, is liable to pay VAT. In addition, VAT is due on certain imported services.

There are special simplification rules in circumstances where businesses purchase goods in one Member State for direct delivery to customers in another Member State. The special rules enable the 'middle man' to avoid VAT registration in the country of dispatch or arrival of the goods.

The European Union

10.42   In theory a harmonised system of VAT applies throughout all member states although rates of tax differ. In practice, however, there may be differences in the way member states interpret the underlying European Union Directives.

UK businesses may recover VAT incurred in another Member State under a reclaim procedure, provided that it would have been recoverable as input tax if incurred in the UK and would be recoverable as input tax under the domestic legislation of that Member State. Recovery is by a claim to the appropriate overseas authority. Businesses in other Member States may similarly reclaim VAT incurred in the UK. Businesses established outside the European Union may also claim recovery of VAT suffered in a Member State, subject to local recovery rules and to the requirement of some states that the claimant's country offers reciprocal VAT recovery provisions for EU businesses.

Groups

10.43   Two or more bodies corporate which are UK resident and which are under common control may apply for a VAT group registration. The companies are then treated as a single entity trading through their representative member which makes a single return and accounts for all the tax although each group member is jointly and severally liable for any tax due. Any transactions between members of the group are disregarded for VAT purposes: changes made in the 1999 'Budget' means that businesses will only be eligible to join or remain in a VAT group if they have a UK establishment. Historically applications made for grouping, degrouping or changing the representative member must be made on 90 days' notice to take effect at the beginning of a VAT period. With effect from royal assent, there will be automatic approval for VAT grouping with a 90 day period for customers to revoke approval if it transpires that the new member is either ineligible or presents a 'revenue risk'. Customs may refuse grouping or degrouping where they consider the object of the grouping or degrouping is tax avoidance. In addition, where transfers of companies or assets into, or out of, a VAT group occur after 28 November 1995, Customs' powers are extended in certain circumstances, to allow them to direct the composition of the VAT group and/or the VAT liability of transactions between group members.

Where a VAT group acquires a business as a going concern and the group is or becomes partly exempt during the VAT (or longer) period in which the transfer takes place, the transfer may be treated as a self-supply and a restriction on input tax recovery could arise.

The advantages of VAT grouping may need to be balanced against the effect of including exempt or partly exempt companies within a group.

At the time of the March 1998 Budget, it was announced that there was to be a consultation on the operation of VAT grouping. One issue to be reviewed is the inclusion of partly exempt companies in VAT groups. Any changes will be implemented from 1 April 1999.

Small companies

10.44 There are two measures available to ease the burden of accounting for VAT by small businesses. For these purposes a small business is defined by the level of its annual turnover (excluding VAT, exempt supplies and supplies of capital assets previously used in the business).

(*a*) *Cash accounting* allows VAT to be accounted for on a cash paid basis and thus provides a measure of immediate relief for bad debts. In contrast, input tax is not recoverable until suppliers have been paid. Cash accounting is not available to businesses with an annual turnover above £350,000. Certain other conditions must also be met.

(*b*) *Annual accounting* allows a business to account for VAT on an annual basis, instead of preparing quarterly returns. However, payments must be made by direct debit in nine equal monthly instalments for 90% of the liability for the current year as estimated by Customs. Any outstanding payment of VAT should accompany the annual return which must be submitted by the last day of the second month following the end of the accounting year. Any VAT reclaimable from Customs as a result of an overpayment will be refunded at this time.

Annual accounting is not available to businesses with an annual turnover above £300,000 and businesses wishing to use this scheme must contact their VAT office to obtain approval.

Property

10.45 The rules relating to property changed significantly in 1989 and further notable changes were introduced in 1995. The rules are detailed and complex. Briefly, the freehold sale of a commercial building or civil engineering work which is new or uncompleted is standard-rated. Most other grants of interests in, or rights over, commercial land and property are exempt. However, a landlord has the right to elect to waive exemption — broadly on a building-by-building basis — and charge VAT at the standard rate on the supplies he makes. An election is irrevocable within 20 years of being made, although it may be withdrawn within a 3 month period, if certain conditions are met. As a result of the election all future grants by that person of interests in the land or property, including its sale, must be standard-rated. From 26 November 1996 the option may not apply in certain specified circumstances.

The grant of a major interest (i.e. a freehold or a lease in excess of 21 years) in a new domestic dwelling, a new building intended for certain residential or charitable uses, or new dwellings arising from the conversion of previously commercial property may be zero-rated if made by the person constructing the building. All other grants of interests in non-commercial properties are exempt, without the landlord having a right to waive exemption.

Appeals

10.46   If any adverse ruling or assessment is received it may be disputed. A formal appeal must be made within 30 days, unless extended by agreement with Customs pending a local review.

Taxation of company cars

10.47   Despite significant increases in tax charges in recent years the company car is still a benefit to most employees when compared with the cost to them of obtaining a similar car themselves.

All directors and all employees who receive remuneration, benefits and expenses at a rate exceeding £8,500 a year are taxable on the benefit of a car or van made available to them or to members of their family for private use (which includes travel from home to work). They are taxed on the cash equivalent of the benefit. The method of calculating the benefit changed with effect from 6 April 1994 and again with effect from 6 April 1999. Brief outlines of the three systems are as follows.

The current and previous systems

10.48   From 6 April 1994, a new system of chargeable benefits was introduced with the cash equivalent calculated from a scale charge based on the car's 'list price', or £80,000 if lower. The Finance Act 1999 revised the existing system slightly. The tax charge is now 35% of the car's list price plus, normally, the price of 'extras' provided with the car or added later. For company car drivers driving between 2500 and 17999 business miles per annum, the tax charge is reduced to 25% of the list price. There is a further reduction to 15% of the list price where annual business mileage exceeds 18,000.

This replaces the previous reduction of one third and two thirds of 35% for annual mileage in excess of 2500 and 1800 respectively. Where an employee is provided with a succession of cars in a tax year, the mileage thresholds are time apportioned between the cars and the taxable benefit is calculated separately for each car by reference to the actual business mileage driven (this means that even though the annual business mileage may entitle the employee to a reduction, he/she may not recover maximum benefits from this where, for example, having changed cars half way through the year, he/she does not have sufficient business mileage in the first half of the year i.e. with the first car). Employers are required to notify the tax office at the end of each quarter of details of cars newly provided to employees and of any 'extras added'. The cost of certain alterations and accessories in vehicles for the registered disabled is excluded from the benefit calculation.

If the car is four or more years old at the end of the tax year, an additional discount of one quarter (before 6 April 1999 one third) is available from the mileage adjusted cash equivalent.

Cars over 15 years old at the end of the tax year with an open market value of more than £15,000 have a tax charge based on 35% of the market value, or £80,000 if lower.

From 6 April 1999 where an employee has two or more company cars, there is a reduction to 25% of the list price in cases where annual business mileage is in excess of 18,000. In previous tax years, the scale charge for second and subsequent company cars doing more than 18,000 business miles per annum was 23.3% (ie 35% less a reduction of one third).

If a car is made available after the beginning of the tax year, or if it ceases to be available before the year end, the benefit is proportionally reduced. The benefit is similarly reduced if the car is not available for continuous periods of over 30 days (e.g. for repairs).

If a condition of the car being made available to an employee is that he is required to make a contribution for his private use, this contribution is deducted from the charges set out above and VAT is chargeable on the employer on the amounts paid by the employee, whether directly or by salary deduction. From 1 August 1995 no VAT is charged on such contributions where they are made in respect of a leased car on which the employer has been able to recover only half of the input tax on the lease rentals. This deduction for contributions by the employee also applied to the calculation of taxable benefits under the old system noted below. A reduction in the taxable benefit is also available to an employee who makes a contribution of up to £5,000 towards the capital cost of a car. Such a contribution is deducted from the 'list price' before calculating the benefit.

The government have announced further, sweeping changes to the taxation of company cars. This is considered further below.

The old system

10.49   For the tax years to 5 April 1994 the cash equivalent was calculated from a scale charge based on engine size. The position for 1993/94 was as follows.

Cylinder Capacity	Original Market Value	1993/94 £
Up to 1400cc		2,310
1401cc–2000cc	Up to £19,250	2,990
2001cc or more		4,800
Any cc	£19,251–£29,000	6,210
Any cc	Over £29,000	10,040

If the car was four or more years old at the end of the tax year, the taxable benefit was reduced by about one-third. If the car was made available after the beginning of the tax year, or it ceased to be available before the year-end, the benefit was proportionally reduced. The benefit was similarly reduced if the car was not available for continuous periods of over 30 days (e.g. for repairs).

Where, in a year of assessment, the car was used by the person to whom it was made available for substantial business travel (18,000 miles or more), the scale charge was halved, but where business travel was 2,500 miles or less the scale charge was increased by one half. The scale benefit covered the cost to the employer of keeping the car on the road, which included depreciation and interest (or leasing payments), road tax, insurance, servicing and repairs. Second and subsequent cars were taxed at 150% of the scale charge regardless of the number of business miles travelled.

Green issues

10.50   With effect from 6 April 1999, the government has removed the employee benefit tax charge on the following 'green' commuting benefits:

- works buses (for one or more employers) with seating capacity of 17 or more, as long as the bus is available generally to employees of the employer (or each employer);

- general subsidies paid directly to public transport bus services as long as employees are treated no more favourably than other members of the public and the service is available generally to employees of the employer (or each employer);

- the provision of bicycles and cycling safety equipment as long as this is available to employees generally;

- workplace parking for bicycles and motorcycles.

Vouchers which may be provided in respect of any of these items (other than general subsidies to bus services) will also be free of income tax.

In addition employees will be able to claim capital allowances if they use their own bicycle for business travel, and obtain a tax-free mileage rate of 12p for business travel.

The existing concession whereby some employer-paid or employer-provided late-night office-to-home travel is not a taxable benefit has been extended to cover car-sharing arrangements, so that a tax charge will not arise if an employer pays for or provides the employee's home journey because the employee due to unforeseen and exceptional circumstances cannot get home in the shared car.

Fuel

10.51   Where a director or higher-paid employee has a car made available and petrol is provided for private use, the cash equivalent of this additional benefit is chargeable to income tax on the following scale:

Cylinder Capacity	Benefit
	£
1999/00	
Non-diesel cars	
Up to 1400cc	1,210
1401cc–2000cc	1,540
2001cc or more	2,270
Diesel cars	
2000cc or less	1,540
2001cc or more	2,270
Cars with no internal combustion engine	2,270
1998/99	
Non-diesel cars	
Up to 1400cc	1,010
1401cc–2000cc	1,280
2001cc or more	1,890
Diesel cars	
2000cc or less	1,280
2001cc or more	1,890
Cars with no internal combustion engine	1,890

There is no provision for increasing the fuel benefit if the car is 'insubstantially' used for business purposes or is a second car. No deduction is made for a partial reimbursement of private fuel; the scale charge applies unless full reimbursement is made, or unless private fuel is not provided.

With a view to reducing vehicle emissions the Government has announced that fuel benefit rates will consistently be increased at 5% ahead of the increase in fuel prices. This policy is reflected in the 20% increase in scale charges for 1999/00.

Vans

10.52   From 6 April 1993 the benefit to an employee of a van available for private use, including the benefit of any fuel provided, depends on the size of the van and its age at the end of the tax year as follows:

Vehicle design weight	Under 4 years old	4 years old or more
	£	£
Up to 3.5 tonnes	500	350
Over 3.5 tonnes	—	—

The benefit is reduced by £1 for every £1 reimbursed by the employee. There are special arrangements for shared vans.

National insurance

10.53   From 6 April 1991, employers have been liable to pay national insurance contributions on cars and fuel provided for the private use of directors or employees earning over £8,500 per annum. (See 10.69 below for further details).

Summary

10.54 Cars remain a popular benefit for employees. Despite the increased tax charge, for many employees it is still more cost effective tohave a company car than to provide a similar car personally out of taxed income. It may, however, be advantageous for the employee with low private mileage to pay for his own private fuel. Many employers consider offering cash alternatives to the company car, not only for tax reasons, but also, for example, to reduce the burden of administering the company car fleet.

In the March 1999 Budget the government announced that a major reform of company car taxation will take effect from April 2002. The existing system is likely to be replaced with adjustments to the amount of the tax charge based on a measure of the car's emissions.

The reform is intended to remove any incentive for unnecessary business miles, to encourage employees to choose more fuel efficient cars and to encourage manufacturers to produce cars with lower carbon dioxide emissions. The Inland Revenue has invited comments on these proposals.

PAYE administration

Duties

10.55 Pay As You Earn ('PAYE') is a tax collection system which requires an employer to calculate the income tax due by his employees in respect of their pay and certain benefits, to deduct this tax from payment to the employees and to account for it to the Inland Revenue. PAYE is generally also regarded as including the system for collection of National Insurance contributions from the employee and employer.

Failure by an employer to observe this duty to operate PAYE, even if instructions have not been received from the Inland Revenue, is likely to result in a liability for the tax which should have been deducted, with no automatic recourse to the employee, plus possibly penalties. It is the employer's duty to determine whether an individual, whom they are paying, is an employee. If in any doubt they should contact their own PAYE district.

Records

10.56 It is the duty of every employer to keep adequate records of his operation of the PAYE system for at least three years. These are liable to inspection by the Inland Revenue at any time.

Documents needed to operate a PAYE system

10.57 The tables and guides required to operate a PAYE system are:

Inland Revenue:	Table A	Pay adjustment
	Tables LR and B–D	Taxable pay
	Expenses and	A Tax Guide (480)
	Benefits	
Inland Revenue and DSS	Employers Quick Guide to PAYE and NICs (CWG 1)	
	Employers Further Guide to PAYE and NICs (CWG 2)	
DSS	NI, SMP and SSP tables CA 35/36, CA 38, CA 39, CA 40, CA 43	
	Employers Manual on Statutory Sick Pay (CA 30)	
	Employers Manual on NI for Company Directors (CA 44)	

The basic forms required are:

P9D	Return of expenses and benefits paid to certain employees
P11	Deductions working sheet
P11D	Return of expense payments and benefits etc. not covered by a dispensation for directors and employees earning at a rate of £8,500 a year or more. (For convenience, such employees are subsequently referred to as 'higher paid employees'.)
P11D(b)	Expenses and benefits statements: declaration
P14/60	Employee end of year return
P35	Employer's annual statement, declaration and certificate
P45	Details of employee leaving
P46	New employee certificate
P46(car)	Notification of a car provided for private use of an employee or director

New business

10.58   A new employer must take the following steps as soon as possible.

(*a*)   Ascertain the correct tax district from the Inland Revenue.

(*b*)   Contact the New Schemes department of the district and explain that a new business is about to commence a payroll.

(*c*)   Complete and return form P223 which will be received from their tax office. To assist in the operation of PAYE a stock of forms, tables and guides will be received from their tax office together with a reference which should be used in all communications. A 'paying-in booklet' (ref P30BC) will also be received from the Collector for payment of the PAYE deducted.

Regular payroll

10.59   It is the employer's duty to operate PAYE from the first instalment of pay. Whether a manual or computerised system isoperated the employer must follow the same basic steps and keep equivalent records. For each employee these steps are as follows:

(*a*)   Calculate the PAYE taxation by reference to PAYE Table A and Tables LR and B–D.

(*b*)   Calculate thc national insurance (NI) contributions due by reference to the NI Tables A–C for those who are not contracted-out and Tables C–G and S for those in contracted-out employment.

(*c*)   Calculate the amount of Statutory Sick Pay (SSP) and Statutory Maternity Pay (SMP) due by reference to CA 35/36.

(*d*)   Record these calculations on a deductions working sheet (P11) or equivalent.

(*e*)   Pay the employee's net pay and retain the total PAYE and NI less the permitted element of any SSP and SMP (see below).

(*f*)   By the 19th of the following PAYE month pay to the Collector of Taxes the total PAYE and NI less SSP and SMP, using the paying-in booklet.

The Percentage Threshold Scheme (PTS) restricts the amount of SSP that employers can recover from the government. Where the SSP payable in a month exceeds 13% of the total NI liability for that month the employer can recover the SSP to the extent of the excess by reducing the monthly NI payment. If the SSP is 13% of the NI liability, or less, no SSP can be recovered.

Only 92% of SMP paid is now recoverable and no NIC compensation is available at the current rate of 6.5% (formerly 5%) unless the Small Employers' Relief scheme applies (see CA29 for details).

New employees

10.60   If a new employee produces or can obtain parts 2 and 3 of a new form P45 from his previous employer, this should be used to prepare a deductions working sheet for recording PAYE. Part 2 should be kept with the company's records; part 3 should be sent to the tax office immediately. The employee should keep part 1A for his own records.

If the employee cannot produce a form P45, a form P46 should be completed and the appropriate declaration signed. Dependent on whether statement A, B or C has been signed, tax should be deducted at basic rate or the appropriate emergency tax coding may be allocated on either a cumulative or non-cumulative basis and the form sent to the tax office.

Employees leaving

10.61   When an employee leaves his employment, a new four part form P45 must be completed from the details recorded on his deductions working sheet. Part 1 must be sent immediately to the tax office and parts 1A, 2 and 3 should be given to the ex-employee. If a lump sum payment is being made, or if there is to be some other special arrangement, further advice should be sought.

Year end procedures

10.62   Following and as at 5 April each year the employer must:

(*a*)   complete a three part form P14/60 for each employee, or magnetic tape equivalent;

(*b*)   complete a form P35 (P35MT), or substitute, for the employer;

(*c*)   pay by 19 April the balance of the PAYE and NI shown by the P35;

(*d*)   complete a form P11D for directors and 'higher-paid' employees recording all benefits and expenses provided to or paid on behalf of employees, and which are not covered by a dispensation from the Inland Revenue. From the tax year 1996/97, employers must attribute values to benefits on the P11Ds and provide employees with a copy of the information declared on their forms P11D;

(*e*)   complete a form P9D for all employees earning at a rate of less than £8,500 per year who receive certain types of benefits;

(*f*)   complete a form P11D(b) in respect of all the forms P11D;

(*g*)   give the P60 to each employee by 31 May following the tax year;

(*h*)   send the P14s and the P35 to their tax office by 19 May. Penalties will apply if these forms do not reach the Inland Revenue on or before this date;

(*j*)   send the P11Ds, the P9Ds and the P11D(b) to their tax office. For the tax year 1997/98, which ended on 5 April 1998, the deadline for submission of these returns is 6 July 1998 by which date the employer must also supply the employee with a copy of the information on his form P11D or P9D, as appropriate; and

(*k*)   in preparation for the new tax year, change any employee who is on week 1/month 1 basis to a cumulative basis.

In addition to the above, the employer may choose to pay a lump sum of tax to the Inland Revenue in accordance with a PAYE settlement agreement ('PSA'). This payment replaces tax which the employees would otherwise have to pay themselves on benefits which the Inland Revenue regard as minor, irregular, or where it is impracticable to operate PAYE. The PSA should be agreed in advance with the Inland Revenue and the tax paid by 19 October following the end of the tax year concerned.

In order to reduce the compliance burden relating to the above returns, many employers apply for a dispensation which allows them to pay their employees non-PIID expenses without operating PAYE.

PAYE audits

10.63 As part of its drive to concentrate resources in areas most likely to lead to the recovery of 'shortfalls to the tax fund' the Inland Revenue has for some time been increasing the number of staff engaged on PAYE audits and control visits. It is the Inland Revenue's aim that each large and medium-sized employer should be visited by a PAYE auditor every five years.

The purpose of PAYE audits and reviews is to confirm that PAYE has been operated properly on all earnings and payments in accordance with the PAYE regulations. Although an audit will frequently concentrate on a few specific areas only, it may involve the inspection of any records relating to the calculation and payment of emoluments, the deduction of tax under PAYE and national insurance contributions.

Personal Service Companies

10.64 The March 1999 Budget announced measures to address tax and NIC avoidance in the provision of personal services.

Although the government are still seeking consultations on this issue, they have issued detailed proposals which suggests that whenever

(*a*) An individual provides personal services to a client through an intermediary, such as a partnership company or agency and

(*b*) the worker is under the client's supervision, direction or control

the client must withhold PAYE and NIC or any payments it makes for those services unless an intermediary undertakes to pay all remuneration to the worker in a form subject to Schedule E and NIC.

Casual labour

10.65 An employer paying £1 a week or more to any employee must deduct income tax at the basic rate from the full payment unless the employee has signed form P46 certifying that he or she has no other employment, in which case tax should be deducted using the current emergency code.

If the casual worker is employed for one week or less, form P46 does not need to be completed, although full details of the individual's name and address should be kept. Tax should be deducted by reference to the current emergency code unless the employee is known to have other employment. In that instance, tax at the basic rate must be deducted from the full payment. The Inland Revenue apply this procedure rigorously and may assess employers to tax and where appropriate national insurance contributions, possibly on the grossed-up amount of such payments, irrespective of whether any tax has actually been lost by them.

Settlement

10.66   Most PAYE audits and reviews reveal some discrepancies and the Inland Revenue will often calculate the tax and national insurance contributions which have been 'lost' by extrapolating the results of a review covering a limited period of up to six years plus the current year, and possibly longer if they suspect that deductions have been deliberately withheld. Penalties may also be sought, but may be partially mitigated depending on the gravity of the matter and the degree of employer's co-operation and disclosure.

National insurance

10.67   National insurance expressed in its simplest form, is a deduction made from gross earnings in relation to a specific earnings period(s). Collection is normally made via the PAYE system by the Inland Revenue. Prior to 1999/00, the legislation was administered by the DSS, Contributions Agency. However, the Contributions Agency has now become an executive office of the Inland Revenue ('the National Insurance Contributions Office').

A change in the way in which NICs for members of Contracted Out Money Purchase (COMP) schemes are worked out, recorded and reported took effect from 6 April 1997. New Contribution Table letters F, G and S were introduced to take account of these changes.

Rates

10.68   The rates of national insurance contributions are reviewed annually and are currently:

1999/00

Employer

Weekly Earnings	Not Contracted Out (on all earnings)	Contracted Out Salary Related Schemes (Note 3)	Contracted Out Money Purchase Schemes (Note 3)
Class 1 – Employers			
Below £64	—	—	—
£64 to £109.99	12.2%	—	1.5%
£110 to £154.99	12.2%	2.0%	3.5%
£155 to £209.99	12.2%	4.0%	5.5%
£210 to £485	12.2%	7.0%	8.5%
Over £485	12.2%	(Note 1)	(Note 2)

Employee (Note 4)	Not Contracted Out	Contracted Out
On first £66	2%	2%
Balance up to £500	10%	8.4%
Over £500	Flat rate maximum of £43.38 per week	Flat rate maximum of £36.64 per week

Note 1
£35.87 per week plus 10.0% on all earnings over £500 per week.

Note 2
£42.18 per week plus 10% on all earnings over £500 per week.

Note 3
Over £66, the first £66 is charged at the appropriate 'contracted in' rate.

Note 4
Men aged 65 or over, and women aged 60 or over do not pay employees' contributions.
Employer's contributions are however still payable.

Liability to national insurance

10.69   In calculating an employee's liability to national insurance, it is gross remuneration which is considered earnings. For this purpose, it is normally cash payments which are considered; in general, benefits in kind are excluded.

Where an employer meets an element of personal debt for the employee, the payment creates a liability for national insurance. In general, if the contract for supply of goods or services is between the employer and the provider then no NI liability arises. However, in recent years anti-avoidance legislation has been introduced to bring certain non-cash payments into the charge of NI, for example — gold, diamonds, unit trusts and gilts.

From 6 April 1991 employers are required to pay Class 1A national insurance contributions for cars provided for the private use of:

(*a*)   most directors; and

(*b*)   employees who are paid at a rate of £8,500 a year, including taxable benefits and expenses.

A charge will also arise on private fuel if supplied. The calculation is based on the income tax car benefit and fuel scale rate multiplied by the highest rate of employers NI for the year the benefit was granted. The amount is payable in arrears by the 19 July following the end of the tax year.

The main difference between 'earnings' for NI purposes and 'pay' and 'benefits in kind' for income tax purposes is that 'earnings' includes all cash payments from employment such as commission, fees, bonuses and cash payments in lieu of 'payments in kind' but certain payments are specifically excluded from 'earnings' for NI purposes.

These include:

(i)   reimbursed receipted business expenses;

(ii)   any genuine redundancy or non-contractual compensatory payment; and

(iii)   payments in kind. These may include vouchers (not exchangeable for cash), use of employer-owned or leased assets (such as houses or furniture), expenses contracted for by the employer, such as season tickets or medical insurance (BUPA) and paid for by the employer. Gilts and other debt instruments, and in certain instances, shares are now liable to NI. It is proposed that from 6 April 1999 vouchers will also be liable to NI.

Employers are now able to take account of all Inland Revenue 'dispensations' in deciding whether NIs should be paid on expense payments to employees.

Self assessment

10.70   Self assessment gives people more responsibility and control over their tax affairs and imposes on employers a number of additional information requirements. The requirement for taxpayers to submit returns and self-assess their income tax liabilities affects mainly:

(*a*)   self-employed people;

(*b*)   business partners;

(*c*)   company directors; and

(*d*)   employees who pay tax at the higher rate.

The main changes apply from the 1996/97 tax year. The first self assessment tax returns were issued to individual taxpayers in April 1997 for submission to the Inland Revenue no later than 31 January 1998.

To enable employees to comply with the tax return requirements under the new regime, employers should, as noted at 10.62 above, provide the employees, by 31 May following the tax year, details of pay and tax deducted on form P 60. In addition, the employer should evaluate benefits in kind provided to the employees, report these on forms PIID (or substitute) and provide a copy to the employees by 6 July following the tax year. The employer is also responsible for providing similar information in respect of benefits the employer had arranged or facilitated from third parties.

The current penalty regime covers the late or incorrect submission of these documents.

Chapter 11

Commercial Considerations

Corporate capacity

Ultra vires

11.1 Sections 108 to 112 of the Companies Act 1989 introduced into the Companies Act 1985 a series of provisions dealing with the capacity of the company and the related issue of the authority of the board of directors to bind the company in relation to contracts made by the company with third parties.

The doctrine of *ultra vires*, as it was developed from the decision of the House of Lords in the case of *Ashbury Railway Carriage & Iron Company Ltd v Riche (1875) LR 7 HL 653*, dictated that a company may only do such acts as were specified in its memorandum of association and any act outside those objects was *ultra vires* and therefore void. This led to the practice of giving the company a comprehensive list of objects, stating that each is to be treated as a separate and independent object of the company by means of an independent objects clause, the effectiveness of which has been recognised by the House of Lords in the case of *Cotman v Brougham [1918] AC 514*. In order to further widen the capacity of the company the memorandum may include a subjective objects clause which would allow the company to carry on any other trade or business which, in the opinion of the directors, could be advantageously carried on in connection with, or ancillary to, the main business of the company. The doctrine was substantially modified by section 9 of the European Communities Act 1972, subsequently re-enacted as CA 1985, s 35, in relation to third parties dealing with the company in good faith.

Section 35 of the CA 1985 was amended by the provisions of sections 108 to 112 of the Companies Act 1989 with the purpose of distinguishing between the company's capacity and the powers of the directors to bind it. The provisions seek to extend the effect of CA 1985, s 35 by abolishing the application of the doctrine of *ultra vires* to third parties, but retaining it in relation to the internal operation of the company, by allowing the members to bring proceedings to restrain an *ultra vires* act by the directors or to hold directors personally liable for the committing of the company to *ultra vires* acts.

The legislation covers the following points:

(*a*)   the capacity of the company to enter into transactions;

(*b*)   the drafting of the company's constitution so as to widen its capacity;

(*c*)   the powers of the directors to bind the company;

(*d*)   the ability of the members of the company to restrain an *ultra vires* act;

(*e*)   the protection of third parties entering into contracts; and

(*f*)   the ability of the members to ratify an *ultra vires* act.

Capacity of the company in contracts

11.2   Section 35 of the Companies Act 1985 as introduced by section 108(1) of the Companies Act 1989 provides that:

> '(1) The validity of an act done by a company shall not be called into question on the ground of lack of capacity by reason of anything in the company's memorandum.'

Thus, any transaction entered into by a company will be valid and enforceable by the company and by third parties involved in the transaction. However, where a company intends to enter into a transaction which is beyond its capacity, any member may bring proceedings to restrain the *ultra vires* act.

It remains the duty of the directors to observe any limitations on their powers flowing from the company's memorandum of association, and therefore the authority of the directors to bind the company continues to be restricted by the objects clause. However, any acts carried out by the directors which would have been *ultra vires* the company, but for section 35(1) of the CA 1985, may be ratified by a special resolution of the shareholders. If such a resolution is passed, however, the directors will remain liable for any losses incurred as a result of the transaction unless relief from liability is agreed to by a separate special resolution (CA 1985, s 35(3)).

The form of company contracts

11.3   Section 36 of the Companies Act 1985 provides that a contract may be made either:

(*a*)   by a company, by writing under its common seal; or

(*b*)   on behalf of a company, by any person acting under its authority, express or implied.

Any formalities required by law in the case of a contract made by an individual also apply to a contract made by or on behalf of a company.

Further provisions apply where a private company having only one member, who is also a director of the company, enters into contracts with that member (see 6.34 THE DIRECTORS).

Sealing of documents

11.4   Section 36A of Companies Act 1985 provides that a document is executed by a company by the affixing of its common seal, but also goes on to state that a company need not have a common seal (see 1.15 THE COMPANY SECRETARY).

The right to use the seal for the purposes of its business is usually vested in the directors. Regulation 101 of Table A provides that the seal shall only be used by the authority of the directors or of a committee of the directors authorised by the directors. The article further provides that the directors may determine who shall sign any instrument to which the seal is affixed and unless they determine otherwise, it shall be signed by a director and the secretary or a second director.

Whether or not a company has a common seal, a document signed by a director and the secretary of a company, or by two directors, and expressed to be executed on behalf of the company has the same effect as if it were executed under the common seal (CA 1985, s 36A(4)). A document executed by a company which makes it clear on its face that it is intended to be a deed has effect upon delivery, as a deed, and unless a contrary intention is proved, it is presumed to be delivered upon its execution (CA 1985, s 36A(5)). In favour of a *bona fide* purchaser for valuable consideration a document is deemed to have been duly executed by a company if it purports to be signed by either two directors or a director and the secretary. It will be valid as a deed, and will be delivered upon execution, that is to say, the signatories bind the company when they sign.

The Law Commission has recommended that s 36A be altered to remove any inconsistencies with other legislation on deeds and to make clear the application of the common seal.

The Foreign Companies (Execution of Documents) Regulations 1994 (SI 1994 No 950) which came into force on 16 May 1994 allow any foreign company to execute a document either by affixing its common seal or by any method valid under its own domestic law. The application of any English company law requirement relating to the execution of deeds by foreign companies need not be considered.

Power of directors to bind the company

11.5   In relation to dealings by a third party with officers of the company, section 35A of the Companies Act 1985 has removed some of the doubts raised by the drafting of the previous legislation. CA 1985, s 35A(1) provides that:

'In favour of a person dealing with a company in good faith, the power of the board of directors to bind the company, or authorise others to do so, shall be deemed to be free of any limitation under the company's constitution.'

Under the previous legislation a person was only protected in respect of 'transactions decided upon by the directors'. A person is now defined as dealing with a company if he is a party to any transaction or other act to which the company is a party. A person shall not be regarded as acting in bad faith by reason only of his knowing that an act is beyond the powers of the directors and shall be presumed to be acting in good faith unless the contrary is proved.

The protection from lack of authority derived from any limitation under the company's constitution is thus now wider than available previously and will include limitations deriving from a resolution of the company in general meeting or from any agreement between the members of the company.

The directors may not, however, use CA 1985, s 35A to enforce a contract against a third party unless the transaction has first been ratified by the company.

Transactions with directors

11.6   Different rules apply when one of the parties to the transaction is a director of the company, its holding company or a person connected with them, and the board of directors exceeds any limitation on its powers under the company's constitution. In such cases the transaction is voidable by the company (CA 1985, s 322A(2)). Whether or not it is avoided, the director who is a party to the transaction and any director of the company who authorised it, are liable to account for any gain to the company and to indemnify it against any loss suffered.

The transaction ceases to be voidable (CA 1985, s 322A(5)) if:

(*a*)   restitution of any money or other asset, being the subject matter of the transaction is no longer possible;

(*b*)   the company is indemnified for any loss or damage resulting from the transaction;

(*c*)   the avoidance would affect a person acquiring rights in good faith who was unaware that the directors were exceeding their powers; or

(*d*)   the transaction is ratified by the company in general meeting.

A person who is not a director of the company but is connected with them is not liable if he can show that at the time the transaction was entered into he did not know that the directors were exceeding their powers.

Section 322 of the Companies Act 1985 is intended to prevent a director acting fraudulently by misusing his power to bind the company to a transaction from which he will benefit.

Constructive notice

11.7   Section 35B of the Companies Act 1985 makes it clear that a party to a transaction with a company is not bound to enquire as to whether it is permitted by the company's memorandum of association or as to any limitation on the power of the board of directors to bind the company or authorise others to do so.

Under the doctrine of constructive notice a person is deemed to have notice of the details disclosed in any document kept at Companies House or made available for inspection by the company.

Section 711A(1) of the CA 1985 will effectively abolish this doctrine, once substituted by CA 1989, in that a person shall not be taken to have notice of any matter merely because of its having been disclosed in any document kept by Companies House, and thus available for inspection, or made available by the company for inspection. Any document includes annual returns, notifications of appointments not just constitutional documents.

It is expressly stated in CA 1985, s 711A(2) that this does not affect the question of whether a person is affected by notice of any matter by reason of a failure to make such enquiries as ought reasonably to be made.

Notice of what is on the public file is, therefore, relevant to someone who has actually read it or in the circumstances ought to have done so. The question of when enquiries reasonably ought to have been made is one which the courts will have to settle. However, CA 1985, s 35B gives an exemption in relation to the question of the capacity of the company or the authority of the directors, as it states that there is no duty to enquire whether the transaction is permitted or as to any limitation on the power of the board to bind the company.

If introduced the abolition of the doctrine of deemed notice will not apply to company charges disclosed in the company charges register or to certain land charges.

The objects clause

11.8   Section 2(1)(c) of the Companies Act 1985 requires a company to set out its objects in its memorandum of association (see 2.19–2.32 THE COMPANY CONSTITUTION). These objects clauses, for reasons of commercial necessity, have tended to extend to several pages.

Section 3A of the CA 1985 has endeavoured to remove this burden and allows a company's memorandum to state that the object of the company is to carry on business as a 'general commercial company' in which case the company:

(*a*)   may carry on any trade or business whatsoever; and

(*b*)   has the power to do all such things as are incidental or conducive to the carrying on of any trade or business by it.

(See 2.25 THE COMPANY CONSTITUTION.)

The clause covers only trade or business activities and may not cover a range of other transactions such as giving guarantees, or the disposal of the whole or part of the business, which will probably still require a specific power to be given in the memorandum of association.

Charitable companies

11.9   Section 111 of the Companies Act 1989 substituted sections 30, 30A to 30C for the original section 30 in the Charities Act 1960. These sections now comprise Part VIII of the Charities Act 1993 following consolidation of the 1960 Act together with Part I of the Charities Act 1992 and the Charitable Trustees Incorporation Act 1872. Section 65 of the 1993 Act limits the protection otherwise given by sections 35 and 35A of the Companies Act 1985 in relation to an act falling outside the objects of the company to a person who knows that he is dealing with a charitable company. This section will only apply in favour of a person who:

(*u*)   gives full consideration in money or money's worth in relation to the act; and

(*b*)   does not know that the act is not permitted by the company's memorandum or is beyond the powers of the directors.

Powers of attorney

11.10   Section 38 of the Companies Act 1985 gives a specific power to appoint attorneys to execute deeds on a company's behalf outside the United Kingdom. The appointment must be under seal (see 11.4 above) and the power of attorney may be either general or for a specific purpose.

Preliminary contracts

11.11   A limited company only comes into existence on the issue of a certificate of incorporation by the Registrar of Companies. If a person purporting to act for a company, or as agent for it, enters into a contract or deed for, or on behalf of, a company at a time when that company has not been legally constituted, then, subject to any agreement to the contrary, the contract takes effect as one made by the person acting for the company or as agent for it and he is personally liable accordingly (CA 1985, s 36C(1)).

To ensure the company subsequently becomes a party to a pre-incorporation contract, the objects clause in the memorandum of association may be drafted in such a way as to bind the directors to accept the contract and execute it upon incorporation.

Provisional contracts

11.12   If a public company enters into a contract before the issue of a certificate to commence business (see 2.47 THE COMPANY CONSTITUTION), and fails to comply with its obligation to obtain a certificate within 21 days of being called upon to do so, the directors of the company are jointly and severally liable to indemnify the other party to the transaction in respect of any loss or damage suffered by him by reason of the failure to comply (CA 1985, s 117(8)).

The contract remains valid and enforceable.

Personal liability of the officers of the company

11.13   If any officer of the company or any person acting on its behalf signs, or authorises the signature, on behalf of the company any negotiable instrument or order for money or goods in which the name of the company is not mentioned in full, he is personally liable to the holder of the negotiable instrument or order for the amount of it if it is not paid by the company. In particular, the words 'limited' or 'public limited company' must not be omitted. 'The holder' is construed to mean, in the case of an order for money or goods, the person to whom the order is addressed.

Care must also be taken to ensure that the person who signs an agreement for the company clearly does so 'for and on behalf of the company' thereby establishing himself as an agent for the company, in order to avoid any personal liability. This is particularly important in the case of negotiable instruments because the agent will only be free from personal liability as far as persons who do not know of his representative capacity are concerned, if the intention to sign as an agent is stated on the instrument or is otherwise implied. Section 26 of the Bills of Exchange Act 1882 provides:

'Where a person signs a bill as drawer, indorser or acceptor and adds words to his signature indicating that he signs for or on behalf of a principal, or in representative character, he is not personally liable thereon; but the mere addition to his signature of words describing him as an agent, or as filling a representative character, does not exempt him from personal liability.'

Authority of directors to act on behalf of the company

11.14   The articles of association generally define the powers of the directors. Express authority is given to the board of directors to exercise all the powers of the company subject to the provisions of the Companies Act 1985 and the articles (Table A, regulation 70). The articles may also allow the delegation of the directors' powers to committees, managers, managing directors or other persons. Such delegation may be expressly given or by implication. The directors can be held liable for breach of duty if they exceed their powers (see 6.36 THE DIRECTORS).

Criminal liability

11.15   Where the entering into a transaction by the company gives rise to a criminal liability, questions arise as to whether the officer of the company is personally responsible or whether the company is vicariously liable for the act of its agent (see 14.33 EMPLOYMENT, HEALTH AND SAFETY). It is a question of law whether, once the facts have been established, a person doing a particular thing is to be regarded as the company or merely as the company's servant or agent.

Retention of company records

11.16   A company's records need to be retained for various statutory reasons, for example, accounting, taxation and employment legislation. Accordingly, it will frequently fall to the secretary of a company to draw up a policy for the retention of records and documents relating to the company's affairs.

In the majority of cases, legislation makes no specific reference to the length of time a particular record should be retained. In view of the increase in the number of records required to be produced by a company in fulfilment of its statutory obligations and the availability of storage space, it is clear that any policy on retention of documents should ensure that records are retained for the shortest possible time.

In order to comply with section 222 of the Companies Act 1985, the accounting records of a company (including all subsidiary records) must be preserved for a period of three years from the date when they were made in the case of a private company, and six years in the case of a public company. They must be kept at the registered office of the company or such other place as the directors think fit.

The length of retention is subject to any provision contained in rules made under section 411 of the Insolvency Act 1986. In addition, a company must ensure it also complies with other statutory requirements such as those contained within the Taxes Management Act 1970, Limitation Act 1980, VAT Act 1983, and PAYE Regulations.

It is therefore desirable to comply with the other statutory requirements, that accounting records should be retained for at least six years even by a private company (see 3.38 THE STATUTORY RECORDS).

All company records relating to the registration of the company, the company's constitution, meetings of the company and resolutions passed, should be retained for the life of the company. Minute books containing the minutes of proceedings of any general meetings of a company held since 1

November 1929 must be kept at the registered office of the company (CA 1985, s 383).

In a few cases, the Companies Act 1985 lays down a specific period of retention for certain documents as follows.

(*a*)   A copy of any contract for purchase of own shares must be kept at the registered office of the company for a period of *ten years* from the date on which the purchase of all shares in pursuance of the contract is completed (CA 1985, s 169(4)).

(*b*)   A report on interests in voting shares following investigation on requisition by the members, must be kept at the registered office for a period of *six years* from the day when it is first available, beginning with the day following that day (CA 1985, s 215(7)).

(*c*)   A register of interests in shares of a public company must be kept for a period of *six years* after the company ceases to be a public company (CA 1985, s 211(7)).

(*d*)   An entry in the register of members relating to a former member of the company may be removed from the register after the expiration of *20 years* from the date on which he ceased to be a member (CA 1985, s 352(6)).

Some further suggested periods for retention of documents are contained in Appendix 11A to this chapter.

Patents, trade marks, copyright and designs

Patents

11.17   An inventor wishing to protect his invention from being exploited by someone else without his consent can do so by acquiring a patent for the invention. In the UK the governing law for the application and enforcement of patents is the Patent Act 1977. All UK patents last for 20 years from the date when the patent is filed. To keep a patent in force for the full 20 years, it is necessary that annual renewal fees are paid from the 4th anniversary of the date of filing. The patent gives the owner (the 'patentee') an exclusive right to the manufacture, use, or sale of the invention within the country or countries for which the patent has been granted. To be patentable an invention must be concerned with the composition, construction or manufacture of something concerned with an industrial process or an article or apparatus of practical use. The invention must be new and not obvious to a person of ordinary skill experienced in the area in which the invention operates. If some other party exploits the invention without the patentee's consent, the patentee has the right to take legal action to prevent such exploitation. The patentee can licence another person or company to exploit the invention in return for royalties, or alternatively the patent can be sold outright by assignment. Note that the patentee himself may require a licence to work his own invention if a third party has a patent which covers his product.

It is not necessary to have a patent in order to put an invention into practice but, if an application is not made, somebody else subsequently making the same invention may be able to obtain a patent for it if the invention has been kept secret in the meantime. If the inventor decides to apply for a patent he must not publicly disclose the invention before filing an application, as this would prevent the grant of a patent or cause its subsequent withdrawal.

The method of application for a patent depends on where the inventor wishes to exploit his invention. If there is no intention of expanding into overseas markets, it is cheaper and simpler to file a national UK patent application. However, if the inventor is also seeking protection abroad, he can either apply for a patent under the European Patent Convention (EPC) or under the Patent Co-operation Treaty (PCT). In both cases the patent can be valid in the UK and, additionally, for certain other designated European or worldwide countries respectively. Further separate national filings may be required for protection in states which are not parties to these treaties. However, usually, a UK application is filed first, and any foreign applications up to twelve months later, based on the first UK application.

Obtaining a patent can be complex and the consequences of error serious. It is advisable to seek the advice of a registered patent agent who can perform the work involved in preparing, filing and processing an application. However, under the Copyright, Designs, and Patents Act 1988 (CDPA 1988), it is no longer the sole right of patent agents and solicitors to apply for or obtain patents on behalf of others.

Trade marks

11.18   A trade mark is a means of identification. It is a symbol which a person can use to his benefit in the course of trade by distinguishing his own goods from similar goods of other traders. To achieve this, the trade mark must be distinctive in itself — in effect, the mark should be separately identifiable from the appearance or form of the goods to which it relates.

Registration of trade marks is not compulsory in the UK and it is not possible to register a trade mark in all cases (for example, where the mark is descriptive or too similar to known marks). Clearly, since registration confers a statutory monopoly, it would not be right to allow the registration of marks which are identical or are able to be confused with words or symbols (whether or not used as trade marks) which other traders in the goods or services are free to use in the ordinary course of business. The benefit of registration of a trade mark is that it confers a statutory monopoly in the use of that mark when related to the goods for which it is registered and the registered owner has the right to sue in the courts for infringement of the mark. The same considerations apply to service marks which may be used to distinguish the providers of certain services.

The Trade Marks Act 1994 regulates the application and registration of trade marks in the UK.

A trade mark is defined as 'any sign capable of being represented graphically which is capable of distinguishing goods or services of one undertaking from those of other undertakings' (TMA 1994, s 1).

Thus, trade marks can consist of the following:

(*a*)   words (including personal names);

(*b*)   designs;

(*c*)   letters, numerals;

(*d*)   shape of goods;

(*e*)   musical sounds, colours, smells (but only where they can be represented graphically);

(*f*)   computer generated images; and

(*g*)   geographical names (where this has acquired a distinctive character, e.g. Champagne).

Under the Trade Mark Act 1994, s 63, the Controller General of Patents, Designs and Trade Marks (referred to as the Trade Marks Registrar) is required to keep a Register of Trade Marks on which details of all trademarks and registrable transactions affecting them are kept. The Act contained transitional provisions dealing with the transfer of existing registrations under the previous system; it allows multi-class applications for goods and services; extends and improves the rights of trade mark owners with regard to trade mark infringement and introduces new rules for registration. The Act now carries a presumption that the trade mark is registrable, renewable every ten years on the payment of a fee (TMA 1994, ss 42–43).

New offences under the Act have been created with regard to the fraudulent use of a mark, resulting in imprisonment for up to ten years and fines exceeding £5,000.

Companies seeking protection abroad can do so in three ways:

(i)   by making an individual application in the chosen country;

(ii)   by making an application which is effective throughout the EU, known as a European Community Trade Mark; or

(iii) by making an application under the Madrid Protocol.

As with patents, it is advisable to instruct a trade mark agent to deal with the application, the processing of which can take between 12 and 18 months in the UK, assuming no objections to the mark are made.

Copyright

11.19   To qualify for copyright under the Copyright, Designs and Patents Act 1988, there must be a work which is original and literary, dramatic, musical or artistic in nature, or a sound recording, film, broadcast, or cable programme, or a typographical arrangement of a published edition. The definition expressly includes computer programs and extends to other work stored on a computer (CDPA 1988, s 3(1)(b)). Copyright will automatically apply and lasts at most for seventy years after the year in which the author dies or, in certain cases from the end of the calendar year in which the work was made (CDPA 1988, s 12 and Duration of Copyright and Rights in Performance Regulations 1995 (SI 1995 No 3297)). Computer generated programs enjoy protection for a period of fifty years from the date of creation.

The author of a work is the owner of the copyright in the first place unless:

(*a*) he is an employee working in the course of employment, when the employer will own the rights (CDPA 1988, s 11(2)); or

(*b*) the work is done under contract requiring transferral of the rights after production of the work.

The primary benefit of owning the copyright is that it gives certain rights to prevent:

(i) copying the whole or a substantial part of a work without permission;

(ii) trading in illicit copies, i.e. street trading of copied goods.

There are exceptions to copyright of which the exceptions for educational purposes are the most important and these are much tighter under the new law.

It is important to note that copyright only protects against actual copying and is not an absolute monopoly right.

'Moral rights' are a new aspect of copyright law. They pertain to the author of copyright material and include:

(A) the right to be identified when a work is published commercially; and

(B) the right of objection to 'derogatory treatment' of the author's work.

(CDPA 1988, s 77.)

Moral rights do not cover computer programs and are not infringed unless the author asserts his right. Copyright contracts should take account of this new right separately from the ownership of the copyright itself, as there are various provisions in the Act relating to employees and contract work. Moral rights are not assignable, but pass under the estate of the author, either as he has directed or, if he has not done so, to the owner of the deceased's copyright.

Rights in performance

11.20 The Copyright, Designs and Patents Act 1988 seeks to prevent amongst others unauthorised films, recordings, broadcasts and cable programmes of artists' performances. This means that consent should be sought before any live transmission or recording of their performances are made. The rights are personal and last 70 years from the year of any performance (CDPA 1988, ss 3–7). With films, the copyright lasts for 70 years from when the last of a number of people connected with the film die e.g. the director, author etc. (Duration of Copyright and Rights of Performance Regulations 1995).

Design right

11.21 The Copyright, Designs and Patents Act 1988 removes industrial designs out of the scope of 'artistic' copyright, but at the same time provides some short-term protection to all original industrial designs. The right, known as unregistered design right, covers industrial articles of an original shape or configuration and applies automatically on either recording of the design or making an article to it and includes computer generated designs. The right lasts for 15 years from the end of the calendar year in which the design was made or was made into an article, whichever is the first, or if the articles made to the design are made available for sale or hire within 5 years of the end of the calendar year, 10 years from the date of availability for sale or hire, giving the owner the opportunity to prevent copying or import of copies. If marketing of a design is delayed beyond 5 years, then the term of protection is 15 years from the date the design was first recorded (CDPA 1988, ss 51 and 213 to 225).

There are some exceptions to unregistered design right and these include 'commonplace' designs (not defined), methods and principles of construction (though these may be patentable), surface decoration and, where the designed article is to fit into another article, the connecting parts. The purpose of the last exception is to exclude protection for spare parts and alternative designs which fit on to other articles. Also excluded are features which depend upon the appearance of another article with which the article is intended to be integral, apparently opening the door for producers of 'pattern' parts. There are also some complex restrictions on design right relating to nationality which excludes certain persons from design rights.

Registered design

11.22 The registration of a design is possible by payment of a registration fee. This gives additional protection to unregistered design right in that it provides protection for five years renewable up to four more times, for five years each, on payment of a prescribed renewal fee. Articles which closely resemble the design, even if they have not been copied from the design, are included. To be registrable, the design must be new and a condition of 'aesthetic appeal' must apply; if an article's aesthetic aspects are not important to buyers, the registration will be refused. The same sort of exceptions apply as for unregistered design right (CDPA 1988, s 265).

Summary of new provisions

11.23 The Copyright, Designs and Patents Act 1988 introduced much new legislation, some of which has far-reaching implications for companies.

The main changes are as follows.

(*a*) The Act covers aspects of computer software and computer generated works which were not specifically covered in previous legislation.

(*b*) The removal of copyright protection for drawings and blueprints for industrial articles and its replacement with unregistered design right makes the consideration of the benefits of registering designs important. This covers all designs and companies should consider the effect regarding competition against their products.

(*c*) Contracts for works covered by the Act should cover all aspects of the legislation, including moral and employee rights, and not just copyright.

Useful addresses

11.24 The Patent Office issues many advisory booklets on Patents, Copyright and Trade marks and these are available at the following address:

The Patent Office
Concept House
Cardiff Road
Newport
South Wales
NP10 8QQ

Telephone: 0645 500505

There is a list of registered patent or trade mark agents available from the following addresses (respectively):

Chartered Institute of Patent Agents
Staple Inn Buildings
High Holborn
London
WC1V 7PZ
Telephone: 0171 405 9450

Institute of Trade Mark Agents
4th Floor, Canterbury House
2–6 Sydenham Road
Croydon
CR0 9XE

Telephone: 0181 686 2052

The addresses for the Trade Marks Registry are as follows:

Head Office:
The Trade Marks Registry
Concept House
Cardiff Road
Newport
South Wales
NP10 8QQ

Telephone: 01633 814 000

Document retention periods

Record	Retention Period	Remarks
Company records (including share registration)		
*Certificate of incorporation	Permanently	CA 1985, s 13
*Certificate to commence business (if any)	Permanently	CA 1985, s 117
*Certificate of change of company name	Permanently	CA 1985, s 28
Board minutes (signed copy)	Permanently	CA 1985, s 382
Written resolutions of board	Permanently	CA 1985, s 382
Minute books	Permanently	
Board committee minutes	Permanently	CA 1985, s 382
Minutes of general & class meetings	Permanently	CA 1985, s 382
Written resolutions of members/sole member	Permanently	CA 1985, s 382A s 382B
*Report & accounts (signed copy) Spare copies (few)	Permanently To meet casual enquiries	
Interim report & accounts	Permanently	
Circulars to shareholders (master copy)	Permanently	
Notices of general & class meetings (master copy)	Permanently	
*Resolutions passed at above meetings (printed copies)	Permanently	CA 1985, s 380
*Memorandum & articles of association (signed original)	Permanently	

Record	Retention Period	Remarks
*Memorandum & articles of association (current)	Permanently	CA 1985, s 19 s 20
Register of sealed documents	Permanently	Attention is drawn to the removal of requirements to have a seal but record of documents sealed is still needed
Proxy forms/polling cards	1 month after meeting if no poll demanded 1 year after meeting if poll demanded	
Proxy forms used at meetings convened by court	At direction of court or 1 year after meeting	
*Register of directors & secretaries (original)	Permanently	CA 1985, s 288
Directors' service contracts	6 years after employment ceases	TMA 1970
*Register of directors' interests in shares & debentures	Permanently	CA 1985, s 325
Register of interests in voting shares	Permanently	CA 1985, s 211
*Register of charges	Permanently	CA 1985, s 411
Register of members	Permanently	CA 1985, s 352 permits records of former members to be removed from register 20 years after cessation of membership

Record	Retention Period	Remarks
Register of debenture or loan stock holders	6 years after stock redemption + permanent microfilmed record	
Forms of share and debenture application (originals)	12 years from share issue + permanent microfilmed record	
Forms of acceptance & transfer	12 years from actioned date + permanent microfilmed record	
Renounced letters of acceptance & allotment	12 years from renunciation + permanent microfilmed record	
Renounced share certificates	12 years from renunciation + permanent microfilmed record	
Fully paid acceptance & allotment letters exchanged for a certificate	1 year after ceasing to be valid	
Share & stock transfer forms	12 years after transfer + permanent microfilmed record	
Requests for designating or redesignating accounts	12 years after request + permanent microfilmed record	

Record	Retention Period	Remarks
Letters of request	12 years after request + permanent microfilmed record	
*Returns of allotments	Permanently	
Redemption discharge forms or endorsed certificates	12 years after date of redemption + permanent microfilmed record	
Forms of conversion	6 years after date of conversion + permanent microfilmed record	
Signed forms of nomination	12 years + permanent microfilmed record	
Letters of indemnity for lost certificates	Permanently	
*Annual return (1 copy) (excluding list of members)	Permanently	
Stop notices & other court orders	12 years + permanent microfilmed record	
Powers of attorney (copy)	12 years + permanent microfilmed record	
Dividend & interest payment lists (before disposal, an extract of outstanding warrants should be made)	Until annual audit, following payment, is complete	

Record	Retention Period	Remarks
Paid dividend & interest warrants	6 years after date of payment	
Dividend & interest mandates	Originals until 3 years after validity ceases	
Cancelled share/stock certificates	1 year from date of registration of transfer	
Notification of change of address (shareholders)	3 years	
Trust deed securing issue of debentures or loan stock	Permanently	
Talisman documents		
Talisman sold transfers	12 years + permanent microfilmed record	
No subsale declaration forms	12 years + permanent microfilmed record	
Talisman bought transfers	12 years + permanent microfilmed record	
Request of rectification of transferee details	12 years + permanent microfilmed record	
Sold transfer schedule	1 year	Since Talisman ceased in April 1997, the life of these documents is numbered
Bought transfer control schedule	1 year	
Certificate despatch note	1 year	
Consignment list	1 year	

Record	Retention Period	Remarks
Sold transfer rejection docket	1 year	
Bought transfer rejection docket	1 year	
Sepon advice	1 year	
Property documents		
Deeds of title	Until sold or transferred	
Leases	12 years after termination & any terminal queries (e.g. dilapidations) have been settled	
Agreements with architects, builders	6 years after completion	
Intellectual property records		
Documents evidencing assignment of trade/ service marks	6 years after cessation of registration	
Certificates of registration of trade/service marks	6 years after cessation of registration	
Intellectual property agreements & licences	6 or 12 years after expiry	
Materials for which copyright protection is claimed: Literary, dramatic and musical works	Life in being + 50 years	Copyright, Designs & Patents Act 1988
Artistic works, recordings, films, photos and broadcasts	50 years	
Accounting records		
To comply with CA 1985, s 221 (this obviously also includes all subsidiary records to support the annual accounts)	PLC—6 years Ltd—3 years	CA 1985, s 222

Record	Retention Period	Remarks
Budgets & periodic internal financial reports, e.g. to board	2 years	
Taxation returns and records	10 years	
VAT records	6 years	VATA 1994, Sch 11
Banking records, including Giro Cheques, bills of exchange & other negotiable instruments	6 years	
Paying-in counterfoils	6 years	
Bank statements & reconciliations	6 years	CA 1985, s 221
Instructions to banks	6 years after ceasing to be effective	
Charitable and political donations Deeds of Covenant (Donee)	6 years after last payment	TMA 1970
Documents evidencing entries in accounts re donations	6 years	CA 1985, s 221
Contractual and trust agreements Contracts under seal	12 years after expiry	
Other contracts	6 years after expiry	
Trust deeds (original & copy)	Permanently	

Record	Retention Period	Remarks
Employee records		
Job applications & interview records	3 months after notifying unsuccessful candidates	Sex Discrimination and Race Relations Acts 1975 & 1976
Personnel and training records	6 years after employment ceases	
Senior executive records	Permanently	
Payrolls & wage records (including details on overtime, bonuses & expenses)	6 years	TMA 1970
Details of benefits in kind	6 years	TMA 1970
Labour agreements	10 years after ceasing to be effective	
Works council minutes	Permanently	
Income tax records (P45, P60, P58, P48 etc.)	6 years	TMA 1970
Annual return of taxable pay and tax paid	6 years	TMA 1970
Time cards	2 years after audit	
Health and safety		
Record of consultations with safety representatives and committees	Permanently	
Assessments under health & safety regulations	Permanently	
Record of reportable accidents/accident book	3 years from date of entry	RIDDOR 1995, reg 7

Record	Retention Period	Remarks
Records of assessments, maintenance, air monitoring, medical surveillance and biological tests under the Control of Lead at Work Regulations 1980	2 years from date of last entry	CLWR 1980, reg 17
General register and other records required to be kept under the Factories Act 1961 where no other provision is made	2 years from date of last entry	FA 1961, s 141
Medical records: Radiation accident assessment	50 years	IRR 1985, reg 14
Radiation dosage summary	2 years from end of calendar year	IRR 1985, reg 13
Under Control of Lead at Work Regulations	2 years from date of last entry to be effective	CLWR 1980, reg 17
Under Control of Asbestos at Work Regulations	40 years	CAWR 1987
Under COSHH Regulations	40 years	COSHH 1994
Classifications data under the Chemicals (Hazard Information and Packaging for Supply) Regulations 1994	3 years	CHIP 1994
Pension records All trust deeds & rules	Permanently or, if merged with another fund, 12 years after merging	

Record	Retention Period	Remarks
Trustees' minute books	Permanently or, if merged with another fund, 12 years after merging	
Records of pensioners	12 years after benefit ceases	
Money purchase details	6 years after transfer or value taken	
Pension scheme investment policies	12 years after final cessation of any benefit payable under the policy	
Individual life policies under 'Top Hat' schemes	12 years after settlement of claim or final cessation of benefit	
'Inland Revenue approved/statutory pension schemes' Accounts & supporting documents	Permanently (accounts)	RBS(IP), 1995, reg 15 6 years from date accounts signed
Inland Revenue approvals	Permanently or, if merged with another fund, 12 years after merging	
Actuarial valuation reports	Permanently or, if merged with another fund, 12 years after merging	RBS(IP) 1995, reg 15 6 years from date report signed
Documents relating to events notifiable under RBS(IP) 1995, regs 6, 8, 10, 11	6 years after the year in which the event took place	RBS(IP) 1995, reg 15

Record	Retention Period	Remarks
Documents re. decision to allow retirement due to incapacity	6 years from end of scheme year in which the benefits began	RBS(IP) 1995, reg 15
Documents relating to events specified in RBS(IP) 1995, reg 15(4)	6 years from end of scheme year in which the event took place	RBS(IP) 1995, reg 15
Insurance		
Public liability policies	Permanently	
Product liability policies	Permanently	
Employers' liability policies	Permanently	
Other policies	Until claims under the policy are barred	
Claims correspondence	3 years after settlement	
Group health policies	12 years after the cessation of benefit	
Group personal accident policies	12 years after the cessation of the benefit	

The Registrar of Companies retains copies of some documents (marked * in the list). Some retention periods can be reduced by taking a power in the company's Articles of Association (marked + in the list).

Notes

CA	Companies Act 1985 (as amended)
CAWR	Control of Asbestos at Work Regulations 1987
CLWR	Control of Lead at Work Regulations 1980
CHIP	Chemicals (Hazard Information and Packaging for Supply) Regulations 1994
COSHH	Control of Substances Hazardous to Health Regulations 1994
FA	Factories Act 1961
IRR	Ionising Radiations Regulations 1985
RBS(IP)	Retirement Benefit Schemes (Information Powers) Regulations 1995
RIDDOR	Reporting of Injuries, Diseases and Dangerous Occurrences Regulations 1995
TMA	Taxes Management Act 1970
VATA	Value Added Tax Act 1994

Chapter 12

Pensions

General

12.1   The UK has one of the strongest occupational pensions movements in the industrialised world. There are a number of reasons for this, among them being:

(*a*)   to recruit and retain staff — a good pension scheme can be helpful in recruiting employees and keeping them subsequently. At the very least, the absence of a scheme may place an employer at a disadvantage to one that has a scheme in place;

(*b*)   to support employment policies and spread cost — employers will wish staff to retire in a planned and orderly way without creating unexpected and substantial financial burdens. Failure to provide a scheme can lead to lower paid employees being reliant on supplementary benefits to enhance the relatively low living standards afforded by the State; and

(*c*)   to help industrial relations and public image — most employees and their representative organisations regard the existence of a pension scheme favourably and the employer's public image can be enhanced if it is seen that sick or elderly retired employees and their dependants are well treated.

What does the State provide?

12.2   The Government does still have a role, albeit a diminishing role, in the provision of retirement and death benefits. These benefits are summarised below.

State pensions

12.3   The State pension scheme is in two parts. The first is a flat rate pension. From 6 April 1999 this is £66.75 a week for a single person and £116.70 a week for a married couple. Most people in employment receive the Basic State Pension, but the figures quoted above are subject to a full national insurance contribution record. The rules for determining a full national insurance contribution record are complex and outside the scope of this Chapter. The only employed people who are not entitled to State pensions are married women who elected to pay national insurance contributions at a reduced rate; this option is no longer available. The Basic

State Pension increases in line with increases in the Retail Prices Index (RPI).

The second part of the State pension scheme is the State Earnings Related Pension Scheme (SERPS). This scheme started in April 1978 and its purpose was to allow employed people to build up earnings related pensions. SERPS gives a maximum pension of 25% of revalued earnings between certain limits, the lower earnings limit and the upper earnings limit. For the tax year 1999/00 the former is £3,432 a year (or £66 a week) and the latter is £26,000 a year (or £500 a week). The earnings limits set increase year by year in line with increases in national average earnings. However, under the requirements of the Social Security Act 1988, this 25% maximum will reduce to 20% over a ten year period from the year 2000.

Assuming that a person on £20,000 per annum has accrued entitlement to the maximum level of SERPS pension (25%), the State pensions together equal just over one third of this salary and the percentages are less for higher salaries. In addition, an employee will have to contribute all his working life (which could be for 49 years) in order to achieve this pension.

The future of State second pensions

12.4   It is proposed to replace SERPS with a new State Second Pension (which is in danger of being called the SSP, at the risk of confusion with Statutory Sick Pay). Most low earners would be expected to remain in the SSP unless they can get a better deal in an occupational scheme. Moderate and higher earners (those earning above £9,000 per annum) will have the choice of the SSP, or of contracting-out, to begin with. However it is envisaged that later (after 5 years?), they will have to be in funded schemes only.

The SSP in its initial form will provide extra benefits for moderate earners (those earning between £9,000 and £18,500 per annum in present terms) compared with SERPS, and rebates for them will also be increased, to encourage take-up of stakeholder schemes. Indicative figures for the SSP, in today's terms, are given below:

- all contributing employees earning less than £9,000 pa would be treated in the SSP as if they had earnings of £9,000 pa;

- Employees' rights to a SSP would build up (on earnings up to £9,000 pa) to a pension of 40% of earnings between the Lower and Upper Earnings Limits over a full working lifetime, i.e. 49 years;

- plus 10% on earnings from £9,000 to £18,500 pa;

- plus 20% on earnings from £18,500 pa to the upper earnings limit;

- National Insurance contribution rebates would continue to be based on earnings, and would reflect this tiered structure; and

- this would apply to future earnings from a given implementation dates, no earlier than April 2002.

Even more radical changes are proposed for later. The new SSP would become a flat-rate scheme after a run-in period, although contracting-out rebated. This might start to take place five years after the introduction of stakeholder schemes, perhaps for those below age 45 at that time.

State death benefits

12.5   It is generally accepted nowadays that any test of benefit adequacy must use, as its chief criterion, the extent to which the benefit is related to earnings. As an example of State death benefit, let us take a look at the provision of lump sum death benefits — the funeral grant and widow's payment. The funeral grant was first introduced in the years following World War II, but its real value was so eroded by inflation that few people shed any tears for its demise in 1988. The funeral grant has been replaced by a lump sum payment, but this payment is not only strictly means-tested, but is also repayable from the estate of the deceased. To obtain help from the Department of Social Security (DSS) towards the cost of a 'simple funeral', the person organising the funeral has to be on income support or entitled to housing benefit or family credit. The payment is made from the Social Fund, which was created in 1988.

The other lump sum that the State pays when someone dies is the widow's payment. This is a tax free benefit of £1,000 and is based on the national insurance contribution record of the deceased. Entitlement to the benefit is restricted to those who are widowed under age 60 and it is not paid at all if the husband was entitled to a state retirement pension when he died.

The main income benefits are the widowed mother's allowance and the widow's pension, although it is not possible to receive both benefits at the same time. The widow's pension begins, for example, when the widowed mother's allowance ends! Both benefits may be supplemented by an additional pension, but this is only based on the husband's earnings since 6 April 1978.

Apart from that earnings related element both the widowed mother's allowance and the widow's pension are flat rate benefits — £66.75 per week in each case, as from 6 April 1999. The widow's pension may be reduced for younger widows and it is not payable at all to those who are widowed under the age of 45.

So, the level of State retirement and death benefits is a powerful reason why companies run pension schemes: very few companies who wish to be seen as good employers in their local communities would be content to let their long serving employees and their dependants live solely on state benefits.

Government incentives

12.6   In common with all Governments in the developed world, the UK Government views with some concern adverse demographic trends, i.e. people are living longer and the birth rate is falling. Therefore, the contributory State pension scheme is likely to come under increasing strain and it is therefore to be expected that future legislation will make it even more attractive for companies and individuals to provide pension schemes. At present:

(*a*)   the Government gives rebates on employees' and employers' national insurance contributions for those pension arrangements which contract out of SERPS;

(*b*)   valuable tax concessions are granted on employers' and employees' contributions to pension schemes, provided that these schemes are approved by the Inland Revenue; and

(*c*)   the progressive reduction in the level of SERPS benefits is itself an encouragement towards private pension provision; more employers are likely to consider that State pensions by themselves are inadequate, in which case the establishment of contracted out pension arrangements could be attractive alternatives.

Types of pension scheme

12.7   In the UK there are two main types of pension arrangements, the defined contribution scheme (also known as 'money purchase') and the defined benefit scheme (also known as 'final salary'). The main difference between them is the degree of risk sharing between the employees and the employer. In addition there are various hybrid arrangements. Risks in this context relate to such things as future salary inflation, future investment conditions (both up to and after retirement) and, to some extent, political risk.

Defined benefit schemes

12.8   Under a defined benefit scheme the member is promised a pension, usually based upon length of service and salary at or close to retirement although it could be either a specific amount of pension (e.g. £50,000 per annum) or a specified ratio of final salary (e.g. ⅔ of final pay). Whatever the promise, the member is assured of that level of pension at retirement (assuming he or she remains with the employer to retirement).

Any variations in future inflation and investment returns will be reflected in the employer's costs of providing the scheme. In some schemes the employee also meets a part of the cost but this is usually at a fixed rate. In recent years final salary schemes have tended to bear a greater share of the impact of political changes than money purchase schemes.

Defined contribution schemes

12.9   Under a defined contribution scheme the employer agrees to make contributions to the scheme on behalf of the employee. These benefits may be defined as a fixed amount, a fixed percentage of pay, or a graded amount (depending, say, on age) or may be arbitrary. The contributions paid in respect of an employee are paid into an individual account for each employee and accumulated, net of any expenses, up to retirement. The rate of accumulation will depend upon the investment vehicle which could be a 'with profits' or 'deposit administration' insurance contract which provides capital guarantees and which smooths out variations in investment return, or a potentially higher yielding unit linked policy which is directly invested in stock exchange securities etc. but is subject to the full and immediate impact of market variations.

In some arrangements the employee may have wide freedom as to how his or her pensions account is invested or this may be at the partial or total discretion of the pension scheme trustees. At retirement, the value of the employee's pension accumulation will then be available to buy a pension in the format that most suits his or her circumstances.

Clearly the employee is exposed to the full risk of variations in future investment performance up to retirement and investment conditions at retirement.

There are two types of defined contribution scheme. The first is an employer sponsored, Inland Revenue approved, arrangement. The second is a group personal pension arrangement. This consists of individual personal pension plans to which the employer may contribute. With this arrangement, employer contributions are not compulsory.

Hybrid arrangements

12.10   The simplest type of hybrid arrangement is one under which the employee is provided a pension which is the better of a final salary pension promise or the pension which can be provided out of a money purchase accumulation.

Such hybrid schemes will either be referred to as a 'final salary scheme with a money purchase underpin (or guarantee)' or a 'money purchase scheme with a final salary underpin'. A money purchase underpin solves the problem of poor early leaver benefits under final salary schemes and thus makes them more attractive to younger mobile employees. A final salary guarantee under a money purchase scheme protects the employee against adverse investment conditions.

Another common variation is to provide money purchase benefits up to, say, 40 and then switch over to final salary benefits. This usually requires two schemes but a problem then has to be solved as to whether the money purchase credits should be translated into final salary benefits at age 40 or whether they should remain as separate additional benefits.

The pros and cons of defined benefit schemes

12.11   The main arguments *for* defined benefits (or final salary) schemes are:

(*a*)   it is the form of pension most commonly provided in the UK;

(*b*)   the employee knows exactly what his retirement benefits will be in terms of his salary at retirement. The security this provides is normally particularly important to older and longer serving employees;

(*c*)   benefits on death in service and disability can be integrated easily into the benefit design, as can integration with State pension provision;

(*d*)   the employer can control the pace of funding (i.e. it can choose a low initial rate of funding in the knowledge that the cost will gradually rise, or can deliberately incorporate generous margins for future contingencies etc.);

(*e*)   the employer can benefit from any investment surpluses etc. to reduce its future pension cost or to improve benefits; and

(*f*)   the scheme can sometimes be used as an element of a redundancy programme although the cost issues involved should be properly appreciated.

Some of the *difficulties* with final salary schemes are:

(i)   high salary inflation increases the cost of benefits already accrued thus resulting in additional costs to the employer. However, high inflation may be linked with increased equity returns from which the employer can benefit. Furthermore, the employer has some control over the level of salaries within his organisation;

(ii)   early leaver benefits are less valuable than benefits at retirement. This creates a divide between people who can receive a retirement pension (usually on leaving at age 50 or over) and those who cannot;

(iii)   final salary schemes provide effective security when a salary can be relied on to increase progressively through a career and the member can expect to stay with the same firm. In changing employment conditions, with changing earnings patterns and more frequent job changes this 'security' can be an illusion;

(iv)   final salary schemes have been more susceptible to political interference; this has tended to increase the costs of operating such schemes; and

(v)   surplus and deficits may arise. This can lead to conflict over the use of any surplus and to sharply fluctuating costs.

The pros and cons of defined contribution schemes

12.12   The main arguments *for* defined contribution (or money purchase) schemes are:

(*a*)   from the employer's perspective the future cost of the scheme is known; it is therefore limited and easier to budget for;

(*b*)   employees can exercise their judgment as to how to invest their own pension monies;

(c)   employees can choose to take their retirement benefits in a manner which best suits their circumstances;

(d)   employees appear to be treated equally regardless of age or sex (depending on the scheme design); and

(e)   an option for the employees to take the promised employer's contribution as salary might be very attractive to younger employees with limited resources.

However, some of the *difficulties* with money purchase schemes are:

 (i)   the employee bears all the risks of poor investment returns and of annuity rates at retirement being poor. This makes some employees feel insecure;

 (ii)   the company may feel it has a residual moral responsibility to make up employees' benefits where these have been badly eroded by high inflation and/or poor investment performance;

(iii)   not all employees feel competent to make the choice of the investment medium and some employers/trustees are reluctant to make it for them;

(iv)   the final pension is not known until retirement. This makes it difficult for the individual to plan his or her retirement benefits;

 (v)   money purchase does not recognise the increasing cost of pensions with age and the higher cost for women (who are expected to live longer). Thus, compared with final salary schemes, too much is provided for younger employees and too little for older employees. This can be corrected by using an age related contribution scale but then the overall cost would be susceptible to changes in the age distribution of the employees and might be seen as unfair by younger employees; and

(vi)   in general it is difficult to provide for the most suitable level of benefits for dependants on death in service under this type of scheme although it can be achieved by complex insurance arrangements.

Stakeholder Pensions

12.13   The Green Paper on pensions reform which was published in December 1998 envisages some significant changes to pension provision, starting in April 2001.

First, state second-tier pensions are changing, probably in April 2002, SERPS will be replaced, for future accrual of benefits, by a new State Second Pension. This will be aimed particularly at lower earners, defined as people earning up to £9,000 pa in today's terms.

Second, Stakeholder Pension Schemes will be introduced in April 2001. Many details of these are still to be discussed, but they are intended to be trustee arrangements, run by any organisation (e.g. mutual societies, trades unions, pensions providers) who will meet the criteria to be laid down. They will be money purchase schemes, with a maximum limit of £3,600 pa on contributions (from employee and employer) per member. There will be specified maximum charges and other criteria which such schemes must meet. They will be able to accept National Insurance contribution rebates in addition to the maximum contribution limit — indeed it is envisaged that most if not all members of stakeholder scheme will be contracted out of the State Second Pension in this way. There will be no compulsion on employers to make contributions to stakeholder pension schemes (other than national insurance rebates), at least not at present.

Employers will be required to offer access to a stakeholder scheme to all employees to whom they do not offer membership of an occupational scheme. 'Offering access' is likely to mean that details of a stakeholder scheme will be made available to such employees, and that each employer will pass contributions (national insurance rebates, and voluntary employee contributions) from his payroll to the stakeholder scheme for all employees.

In designing a new occupational pension scheme, we must consider the eligibility conditions for membership of the scheme, since an employer may become involved in stakeholder pensions for all non-eligible employees in due course. Of course, he may review his occupational arrangements in 2001, by which time we should know the full details of how stakeholder schemes will work and how they will interact with occupational schemes.

Some employers may wish to reconsider the future of their occupational schemes in the light of stakeholder schemes. At present it is not envisaged that stakeholder schemes as being replacements for good occupational schemes. They will not be adequate for medium/higher earners, and are unlikely to be as flexible. Indeed, the Green Paper States that 'occupational pension schemes sponsored by employers are one of the great welfare success stories'.

Legal and regulatory background

12.14   Apart from European law, which will be covered at 12.30 below, there are many areas of the law which impact upon the operation of pension schemes in the UK including the Pensions Act 1995 which received Royal Assent on 19 July 1995; among the most important areas are those to do with:

(*a*)   trusts;

(*b*)   tax;

(*c*)   social security;

(*d*)   employment;

(*e*)   financial services; and

(*f*)   data protection.

Trust law and trustees' duties

12.15   Most pension schemes in the UK are set up under trusts and therefore managed by trustees. There are three main reasons for this:

(*a*)   the pension scheme's assets are legally separated from those of the sponsoring employer. They are, therefore, protected from creditors should the company go into liquidation;

(*b*)   it is a requirement of the Inland Revenue that a scheme is established under an irrevocable trust in order to be treated as an exempt approved scheme. Exempt approval removes tax penalties and confers valuable tax advantages; and

(*c*)   a pension scheme must also be established under an irrevocable trust in order to qualify for a contracting out certificate.

A trust is where someone owns the assets but someone else is entitled to benefit from them. Trusts are administered by trustees. They are so called because they are trusted to look after the trust property. Over the centuries trust law has evolved so as to impose high standards of behaviour upon those who are placed in positions of trust. In a pension scheme the trustees own the assets and administer the scheme, but they do so solely for the benefit of the scheme members and their beneficiaries.

Leaving aside the legislative and regulatory points that have already been made, the role of trust law in pension provision has frequently been questioned. After all, the concept of a trust dates from medieval times, and derives from equitable, rather than common law rules. Is such a device appropriate for the 1990s? Should not pension rights be incorporated into the contract of employment, for example?

The Goode Committee, which was set up by the Government to enquire into, and to propose regulations for, the operation of pension schemes in the wake of the Robert Maxwell affair, considered this question and concluded that:

> 'trust law in itself is broadly satisfactory and should continue to provide the foundation for interests, rights and duties arising in relation to pension schemes'.

Why did the Committee come to this conclusion? There are several reasons for this, among them being:

(i)   while trust law is indeed of considerable antiquity, it has shown a remarkable ability to adapt to modern commercial requirements;

(ii)   a trust is not only a means of segregating assets for the protection of the beneficiaries, thus insulating them from the bankruptcy of the settlor, i.e. the employer, but it also provides a mechanism for the collective protection and representation of a group of people linked by a common interest;

(iii)   trust law provides for a high degree of fiduciary responsibility, i.e. the trustees have to act in good faith in the best interest of all the beneficiaries; it is surely right that this requirement be preserved; and

(iv) contract law is in fact not sufficient to take over the obligations under a trust. Individual employment contracts do not, of themselves, provide the security resulting from a segregation of assets nor the collective mechanism that is important for the running of pension schemes. Additionally, contract law does not provide protection to all the beneficiaries of a pension scheme, e.g. the dependants of current members and early leavers who have deferred pensions under the terms of the scheme.

This viewpoint has been reinforced by the Pensions Act 1995. Thus, it can be confidently predicted that trust law will, with some modification, continue as the basis of pension provisions in the UK for the foreseeable future.

Pension scheme trustees can be individuals, but it is possible to have corporate trustees and trust corporations. It is also common, especially with executive benefit schemes, for the sponsoring employer to act as trustee. This is not generally to be recommended because of possible conflicts of interest. (See also 12.34 for discussion of Pensions Act 1995 requirements for member-nominated trustees.)

All resignations and new trustee appointments have to be documented by means of deeds. This procedure, laborious though it may appear, is advantageous because it allows for the immediate vesting of the trust property in a new trustee.

Individual trustees are often directors or senior employees of the sponsoring organisation, but there is a trend towards the appointment of employee trustees who are selected, in some manner, by the scheme members. Also, some schemes have appointed independent trustees either to act alone or in addition to company and member appointed trustees.

Trustees' duties

12.16 Besides being responsible for ensuring that contributions are collected and that employees are admitted to membership when they become eligible to join the scheme, trustees have a wide range of other equally important duties. The main duties can be summarised as follows:

(*a*) familiarisation with the provision of the scheme;

(*b*) duty to carry out the provisions of the trust deed and rules of the scheme;

(*c*) duty not to discriminate;

(*d*) not to delegate unless authorised to do so;

(*e*) to act jointly;

(*f*) duty to invest;

(g)   duty to keep accounts and other records e.g. payment and transfer details and minutes of meetings;

(h)   duty not to make a profit; and

(j)   duty to be discreet.

Trustees' conduct in practice

12.17   The trust deed governing the pension scheme will normally state how the trustees should carry out their duties. It usually specifies the following:

(a)   where a majority decision should prevail;

(b)   how many trustees can constitute a quorum;

(c)   whether written resolutions can be passed without a meeting;

(d)   the procedure for appointment of a secretary; and

(e)   the procedure for appointment of a chairman and whether the chairman is to have a casting vote.

At meetings the trustees will discuss how they should exercise their discretion. They will receive and discuss reports from professional advisers such as the actuary, auditor and investment manager. They will adopt accounts and minute the decisions taken in meetings.

Trustees' powers

12.18   Trustees are given limited powers under general law and statute, for example certain restrictive powers of investment and limited powers to insure the trust property and to delegate administrative functions. Wider powers are generally given in a pension scheme trust deed. Examples are as follows:

(a)   power of alteration;

(b)   power to invest;

(c)   power of delegation;

(d)   power to act by majority vote;

(e)   power to augment benefits;

(f)   power to accept incoming transfer values;

(g)   power to wind up schemes; and

(h)   discretionary powers.

There are certain discretionary powers which must be exercised by trustees. They can, and indeed must in some circumstances, call in advice, but must exercise the discretion themselves. Areas where trustees have to exercise discretion include:

(i)   payment of lump sum death benefits;

(ii) approval of ill health early retirements; and

(iii) consenting to amendments proposed by the employer.

Trustees' hazards

12.19   Remedies for errors by trustees are enforceable by court action by a beneficiary for breach of trust. Breach of trust can be deliberate, negligent or accidental but there can be no successful action unless the beneficiary has suffered some loss.

The Trustee Act 1925 gives some protection to trustees, for example:

(*a*)   section 30 states that no trustee can be held personally liable except in the case of wilful default (in trust law this includes carelessness). Some trust deeds extend this further to state that a trustee will be indemnified unless the breach is a result of conscious, wilful default; and

(*b*)   section 61 gives the court power to relieve a trustee's liability where he acted honestly and reasonably.

Companies should also give careful consideration to other ways of protecting trustees and scheme assets through indemnity insurance schemes.

Trustees can and have been sued. Prior to 1996, many cases against trustees concerned the matter of who owned a surplus in a pension scheme. It had been held in several cases that, complaints by pensioners who objected to surpluses being remitted back to the company, rather than being used to increase members' benefits, were unfounded, except in the case of fraud. However, the Occupational Pension Schemes (Payments to Employers) Regulations 1996 (SI 1996 No 2156), which came into effect on 6 April 1997, changed the former position. Pension scheme trustees now need to meet new statutory conditions before transferring surplus pension scheme assets to an employer. Members who object to such a transfer will be able to refer the trustees' decision to the Occupational Pensions Regulatory Authority (OPRA) (see 12.32). OPRA can prohibit payments to employers, order the money to be returned to the scheme, or fine the trustees if the statutory rules are not met. The aim of these regulations is to strike a fairer balance between the interests of the members whilst continuing to allow employers access to surplus funds not needed to meet promised pensions. Trustees will need to be aware of the possibility of challenge in these situations, and the need to comply with the regulations.

Additionally, the Pensions Ombudsman has made several published decisions against trustees. Some of these findings have resulted from complaints about maladministration where trustees have been ordered to reconsider decisions; others have resulted in trustees being forced to make compensatory payments. The Ombudsman can rule on complaints made by individuals against employers, trustees and administrators, e.g. insurance companies. Appeals against his decisions are to the High Court and can only be made on points of law.

Tax law

12.20   It was the Finance Act of 1921 which first set out the general principle that tax relief could be claimed in respect of occupational pension schemes for contributions made by companies and by employees.

Since then, the legislation, both primary (by way of Acts of Parliament) and secondary (by way of regulations), has developed steadily andrelentlessly. The general principle has, however, not changed a great deal since 1921, and may be summarised as follows:

> 'in return for generous tax reliefs given for employee and company contributions to pension schemes, benefits and contributions must be limited'.

Exempt approved pension schemes, i.e. those which have been approved by the Inland Revenue, enjoy the following tax privileges:

(*a*)   the company obtains full corporation tax relief on its contributions;

(*b*)   the members are entitled to full tax relief (*currently* at their highest marginal tax rates) on their contributions;

(*c*)   the fund which backs the pension promises accrues free of all income and capital gains taxes, although tax credits on dividends from UK Equities received on and after 2 July 1997 cannot be reclaimed; and

(*d*)   cash taken at retirement is tax free, within certain benefit limits.

These tax advantages are generous; at the same time, exempt approval also removes possible tax penalties. Contributions paid by a company to a pension scheme which is neither approved nor exempt approved are deemed to be part of the income of the employees and taxed accordingly.

In return for these generous tax advantages, benefits and contributions are limited. The whole area of limits on benefits has become incredibly complex because it is possible, under one scheme, to have members who are subject to three different tax approval regimes, namely:

(i)   Pre 17 March 1987;

(ii)   17 March 1987 to 31 May 1989; and

(iii)   1 June 1989 onwards.

However, the limits can be simplified as follows:

(A)   pensions cannot exceed ⅔ of annual remuneration;

(B)   cash at retirement cannot exceed 1½ times final remuneration;

(C)   lump sum benefits on death in service cannot exceed four times final remuneration;

(D)   spouses' pensions on death in service or death after retirement cannot exceed ⅔ of the members' maximum approval pensions;

(E)   pensions cannot increase at a rate greater than the rate at which the cost of living increases but can be subject to a minimum increase of 3% per annum;

(F)   employees' contributions cannot exceed 15% of their annual pay; and

(G)   companies may not pay contributions that are so high as to deliberately 'overfund' their schemes.It is the function of the Pension Schemes Office of the Inland Revenue (the PSO) to police pension schemes in order to ensure that these limits are not exceeded; it can, and often does, call for compliance checks on individual pension schemes. The PSO acquired new powers at the beginning of 1996. These powers enable officials to carry out checks on pension schemes in order to ensure that they are being managed in line with PSO requirements. At present 28 days notice is needed before such visits can take place. Those who administer pension schemes are required to keep such books and records as will enable compliance checks to be carried out; in most cases, these books and records are required to be kept for six years.

The ultimate sanction that the PSO can impose is the withdrawal of exempt approval for the offending scheme. However, it acknowledges that such a drastic step would have unfortunate consequences on the members, who are probably unaware that PSO limits have been exceeded. So the PSO prefers other less drastic means of enforcement. However, it is not unknown for penalties to be imposed e.g. where trustees failed to comply with PSO deadlines on a scheme merger, the PSO imposed the loss of exempt approval for 12 months.

Employment law

12.21   The Employment Rights Act 1996, s 1 provides that pensions and pension schemes should be among the written details of the terms of employment given to employees within two months of starting employment. (See 14.13 EMPLOYMENT, HEALTH AND SAFETY.)

However, more needs to be mentioned under this heading. There have been signs recently that employment tribunals are hearing more and more cases to do with pension rights. While decisions of employment tribunals carry no legal precedent (appeals against decisions are made to the Employment Appeals Tribunal) pensions are today being seen increasingly as part of the employment package. The major issue is the extent to which pension rights are transferred when employments are transferred, especially in compulsory competitive tendering situations. European Council Directive 77/187 provides that, when a business is sold, the purchaser must maintain the existing terms and conditions of employment of the employees of the business. In the UK, the Transfer of Undertakings (Protection of Employment) Regulations 1981 (SI 1981 No 1794) 'TUPE', brought the requirements of the Directive into UK law. Both TUPE and the Directive excluded pensions from the scope of their requirements. (See 14.28 EMPLOYMENT, HEALTH AND SAFETY.)

Originally, the UK Government took the view that, where transfers of undertakings from the public to the private sector took place, pension rights did not have to be maintained. However, in April 1995, there was something of a volte-face on the part of the Government. It issued a circular to local authorities stating its view that a failure to maintain pension rights could render an authority liable to claims for constructive dismissal. The case of *Adams and Others v Lancashire County Council and BET Catering Services Limited [1996] IRLR 154*, is the 'lead' case on this issue. The decision of the High Court on 17 January 1996 was that pensions were excluded both from the Directive and from the Regulations, although EU law did require Member States to adopt measures to protect employees' (and ex-employees') accrued pension rights. The Court of Appeal have since upheld this decision (*The Times, 19 May 1997*). By the passage of legislation relative to revaluation and preservation of deferred pensions, the UK Government had complied with this requirement.

Under the Pension Schemes Act 1993, s 124(1) (PSA) the Secretary of State may make payments out of the National Insurance Fund into an occupational pension scheme if he is satisfied that an employer has become insolvent and that at the time he became insolvent there remained unpaid relevant contributions falling to be paid by him into the scheme. 'Relevant contributions' are defined as contributions to be paid by the employer on his own behalf or on behalf of an employee from whose pay a deduction has been made for that purpose (PSA 1993, s 124(2)).

Financial services law

12.22   Under this heading reference is made to the Financial Services Act 1986. This Act states, among other things, that it is a criminal offence for anyone to give investment advice or to deal in investments unless he or she is registered to do so.

Therefore, pension scheme trustees run two risks, namely that:

(*a*)   they will handle the scheme investments themselves without being registered; and

(*b*)   they will, albeit unwittingly, find themselves in situations where they are giving investment advice to members.

The first of these can be overcome. Trustees can register under the Act but they normally choose to delegate the investment of the assets to an investment manager who is registered. It is a fact that only the very largest pension schemes handle the investments 'in house', simply because they can afford to employ 'in house' investment experts.

It is the second risk that is perhaps more dangerous. If trustees give general advice to new employees as to whether they should join pension schemes they are not committing an offence because pension schemes themselves are not classed as investment under the Act. However, if a member comes along and asks 'what do you think of the personal pension contract offered by ABC Insurance PLC?' a trustee can only give general advice on the merits of the company pension scheme against a personal pension policy. If a trustee comments about, for example, the past performance of ABC Insurance PLC whether this is likely to be repeated in the future and the charging structure of ABC's contract etc., then he or she is giving investment advice.

Similarly, if a scheme has a choice of AVC providers, e.g. P&R Building Society and ABC Insurance PLC, a trustee must not attempt to comment on the relative merits of the two alternatives by way of charges, investment performance, etc. A trustee can only give general advice as to the advantages of building society investments over insurance based investments or vice versa.

Social security law

12.23   Along with tax law, social security law is one of the most important areas of law affecting occupational pension schemes, if only because of the plethora of both primary and secondary legislation emanating from the Department of Social Security! This is summarised below.

Social Security Act 1973

12.24   This legislation:

(*a*)   established the Occupational Pensions Board (OPB) (which has been replaced by the Occupational Pensions Regulatory Authority — see 12.32 below) and defined its powers;

(*b*)   gave the OPB powers to modify trust deeds and rules of pension schemes for specific purposes; and

(*c*)   established the rules dealing with the preservation of benefits for early leavers from pension schemes.

Social Security Pensions Act 1975

12.25   This Act, some of the provisions of which were enacted subsequently, established the law by which occupational pension schemes may contract out of SERPs. The legislation also:

(*a*)   established the law on how the preserved pensions of early leavers must be revalued during the period of deferment (sections 52A and 52B);

(*b*)   allowed occupational pension schemes to extinguish pension liabilities by using buy-out insurance contracts (section 52C and 52D);

(*c*)   established the law on equal access by men and women to pension schemes (sections 53 to 56);

(*d*) established the requirement that occupational pension schemes must disclose information to their members (section 56A);

(*e*) established the requirement to lodge details of occupational pension schemes with an official registry (section 56E);

(*f*) established requirements relating to auditors of pension schemes (section 57A);

(*g*) restricted occupational pension schemes on how they can invest their assets (section 57A);

(*h*) allowed the OPB to fund bodies such as the Occupational Pensions Advisory Service (OPAS) (section 57B);

(*j*) established the Pensions Ombudsman;

(*k*) required the appointment of an independent trustee when the sponsoring employer becomes involved (sections 57C and 57D);

(*l*) set out compulsory limited prices indexation of pensions (section 58A) (but this is not yet in force); and

(*m*) provided that the making up of pension scheme deficiencies on the winding up of a scheme a debt of the sponsoring employer (section 58B).

It has taken nearly 20 years for all the provisions of the Act to be brought into law. In some cases, further legislation has had to be passed, for example the Social Security Act 1990, in order to do this.

Social Security Act 1985

12.26 This Act provided a statutory right to a cash equivalent on the termination of pensionable service on or after 1 January 1986. A cash equivalent, otherwise known as a transfer value, should be calculated and verified in accordance with actuarial guidelines. Previously, it had not been obligatory for pension schemes to provide transfer values. Interestingly, there is no legislation which compels pension schemes to receive transfer values.

Social Security Act 1986

12.27 The Act served to:

(*a*) establish the law relating to Contracted Out Money Purchase Schemes;

(*b*) introduce guaranteed minimum pensions for widowers;

(*c*) make it compulsory for pension schemes to provide AVC facilities;

(*d*) end the ability of employers to make membership of occupational pension schemes compulsory; and

(*e*) introduced personal pensions.

Social Security Act 1989

12.28 This Act made prospective changes to the law relating to equal treatment of men and women in occupational pension schemes. Much of this was overtaken by the European Court of Justice in its judgment in the case of *Barber v Guardian Royal Exchange*, 17 May 1990, but from 23 June 1994 the Government quite unexpectedly brought into force Schedule 5 of the Act. This says that women on paid maternity leave have the right to continue in membership of a pension scheme and to accrue rights based on their 'normal' remuneration. They can only be required to pay contributions, however, on the maternity pay (be it statutory or contractual) actually received.

Social Security Act 1990

12.29 The Act provided for:

(a) all deferred pensions for those leaving pensionable service after 1 January 1991 to be revalued for all past pensionable service;

(b) the appointment of the Pensions Ombudsman and the establishment of the Pensions Registry;

(c) restrictions on the investments of pension schemes in employer related assets; and

(d) annual increases to pensions in payment (Limited Price Indexation or LPI) in excess of any GMP entitlements from a day yet to be prescribed.

In connection with LPI, it should be noted that where an actuarial valuation of a pension scheme as at the 'appointed day' reveals a surplus, the surplus must be used to provide increases to pensions in respect of pensionable service before the 'appointed day'.

Pension Schemes Act 1993

12.30 The purpose of the Act is to consolidate into one piece of legislation the various Social Security Acts which have been passed over the last 15 years. It is useful to be aware of different references and sections; for instance, Section 57C of the Social Security Act 1975, dealing with the requirement to appoint independent trustees, now becomes section 119 of the Pension Schemes Act 1993. Schedule 6 of the Health and Social Security Act 1984 (the 'anti-franking' requirements) now becomes Chapter III of Part IV of the Pension Schemes Act 1993. All this is explained in a Table of Derivations at the back of the Act.

There is also a welter of secondary legislation, enacted through Regulations.

The Pensions Act 1995

12.31 This major piece of legislation received Royal Assent on 19 July 1995 and came into force on 6 April 1997. The following paragraphs summarise changes to pensions law and practice made by the Act.

Occupational Pensions Regulatory Authority (OPRA)

12.32   A new regulatory authority, the Occupational Pensions Regulatory Authority (OPRA) has been established. It replaces the Occupational Pensions Board and, apart from the Pension Schemes Office of the Inland Revenue, is the principal authority for the regulation and supervision of occupational pension schemes in the UK.

The powers of OPRA can be summarised as follows:

(*a*)   it may suspend, for up to twelve months, or remove from office, trustees whom OPRA consider to be in serious breach of their duties. 'Duties' in this context refers not only to duties under general trust law, but also to duties under the provisions of the Act. Before making a removal order, one month's notice must be given to the person concerned and to the other trustees. It will be an offence for anyone to act as a pension scheme trustee while suspended or removed;

(*b*)   it may appoint a new trustee to replace the removed or disqualified trustee; it may also appoint new trustees if it is satisfied that by doing so the scheme can be administered in a proper manner and that its assets can be well managed;

(*c*)   if OPRA is satisfied that, for example, it is in the best interests of the majority of members that a scheme be wound up, it will be empowered to issue the necessary order. An amendment to the original Bill at Committee stage makes it clear that such an order will override any provision in the trust deed of a scheme that prevents a winding-up taking place in this situation. OPRA will also have powers to modify the rules of schemes in situations where, for example, surplus monies cannot be repaid to the employer despite the fact that all necessary statutory requirements have been satisfied; and

(*d*)   OPRA may apply to the High Court for an order requiring restitution of scheme assets where it feels that they have been misappropriated, e.g. where assets have been paid or loaned to the employer in contravention of the legal requirements. It will also be able to apply for an injunction if it feels that someone is about to misappropriate the assets.

Trustees, managers, employers and professional advisers will be required, on a request from OPRA, to provide OPRA with any document relevant to the discharge of OPRA's functions in relation to the scheme; OPRA's inspectors will have powers to enter premises e.g. a company's pensions office and inspect all relevant documents.

The role of pension scheme trustees

12.33   The intention of the legislation is to both clarify the powers and duties of the trustees of occupational pension schemes and to give to them new powers and duties. As examples of the former, trustees are required to:

(*a*)   have proper regard to the need for diversification of the scheme's investments as appropriate to the circumstances of the scheme;

(*b*)   maintain a separate scheme bank account; and

(*c*)   keep proper account books and records of their meetings, of any payment of pensions and benefits and of transfer details (Occupational Pension Schemes (Scheme Administration) Regulations 1996 (SI 1996 No 1715)).

These provisions are not new; they have always been present under trust law. The intention behind the legislation was to make the existing machinery work more effectively by inserting such provisions into the Act.

The Act gives to trustees certain powers that formerly could only be exercised by employers or employers with the consent of trustees, or trustees with the consent of employers.

Trustees are required to appoint the scheme actuary and auditor. While the latter appointment is usually made by trustees under the terms of their trust deed, it is quite common for employers to appoint scheme actuaries, who may, in practice, advise both the trustees and the employer in relation to the scheme. There is nothing in the legislation which forbids employers to appoint actuaries for the purpose of advising them on financial matters relating to pension schemes, but scheme valuations and the statutory certification process have to be conducted by actuaries who are appointed by the trustees.

In the matter of pension scheme investments, trustees must prepare, and revise where necessary, in conjunction with their investment advisors, a written statement of the principles governing their decisions about investing the assets of the scheme. The statement should cover the trustees' policy for complying with, among other things:

(i)   the requirement for diversification of the investments in line with the scheme's circumstances; and

(ii)   the minimum funding requirement (see 12.35 below).

They will also have to state, amongst other things:

(A)   their policy relative to risk;

(B)   the balance between different types of investment; and

(C)   the expected returns on investments.

Before such a statement is produced, the legislation requires the trustees to consult the employer. Trustees have the sole power to determine how their decisions are to be taken i.e. whether unanimously or by majority vote. This power is currently subject to the terms of individual pension scheme trust deeds; the Act overrides anything to the contrary in the relevant documents.

Trustees have the sole power to refund ongoing scheme surpluses to employers, subject to any restrictions imposed by scheme rules. Among other things, trustees must be satisfied that this is in the interests of the generality of members. No other person (including the employer, and, in wind-up situations, the liquidator or receiver) can exercise this power. Trustees must set a schedule of contribution payments, sufficient to ensure that at all times their scheme conforms to the minimum funding requirement (see 12.35 below) in agreement with the employer. It is for them to determine the frequency of contributions. They are required to notify OPRA if contributions are not paid in accordance with the agreed schedule.

Trustees are also be required to set up and maintain procedures for settling disputes in occupational pension schemes. It is common at present for the trustees to have the sole power to determine disputes about benefit calculations etc.

No trustee, or anyone who is connected with him or her, can act as the auditor or actuary to the same scheme. However, there are exceptions for firms of actuaries who also own trustee companies. Furthermore, no person can act, or continue to act, as a trustee if, among other things, he has been made bankrupt or has been convicted of an offence involving dishonesty. Trustees cannot be indemnified out of scheme assets for any fines that may be imposed on them, nor are they able to effect insurance to cover these instances.

Trustees are also responsible for ensuring that their schemes comply with the requirements for equal treatment between men and women. (See 12.43 below.)

Member-nominated trustees

12.34 Trustees must ensure that arrangements are made for people nominated by the members to be trustees. Member-nominated trustees may only be removed with the consent of all the other trustees. The powers and duties of member-nominated trustees must not differ from those of any of the other trustees. The number of member-nominated trustees must be:

(*a*)   at least two (or at least one if the scheme has less than 100 members); and

(*b*)   at least one-third of the total number of trustees.

The people selected as member-nominated trustees must serve for not less than three years, nor more than six years, and must be eligible for re-election.

Employers had until 5 May 1997 to propose non-statutory arrangements for their pension scheme. Those who missed this deadline or who decided against alternative arrangements have to follow the statutory route.

Under the statutory arrangements it is the trustees who are responsible for the process and who decide on the rules for nomination or selection of member-nominated trustees. For this purpose they may follow rules which are prescribed by Regulations or propose alternative rules. In the latter case there must be a statutory consultation procedure and if the proposals are rejected by members, the prescribed rules must be followed.

Minimum funding requirement (MFR)

12.35 Every occupational pension scheme, other than money purchase arrangements and certain statutory schemes, are subject to a minimum funding requirement. The precise detail of the test is the subject of regulations and guidance notes from the actuarial profession. The Government has however conceded that the requirement will not guarantee solvency on a winding-up.

Trustees are under tight time schedules to obtain the necessary valuations from their appointed actuaries. There is a prescribed initial period within which a valuation must take place; further valuations will need to be carried out at prescribed intervals. At each valuation, the scheme actuary is required to prepare a certificate stating whether or not, in his opinion, the contributions payable are sufficient to ensure that the MFR will continue to be met throughout the period to the next valuation or, if it appears to him that it is not met, will be met by that date. If the actuary states in the certificate that the contributions are not adequate to achieve this, a further valuation (and a further certificate) will be required within six months unless the value of the assets is not less than 90% of the value of the liabilities and, since the date on which the certificate was signed, the contribution schedule has been revised as agreed by the trustees and the employer and certified by the actuary.

If the value of the scheme's assets, at the date of the valuation, is less than 90% of the value of its liabilities, the employer must take steps to bring the value of the assets up to 90% of the value of the liabilities within a prescribed period; this will be one year. If the employer fails to take this action, the scheme trustees will be duty bound to inform OPRA and the members. The shortfall will be treated as a debt, although not as a preferential debt, from the employer to the trustees. If the value of the scheme's assets, at the date of the valuation, is between 90% and 100% of the value of the liabilities, the employer must take steps to bring the value of the asset up to 100% within another prescribed period; this period will be five years.

Trustees must ensure that a schedule of contributions is prepared, kept up-to-date, and if necessary revised, in accordance with the recommendations of the scheme actuary. The schedule must be agreed between the trustees and the employer, but, if no agreement can be reached, the trustees must implement it.

New contracting-out terms

12.36 Defined benefit schemes are subject to a new test before they can retain their contracted-out status. The requirement will be that they must provide benefits that are broadly equivalent to, or better than, a reference scheme (the scheme actuary will be required to provide the necessary certification every three years). It is difficult to see how the test of 'broad equivalence' will be successfully maintained during the period between certificates. Much will depend on the flow of information between employers, trustees and actuaries. The Act sets out the benefits that the reference scheme must provide. They are:

(a) pensions at 65 of 1.25% of average qualifying earnings in the last three tax years of service multiplied by the number of year's service (with a maximum of 40 years to count); and

(b) spouses' pension of 50% of the members' accrued pensions, on death before and after 65.

'Qualifying earnings' in any tax year are defined as 90% of the amount by which members' earnings exceed the 'lower earnings limit' and do not exceed the 'upper earnings limit'.

The Act gives the Government powers to introduce other contracting-out criteria by way of regulations and also gives it the power to restrict or prohibit transfers or cash commutation from a contracted-out scheme. All pensions accrued by reference to pensionable service after 6 April 1997 have to be increased in payment in line with increases in the RPI, subject to a ceiling of 5% each year.

The Act provides for changes to be made to the basis on which National Insurance contribution rebates are calculated in the light of new arrangements. It also heralds the introduction of age related National Insurance contribution rebate for people who contract by means of money purchase pension schemes and personal pension arrangements. The Government has, however, capped the maximum rebate at 9% of relevant earnings i.e. earnings between the 'lower' and 'upper' earnings' limits.

Under the proposed new contracting-out regime, it is still possible for people to be brought back into the State Earnings Related Pension Scheme (SERPS) in exchange of contributions equivalent premiums.

Where a contracted-out scheme is wound-up and the resources are insufficient to secure members' SERPS rights, members may be treated as having been in SERPS (to an extent to be determined by subsequent regulations).

Pensions and divorce

12.37 The Pensions Act introduces new provisions for dealing with pension rights in all divorce, nullity and judicial separation proceedings. The new requirements apply to all petitions filed or actions brought under English law on or after 1 July 1996. Courts will be able to issue attachment orders instructing pension schemes to pay benefits to ex-spouses. Under English law the orders may apply to pension payments and lump sum benefits (e.g. benefits payable on retirement or death). Court orders apply to any pension payments made after 6 April 1997; attachment orders on lump sums can also be made. According to regulations issued under the Pensions Act, the value of pension benefits is based on cash equivalents; existing clean break settlements remain as courts seek to split other assets before issuing attachment orders to pensions; the ex-spouse does not become a scheme member; the courts have the power to override trustees' discretion or member's nomination regarding the payment of lump sum death benefits; and schemes will be able to charge for complying with requests from the courts for information on the pension rights of the parties.

The previous Government had issued a Green Paper seeking comments on likely future changes in this area. A provision to allow a fundamental change in this area was incorporated into the Family Law Act 1996, but further legislation will be necessary to implement it.

The present Government came into office with a commitment to further reform the law concerning pensions on divorce. It is anticipated that, following consultation, legislation will permit the courts to order that pension rights are split at the point of divorce rather than when the benefits became payable.

The role of professional advisers

12.38   The 'whistle-blowing' role, which was originally to be reserved for scheme auditors and actuaries only, has now been extended so that other professional advisers, scheme managers and trustees may, if the circumstances so justify, report relevant matters to the Occupational Pensions Regulatory Authority (OPRA). However, unlike auditors and actuaries, the legislation will not impose a duty on these people to report to OPRA. The Government has accepted that there is a wider range of professional people involved in the day-to-day administration of pension schemes, and has further accepted that, due to their closer involvement on a day-to-day basis, they may become aware of maladministration (or potential maladministration) earlier than actuaries and auditors.

Change to the calculation of SERPS

12.39   Under the present method which is used for the calculation of SERPS entitlement, total earnings up to the 'upper earnings limit' are revalued each year in line with increases in national average earnings. At an individual's State pension age, the 'lower earnings limit' for the last complete tax year to the State pension age is deducted, in order to arrive at the earnings on which the SERPS entitlement is based. The Act requires the 'lower earnings limit' figure to be deducted from earnings before revaluation takes place. This change, which is intended to assist in reducing the Government's bill for SERPS, will lead to a progressive reduction in SERPS benefits.

The Act allows rights to guaranteed minimum pensions, as well as those which derive from protected rights to be held under the same pension scheme. This is a significant development in that it allows schemes some flexibility in their treatment of incoming transfer values.

Compensation scheme

12.40 The Act establishes the Pensions Compensation Board and prescribes circumstances in which compensation may be payable. It covers schemes where the sponsoring employer is insolvent and where:

(*a*) the value of the assets has been reduced by a prescribed offence;

(*b*) (in the case of a final salary scheme) the value of the assets is less than 90% of the value of the liabilities; and

(*c*) it is reasonable that the members of the scheme should be compensated.

The Act provides for advance payments to be made by the Board where circumstances so justify. The Board (as well as OPRA) will be financed by a levy on pension schemes generally.

Equalisation of State pension ages

12.41 The Act provides for State pension ages to be equalised at the age of 65. This will be brought in on a gradual basis, the intention being that the process shall be complete by 2020.

Data protection law

12.42 The Data Protection Act 1984 exempts from its requirements personal data held only for payroll and accounting purposes. The exemption is not, however, absolute. It is conditional upon the personal data not being used for any other purpose. A data user cannot therefore claim exemption because the data is held for payroll reasons and then use the data for personal reasons.

Personal data held for one or more payroll purposes may be disclosed, *inter alia*:

(*a*) to any person by whom the person is payable (for example a pension provider); and

(*b*) for the purposes of obtaining actuarial advice.

Nevertheless, it is considered by many that the exemptions are too narrow and it is therefore usual for pension scheme trustees to register under the Act, especially if pension scheme data is held on a computerised system.

The influence of European law

12.43 As a member of the European Union (EU) the UK has a binding commitment (by virtue of the European Communities Act 1972) to uphold the principles contained in the Articles of the Treaty of Rome which the UK signed in 1973. The EU is conscious of the variety and differences in laws from one Member State to another and the ultimate intention of the Treaty of Rome is to harmonise the laws of the Member States.

By way of background, EU law takes three main forms:

(*a*)   Treaty Provisions — these are direct application through the EU and may be enforced against Governments of Member States, private sector employers and individuals;

(*b*)   Directives — these are laws binding on the Member States and are designed to impose objectives which each Member State must introduce into its national legislation in whatever manner it chooses. If a directive is sufficiently precise in its terms it may be relied upon by an individual against the other individuals or private sector employers; and

(*c*)   Decisions — these are issued by the Council, the Commission and the European Court of Justice (ECJ) and are binding only on those to whom they are addressed. Decisions can be addressed to Member States, national courts and individuals but are usually addressed to corporate bodies.

EU law has become very relevant to the pensions industry in recent years, particularly the application of Article 119 of the Treaty of Rome. This states:

'Each Member State shall during the first stage ensure and subsequently maintain the application of the principle that men and women should receive equal pay for equal work.'

The case of *Barber v Guardian Royal Exchange Assurance Group (1990)* significantly extended the equal treatment requirements for pension schemes. In the *Barber* case the GRE pension scheme had a normal pension age of 62 for men and 57 for women. Mr Barber was made redundant at age 52. Under the scheme rules he was not entitled to an immediate early retirement pension although a female employee made redundant at age 52 would have been so entitled. The court held that benefits from a contracted out occupational pension scheme were 'pay' for the purposes of Article 119 provided they were derived from contract. There was clear discrimination so Mr Barber's estate (Mr Barber having died meanwhile) was entitled to receive compensation.

Unfortunately, it was not immediately clear to what extent the ECJ's judgment was intended to be retrospective. In order to clarify the position, the Maastricht Protocol (1991) contained a provision to the effect that scheme benefits relating to employment before the date of the *Barber* Judgment (17 May 1990) should not be considered as 'pay' and therefore are not required to be equalised (unless legal proceedings have already commenced).

While the issue of whether or not the *Barber* decision was intended to be retrospective is crucial, many other questions relating to pension provision were raised by this decision, some, but by no means all of which have been answered by subsequent test cases.

It would take too long to go through all the cases, but in summary:

(i)   the *Barber* judgment applies to all occupational pension schemes, whether or not they are contracted out;

(ii)   equal treatment in occupational pension schemes is only required for service from 17 May 1990;

(iii)   both employers and pension scheme trustees are responsible for ensuring conformity with the equal treatment requirements;

(iv)   where men have a normal retirement age of (say) 65 and women 60, companies have to reduce the retirement age for men to 60 for service between 17 May 1990 and the date from which a common retirement age is adopted;

(v)   the use of sex based actuarial factors (for calculating transfer values for example) is permitted;

(vi)   part-time employees should be granted access to pension schemes along with their full-time colleagues. However, employers can exclude them if they can demonstrate objective grounds for so doing which are not related to gender; and

(vii)   if a transfer is made from scheme A to scheme B, and the transfer value is not calculated in accordance with equal treatment principles, it is scheme B's responsibility to make sure that the transfer value is appropriately increased.

Small Self-Administered Schemes (SSAS)

12.44   Since the 1973 Finance Act, controlling directors have been allowed to become members of exempt approved pension schemes, and thus enjoy a tax efficient build up of pension benefits on the same terms as other workers. The PSO allows directors' schemes to be set up on a self-administered basis. This means that, in addition to the tax advantages, there is no longer any need to pay all the pension scheme contributions to an insurance company. The directors, through the scheme trustees, are able to control their own pension scheme investments, and even direct them towards helping the company's business.

To prevent abuse of the tax advantages by these directors' pension schemes (normally less than twelve members), the PSO imposes certain conditions on their operation, chiefly in relation to permitted investments. The PSO also imposes strict reporting requirements on trustees of SSAS.

An SSAS is established by a trust deed and rules and operated by trustees. One requirement is that one of the trustees must be a 'pensioner trustee', which is somebody known to and accepted by the Inland Revenue for this purpose. The role of the pensioner trustee is to block any proposal that the trust be terminated and the assets distributed among the beneficiaries other than in accordance with the scheme winding-up rule.

The PSO permits wide powers of investment. The only restrictions are designed to preclude possible abuse of the tax privileges accorded to pension schemes and to ensure that investments are not totally mismatched to the need ultimately to provide benefits to members and their dependants. For example, a substantial investment in property which may be difficult to sell at the required time would be considered unsuitable.

Prohibited investments are:

(*a*)   those which may give members, their families or other individuals some kind of personal benefit, whether tangible or intangible;

(*b*)   loans to individuals;

(*c*)   investments in residential property, cars, yachts etc; and

(*d*)   significant investments in works of art, jewellery and other non-income producing assets.

The pension fund should also 'invest' rather than 'trade'. Thus the purchase of commodities, commodity futures, plant and machinery for hiring out may be regarded as unacceptable to the PSO. New regulations came into force in 1991 which govern the operation of these arrangements. They change, and to some extent tighten up, the PSO's requirements. The regulations restrict investments in the assets of the sponsoring company (this includes loans to the sponsoring company) during the first two years of a scheme to 25% of the market value of those assets which are derived wholly from contributions made to the scheme since it was established. At the end of the two-year period, this increases to 50% of the market value of all the assets of the scheme.

Trustees may borrow funds to the extent that their borrowings do not exceed the total of:

(i)   three times the ordinary annual contribution paid by the company;

(ii)   three times the annual amount of contractual contributions paid by the members; and

(iii)   45% of the market value of the investments.

All income and capital gains deriving from investments held in an exempt approved pension scheme are free from tax under current legislation.

The Government has recently relaxed the requirement that annuities be purchased as soon as members of SSAS retire; annuity purchase may be deferred until age 75.

The 1998 Budget introduced further changes to the regulatory environment surrounding SSAS. These changes were a part of the stated intention of the Government to clamp down on 'tax avoidance'. Detailed changes have been made to the list of permitted investments, the determination of ordinary annual contributions (for tax relief purposes) and the role of pensioneer trustees.

Chapter 13

Insurance administration

Risk management and insurance

13.1   The company secretary may be responsible for risk management or, more specifically, insurance which is one component of risk management.

Risk is a combination of events and likelihoods and is concerned with any situation in which unanticipated events result in the non achievement of the organisation's objectives.

Risk management may be defined as the identification, assessment, economic control and financing of those risks which threaten the assets or earning capacity of an organisation.

Assets not only include physical assets of the organisation but also intangible assets such as goodwill, intellectual property, trade marks, copyright etc. and human resources. Threats to earning capacity include not only events causing a reduction in income, but also incidents resulting in an increase in costs, whether payable to maintain operations, or due to breach of legislation or contractual obligations arising from goods sold or services performed.

Risk management is an integral part of management in an organisation and can be a positive mechanism to operational managers in assisting them to achieve their objectives. It is a multi-stage process. The first stage is risk identification where one determines how the assets or the earning capacity of the organisation may be threatened. Only if such threats are recognised can one successfully deal with them.

The second stage is risk assessment where:

(a)   the impact of the risk is quantified to determine its potential severity; and

(b)   the likelihood of the risk occurring is established to measure its potential frequency.

The principal objective here is to measure the relative importance of the risk, which enables decisions to be made on priorities, and the most appropriate form of treatment adopted.

Following measurement of the exposure the next step is to ascertain how it may be eliminated or reduced. Loss reduction may take the form of:

(i)   pre-loss reduction — action taken following identification of a risk, but prior to the event occurring. Pre-loss risk control concentrates on reducing the frequency of an occurrence (e.g. ensuring guards on dangerous machinery); and

(ii)   post-loss reduction — focusing on reducing severity once the event has taken place (e.g. the installation of a sprinkler system).

Risks may also be controlled through non-insurance contractual transfer. Such transfers may be in the form of:

(A)   risk control transfers — requiring the transferee to perform and complete the action giving rise to the risk (e.g. subcontracting hazardous construction work); and

(B)   risk financing transfers — requiring the transferee to accept financial responsibility for losses arising from a particular exposure (e.g. indemnity agreements).

Once a risk has been identified and either avoided or reduced to the greatest extent practicable and economically viable, a decision has to be made as to whether the financial consequence of any residual risk can be:

 (I)   retained by the organisation; or

(II)   transferred to the insurance market (assuming coverage exists).

The levels of risk which a company is able to retain depends upon:

(1)   the financial strength of the organisation;

(2)   the shareholders and the markets expectations;

(3)   the characteristics of the company; and

(4)   the post-loss goals of the operation.

The major benefits of risk retention are obtained by retaining the financial consequences of high frequency, low severity, and predictable losses, the costs of which are generally uneconomic to transfer.

For exposures which cannot be economically:

(*aa*) avoided or eliminated;

(*bb*) reduced through risk control and contractual risk transfer; or

(*cc*) retained by the organisation,

consideration may be given to insurance, providing coverage is available.

Insurance is a risk transfer mechanism which transfers the financial consequences of loss to a third party. If insurance protection is not available, consideration should be given to whether the activity giving rise to the risk should be continued.

The key features of an insurance contract are:

(*gg*) it is arranged in advance of an event and the agreement is documented in writing in the insurance policy; and

(*hh*) the financial consequences of the loss are transferred to the insurer at the time of the incident.

There are a number of benefits of insurance which include:

(*mm*) compliance with legal or statutory requirements to insure;

(*nn*) indemnification against unexpected events and losses;

(*oo*) reduction in uncertainty through the substitution of the unknown costs of losses with the certainty of the known cost of the premium in that year;

(*pp*) release of funds held in reserve for unknown losses for more productive use; and

(*qq*) access to specialist risk management services provided by insurers.

However, the use of insurance as a risk financing tool is not without its criticisms. Most importantly, it may not provide full financial compensation in the event of a loss because of delays in restoration to full capacity and claim settlement; nor full compensation for permanent loss of market share and effect on public image etc.

Additionally, there may be practical problems such as financial failure of insurers, inadequate and inappropriate insurance arrangements, poor quality of service, volatility of premium costs and non-availability of the cover sought.

Risk transfer to insurers

13.2   Risk transfer to insurers will normally take place in circumstances where:

(*a*)   there is a legal or statutory obligation to insure;

(*b*)   the size of the potential loss is such that it cannot be retained by the organisation; or

(*c*)   this is the most cost-effective method of handling the risk (subject to insurance coverage and capacity being available up to the limits required).

Insurance available

13.3   There are three general areas of insurance covering:

(*a*)   loss or damage to the assets of the company;

(*b*)   loss of earnings; and

(*c*)   protection against statutory or common law liabilities.

Most insurance companies offer packages to cover these risks and in assessing the merits of them, consideration should be given as to whether they adequately provide protection for the organisation's assets, liabilities, risks and exposures which might include:

  (i) buildings, machinery and plant;

  (ii) stock;

  (iii) goods in transit;

  (iv) loss of income or increased costs;

  (v) crime;

  (vi) computer equipment;

  (vii) legal liability arising out of the operation of the business; and

  (viii) terrorism.

Insurance policies should be carefully scrutinised to ensure that they cover the appropriate risks. It should also be considered whether insurance is, in fact, the optimum approach. Many risks can be managed without the use of insurance by identifying the risk and taking the appropriate preventative action.

The insurance broker

13.4   Although all of the large insurance companies can offer expert guidance on many insurance issues and policies on a direct basis, they only offer their own policies for sale. There are advantages for the small company in the use of an insurance broker or consultant to reduce the overall cost of an insurance package and to advise on insurance needs. For larger companies or where complex risk issues are involved, it is usual for an insurance broker or consultant to be employed.

There are two main advantages in seeking this advice:

(*a*)   the broker or consultant has the experience of identifying risks and insuring against them that a company's own personnel may lack; and

(*b*)   the broker or consultant will be independent of the insurers and thus will be able to undertake a more objective assessment of a company's insurance requirements.

Insurance brokers are remunerated by a commission, included in the insurance premium, or by an agreed fee basis.

The loss adjuster and loss assessor

13.5   In the event of a significant loss which is covered by the insurance arrangements it is normal practice for the insurers to appoint a loss adjuster to handle the negotiation of the claim.

The loss adjusters fees are paid by the insurer but he has a professional duty to:

(*a*)   be independent and impartial; and

(*b*)   assist the insured if he is unrepresented.

A loss assessor is appointed by and acts solely on behalf of the insured. It is the insured who is responsible for the payment of the loss assessor's fees, which may be based on time spent or on a success basis. To some extent, the appointment of a loss assessor by the insured removes some of the responsibilities that would otherwise fall on the loss adjuster. Insurance policies do not generally cover loss assessor's or claim preparation costs.

General principles and practice of insurance

13.6   The following are key general principles and practices of insurance:

Utmost good faith

13.7   The principle of utmost good faith forms the basis of the insurance contract. This places a responsibility on the insured to disclose any circumstances which are relevant or material. A material fact is one which would influence the judgment of a prudent insurer in setting the premium or determining whether to accept the risk.

Insurable interest

13.8   Insurance may only be purchased in situations of risk where an 'insurable interest' exists. An insurable interest could be described as existing where:

(*a*)   there is a property or interest to insure (subject matter);

(*b*)   there is a relationship recognised at law between the insured and the subject matter; and

(*c*)   the happening of an insured event would cause the insured financial loss.

Indemnity

13.9   Contracts of insurance are generally contracts of indemnity. Indemnity can be defined as returning an insured party to the same financial position it was in prior to the insured loss occurring. Neither profit nor betterment are allowed.

In property insurance the measure of indemnity is the lesser of the cost of repair of the damaged property or its value at the time of the loss. In practice, the insurers may pay for the cost of replacement on a new for old basis providing more than an indemnity settlement.

In respect of liability the measurement is the insured's legal liability to the employee or third party.

Average

13.10   Average normally applies to material damage insurance and may sometimes be applicable to business interruption insurance. In circumstances where an average provision applies an insured will be considered their own insurer for any underinsurance and shall bear a rateable share of the loss. For example, if an insured only insures 90% of the total value at risk and an average provision operates any claim settlement will be reduced by 10%. Underinsurance must therefore be avoided to ensure an adequate indemnity.

Warranty

13.11   A warranty imposes a duty upon an insured to maintain specific conditions which might otherwise give rise to an increase in risk. A breach of warranty, whether or not it is the cause of any loss, enables the insurer to void the policy at their option from the date of the breach. Warranties must therefore be strictly complied with.

An example is cash warranted to be kept in a safe overnight.

Excess

13.12   This is the amount of loss to be borne by the insured, first, before the insurers pay. It may be stipulated as a monetary amount or, for business interruption insurance, a period of time. Only loss suffered beyond the excess will be met by the policy e.g. loss £500,000 with an excess of £100,000 — policy pays £400,000.

Franchise

13.13   A franchise operates as a threshold. It is necessary for the total loss to exceed the threshold before it can be claimed in full e.g. loss £500,000 franchise £100,000 — policy pays £500,000. If the loss falls below the franchise no cover operates. A franchise may similarly be specified as a monetary amount or a period of time.

The insurance policy

Statutory policies — insurance policies required by law

13.14   All businesses in the UK are legally obliged to have employer's liability insurance and motor third party insurance.

These compulsory insurances must be insured with an approved insurance company authorised to insure these risks. Approval is granted by the Department of Trade and Industry which supervises insurance companies who transact business in the UK. Companies may now, if they so choose, obtain insurance from an insurer who is authorised to insure these risks in another EU Member State and has notified the DTI that it wishes to provide insurance in the UK.

Employers' liability

Legal requirement

13.15   Under the Employers' Liability (Compulsory Insurance) Act 1969, every employer carrying on business in the UK must insure against legal liability for death, bodily injury or illness sustained by employees, while serving under a contract of service or apprenticeship, which arises out of and in the course of their employment.

Policy coverage

13.16   The purpose of employers' liability insurance is to protect an employer against claims for damages brought by employees. The policy covers the employer's legal liability including:

(*a*)   negligence in failing to use reasonable care and skill in:

   (i)   providing suitable and safe plant;

  (ii)   providing a safe system of work;

 (iii)   providing a safe place of work; and

 (iv)   engaging suitable and competent employees;

(*b*)   breach of statutory regulations e.g. Health and Safety at Work Act 1974; and

(*c*)   negligence of fellow employees (an employer will be vicariously liable if one employee negligently injures a fellow employee during the course of his/her employment).

The employers' liability policy responds to death, bodily injury or illness caused during the period of insurance. There may be a significant time period between the cause and the onset of the injury or illness, particularly in relation to exposure to toxic materials or the effects of noise. There may be a further period of time before the employee makes a claim. It is therefore important to retain records of historic policies to ensure that claims can be recovered under the appropriate policy.

The territorial limits operative on employers' liability insurance are Great Britain, Northern Ireland, the Channel Islands and the Isle of Man but cover also operates for employees who sustain death, bodily injury or illness whilst temporarily elsewhere in the world. Normally any action for damages must be brought within Great Britain, Northern Ireland, the Channel Islands and the Isle of Man.

The policy extends to indemnify any principals in like manner to the insured if it is necessary to do so to meet the requirements of any contract entered into by the insured with the principal.

A copy of the certificate confirming the insurance is in place is required to be displayed in a prominent place (e.g. a notice board) at each place of business.

Limit of indemnity

13.17   The amount for which an employer is required to insure is £2 million for any one occurrence. It was common practice for insurers to provide cover, unlimited in amount, but with effect from 1 January 1995 insurers have generally imposed a limit of indemnity of £10 million for any one occurrence. Costs and legal expenses incurred in defending negligence claims made against the company by employees are inclusive of the limit of indemnity.

If the standard limit of indemnity is insufficient to cater for the maximum damages and costs which might arise from a single occurrence additional coverage will need to be sought.

Restrictions

13.18   Legislation prohibits insurers avoiding liability due to an insured breaching a policy condition. In such circumstances the insurers will have to deal with the claim and compensate the injured employee. They will then have the right to recover from the insured the sum so paid any of which they have been obliged to pay under the provisions of the Employers' Liability (Compulsory Insurance) General Regulations 1971.

Excesses are not permitted under the Act, but it is permissible to include a policy term requiring the insured to reimburse insurers up to a stipulated sum in respect of any claim.

Motor

Legal requirement

13.19   The Road Traffic Act 1988 requires that insurance exists for all vehicles used on the road against liability to any third party for death or bodily injury and damage to property. There is no requirement to cover damage to the insured vehicle.

Policy coverage

13.20   There are three principal bases of motor insurance.

(*a*)   Third Party only — unlimited liability to third parties in respect of death, bodily injury or damage to property arising out of the use of a vehicle. Property damage arising out of the use of commercial vehicles or vehicles bearing trade plates is normally limited.

(*b*)   Third Party Fire and Theft — as above extended to include fire damage to and theft or attempted theft of the vehicle itself.

(*c*)   Comprehensive — as above extended to include accidental damage of the vehicle itself and other specified extensions.

It is a requirement of the Road Traffic Act 1988 that a certificate of insurance or cover note has been issued by the insurer.

Third party coverage includes legal fees for representation and for defence. In addition, motor insurance policies normally pay costs of defence against a charge of manslaughter or causing death by reckless or dangerous driving in the UK if the charge arises out of an accident which is subject to indemnity under the policy.

Insured use

13.21   There are two main classifications of insured use as far as a company is concerned:

(*a*)   social, domestic and pleasure purposes and for the business of the policyholder excluding use for hiring, commercial travelling or for any purpose in connection with the motor trade; and

(*b*)   as in (*a*) above but including carriage of passengers for hire or reward and use in connection with the motor trade.

It is normal practice to exclude use for racing, competitions, rallies or trials.

There may be restrictions on young or inexperienced drivers or persons convicted of serious motoring offences. Some policies severely restrict the cover provided if at the time of the accident the driver is under the influence of drink or drugs.

Foreign use

13.22   Policy coverage applies in respect of an accident occurring in Great Britain, Northern Ireland, the Isle of Man and the Channel Islands and during sea transits between ports in these areas. In accordance with the EU Directive the policy includes cover in respect of the minimum requirements of those European Countries which have signed the Directive.

However, the insurer should be notified early of any proposed journey abroad to extend full policy coverage and for the issue of an international green card, for countries which are not party to the EU Directive. This green card is evidence that the insurance meets any local statutory requirements, so exempting the policyholder from having to effect insurance locally in most European countries. For countries which do not subscribe to the international green card system, insurance should be arranged locally.

For visits to Spain a bail bond is recommended. This is a guarantee provided by an insurer to secure the release of the policyholder or their vehicle from the custody of the authorities following an accident by the bearer. The bond is a guarantee and not insurance, and so is refundable by the bearer to the insurer if retained permanently by the authorities.

Minimum extensions

13.23   It is usual to extend the policy to include:

(*a*)   Contractual Liability to Principal — liability assumed under an agreement with a principal for the execution of work or services;

(*b*)   Unauthorised Use — indemnity in the event of an accident occurring whilst a vehicle is being used without the knowledge of the insured for a purpose not permitted under the insurance policy; and

(*c*)   Unauthorised Movement — liability incurred in moving an obstructing vehicle without the authority of the owner.

Motor third party contingency cover

13.24   Circumstances may arise where an employee uses his own vehicle on company business. Any claims from third parties arising out of this use may be covered by the employee's own insurance if business use is included. If not, then the employer may be vicariously liable. Contingent third party insurance covers this vicarious liability and indemnifies the employer. It does not cover the employee. Before giving permission to an employee to use his own vehicle on company business it is advisable to check that his insurance covers such business use by him.

Uninsured losses

13.25   There are certain types of losses which may be incurred following a motor accident which are not covered under the insurance policy e.g. hire charges of an alternative vehicle.

Legal expenses insurance can be arranged to meet the legal costs of seeking to recover uninsured losses suffered following a collision with a negligent third party.

Insurance policies to protect the business

13.26   Common insurance policies include 'Material Damage', 'Business Interruption' and 'Third Party Liability' insurance.

Material damage

The risk

13.27   The assets of a business will generally fall into three categories:

(*a*)   buildings;

(*b*)   plant, machinery and other contents; and

(*c*)   stock.

All are subject to possible loss, destruction or damage.

Policy coverage

13.28   The material damage policy seeks to indemnify the insured in respect of loss, destruction or damage of physical assets. This indemnification may take the form of the insurer:

(*a*)   paying the value of the property at the time of the loss, destruction, or damage, in the event of a total loss;

(*b*)   paying the amount of the damage or the cost of repair in the event of partial damage; or

(*c*)   at its option reinstate or replace the property which has suffered damage.

Material damage insurance may be arranged to respond to loss, destruction or damage either from specified events or for all risks.

(i)   Fire and special perils

The standard fire policy covers fire, lightning and to a limited extent explosion. At the insured's option the standard policy can be extended to include additional special perils such as:

(A)   explosion;

(B)   earthquake;

(C)   riot and civil commotion;

(D)   malicious damage;

(E)   storm, tempest and flood;

(F)   burst pipe; and

(G)   impact.

The insurer may also be prepared to grant cover for loss or damage arising out of:

 (I)   accidental damage;

 (II) theft (normally restricted to that involving forcible and violent entry or exit);

(III) explosion, collapse and overheating of boilers, economisers and vessels;

(IV) sprinkler leakage; and

 (V) subsidence.

(ii) All Risks

The all risks policy covers loss, destruction or damage from any cause which is not specifically excluded. The standard all risks wording broadly covers fire, the special perils listed above (A–G) and accidental damage subject to some exclusions. Some of these exclusions may be avoided by the payment of an additional premium.

They include:

(1) explosion of steam pressure vessels;

(2) mechanical or electrical breakdown;

(3) theft or attempted theft;

(4) subsidence, ground heave and landslip; and

(5) collapse and overheating of boilers, economisers etc.

Terrorism

13.29   Cover for terrorist fire and explosion in the UK is limited in amount by insurers under their standard policy wordings. Full policy limits can be attained by purchasing terrorism cover from the material damage insurers, who then reinsure the risk with a facility set up by UK Insurers, Pool Re. This will attract an additional premium at standard rates established by Pool Re. The UK Government acts as a reinsurer of last resort to this facility. Depending on market conditions there may be alternative sources of terrorism insurance which can be explored.

Additional insurance

13.30   The basic material damage policy may be extended to include:

(*a*) goods in transit; and

(*b*) money.

Goods in transit insurance can cover consignments by post, rail, road, sea or air carrier within preselected territories. Money insurance can cover cash and non negotiable instruments in transit and at own premises in and out of business hours. Money insurance may additionally be extended to include personal accident assault to employees carrying cash.

Average

13.31   Material damage policies are normally subject to average. In the event of underinsurance the insured will be penalised in any claim settlement.

In respect of buildings, machinery and plant, underinsurance caused by inflation can be avoided by utilising the 'day one basis'. The insured declares the cost of reinstating the property insured at the level of costs at the start of the period of insurance. An inflation provision is then applied to this figure. Providing the value declared at the commencement of the policy is adequate and the inflation provision sufficient the claim settlement will not be reduced by average.

Underinsurance on stock is most appropriately avoided by setting the sum insured at the absolute maximum which is envisaged will be held at any one time during the period of insurance and then agreeing with insurers that the premium they charge reflects this fact.

Reinstatement

13.32   Being a contract of indemnity the measure of loss under the material damage policy is the value of the property at the time of loss or damage. This would include an appropriate reduction to allow for wear and tear. The indemnity contract can be amended so as to provide the full cost of reinstatement of buildings or machinery (but not stock) on a new for old basis (but not to include betterment). Consequently there would be no deduction to allow for the effects of wear and tear. Otherwise the insured should not be better off as a result of insurers meeting the full cost of reinstatement.

Minimum requirements

13.33   It is recommended that the material damage policy includes the following.

(*a*)   Automatic reinstatement — automatic reinstatement of the sum insured in the event of loss.

(*b*)   Debris removal — the cost of removing building debris, damaged machinery and stock.

(*c*)   Professional fees — architects, surveyors and consulting engineers fees incurred in the reinstatement of property.

(*d*)   Public authorities — additional costs of reinstatement incurred in complying with building or other regulations.

(*e*)   Capital additions — automatic cover for alterations, additions and improvements to existing property.

The sum insured should be increased to include an estimated price for items (*b*) to (*e*) inclusive.

Areas to consider

13.34   Some particular issues that should be considered are detailed below.

(*a*)   Buildings — in respect of leased premises, the insurance obligations of the landlord and the tenant should be examined carefully. It is also necessary to take into account any obligations to maintain the premises and/or the landlord's fixtures and fittings and ensure appropriate insurance is arranged. The landlord may be obliged to insure only against loss or damage to the basic structure of a building, caused by fire or related damage. Items such as flood or subsidence are not always required to be covered and a tenant should thus take particular care to ensure that his business is protected against these eventualities.

When insuring a building, it is advisable to insure on a re-instatement basis and to account for items such as architects' and surveyors' fees, demolition of the damaged structure and costs of meeting local authority requirements.

(*b*)   Plant, machinery and other contents — where plant and machinery are hired, clarification of the hirer's risks should be sought. It is common for the hirer to be responsible for all loss or damage to such equipment.

Computer equipment is another area requiring particular attention. Risks to be assessed here are the costs of repairs falling outside any maintenance agreement and the cost of replacing any information corrupted or lost following a malfunction of the system.

(*c*)   Stock — an important consideration with stock is in relation to its transportation and storage. To avoid gaps in cover which could result in a loss to the company one should clarify the point at which stock becomes the company's liability on inwards transit.

(*d*)   Rent — ideally rent should be insured under the business interruption insurance arrangements which provides more appropriate and wider cover for rent than material damage insurance.

Business interruption

The risk

13.35   Although a material damage policy is designed to cover such expenses as the cost of clearing debris, rebuilding premises and replacement of other physical assets, it is not intended to cover loss of income whilst replacements, repair or rebuilding are carried out. Neither does the material damage policy cater for the burden of extra expenses incurred in keeping the business in operation.

Overview of policy

13.36   Business interruption insurance provides compensation to an insured who suffers loss of income following physical damage by an insured event.

The standard policy wording can be designed to cover both loss of income and costs incurred in avoiding such loss or can merely cover costs only. The trigger for the business interruption policy is an insured contingency causing damage to property used by the insured at their premises which causes interruption to their business.

Extension of the basic policy coverage may be required to cover certain scenarios and types of financial loss which are not covered under the standard wording. Business interruption insurers limit coverage under their standard policy wording in respect of terrorist fire or explosion. Full policy limits may be achieved by selecting the appropriate extension in a similar manner to material damage insurance.

Principles of business interruption insurance

13.37   There are certain general principles to business interruption insurance which limit policy coverage and which need to be understood when arranging business interruption cover. These include the following.

(*a*)   Business definition — the business interruption policy only covers business activities which are defined. It is necessary for the business description to embrace all activities undertaken.

(*b*)   Premises definition — the standard business interruption policy only caters for consequential loss suffered as a result of insured damage occurring to premises which are defined. Therefore the standard business interruption policy does not cover loss suffered as a result of damage:

   (i)   to the insured's premises which are not defined and included in the 'premises' definition; or

   (ii)   to third party facilities.

However, the policy can be extended to cover such losses arising from damage to other premises upon which there is a dependency and property away from own premises.

(*c*)   Material damage insurance provision — it is a condition of business interruption insurance that there must be a material damage insurance in force:

   (i)   protecting the interest of the insured;

   (ii)   covering the property which has suffered damage; and

   (iii)   the material damage insurers must have accepted liability.

(*d*)   Material damage provision waiver — the material damage insurance provision does not apply:

   (i)   in circumstances where the material damage insurers avoid liability under their policy solely because the material damage loss falls below an excess or franchise and is therefore not recoverable under the policy; and

(ii)   to property in which the insured has no insurable interest e.g. property owned by a third party.

Policy coverage

13.38   There are three main types of business interruption policy.

(*a*)   Increased Cost of Working Only Policy — this type of policy covers the additional expenditure reasonably incurred by the insured in order to minimise interruption to the business. It offers no protection for loss of income suffered. This basis of cover is only appropriate if it is possible to continue operating, at increased cost, following an incident without any effect on turnover.

(*b*)   Gross Revenue Policy — this type of policy covers loss of revenue and any increased costs incurred to avoid or reduce a loss of revenue which would otherwise be incurred. It is necessary for such costs to be economic (i.e. costs incurred do not exceed revenue loss avoided). Insurers will normally exclude the element of variable costs which may reduce after an incident (e.g. savings in electricity consumption costs).

(*c*)   Gross Profit (or Net Revenue) Policy — this type of policy covers loss of gross profit and any increased costs incurred in avoiding or reducing a loss in gross profit providing such costs are economic. Under a gross profit policy, it is necessary to specify these costs payable out of turnover that will be uninsured. To avoid underinsurance it is necessary to deduct only costs which are directly and proportionally variable with turnover under both a total and partial loss scenario (i.e. a 10% decrease in turnover should be accompanied by the same percentage reduction in the cost). Insurable gross profit is different to accounting gross profit, particularly in the treatment of wages, as all salaries and payroll are insured in full.

Average

13.39   The insurance for increased cost of working only does not include either an average provision or an inflation provision. Business interruption insurance covering revenue or gross profit comes in two forms; one subject to average and one with no such provision.

The conventional form of cover in respect of gross profit and revenue includes an average provision. Therefore, if the sum insured is inadequate the insured will bear a share of the loss. There is no in-built provision for inflation during the period of insurance or the indemnity period.

Both gross profit and revenue cover may also be written on a non-average form known as the declaration linked approach. This method requires an estimate, calculated on a basis laid down in the policy, to be declared to insurers at the start of the period of insurance. The insured then benefits from an inflation provision up to 133 1/3% of declared value.

The non average declaration linked form has significant advantages which include:

(*a*)   no penalty for underinsurance providing the declared value has been arrived at in accordance with the policy terms;

(*b*)   automatic provision for inflation during both the period of insurance and the indemnity period;

(*c*)   values based on current financial forecasts avoiding the need to accurately project income in future years; and

(*d*)   possibly, lower premiums because of a lower value declared to insurers.

Maximum indemnity period

13.40   In addition to a monetary limit, the sum insured or limit of liability, there is a time limit, the maximum indemnity period. The indemnity period commences on the date of the damage and ceases when the results of the business are no longer being affected, providing this does not exceed a predetermined limit known as the maximum indemnity period. Hence it is not possible to claim for an indefinite interruption.

To establish an adequate maximum indemnity period consideration should be given to the period in which not only loss of income might be suffered but also additional costs incurred. The period needs to assume a catastrophic incident occurs (such as a major fire or explosion), and make allowance for:

(*a*)   debris removal, planning application and rebuild (where buildings are involved);

(*b*)   lead times for delivery (where machinery and equipment are involved);

(*c*)   additional allowance for any statutory or public authority requirements and any testing and commissioning; and

(*d*)   any additional period for recapture of lost market share.

The maximum indemnity period also needs to cater for on going expenses for which there are contractual obligations e.g. lease and rent payments, to ensure such payments are protected for the maximum period contractually required.

The maximum indemnity period is normally defined in multiples of six months (e.g. 12, 18, 24 months etc.) but there are generally no premium savings in selecting an indemnity period of less than 12 months.

Minimum requirements

13.41 It is recommended that, as a minimum, the business interruption policy provides the following:

(*a*) automatic reinstatement — automatic reinstatement of sum insured after a loss;

(*b*) payments on account — interim payments throughout the indemnity period; and

(*c*) professional accountancy fees — costs payable to professional accountants in providing and certifying particulars requested by insurers which form the basis of claim.

Extensions

13.42 The standard business interruption policy covers consequential loss during the indemnity period as a result of:

(*a*) physical damage which is insured;

(*b*) to property used by the insured;

(*c*) which is at the premises of the insured.

There are a number of types of scenarios which are not covered by the standard policy wording but which can be covered by specific extensions at additional premium. These include interruption suffered as a result of:

(i) a non damage incident such as bomb threat;

(ii) damage in the vicinity of the premises causing denial of access or a reduction in the number of customers in the area;

(iii) damage to customer premises resulting in a reduction in demand for the product;

(iv) damage to a suppliers' premises causing a shortfall in raw material or services provided; and

(v) failure of utility supplies such as electricity, telecommunications, gas and water.

There are certain financial losses not catered for adequately by the standard business interruption policy but which also can be covered by specific extension at additional premium. These include:

(A) delay to income as a result of damage to property to be used at a future date;

(B) uneconomic additional expenditure incurred in maintaining the business;

(C) fines and penalties payable to third parties as a result of non performance of contract terms because of the insured damage;

(D)   continuing research and development costs; and

(E)   inability to recover outstanding debts because of destruction of debtor records.

Third party liability

The risk

13.43   An organisation may incur liability in a number of ways which include:

(*a*)   negligence — omission to do something which a reasonable person would do or doing something which a prudent person would not do;

(*b*)   nuisance — unlawfully disturbing a person's enjoyment of their property;

(*c*)   trespass — an unlawful act committed with force on the person or property of another;

(*d*)   strict liability — where the defendant will be liable even though reasonable care has been exercised;

(*e*)   contractual liability — amendments to common law liability assumed under the terms of a written contract;

(*f*)   statutory liability — liabilities created by Acts of Parliament; and

(*g*)   vicarious liability — where responsibility is assumed for the torts of others.

Policy coverage

13.44   Public liability insurance protects an insured against legal liability for death of or bodily injury to third parties or loss of or damage to their property which happens in connection with the insured's activities. Product liability insurance indemnifies an insured against legal liability for death or bodily injury to third parties, or loss of or damage to their property caused by goods sold, supplied, repaired or serviced by the insured. The policies are commonly linked.

The policies will also indemnify the insured in respect of costs which the claimant has incurred as a result of the incident. This amount is usually in addition to the limit of indemnity (other than in North America).

Public and product liability insurance are both subject to territorial limits which stipulate where the death, injury or damage must occur for the policy to apply. It is important for the territorial limits to be sufficiently wide and ideally to be worldwide. Additionally, cover may be subject to a jurisdiction clause making reference to where actions by claimants against the insured may be covered by the policy. Similarly, the jurisdiction clause should be as wide as is possible to negotiate.

Most insurers exclude all claims arising out of pollution or contamination in North America. For other parts of the world, cover will normally not apply unless the claim arises out of a sudden, unintended, unexpected or unforeseen occurrence which takes place entirely at a specific time and place. Additionally any pollution and contamination cover will be subject to a limit of indemnity for the entire period of the insurance.

Basis of cover

13.45   Public and product liability insurance can be available on a claims made or loss occurring basis. There are significant differences between the way these two types of coverage respond to claims:

(*a*)   the claims made basis provides cover for claims made in writing to the insured during the policy period irrespective of when the incident or cause giving rise to the claim occurred; and

(*b*)   the loss occurring basis responds to death, injury or damage caused to third parties during the period of insurance. The claim on the insured does not need to be made during this period.

The loss occurring basis is the form which is normally utilised in the UK.

Limit of indemnity

13.46   Both public liability insurance and products liability insurance are subject to limits of indemnity, but the way in which these operate differs:

(*a*)   under public liability insurance the limit of indemnity is the maximum that the insurer will pay out in respect of any one event which gives rise to a claim; and

(*b*)   in respect of product liability insurance the limit of indemnity is the maximum that will be paid in respect of all events in any one period of insurance.

Minimum requirements

13.47   As a minimum the public/product liability coverage should include:

(*a*)   additional insureds — individual indemnity should be provided to directors, officers and employees, sport, social, first aid or medical staff, ambulance and fire services;

(*b*)   cross liabilities — where the policy is in the name of more than one insured this makes it clear that liability of one insured to another is covered;

(*c*)   indemnity to principals — where contractual obligations require this provides indemnity to a principal;

(*d*)   tenant's legal liability — legal liability in respect of premises leased or rented to the insured;

(*e*)   Defective Premises Act 1972 — liability for newly built, converted or adapted dwellings and landlord's liability for defects in premises;

(*f*)   Consumer Protection Act 1987 — strict liability in respect of products supplied where an injured party need only prove that he has suffered injury caused by a defective product to be able to claim against the producer;

(*g*)   Data Protection Act 1984 — liability arising out of the misuse of information retained about individuals on computer systems;

(*h*)   overseas personal liability — personal liability for the insured's employees when outside the UK on business.

Extensions

13.48   There are a number of types of liability which are excluded from the standard public/product liability policy but which can be included in certain circumstances. These include, *inter alia*:

(*a*)   contractual liability — liability assumed under contract which would not otherwise have existed;

(*b*)   property in insured's charge or control — inclusion of property belonging to others on which the insured is temporarily performing work;

(*c*)   financial loss — liability for financial loss not dependent upon injury to persons or damage to property;

(*d*)   contingent motor liability — legal liability arising out of a vehicle not owned or provided by the insured but used on the insured's behalf;

(*e*)   design, plan or formula — liability arising out of defective design, plan, formula or specification of goods;

(*f*)   labels and instructions — liability arising out of labels, pamphlets, instructions or other written material;

(*g*)   product recall — expenses incurred in recalling or withdrawing a defective product from the market; and

(*h*)   product guarantee — liability arising out of failure of a product to perform its intended purpose.

Professional indemnity

The risk

13.49   Liability may arise from a breach of contract for services between a professional party and a client. It is implied in a contract for professional services that the professional will exercise a fair, reasonable and competent degree of care and skill. Any failure to do so which causes a loss to the client may result in the professional being sued for professional negligence. Case law has established that a professional may also owe a duty of care to another party who relies on the advice given. The standard of care expected of a professional person is the standard expected of an average member of his particular profession.

It is increasingly common for professionals to seek insurance to cover liability which may arise from a damages claim brought by a client. In the past such cover only tended to be sought by accountants, solicitors and architects. In the increasingly litigious climate, very few professionals now consider themselves safe. The number of actions for professional negligence has increased dramatically over recent years and damages and costs have spiralled, resulting in escalating costs of insurance and reduced availability in relation to certain professions.

Policy coverage

13.50   The professional indemnity policy is designed to protect professional persons or others, who supply a skill or service, against their legal liability to compensate any third party who has sustained some form of injury, loss or damage due to their professional negligence. Cover is intended to apply to unintentional forms of conduct and does not include dishonest, fraudulent, criminal or malicious acts.

The professional indemnity cover provided is subject to claims arising within specific geographical limits. The geographical limits within a professional indemnity policy should be sufficiently wide to include all territories where a claim could arise.

Basis of cover

13.51   Professional indemnity insurance is provided on a claims made basis. Provided the actual claim is made during the period of insurance it does not matter when the act of negligence giving rise to the claim took place. The policy may provide retrospective cover for acts of negligence committed prior to a specified date. Consequently an insured will be required to disclose all potential occurrences which may give rise to a claim in the future. Similar strict reporting requirements apply at each renewal. Failure to disclose a potential occurrence could prejudice cover.

The policy may also cover claims intimated during a discovery period after the expiry date of the policy. This is in respect of negligence occurring during the period of insurance for which claims are not made until after the policy ends.

Limit of indemnity

13.52   The limit of indemnity will normally be a total limit for the entire period of insurance. In the event of a claim it is therefore necessary to reinstate the limit which has been eroded. Some insurers will offer a prepaid reinstatement at the time of setting up the policy. Costs and expenses incurred in the defence or settlement of any claim may be in addition to this limit, or included. It is common practice for policies to impose a degree of financial involvement by the professional should any damages claim be upheld.

Extensions

13.53 There are a number of types of exposure which are not covered under the standard professional indemnity policy but which may be included in certain circumstances. These include:

(*a*) dishonesty of employees — legal liability to others arising out of the dishonesty of employees (but not partners or directors);

(*b*) libel and slander — legal liability in respect of libel or slander to title of goods and infringement of trademark, copyright or patent from matter contained in publications;

(*c*) breach of warranty of authority — liability to a third party if the insured caused the third party to act on the strength of the insured's supposed authority;

(*d*) loss or damage to documents — all risks cover on documents belonging to the insured or for which the insured is responsible; and

(*e*) incoming/outgoing partners — liability for partners in respect of work performed in a previous practice/continuing liability for work performed once they have left.

Directors' and officers' liability

The risk

13.54 Both executive and non-executive directors owe a duty of skill and care to both the company and to others.

Legal liability may arise from breaches of this duty such as:

(*a*) negligent misstatements;

(*b*) failure to carry out statutory responsibilities;

(*c*) making unauthorised payments or allowing excessive company borrowing;

(*d*) errors of judgement arising from a conflict of interest; and

(*e*) through guarantees given in the course of business.

There are a variety of people or groups of people who can bring actions against directors and officers. These include:

(i) shareholders;

(ii) the company;

(iii)   the Department of Trade and Industry;

(iv)   a receiver/liquidator;

 (v)   company creditors; and

(vi)   regulatory bodies.

The Companies Act 1985 provides that a company may indemnify any director or officer of the company against any indemnity incurred by him in defending any proceedings (civil or criminal) in which judgment is given in his favour or he is granted relief by the court.

Prior to the Companies Act 1989, there was doubt as to whether it was lawful for companies to purchase and maintain such indemnity policies on behalf of their directors or officers. However, companies may now purchase such policies, subject to the disclosure of their existence in the directors' report to the annual accounts.

Policy coverage

13.55   A directors' and officers' policy provides cover under two sections:

(*a*)   one part protects the directors and officers in their personal capacity in circumstances where they cannot claim an indemnity from the company; and

(*b*)   the second part indemnifies the company in respect of costs and expenses it may have incurred in successfully defending a director or officer under the relevant sections of the Companies Act.

Basis of cover

13.56   Directors' and officers' insurance operates on a claims made basis protecting directors and officers in respect of claims made against them during the period of insurance arising out of any wrongful act committed in their respective capacities.

Limit of indemnity

13.57   The limit of indemnity is a total limit for all claims under the policy during the period of insurance and is inclusive of costs and expenses incurred in the defence or settlement of any claim.

Basic requirement

13.58   The directors' and officers' insurance should ideally reflect the following:

(*a*)   insured persons — the policy should provide blanket coverage for all past, present and future directors and officers of the company;

(*b*) company — the policy should include all subsidiary companies created or acquired on or before the inception date of the policy period;

(*c*) legal costs — the policy should include the provision for insurers to provide payment of defence costs as these are incurred; and

(*d*) directors' estates — the policy should automatically provide indemnity for claims made against the estates, heirs, legal representatives of the insured persons in the event of their death, incapacity or bankruptcy.

The standard directors and officers liability policy can be extended to include other areas of cover such as:

(i) protection for individual directors or officers of the company whilst acting in the capacity of a director or officer of another unrelated company; and

(ii) employment practices liability, such as claims arising from unlawful dismissal, sexual harassment, sexual/racial discrimination etc.

Exclusions

13.59 Cover does not apply to losses arising out of dishonesty, fraud or illegal personal profit. Additionally, standard exclusions include:

(*a*) pollution and contamination;

(*b*) bodily injury/property damage;

(*c*) libel and slander;

(*d*) insured versus insured (i.e. the company suing a director or one director suing another);

(*e*) guarantees and warranties;

(*f*) professional liability; and

(*g*) fines and penalties.

Exclusions may vary between insurers, and it may be possible to modify these exclusions to some extent through negotiation and the payment of an additional premium.

Crime insurance

The risk

13.60 A fraudulent or dishonest action of an employee or third party may result in loss of money or property. The risk may vary from low level pilferage by individuals to a major conspiracy between a group of employees, or a major funds transfer fraud carried out by a member of the public.

Policy coverage

13.61   Crime insurance is designed to indemnify the insured against direct financial loss arising from the deliberate fraud or dishonesty of an employee or third party.

Basis of the cover

13.62   The crime policy provides cover for direct financial loss arising from fraud or dishonesty committed during the period of indemnity, which is discovered either during the period of indemnity, or within a stipulated time period, normally 24 months after expiry of the period of indemnity or the cessation of the employment of the employee, whichever occurs first. The period of indemnity is the time during which the policy has been in force, not only the current year, but also any preceding years.

In addition to payment of the loss, insurers generally accept fees and expenses incurred in connection with a claim. The limit of indemnity under the policy will be inclusive of such costs.

When arranging crime insurance, it is usual for insurers to request the completion of a proposal form which sets out the systems of check that are in place to protect the business against the consequences of fraud or dishonesty.

In addition to electronic funds transfer fraud, a crime policy can be extended to cover other forms of loss such as:

(*a*)   loss or damage to money or other property including that arising from theft, mysterious unexplained disappearance; and

(*b*)   loss or damage to money or property whilst in transit.

Limit of indemnity

13.63   The usual practice is to limit the indemnity to a specified amount.

Engineering

The risk

13.64   Many organisations incur risks and responsibilities arising out of the use of boiler and pressure plant, lifting equipment, electrical equipment, mechanical machinery and computers.

The movement and installation of plant and machinery can additionally result in the loss of assets, the interruption of activities or liabilities being incurred.

Policy coverage

13.65   Engineering policy coverage may be subdivided between:

(*a*)   the inspection of plant to comply with legislation; and

(*b*)   the insurance of plant and equipment against damage or breakdown.

Basis of cover

13.66   The usual basis of cover will depend on the type of plant being insured.

(*a*)   Inspection — periodical inspection of plant may be required:

    (i)   to ensure the plant complies with the statutory requirements;

    (ii)   to meet the Health and Safety Commission's Guidance Notes, and Industry Codes of Practice;

    (iii)   to meet the operator's own needs to avoid faults, breakdowns and stoppages; and

    (iv)   to ensure the plant is in a suitable state of repair and adequately maintained for insurance purposes (if it is insured).

Legislation stipulates the maximum periods between inspection of particular types of plant. An insured may elect for more frequent inspection and the inspection of plant not subject to statutory inspection, particularly in circumstances where the plant is of a critical nature. Inspection services are available for most types of plant, whether or not the plant is actually insured.

(*b*)   Boiler/pressure plant — this covers all types of boiler and vessels which are subject to internal pressure. Cover may either operate:

    (i)   on a limited basis covering explosion or collapse only; or

    (ii)   on a wider basis covering sudden and unforeseen damage arising from any cause not specifically excluded.

In respect of steam plant, the policy should also cover damage to own surrounding property and third party liability arising from a steam explosion.

(*c*)   Lifts and lifting equipment — this covers lifts, cranes, hoists and all types of lifting and handling equipment. Cover is available for sudden and unforeseen damage arising from any cause not specifically excluded and/or breakdown.

Cover can additionally be extended to include:

    (i)   damage to own surrounding property (either in consequence of damage to the equipment or arising out of the use of the equipment); and

(ii)   goods being lifted or carried by the equipment (either in consequence of damage to the equipment or arising out of the use of the equipment).

(*d*) Electrical and mechanical machinery — this covers all types of electrical and mechanical equipment including alternators, electric motors, engines, switchgear, compressors, electric pumps, turbines and fans. Cover is available for sudden and unforeseen damage arising from any cause not specifically excluded and/or breakdown. For high speed rotational items of plant the coverage can be extended to include own surrounding property.

(*e*) All plant and machinery — where an insured utilises boiler/pressure plant, lifts and lifting equipment and electrical and mechanical machinery, it is common practice to insure all plant at the premises on a sudden and unforeseen basis and breakdown.

(*f*) Computers — this covers all computer equipment, interconnecting cabling, telecommunication equipment, ancillary equipment and computer media. Cover is generally available in respect of:

(i)   hardware and associated plant;

(ii)   computer system records;

(iii)   reinstatement of data; and

(iv)   increased cost of working or business interruption.

Many computer policies specifically include additional benefits such as:

(A)   accidental or malicious erasure, distortion or corruption of information on computer system records (e.g. by computer virus or disgruntled employees);

(B)   incompatibility of computer systems records with replacement hardware;

(C)   consulting engineers' repairs and investigations;

(D)   avoidance measures impending loss;

(E)   temporary repairs;

(F)   property in transit/away for own premises;

(G)   continuing rental costs;

(H)   denial of access;

(I)   failure or fluctuation in electricity supply;

(J)   failure in distribution wiring; and

(K)   failure of telecommunications and data transmission systems.

(*g*) Machinery movement — this cover can be tailored to cater for damage to machinery whilst being dismantled, erected or whilst in transit. Cover can either operate on a 'one off' basis for a specified period of time or as an annually renewable contract. Special consideration needs to be given where the transit is by sea or air.

(*h*)   Erection, all risks — this provides cover against physical loss, destruction or damage to machinery and plant during transit/delivery to site, installation, erection and testing up until completion. Cover may specifically extend to include the maintenance period.

(*j*)   Machinery, consequential loss — this covers loss of gross profit and/or increased cost of working following sudden and unforeseen damage and/or breakdown to plant or machinery. Cover can either be arranged on all plant and machinery or be restricted to specified items. In circumstances where loss, destruction or damage to new plant prior to use and production could result in delayed or lost income and increased costs, consideration should be given to advance profit cover.

Personal accident

The risk

13.67   Everybody faces the risk of death and disablement arising out of an accident at work or home, whilst travelling or participating in hobbies or sports. Such an incident can cause the injured person and/or their dependants to suffer loss of income and/or incur extra costs. If the injured person is temporarily disabled their employer may have to maintain salary payments and employ a temporary replacement.

Policy coverage

13.68   In the event of accidental bodily injury resulting in an insured person's death or permanent total disablement from any occupation within a specified time period (normally 12 or 24 months), the policy pays a fixed monetary sum or multiple of salary. A percentage of the lump sum is paid in the event of permanent partial disablement such as total loss of sight in one eye or total loss of one limb. Weekly benefits are payable, normally for a maximum of 104 weeks, in the event of temporary, total or partial disablement. The weekly benefits may be subject to a time excess or franchise before they become payable. Coverage may either be provided by way of a stand alone personal accident policy or an extension of other insurance policies such as motor or money policies.

Basis of cover

13.69   Coverage is normally arranged on a group scheme basis to cover all employees of specified categories under a certain age and operates world-wide. Whilst benefits are normally based on multiples of salary, or percentages thereof, there will usually be a maximum limit in respect of any one person, and a separate limit in respect of an accumulation of employees killed or injured whilst travelling in an aircraft.

Coverage can be arranged on a 24 hour basis or be restricted to specified times and events, such as occupational accidents, non-occupational accidents, travel excluding commuting, sports, hobbies, criminal violence etc.

Coverage may extend to include legal expenses to pursue actions against negligent third parties causing bodily injury.

The lump sum payment for permanent total disablement will be dependent on the extent of coverage. The permanent total disablement may be:

(*a*)   from gainful employment of any and every kind;

(*b*)   from the insured's usual occupation and any other occupation for which the insured person is fitted by knowledge and training; or

(*c*)   from the insured person's usual occupation.

Extension to basic policy coverage may be available in respect of:

 (i)   risks arising out of business travel outside the UK, such as medical expenses, baggage, personal effects and money, personal liability, cancellation and curtailment and replacement/rearrangement costs; and

(ii)   sickness resulting in temporary total disablement of the insured person from their usual occupation.

Key man

The risk

13.70   Many companies rely heavily on certain key directors and employees. Loss of such persons due to ill-health, disability or death can have a dramatic effect on a company due to:

(*a*)   lost orders from personal contacts;

(*b*)   loss of investor and bank confidence;

(*c*)   costs incurred in finding and training a replacement;

(*d*)   disablement costs such as salary and pension contributions; and

(*e*)   general loss of confidence.

Overview of policy

13.71   A policy can be taken out to cover these risks provided there is an insurable interest (i.e. the key man's function is vital) and that the level and period of cover is reasonable. The level of cover will normally be set at a multiple of salary.

The policy is not normally a personal benefit for the key person or the estate but a method of protecting the company. It can take the form of term assurance, life endowment assurance, health assurance or disability cover. The benefits can be taken in the form of a lump sum on death, instalments, or a regular income for disability.

Chapter 14

Employment, Health and Safety

Employment legislation

14.1   Employment law is today recognised by company administrators as being of the greatest importance. Legislation in recent years has transformed the law in this area, and has created new statutory rights for employees and obligations for employers. The European Union (EU) and the decisions of the European Court have had, and will continue to play an important role in the development of the UK's domestic employment law. The employment section of this chapter seeks to outline the legislation governing individual employment i.e. that directly applying between employees and employers, along with the common law and EU law on relevant employment matters.

The legal rules governing employment law are derived from three principal sources:

(*a*)   the common law — including the law of contract pursuant to which the contract of employment is enforced, and the law of torts (wrongful acts which cause damage or loss) which governs, for example, an employer's liability for the acts of his employees, and civil liability for industrial accidents and for forms of industrial action;

(*b*)   statute law — i.e. Acts of Parliament and regulations (statutory instruments), which operate outside the contract; and

(*c*)   European legislation and judgments of the European Court of Justice (ECJ).

The Employment Rights Act 1996 (ERA 1996) and the Industrial Tribunals Act 1996 (now known as the Employment Tribunals Act 1996 (ETA 1996)) received Royal Assent on 22 May 1996 and came into force on 22 August 1996. These Acts make no substantive changes to employment law as it stood prior to 22 August 1996, but collected together previous legislation on 'individual' employment rights which were previously scattered across various statutes. The Acts repeal, either in whole or in part, the following statutes:

(i)   Employment Protection (Consolidation) Act 1978 (EP(C)A 1978);

(ii)   Wages Act 1986 (WA 1986);

(iii)   Trade Union Reform and Employment Rights Act 1993 (TURERA);

(iv)   Sunday Trading Act 1994.

Certain legislative provisions remain unaffected by the ERA 1996 consolidation exercise, including:

(A)   Equal Pay Act 1970 (EPA 1970);

(B)   Sex Discrimination Act 1975 (SDA 1975);

(C)   Race Relations Act 1976 (RRA 1976);

(D)   Transfer of Undertakings (Protection of Employment) Regulations 1981 (TUPE 1981); and

(E)   Disability Discrimination Act 1995 (DDA 1995).

The main legislation dealing with 'collective' employment rights i.e. trade unions and trade disputes is the Trade Union and Labour Relations (Consolidation) Act 1992 (TULR(C)A 1992), as amended by the Trade Union Reform and Employment Rights Act 1993 (TURERA 1993). Other relevant employment legislation now in force includes the Employment Rights (Dispute Resolution) Act 1998, the National Minimum Wage Act 1998 (see 14.71 below), the Public Interest Disclosure Act 1998 (see 14.77 below), and the Working Time Regulations 1998.

On 27 July 1999, the Employment Relations Act 1999 received Royal Assent. Among other matters, the Act will give trade unions a statutory right to recognition by an employer for collective bargaining purposes; make provision for maternity and parental leave, in accordance with the requirements of the EU Parental Leave Directive; extend the protection against unfair dismissal for employees dismissed for taking official industrial action; and increase the maximum compensatory award in unfair dismissal cases from £12,000 to £50,000. At the time of writing, none of the Act's provisions are in force; different sections of the Act are likely to come into force on different dates. The main provisions of the Act are summarised in an Appendix at the end of this chapter.

Also on 27 July 1999, the Disability Rights Commission Act 1999 received Royal Assent. It will set up a Disability Rights Commission with statutory powers similar to those enjoyed by the Commission for Racial Equality and the Equal Opportunities Commission. Again, this Act is not yet in force.

Finally, another Act which is likely to be of considerable relevance to employment law is the Human Rights Act 1998, which will incorporate the European Convention on Human Rights and Fundamental Freedoms into UK law. At the end of May 1999, the Home Secretary announced that the Act would be brought fully into force on 2 October 2000.

Administration of employment legislation

14.2   Employment law is primarily administered by tribunals as opposed to the courts. These tribunals, previously called industrial tribunals, were renamed employment tribunals by the Employment Rights (Dispute Resolution) Act 1998. There is a right of appeal from employment tribunals to the Employment Appeal Tribunal (EAT) and from there to the Court of Appeal and the House of Lords. The employment tribunals were established to act as informal courts consisting of a legally qualified chairperson and two members, representing the interests of the employer and the employee. A considerable body of tribunal decisions has grown up around the interpretation of the legislation.

The Employment Tribunals Act 1996 consolidated the previous law on employment tribunals. The Act covers amongst other matters the composition of tribunals (ETA 1996, s 4), procedure adopted in tribunals (ETA 1996, ss 6–15) and the membership, procedure and jurisdiction of the Employment Appeal Tribunal (ETA 1996, ss 20–37).

The Advisory, Conciliation and Arbitration Service (ACAS) was established by the Employment Protection Act 1975, s 1 (now consolidated as ss 247–253, Trade Union and Labour Relations (Consolidation) Act 1992). Its role is primarily to bring about an improvement in industrial relations between workers and employers. It does this both by conciliating on trade disputes and on matters which may be brought before an employment tribunal.

The Employment Rights (Dispute Resolution) Act 1998 received Royal Assent on 8 April 1998 and most of its provisions are now in force. As mentioned above, the Act has renamed industrial tribunals as 'employment tribunals'. With effect from 1 January 1999, the Act also empowers tribunals to increase or decrease compensation in unfair dismissal cases where the employee was denied, or did not make use of, an internal appeal procedure where the effective date of termination was on or after that date. In addition, the Act contains provisions for ACAS to draw up a voluntary binding arbitration scheme as an alternative to tribunal proceedings in unfair dismissal cases. However, at the time of writing, the scheme for arbitration has yet to be published in its final form and, at that stage, an Order by the Secretary of State will need to be made to give legal effect to the scheme.

An employee or not?

14.3   Whether an individual is, in law, an employee or not is one of the most regularly reviewed, and yet least clear issues in employment law. Every company secretary must know which persons employed are 'employees' for the purposes of his/her company's rights and obligations under employment law. Whether an employee is an 'employee' has a crucial bearing on various matters such as the tax treatment of the employee's remuneration, the coverage of employers' liability insurance policies, and the application of health and safety law. Whilst an individual's status as an employee or not has always been important in determining the ability to claim unfair dismissal or a statutory redundancy entitlement (see 14.74 and 14.76 below), it has become even more important due to certain developments including:

(*a*)   the fact that the hours threshold for claiming such employment protection (i.e. unfair dismissal and redundancy entitlement — see 14.74, 14.76 below) has been removed following the House of Lords' decision in *R v Secretary of State for Employment ex parte Equal Opportunities Commission* [*1994*] *IRLR 176;*

(*b*)   the introduction of the right to claim automatic unfair dismissal without the need to establish any length of service, for instance, on the grounds that the dismissal was occasioned by:

   (i)   the employee's assertion of a statutory right (ERA 1996, s 104);

   (ii)   the employee's performance of his duties as a health and safety representative (ERA 1996, s 100);

(*c*)   the recent reduction of the qualifying period of continuous employment for an employee to qualify for protection against unfair dismissal, from two years to one year (see 14.74 below).

(See also 14.27 below, which considers the position of temporary and fixed contract employees.)

The traditional test of whether an individual is an employee is whether he works under a contract of employment or a contract of service. Others, e.g. consultants and independent contractors who work under contracts for services, are not employees. The labels which the parties adopt for their relationships are not conclusive. In *Hall v Lorimer* [*1994*] *ICR 218* the Court of Appeal decided that there is no single approach which is appropriate. The following 'tests' are looked at by the courts in determining the relationship.

(A)   The control test — this looks at the extent that the employer controls the worker i.e. his ability to tell the individual how and when to do his work (*Performing Rights Society v Mitchell and Booker* [*1924*] *1 KB 762*). This test, however, is only seen as being of real assistance in relation to unskilled workers.

(B)   The organisational test — this looks at whether the individual was part of, as opposed to accessory to, the employer's business (*Stevenson Jordan and Harrison Ltd v MacDonald and Evans* [*1952*] *1 TLR 101*).

(C)   The mixed test — this looks at the entire relationship and its circumstances, in which control is only one element (*Ready Mixed Concrete (South East) Ltd v Minister of Pensions* [*1968*] *2 QB 497*).

Relevant factors include:

   (I)   the parties' practice concerning tax;

   (II)   the responsibility for expenses and equipment;

   (III)   whether the employee performs exclusive service for the person for whom he works;

   (IV)   whether there is any obligation to provide or perform work;

(V)   the opportunity for the individual to profit from the performance of the organisation for which he works;

(VI)   his degree of financial risk; and

(VII)   his responsibility for investment and management.

Recently, the Court of Appeal held in *Express and Echo Publications Ltd v Tanton [1999] IRLR 367* that in the absence of a personal obligation on the worker to do work (i.e. where the worker can provide a substitute), the contract is not a contract of employment.

Employing new staff

The advertisement

14.4   Generally, anything said in an advertisement does not form part of the employment contract. However, in some cases the courts have used advertisements as an aid to interpreting the contract, when the contract was silent on an important term, or where a term was ambiguous. For instance, in *Financial Techniques (Planning Services) Ltd v Hughes [1981] IRLR 32*, the contract of employment (see 14.13 below) failed to mention a profit-sharing scheme that had been described in detail in the advertisement, so the Court of Appeal implied a term (see 14.14 below for further details on implied terms).

Interviews — asking the right questions

14.5   In employment law there is a difference in law between lying when asked direct and specific questions and failing to offer information which may otherwise be relevant. As a general rule there is no obligation on a job candidate to offer information, the onus is on the employer to ask the right questions. In *Walton v TAC Construction Materials Ltd [1981] IRLR 357*, the EAT held that 'it would not be said that there is any duty on the employee in the ordinary case, though there may be exceptions, to volunteer information about himself otherwise than in response to a direct question'. Company secretaries conducting interviews should diligently read submitted CVs or application forms for 'gaps' or unexplained occurrences, and ask the candidate directly about the circumstances.

The provisions of the Rehabilitation of Offenders Act 1974 should also be considered in this context. This Act sets limits on the extent to which an employer may take into account the criminal convictions of an applicant when making an appointment. Subject to certain exceptions, where a conviction is 'spent' within the terms of the Act, a question put to an applicant at an interview (or on an application form) about his past criminal convictions may be answered on the basis that it does not refer to a spent conviction, and it is not lawful to exclude an applicant from employment if he has failed to disclose a spent conviction. The exceptions (specified by various statutory instruments) broadly relate to entry into certain professions, such as doctors, nurses, dentists, lawyers and accountants, and employment (i) in specific areas of the financial sector, (ii) in jobs connected with the administration of justice, and (iii) in the social and health services, and in teaching, where there is access to clients, patients and children. Where an applicant is being interviewed for a post which is covered by one of the specified exceptions, then provided that the questions being asked in the interview are in order to assess the suitability of the applicant for the post and he is informed that spent convictions must be disclosed, the applicant will be obliged to answer any questions about previous convictions, whether or not they are spent, and failure to disclose them would constitute a valid reason not to employ him.

Employees lying at interview

14.6   Lying at an interview can be grounds for fair dismissal by an employer. In the case of *O'Brian v Prudential Assurance Co Ltd* [*1979*] *IRLR 140*, Mr O'Brian was held to have been fairly dismissed after lying at his medical about his previous mental illness. When his employers found out about it, they dismissed him as he was an insurance salesman visiting people's homes. Even though he had two years of exemplary service the Employment Appeal Tribunal (EAT) did not overturn the original decision of fair dismissal. In *Torr v British Railways Board* [*1977*] *IRLR 174*, Mr Torr was held to have been fairly dismissed from his job as a railway guard, when his employers discovered that he had been sent to prison for three years. The EAT held that 'It is of the utmost importance than an employer seeking an employee to hold a post of responsibility and trust should be able to select for employment a candidate in whom he can have confidence. It is fundamental to that confidence that the employee should truthfully disclose his history so far as it is sought by the intending employer'.

Checking credentials

14.7   Recruiters cannot rely upon intuition of the interviewing panel or the 'old school tie'. Apart from the issues of sex, race and disability discrimination (see 14.35–14.40 below), recruiters may need to play detective about a candidate's background. Some employers require candidates to bring with them to their interview, their certificates of school and higher education qualifications. It may also be regarded as a criminal offence for an employee to lie about a qualification in order to obtain or keep his employment, especially where professional qualifications are required to do the job (*R v Callender* (unreported)). Professional qualifications can often be checked by searching the relevant professional register.

Until 1984 employers were only vicariously liable for the negligent acts their employees committed in the course of their employment (see 14.33 below). However, in 1984, the High Court ruled that the employer was liable for criminal acts. In *Hicks v Pier House (Cheyne Walk) Management Co Ltd* (*unreported*), a porter had been employed in a position of trust, yet his references had not been taken up. Had the employers done any form of check, they should have discovered large periods of unemployment due to being in prison. The employers were held vicariously liable for the cost of jewellery, and the interest on that sum, stolen from Mrs Hicks.

Making promises at interviews

14.8   Assuming the recruiter has the authority to make offers or promises about the job at the interview, an oral promise may be binding. Company secretaries should pay particular attention to this point to avoid binding the company. For illustration, in the case of *Hawker Siddeley v Rump* [*1979*] *IRLR 425*, Mr Rump's oral promise at his interview that he would not have to be mobile was held to be a binding term. This was despite the fact that the written term of his contract which he later signed stated that he did have to be mobile. The court held that since nobody had pointed out that the earlier term no longer applied, that this was an implied promise and took precedence over the conflicting written term (see 14.14 below for implied terms).

Making representations

14.9   In normal cases where a person applies for a job advertised in the media, he/she is deemed to hold themselves out to be competent for that job. However, where a job is barely described in the advertisement and is one for which an applicant could not be expected to know whether he is or is not competent, interviewing managers must take care not to make misrepresentations about the job or the ability of the applicant to do it. A recruiter who makes a misrepresentation which induces a person to enter into a contract may be sued for any losses sustained by him as a result of that misrepresentation, under the Misrepresentation Act 1967. The misrepresentation does not need to be fraudulent for the plaintiff to succeed, but there is a defence that, at the time the person made the representation, he had reasonable grounds to believe and did believe, up until the contract was made, the facts represented were true.

References

14.10   Employers usually make offers of employment subject to the receipt of 'satisfactory' references. On the face of it, it appears that there should be no dispute if the reference(s) do not satisfy the prospective employer. In fact, an employer has a duty to review the reference 'in good faith'. (See also 14.25 below.) In *Wishart v National Association of Citizens' Advice Bureaux (NACAB)* [*1990*] *IRLR 393*, Mr Wishart was turned down for a job of information officer because his references disclosed an alarming history of sickness absence. His explanation for this was that he had Hepatitis B. However, upon investigation, it was discovered that he had tested negative. In the light of the inconsistent explanations, his job offer was withdrawn on the basis of unsatisfactory references. He then sought an interlocutory injunction seeking to restrain the alleged breach of contract. The Court of Appeal held:

'Where an offer of employment is conditional upon "satisfactory" references being furnished, it is likely to have a subjective meaning to the defendant. It is highly probable that no objective test is applicable and that there is no obligation in law upon the employer in considering the reference other than to consider it in good faith, whether they were satisfactory to them. The natural reading of a communication, the purpose of which is to tell the prospective employee that part of the decision on whether he is firmly offered thepost has yet to be made, is that the employer is reserving the right to make up his own mind when the references have been received and studied. Although it is possible for an employer to make an offer conditional on something to be objectively determined (e.g. passing an examination) it is very hard to see that the defendant's letter in this case fell into that category. Therefore, it was unlikely that the plaintiff would be able to show that the test was objective in the sense that a reasonable person in the position of the defendants, with the particular post to fill, would not regard the references as a satisfactory basis on which to appoint the plaintiff'.

Employers reneging on job offers

14.11   Once an offer of employment is made and accepted, a collateral contract has been formed, i.e. a contract to employ, as the EAT decided in *Sarker v South Tees Acute Hospitals NHS Trust [1997] IRLR 328*. In this case, an employee whose contract of employment was terminated before she had even started work was entitled to bring a claim for breach of contract before the employment tribunal.

In other words, the prospective employer makes a warranty of employment to the other party that if he gives up his current employment, he will be given the new employment. In reliance on this warranty, the other party gives up his existing employment. Thus, if the prospective employer reneges on that contract, the other party may sue on it. Damages will be awarded on the basis of the financial loss suffered as a result of the breach by the prospective employer. The employee could claim loss of earnings until he obtains further employment (subject to his duty to mitigate his loss).

If employers wish to make offers of employment subject to the job applicant successfully passing an examination whose results are not known at the time of the interview, it is essential that such conditions are expressly stated in the letter offering employment (*Stubbes v Trower Still & Keeling [1987] IRLR 321*).

Employee reneging on a job offer

14.12   In the case where a prospective employee refuses to join the employer after originally having accepted the appointment, it is possible to sue that individual for the loss suffered by the employer as a direct result of the breach of contract. In most cases, this will be the cost of re-advertising and all recruitment costs. The feasibility of this approach, will naturally depend on an analysis of the individual's ability to pay.

The statutory contract of employment

General requirements

14.13   A contract of employment made between an employer and an employee need not necessarily be in writing. An oral contract is as valid in law as one reduced to writing. However, under the provisions of the Employment Rights Act 1996, s 1, there is now a requirement for most categories of employee to be provided with a written statement of their main terms and conditions of employment, within two months of their beginning employment. Prior to 1995, employees who worked less than eight hours a week did not have the right to a Section 1 statement of employment. The Employment Protection (Part-time Employees) Regulations 1995 (SI 1995 No 31), which came into force on 6 February 1995, provided that the exclusion of part-time employees was no longer valid. The 1995 Regulations were revoked by the ERA 1996, which incorporated their provisions. The individual employment rights contained within the ERA 1996 apply equally to full and part-time employees unless specifically stated not to. (See also 14.26 and 14.74 below).

Under the Employment Rights Act 1996, certain excluded classes of employees will not have a right to a Section 1 statement of employment (ERA 1996, s 5). These include employees who are engaged in work wholly or mainly outside the UK (ERA 1996, s 196), and persons employed for less than one month (ERA 1996, s 198).

The terms and conditions of employment provided in the written statement must now include details of the following.

(*a*)   The names of the employer and employee.

(*b*)   The date when the employment began.

(*c*)   The date when the employee's continuous employment began (including any employment with a previous employer which counts towards the period).

(*d*)   Scale or rate or method of calculating remuneration and the intervals at which remuneration is paid.

(*e*)   Hours of work, and any terms relating to hours of work.

(*f*)   Entitlement to holiday, including public holidays and holiday pay.

(*g*)   Sick pay rights.

(*h*)   Pension arrangements.

(*j*)   Length of notice the employee is obliged to give and is entitled to receive from his employer to terminate employment.

(*k*)   Where the employment is not intended to be permanent, the period for which it is expected to continue, or if it is for a fixed term, the date it is expected to end.

(*l*)   The title of the job and a brief description of the work that the employee is employed to do.

(*m*)   The place of work or, where the employee is required or permitted to work at various places, an indication of that and the name of the employer.

(*n*)   Any collective agreements directly affecting terms and conditions.

(*o*)   If the employee must work for more than one month outside the UK, the period for which he must work, the currency in which he will be paid and any additional remuneration or benefits resulting from overseas work and any terms and conditions relevant to his return must be added.

(Employment Rights Act 1996, s 1.)

A Section 1 statement must also include a note of the disciplinary rules applicable to the employee, or must refer to a document, accessible to the employee, where such rules are contained. The statement must specify:

(i)   a person to whom the employee can apply if dissatisfied with any disciplinary procedure relating to him;

(ii)   a person to whom the employee can apply for the purpose of seeking redress of any grievance relating to his employment; and

(iii)   the manner in which it should be made.

(ERA 1996, s 3(1)).

Small companies employing less than 20 people also need to comply with points (ii)–(iii) above (ERA 1996, s 3(3)).

Section 1 statements, and statements under ERA 1996, s 3, may not be changed without written notice being given to the employee at the earliest opportunity and, in any event, not more than one month after the change. (ERA 1996, s 4.)

A written statement containing sickness and pension particulars may simply refer employees to other documents which they have reasonable opportunities to read in the course of their employment or which are made reasonably accessible to them in some other way (ERA 1996, s 2.) An employer may, in a Section 1 statement, refer the employee to a collective agreement for notice of the particulars.

It is generally accepted in practice that if the employee is given a written contract of employment which contains all the particulars covered by a Section 1 statement, that the employer is not obliged to provide him with a further, separate Section 1 notice.

Where an employer does not provide an employee with a Section 1 statement, or provides a statement which is inaccurate or incomplete, the employee may apply to an employment tribunal (ERA 1996, s 11(1)(2)). Unfortunately, the employment tribunal has no power to fine the offending employer, but can determine what the particulars should have been. These will then be taken as having actually been given to the employee by the employer.

Implied terms

14.14   The employment relationship is governed not only by any express terms in the contract of employment, but also by terms which the law implied into the employment relationship. Implied terms which are commonly imposed upon employees include duties of fidelity and obedience, disclosure of information, performance of duties with due diligence and care, and not to make a secret profit. Both parties are also under a duty to give reasonable notice of termination if no notice period has been specified, and to maintain a relationship of mutual trust and confidence between themselves.

There are various bases upon which courts may imply terms into contracts of employment. These include the following.

(*a*) *Conduct* — which may evidence an agreement between the parties on a certain matter.

(*b*) The *'officious bystander' test* — a term may be implied if the court holds that it is so obvious that the parties are taken to have agreed to it.

(*c*) *Custom* — terms which are regularly adopted in a particular context may be taken to have obviously been implied into every contract in that area.

(*d*) *'Business efficacy'* — terms may be implied if it is necessary to give business efficacy to the contract i.e. to make it work properly.

(*e*) *Common characteristic* — a term may be implied if it is so characteristic of employment relationships that the employer and employee are taken to have necessarily accepted such a term.

The law, however, will not simply imply a term into a contract only because it is reasonable. It will only imply a term which is reasonably seen as a necessary condition of the modern employment relationship (*Lister v Romford Ice and Cold Storage Co Ltd [1957] AC 555*). Company secretaries should be aware of the possibility of relying on implied terms in relations with employees, or that employees may rely on them. For instance, where there is no contractual provision concerning mobility of an employee, the courts have held that there is an implied term in employment relationships which require the employee to work anywhere within reasonable travelling distance of home (*Courtaulds Northern Spinning Ltd v Sibson [1988] IRLR 305*). In *Aspden v Webbs Poultry and Meat Group (Holdings) Ltd [1996] IRLR 521*, Sedley J incorporated an implied term into the contract of a sick employee that his employers would not terminate the contract while he was incapacitated and negate the benefit of the permanent health insurance scheme.

In a landmark decision *(Malik and another v Bank of Credit and Commerce International (in compulsory liquidation) [1997] ICR 606*, the House of Lords held that dishonest business conduct by an employer potentially amounts to a breach of the implied contractual term of mutual trust and confidence enabling an employee to recover 'stigma damages' for the damage to his reputation where the employer's conduct makes it more difficult for the employee to obtain work in the future.

However, a number of cases subsequent to *Malik* have made clear that there are limitations to the scope of the implied term of trust and confidence. In *Hill v General Accident Fire and Life Assurance Corporation Ltd* [*1998*] *IRLR 641*, the Court of Session in Scotland held that there is no overriding obligation for the contract of employment to be interpreted in a way which furthers the principle of mutual trust. The Court in *Hill* also considered the *Aspden* decision referred to above. It held that Sedley J in *Aspden* had been justified in holding that, on the facts of that case, it was not open to the employer to dismiss the employee merely because he was sick, or for no reason whatever. However, there is no implied term that gross misconduct is the only cause warranting the dismissal of an employee whilst in receipt of sick pay. Thus in *Hill*, a dismissal for redundancy was not in breach of the implied term of trust and confidence.

In *Bank of Credit and Commerce SA v Ali and others* [*1999*] *IRLR 226*, Lightman J in the High Court held that the term of mutual trust and confidence implied in *Malik* did not have the effect of giving rise to a duty of disclosure of breaches of contract by an employer where they may give rise to risks to the 'physical, financial and psychological welfare of an employee'. Lightman J pointed out that the duty of trust and confidence is a mutual obligation, and that a duty to disclose wrongdoing is likely to place an intolerable burden on both employer and employee.

Changing the contract terms

14.15   Employment contracts can be changed at any time, but only with the agreement of both parties. Employers cannot unilaterally vary an employee's terms of employment. Employers who unilaterally impose changes in a contract can be sued for the loss of earnings involved, or may face an employment tribunal defending an unfair dismissal complaint. Imposed changes by the employer to one of the main terms of the contract amounts to a fundamental breach, giving the employee the right to resign and claim damages for breach of contract (limited to the notice period) or to continue working under the old terms. In practice, the terms of employment may not be contained in one single document (see 14.13 above), but may be contained in a pot-pourri of sources, including, typically, an offer letter, a 'contract' of employment, a staff handbook, various policies/memoranda, collective agreements and custom and practice. Not all of these will necessarily be contractual, for instance, policies in staff handbooks are often specifically stated to be non-contractual. Whether a proposed change affects a contractual clause or a policy may be of importance, the courts usually holding that employers can make changes in policy unilaterally. However, in some cases, radical changes in policy may lead to a breach of an implied 'trust and confidence' provision in the contract of employment proper.

In the absence of carefully drafted provisions in a contract of employment which allow an employer the necessary flexibility to make changes, the employer requires the employee's consent to make changes. Obviously, express consent is the ideal. Consent may, however, result from implication, typically the employee continuing to work after what is otherwise a unilateral imposition of changes, to the extent that the employee's conduct may be said to be evidence of acceptance. This approach is not recommended, especially where a change does not have an immediate effect. In this case the courts may be slow to conclude that continued working on the part of the employee without objection is evidence of consent. In *Aparcau v Iceland Frozen Foods* [*1996*] *IRLR 119*, the EAT made a distinction between contractual terms which have immediate application, such as pay rates, and those such as mobility which do not, and upheld a cashier's claim of constructive dismissal when she was required to move to another store, even though a mobility clause had been introduced into her contract twelve months earlier.

Employers should be particularly careful with variations relating to remuneration. An employee facing a unilateral cut in wages can, as a matter of contract, refuse to accept the cut whilst working on, and claim contractual entitlement to be repaid the lost pay (*Burdett-Coutts v Hertfordshire County Council* [*1984*] *IRLR 91*). Under the ERA 1996, s 13 (see 14.65 below), reductions in wages, overtime rates and the abandonment/modification of contractual bonus schemes would all result in a 'deduction' contrary to the Act and would be actionable (*Bruce v Wiggins Teape (Stationery) Ltd* [*1994*] *IRLR 536*). Also, according to the ERA 1996, s 104(1), any employee who is dismissed for asserting a statutory right is automatically unfairly dismissed. Arguably, an employee faced with a cut who resigns, claiming constructive dismissal (see 14.74 below), or who is given notice under the existing contract and an offer is made of a new contract, on reduced pay, could be regarded as having been dismissed in the context of a statutory right under the ERA 1996 to continue to be paid at the agreed rate. In *Rigby v Ferodo* [*1987*] *IRLR 61*, the employer unilaterally imposed a reduction in wages. The court held that the employee, in continuing to work and receiving a reduced payment under protest, had not accepted the variation in terms and was therefore entitled to recover the difference between his contractual entitlement and the amount actually paid. The period of the damages was not restricted to the notice period because the employer had not sought to terminate the employment on notice (or at all).

More scope exists for changing contractual terms, where particular terms being altered are incorporated from a collective agreement. There will be no breach of contract where the employer has the right to vary the contract unilaterally, as in *Airlie and others v City of Edinburgh District Council* [*1996*] *IRLR 516*. Here, an employer reduced the bonuses payable under a collective agreement without the consent of the employees, but the agreement contained a code of practice allowing him to alter the bonus scheme. An employee's objection to changes negotiated with a union or already contained within the collective agreement will not prevail where the terms are expressly incorporated into the contracts of employment, irrespective of whether the employee was ever a member of the union, or has left (*National Coal Board v Galley* [*1958*] *1 AER 91*). Also, the employer is not free to abandon the application of collectively derived but individually incorporated terms, even where the original collective agreement terminates (*Robertson and Jackson v British Gas Corporation* [*1983*] *IRLR 302*). It is lawful for an employer to offer financial inducement to workers to gain their consent to substitute terms and conditions which were collectively negotiated for an 'individual' contract (*Associated Newspapers Ltd v Wilson* [*1995*] *IRLR 258*).

Thus, it is preferable when proposing changes to contracts of employment to which consent cannot be obtained to give proper contractual notice to terminate (see 14.73 below), together with an offer of re-employment on the new terms and conditions, rather than run the risks inherent with the imposition of unilateral changes. This should only follow:

(*a*)   the adoption of a fair procedure; and

(*b*)   consultation.

Whether the dismissals will be unfair or not (see 14.74 below) will be determined by applying principles established in *Hollister v NationalFarmers Union [1979] IRLR 328*, where it was held that an employer could fairly dismiss where there were 'sound, good business reasons' for introducing changes to terms and conditions. Employers must avoid statements such as 'Accept these terms or you will be dismissed'. Duress of this kind has been held to be an anticipatory breach of contract by the employer, entitling the employee to claim constructive dismissal. Employers must therefore ensure adequate consultation about the intended changes, without threatening to give contractual notice of termination of the existing contract if this does not meet with success (*Greenaway Harrison Ltd v Wiles [1994] IRLR 380*).

Employers must remember that a special regime applies to changes to employment contracts in the context of transfers of undertakings (see 14.28–14.31 below).

Unenforceable terms and illegal terms

14.16   Any terms which seek to contract the employee out of minimum statutory rights (e.g. those covering discrimination, equal pay, redundancy rights and unfair dismissal) are unenforceable. Illegal terms on the other hand e.g. an agreement not to declare wages for tax, can make the contract itself unenforceable.

Promotions

14.17   Employees who are promoted are effectively accepting an offer of employment under a new contract. Continuity is not broken and the new contract immediately succeeds the previous one. Normally one or more of the fundamental terms of a contract are changed by the offer of promotion: position, duties, pay, overtime, benefits, mobility etc. The promotion gives the employer the opportunity to change the contract and for the employee to accept it. A promoted employee is entitled to rely on the terms of the original contract where these have not been revised or altered in the offer of promotion.

Directors' service contracts

14.18   Company directors are not automatically employees of a company. However, it is common for many directors to hold executive office within the company, thus effectively becoming an employee. In (1) *Buchan v Secretary of State for Employment* (2) *Ivey v Secretary of State for Employment* [*1997*] *IRLR 80* two company directors owning a controlling interest in their companies were held not to be employees and could not claim unfair dismissal or a redundancy payment following the insolvency of their businesses since the decision to dismiss them could only be taken with their agreement. However, in *Fleming v Secretary of State for Trade and Industry* [*1997*] *IRLR 682*, the Court of Session in Scotland, while upholding on the facts the employment tribunal's view that the managing director was not an 'employee' and therefore not entitled to a redundancy payment, went on to state that there was no rule of law to the effect that the fact that a person is a majority shareholder implies that that person cannot be regarded as a employee. This *dictum* was followed by the Court of Appeal in *Secretary of State for Trade and Industry v Bottrill* [*1999*] *IRLR 326*, where a director who temporarily held 100 per cent of company shares was held to be an employee of the company. The Court of Appeal specifically upheld the approach in *Fleming*, and rejected that in *Buchan and Ivey*.

Where directors are regarded as employees the above provisions relating to the contract of employment apply, together with the Companies Act 1985 which introduces further requirements (see 14.52 below). A director may be employed under the authority of Article 84 of Table A (or a similar article), by a resolution of the board containing the terms of appointment, by a letter written under the authority of the board or in a service agreement approved by it.

Under section 318 of the Companies Act 1985, a company is required to keep at its registered office (or the place where the register of members is kept) a copy of each director's service contract where it is in writing. Where the contract is not in writing, a written memorandum of its terms (for example The Written Statement of the Terms and Conditions of Employment) must be kept. These copies are open to inspection by the members at the place where they are kept. A slight exception to this rule is given by section 318(11) of the Companies Act 1985 where the contract is in force for a period of less than twelve months, or where the contract can within the next twelve months be terminated by the company without the payment of compensation. The requirements are also modified if the contract requires the director to work wholly or mainly outside the UK. In such cases, a copy need not be kept. If the company is listed, then the Listing Rules of the Stock Exchange (often referred to as the Yellow Book) requires that directors' service contracts, or memoranda of their terms, be available for inspection by any person at the company's registered office at all times during business hours and at the annual general meeting for 15 minutes prior to the holding of the meeting.

Under section 319 of the Companies Act 1985, a company is forbidden to enter into service contracts with its directors for periods exceeding five years where the contract is not capable of being terminated by notice, or can only be terminated in specified circumstances, unless the term is first approved by a resolution of the company in general meeting, or, where it is for the employment of a director of a holding company, by resolution of the holding company in general meeting. Before any such a term is passed, a written memorandum setting out the proposed agreement incorporating the term must be available for inspection by members of the company both at the company's registered office for not less than 15 days ending with the date of the meeting, and at the meeting itself (section 319(5)). Any such contracts not so approved are deemed void and the director's employment may be terminated on reasonable notice.

The report of the Cadbury Committee, published in December 1992, recommended that directors' service contracts should not normally exceed three years without shareholders' approval. The Greenbury Code, Part D 'contracts and compensation', published in July 1995, recommended that there is a strong case for setting contract periods at, or reducing them to, one year or less. This statement was repeated in the Combined Code (a consolidation of the Cadbury and Greenbury Codes published in June 1998, and now annexed to the Listing Rules — see 6.12 DIRECTORS). The Listing Rules now require the disclosure to shareholders, in the company's annual report (as part of a report to the shareholders by the board of directors), of details of any directors' service contract with a notice period in excess of one year, giving the reasons for such notice period.

A further point worth noting is in relation to the position where a director's service contract conflicts with the company's articles of association. In such circumstances, the provisions of the articles will prevail, as the board may not override them. Articles of association will usually delegate the power to fix the terms and conditions of a director's employment to the board of directors. However, the power may be further delegated by the board to a committee of it, or to an individual director, for example, the managing director. In *Guinness plc v Saunders [1990] 1 AER 652*, a committee of the board purported to grant special remuneration to a director. The alleged oral contract between the director and the committee was held by the House of Lords to be void as the board had no power under the articles to delegate the power to a committee. A director cannot rely on ostensible authority or implied authority on the part of other members of the board; as the provisions of any resolution of the board or a committee are deemed to be known by each director.

An announcement must be made to the Company Announcements Office, of the appointment or resignation (or removal or retirement) of a director and of any important change being made in the functions or executive responsibilities of a director.

Sunday working

14.19   The Sunday Trading Act 1994 which came into force on 26 August 1994, reformed the law of England and Wales in regard to Sunday trading. The Act reformed the provisions of the Shops Act 1950. The Act permits large shops (those with a floor area of more than 280 square metres) to open for up to six hours a day between 10 a.m. and 6 p.m. on Sunday (except Easter Day and Christmas Day) by giving 14 days' notice to the local authority. The Act contained important provisions covering the employment rights of shop workers. The rights were conferred by Schedule 4 to the Act, but have now been repealed and incorporated into the Employment Rights Act 1996. These rights are that:

(*a*)   the dismissal of 'protected shop workers' and (after a three-month period) 'opted-out shop workers' for refusing to work on Sundays is automatically unfair; and

(*b*)   that such workers have the right not to suffer any other detriment for refusing to work on Sunday.

A 'protected shop worker' is a person who was employed as a shop worker when the Act came into force (26 August 1994), and continues to be so employed (until the date on which he was dismissed or suffered a detriment for refusing to work on Sunday); or a worker, irrespective of whether he was employed when the Act came into force, whose contract of employment is such that he is not required to work on Sunday. The Act does not protect 'Sunday only' shop workers, nor does it prevent discrimination against those who are applying for shop work which may entail working on Sundays and who appear reluctant to do such work. A worker ceases to be 'protected' by giving his employer an 'opt in' notice, stating that he wishes to work on Sunday and, after giving that notice, expressly agreeing to do work on Sunday or a particular Sunday. A shop worker who, under his contract, may be required to work on Sunday (but who is not employed to work only on Sunday), may give his employer an 'opting-out notice' i.e. a written statement that he objects to working on Sunday. After a three-month period starting with the date the notice was given, the employee has the same protection against unfair dismissal or suffering detriment as a protected shop worker. Employers must provide a statutory explanatory statement to employees who are or may be required to work on Sundays, within two months of their employment. This statement describes the employment protection available and the ability to 'opt-out'. Thus, new employees and existing employees who have opted in can be forced to work on Sundays. Existing employees who have not opted in, and new employees who have opted out, cannot be forced to work on Sundays.

Time off

14.20   There are various instances when employees have a statutory right to time off. These rights are now contained in the ERA 1996, Part VI along with various other Acts detailed below.

(*a*) *Trade union officials and members* — Officials of recognised trade unions have the right, under the Trade Union and Labour Relations (Consolidation) Act 1992, ss 168–169, to time off with pay to carry out official union duties. Members of recognised trade unions have under the Trade Union and Labour Relations (Consolidation) Act 1992, s 170, rights to reasonable time off without pay, to take part in trade union activities. There are no service requirements for these rights. An employee who is an official of, or member of, a recognised trade union may present a complaint to an employment tribunal that his employer has failed to permit him to take time off to carry out such duties, or (as the case may be) to take part in such activities (TULRCA 1992, ss 168(4), 170(4)). In addition, an employee who is an official of a recognised trade union may present a complaint to an employment tribunal that his employer has failed to pay him for time off to carry out such duties (TULRCA 1992, s 169(5)).

(*b*) *Public duties* — Employees who hold certain public offices including being a justice of the peace (ERA 1996, s 50(1)), a member of: a local authority; a statutory tribunal; a police authority; a board of prison visitors; a relevant health body; a relevant education body or the Environment Agency (ERA 1996, s 50(2)) have the right to take time off without pay to perform duties. The amount of time off which the employer permits the employee will depend on the occasion and what is reasonable in the circumstances. Employers can pay regard to: how much time off is required for the performance of the particular duty; how much time the employee has already been permitted under the ERA 1996, s 50 or time off for trade union activities under the Trade Union and Labour Relations (Consolidation) Act 1992 (see (*a*) above); and the circumstances of the employer's business and the effect the employee's absence will have on the running of that business. An employee may present a complaint to an employment tribunal if his employer fails to permit him to take time off as is allowed under ERA 1996, s 50 (ERA 1996, s 51).

(*c*) *Health and safety representatives* — Under the Safety Representatives and Safety Committees Regulations 1977 (SI 1977 No 500), safety representatives must be permitted time off with pay to undertake their duties or to undergo training. These rights are now contained in the Employment Rights Act 1996, s 44, providing protection for such employees not to suffer detriment in the exercise of these duties. From 1 October 1996, the Health and Safety (Consultation with Employees) Regulations 1996 (SI 1996 No 1513), applicable to employees not represented by safety representatives (i.e. non-unionised workplaces) require employers to consult either with elected 'representatives of employee safety' or directly with employees. These representatives of employee safety have similar rights, as do safety representatives under the 1977 Regulations, to time off with pay for their duties, and the right (again set out in ERA 1996, s 44) not to suffer detriment as a result of the conduct of those duties. In addition, an employee has the right not to suffer a detriment where he took part (or proposed to take part) in consultation with the employer pursuant to the 1996 Regulations or in an election of representatives of employee safety under those Regulations, whether as a candidate or otherwise. A safety representative under the 1977 Regulations, or a representative of employee safety under the 1996 Regulations, may present a complaint to an employment tribunal that his employer has failed to permit him to take time off, or to pay him, for undertaking his duties or undergoing training (1977 Regulations, Reg 11; 1996 Regulations, Sch 2).

(*d*) *Pension trustees* — The Pensions Act 1995 which received Royal Assent on 19 June 1995 introduced a new statutory right to time off for an occupational pension scheme trustee to perform his or her duties and to undergo training, with pay at his or her average hourly earnings. These rights have been consolidated into the Employment Rights Act 1996, ss 58–60. As with time off for public duties, the circumstances of the employer's business and the effect of the employer's absence on the running of the business will be taken into account. There is a similar remedy of complaint to an employment tribunal, normally within three months of an employer's failure to permit the time off. Pension fund trustees have the same rights as safety representatives not to suffer detriment in employment as a consequence of the conduct of their duties. Dismissal as a result of carrying out such duties will be automatically unfair.

(*e*) *Employees looking for work* — Employees who have been given notice of dismissal by reason of redundancy (see 14.76 below) are entitled to time off during normal working hours in order to look for new employment or make arrangements for training for future employment. This only applies to employees who have had two years continuous service at the time the notice of dismissal by reason of redundancy is due to expire. Employees taking time off in these circumstances are entitled to remuneration at their normal hourly rate, and can also apply to an employment tribunal if an employer fails to permit the time off.

(*f*) *Employee representatives* — An employee who is an employee representative for the purposes of Chapter II of Part IV of the Trade Union and Labour Relations (Consolidation) Act 1992 or a representative for the purposes of the Transfer of Undertakings (Protection of Employment) Regulations 1991 (SI 1991 No 1794), Regs 10–11, or a candidate in an election in which any person being elected will be such an employee representative is entitled to take reasonable time off for him to be able to perform the functions of employee representative or candidate (ERA 1996, s 61). The representative has the right to remuneration at his normal hourly rate (ERA 1996, s 62) and the right to complain to an employment tribunal if this right is denied by his employer (ERA 1996, s 63). Like safety representatives and pension fund trustees, employee representatives have the right not to suffer detriment as a result of their position and exercise of their duties. Dismissal for such activities is also automatically unfair.

(*g*) *Ante-natal care* — An employee who is pregnant and has, on the advice of a medical worker (e.g. doctor or midwife) made an appointment to attend a clinic for the purpose of ante-natal care is entitled to be permitted by her employer to take time off during normal working hours to attend the appointment (ERA 1996, s 55(1)). To exercise this right the employee has to provide a certificate from a doctor, midwife or health visitor stating that the employee is pregnant, and an appointment card or some other document showing the appointment has been made. (ERA 1996, s 55(2)). The employee is entitled to her normal hourly remuneration to attend such an appointment (ERA 1996, s 56) and has the right to complain to an employment tribunal if this right is denied (ERA 1996, s 57).

(*h*) *Young persons undergoing study or training* — A new right for young persons in employment to take paid time off work for study and training, by virtue of ERA 1996, ss 63A-63C (inserted by the Teaching and Higher Education Act 1998, s 32), came into effect on 1 September 1999 (see SI 1999 No 987). An employee who (*a*) is aged 16 or 17, (*b*) is not receiving full-time secondary or further education, and (*c*) has not attained the prescribed standard of achievement (as to which, see SI 1999 No 986) is entitled to be permitted by his employer (or principal, where he has been sub-contracted) to take time off during the employee's working hours in order to undertake study or training leading to a relevant qualification (as defined). An 18 year-old employee who is undertaking study or training leading to a relevant qualification which he began before attaining that age has a similar right to time off.

The amount of time off that an employee is to be permitted to take is that which is reasonable in the circumstances having regard, in particular, to (*a*) the requirements of the employee's study or training, and (*b*) the circumstances of the business of the employer (or the principal) and the effect of the employee's time off on the running of that business. An employee who is allowed time off is entitled to be paid for the time taken off at the 'appropriate hourly rate', and has the right to complain to an employment tribunal if the employer (or principal) has unreasonably refused the employee time off or has refused to pay him. An employee entitled to time off and to remuneration under these provisions also has the right (by virtue of ERA 1996, s 47A) not to suffer detriment in employment on the ground that the employee exercised (or proposed to exercise) that right, or received (or sought to receive) such remuneration.

Other terms and conditions

14.21   In addition to statutory rights, like Statutory Maternity Pay (SMP) (see 14.48 below) and Statutory Sick Pay (SSP) see (14.50 below), employees may have other legal entitlements provided for in the contract. As will be seen below, the Working Time Regulations 1998 have made provision for statutory entitlements in certain areas that previously were purely contractual.

Hours of work

14.22   Traditionally, prior to the coming into force of the Working Time Regulations 1998 (see below), this area was left to collective bargaining. However, some professions such as truck drivers, and the hours that children may work, were individually regulated. The law protecting children was extended following the adoption of EU Directive 94/33/EC (the Young Workers Directive) in June 1994 (see the Children (Protection at Work) Regulations 1998 (SI 1998 No 276), which came into force on 4 August 1998). The Health and Safety (Young Persons) Regulations 1997 (SI 1997 No 135) implemented articles 6 and 7 (Risk Assessment and Prohibition of Work by Young People) in the UK from 3 March 1997.

An EU Directive on Working Time (No 93/104), dealing with hours of work, breaks and holidays for adult workers, was due to take effect on 23 November 1996, and did so throughout the EU except in the UK. The provisions of this

Directive, together with the remaining provisions of the Young Workers Directive (which made similar provision in relation to young workers, i.e. those between 16 and 18 years of age) were finally implemented in the UK by the Working Time Regulations 1998 (SI 1998 No 1833),with effect from 1 October 1998. Very broadly, and subject to numerous detailed exceptions which are beyond the scope of this book, these Regulations provide for: a maximum 48 hour working week; a minimum daily rest period of 11 consecutive hours; a rest break where the working day is longer than 6 hours; a minimum uninterrupted rest period of 24 hours (in addition to the above rest periods of 11 hours) every week; paid annual leave of at least four weeks (three weeks until 23 November 1999); and an average limit of 8 hours in any 24-hour period on night work. Although under the Regulations, young workers are subject to the same broad limits on working time as adult workers, there are certain special entitlements applicable to them (again subject to exceptions).

Apart from their obligations under the Working Time Regulations 1998, employers should in any case take care to avoid employees working excessive hours. The case of *Walker v Northumberland County Council [1995] IRLR 35*, illustrates the duty of care placed on employers as regards their employees. The High Court held that the defendant council were in breach of their duty of care which they owed to the plaintiff employee as his employer in respect of a second mental breakdown which he suffered as a result of stress and anxiety caused by his job as a social worker. The court held that an employer owes a duty of care to his employees not to cause them psychiatric damage by the volume or character of work that they are required to perform. The judge stated that there was no logical reason why the risk of injury to an employee's mental health (as against physical) health should be excluded from the employer's general duty to provide an employee with a safe system of work and to take steps to protect him from reasonably foreseeable risks. This re-inforced the previous case of *Johnstone v Bloomsbury Health Authority [1991] 2 AER 293*, where the Court held that whilst a contract of employment could impose a requirement on a hospital doctor to be available for 48 hours' overtime above the 40-hour week this had to be exercised in such a way as not to cause injury or damaged health. Employers should be aware of the liability that may arise from expecting workers to work excessively long hours.

Holidays

14.23   Until the end of September 1998, there was no statutory provision for holiday entitlement. However, with effect from 1 October 1998, the Working Time Regulations 1998 (SI 1998 No 1833) (see 14.22 above) introduced a legal right to at least three weeks' paid leave a year, rising to four weeks from 23 November 1999. Note that a payment in lieu of the statutory entitlement cannot be made, except where the worker's employment is terminated. In such a case, compensation is payable, with the amount being determined by a statutory formula. There are detailed requirements in the Regulations as to the dates on which leave can be taken, and as to notice.

Miscellaneous

14.24   Other rights to which employees may be contractually entitled are membership of the company pension scheme, subsidised sickness insurance, arrangements for time-off for medical appointments etc., stress counselling, provisions for London weighting, and relocation packages.

References

14.25   Employers are under no legal obligation to provide a reference for a departing employee. However, where they do, then, according to the House of Lords in *Spring v Guardian Royal Exchange [1994] IRLR 460*, there is a general duty of care in negligence in relation to the contents of the reference. Mr Spring brought an action for negligence against Guardian Assurance plc following a reference written about him by two directors stating that: '. . . this man has little or no integrity andcannot be trusted . . .'. The High Court accepted Mr Spring's description of the reference as 'the kiss of death'. The House of Lords ruled that a duty of care was owed both to the recipient and to the subject of the reference, saying that it was indeed a negligent reference as Mr Spring was undoubtedly 'a fool but not a rogue'. Mr Spring therefore won his claim that the reference was negligent and compensation for the fact that he suffered financial loss.

In relation to references and employers' liability for defamation, the *Spring* case also assists. Mr Spring lost his case for libel and malicious falsehood. A defamatory statement is one that is published, is false and derogatory without lawful justification. Such a statement must lower that person's reputation in the estimation of right-thinking people; expose him to ridicule or hatred or contempt and have a tendency to injure him in his office, profession or trade. The key to a successful claim for defamation is that the plaintiff must be able to show that the author of the statement was prompted by malice. Very few statements made about ex-employees or employees would fall into this category.

Part-time employees

14.26   Until 1994, the legislation required part-time employees (i.e those who worked less than 16 hours a week) to have longer service requirements (i.e. five years instead of two years) in order to avail themselves of rights enjoyed by full-time workers (e.g. unfair dismissal and redundancy pay). Employees working less than eight hours a week were completely excluded from these rights. However, all employees, regardless of length of service, were always entitled to protection under the Equal Pay Act 1970, the Sex Discrimination Act 1986, the Race Relations Act 1976 and the former Wages Act 1986 (now repealed and consolidated into the Employment Rights Act 1996). The growth of part-time employment lead to the introduction of new legislation designed to give part-timers equal rights as those in full-time employment. In *R v Secretary of State for Employment ex parte Equal Opportunities Commission [1994] IRLR 176*, the House of Lords ruled that the qualifying thresholds for claiming redundancy pay and unfair dismissal were in breach of European law because they indirectly discriminated against women who are the majority of part-time workers. As a result the Employment Protection (Part-time

Employees) Regulations 1995 (SI 1995 No 31) were introduced to implement the House of Lords' decision. These regulations, which came into force on 6 February 1995, established that, irrespective of the number of hours worked, employees are entitled to the following rights enjoyed by full-time workers. The regulations were revoked by the Employment Rights Act 1996, which incorporated its provisions. Part-time workers have the rights to:

(*a*)　claim unfair dismissal after one year's continuous employment (see 14.74 below);

(*b*)　claim statutory redundancy pay after 2 years' continuous employment;

(*c*)　claim 40 weeks' maternity leave after 2 years' continuous employment (ERA 1996, s 79);

(*d*)　a written statement of terms and conditions of employment to be given within two months of joining (ERA 1996, s 1);

(*e*)　itemised pay slips (ERA 1996, s 8);

(*f*)　written reasons for dismissal, after one year's continuous employment (ERA 1996, s 92);

(*g*)　a minimum period of notice of dismissal (ERA 1996, s 86);

(*h*)　time off for trade union duties and activities (TULR(C)A 1992, ss 168 and 170);

(*j*)　time off for public duties (ERA 1996, s 50);

(*k*)　time off to look for alternative work or to arrange training when under notice of redundancy, after two years' continuous employment (ERA 1996, s 28);

(*l*)　a statutory guarantee payment (ERA 1996, s 28); and

(*m*)　medical suspension pay (ERA 1996, s 64).

In *London Borough of Hammersmith and Fulham v Jesuthasan [1998] IRLR 372*, the Court of Appeal ruled that a male part-time worker employed in the public sector was entitled to claim unfair dismissal and a statutory redundancy payment on the basis of the EOC decision.

Even before the 1995 Regulations, the Trade Union Reform and Employment Rights Act 1993 introduced some reforms which were also extended to part-time employees. These rights, also consolidated in the Employment Rights Act 1996, include rights to:

(1)　14 weeks' maternity leave (ERA 1996, s 73);

(2)　protection against dismissal on the grounds of pregnancy, childbirth or the taking of maternity leave (ERA 1996, s 99);

(3)　not be dismissed, to be selected for redundancy or to suffer detriment where health and safety matters are at issue (ERA 1996, s 100); and

(4)　protection against dismissal for asserting a statutory right (ERA 1996, s 104).

Temporary/fixed contract employees

14.27   In the last decade many employing organisations have been re-assessing working time, especially contract length, to ensure flexibility. Company secretaries should remember that, even if staff are classified internally as 'temps', fixed-term workers, seasonal workers etc., in law there are only two categories of employment status, employee and self-employed (see 14.3 above). The position of casual workers might suggest that such workers have a closer affinity to self-employed workers than the typical employee. The employment tests at 14.3 above should be applied to define whether a temporary worker is an employee or self-employed. It has to be remembered that self-employed workers are not covered by most employment legislation, especially job security laws. On the other hand, the employer does not have to pay SSP when such workers are ill (see 14.50 below) and is not usually vicariously liable if a worker causes damage to third parties through negligence (see 14.33 below).

The key issue with workers who are casuals, fixed-term workers, seasonal, freelance and 'contract' labour is whether the length of an engagement, its regularity (or otherwise) or the type of work done affect their employment status. It is important to note that simply declaring a 'casual' to be self-employed or concluding an agreement that is their status, will not suffice. The law will declare the 'legal realities'; if, say, the label of self-employment is challenged by the Inland Revenue or a claim arises in an employment tribunal. The following two cases provide examples of the courts' reasoning. In *Catamaran Cruisers v Williams [1994] IRLR 386*, a worker on a river boat company set up a limited company with a view to being treated as self-employed. However, as the 'realities' were that he worked regularly, invested nothing in Catamaran Cruisers, received sick pay when ill etc., he was found to be an employee. However, in *Hall v Lorimer [1994] IRLR 171*, a 'freelance' vision mixer worked on a series of short-term contracts in studios. He was required to carry out the work personally and not 'sub-contract'. Nonetheless, his pattern of working indicated self-employment. He worked for up to 20 companies a year and did his own paperwork, and was thus found to be self-employed.

An agency 'temp' is usually on the books of an agency, works for the client, but is employed by the agency (formally an 'employment business'). Day-to-day control rests with the client but the contractual relationship is only with the agency. English law does not allow for joint or delegated employment contracts. The following cases shed light on the legal position of an employer. In *Wickens v Champion Employment [1984] ICR 365*, the EAT decided that there was no binding 'mutuality of obligation' to provide assignments by the agency or to accept those on offer by the temp and, thus, temps were not employees of an agency. This seemed to settle the situation. Although agencies could choose to make temps their employees, most did not, and therefore temps were unprotected by key aspects of employment legislation. They could not make claims against their agency or the client, even in the face of long-standing relationships. This matter was, however, recently opened up in the case of *McMeechan v Secretary of State for Employment [1995] IRLR 461*.

The work of a long-service agency temp came to an end due to the insolvency of the agency. The temp had been explicitly told in documentation that he was not an employee, however, he could also be dismissed for misconduct. The temp claimed that he was made redundant and entitled to compensation, and won the case. The decision was upheld on a narrower basis by the Court of Appeal (*[1997] IRLR 353*) which held that the agency worker was an employee of the agency for the duration of an engagement with one of its clients since there was a contractual grievance procedure and the agency had the power to dismiss the worker for misconduct. However, the Court left open the issue of whether the applicant also derived employee status from the terms of his general engagement with the agency. Conversely, in *Knights v Anglian Industrial Services (EAT 640/96)* the EAT agreed with a tribunal finding that an agency worker placed exclusively with one company for three years and whose tax and NICs were deducted from his wages by the agency via PAYE was not an employee of the agency.

The sex, race, and disability discrimination legislation applies to all situations where work is 'personally executed', and thus applies to most casual, freelance and short-term contract employees. Many rights however, e.g. time off, guarantee pay etc. are dependent on a minimum period of continuous employment and thus do not apply to temporary workers. Recent changes, however, have reduced many of these qualifying periods. Rights which are not dependent on a qualifying period, and thus apply to temporary employees now include: discriminatory and maternity dismissals; victimisation dismissals and rights under the former Sunday Trading Act 1994, now consolidated in the Employment Rights Act 1996. The usual grounds for fair dismissal apply to fixed-term contracts e.g. redundancy (see 14.76 below).

Employment law establishes the major duties regarding employees, but employers also owe duties to 'others' i.e. the self-employed, some freelancers and agency temps under the Management of Health and Safety at Work Regulations 1992 (SI 1992 No 2051) (see 14.55 below). These workers should be included in risk assessments conducted.

Transfers of undertakings

14.28   The Transfer of Undertakings (Protection of Employment) Regulations 1981 (SI 1981 No 1794) 'TUPE' give employees continuous employment rights when a trade or business is transferred by sale or other disposition.

TUPE was intended to cover the requirements of the EU Directive 77/187/EEC, usually known as the 'Acquired Rights Directive (ARD)'. The regulations state that they cover the 'rights and obligations on the transfer or merger of undertakings, businesses or part of businesses'. TUPE came into force on 1 May 1982. Its three principal aims are:

(*a*)   the protection of existing employment rights;

(*b*)   obliging employers to consult over transfers; and

(*c*)   the protection of employees against dismissal.

The types of transfer to which TUPE applies depend upon their classification as a 'relevant transfer' (Reg 3). These are defined as transfers:

(i)   from one person to another of an undertaking situated in the UK;

(ii)   effected by sale or some other disposition;

(iii)   which may be effected by two or more transactions; or

(iv)   which takes place whether or not any property is transferred.

Thus, transfers of franchises and leases also come within the definition, but transfers to a wholly-owned subsidiary do not. It is also worth noting that it is not necessary for assets to be transferred for the Regulations to apply (e.g. a service contract). There must, however, be a stable economic entity that is transferred — therefore, meaning that all the circumstances of each particular case must be looked at (*Ayse Süzen v Zehnacke Gebäudereinigung GmbH Krankenhausservice [1997] IRLR 255* and *Betts v Brintel Helicopters [1997] IRLR 361*; see also *ECM (Vehicle Delivery Service) Ltd v Cox [1998] IRLR 416 (EAT)*).

The transferee is solely liable for any pre-transfer unfair dismissal. There is no joint liability with the transferor according to the Court of Session in *Stirling District Council v Allan and others [1995] IRLR 301*.

Effects of transfers on contracts of employment

14.29   The effect is to place those employed immediately before the transfer in the same position as they would have held had it not been for the transfer itself. Employment rights and duties that automatically transfer to the employer following a relevant transfer include:

(*a*)   terms and conditions of employment;

(*b*)   claims regarding the payment of arrears;

(*c*)   outstanding legal claims (e.g. any discrimination claims before employment tribunals);

(*d*)   outstanding personal injury claims;

(*e*)   disciplinary records; and

(*f*)   contractual requirements concerning confidentiality, the status of patents etc.

The ECJ has defined 'immediately before' as not confined to events at the time of the transfer but includes cases where employees are dismissed some time before a transfer, but solely or principally because of it (*P Bork International v FAD [1989] IRLR 41*). In *Litster v Forth Dry Dock Engineering Co [1989] IRLR 161*, the House of Lords held that individuals dismissed in such circumstances have the right to pursue unfair dismissal claims against the transferee who has acquired the business. In *D'Urso v Ercole Marelli Elettromeccanica Generale SpA [1992] IRLR 136*, the European Court confirmed that all contracts of employment or employment relationships existing at the date of the transfer are automatically transferred to the new employer.

The new employer after a transfer is, in law, in exactly the same position as was the previous employer and is therefore subject to the same legal restrictions in any attempt to change employment contracts. In the case of *Daddy's Dance Hall*, the court held that if the variation is connected with a transfer then it is ineffective as it would infringe the Acquired Rights Directive. In *Wilson and others v St Helens Borough Council; Meade and another v British Fuels Ltd [1998] IRLR 706*, one of the issues before the House of Lords was whether transferees had any scope to vary the terms of employment after a transfer, by agreement with the employers. In view of the conclusion which they had reached on the dismissal issue (see 14.31 below), the Lords stated that it was not strictly necessary to deal with the variation issue. However, Lord Slynn (with whom the other Law Lords agreed) stated that he did not accept the argument that a variation was only invalid if agreed on as part of the transfer itself. It might still be due to the transfer even if it came later. However, there must (or, at least, might) come a time when the link with the transfer was broken or treated as no longer effective. Lord Slynn also stated that, where the variation was not due to the transfer, it could validly be made, although he accepted that it may be difficult to decide whether the variation is due to the transfer or attributable to some separate cause.

In general, transfers of contracted-out undertakings are covered by the regulations.

TUPE does not apply to the transfer of pension benefits. In *Walden Engineering v Warrener [1993] IRLR 420*, the court held that there was no obligation on the part of a new employer to provide equivalent benefits, or pay an equivalent pension. This finding was confirmed by the Court of Appeal in *Adams v Lancashire County Council and BET Catering Services Ltd [1997] IRLR 436*.

Consultation

14.30   TUPE also gives recognised trade unions or employee representatives elected for the purpose, rights to information and consultation before the transfer takes place. If it is believed that the transfer will result in 'measures' (i.e. redundancies), consultation must take place. The Collective Redundancies and Transfer of Undertakings (Protection of Employment) (Amendment) Regulations 1995 (SI 1995 No 2587) and 1999 (SI 1999 No 1925) also apply in transfer cases. They make it permissible for employers to consult with separately appointed or elected employee representatives, but by virtue of the 1999 Regulations (which apply to transfers completed on or after 1 November 1999), only where there is no recognised trade union. (In relation to transfers completed before that date, the employer can choose whether to consult with a recognised union or with employee representatives.) TUPE, Regs 9–10 place an obligation on the old employer to consult 'long enough before the relevant transfer', and to inform the representatives of:

(*a*) the fact that the relevant transfer is to take place, and the reasons for it;

(*b*) the legal, economic and social implications of the transfer for affected employees; and

(*c*) the measures which the employer envisages will, in connection with the transfer, take place in relation to those employees, or if he envisages no action, that fact.

If an employer fails to consult, can apply to a tribunal for compensation for the failure to consult. Compensation is set at a maximum of four weeks' pay (increased to 13 weeks' pay in respect of transfers completed on or after 1 November 1999), the actual award being set by the employment tribunal considering all the circumstances. The ability to enforce this right is vested in employee representatives only (unless there are none). Where there are employee representatives for information and consultation purposes, individual employees may not bring tribunal claims alleging a failure to consult properly. (*Keane v Clerical Medical Investment Group Ltd* Case No 2900491/97).

Dismissal following transfer

14.31 Dismissal following a transfer is automatically unfair unless connected with an economic, technical or organisational change. If dismissal falls under one of the exceptions in TUPE, reg 8(2) the tribunal still has to decide, using the criteria of reasonableness, whether in all the circumstances the decision to dismiss was reasonable. The EAT decision in *Milligan and another v Securicor Cleaning [1995] IRLR 288*, which held that there was no service requirement in TUPE cases, has been reversed by an amendment made in the Collective Redundancies and Transfer of Undertakings (Protection of Employment) (Amendment) Regulations 1995 (SI 1995 No 2587). Unfair dismissal claims have been successfully pursued by employees dismissed before a transfer to make the business look more attractive, or where terms and conditions have been changed to standardise arrangements.

In *Wilson and others v St Helens Borough Council; Meade and another v British Fuels Ltd [1998] IRLR 706*, the House of Lords held that under Regulations 5 and 8 of TUPE (and under Articles 3 and 4 of the EU Acquired Rights Directive):

(*a*) dismissal of an employee before, on or after a transfer was effective and not a nullity; and

(*b*) the employee had no right as against the transferee to continue in his employment on the same terms and conditions.

Lord Slynn (with whom the other Law Lords agreed) stated that the provisions of Regulation 8 of TUPE pointed to the dismissal being effective and not a nullity. Nor was there an automatic obligation on the part of the transferee under Regulation 5 to continue to employ the dismissed employee. The effect of articles 3 and 4 of the EU Acquired Rights Directive was that the existing rights of employees were to be safeguarded if there was a transfer, i.e. that the employee could look to the transferee to perform those obligations that the employee could have enforced against the transferor. The precise rights to be transferred depended on national law; there was no separate Community law right to continue in employment. It followed that TUPE gave effect to and were consistent with the Directive. It was unnecessary to refer a question to the ECJ on the matter.

On 29 June 1998, the EU Social Affairs Council adopted a new Directive, which amends the Acquired Rights Directive by entirely replacing Articles 1 to 7. Member States have until 17 July 2001 to implement agreed amendments to the Directive into domestic law. In the meantime, the Directive and existing Regulations apply in their present form.

Employees' rights and employers' duties

14.32 Employers are bound by a wide range of duties and obligations to their employees both by statute (e.g. The Health and Safety at Work etc. Act 1974) (see 14.54 below) and by common law, most notably, vicarious liability (see 14.33 below). Employees also have many rights, most of which have been introduced by statute.

Vicarious liability

14.33 This is a duty imposed upon employers by the common law which has the effect of making employers liable to third parties injured by the tortious acts of an employee in 'the course of the employee's work'. For the purpose of ascertaining whether an employer is vicariously liable for torts of an individual engaged by him to perform certain duties, it is essential to determine whether that individual is an employee or an independent contractor. If the individual is an employee, then the employer will be vicariously liable for the torts committed by the employee *in the course of his employment*. If, however, the individual is an independent contractor, then the employer will only be liable for acts which come within his non-delegable duties. The employer does, however, have an option of obtaining an indemnity from the employee who committed the act which gave rise to the liability or, in certain circumstances, to dismiss him if the dismissal is fair; an example would be serious misconduct (see 'Unfair dismissal' 14.74 below).

There are some statutes which provide specifically for vicarious liability to be imposed on employers (e.g. section 41(1) of the Sex Discrimination Act 1975 and section 32(1) of the Race Relations Act 1976).

Employers are also usually liable for acts of race or sex discrimination which occur in the workplace. In *Tower Boot Company Ltd v Jones* [1995] *IRLR 529* Mr Jones complained that he had been racially abused by other employees at work, including being called names, being branded with a hot screwdriver, whipped with pieces of leather and being pounded with metal bolts. He maintained that his employers were vicariously liable for the acts of their employees. However, his employers argued that the acts of harassment were not carried out in the course of their employment — they were not employed to physically and verbally abuse other staff — and thus were not liable. The EAT held that the meaning of 'in the course of employment' under the RRA 1976, s 32(1) meant that an employer would only be vicariously liable if the employee is carrying out an authorised act, albeit in an unauthorised fashion. Only if employers become aware of the fact that their employees are acting in a way which is discriminatory, and do nothing about it, can they be found liable. In an important judgment which has implications for sex and disability discrimination as well as race discrimination, the Court of Appeal (*[1997] ICR 254*) rejected the approach of the employers that had found favour with the EAT, and held that section 32 of the Race Relations Act 1976 did not require the employee to prove that the acts of harassment came within the common law concept of vicarious liability. The words 'in the course of his employment' should be given their natural everyday meaning. In short, harassment of all kinds while at work is likely to be 'in the course of employment'.

Employers' Liability (Compulsory Insurance) Act 1969

14.34   This Act imposes upon an employer an obligation to maintain insurance against claims by employees injured in the course of their employment. The insurance must be maintained under one or more approved policies with an authorised insurer against liability for bodily injury or disease sustained by employees arising out of and in the course of their employment in Great Britain. A copy of the current certificate of insurance must be displayed at each business premises in a position where it may be easily seen and read by employees (e.g. a noticeboard).

Until recently it was current practice for most employers' liability insurance policies to be issued with an unlimited amount of insurance cover. Where this was not the case, the Employers' Liability (Compulsory Insurance) General Regulations 1971 (SI 1971 No 1117) required that cover must be at least £2 million (Regulation 3). Companies had to insure £2 million worth of insurance for each of their subsidiaries. In September 1994 the Association of British Insurers (ABI) announced that from January 1995 any policies issued would be limited to an indemnity of £10 million. Although cover of £10 million would be sufficient for the majority of companies, employers such as holding companies and multinationals whose insurance covered a number of companies within the same group had problems complying with the requirements of Regulation 3. The Employers' Liability (Compulsory Insurance) General (Amendment) Regulations 1994 (SI 1994 No 3301) which came into force on 1 January 1995, provided a stop-gap measure by providing that Regulation 3 of the 1971 Regulations would be deemed to have been satisfied if the company insured and maintained insurance (where required) for itself and on behalf of its subsidiaries for that amount in respect of claims relating to any one or more of its own employees and to any one or more employees of its subsidiaries arising out of any one occurrence i.e. that a £2 million limit for a group would comply.

In April 1995 the Department of Employment issued a consultation paper 'Review of the Employers' Liability (Compulsory Insurance) Act 1969 and related legislation', to review the whole area. Following this review, the Employers' Liability (Compulsory Insurance) Regulations 1998 (SI 1998 No 2573) were enacted. They came into force on 1 January 1999, consolidating (with amendments) the 1971 Regulations referred to above (including the 1994 Amendment Regulations also referred to). The 1998 Regulations require that the aggregate amount of insurance that an employer must maintain under the 1969 Act must be not less than £5 million. However, where an employer is a company with one or more subsidiaries, that requirement will be taken to apply to that company and its subsidiaries together, as if they were a single employer. (See Regulation 3.) Certain employers (specified in Schedule 2) are exempted from the requirement to maintain insurance cover. There are various transitional provisions; in particular, in the case of an insurance policy commenced before (and current at) 1 January 1999, the provisions of the 1971 Regulations (Regulations 2 to 6, and Schedule) rather than those of the 1998 Regulations (Regulations 2 to 6, and Schedule 1) will apply until the expiry or renewal of that policy, or until 1 January 2000 (whichever is the earlier).

Discrimination

14.35   A wide body of statutes prohibit the discrimination by employers against anyone on the grounds of sex (Sex Discrimination Act 1975), race (Race Relations Act 1976), 'spent' convictions (Rehabilitation of Offenders Act 1974 — see 14.5 above), or disability (Disability Discrimination Act 1995) at any time from before the commencement of employment and during employment. The Trade Union and Labour Relations (Consolidation) Act 1992, s 137(1) makes it unlawful for an employer to refuse a person employment on the grounds that they are, or are not, a member of a trade union or that they refuse to become a member of, or refuse to resign from, a trade union. The Act effectively removes the legal protection of a 'pre-entry' closed shop. Advertising for union, or non-union members, or instructing an employment agency to supply only one type of employee is also acting unlawfully. After employment has commenced, the Employment Rights Act 1996 contains provisions for the protection of employees from suffering detriment in employment (ERA 1996, ss 44–47). These protections include the right not to be discriminated against for:

(*a*)   carrying out health and safety duties (and certain other specified circumstances relating to health and safety);

(*b*)   refusing to work on Sundays;

(*c*)   acting as a trustee of an occupational pension scheme;

(*d*)   activities as an employee representative, or as a candidate for election as such;

(*e*)   making a protected disclosure (within the meaning of the Public Interest Disclosure Act 1998 — see 14.77 below);

(*f*)   asserting certain rights under the Working Time Regulations 1998 (see 14.22 and 14.23 above) or the National Minimum Wage Act 1998 (see 14.71 below); or (*g*)   exercising the right to time off for study or training (see 14.20 above).

Discrimination on the grounds of sex or race can be either direct or indirect (the concept of indirect discrimination does not feature in the Disability Discrimination Act 1995). Direct discrimination is the less favourable treatment of one person compared with another on any of the above grounds, whereas indirect discrimination is the imposition of requirements or conditions which:

(*a*)   are such that the proportion of persons who can comply with them of one sex or race are considerably less than that of the other sex or another race; and

(*b*)   are such that the conditions are detrimental to the other sex or another race and cannot be justified on other grounds.

In *Marshall v Southampton and South West Hampshire Area Health Authority (No 2) [1993] IRLR 445*, the ECJ ruled that it was contrary to Article 6 of the EU Equal Treatment Directive 76/207 to lay down an upper limit for compensation for sex discrimination, as the financial compensation must be adequate depending on the facts of the case. The Government implemented these rulings. In late 1993 the upper limit (£11,000) was removed, and in July 1994 this was extended to race discrimination cases. From March 1996, employment tribunals have been able to award compensation in unintentional and indirect discrimination cases.

Equal pay

14.36   The Equal Pay Act 1970 further operates to reduce discrimination between the sexes by imposing a duty upon employers to pay equal rates of pay to both sexes involved in 'like work' or work rated as equivalent, or work of equal value, unless differences of practical importance exist. A job evaluation scheme must have been made for work to be rated as equivalent. The methods for job evaluation are laid out in ACAS Guide No. 1. In the event of a dispute, it would fall to an employment tribunal to determine whether or not the work was 'like work', work rated as equivalent, or of equal value. In the case of work of equal value, the evidence of a member of an independent panel of experts will also be required. If an equal pay claim is successful up to two years' back pay, including interest, can be claimed. Applicants in equal pay cases can either rely on the Equal Pay Act 1970 or can directly rely upon EU law (Article 141, Treaty of Rome — as renumbered by the Treaty of Amsterdam (formerly Article 119)). Applications under Article 141 are also heard by employment tribunals. The relationship between EU law and the Equal Pay Act 1970 is that the former is dynamically developing, and as it does so it amends the latter by judicial precedent. If UK law is more favourable to an appellant's claim, then it should be made under the Equal Pay Act, if the converse is true then the applicant can rely directly on Article 141. The European Court of Justice has given a wide interpretation to the meaning of 'pay' which falls within Article 141. This includes:

(*a*)   sick pay;

(*b*)   pension schemes supplemental to State provision; and

(*c*)   occupational pension schemes linked to State retirement age (*Barber v Guardian Royal Exchange [1990] IRLR 240*); and

(*d*)   an award of compensation for unfair dismissal (*R v Secretary of State for Employment, ex parte Seymour-Smith and Perez [1999] IRLR 253*).

A Code of Practice on Equal Pay (issued by the Equal Opportunities Commission) came into force on 26 March 1997 and although not compulsory can be admitted as evidence in tribunal proceedings.

Certain exceptions to the basic principle of non-discrimination, however, are introduced by both the Sex Discrimination Act 1975 and the Race Relations Act 1976, examples of which are given below.

Sex Discrimination Act 1975 exceptions

14.37

(*a*)   Where the employee will work wholly or mainly outside Great Britain.

(*b*)   Where sex is a genuine occupational qualification e.g:

  (i)   for physiological reasons (e.g. a male model);

  (ii)   to preserve decency or privacy;

  (iii) where communal premises are provided by the employer and it is not reasonable for the employer to make provision for women;

  (iv)   where the nature of the establishment requires the job to be held by a man.

Race Relations Act 1976 exceptions

14.38

(*a*)   Where the employee will work wholly or mainly outside Great Britain.

(*b*)   Where the employment is in a private household.

(*c*)   Where a genuine occupational qualification exists, e.g:

  (i)   for authenticity in a dramatic or artistic performance;

  (ii)   for the provision of personal services to a racial group;

  (iii) for the service of food and drink to the public in a particular setting where authenticity is required (e.g. a Chinese restaurant).

Employers should also take care not to discriminate against certain races when seeking to comply with the Asylum and Immigration Act 1996 (see 14.39 below).

Asylum and Immigration Act 1996 — employers' liability for illegal workers

14.39   With effect from 27 January 1997, section 8 of the Asylum and Immigration Act 1996 makes it an offence for an employer to engage a person who is not entitled, under the immigration rules, to work in the UK. Employers have a statutory defence if they have checked that a potential employee has a National Insurance (NI) number and have kept a record of that number. When no NI number is available, employers will need to obtain specified documentation, such as a passport or identity card, which demonstrates entitlement to live and work in the UK. Criminal liability for the offence rests with the employer and will be punishable by a fine.

Requests for documentary proof of the right to work in the United Kingdom must be made each and every time to an applicant who is considered for employment. Not to do so is racial discrimination. It is also recommended that staff responsible for hiring employees should know what to look for when asking for proof of a prospective employee's right to work. The stamp, 'Given leave to enter the United Kingdom for an indefinite period', places no restrictions on an applicant's right to stay in the United Kingdom and the applicant is not subject to any alien registration requirements or any restrictions with regard to employment. The Government is issuing a Code of Practice (which, at the time of writing, has been issued in draft form) 'to provide employers with guidance on meeting their obligations and securing the defence available under section 8 ... in a way that does not result in unlawful racial discrimination'.

It should be noted that the legislation only refers to **new** employees engaged after 27 January 1997, although it is an offence to knowingly employ a person without permission to work in the UK.

Disability Discrimination Act 1995

14.40   The Disability Discrimination Act 1995 received Royal Assent on 9 November 1995. The provisions of the Act have gradually come into force since then, via the issuance of regulations. The Act's employment provisions came into force on 2 December 1996. The 1995 Act makes it illegal for UK employers of 15 or more persons to discriminate on the grounds of disability when persons are applying for employment or during the course of employment. Previous legislation in this area was limited to the Disabled Persons (Employment) Act 1944 which established that employers of a substantial number of employees were under a duty to employ a quota of persons registered as disabled. The Companies Act 1985 continues to require companies to disclose in their annual reports details of the training and employment of disabled persons.

The 1995 Act makes it unlawful to discriminate against a disabled person in connection with employment, the provisions of goods, facilities and services or the disposal or management of premises. The DDA 1995, s 1 defines disability by stating that a person has a disability if they have a physical or mental impairment which has a *substantial and long-term adverse effect* on their ability to carry out normal day-to-day activities. DDA 1995, s 2 widens the definition to include for the purposes of those provisions concerned with employment and the provision of goods, facilities and services, those persons who have had a disability but no longer have one, for instance, where someone has had cancer but is now in remission. The Disability Discrimination (Meaning of Disability) Regulations 1996 (SI 1996 No 1455) exclude from the definition of 'disability' addictions (other than those medically caused) (Reg 3); certain personality disorders, e.g. tendencies to steal, cause fires, physically/sexually abuse others (Reg 4(1)); and hayfever and similar conditions (Reg 4(2)). DDA 1995, Sch 1, para 3 states that a severe disfigurement is to be treated as having a 'substantial adverse effect'. Sensory impairments are not specifically referred to in the Act and it is considered that they will be treated as falling within the physical impairment definition.

DDA 1995, Sch 1 defines mental impairment as impairment resulting from or consisting of mental illness only if it is clinically well recognised. Any impairment is likely to be 'long-term' if it is likely to last or has lasted for 12 months. DDA 1995, Sch 1, para 4(1) sets out what are considered to be normal day-to-day activities. These include: mobility; manual dexterity; physical co-ordination; continence; ability to lift, carry or otherwise move everyday objects; speech, hearing or eyesight; and memory.

The Act makes it unlawful for an employer to discriminate against a disabled person in relation to:

(*a*)   selection arrangements;

(*b*)   recruitment;

(*c*)   terms on which employment is offered;

(*d*)   opportunities for promotion, transfer or training;

(*e*)   employee benefits; or

(*f*)   dismissal or any other detrimental treatment.

DDA 1995, s 5 sets out the discrimination test. This states that an employer discriminates against a disabled employee if:

(i)   for a reason which relates to the disabled person's disability he treats him less favourably than he treats or would treat others to whom that reason does not or would not apply; and

(ii)   he cannot show that the treatment in question is justified.

Unlike the RRA 1976 and the SDA 1975 the 1995 Act does allow positive discrimination in that it will not be unlawful to discriminate against someone because they are able bodied.

The Act does provide the employer with a defence, in section 5(3), which is that discriminatory treatment will be justified if the reason for it is both material to the circumstances of the particular case and substantial. The Act does not define 'material' or 'substantial', thus employers will have to wait for case law clarification on the point. Employers should, however, be careful not to impose unnecessary job requirements, for example, requesting the employee has a full driving licence when the job requires very little driving.

The DDA 1995, s 6 imposes upon an employer a duty to make adjustments. Section 6 requires that where any arrangements made by or on behalf of an employer or any physical feature of the premises occupied by the employer, place a disabled person at a substantial disadvantage in comparison with persons without a disability, the employer has a duty to take such steps as are reasonable in all the circumstances for him to take in order to prevent the arrangements having that effect. Section 6(3) sets out some examples of the steps which the employer may have to take. These include:

(A)   making adjustments to premises;

(B)   allocating some of the disabled person's duties to another person;

(C)   transferring him to fill an existing vacancy;

(D)   altering his working hours;

(E)   assigning him to a different place of work;

(F)   allowing him to be absent during working hours for rehabilitation or treatment;

(G)   giving him training;

(H)   acquiring or modifying equipment;

(I)   modifying procedures for testing or assessment;

(J)   providing a reader or interpreter; and

(K)   providing supervision.

The Disability Discrimination (Employment) Regulations 1996 (SI 1996 No 1456) which came into force on 2 December 1996, provide for circumstances where the treatment of a disabled employee (or a failure to make an adjustment to premises) is justified. These include:

(I)   where pay is linked to performance (Reg 3);

(II)   where there are uniform rates of contribution to an occupational pension scheme regardless of the benefits received (Reg 4); and

(III)   where building works complied with (and continue to comply with) the building regulations in relation to access and facilities for disabled people at the time the works were carried out (Reg 8).

Like the RRA 1976 and the SDA 1975, the DDA 1995 makes it unlawful to discriminate by way of victimisation. The DDA 1995 also makes the employer vicariously liable for contravention of the Act by his employees, unless the employer can show that they took such steps as were reasonably practicable to prevent the discriminatory act (see 14.33 above). Complaints should be presented to an employment tribunal within three months of the act complained of. Compensation which can be awarded by employment tribunals will be unlimited. They will also be able to recommend action to be taken by the employer within a specified time.

For a case in which the EAT set out detailed guidance as to the approach which employment tribunals should take in determining whether an applicant is disabled within the meaning of the DDA 1995, see *Goodwin v Patent Office* [*1999*] *IRLR 4*. In *Clark v Novacold Ltd* [*1999*] *IRLR 318*, the Court of Appeal (in its first decision in respect of the DDA 1995) considered the issue of what constitutes discrimination in employment. Among other conclusions, the Court held that in order to establish less favourable treatment, it is not necessary for a disabled person to identify an able-bodied comparator who has (or would have) been treated differently. The test of less favourable treatment is based on the reason for the treatment of the disabled person and not the fact of his disability.

Equal treatment and pensions provision

14.41   On 28 September 1994, the decision in six cases being heard together before the European Court of Justice (ECJ) was announced. All involved the issue of sex equality and pension schemes. The cases arose from the ECJ's ruling of May 1990 in *Barber v Guardian Royal Exchange* [*1990*] *IRLR 240*. The case held that EU law outlawed pay discrimination between men and women, and that this also applied to benefits under private occupational pension schemes and retirement ages. In *Ten Oever v Stichting Bedrijfspensionenfonds voor het Glazenwassers en Schoonmaakbedrijf* [*1993*] *IRLR 601* (the 'Ten Oever' case) the ECJ ruled that the *Barber* judgment did not apply retrospectively. In *Coloroll Pension Trustees Ltd v Russell* [*1994*] *IRLR 586* the ECJ ruled that both employers and trustees are bound to apply the equal treatment rules, and employers could continue to rely on sex-based actuarial rates for the calculation of transfer values and commutation values for those leaving the scheme. It was not sexually discriminatory to take into account the actuarial assumption that women tend to outlive men, and consequently give rise to lower pension payments for men. In *Vroege v NCIV* [*1995*] *ICR 635* the ECJ ruled that employers will need to admit part-time workers to pension schemes, if barring them constituted discrimination. The ECJ reasoned that employers should have realised from its judgments in 1976 (in *Defrenne v Sabrena (No 2)* [*1976*] *ECR 455*) that barring part-time workers from pension schemes is frequently discriminatory and should have ended the practice long ago. This right is not limited by the *Barber* judgment and retrospective claims can be made back to April 1976.

In *Preston v Wolverhampton Healthcare NHS Trust* [*1998*] *IRLR 198*, the House of Lords referred to the ECJ the issue of whether the two domestic time limits outlined below were compatible with EU law:

(*a*)   section 2(4) of the Equal Pay Act 1970, whereby a claim for membership of an occupational pension scheme must be brought within six months of the end of the employment to which the claim relates; and

(*b*)   section 2(5) of that Act, which limits an employee's entitlement to arrears of compensation to a two-year period prior to the date on which proceedings were instituted.

The decision of the ECJ in *Preston* is awaited at the time of writing. However, in *Levez v T H Jennings (Harlow Pools) Ltd [1999] IRLR 36*, the ECJ held (following a reference to it from the EAT in that case) that the application of section 2(5) is precluded by EU law:

(i)   where the delay in bringing the claim is due to the employee being provided with inaccurate information by the employer, so that she had no way of determining whether (and, if so, to what extent) she was being discriminated against); and

(ii)   even where another remedy is available, if that remedy is likely to entail procedural rules or other conditions which are less favourable than those applicable to similar domestic actions — it is for the national court (in this case, the EAT) to determine whether that is the case.

The decision of the EAT is awaited, but it has been suggested by certain commentators that the result of the ECJ's judgement in *Levez* will be the ending of the two-year limitation in section 2(5).

Readers should also refer to Chapter 12 'Pensions'.

Statutory maternity rights

14.42   Statutory maternity rights are currently contained in several pieces of legislation, comprising, for example, the Employment Rights Act 1996, the Social Security (Contributions and Benefits) Act 1992, the Social Security Act 1989 and regulations under the Health and Safety at Work etc. Act 1974 (notably the Management of Health and Safety at Work (Amendment) Regulations 1994 (SI 1994 No 2865)).

The legislation provides for statutory rights in four specific areas:

(*a*)   time off for ante-natal care;

(*b*)   protection against unfair dismissal on maternity-related grounds;

(*c*)   maternity leave and maternity absence (see 14.43(*b*) and (*c*) below for the distinction); and

(*d*)   maternity benefit.

Note that the Employment Relations Act 1999 (for an outline of which, see the Appendix to this chapter) will replace, with new provisions supplemented by regulations, the current provisions in the Employment Rights Act 1996 relating to maternity leave, and unfair dismissal on maternity grounds. These new provisions are expected to come into force in December 1999. The current provisions are outlined below.

Requirements

14.43   The Employment Rights Act 1996, ss 71–78 provides maternity rights for women:

(*a*) to time off for ante-natal care (no service qualification exists for this right) (ERA 1996, s 55);

(*b*) to return to work up to 29 weeks after beginning of the actual week of confinement, subject to a service qualification of two years immediately prior to the 11th week before the expected week of confinement (ERA 1996, s 79), known as 'maternity absence';

(*c*) to maternity leave of 14 weeks, applying to all women regardless of length of service (ERA 1996, s 73);

(*d*) to complain of unfair dismissal on account of pregnancy (dismissal by reason of pregnancy is automatically unfair, see 14.74 below);

(*e*) to entitlement to the benefit of the terms and conditions of employment which would have been applicable to her if she had not been absent (and had not been pregnant or given birth to a child). This is subject to the employee fulfilling certain requirements (see (A)–(C) below) (ERA 1996, s 71).

As a result of EU Directive 92/85/EEC, all pregnant workers have a right to 14 weeks' maternity leave, regardless of length of service and hours worked. This right has applied to any pregnant worker with an expected week of confinement (EWC) commencing on or after 16 October 1994. The maternity leave period starts from:

(i)   the notified date of confinement;

(ii) the start of the 6th week before the EWC if the employee is already absent with a pregnancy related illness;

(iii) the first day she becomes sick with a pregnancy related illness if this is after the start of the sixth week before the EWC, whichever is the later; and

(iv) the date of the childbirth;

and continues for 14 weeks or until the end of two weeks' compulsory leave, whichever is the later.

In order to enjoy the right to maternity leave, the employee must conform with the following requirements:

(A) give advance notice of 21 days (or as soon as reasonably practicable), in writing if the employer so requests, giving the date of the start of absence (which must be no earlier than the beginning of the eleventh week before the EWC); or

(B) where she is first absent wholly or partly because of pregnancy or childbirth before the notified leave date (or before she has notified such a date) after the beginning of the sixth week before the EWC, notify her employer (in writing, if he so requests) as soon as is reasonably practicable that she is absent for that reason; and

(C) give advance notice in writing 21 days (or as soon as is reasonably practicable) before the start of the maternity leave period that she is pregnant, and of the expected week of childbirth (or, if childbirth has occurred, the date on which it occurred); and

(D)   if requested to do so by her employer, produce for his inspection a certificate from a registered medical practitioner, or a registered midwife, stating the expected week of childbirth.

The Maternity Rights (Compulsory Leave) Regulations 1994 (SI 1994 No 2479) which came into force on 19 October 1994 prohibit, by Regulation 2, an employee who is entitled to maternity leave in accordance with Part VIII of the Employment Rights Act 1996, from working during the period of two weeks which commence with the day on which childbirth occurs. An employer who breaches this requirement (i.e. who allows the employee to work within 14 days of childbirth) can be fined up to a maximum of £500.

Protection from dismissal

14.44   A woman who is pregnant on maternity leave has the absolute statutory right not to be dismissed because of her pregnancy or for any pregnancy-related reason. This right applies regardless of the hours she works or how long she has worked. The ERA 1996 also requires employers to provide written reasons for any dismissal of a woman who is pregnant or on maternity leave, regardless of the reason for the dismissal and even if totally unconnected with her condition. Although a woman dismissed on these grounds can pursue an unfair dismissal claim (see 14.74 below), she is not precluded from taking her claim under sex discrimination law (see 14.35 above). The advantages to her of seeking to establish a claim on that basis is that any compensation awarded under a heading of discrimination is now not subject to any statutory maximum.

In the case of *Webb v EMO Air Cargo (UK) Ltd [1995] IRLR 645*, the House of Lords adopted a ruling of the ECJ that an employer who has dismissed a woman employed to cover for a pregnancy absence when it was discovered that she too was pregnant was acting contrary to the EU Directive on equal treatment. Also, an employer refusing to take a woman back after her maternity leave, because her replacement was more suitable, was also guilty of unfair dismissal (*Rees v Apollo Watch Repairs plc [1996] ICR 436*).

It may be fair to dismiss a pregnant employee, or one on maternity leave, for reasons of redundancy provided that this was not the reason for her selection. In all redundancy cases where a woman is pregnant or on maternity leave there is now a requirement under the ERA 1996, s 77 to offer a suitable position where there is a vacancy. The new contract has to be suitable to the employee, with work appropriate for her to do in the circumstances, and on terms and conditions which are not substantially less favourable.

Suspension on the grounds of pregnancy

14.45   The Suspension from Work (on Maternity Grounds) Order 1994 (SI 1994 No 2930) introduces the new employment protection rights for women in relation to suspension from work on maternity grounds. The regulations have been effective since 1 December 1994. The rights protect women who are pregnant, who have recently given birth or are breastfeeding, if they have to be suspended from work because their job poses a risk to their health and safety. The rights, contained in the ERA 1996, ss 66–67 include the following:

(*a*)   the right to be offered suitable alternative work where this is available;

(*b*)   where there is not suitable alternative work and where the employee is therefore suspended, the right to be paid her normal remuneration (except where the employer has offered her suitable alternative work and she has unreasonably refused it); and

(*c*)   it is automatically unfair for an employer to dismiss a woman rather than move or suspend her under the new provisions.

Women who consider that their rights have been infringed can take their complaint to an employment tribunal, regardless of the length of service.

Return to work

14.46   A woman who has the 14-week leave entitlement need do nothing at the end of her leave other than present herself for work. She is not obliged to give advance notice of her return date. However, if she wishes to return before the end of 14 weeks, then she has to give at least 7 days' notice. Women exercising their rights to the 29 weeks' leave, which is additional to a leave of up to 11 weeks before the expected date of the baby's birth (see 14.43 above), must confirm their intention to return in writing if so requested. Any time during the 11 weeks after the beginning of her leave her employer may write asking if she intends to come back to work. She must reply in writing within 14 days or she may lose the right to return. In addition, a woman with the 29 weeks' leave must also separately give 21 days' notice of the date she intends to return. Her employer can postpone this return by up to four weeks. In the joined appeal cases of *Crees v Royal London Insurance Soc. Ltd* and *Greaves v Kwik Save Stores Ltd [1998] IRLR 245*, the Court of Appeal decided that a woman completes the process of exercising her right to return to work by giving the appropriate 21 days' written notice and it is not necessary to physically attend work to protect her rights. (See also *Halfpenny v IGE Medical Systems Ltd [1999] IRLR 177.*)

The one exception to the right to return to work is where a woman is entitled to the longer leave, but her employer employs five or fewer employees and shows that it was not reasonably practicable to allow her to return or to offer suitable alternative employment. Under ERA 1996, s 96 this would not give rise to an unfair dismissal claim. However, even in cases of small employers, the right to return after 14 weeks' leave would continue. A woman with a statutory entitlement to the longer leave but who works for a small employer can choose only to exercise her rights to the restricted leave and thereby guarantee her right to return.

Contractual rights during maternity leave

14.47   During the first 14 weeks' leave, under ERA 1996, s 71 a woman is entitled to benefit from all of her contractual terms save those covering remuneration. This means that she will continue to accrue rights to conditions like holidays, pension credits, service-related benefits, company cars and other perks. The rights to these entitlements do not extend beyond the first 14 weeks' leave, and tribunals will not look to see how male employees have been treated whilst not at work to determine other non-pay entitlements. The ECJ (in *Gillespie* — see 14.48 below) have rejected the concept of comparing the treatment of women while on maternity leave and that of men on sick leave. This means that rights like entitlement to accrued holidays would not automatically extend to women on maternity leave, particularly those on the longer maternity leave.

Under the Statutory Maternity Pay (General) Regulations 1986 (SI 1986 No 1960), regulation 26, employers must keep records for the three-year period following the end of the tax year in which a maternity pay period ends.

Statutory maternity pay (SMP)

14.48   All employees who by the 15th week before the week that their baby is due:

(*a*)   have worked for at least 26 weeks continuously; and

(*b*)   have earned at least £66 a week (1999/2000),

have the right to Statutory Maternity Pay (SMP) irrespective of whether or not they intend to return to work.

SMP is payable for a maximum of 18 weeks and is set at the following rates:

(i)   6 weeks' pay at 90% of average earnings; plus

(ii)   12 weeks at a flat rate of £59.55 a week (1999/2000).

If a backdated wage increase is agreed during the employee's period of maternity pay, the amount due has to take account of the increase, according to the ECJ in the case of *Gillespie and others v Northern Ireland Health and Social Services Board [1996] IRLR 214*. The Statutory Maternity Pay (General) Amendment Regulations 1996 (SI 1996 No 1335) gave effect to this. However, the court also held that the claim that employees on maternity leave should be entitled to the same level of pay as would have been met had their absence been on account of sickness was not a requirement of European law.

To gain her entitlement to SMP a woman must have complied with the notification rules which are:

(A)   she must have given her employer 21 days' notice in writing of her intention to stop work and claim SMP;

(B)   she must have produced a copy of her maternity certificate (MATB1); and

(C)   she must have stopped work.

She can decide when to begin her leave and start receiving her SMP but can do this no earlier than 11 weeks before the expected week of birth. She can, however, work up to the expected week of birth provided that she has not had to go on leave due to a pregnancy-related sickness in the final six weeks of the birth. Any sickness (even if pregnancy-related) prior to the six-week period should be treated as normal sickness and SSP should be paid. Non-pregnancy related sickness in the last six weeks may also be treated as part of SSP if the employee has not indicated her intention to begin her maternity leave.

Once she has returned to work, entitlement to SMP ends. This means that a woman with just 14 weeks' leave must forfeit the remaining four weeks' SMP by returning to work at the end of 14 weeks. The only exception to this rule is where she falls sick after a return to work but within 18 weeks. In this case she reverts, not to SSP, but to SMP.

Employers may no longer reclaim all that they have to pay out in SMP. For payments of SMP which fell due on or after 4 September 1994, employers other than 'small employers' (broadly those whose NI contributions for the qualifying tax year do not exceed £20,000) will only be able to recover 92% of such payments. The Statutory Maternity Pay (Compensation of Employers) Amendment Regulations 1999 (SI 1999 No 363), which came into force on 6 April 1999, reduced the percentage that small employers can recover for paying statutory maternity pay from 7% to 5%.

Statutory maternity allowance (SMA)

14.49   Women who have worked and paid National Insurance contributions in 26 out of the 66 weeks ending with the week before the expected week of childbirth are entitled to claim a maximum of 18 weeks of SMA. There are two rates of SMA — the lower rate is £51.70 for 1999/2000 and the higher rate is £59.55.

Statutory sick pay (SSP)

14.50   Statutory sick pay (SSP) was introduced by the Social Security and Housing Benefits Act 1982 as a means of reducing the administrative burden on the state of paying sickness benefit. The main set of regulations is the Statutory Sick Pay (General) Regulations 1982 (SI 1982 No 894), as amended. SSP is payable to all eligible employees for periods of absence exceeding three days and up to 28 weeks. The SSP scheme applies to all employers regardless of size.

Employers used to be able to reclaim 80% of their payments made under SSP by deducting them from their monthly national insurance contributions

(Statutory Sick Pay Act 1991, s 1). However, the Statutory Sick Pay Act 1994, which came into force on 6 April 1994, has abolished the 80% rebate large employers receive in respect of SSP and has restricted the employers' right of recovery to companies receiving small employers' relief. Basically, the government shifted the cost from themselves to employers.

Employers whose contributions in a qualifying tax year did not exceed £20,000 (employers' and employees' share), used to be able to reclaim if the employee had been off sick for four weeks or more (the Statutory Sick Pay (Small Employers' Relief) Amendment Regulations 1994 (SI 1994 No 561)). On 6 April 1995 the new percentage threshold scheme (PTS) came into force and replaced the small employers' relief scheme for the recovery of statutory sick pay. The rules are contained in the Statutory Sick Pay Percentage Threshold Order 1995 (SI 1995 No 512). The Order allows any employer to recover the amount of SSP paid in a tax month which exceeds a specified percentage (13% for 1999/2000) of gross liability in the same tax month. A simple calculation is therefore required to ascertain whether or not there is an amount of SSP which can be recovered in a tax month:

(*a*)   establish the gross Class 1 NICs liability for the tax month (exclude Class 1A NICs)

(*b*)   multiply the figure by 13%

(*c*)   establish the total SSP payments in the same tax month

(*d*)   if the amount at step 3 exceeds the amount at step 2, the difference can be recovered.

The amount an employer may pay his employees whilst they are absent from work will depend on the terms and conditions of employment. Most employees are entitled to receive SSP which is paid at predetermined rates.

1999/2000 rates

14.51   The rate of statutory sick pay from 6 April 1999 for employees earning £66.00 or over is £59.55 a week (Social Security Benefits Up-rating Order 1999 (SI 1999 No 264)).

Certain categories of employee are not entitled to SSP, generally those who:

(*a*)   are aged 65 or over or under 16 years of age on the first day of the period of incapacity for work (PIW);

(*b*)   are employed for a period of less than 13 continuous weeks or engaged on a fixed term contract of three months or less;

(*c*)   are earning less than the lower level of weekly earnings for national insurance (£66.00 per week);

(*d*)   are sick during the period of a stoppage due to a trade dispute;

(e)   are sick whilst in legal custody;

(f)   have done no work for their employer under the contract of service;

(g)   are abroad in a country outside the EEA;

(h)   have already received 28 weeks' SSP from his employer in any one PIW, or in any two or more linked periods (two or more PIWs separated by 8 weeks or less are 'linked' and are counted as one PIW);

(j)   have provided a leaver's certificate showing that they have had 28 weeks' SSP from a former employer, the final payment of which was made within the last 56 days;

(k)   are or have been pregnant and have received or would have received maternity pay or allowance in the same period had they been entitled. An employee cannot receive SSP for 18 weeks starting from the beginning of the week she is first entitled to SMP or SMA.

Eligible employees become entitled to SSP once they have been sick through illness for at least four days in a row and this period of absence includes three qualifying days. They must also have complied with the agreed notification procedures. Notification of absence through illness can be required by the end of the first day of the illness, but if the employer does not specify a date, then the employee has seven days before he needs to notify his employer in writing. Notification arrangements are usually agreed between the employer and the worker or workers' representatives and normally include a self-certification form for the first seven days' absence.

Companies Act 1985

14.52   The Companies Act 1985 (CA 1985) contains a number of provisions relating to employment mostly relating to duties which the directors owe to employees and the disclosure of information.

(a)   *Employees' interests*
Section 309(1) of the CA 1985 states that the directors of a company must have regard in the performance of their functions to the interests of employees as well as those of the company's shareholders. However, CA 1985, s 309(2) somewhat narrows this obligation by stating that the duty of the directors is owed to the company alone and not to the employees. Thus, employees have no right of redress if in disagreement with any of the directors' decisions.

(b)   *Directors' report*
Schedule 7 to the CA 1985 contains a number of provisions concerning the disclosure of certain items in the directors' report on a company's annual financial statements, where the average number of persons employed by the company in each week during the financial year exceeds 250.

Items that must appear in such circumstances are as follows.

(i)   A statement of the company's policy on the employment, training, career development and promotion of disabled persons (CA 1985, Sch 7, Part III).

(ii) A statement describing action taken by the company to introduce, maintain and develop arrangements on:

(A)   the provision of information on matters of concern to employees;

(B)   the consultation of employees;

(C)   employee involvement in the company's performance;

(D)   the awareness of the employees of the financial and economic factors which affect the company.

(CA 1985, Sch 7, Part V).

Health and safety legislation

14.53   The basis of UK health and safety law is the Health and Safety at Work etc. Act 1974 (HSWA). The Act sets out the general duties which employers have towards their employees and members of the public, and those duties that employees have to themselves and to each other. These duties are qualified by the principle of 'so far as is reasonably practicable'. In other words, the degree of risk in a particular job or workplace needs to be balanced against the time, trouble, cost and physical difficulty of taking measures to avoid or reduce the risk. The law requires that management look at what the risks are and take sensible measures to tackle them. The Management of Health and Safety at Work Regulations 1992 (SI 1992 No 2051) generally make more explicit what employers are required to do to manage health and safety under the Health and Safety at Work etc. Act. Like the Act itself they apply to every work activity.

The area of health and safety law has been one of considerable change in recent years, mainly because of legislative developments emanating from the European Union. Directives have resulted in a host of regulations in the UK. The HSWA 1974 has been supplemented by the so-called 'six pack' of regulations (as amended). These are:

(*a*)   Management of Health and Safety at Work Regulations 1992 (SI 1992 No 2051);

(*b*)   Health and Safety (Display Screen Equipment) Regulations 1992 (SI 1992 No 2792);

(*c*)   Manual Handling Operations Regulations 1992 (SI 1992 No 2793);

(*d*)   Provision and Use of Work Equipment Regulations 1998 (SI 1998 No 2306);

(*e*)   Personal Protective Equipment at Work Regulations 1992 (SI 1992 No 2966); and

(*f*)   Workplace (Health, Safety and Welfare) Regulations 1992 (SI 1992 No 3004).

These regulations came fully into force on 1 January 1996 (except for the Regulations referred to in (*d*) above, which came into force on 5 December 1998, replacing the 1992 Regulations of the same name). These and any other relevant regulations are detailed below.

In addition to EU developments, there will also be many forthcoming changes as a result of the review of the Health and Safety Commission (HSC) which reported in May 1994. As a result of the review, the HSC has set out a programme to simplify and modernise existing health and safety law over the next four to five years. This will result in the repeal of seven Acts and around 100 sets of regulations. Most of the repeals deal with legislation which was enacted before HSWA 1974, such as the Offices, Shops and Railway Premises Act 1963 and the Factories Act 1961. Much of this legislation has already been incrementally repealed by new EU sourced Regulations, such as those listed above. In such a fluid situation readers should therefore ensure that they check the current situation.

The Health and Safety at Work etc. Act 1974

14.54   HSWA is the main legislation covering health and safety applying to virtually all workers and workplaces in the UK. It lays down the general principles for the health and safety of employees and others affected by work activity, and established the Health and Safety Executive (HSE). The Act lays down broad general duties and acts as a framework, with detailed health and safety regulations and Approved Codes of Practice (ACOPs) (including those that implement EU Directives) being made under the Act. The Act:

(*a*)   imposes duties on employers, the self-employed and employees;

(*b*)   outlines the role of the Health and Safety Executive (HSE), and the Health and Safety Commission (HSC) — the HSE's enforcement arm;

(*c*)   sets out enforcement provisions; and

(*d*)   details the penalties for non-compliance.

Employers' duties — Section 2 of HSWA requires every employer to ensure, so far as is reasonably practicable, the health, safety and welfare of his employees. Employers must provide and maintain plant and safe systems of work so that they are, so far as is reasonably practicable, safe and without risks to health. They must make arrangements to provide the necessary information, instruction, training and supervision to ensure the health and safety of employees. Employers must also maintain a safe working environment with adequate facilities and welfare arrangements (including safe access and egress). Section 2 does not detail what constitutes a 'safe system of work'.

In *R v Gateway Foodmarkets Ltd* [*1997*] *IRLR 189*, the Court of Appeal held that a company was in breach of its duty under section 2 for a failure at store management level to take all reasonable precautions to avoid the risk of injury to an employee, even though at senior management or head office level, all reasonable precautions had been taken. Section 2 of the HSWA was also relevant to an important decision on smoking at work. In *Waltons and Morse v Dorrington [1997] IRLR 488,* the EAT held that there is an implied contractual term that an employer will provide and monitor for employees a working environment that is reasonably suitable for the performance of their duties. An employee was constructively dismissedwhen her employers failed either to provide a smoke-free environment or to deal adequately with her complaints about colleagues who smoked at work. The HSE advocates that clear procedures should be adopted, and for serious hazards a written 'permit to work' system should be adopted. The duties under section 2 are qualified by the phrase 'so far as is reasonably practicable'. This has been interpreted in the courts as meaning that the costs of carrying out the health and safety measures must not be grossly disproportionate to the benefits to be obtained from doing it.

Section 2 also requires every employer with five or more employees to prepare a written health and safety policy. It should detail the hazards present at the workplace, and the organisation and arrangements in force for implementing the policy. It should be revised 'as often as appropriate', be brought to the notice of employees, and state all persons within the organisation with health and safety responsibilities.

Section 2(6) provides for employers to consult with safety representatives to enable co-operation to effectively promote health and safety, and to check the effectiveness of current arrangements. Where requested by two or more safety representatives, the employer must establish a safety committee. The Safety Representatives and Safety Committees Regulations 1977 (SI 1977 No 500), as amended by the Management of Health and Safety at Work Regulations 1992 (see 14.55 below) set out in detail the function of such representatives and committees where a trade union is recognised by an employer, and employers' duties to consult with them. With effect from 1 October 1996, the Health and Safety (Consultation with Employees) Regulations 1996 (SI 1996 No 1513) require an employer to consult all employees on health and safety issues, regardless of whether the employer recognises a trade union. Where there is no recognised union, these Regulations require an employer to consult either with elected 'representatives of employee safety' or directly with employees. (For the right of safety representatives and representatives of employee safety to time off work with pay, and the right not to suffer a detriment, see 14.20 above; and for protection against unfair dismissal, see 14.74 below.)

Section 3 of the HSWA requires employers and self-employed persons to conduct their undertakings so as to ensure that persons other than employees are not exposed to risks to their health and safety. For cases regarding an employer's liability under this provision, see e.g. *R v British Steel plc [1995] IRLR 310* (employer still liable even though senior management were not involved) and *R v Associated Octel Co Ltd [1997] IRLR 123* (employer liable for negligence of independent contractor).

Section 9 prohibits employers from charging employees for items of equipment or protective clothing required by law.

Employees' duties — Section 7 of HSWA sets out that every employee must take reasonable care for the health and safety of himself and other people at work. If there is a legal requirement on an employer to undertake safety measures, the employee must co-operate with his employer to fulfil his legal duty.

Management of Health and Safety at Work Regulations 1992 (as amended)

14.55   The general duties outlined in HSWA have been made clearer by the Management of Health and Safety at Work Regulations 1992, which came into force on 1 January 1993. These Regulations arose from the European 'Framework Directive' (89/391/EEC) 'on the introduction of measures to encourage improvements in the health and safety of workers at work', which mirrors HSWA but contains more specific requirements. The main requirements under the Regulations are for employers to:

(*a*)   carry out risk assessments;

(*b*)   make and record arrangements for implementing the health and safety measures identified as being necessary in the risk assessment;(*c*)   appoint competent people to help implement the health and safety arrangements;

(*d*)   establish emergency procedures;

(*e*)   provide understandable information and adequate training for employees; and

(*f*)   co-ordinate health and safety measures with other employers sharing the same workplace.

The central requirement is to carry out a 'suitable and sufficient' risk assessment (Regulation 3), in order to decide what health and safety measures are needed. HSE guidance indicates that the level of detail in the risk assessment should be determined by the risks. Risk assessments must be recorded where five or more people are employed.

The Management of Health and Safety at Work (Amendment) Regulations 1994 (SI 1994 No 2865) came into force on 1 December 1994. The Regulations amend the 1992 Regulations requiring employers to assess the risks to the health and safety of 'new and expectant mothers' to ensure that they are not exposed to risks. The Regulations apply to employees who are pregnant, who have given birth or miscarried within the previous six months, or who are breastfeeding. Employers must assess risks, and ensure that workers are not exposed to risks identified by the risk assessment which would present a danger to their health and safety. The HSE has provided a list of known risks and agents. If there is still a significant risk, after taking reasonable preventative action, the employer must: temporarily adjust the worker's hours or conditions of work to avoid the risk; offer her alternative work; or if neither of the former is appropriate give her paid leave from work for as long as it is necessary to protect her health and safety. The ERA 1996, s 66(3) requires that any alternative work offered under the

Regulations is no less favourable than her normal terms and conditions. (See also 14.45 above.)

Regulations on health, safety and welfare at workplace premises

14.56 Under the framework established by HSWA 1974 and the Management of Health and Safety at Work Regulations 1992, specific regulations deal with health, safety and welfare at workplace premises. The main statutory requirements of which readers should be aware are as follows:

(*a*) Workplace (Health, Safety and Welfare) Regulations 1992 (SI 1992 No 3004);

(*b*) Health and Safety (Safety Signs and Signals) Regulations 1996 (SI 1996 No 341);

(*c*) Fire Precautions Act 1971 (as amended by the Fire Safety and Safety of Places of Sport Act 1987) and the Fire Precautions (Workplace) Regulations 1997 (SI 1997 No 1840);

(*d*) Electricity at Work Regulations 1989 (SI 1989 No 635);

(*e*) Gas Safety (Installation and Use) Regulations 1998 (SI 1998 No 2451); and

(*f*) Health and Safety Information for Employees (Modifications and Repeals) Regulations 1995 (SI 1995 No 2923).

Regulations on equipment, plant and machinery

14.57 Regulations made in this category cover employers' responsibilities for equipment, plant, machinery used at work (including display screen equipment) and personal protective equipment (PPE). The main statutory requirements of which readers should be aware are as follows:

(*a*) Provision and Use of Work Equipment Regulations 1998 (SI 1998 No 2306);

(*b*) Supply of Machinery (Safety) Regulations 1992 (SI 1992 No 3073) as amended by the Supply of Machinery (Safety) (Amendment) Regulations 1994 (SI 1994 No 2063);

(*c*) Personal Protective Equipment at Work Regulations 1992 (SI 1992 No 2966) as amended by the Personal Protective Equipment (EC Directive) Regulations 1992 (SI 1992 No 3139), the Personal Protective Equipment (EC Directive) (Amendment) Regulations 1994 (SI 1994 No 2326) and the Personal Protective Equipment (EC Directive) (Amendment) Regulations 1996 (SI 1996 No 3039); and

(*d*) Health and Safety (Display Screen Equipment) Regulations 1992 (SI 1992 No 2792).

Regulations on physical hazards

14.58 Regulations made in this category cover noise, radiation, manual handling, major accident hazards, work related upper limb disorders

(WRULDs)/repetitive strain injury (RSI), and vibration. The main statutory requirements are:

(*a*)   Noise at Work Regulations 1989 (SI 1989 No 1790);

(*b*)   Ionising Radiations Regulations 1985 (SI 1985 No 1333) as amended by the Ionising Radiations (Outside Workers) Regulations 1993 (SI 1993 No 2379);

(*c*)   Manual Handling Operations Regulations 1992 (SI 1992 No 2793); and

(*d*)   Control of Substances Hazardous to Health Regulations 1999 (SI 1999 No 437) ('COSHH'); and

(*e*)   Control of Major Accident Hazards Regulations 1999 (SI 1999 No 743) ('COMAH').

Regulations on first aid

14.59   The Health and Safety (First-Aid) Regulations 1981 (SI 1981 No 917) impose a general duty on employers to make adequate and appropriate first-aid provision for employees if they are injured or become ill at work. This includes providing first-aid equipment and arranging for first-aiders or an appointed person to administer first aid.

The accompanying Approved Code of Practice (ACOP) to the regulations was revised in 1997, giving employers greater flexibility in determining their own workplace first aid provision. The Regulations require the employer to make an assessment of first-aid requirements, and he should provide a suitable first-aid room or rooms should the assessment identify this as necessary. The ACOP states that at least one suitably stocked and properly identified first-aid container should be provided, which should be easily accessible and placed near to handwashing facilities where possible.

Regulations on reporting of accidents and injuries at work

14.60   The Reporting of Injuries, Diseases and Dangerous Occurrences Regulations 1995 (SI 1995 No 3163) 'RIDDOR' require certain events relating to accidents and ill-health at work to be recorded, notified and reported by a 'responsible person' to the enforcing authority, which may be the Health and Safety Executive or the local authority environmental health department. Under RIDDOR 'responsible persons' (normally employers) must notify enforcing authorities by the quickest possible means of the following:

(*a*)   the death of a person as a result of an accident arising out of or in connection with work;

(*b*)   a major injury suffered as a result of an accident arising out of or in connection with work;

(*c*)   an injury suffered by a person not at work (e.g. a visitor, customer, client, passenger or bystander) as a result of an accident arising out of or in connection with work;

(*d*)   a major injury suffered by a person not at work, as a result of an accident arising out of or in connection with work at a hospital; and

(*e*)   a dangerous occurrence.

Accidents now include non consensual physical acts of violence done to a person at work, and suicides on, or in the course of the operation of a railway, tramway, vehicle system or guided transport system. Deaths or major injuries arising from gas incidents must now be notified, as must injuries or deaths where a vehicle was involved.

In addition to the notification, the employer must submit a written report within ten days of the incident to the relevant enforcing authority. A report must also be submitted where by reason of an accident at work, a person has been incapacitated for his normal work for more than three consecutive days. Gas incidents must be reported within 14 days. Cases of disease must be reported forthwith if the employer has received a written statement by a doctor which diagnoses the disease as one listed as reportable in Schedule 3 to the Regulations. The employer must also report the death of an employee if it occurs within a year of that employee suffering a reportable injury.

RIDDOR, Reg 7 outlines the record-keeping requirements imposed on the employer.

In addition to the requirements under RIDDOR, employers must also ensure that all injuries, regardless of how minor, are recorded in an accident book. An accident book is required under the Social Security (Claims and Payments) Regulations 1979 (SI 1979 No 628) for all premises covered by the Factories Act 1961 or where ten or more people are employed at any one time. The book must contain the following information:

 (i)   full name, address and occupation of the injured person;

(ii)   date and time of the accident;

(iii)   place where the accident happened;

(iv)   cause and nature of the injury; and

 (v)   name, address and occupation of the person giving notice, if other than the injured person.

Accident books are required to be kept for a period of three years from the date of the last entry.

Major injuries. Major injuries are listed in RIDDOR, Schedule 1 as including:

(*a*)   any fracture;

(*b*)   dislocation of the shoulder, hip, knee or spine;

(*c*)   any amputation;

(*d*)   loss of sight (whether temporary or permanent);

(*e*) a chemical or hot metal burn to the eye or any penetrating injury to the eye;

(*f*) any injury resulting from an electric shock or electrical burn (including one caused by arcing or arcing products) leading to unconsciousness or requiring resuscitation or admittance to hospital for more than 24 hours;

(*g*) any other injury leading to hypothermia, heat induced illness or unconsciousness; requiring resuscitation or admittance to hospital for more than 24 hours;

(*h*) acute illness requiring immediate medical treatment, or loss of consciousness, resulting from the absorption of any substance by inhalation, ingestion or through the skin; and

(*j*) acute illness requiring medical treatment where there is reason to believe that the illness resulted from exposure to biological agents or its toxins or infected material.

Enforcement of legislation

14.61 Enforcement of the HSWA is by the Health and Safety Executive, who appoint inspectors with powers to inspect workplaces, to institute prosecution proceedings for breaches of safe practices and to issue improvement notices for and prohibition notices against the carrying out of certain practices.

Improvement notices direct the employer to take certain actions or make improvements within a given time (not less than 21 days) when a health and safety law has been broken and is likely to be broken again. An employer can appeal to an employment tribunal, in which case the notice is suspended until the appeal is heard. New procedures have recently been introduced for the serving of improvement notices. An inspector must now give the employer two weeks' notice of his/her intention to serve an improvement notice. The employer can then make informal representations, before the notice is served. Prohibition notices are served where a process carries a possibility of serious imminent danger. The notice forbids the process until the faults specified in the notice are rectified. If an appeal is made against a prohibition notice, it remains in force, unless the tribunal otherwise directs.

Other bodies which have powers of enforcement include the local authorities and fire authorities. It is quite possible that more than one body may have responsibility for the health, safety and welfare aspects of an employer's premises or operation. The local office of the HSE is able to determine who has responsibility for any particular part of an employer's premises or operations.

Wages and salary

14.62 Pay is a basic element in the contract of employment, and the contract is therefore a key to determining pay rights. The rights contained in the Wages

Act 1986 are now consolidated into the Employment Rights Act 1996, the former statute thus being repealed. As part of an employee's Section 1 statement of particulars of employment, the employer is under an obligation to provide the following details (which are applicable at a specified date no more than seven days before the Section 1 statement):

(*a*)   the scale or rate of remuneration or the method of calculating remuneration; and

(*b*)   the intervals at which the remuneration is paid (i.e. weekly, monthly etc.).

Pay

14.63   The method of pay is now a matter of agreement between the employer and employee. However, if employees have always been paid in cash and there is no provision within the employees' contracts allowing the employer to vary the method of payment, a unilateral change to cashless pay could amount to a breach of contract.

All employees are entitled to an itemised pay statement by virtue of ERA 1996, s 8. The statement shall contain particulars of:

(*a*)   the gross amount of wages or salary;

(*b*)   the amounts of any variable and fixed deductions from that gross amount and the purposes for which they are made (unless a standing statement of fixed deductions has been given to the employee in writing, pursuant to ERA 1996, s 9);

(*c*)   the net amount of wages or salary payable; and

(*d*)   where different parts of the net amount are paid in different ways, the amount and method of each part-payment.

If an employer fails to give a statement, then the employee can apply to an employment tribunal to get one.

Pay period

14.64   The period is not regulated. However, the period must be stated in the contract of employment and included in the written particulars of terms of employment (ERA 1996, s 1(4)(b)). Again, it cannot be unilaterally changed without the change constituting a breach of an employee's contract of employment. This could entitle the employee to present a claim for constructive dismissal to an employment tribunal.

Restrictions on deductions made from wages by employers

14.65   The ERA 1996, Part II states that an employer shall not make any deduction from any wages of any worker employed by him unless the deduction satisfies one of the following conditions:

(*a*)   it is required or authorised to be made by virtue of any statutory provision or any relevant provision of the worker's contract; or

(*b*)   the worker has previously signified in writing his agreement or consent to the making of it. (ERA 1996, s 13.)

Deductions by statutory power include income tax and national insurance contributions.

A relevant provision means any express or implied provision of the employee's contract, or one or more written terms of the contract, the effect of which the employer has notified to the employee in writing at any time prior to the employer making a deduction and the employee has given written permission for the deduction to be made.

Deductions cannot be backdated and made lawful by later agreement or consent. (ERA 1996, s 13(5).)

Thus, according to the ERA 1996, s 13, a worker has the right to be paid wages properly due and any shortfall on such payment is effectively a deduction unless it is an error of computation. The case of *Yemm v British Steel Plc* [*1994*] *IRLR 117* makes clear that employers who make conscious decisions not to make a payment because they believe there is no contractual entitlement to it, are not making an 'error of computation'. 'Wages' includes fees, bonuses, commission, holiday pay, sick pay and maternity pay (*Delaney v Staples* [*1992*] *IRLR 191*). However, ERA 1996, Part II cannot be used to claim notice pay or pay in lieu, nor can it be used to claim a car mileage allowance where the employer has unilaterally changed the contract and reduced the allowance. According to the EAT such allowances are not part of wages (*Barrier v Rochdale MBC* [*1996*] *IRLB 538*). ERA 1996, Part II can also be used to claim shortfalls, for example, non-payment of shift allowance or non-payment of a 'discretionary' bonus or commission (*Kent Management Services Ltd v Butterfield* [*1992*] *ICR 272*). An industrial tribunal has also held that an employer's decision to erode a cashless pay supplement would be classified as an unlawful deduction (*McCree v London Borough of Tower Hamlets* [*1992*] *IRLR 56*).

The above also applies to situations where the employer might demand a payment from an employee, for example, the payment of a fine. Such demands must also conform with similar requirements (ERA 1996, s 15).

However, there are certain specified deductions and payments to which the requirements of sections 13 and 15 of the ERA 1996 do not apply; see sections 14 (excepted deductions) and 16 (excepted payments) respectively, and 14.69 below.

Retail employment — cash shortages etc.

14.66   In addition to the above, there are extra provisions covering employees in retail employment. These apply when an employer makes deductions from an employee's wages or salary on account of one or more cash shortages or stock deficiencies. Any deduction(s), in aggregate, from any wages payable to the employee on a pay day shall not exceed 10% of the employee's gross pay due to the employee on the day of payment. (ERA 1996, ss 17–18).

Employees who leave their employment are not subject to the 10% limitation. In this particular circumstance an employer can make deductions from the following:

(*a*)   final pay due under contract for the last period of work prior to its termination for any reason (excluding payments relating to an earlier period); and

(*b*)   pay in lieu of notice paid to an employee after the payment of final pay,

whether the amount in question is paid before or after the termination of the employee's contract (ERA 1996, s 22).

The deductions and payment received include those arising out of the dishonesty or conduct of the employee resulting in the cash shortage or stock deficiency, or any other event for which the employee was contractually liable.

Before a retail employer can make deductions on account of cash shortages or stock deficiency the employer must have:

(i)   written to the employee stating the total liability; and

(ii)   required the employee to make the payment by means of a written demand issued to the employee on a pay day, or if this is not a working day, the first working day following that pay day.

The demand for payment must not be made earlier than the first pay day after the employee was notified of the total liability and no later than twelve months after the employer established the existence of the loss (ERA 1996, s 20).

Retail employment — definition

14.67   Retail employment means carrying out retail transactions directly with, and collecting amounts payable in connection with retail transactions by members of the public or fellow employees or other individuals acting in their personal capacities. This does not have to be the employee's principal duty or carried out by the employee on a regular basis. 'Retail transaction' means the sale or supply of goods or the supply of services (including financial services). Retail employment includes, for example, car park attendants, bus and rail conductors etc. (ERA 1996, s 17(2)).

Wages

14.68   Wages means any sum payable to the employee by the employer in connection with his employment including:

(*a*)   any fee, bonus, commission, holiday pay or other emolument referable to his employment, whether payable under his contract or otherwise;

(*b*)   statutory sick pay under Part XI of the Social Security Contributions and Benefits Act 1992;

(*c*)   statutory maternity pay under Part XII of the 1992 Act;

(*d*)   a guarantee payment (under s 28 of ERA 1996);

(*e*)   any payment for time off under Part VI of the ERA 1996, or s 169 of the Trade Union and Labour Relations (Consolidation) Act 1992 (i.e. payment for time off for carrying out trade union duties);

(*f*)   remuneration on suspension on medical grounds (under ERA 1996, s 64) and remuneration on suspension on maternity grounds (under ERA 1996, s 68);

(*g*)   any sum payable in pursuance of an order for reinstatement or re-engagement under ERA 1996, s 113;

(*h*)   any sum payable in pursuance of an order for the continuation of a contract of employment under ERA 1996, s 130 or under section 164 of the 1992 Act; and

(*j*)   remuneration under a protective award under s 189 of the 1992 Act.

(ERA 1996, s 27(1).)

Excluded from the definition are:

(*a*)   any payment by way of an advance under an agreement for a loan or by way of an advance of wages (but without prejudice to the application of section 13 to any deduction made from the worker's wages in respect of any such advance);

(*b*)   any payment in respect of expenses incurred by the worker in carrying out his employment;

(*c*)   any payment by way of a pension, allowance or gratuity in connection with the workers retirement or as compensation for loss of office;

(*d*)   any payment referable to the worker's redundancy; and

(*e*)   any payment to the worker otherwise than in his capacity as a worker.

(ERA 1996, s 27(2).)

It should be noted that a non-contractual bonus paid to an employee by an employer shall be treated as wages payable on the day on which payment is made. Also vouchers, stamps or similar documents which are expressed as a fixed monetary value and are capable of being exchanged for money, goods or services are also counted as wages. (ERA 1996, s 27(3) and (5)).

Deductions and demands not covered by the ERA 1996, Part II

14.69   Deductions and demands not covered by the Act are those made in respect of the following ((d) to (f) apply to deductions only):

(a)   reimbursement of an overpayment of wages;

(b)   reimbursement of an overpayment of expenses;

(c)   disciplinary proceedings if those proceedings were held by virtue of statutory provisions;

(d)   deductions made under a court order for an attachment of earnings for sums due to a public authority;

(e)   where the deduction is in accordance with a provision of his contract of employment and the employee has signified his agreement or consented in writing;

(f)   where there was no prior agreement, but the employee has agreed to the deduction by consent in writing (e.g. other attachment of earnings orders);

(g)   taking part in a strike or other industrial action, and the deduction is made (or the payment is required) by the employer on account of the worker's having taken part in that strike or other industrial action; and

(h)   where (in the case of a deduction) it is made with the prior consent of the employee, and the deduction or payment is for the satisfaction (whether wholly or in part) of an order of a court or tribunal requiring the repayment of an amount by the worker to the employer.

(ERA 1996, ss 14, 16.)

Note that union dues deducted after an employee has certified to the employer that he has resigned from a trade union are unlawful.

Unauthorised deductions

14.70   If an unauthorised deduction is made from the pay of an employee (or the employer receives an unauthorised payment from the employee) under ERA 1996, the employee can complain to an employment tribunal. The claim must be presented to the tribunal within three months of the date the deduction was made. In the case of a series of deductions the claim must be presented within three months of the last deduction. The time limit can be extended by a tribunal where it was not practicable for the employee to present the claim in time. Where a tribunal finds a complaint well founded it shall order the employer to repay in full any unauthorised amounts received. Where only part of the deduction was unauthorised, or where the employer has already reimbursed the employee, the amount will be reduced accordingly.

(ERA 1996, ss 23–26.)

An employer who has been ordered to repay a deduction cannot recover the payment from an employee at a later date.

National minimum wage

14.71   The National Minimum Wage Act 1998 (NMWA 1998) received Royal Assent on 31 July 1998, and most of its provisions came into force on 1 April 1999 (as amended, with effect from that date, by the National Minimum Wage Act 1998 (Amendment) Regulations 1999 (SI 1999 No 583)). The Act sets out the powers of the Secretary of State to implement and set the level of the statutory national minimum wage (NMW), establishes a Low Pay Commission, and provides for the appointment of enforcement officers (who will be from the Inland Revenue) to enforce the Act's provisions.

From 1 April 1999, the NMW applies to all workers over school leaving age working in the UK other than 'voluntary workers' at the following rates (subject to variation), before deductions:

(*a*)   £3.60 per hour (except where either (*b*) or (*c*) below applies);

(*b*)   £3 per hour for 18 to 21 year olds;

(*c*)   £3.20 per hour for accredited trainees aged 22 or over in the first six months of a new job with a new employer.

The Act excludes certain workers such as servicemen, share fishermen and prisoners; the genuinely self-employed are also excluded. The National Minimum Wage Regulations 1999 (the NMW Regulations) (SI 1999 No 584), in force from 1 April 1999, also exclude workers who have not attained the age of 18, certain apprentices, certain trainees on Government training schemes, students on sandwich courses and teacher trainees while doing work experience, and homeless workers who do some work in exchange for being provided with shelter. The NMW Regulations also prescribe (in a detailed set of provisions) how to calculate a worker's hourly rate of remuneration to ensure it is at least the NMW.

Employers are required by the NMW Regulations to keep records to show that they are paying workers at a rate at least equal to the NMW. There is no prescribed format, but they must be capable of being produced in a single document. They must be kept for at least three years, and access to them must be granted to a worker or enforcement officer, on request. Enforcement officers may enforce payment of the NMW by serving an 'enforcement notice' on an employer (subject to a right of appeal to an employment tribunal), followed, if the enforcement notice is not complied with, by:

(i)   a 'penalty notice' (the penalty being double the amount of the applicable NMW in respect of each worker in respect of whom it applies), and

(ii)   proceedings on the worker's behalf (which can also be brought by the worker himself) to enforce payment of the NMW in the employment tribunal as an unauthorised deduction from wages, or by bringing a civil action for breach of contract.

There are also rights for the worker not to suffer detriment or to be unfairly dismissed in certain specified circumstances connected with the NMW, which have been in force since 1 November 1998.

Six new criminal offences are created, which are set out in section 31 of the NMWA 1998. It is an offence for an employer:

(A)   to refuse or wilfully neglect to remunerate the worker for any pay reference period at a rate which is at least equal to the NMW;

(B)   to fail to keep or preserve any record relating to the NMW;

(C)   to make, or knowingly cause or allow to be made, any false entry in an NMW record;

(D)   to produce or furnish, or knowingly cause or allow to be produced or furnished, any record or information which he knows to be false;

(E)   to intentionally delay or obstruct an enforcement officer; or

(F)   to refuse or neglect to answer any question, furnish any information or produce any document when required to do so by an enforcement officer.

The maximum penalty will be a £5,000 fine on summary conviction.

Termination of employment

14.72   The termination of a contract of employment can be brought about either unilaterally by an employee, or by an employer, by mutual agreement, or by the expiry of the term of a fixed term contract. In each case, a considerable body of law, both statutory and at common law has grown up.

Notice of termination

14.73   The period of notice required to terminate a contract of employment will usually be specified in the contract and has to be specified in the written terms and conditions of employment to which employees are entitled.

The ERA 1996, s 86 provides for statutory minimum periods of notice of termination to which employees are entitled, notwithstanding anything to the contrary in their contract, or written terms or conditions of employment. An employee is also entitled to be paid during a period of notice whether there is work provided for him or not, or if he is off sick (normally for a specified period of time and subject to conditions) or on holiday under his contract of employment.

The statutory periods of notice start at a minimum of one week for one month's service up to a period of two years' service. Thereafter, an additional week's notice is required for each additional year's continuous service up to a maximum of twelve weeks' notice for service of twelve years or more. (ERA 1996, s 86(1)). The statutory period of notice may be waived by an employer if the employee requests it. An employer may also give pay in lieu of notice. This can be given free of tax and national insurance deductions, but only where there is no right to pay in lieu in the employee's contract (see *EMI Group Electronics Ltd v Coldicott, The Times, 31 August 1999 (CA)*).

An employer who dismisses an employee without the requisite statutory notice period will be liable for an action of wrongful dismissal (see 14.75 below).

Unfair dismissal

14.74   The right of an employee not to be unfairly dismissed was originally introduced into legislation in 1971 and is now found in Part X of the Employment Rights Act 1996 — Unfair Dismissal.

An employee must have been continuously employed by the company for a period of at least one year in order to qualify for protection from unfair dismissal. The qualifying period for the right to claim unfair dismissal was reduced from two years to one year by the Unfair Dismissal and Statement of Reasons for Dismissal (Variation of Qualifying Period) Order 1999 (SI 1999 No 1436). This change takes effect in cases where the effective date of termination falls on or after 1 June 1999.

For employees employed under contracts requiring between 8 and 16 hours work per week, the qualifying period was at one time extended to five years. The employee must also have been employed under a contract of service. The House of Lords ruled (March 1994) in *R v Secretary of State for Employment ex parte Equal Opportunities Commission* [*1994*] *IRLR 176* that the hours per week qualifying thresholds excluding part-time workers from the rights to claim unfair dismissal was incompatible with European Law and therefore void. It further ruled that the Equal Opportunities Commission had locus standi to challenge domestic UK legislation by reference to EU law. The qualifying periods were formally removed by The Employment Protection (Part-time Employees) Regulations 1995 (SI 1995 No 31) which came into effect on 6 February 1995. The Employment Rights Act 1996 revokes these Regulations, having incorporated its provisions. Thus there are now no extended length of service barriers for part-time employees bringing unfair dismissal claims (ERA 1996, s 94). (See also 14.26 above.)

The previous qualifying service period of two years was challenged as indirectly discriminatory in *R v Secretary of State for Employment ex parte Seymour-Smith and Perez*. The House of Lords heard an appeal and referred several questions to the ECJ in March 1997 ([*1997*] *IRLR 315*). The European Court of Justice has now ruled upon a number of matters ([*1999*] *IRLR 253*), including a decision that an award of compensation for unfair dismissal constitutes 'pay' under what is now Article 141 (see 14.36 above). However, the essence of the case, whether or not the two-year qualifying period had such a disparate effect between men and women as to be indirectly discriminatory, was referred back to the national court (the House of Lords) to decide.

The ERA 1996 treats all dismissals as potentially unfair unless they fall within the range of what are known as 'fair dismissals' (see below). Some dismissals are automatically unfair; these are where the dismissal:

(*a*)   is pregnancy related;

(*b*)   is on the grounds of trade union membership or non-membership;

(c)   occurs because an individual has attempted to enforce a 'relevant statutory right';

(d)   in circumstances where the worker left, or proposed leaving work, because of a serious imminent danger (and certain other specified circumstances relating to health and safety);

(e)   is of a protected or opted out shop or betting worker, for refusal to work on a Sunday;

(f)   is related to the fact the employee is a pension fund trustee;

(g)   is on the grounds that the employee is an employee representative or a candidate for election as an employee representative;

(h)   making a protected disclosure (within the meaning of the Public Interest Disclosure Act 1998); or

(j)   asserting certain rights under the Working Time Regulations 1998 or the National Minimum Wage Act 1998.

Where an employee is claiming unfair dismissal, he must present his claim to an employment tribunal within three months from the date of dismissal.

From the employer's perspective, to avoid claims for unfair dismissal employees should not be dismissed without sufficient verbal and written warnings being given and the employer should be able to show that he has acted fairly and reasonably in the circumstances surrounding the dismissal. In general, one formal oral (or written warning) followed by a further final written warning and possibly a disciplinary suspension would be deemed sufficient. In any event, reference should be made to the ACAS Code of Practice No 1: Disciplinary Practice and Procedures in Employment reissued in February 1998 (SI 1998 No 44).

Summary dismissal of an employee is seldom fair, but acceptable circumstances for dismissal are:

(i)   serious or consistent misconduct by the employee;

(ii)   redundancy (provided that a fair procedure for selection for redundancy has been agreed and used) (see 14.76 below);

(iii)   contravention of an enactment whereby continued employment would constitute an offence;

(iv)   lack of capability of the employee to carry out the work for which he is employed (adequate training must however have been given); or

(v)   any other substantial reason.

(ERA 1996, s 98.)

In cases of dismissal, in determining whether the above circumstances in particular cases constitute fair dismissal, an employment tribunal will look at:

(A)   whether in the circumstances, the employer acted reasonably or unreasonably in treating the event as sufficient reason for dismissing the employee (taking into account the size and administrative resources of the employer's undertaking); and

(B)   the equity and substantial merits of the case.

(ERA 1996, s 98(4).)

The outcome of a claim put to an employment tribunal, assuming the claim for unfair dismissal is upheld, can be either an award of compensation (see below) to the employee or an order to re-engage or reinstate the employee. Compensation is also available for breach of an order to reinstate or re-engage an employee.

Where a tribunal makes an award of compensation it must consist of two components for which statutory limits exist.

(I)   *Basic award*
The calculation of this award depends upon the basic weekly pay (maximum £220, 1999/2000), length of service (maximum 20 years) and age of the employee and in summary is:

   (i)   one and a half weeks' pay for each year of employment in which the employee was not below the age of 41;

   (ii)   one week's pay for each year of employment not falling within (i) in which the employee was not below the age of 22;

   (iii) half a week's pay for each such year of employment not falling within either (i) or (ii).

The basic award maximum for 1999/2000 is £6,600.

(II)   *Compensatory award*
The maximum amount of any compensatory award which may be awarded is currently £12,000, 1999/2000.

Note that when the relevant provisions of the Employment Relations Act 1999 come into force, the statutory maximum of £12,000 referred to in (II) above will be increased to £50,000. In addition, that sum will be linked to the retail prices index (RPI), as will (amongst other sums) the maximum basic weekly pay and the maximum basic award referred to in (I) above. Depending on the upward or downward movement of the RPI in the previous twelve months, those sums will be increased (or, as the case may be, decreased) by the appropriate percentage in September of each year.

Where the employee is over the age of 64 the amount payable is reduced by one-twelfth for each month by which the employee's age exceeds 64.

Certain breaches of law relating to pregnancy, union membership, health and safety and breach of statutory duty have higher compensation amounts and, as stated above, are also automatically unfair dismissals. When the relevant provisions of the Employment Relations Act 1999 come into force, the compensatory limit will be removed where dismissal (or selection for redundancy) is automatically unfair for reasons of health and safety (ERA 1996, ss 100 and 105(3)) or for making a protected disclosure within the meaning of the Public Interest Disclosure Act 1998 (ERA 1996, ss 103A and 105(6A)).

Wrongful dismissal

14.75   Wrongful dismissal is essentially a common law liability which arises when an employee is dismissed by an employer who acts in breach of his obligations to the employee under the contract of employment. Thus, the claim is basically one for breach of contract. A claim for wrongful dismissal will usually arise in the context of not enough notice being given to the employee, with the usual remedy being damages.

From the employer's perspective, a defence to a claim of wrongful dismissal is that the behaviour of the employee constituted a breach of contract that in itself justified dismissal without notice.

A claim for wrongful dismissal does not impede an employee's statutory right to also claim unfair dismissal. Actions for wrongful dismissal may be heard in employment tribunals, subject to a £25,000 limit. (Employment Tribunals Act 1996, s 3(2)).

Redundancy

14.76   The Employment Rights Act 1996 sets out the right for employees to receive a statutory redundancy payment where certain qualifying conditions are fulfilled. Employees' statutory rights also include the right to be consulted and/or for the employer to consult with a recognised union or employee representatives elected for consultation over the proposed redundancy. Statutory notice periods must also be complied with. The legal requirements on redundancy consultation changed as a result of the Collective Redundancies and Transfer of Undertakings (Protection of Employment) (Amendment) Regulations 1995 (SI 1995 No 2587) which introduced a new obligation on employers to consult employee representatives where at least 20 employees are to be made redundant at an establishment within 90 days, even when there is no recognised union. Where there is a union, the Regulations currently allow the employer to choose whether to consult the union or a specifically appointed workplace representative body. However, in relation to dismissals taking effect on or after 1 November 1999, the position will be further altered by the Collective Redundancies and Transfer of Undertakings (Protection of Employment) (Amendment) Regulations 1999 (SI 1999 No 1925), whereby an employer will be required to consult with a recognised trade union, where there is one.

Broadly, an employee can be said to have been made redundant where the employer has ceased to carry on a business at the employee's workplace, or where the requirements of the business for the employee to carry out work of a particular kind have ceased or diminished or are expected to do so (ERA 1996, s 139).

To qualify for statutory redundancy pay, the employee must have been employed continually for a period of two years (service under the age of 18 years is not included in such a calculation).

The amount of statutory redundancy pay to which an employee is entitled is based upon the employee's age, length of continuous employment (maximum 20 years), gross average weekly pay (maximum £220 per week, 1999/2000) at the date of his redundancy and is calculated as follows:

(*a*)   one and a half weeks' pay for each year of employment in which the employee was not below the age of 41;

(*b*)   one week's pay for each year of employment not falling within (*a*) in which the employee was not below the age of 22;

(*c*)   half a week's pay for each year of employment not falling within (*a*) or (*c*).

(Note that when the relevant provisions of the Employment Relations Act 1999 come into force, the maximum weekly pay figure referred to above will be linked to the RPI. Depending on the upward or downward movement of the RPI in the previous twelve months, that sum will be increased (or, as the case may be, decreased) by the appropriate percentage in September of each year.)

Where the employee is over the age of 64 the amount payable is reduced by one-twelfth for each month by which the employee's age exceeds 64.

The time limit for claiming redundancy pay is six months.

Statutory redundancy pay is allowable for corporation tax purposes and is not liable to income or capital gains tax in the hands of the recipient. The House of Lords in *Mairs (Inspector of Taxes) v Haughey [1993] 3 AER 801*, held that enhanced redundancy payments (up to £30,000) should be tax-free. The fact that, on previous occasions when redundancies were carried out, an enhanced redundancy pay scheme had been offered, does not establish custom and practice entitling employees to the same enhancement in a future round of redundancies (*Quinn v Calder Industrial Materials [1996] IRLR 126*).

Certain categories of employee are excluded from the right to receive a statutory redundancy payment, broadly these are employees:

(i)   who have attained the normal retiring age;

(ii)   who ordinarily are employed outside Great Britain; or

(iii)   who have been offered suitable alternative employment by the employer.

If an employee is offered alternative employment which is different in nature or has different terms and conditions of employment, the employee is entitled to a four-week trial period in the new job. If, during or at the agreed end date of the trial period, either the employer or employee wishes to terminate the employment, the employee must be treated as having been dismissed for the reason that caused the original contract to end (ERA 1996, s 138(2)(4)).

However, the employee will not be entitled to a redundancy payment if the alternative employment is suitable in relation to him, and:

(*a*)   he unreasonably refuses the offer of alternative employment; or

(*b*)   during the trial period he unreasonably terminates the contract, or unreasonably gives notice to terminate it and it is in consequence terminated.

(ERA 1996, s 141).

Public interest disclosure by employees

14.77   The Public Interest Disclosure Act 1998 came into force on 2 July 1999. This Act (which inserts sections 43A to 43L into the ERA 1996) will protect workers (defined so as to include contractors under the control of an employer, persons on training courses, and doctors, dentists, opticians and pharmacists providing services under statutory schemes) who report wrongdoing, in an authorised manner, in one of six specified categories (a 'qualifying disclosure') set out below:

(*a*)   that a criminal offence has been committed, is being committed or is likely to be committed,

(*b*)   that a person has failed, is failing or is likely to fail to comply with any legal obligation to which he is subject,

(*c*)   that a miscarriage of justice has occurred, is occurring or is likely to occur,

(*d*)   that the health or safety of any individual has been, is being or is likely to be endangered,

(*e*)   that the environment has been, is being or is likely to be damaged, or

(*f*)   that information tending to show any matter falling within any one of the preceding paragraphs has been, or is likely to be deliberately concealed.

A worker will only be protected if the qualifying disclosure is also a 'protected disclosure'. The first category of 'protected disclosure' is to the worker's employer. However, where the worker reasonably believes that the relevant failure relates solely or mainly to (i) the conduct of a person other than his employer, or (ii) any other matter for which a person other than his employer has legal responsibility, disclosure may be made to that other person. A worker who, in accordance with a procedure whose use by him is authorised by his employer, makes a disclosure to a person other than his employer, is to be treated for these purposes as making the disclosure to his employer.

A qualifying disclosure is also a 'protected disclosure' if it is made to an authorised regulator. The Public Interest Disclosure (Prescribed Persons)

Order 1999 (SI 1999 No 1549) (which also came into force on 2 July 1999) authorises regulators for this purpose. The effect is that a worker will be protected if he makes a qualifying disclosure in good faith to a person specified in the Order, reasonably believing that (i) the failure disclosed falls within the matters in respect of which that regulator is prescribed, and (ii) that the information disclosed, and any allegation contained in it, are substantially true.

The other four ways in which a 'qualifying disclosure' will be a 'protected disclosure' are disclosure:

(1)   to a legal adviser, in the course of obtaining legal advice;

(2)   to a Minister of the Crown, where the worker's employer is either an individual appointed under any enactment by a Minister, or a body whose members are appointed by a Minister;

(3)   to another person other than those previously mentioned, but only if the worker makes the disclosure in good faith, reasonably believes the information to be substantially true, satisfies one of a number of stringent conditions (see ERA 1996, s 43G(2) to (4)) and in all the circumstances it is reasonable to make the disclosure;

(4)   in the case of 'exceptionally serious failures', to another person where the worker makes the disclosure in good faith, he reasonably believes that the information disclosed (and any allegation contained in it) are substantially true, he does not make the disclosure for purposes of personal gain, the relevant failure is of an exceptionally serious nature, and in all the circumstances of the case, it is reasonable for him to make the disclosure (in determining this last point, particular regard will be had to the identity of the person to whom the disclosure is made).

Workers will have the right to complain to an employment tribunal if they have suffered any detriment as a result of making a protected disclosure, and dismissal for making a protected disclosure will be automatically unfair. (In this connection, note that when the relevant provisions of the Employment Relations Act 1999 come into force, the compensatory limit will be removed where dismissal (or selection for redundancy) is automatically unfair on the ground that a worker made a protected disclosure within the meaning of the Public Interest Disclosure Act 1998 (ERA 1996, ss 103A and 105(6A)).)

It should be noted that any provision in an agreement (including a contract of employment) which purports to prevent a worker from making a protected disclosure is rendered void.

Appendix 14A

Employment Relations Act 1999

The Employment Relations Act 1999 (the Act) received Royal Assent on 27 July 1999 and at the time of writing awaits commencement orders to bring its provisions into force. The provisions of the Act cover a number of areas and affect many aspects of employment law, including several that are not currently dealt with in this chapter. However, because of the Act's importance, an outline of its main provisions is set out below.

Copies of the Act can be obtained from The Stationery Office, price £12.35, and now available on the Internet (www.dti.gov.uk/public/search.html).

Trade Unions

Section 1 of the Act amends the Trade Union and Labour Relations (Consolidation) Act 1992 (TULRCA 1992) by inserting a new Schedule A1.

This Schedule sets out the legal procedures for obtaining union recognition and derecognition for collective bargaining purposes (for employers of 21 employees or more). Paragraph 156 of Schedule A1 also provides that a worker has a right not to be subjected to any detriment by an act or deliberate failure to act by his employer if the act or failure is on the grounds that the worker:

(a) acted with a view to obtaining or preventing recognition of a union by the employer;

(b) indicated that he supported or did not support recognition of a union by the employer;

(c) acted with a view to securing or preventing the ending of bargaining arrangements;

(d) indicated that he supported or did not support the ending of bargaining arrangements;

(e) influenced or sought to influence the way in which votes were to be cast by other workers in a ballot;

(f) influenced or sought to influence other workers to vote or to abstain from voting in such a ballot;

(g) voted in such a ballot; or

(h) proposed to do, failed to do, or proposed to decline to do, any of the above.

If a worker suffers a detriment for any of the above reasons, he has a right to present a claim within three months to an employment tribunal. However, this does not apply if the action or failure to act by the worker constitutes an unreasonable act or omission by the worker. If such a complaint is upheld, the tribunal may award such compensation as it considers just and equitable in all the circumstances, having regard to any loss (para 159). The usual rules of mitigation apply. Compensation is subject to a limit of the total of the basic award for unfair dismissal (under ERA 1996, s 119) plus the maximum amount of possible compensation under ERA 1996, s 124(1) (to be raised to £50,000 under the Act — see below).

If the worker is an employee and the detriment amounts to a dismissal within the meaning of the ERA 1996, he may bring a claim to a tribunal on the grounds that he was unfairly dismissed and the reason or principal reason for his dismissal was one of the above grounds (paragraph 161). There is no qualifying period or upper age limit to bring a claim under this section.

In addition, the dismissal of an employee is unfair if the reason or principal reason for the dismissal was that he was redundant but it is shown that:

(i)   the circumstances constituting the redundancy applied equally to one or more other employees in the same undertaking who held similar positions to the employee and who have not been dismissed by the employer; and

(ii) the reason or principal reason that he was selected for redundancy was one of those reasons outlined at (*a*)–(*h*) above.

Further, extended protection has been provided against dismissal for those taking part in lawfully organised industrial action, by virtue of a new section 238A inserted into TULRCA by Schedule 5 to the Act.

Maternity and Parental Leave

The Act also makes provision for maternity and parental leave, in accordance with the requirements of the Parental Leave Directive. Schedule 4 to the Act grants the Secretary of State the power to make regulations on this issue.

Subsequent to this, the Department of Trade and Industry has published a consultation paper which proposes that:

(*a*) mothers, fathers and adoptive parents will have the right to take up to 13 weeks' unpaid leave whilst their children are under five;

(*b*) ordinary maternity leave will be extended to 18 weeks (from 14) and the qualifying period for additional maternity leave will be reduced from two years to one;

(*c*) parents will be entitled to a short amount of time off to deal with family emergencies, including situations in which:

  (i)   a child or dependant has fallen ill, is injured or assaulted, or gives birth;

  (ii) the employee needs to deal with the consequences of the death of a dependent (e.g. arranging a funeral etc.);

(iii)   a child is involved in a serious incident at school or during school hours; or

(iv)   childcare or other arrangements break down (e.g. if the childminder fails to turn up etc.); and

(*d*)   fathers will be entitled to take time off straight after a baby is born or a child is adopted, providing that at least three months' notice is given before the week in which the birth or adoption is expected.

Responses to the consultation paper are requested by 1 October 1999, with the results expected to be published on 15 October 1999. The resulting regulations are expected to come into force in December 1999.

Disciplinary and Grievance Hearings

Section 10 of the Employment Relations Act 1999 grants workers the right to reasonably request to be accompanied to a disciplinary or grievance hearing. The employer must then allow the worker to be accompanied by a single companion, who is either an official of a trade union (either within the meaning of TULRCA 1992, ss 1 and 119, or whom the union has reasonably certified in writing as having experience of, or as having received training in, acting as a workers' companion at disciplinary or grievance hearings) or a fellow worker. The worker has the right to choose his companion. Further, the elected companion may address the hearing and he and the worker may confer throughout the course of the hearing.

Workers are protected from suffering detriment by any act or any deliberate failure to act by their employers on the grounds that they chose to exercise this right (section 12). If a worker has such a right to be accompanied and his chosen companion is not available at the proposed time of the hearing, the worker may request a reasonable alternative time which falls before the end of the period of five working days beginning with the first working day after the proposed date and the employer must postpone the date as requested.

Employers must permit workers to take time off during working hours for the purpose of accompanying another of the employer's workers. If the employer fails, or threatens to fail, to allow the employee to be accompanied, the employee may complain to a tribunal within three months and may receive compensation of up to two weeks' pay.

Fixed Term Contracts

Section 18 of the Act provides that section 197 of the ERA 1996 shall be amended such that fixed term contracts can no longer include unfair dismissal waivers.

Part Time Workers

The Secretary of State is granted the power under section 19 of the Act to make regulations to ensure that part-time employees are treated no less favourably than those in full-time employment. Further, he will have the right to issue codes of practice containing guidance in order to eliminate discrimination against part-time workers and facilitate the development of opportunities for part-time work.

National Minimum Wage

Section 22 of the Act adds a new section 44A to the National Minimum Wage Act 1998, which extends the exclusion from the Act for voluntary workers to include certain resident workers in religious and other communities. A worker will be exempt from the right to receive the minimum wage if he is a member of a community which:

(*a*)   is a charity or is established by a charity;

(*b*)   has as its purpose the practising or advancing of a religious or similar nature; and

(*c*)   has all or some of its members living together for this purpose.

This excludes, however, independent schools or institutions which provide courses of further or higher education.

Employment Agencies

Schedule 7 to the Act adds new provisions relating to the conduct of employment agencies, amending the Employment Agencies Act 1973, including granting a power for regulations to be made to regulate the way in which and the terms on which such services may be provided by persons carrying on such agencies and businesses as well as the fees charged. Further, the rules relating to fees for finding or seeking to find employment are amended such that fees shall not be requested or received directly or indirectly for finding any person employment or attempting to find such employment.

Compensatory Awards

Section 117 of the Employment Rights Act 1996 is amended by section 33 of the Act so that if an employment tribunal makes an award of compensation and the applicant has not been re-engaged or reinstated, the amount of compensation shall include an additional award of not less than 26 nor more than 52 weeks' pay (unless that section does not apply — ERA 1996, s 117(4)). The special award is to be abolished.

Further, section 34 of the Act provides for the following sums to be index linked to the RPI:

(*a*)   guarantee payments (ERA 1996, s 31);

(*b*)   unfair dismissal awards (basic and compensatory) (ERA 1996, ss 120(1) and 124(1), and TULRCA 1992, s 156(1);

(*c*)   the maximum amount payable on insolvency of employer (ERA 1996, s 186(1)(a) and (b));

(*d*)   the maximum amount of a week's pay for purposes of certain calculations (ERA 1996, s 227(1)); and

(*e*)   remedies for the right to membership of a trade union (TULRCA 1992, s 176(6)).

In addition, ERA 1996, s 124 is amended so that it provides that the amount of compensation for unfair dismissal awarded under section 117(1) or 123 shall not exceed £50,000 (previously £12,000).

Finally, the compensatory limit has been removed for claims of unfair dismissal for reasons of health and safety (ERA 1996, ss 100 and s 105(3)) and for making a protected disclosure under the meaning of the Public Interest Disclosure Act 1998 (ERA 1996, ss 103A and s 105(6A)).

Chapter 15

Car Scheme and Property Administration

Car scheme administration

Introduction

15.1   Recent years have seen a steady erosion of the tax benefits of company cars. Despite this the company car remains as one of the most popular benefits for employees as the cost to the employee of being provided with a company car is, in many instances, still less than providing themselves with a similar car. Accordingly, especially in the small to medium-sized company, the company secretary can commonly find him or herself responsible for car scheme administration.

Acquisition

15.2   The best method of the acquisition of company cars is a question which raises many different points for the company secretary. Currently, outright purchase is the most common means of purchase of a company car. However, other means are available, being hire purchase, contract hire and finance leasing. The pros and cons of each are examined below.

Outright purchase

15.3   Financing the purchase of a fleet of cars can provide a cash flow problem for companies, even where the fleet comprises only a few cars. Unless a business has unused cash resources and can use the benefit of capital allowances (given at the rate of 25% on a reducing balance basis up to a maximum of £3,000 per car per year), outright purchase has several disadvantages.

First, there is the question of a company's cash resources being invested in an asset which quickly depreciates; usually at an unpredictable rate. Also, a business is generally unable to reclaim the VAT paid on the purchase. From 1 August 1995, VAT is recoverable on cars purchased *exclusively* for business purposes but this is a very restrictive test which will not be satisfied if the cars are available for any private use. The main beneficiaries of the change are likely to be car leasing companies although genuine pool cars may qualify.

Where VAT is recoverable on purchase, it must also be charged on the full selling price.

Then there is the question of the administration of the fleet. In most small companies, this is a responsibility which will commonly fall to the company secretary who then has to devote considerable staff time to matters such as buying and selling the cars, arranging insurance cover, organising servicing and repairs, as well as attending to the financial recording aspects.

A possible advantage of outright purchase is the possibility of being able to negotiate discounts with a seller. This is especially true when purchasing a large fleet.

A variation on outright purchase is hire purchase. Although the administrative problems are much the same as for outright purchase, a financing advantage is that interest payable on hire purchase is tax deductible. Also, capital allowances are available to the business from the outset of the hire purchase contract and the cost is spread over the period over which ownership is transferred.

Finance leasing

15.4   Finance leases offer many advantages to a business. In general, leasing payments are deductible as trade expenses, subject to a restriction where the car costs more than £12,000, in which case a proportion of the rental is disallowed. Capital allowances are available to the lessor and the leasing rates reflect this. The lessor does not supply, maintain or sell the cars, but simply provides the finance to acquire the cars chosen by the lessee who bears the risk of their residual value (i.e. profit or loss). Accordingly, the administrative burdens of running a fleet to a large extent remain the problem of the lessee.

The two main forms of finance lease are:

(*a*)   the *open ended lease*, which is typically for a three-year period, but with an option to terminate at any time after a minimum period at a predetermined figure. The lessee pays or receives the difference between the sale proceeds and the predetermined settlement figure;

(*b*)   the *'balloon' lease*, which can be used if it is reasonably certain that the car will be retained until the end of the lease period. In addition to rental payments, a 'balloon' payment equivalent to the expected residual value of the car is payable at the end of the lease, whether or not the car is sold.

Contract hire

15.5   Contract hire differs from finance leasing in that the lessor supplies and maintains the car, usually leaving the lessee with only insurance and fuel costs to pay, in addition to the hire charge which is tax deductible. The lessor also disposes of the car at the end of the contract. Bulk buying discounts and the expertise of the lessor in controlling maintenance costs and disposing of cars for the best prices, make contract hire competitive with the combined cost of finance rentals and maintenance incurred by the company itself.

The services which are offered by the lessor to the lessee under a contract hire agreement are usually a combination of the following:

(*a*)   buying the cars of the lessee's choice;

(*b*)   servicing and repair costs;

(*c*)   licensing the cars;

(*d*)   provision of replacement cars;

(*e*)   roadside assistance;

(*f*)   selling the car at the end of the hire period.

Accordingly, the majority of the car scheme administration is borne by the lessor rather than the lessee, which can be a considerable attraction to a company.

Property administration

Choosing and financing commercial premises

15.6   It is essential that the location of a company be carefully researched to keep financial burdens to the minimum and to allow the business to develop successfully.

The main factors that should be considered when weighing up possible sites are:

(*a*)   availability of financial incentives (see 15.7 below);

(*b*)   costs and funding;

(*c*)   availability of labour;

(*d*)   availability of housing;

(*e*)   relocation of key staff;

(*f*)   preferred type of premises and availability;

(*g*)   time span for relocation; and

(*h*)   facilities, site access and communications.

It should be noted that the Building Regulations 1991 (SI 1991 No 2768) contain provisions applying to new buildings and conversions which include new stricter fire safety requirements. This is in addition to the Workplace (Health, Safety and Welfare) Regulations 1992 (SI 1992 No 3004) which came into force on 30 December 1993 (see 14.56

EMPLOYMENT, HEALTH AND SAFETY. Access and facilities for disabled people must be complied with, and the Disability Discrimination Act 1995 and its subsequent Disability Discrimination (Employment) Regulations 1996 (SI 1996 No 1456) should also be considered (see 14.40 EMPLOYMENT, HEALTH AND SAFETY).

Financial incentives

15.7   Government-backed financial incentives can be analysed into two main categories, namely tax relief and assistance with building costs.

Leasehold or freehold?

15.8   The following options should be considered:

(*a*)   'short' property interests — e.g. a lease of less than 50 years;

(*b*)   'long' property interests — freehold or long leasehold.

In some instances there may be no choice since the 'long' interest may not be available or affordable, or the premises may have to be taken on whatever terms are available.

The main advantages of freehold ownership are:

  (i)   elimination of uncertainty of future rent reviews;

 (ii)   freedom from landlords' restrictions;

(iii)   availability of an asset which can be used to generate liquid funds by borrowing on its value;

(iv)   capital appreciation of the asset.

The main advantages of acquiring a lease are:

(A)   cash flow;

(B)   no necessity to obtain long-term mortgage funding.

Lease terms

15.9   Leases are invariably long and complicated and somewhat difficult to understand. The following clauses will usually constitute the main terms of such documents.

(*a*)   *Rent payable and rent review* — this clause details the amount of rent payable to the landlord at the commencement of the lease together with the dates at which the rent may be increased during the lease.

(*b*)   *Break clause* — this clause will state whether the tenant can leave the premises and therefore maintain some degree of flexibility. Such a clause may also allow for the redevelopment of the premises.

(c)   *The obligation to repair* — this is an important clause as where the obligation is stated to be a 'full repairing and insuring one' the cost of carrying out repairs will fall entirely upon the tenant.

(d)   *Alterations/improvements* — a tenant may not be allowed to carry out alterations or improvements either at all, or at least without the landlord's consent. Under the Landlord and Tenant Act 1927, where a landlord's consent is required, the Act states that such consent may not be unreasonably withheld.

(e)   *Assignment and subletting* — the right to assign the lease is important as it will allow a tenant to market the remainder of the lease should the company no longer require the property.

(f)   *The obligation to insure* — if the landlord insures on a block policy, it is important that the tenant's interest is noted on it.

Licences

15.10   A licence is a contractual document granting a company the right to occupy premises on the conditions set out in the contract. A potential disadvantage of a licence is that the normal rules on security of tenure as conferred by Part II of the Landlord and Tenant Act 1954 do not apply. However, in reality, few licences of business premises are not protected tenancies as, in general, the courts tend to dislike occupational insecurity for business tenants.

Commercial mortgages

15.11   As with any request for mortgage finance, lenders consider both the type of property and the ability of the borrower to service the loan. There are many companies in the commercial mortgage market, comprising a mixture of banks, finance companies and insurance companies. Each has its own particular likes and dislikes, with regard to the type of property, and each has its own range of terms and conditions. The insurance companies tend not to lend against properties such as hotels, nursing homes, sports facilities and other restricted use sites, whilst banks and finance companies are often prepared to consider a wider range of buildings.

The borrower will usually be expected to produce accounts for the previous three to five years to prove a track record but, in addition, many lenders also seek personal guarantees from the directors. The interest rate charged may be fixed or variable; the banks will generally offer the choice to the borrower.

Lease renewal

15.12   Under the Landlord and Tenant Act 1954 (Part II), business tenants are given the right to renew their tenancies at the expiry of the former lease where the provisions of the Act apply. Pursuant to section 23(1) of the Act, the Act applies so long as 'the property in the tenancy is or includes premises which are occupied for the purposes of a business carried on by him or for those or other purposes'. This will cover almost all types of business activity.

Termination of a business lease

15.13   The Landlord and Tenant Act 1954 states that no lease may be brought to an end except in accordance with the Act. The effect of this statement, combined with the fact that most business leases are for a fixed term, means that a landlord must pursue the method of termination set down in the Act before he can regain possession.

To initiate the procedure, the landlord must service a notice of termination of the lease on the tenant under section 25 of the Act which will expire not earlier than the date of expiry of the tenancy under the lease. The notice can be served not less than six or more than twelve months before the date of the end of the lease and must be in the prescribed form and set out whether the landlord intends to oppose the grant of a new tenancy and, if so, on what grounds.

It is important to make sure that the section 25 notice is accurate. In *Morrow v Nadeem [1978] 1 AER 237*, the notice was served in the name of an individual, whereas the lease was held in the name of a company and in *Yamaha-Kemble Music (UK) v ARC Properties [1990] 1 EGLR 261* the landlord was mistakenly named as ARC whereas the parent company PD was the lessor. Both notices were held to be invalid as the landlord's name is the most relevant piece of information.

A tenant must reply to the notice by issuing a counter-notice stating whether or not he is willing to give up possession of the property. This must be done within two months of the receipt of the notice. If such a counter-notice is not given, the tenant loses his right to apply to the court for a renewed tenancy (in default of a negotiated renewal).

Where negotiations for a renewal are proceeding but not yet finalised, the tenant must apply to the court for a renewed tenancy or he will lose the right to a new lease. This must be done not less than two months nor more than four months after service of the section 25 notice.

Should the parties fail to come to an agreement, the terms of the tenancy will be settled by the court under section 29 of the Act.

Should the landlord wish to modify the terms of the lease, he must have a 'fair and reasonable' case for doing so.

Once the landlord has given a section 25 notice to the tenant and the tenant has also replied that he would like to have a new tenancy, the landlord may apply to the court for an interim rent which will run from the date specified in the notice or the date of the tenant's request for a new tenancy, whichever is the later. The court must have regard to the existing rent, assuming an annual tenancy on values existing at the date when the interim rent starts to run (Landlord and Tenant Act 1954, s 24A).

New leases

15.14 Should a landlord not wish to grant a renewed tenancy to a tenant, then he is restricted in his opposition by the terms of section 30(1) of the Landlord and Tenant Act 1954.

Section 30(1) of the Act defines the only reasons upon which a landlord may oppose a renewed tenancy as being:

(*a*) the failure by the tenant to comply with repairing or other obligations;

(*b*) the persistent delay in the payment of rent;

(*c*) breaches by the tenant of other substantial lease obligations;

(*d*) alternative accommodation has been offered by the landlord to the tenant;

(*e*) a better return if the premises were let as a whole (in situations where the premises concerned are currently sub-let);

(*f*) the landlord intends to demolish or reconstruct the premises*;

(*g*) the landlord wishes to occupy the premises.

*Evidence of this intention will be required at the hearing. The landlord must have a fixed and *settled desire* to do what he claims and he must have a *reasonable prospect* of being able to do it and, in particular, that he has or will be able to obtain planning permission for what he intends to do. Planning permission will soon also be required for demolition.

Should the landlord obtain possession on any of the last three grounds specified above, the tenant may be able to claim compensation for the disturbance of his business and for any improvements which the tenant may have made to the premises.

Compensation

15.15 As mentioned in 15.14 above, compensation may be paid by a landlord to a tenant in certain circumstances, and will be payable by the landlord to the tenant as soon as the tenant has quit the premises.

Calculation

15.16 The amount of compensation payable was traditionally calculated by reference to the rateable value of the occupied premises at the date on which the landlord's notice is given, times the appropriate multiplier. This multiplier was announced from time to time by the Secretary of State for the Environment by way of statutory instrument. If premises are occupied by the tenant or predecessors carrying on the same business for a period of at least 14 years, the tenant was paid twice the rateable value times the appropriate multiplier.

Prior to 1 April 1990, all premises, whether used for domestic or business purposes, were valued for rating purposes and the rateable value was easily obtainable. The appropriate multiplier was, until that date, three.

Following the introduction of the uniform business rate and the community charge, concern was expressed as to how compensation could be calculated under the new regime, particularly in relation to mixed premises i.e. a combination of business and residential properties. Also, if the premises were used for business purposes only, the new uniform rate times the then existing multiplier of three led to concern amongst landlords.

It is clear that, as previously, the amount of compensation payable is calculated at the date the landlord serves his section 25 or section 26(6) notice. The rule relating to double compensation for businesses carried on at the premises for at least 14 years still exists in all cases. The compensation for business premises is calculated by reference to the new uniform business rate times the appropriate multiplier. This multiplier is discussed further below.

Mixed properties

15.17   Subsections (5A) and (5B) of section 37 of the Landlord and Tenant Act 1954 (LTA 1954), introduced by the Local Government and Housing Act 1989 (LGHA 1989), state that if part of the holding is domestic property, one should disregard that part, take the uniform business rate valuation on the remainder of the property, add a sum equal to the tenant's reasonable expenses in moving out of the domestic property, and then apply the multiplier to the total sum. If the parties cannot agree upon the removal expenses, the courts will be asked to determine the sum.

Domestic properties

15.18   Subsections (5C) and (5D) of section 37 of the LTA 1954, introduced by LGHA 1989, state that if the whole of the holding is domestic property, the rateable value shall be equal to the rent at which it is estimated it might reasonably be expected to let the premises from year to year when the tenant undertakes to pay all usual tenant's rates and taxes and bears the cost of repair and insurance. The calculation is again made as at the date the landlord served his section 25 or section 26(6) notice. If the parties cannot agree the calculation, the matter is to be referred to a valuation officer at the

Commissioners for the Inland Revenue with the right of appeal to the Lands Tribunal.

The appropriate multiplier

15.19   If the landlord served a notice under section 25 of the LTA 1954 (or section 26(6)) prior to 1 April 1990, the appropriate multiplier remains at three times the rateable value.

If the landlord serves his notice on or after 1 April 1990, the appropriate multiplier is one, unless the tenant has exercised an option introduced to him by LGHA 1989, Schedule 7 (see below). In the event that such an option has been exercised, the appropriate multiplier will be eight times the rateable value of the premises as on 31 March 1990.

The 1989 option

15.20   Paragraph 4 of Schedule 7 to the LGHA 1989 uses the words 'in any case'. However, these words follow references to other parts of Schedule 7 which relate to mixed or domestic property. The debate which has arisen is whether the general words relate to any property protected by the LTA 1954. It is understood that the Department of the Environment is of the view that it does relate to all protected properties, but a representative of the DoE has stated that it is not for the department to interpret statutes. The courts have not yet been given the opportunity to consider the matter. For the sake of safety it must be assumed, for the time being, that the section does relate to all business premises protected by the LTA 1954.

What is clear, is that the tenancy has to have been entered into before 1 April 1990, or entered into on, or after, that date pursuant to a contract made before 1 April 1990; the landlord's notice under section 25 or section 26(6) of the LTA 1954 must be given before 1 April 2000 and the tenant must give notice to the landlord that he wants to exercise his option. This notice must be given within the period the tenant has under the LTA 1954 for making an application to the court for a new tenancy. As stated above, if exercised, the tenant is entitled to eight times the rateable value registered on 31 March 1990.

Rent review

15.21   In order to protect landlords from the effects of inflation, most new leases of business premises contain a clause allowing the rent to be reviewed periodically, thus enabling a landlord to increase the level of rent paid during the term of the lease.

In negotiating a lease a company should consider the following.

(*a*)   The time period between reviews (e.g. every five years).

(*b*)   The formula and method of determining the new rent.

(*c*)   The provisions for arbitration in the event of failure to reach agreement about a rent (e.g. reference to an independent surveyor).

(*d*)   Rent reviews will normally be initiated by the service of a notice. If the lease specifies that time is of the essence in a rent review, a landlord may lose his review right if he fails to deliver the appropriate notice at the appropriate time.

Repairs

15.22   Leases will usually impose upon the tenant the obligation of repairing the property. In this connection there are several different terms that are commonly used. These are as follows.

(*a*)   *To keep in repair* — the tenant has to repair the premises and maintain them during the period of the lease.

(*b*)   *To leave in repair/good tenantable repair* — the premises must be left in repair at the end of the lease to the standard that they were in at the time of grant of the lease.

(*c*)   *Full repairing and insuring* — the premises must be repaired and insured at all times by the tenant.

Where a landlord is obliged to do repairs, the lease will normally state that a notice of disrepair must be served on the landlord before his obligation will arise. Where the obligation to repair falls on the tenant, the landlord will normally have the right to enter and inspect the premises at least once each year.

Assignment

15.23   A landlord may prevent a lease being assigned by inserting a bar against assignment in the lease. This will obviously affect the marketability, and accordingly the value, of the lease. Thus, it is more usual to find a clause in leases not barring assignment, but requiring the surrender of the lease to the landlord before assignment. Where the bar is qualified, the Landlord and Tenant Act 1927 provides that the landlord's consent shall not be unreasonably withheld.

Restrictive use

15.24   There may be a provision that restricts the use to which the premises can be put. Where the clause is highly restrictive, it is likely to have a depressing effect on the rent payable.

Such restrictions are additional to any planning consent that may be required from the local planning authority to carry on a particular business.

The Uniform Business Rate

General

15.25 The introduction of the National Non-Domestic Rate (Uniform Business Rate) on 1 April 1990, coupled with the first revaluation of non-domestic properties since 1973, affected all those concerned with the payment of rates on business premises in England and Wales. Business rates are now set by central government, and all businesses now pay the same amount of UBR, irrespective of where they are located.

The combined redistribution effect of the Uniform Business Rate and the revaluation was dramatic. The total amount of money raised by the Government from the business rate remained broadly similar, but the changes will produce a big shift, with some small businesses in London paying up to three times more and some in the North and Midlands paying substantially less.

The new regime

15.26 All non-domestic properties in England and Wales have now been revalued for rating purposes. The revaluation fixes a new rateable value for every business premises, based on Open Market Rental Value on fully repairing and insuring terms as at 1 April 1993.

From 1 April 1990 the Uniform Business Rate has been payable on all non-domestic properties. The Local Government Finance Act 1988 and ancillary regulations replaced the General Rate Act 1967.

The Uniform Business Rate is calculated by multiplying the new rateable value of a property by a Multiplier set centrally by Government (see 15.27 below).

Rating Lists are available for inspection at borough or district council offices or, in the City of London, at the offices of the City Corporation.

The Multiplier

15.27 Under the Uniform Business Rate, the Central Government fixed a single rate poundage (Multiplier) for England and for Wales; previously this was done by each local authority.

The Multiplier for the rating year commencing 1 April 1997 is 45.8p in the pound in England. The 1988 Act provides for the Multiplier for subsequent rating years to be linked to the Retail Prices Index. In Scotland, local authorities will continue to have individual figures but the Government intends to bring them broadly into line over the next five years.

The City of London sets its own rates poundage which may be different from the Multiplier applying elsewhere in England.

Right of appeal

15.28   The Government in 1990 introduced, for the first time, a six-month limit on appeals against new rateable values. For the 1995 revaluation, the Government introduced new regulations to enable ratepayers to appeal on any one of the permitted grounds, at *any* time during the Rating List. Any appeal must be made to the local Valuation Agency Office for determination by a Valuation Officer, but the help of an independent professional valuer will probably be needed. If the VAO does not believe a proposal to be well-founded, or is unable to reach agreement with the ratepayer, the VAO has a duty to refer the proposal to the Valuation Tribunal. In due course, the appeal will be sent for hearing.

Until the determination of an appeal, rates are payable in full on the basis of the new assessment. Under the regime, interest will be payable where sums are refundable following a retrospective alteration to the Rating List. Interest is payable on the refund at 1% below bank rate. Interest is received net of standard rate tax, and a tax certificate should be obtained from the VAO.

On appeal, the rateable value may be increased as well as decreased. It is inadvisable, therefore, to proceed with an appeal without professional advice as to the chances of success. In the first instance, a second opinion from a Trade Association or Chamber of Commerce which may have an overview of comparable local rates is useful.

The relevant regulations are expected to provide that only the owner or the occupier or others having an interest in the property will be able to appeal against an assessment.

Transitional arrangements

15.29   Transitional arrangements were introduced at the outset, with the introduction of the UBR for those facing large rate increases or decreases. The 1995 revaluation again resulted in some people facing large increases and others large decreases. The transitional arrangements introduced at the outset of the UBR have been extended. Transitional benefits and liabilities are now attached to the property and are not affected by any change in the owner or occupier of the premises. There are detailed rules defining those properties which will benefit or suffer as a result of the transitional arrangements but, broadly, any property which was at any time in the 1990 Rating List, and is either in the 1995 Rating List, or has been entered into the List at a later date, is subject to the regulations. New property brought into assessment for the first time after 1 April 1995 is not subject to transitional arrangements.

For 1997/98, real annual increases will be restricted to a maximum of 10%, the real increase will be −2% for properties with revised rateable values of less than £10,000 (£15,000 in London), and −2% for small shops with living accommodation (rateable values below £10,000 or £15,000 in London). The Government has also determined the maximum decrease in rate liability as follows:

	1997/98	**1998/99**	**1999/2000**
Large property	15%	30%	30%
Small property	22%	35%	35%

The rules relating to downward transition are to be reviewed at the start of each financial year.

If a property changes hands, the new owner is entitled to take over the previous owner's entitlement to transitional relief.

Table of Cases

Table of Statutes

Italicised references to paragraph 9.15 refer to substituted sections of the Companies Act 1985 which overlap with existing provisions and are not yet in force.

Table of Statutory Instruments

Index